ORIGINS of the INFANT'S SOCIAL RESPONSIVENESS

ORIGINS of the INFANT'S SOCIAL RESPONSIVENESS

The Johnson & Johnson
Baby Products Company
Pediatric Round Table, II

Edited by
EVELYN B. THOMAN
The University of Connecticut

LAWRENCE ERLBAUM ASSOCIATES, PUBLISHERS
1979   Hillsdale, New Jersey

DISTRIBUTED BY THE HALSTED PRESS DIVISION OF
JOHN WILEY & SONS
New York   Toronto   London   Sydney

Lawrence Erlbaum Associates, Inc., Publishers
365 Broadway
Hillsdale, New Jersey 07642

Distributed solely by Halsted Press Division
John Wiley & Sons, Inc., New York

Library of Congress Cataloging in Publication Data

Main entry under title:
Origins of the infant's social responsiveness.

(The Johnson & Johnson Baby Products Company pediatric round
table, II)
Includes bibliographical references and index.
1. Infant psychology. 2. Parent and child.
3. Social interaction. I. Thoman, Evelyn B. II. Series: Johnson & Johnson Baby Products Company. Johnson
& Johnson Baby Products Company pediatric round table
series, II. [DNLM: 1. Child development—Congresses.
2. Socialization—Congresses. 3. Infant—Congresses.
4. Mother-child relations—Congresses. W3 J0155 v.1
1978/WS105.5.S6 069 1978]
BF723.I6074   155.4'22   79-16625
ISBN 0-470-26813-1

Printed in the United States of America

Contents

Foreword

This conference comes at the beginning of a scientific revolution. Twenty years ago, the newborn infant's central nervous system was thought to be capable of producing only reflex behaviors with the higher centers not yet developed. Now our understanding has been completely altered by naturalistic observations such as those of Peter Wolff who made the monumentally important discovery that the normal newborn has six states of consciousness.

Once these states were discovered, consistent behaviors were found in each state, and the infant's abilities and potential could be explored. The change in our perspective of the newborn that has resulted from this is as striking as the contrasting portrayals of human infants when paintings from the 11th and 15th centuries are compared. In the 11th century, painters depicted the infant as a miniature adult while after the 15th century it was painted in more accurate proportion with a much larger head and shorter limbs—a new and truer image.

Just as painters altered the portrayal of the infant, the authors in this volume grapple with a new model of how the newborn develops and interacts with his parent. We now perceive the human infant as a very different organism.

This book reports exciting, thoughtful, and perceptive work by investigators who have made major contributions to our understanding of this new infant and his parents. The complex abilities of the young infant have been further elaborated in their reports. To fully enjoy this volume, I encourage all readers to immerse themselves in the discussions where differences and debate so enriched the sessions.

The discovery of the human infant as a gorgeously responsive creature who is able to interact in a complex manner on multiple sensory levels forces on us many questions, such as whether the normal newborn should be placed with many other neonates in a noisy, brightly lit nursery away from its parents where often only a single nurse is available to meet the special individual needs of a dozen or more infants.

The research described in this book will help those concerned with parents and infants—pediatricians, psychologists, obstetricians, midwives, nurses, and, of course, parents—to re-evaluate our present practices, which affect both the infant and its care giver.

MARSHALL H. KLAUS

Preface

The origin of this meeting for me was a visit to Storrs, Connecticut, by Robert B. Rock, Jr., director of professional relations, and Steven Sawchuck, M.D., director of medical services for the Johnson & Johnson Baby Products Company. Over a very fine lunch, they proposed a conference in their company's Pediatric Round Table educational series concerning the mutual influence of mothers and babies. Since this is my major area of interest, I was delighted with the idea and agreed to organize the meeting. The title, "Origins of the Infant's Social Responsiveness," was selected to provide a relatively broad context for including the varied interests of researchers who are at the forefront in the study of early infancy. The general objective was to bring together such a group of people to report on their most recent findings and for an exchange of ideas that might provoke new conceptualizations and questions concerning characteristics of the infant from the time of birth and how these characteristics interact with the environment during the early months of life.

It was a very great personal pleasure to invite the participants in this conference, as I knew very well that each of them would be outspoken in their considered opinions but open to the views of others as well. The enthusiasm with which each of them agreed to come was truly gratifying—it was clear that their high level of regard for all of the other invited participants was a major factor of their eagerness to come (I'll not disclose my strategies for arranging this momentum).

The members of this conference have made contributions to the field of early infancy research in many diverse areas ranging from the most rigorous laboratory studies to naturalistic observations in the home; and from highly focused studies of processes including perception, learning, and motivation to more broadly focused research on social behavior. It was anticipated that because of their heterogeneity in research interests, these people would bring broad perspectives to the discussion of issues that could be expected to emerge.

A decision was made to provide the participants with very little structure for their presentations. The purpose of the conference was very generally stated to them: to explore the developing characteristics and capabilities of the infant during the first year, with a primary concern for the ontogeny of the infant's role as a member of the mother–infant relationship. The framework provided for the conference sessions constitutes the three major sections for the present book:

I   The infant's rhythms and responses as preparation for partnership
II The developing designs for viewing the infant as a social being
III Ontogeny of the mother–infant relationship

Prior to the conference, some methodological and philosophical issues were proposed to the members for their consideration; however, during the course of the discussions, some of these questions were not considered at all, and some were discussed repeatedly—and heatedly. Also, new issues arose, such as, Does the infant acquire expectancies, conditioned responses, or entrained rhythms from its interactions with the mother? Can the development of sensory–motor functions be delayed by too-early practice? Can we meaningfully separate the effects of a mother's behavior on the infant from the infant's influence on the mother? Is the newborn infant capable of expressing a positive affect in response to environmental experience? There was a sharp divergence of views on the nature of the concepts required for exploring the nature of the infant and the impact of the environment on the developing baby. Still, all agreed that the newborn infant is uniquely adapted for its stage of life and that it has amazing capabilities yet to be explored before we can more fully comprehend how the infant is designed to function as a responsive social being from the time of birth.

The format for this book includes the complete conference proceedings, including the manuscripts prepared by each participant, additional material presented at the meetings, and the discussions following the presentations as they actually occurred during the conference sessions. A final chapter briefly attempts to highlight the commonalities and variations in current views of the infant and the importance of continuing the search for an understanding of the development of the infant's social responsiveness.

EVELYN B. THOMAN

ORIGINS of
the INFANT'S
SOCIAL RESPONSIVENESS

THE INFANTS' RHYTHMS AND RESPONSES AS PREPARATION FOR PARTNERSHIP

1 Stimulus Significance as a Determinant of Infant Responses to Sound

Rita B. Eisenberg
Albert Einstein College of Medicine

INTRODUCTION

During discussions preceding this conference, it was suggested that the auditory component underlying social responsiveness in infants might be considered under the title: The Mother's Voice as a Prepotent Stimulus for the Infant. This is a decidedly intriguing title, and it would be very nice indeed if there were some hard data to support using it. Unfortunately, there are not, and so it seems more prudent to consider instead how the infant responds to different kinds of acoustic signals and whether his modes of response to them can cast any light on the questions with which this conference is concerned. When we do consider these matters, the data at least suggest that even in newborn life, the human auditory system may be so organized that the mother's voice *can become* a prepotent stimulus as a natural consequence of the care-giving process.

I would like to focus on newborn life not only because I have spent a great many years learning about the effects of sound during this period, but also because I believe that the effects of environmental experience vary according to the infant's intrinsic organization. That the normal full-term infant is well organized no longer seems subject to doubt. His states of arousal vary in regular ways (Prechtl, this conference). He responds positively to some stimuli and negatively to others (Peiper, 1963). He demonstrates differential capacities to smell (Engen, Lipsitt, & Kaye, 1963) and to taste (Crook & Lipsitt, 1976; Nowlis & Kessen, 1976) and to see (Cohen & Salapatek, 1975) and to hear (Eisenberg, 1976).

It is my purpose at this conference to discuss the differential auditory capacities of human newborns. In doing so, I will try to relate these capacities

1

to the adaptive functions they serve and the mechanisms that underlie them "in ways that satisfy the test for representing reality" (Lemkau, Note 1). Although, in my view, auditory adaptations in man have to do primarily with the organization of verbal information, they bear importantly upon nonverbal functions as well. Among these, surely, is the development of social responsiveness. Mothers probably have soothed their babies by humming or singing to them since time immemorial. Many, if not all, adults have a nonverbal vocabulary of cooing and chuckling and nonsense sounds that they trot out, consciously or unconsciously, only for communication with the very young. All of us, in everyday life, respond on an emotional level to environmental sounds and to nuances of voice that color, and sometimes even contradict, the verbal contents of speech.

With this introduction, let me now spell out some of the realities of human hearing. First, hearing and listening are not the same thing, since as we all know from experience, it is perfectly possible to hear without listening. Second, in man, as in lower species, there is a systematic relation between what goes into the ears and what comes out of the mouth, that is, the sounds processed by our auditory mechanisms and produced by our vocal mechanisms are physically matched. Third, it is a fact of life that people automatically sort out environmental and speech sounds, process them differentially, and respond to them, in a number of voluntary and involuntary ways and on a number of levels. In other words, we somehow hear different things in different ways at the same time. What these realities add up to, then, is that hearing is a hierarchy of auditory functions that presumably must be served by a hierarchy of special-purpose mechanisms.

A Frame of Reference for Studying Infant Responses to Sound

The aim of the research I will discuss today is to determine whether, by systematically varying the conditions of acoustic stimulation and studying the responses associated with each condition, one can arrive at a *testable* model of the auditory system that accords with what we know about the endowment of the human organism, the course of developmental events, and the realities of man's communicative behavior.

In my view, even a tentative model must address at least five basic questions: What properties of the central nervous system (CNS) permit us to hear different things in different ways at the same time? What mechanisms underlie our extraordinary auditory competence? What sensory specializations underlie our use of verbal codes? Are these mechanisms and specializations uniquely human? Are they present at birth or acquired during the course of development?

These are questions that have important practical implications, some of which bear upon the concerns of this conference. Therefore, before proceeding further, it may be well to consider the strategy guiding research at my laboratory.

The basic factual question towards which procedures have been geared is whether coding operations prerequisite to language perception later in life are demonstrable in the form of differential auditory behavior during earliest life. For this reason, all of the acoustic stimuli used have been selected for their specific bearing upon verbal communication, and work has proceeded systematically from the simple to the complex. We have advanced from studying the effects of discrete parameters, such as frequency, to studying the effects of multidimensional signals, such as tonal patterns and synthetic speech sounds. We have advanced from defining thresholds to presenting signals at conversationally loud levels. We have added correlative measures of heart rate (HR) and brain wave (EEG) change to our original behavioral indices (Eisenberg, 1965) and explored the effects of different kinds of stimulus schedules upon state and system(s) dynamics. We have studied normal babies and those in various risk categories; and throughout this work, we have sought diligently to relate our findings to underlying mechanisms as well as to correlates in the performance of adult humans and lower animals.

These labors have brought forth a body of data on newborn responses to sound, some correlates I never expected when I started out some 15 years ago, and a tentative model for the intrinsic organization of the auditory system. They also have forced our group to think carefully about how the organization of a stimulus envelope relates to auditory coding in the nervous system and to communicative behavior in everyday life; and because this thinking has determined the directions our research has taken, I would like to consider our notions in some detail.

To start with, then, let me specify what "organization of a stimulus envelope" connotes. If we define envelope, rather unscientifically, simply as the physical composition of signals during some period of time that they're ON, all acoustic stimuli can be divided into two broad classes according to whether their physical properties vary over time.

When signals have fixed dimensions, as in the case of pure tones and filtered noises that commonly are used for auditory testing, they can be considered "constant" because their *physical properties are invariant over time.* For instance, a pure tone, which looks like a series of sine waves on an oscilloscope, or a band noise, which looks rather like a "shaded in" area, are constant because you can chop off any segment of either signal at any point in time and it looks the same no matter which segment you happen to choose. This means that the nervous system need code such sounds only in "bits", according to frequency, intensity, phase, and other discrete parameters. It also means, since fixed dimension signals are abstract and rarely, if ever, found in the real world, that their significance for a hearer depends heavily upon such factors as learning or the " set" induced by instructions.

When signals are multidimensional, as in the case of spoken language or synthetic speech, on the other hand, they can be considered "patterned" because *their component physical parameters are invariant only in relation to each other.* Thus, if you look at these sounds on an oscilloscope, they are full of peaks and valleys, some points that are dense with energy and others that have very little or none, and so on. In other words, they are stimuli characterized by high variability over time, and if you examine one segment of them on the scope, you can't predict the properties of other segments in your sample. This means that the nervous system somehow must code these stimuli not only according to their component parameters, but also according to their temporal relations. That is to say, they must be treated, in some organized way, as "chunks" or "ensembles". Patterned signals of one kind or another, then, insofar as they approximate sounds in the natural environment, may have varying degrees of built-in significance.

Methods of Studying Infant Responses to Sound

Now, before considering the effects of these different kinds of signals on infants, let me first spell out how our correlative measures are employed. In studying overt behavior, we are concerned with operational definitions of both hearing capacities and listening abilities. Our response indices accordingly refer both to specified effector systems that bear upon verbal communication and to nonspecific mechanisms that bear upon attentional behavior. We classify *motor reactions* because vocal utterance in infancy, like speech in later life, can be considered a subset within this category. We classify *visual reactions* because sight and hearing are interrelated distance senses. We focus in various ways on state-dependent reactions that presumably reflect excitatory and inhibitory mechanisms in the reticular activating system (RAS). Responses falling within this category are defined specifically as stimulus-bound changes in behavior involving either a significant increase or a significant decrease in the level of ongoing activity. If activity increases markedly with signal presentation, the response is scored as arousal. If it decreases, the response is scored as "orienting-quiet" (OQ) during early infancy, and as "orienting" (OR) thereafter. The distinction is made because directional head turning or other clear-cut behavioral correlates of the orienting response rarely are seen in the first weeks of life.

In studying electrophysiologic responses, we are concerned with stimulus-bound changes in waveform that can be measured in terms of latency, amplitude, direction of change, and so forth. We focus on attention-related reactions by examining the effects of defined prestimulus states upon such measures, and also by deriving a curve to show the manner in which state varies over the course of a stimulus schedule. The premise underlying this second maneuver is that stimulus-bound changes in system dynamics can constitute both an implicit measure of hearing and an explicit measure of differences in organization among individuals or groups.

These, then, are the measures—and the burden of all our data is that the human organism emerges from the womb rather neatly equipped to organize his auditory world. Nonspecific mechanisms governing attentive behavior seem to be operational. Functionally differentiated channels for processing acoustic information according to discrete parameters and also according to the organization of a stimulus envelope seem to exist.

The auditory findings should come as no great surprise, since it is known that the human newborn, in comparison with other species, has an exceedingly well developed auditory system. The cochlea is functional by the fifth month of gestation, and the auditory apparatus of a 20-week fetus is structurally comparable with that of an adult. The six-month fetus responds autonomically to pure tones, and the seven-month premature responds both autonomically and behaviorally to a number of acoustic parameters. The list of discriminative abilities for the full-term infant has grown with each new signal studied.

Functional Properties of Sounds and Their Ontogenetic Implications

Since the relevant data have been reviewed in detail elsewhere (Eisenberg, 1976), I will restrict myself here to certain salient findings that cast some light upon relations between stimulus conditions and auditory coding operations. In brief, I first will discuss the effects of two parameters that have been studied fairly extensively—that is, frequency and sound pressure level (SPL)—and then consider the functional properties of those two signal classes I defined earlier as constant and patterned.

(a). Frequency. Getting down to cases, let me begin by reviewing the effects of frequency. This is a logical starting point because range-dependent differences might be predicted on several counts (Eisenberg, 1976), and, in fact, there seems no developmental stage during which low and high frequencies exert similar effects.

During newborn life, almost any index of auditory behavior shows range-dependent frequency effects. As can be seen from Fig. 1.1, sleeping or waking, signals in the range below 4,000 Hz evoke response two or three times more often than those in the range above 4,000 Hz. Responses to low-frequency or side-band signals best can be elicited during doze or light sleep, and stimuli in the carrier range for speech are associated with relatively higher potency as well as differential patterns of electrophysiological activity (Hutt & Hutt,

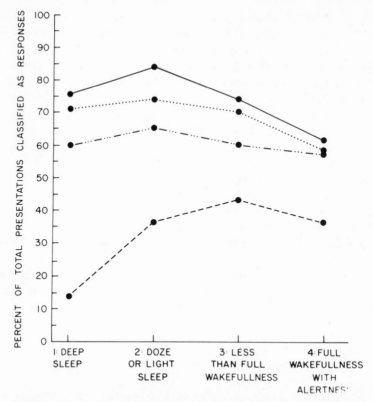

FIG. 1.1.   Overt responsivity as a function of state and signal variables. State, graded on a four-point continuum, is shown on the abcissa, while the ordinate refers to the percentage of total stimulus presentations classified as behavioral responses to each of four noisemaker signals. The functions graphed refer, in decending order, to ▬, a 1.3 sec wide-band noise; ......a 300 msec narrow-band low-frequency (500–900 Hz) noise; ▬...▬, a 200 msec wide-band noise; and ---, a 250 narrow-band high-frequency (4000–4500 Hz) noise. (From Eisenberg, 1976 © 1976 by University Park Press, Baltimore, Md. Reproduced by permission.)

1970; Hutt, Hutt, Lenard, Bernuth, & Muntjewerff, 1968; Lenard, Bernuth, & Hutt, 1969). Responses to high frequency signals best can be elicited during wakeful states. Low frequencies, which are effective inhibitors of infant distress, generally evoke gross motor activity. High frequencies, which are associated with relatively shorter cardiac latencies and tend more to occasion distress than to inhibit it, elicit a high proportion of "fixation" OQ responses much like the freezing reactions one sees in lower animals.

These range-dependent frequency differences found in newborns—and also reported for older infants—have correlates that, later in life, relate to what commonly is termed *affect.* They are reflected in the electrophysio-logical responses of adult subjects, in the acoustic properties of our musical instruments and alarm signals, in the kinds of sounds we find annoying, in the words we use to describe our reactions, and perhaps even in the ways we store acoustic information. In sum, whatever the context in which psychological responses to sound are studied, low frequencies invariably seem to have "good" or "pleasure" connotations, and high frequencies the reverse.

These findings have three important implications for our thinking about developmental processes in hearing. First, they suggest that differential "tuning" to the carrier frequencies of language may be built in during intrauterine life. Second, they suggest that the neonate's unique response to high-frequency signals may be as much a phylogenetic relic as the Moro reflex. Third, they suggest that *qualitative* judgments of sound in adult life—those relating to "noisiness," "pleasantness," and the like—may have their roots in preadapted mechanisms referable to phylogenetic history.

(b). Sound Pressure Level.   If we now consider findings on SPL, it seems possible that *quantitative* responses to sound reflect another class of historical determinants. There is, for instance, a growing body of information—on visual, as well as auditory, functions in infancy—to suggest that parameters having to do with our orientation in space may be processed in much the same way throughout life. The data on audition are fairly consistent: Band-noise thresholds for 2-week-old infants are roughly comparable with adult norms (Eisenberg, 1976, p 124); the potency of many acoustic stimuli has been shown to increase directly with stimulus intensity; the amplitude of certain components of the sound-evoked potential seems to vary more or less linearly with SPL; and loudness functions may follow the same power-law relations at all developmental stages.

Taken as a whole, then, data on SPL effects during early life have two further implications for our thinking about developmental auditory processes. First, neuronal mechanisms for processing intensity may be fully operational at birth. second, it seems possible that loudness and other so-called natural dimensions of sound may have their roots in preadapted mechanisms referable to species history.

The findings just discussed derive almost entirely from studies with signals such as pure tones and band noises, and as I noted earlier, such stimuli differ importantly from multidimensional signals both in their manner of coding within the nervous system and in their bearing upon communicative behavior in everyday life. Nonetheless, in considering the effects of constant and patterned signals as general classes of stimuli, let me note that they have some common functional properties that bear upon organization in the CNS as well as a number of differential properties that bear—very importantly, in my opinion—upon organization in eighth nerve channels.

The functional properties they share have to do with the effects of state, and they form the basis for my earlier statement that mechanisms governing attentive behavior are present at birth. Incidence of neonatal responses to randomly presented sounds varies with state in much the manner adult detection scores vary during vigilance experiments. The curve describing these relations (see Figure 1.1), like that showing incidence of OQ responses during habituation, assumes an inverted-U "cue function" predicted by activation theory. Under any conditions of stimulation—including schedules containing interspersed photic stimuli (Unpublished Bioacoustic Laboratory data)—the curve describing changes in dynamic equilibrium over time, however measured, assumes a similar shape in infants and adults. (See Fig. 1.2) Except perhaps in the case of speech-like signals, modes of overt response vary systematically according to an "awake-alert-aware" continuum frequently postulated for the RAS. (see Fig. 1.3)

(c). Dimensionality. The differential functional properties of constant and patterned signals are as varied as they are suggestive. During newborn life, they are demonstrable in the kinds and amounts of overt response one can elicit. During adult life, they are demonstrable in certain kinds of psychophysical measures. During all stages of development explored at my laboratory, they are demonstrable in differential electrophysiological patterns.

During early infancy, *the outstanding functional property of constant signals is nonspecificity.* As a matter of fact, the auditory behavior evoked by such signals as pure tones and noise bands differs so little from nonstimulus behavior or from other kinds of perceptual behavior that differentiating response events reliably poses serious problems. Overt reactions consist mostly of gross body movements, cessation of such movements, or components of the startle reflex. Although decelerative HR changes occasionally may be evoked during waking states, cardiac responses to a wide variety of constant signals almost uniformly have been found to be *accelerative.* Relations between response magnitude and prestimulus indices of arousal agree with the so-called "law of initial values" (LIV), which holds that stimulus-bound behavior is directed towards homeostasis. Large HR changes and intense motor responses characteristically occur during sleep states; smaller cardiac changes and minor body movements usually are found during wakeful states. The potency of pure tones or band noises is essentially a function of specific parameter variables, and within limits bearing upon the physical attributes of spoken language, can be enhanced by increases in one or more of those parameters. Vocal responses almost never can be elicited, however, and the most sophisticated visual reaction found is a kind of wide-eyed "what-is-it?" look usually considered to be orienting behavior.

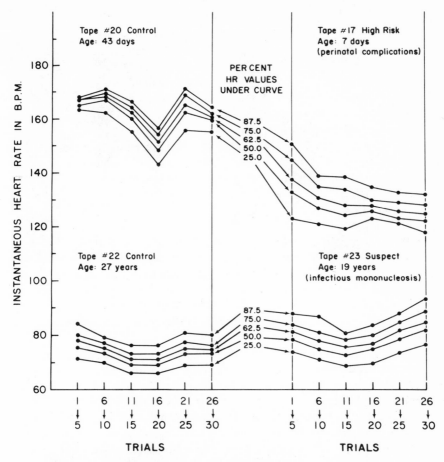

FIG. 1.2. Heart rate change as a function of stimulation with a synthetic "ah" sound presented at fixed 90-sec intervals. The abcissa refers to six consecutive five-trial blocks comprising a 30-signal schedule and the ordinate to instantaneous HR in pbm. The functions shown, which derive from two representative infants (the upper graphs) and two representative adults (the lower graphs), represent mean changes in HR levels over trials, as derived from interval histograms. In the diagram, the lower boundary of the cardiac range is defined as that below which 25% of the HR values fall; and the upper boundary as that above which 12.5% of the values fall. As can be seen, the normal infant in the upper-left-hand graph, despite maturational differences that are reflected in higher HR levels and greater lability, behaves very similarly to the normal adult in the bottom-left-hand graph; that is, HR boundaries tend to fall during middle trials and then to return towards the initial range. (From Eisenberg, 1976. © 1976 by University Park Press, Baltimore, Md. Reproduced by permission.)

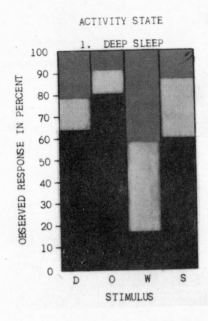

ACTIVITY STATE

1. DEEP SLEEP

OBSERVED RESPONSE IN PERCENT

D   O   W   S

STIMULUS

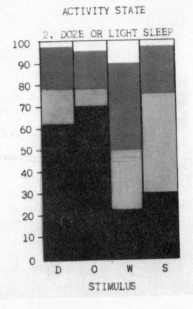

ACTIVITY STATE

2. DOZE OR LIGHT SLEEP

D   O   W   S

STIMULUS

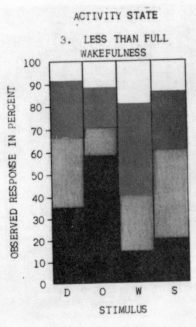

ACTIVITY STATE

3. LESS THAN FULL
WAKEFULNESS

OBSERVED RESPONSE IN PERCENT

D   O   W   S

STIMULUS

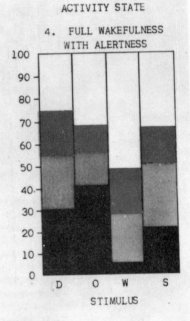

ACTIVITY STATE

4. FULL WAKEFULNESS
WITH ALERTNESS

D   O   W   S

STIMULUS

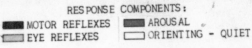

RESPONSE COMPONENTS:

MOTOR REFLEXES   AROUSAL
EYE REFLEXES   ORIENTING - QUIET

The patterned signals explored thus far include matched pairs of ascending and descending tonal sequences as well as a number of synthetic speech sounds, and all of these signals seem to have similar happy properties.

In newborn life, as in later infancy, the effects of these multidimensional signals are so distinctive that naive observers can detect response reliably. If current data are a valid index, the overt behaviors evoked by speech-like sounds differ little, if at all, from those evoked by tonal sequences. Reactions consist mainly of arousal or orienting behaviors; and motor reflexes, which are relatively few, usually take such differentiated forms as facial grimacing or displacement of a single digit. Moreover, the response repertoire associated with these signals includes such discriminative behavior as responsive crying or cessation of crying, pupillary dilatation, and, on rare occasions, a turning of the head in association with visual search.

Response magnitude, however measured, shows no systematic relation with prestimulus indices of arousal, so that LIV seemingly does not apply. Further, whatever the state of arousal, both tonal sequences and synthetic speech sounds prove remarkably potent. In some newborns studied, as in most adults, anticipatory HR and brain wave changes have been found after only 3 or 4 trials with either kind of stimulus. The average newborn responds overtly to at least 3 consecutive trials with these signals, even in deep sleep; the quiet–wakeful baby may respond to as many as 8 or 10. Both types of stimuli are associated with longer latencies than any we have found for constant signals.

The cardiac reactions evoked by patterned signals seem to differ according to whether the pattern presented is a tonal sequence or a synthetic speech sound. All of the tonal sequences explored thus far have been associated mainly with *diphasic* changes, that is, acceleration followed by deceleration, or the reverse. Synthetic speech sounds, on the other hand, have been associated almost entirely with *decelerative* changes, characterized by longer latencies and more prolonged response activity than any other kind of signal. Moreover, these properties seem to be independent of both maturational status and level of arousal.

Current data on infant brain-wave responses to patterned signals are so sparse there seems little point in detailing them. All that can be said with

FIG. 1.3. Effects of signal variables upon the distribution of overt responses. The graphed percentages, based upon the distribution of responses shown in Figure 1.1, indicate, for each of the four noisemaker stimuli presented during a specified activity state, the proportion of behaviors classified as motor, visual, arousal, and OQ. Signals are indicated on the abscissa as D (low-frequency band), O (1.3 sec wide band), W (high-frequency band), and S (200 msec wide-band). As can be seen, each signal is associated with a differential distribution of behaviors and all signals are affected similarly by state variables. (From Eisenberg, 1976. © 1976 by University Park Press, Baltimore, Md. Reproduced by permission.)

assurance at this time is that speech-like sounds are extremely potent at all stages of development and consistently associated with longer latencies than have been reported for any constant signals.

How these infant responses to different kinds of patterned signals relate to language processing later in life is far from clear at present. However, given the results of some preliminary fishing expeditions, I am confident that sharper correlates in adult behavior will emerge. Adult listeners perceive patterned signals as psychologically "softer" than constant ones—and by approximately the difference between pure tone and speech-hearing thresholds. They perceive tonal sequences differently according to starting frequency, the direction of a frequency sweep, and its duration. They attribute meanings to both tonal sequences and prolonged synthetic vowels, though never to constant signals. All things considered, then, data now on hand suggest that the various kinds of selective behavior evoked by tonal patterns and synthetic speech sounds may reflect relatively plastic mechanisms and relatively high levels of neuronal organization.

This pretty much sums up what substantive findings we have to think with right now. They show, contrary to popular belief, that the human newborn is perceptually mature in a great many respects and far better organized than casual inspection would suggest. His auditory behavior depends upon both central and sensory phenomena, and it follows orderly rules, some of which apply throughout life. Moreover, different rules, that evidently refer to different biological determinants and surely must reflect differential coding mechanisms for sound, refer to high frequencies, constant signals, and patterned stimuli.

There is reason to suppose that the biological determinants cover a past-to-future time span. Frequency-bound behavior, which in the newborn period has correlates in the performance of lower animals, bears upon qualitative judgments of sound in adult life. Intensity-bound behavior, as measured by threshold and loudness functions, seems to have species-specific character-istics that are independent of developmental status. Pattern-bound behavior, though lacking clear-cut correlates either in adult or animal performance, is uniquely selective in the newborn period and associated with vocal activity. Further, since it seems possible that the rules governing such behavior may vary according to whether or not the evoking stimuli are speech-like in nature, certain aspects of pattern-bound behavior may bear directly upon the development of communicative functions.

Some Notions About the Organization of Hearing Functions.   Given these correlates, we have developed three specific postulates permitting some general inferences about the intrinsic architecture of auditory pathways and the possibilities for developmental change (Eisenberg, 1970). Our first proposition is that the developmental timetable for any given function is a historically determined "best fit" between a given organism and the particular environment in which he grows up. This implies that "landmark" changes in auditory behavior—and in vocal utterance as well—reflect preprogrammed alterations in neuronal organization that are triggered by "suitable" environmental demands. Our second proposition is that most changes occurring during gestation are directed towards equipping an organism with mechanisms geared to long-term species-specific adaptive requirements. This implies that auditory specializations prerequisite to language perception will be present, at least in *anlage* form, during the newborn period. Our final proposition is that perceptual channels are organized in a functional hierarchy such that the degree of built-in indeterminancy increases directly with the order of phyletic and neuronal development. This implies that man, as the most complex of creatures and the only organism to communicate by verbal codes, will have a variety of low-level auditory coding mechanisms he shares with other species as well as certain uniquely specialized higher-level mechanisms for coding speech sounds.

To account for developmental changes in communicative behavior, one need only assume various kinds of lateral and centrifugal associations between decoding and encoding mechanisms for sound. Such associations, which increasingly are suggested by physiological data and comparative findings, are the basis for a tentative schema, as shown in Figure 1.4. What we have postulated here is a hierarchy of functionally differentiated channels that reflects the presumed evolutionary order of coding mechanisms for sound. In line with current data, each of these channels refers to specified stimulus conditions and primary modes of response, the most significant of which have been discussed.

In line with current thinking, lateral organization in the model incorporates a number of specific notions. First, both direct and indirect pathways are involved in the decoding of acoustic information. Second, centrifugal controls act at all levels of the nervous system. Third, additional channel capacity for coding acoustic information is provided in nonspecific systems. Fourth, mechanisms for ensemble processing serve to increase the resolving power of the auditory system. Fifth, mechanisms for storage, processing, and encoding are found at all levels of the CNS. Finally, it is assumed, though not shown diagramatically, that auditory mechanisms have their counterparts in motor specializations required for speech and in central specializations required for language.

The auditory channels are shown systematically in Figure 1.5. Each of the four levels in the model refers to an indeterminate series of neuronal networks, which under the influence of normal growth and environmental forces, are incorporated into organized feedback systems.

Implicit in this organizational scheme is the idea that the degree of correspondence with peripheral input decreases at successive levels of the

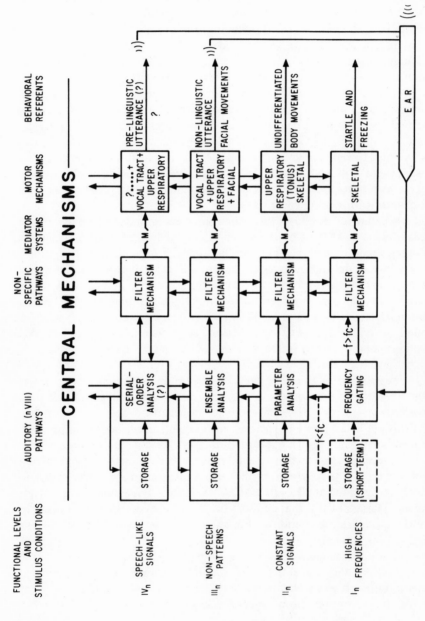

FIG. 1.4. Schematic showing systems involved in auditory processing.

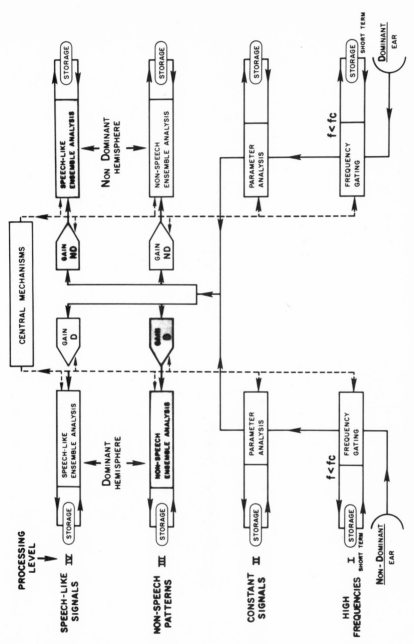

FIG. 1.5. A model for the intrinsic organization of hearing mechanisms. (From Eisenberg, 1976. © 1976 by University Park Press, Baltimore, Md. Reproduced by permission.)

hierarchy, each processing operation yielding a product that is some derivative of the transmitted signal. In a sense, then, what is postulated is a form of "neural funneling" having specific functional consequences: Acoustic information that is stored or processed at a given level of the system cannot be retrieved or processed in the same form at a higher level, and processing may proceed in parallel at several levels of the hierarchy.

The lowest level in the hierarchy is essentially a *frequency-dependent gating circuit,* which, for physiologic reasons, one would be inclined to place at the cochlear level. Assuming some critical cutoff point, it provides a mechanism whereby low frequencies can be filtered upward for specific coding and high frequencies can be filtered through nonspecific channels for low-level storage, or processing, or both. The circuit, present at birth as a phylogenetic relic of approach–withdrawal behavior, is elaborated into an organized "affective" system during the course of development. Given physiologic information currently available, one might speculate that this lowest channel might involve old brain mechanisms, and particularly the limbic system.

Whether long-term storage normally is possible at this lowest level seems debatable for several reasons (Eisenberg, 1976). Whether it is possible under *pathological* conditions may be an important area for study, however: Psychotics, for instance, tend to be vastly disturbed by high-frequency sounds (Coleman & Eisenberg, Note 3), and children with developmental disorders of communication sometimes respond to high frequencies when they seem totally insensitive to other portions of the sound spectrum (Unpublished Bioacoustic Laboratory data, Note 4).

The second level in the diagram represents a series of parameter-coding circuits that collectively serve as a kind of *species-specific adaptor.* Inasmuch as the eighth nerve system is tonotopically organized, such circuits must be time locked. Therefore, assuming critical limits for individual parameters, they provide a mechanism whereby, through successive recoding operations, incoming signals can be refined: Significant perceptual elements can be extracted for further resolution at higher levels in the system; insignificant elements, filtered through nonspecific channels, can be stored or processed in a variety of ways. The circuits, present at birth in the form of "grading" or "scaling" mechanisms, are elaborated into an organized subceptor system as new networks become operational during development.

In light of the strong possibility that many parameter-coding mechanisms may be preadapted, it seems probable that operations at this second level bear, at least indirectly, upon language acquisition. Selective tuning to the carrier frequencies of language, for instance, would lead to selective reinforcement of language cues. A graded response to intensity would permit the developing child to orient himself preferentially towards language sounds. Hierarchal mechanisms, affording a time base for related decoding and encoding operations, might serve in toning up units of the speech apparatus for articulatory tasks.

The organization of higher levels must remain largely speculative until a great deal more substantive information on neonatal responses to patterned stimuli of various kinds has been accumulated. All we have now is some sparse preliminary evidence (Barnet, deSotillo, & Campos, Note 5; Crowell, Jones, Kapuniai, & Nakagawa, 1973; Molfese, Note 6) to suggest that functional asymmetries in perceptual processing may be present during early life. Figure 1.5, then, sketches out a first-guess notion (Eisenberg, 1974) that mechanisms for processing speech-like and nonspeech ensembles are present at birth in both hemispheres. A differential exists, however, such that one hemisphere—usually the left—is specialized for processing speech-like signals, whereas the other hemisphere is specialized for processing other kinds of ensembles. This is shown schematically by the introduction of "gain" elements to control the distribution of coding processes: The shaded areas in each hemisphere represent "inhibitory" mechanisms of one kind or another, so that functional asymmetry is achieved.

Whatever the basis of functional asymmetry in man, the model, in its current skeletal form, postulates only that some sort of "fourth-level" specializations for processing speech sounds contribute differentially to hemispheric dominance in language functions. These specializations normally are present at birth as part of man's species-specific endowment; and they facilitate the establishment of specific neuronal connections, which during the normal course of development, become elaborated into an organized "communicative" network. However, since such mechanisms, like the proposed "third-level" specializations, are represented redundantly, the schema allows for certain eventualities. For instance, the effects of central auditory damage presumably would vary according to the stage of development at which pathology occurs: The earlier damage appears, the greater the chance that either hemisphere can assume dual functions and/or that alternate neuronal connections can be established. By the same token, assuming the best possible outcome of central auditory damage early in life, one must suppose that a major reduction in the channel and storage capacities of eighth nerve systems would be reflected not only in reduced auditory abilities of some kinds, but also perhaps in more generalized sensory-motor dysfunction.

Our present working hypothesis is that third-level mechanisms, here tentatively placed in the nondominant hemisphere, somehow act as a kind of *species-specific ensemble discriminator,* which after detecting and processing nonspeech chunks of acoustic information, funnel speech-like chunks to fourth-level mechanisms presumably located in the dominant temporal lobe. Since all of the tonal patterns explored thus far have evoked some amount of vocal utterance, it is assumed that certain of the individual networks may serve in the development and reinforcement of motor-speech plans. Similarly, since matched pairs of ascending and descending sequences have been associated with differential response patterns, it is assumed that some networks may bear upon perceptions of musical form, intonation, and the like.

Let me stress that this is a very tentative model. Its major purpose at this time is to provide a systematic framework within which one can deal concretely with the immensely complicated facts of communicative behavior in man. We assume that our notions about the hierarchal organization of auditory mechanisms are valid because, so far at least, they've held up under experimental testing. On the other hand, whether our notions about hemispheric specialization are valid remains to be confirmed by experiments now under way.

Whether the model, discussed here is partially, or even wholly, correct is secondary to whether it is useful as it stands. I would like to suggest that it is useful because it affords a concrete, yet flexible, approach to questions about perceptual function in general and auditory function in particular. Stimulus-bound behavior refers to specified perceptual operations and specified functional levels. The stimulus, as a trigger for underlying events and a common denominator permitting comparison among individuals or groups, becomes a key determinant of strategy. The only requirement for productive procedures is to select stimuli that are pertinent to the questions one is asking.

SOME NEW DIRECTIONS

I would like to talk a bit about one of these experiments, which is different from anything we've done previously, terribly exciting (in my biased opinion, at least), and perhaps more relevant to the concerns of this conference than some of our earlier experiments.

It's a rather complicated study and, in order for you to understand what we're doing and why we're doing it, I think it might be well to go a little deeper into psycholinguistics. Let me see, then, whether I can explain in a simple way how the physical properties of sound bear upon speech perception.

First of all, suppose we look at the physical structure of the sounds /bae/ and /ae/ as they're shown in Figure 1.6. In both the schematics, we find localized bands of energy concentration that reflect the natural resonant modes of a vocal tract. The lowest band of any speech sound, the *fundamental,* depends upon the size of a given vocal apparatus, and it is fundamental frequency that permits us to distinguish male from female voices. Higher energy bands, or *formants* , which, by convention, are designated numerically on a low–to–high frequency continuum as f_1, f_2, and so on, depend upon the positioning of the tongue, lips, and other articulators. It is the relation between these energy bands that constitutes their *formant structure*; and it is formant structure that determines whether a vowel sound, for instance, is perceived as /ae/ or /oo/ or /ee/ or something else. By the

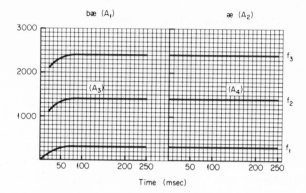

FIG. 1.6. Schematic representation of the speech sounds /bae/ and /ae/. The additional experimental conditions discussed consist of the middle bars, marked f_2, in each diagram.

same token, given the 250 msec time span shown in the figure, it is the presence or absence of a *transition* that determines whether a given utterance is heard as a consonantal–vowel (CV) combination rather than merely as a vowel. Transitions, then, as can be gleaned from the left hand side of Fig. 1.6, are time–dependent frequency shifts that reflect movements of the speech organs; and I want to stress their extreme importance in speech perception. Such transitions, which seldom exceed 40 msec in duration, are critical because they carry information about both the consonantal and the vowel portion of an utterance. In other words, given the two sounds in the schematic, which have a common formant structure except during a very short initial period of time, the presence of the particular transition shown determines that the stimulus labelled "A1" will be heard as /bae/; while its absence determines that the stimulus labeled "A2" will be heard as /ae/. I might note certain important clinical implications here in that any CNS defect such that temporal differences on the order of 40 msec might go undetected obviously would interfere with both comprehension and acquisition of language.

Now, having given you this very sketchy rundown on some matters that are of particular concern for my purposes, let me proceed further.

There has been a great deal of emphasis lately on experimental results, particularly those deriving from dichotic listening studies, showing that language sounds lateralize to the left hemisphere of the brain'and that music, nonlinguistic aspects of speech such as intonation, and various kinds of nonspeech signals lateralize to the right hemisphere. There also have been any number of theories to explain these results and, not to be outdone, we've come up with a theory of our own. Briefly, the hypothesis we've adopted is that lateralization of language functions relates in some part to specializations in the auditory system such that speech-like signals containing transitions within a critical range of durations are processed by a short-time constant system (Gersuni, 1971) that projects to the left temporal lobe; while longer–than–critical signals, processed by a long-time constant system project to the right temporal lobe.

Leaving aside for the moment the problem of what kinds of measures to use, let us consider how this hypothesis can be tested. The most economical approach, obviously, would be to select stimulus conditions on two bases: (1) according to whether or not they contain transitions; and (2) according to whether or not they are speech–like in nature.

Two of the conditions we've chosen are shown in Figure 1.6, – that is, /bae/, which is speech–like in nature and contains a transition; and /ae/, which is speech–like in nature but lacks a transition.

The question then arises as to what kinds of nonspeech signals can be matched to /bae/ and /ae/, and this poses more problems than you might suppose. Our original notion, which seemed entirely workable, was to make up noisebands in which the formant structure of /bae/ and /ae/ could be embedded. Unfortunately, when these conditions were generated at Haskins Laboratories (which supplied the master tape from which our current experiments derive), we discovered, by listening to them, that such structured noisebands sounded enough like the synthetic speech signals with which they would be compared that we might well be biasing the investigation against our hypothesis. At the suggestion of Haskins Lab. personnel, (Note 7), therefore, we decided instead to use as our comparison signals only the second formants of /bae/ and /ae/: These signals, both of which are bandnoises, provide contrast stimuli with and without transitional components.

To summarize our experiment, then, we are concerned with 4 well defined stimulus conditions: (1) a transition-containing synthetic speech sound, /bae/; (2) a steady-state synthetic speech sound, /ae/; (3) a transition-containing noiseband, the second formant of /bae/; and (4) the second formant of /ae/.

Under these conditions, we are testing our model by using both EEG and behavioral measures to approach a number of critical questions. First, by placing our EEG electrodes symmetrically at temporal (T_3 vs T_4) and central (C_3 vs C_4) sites on the scalp (Note 8), we are trying to find out whether hemispheric asymmetry in humans is demonstrable within the first 2 weeks of life. Second, assuming that asymmetry can be found,—which is far from certain,—we can relate it to the presence or absence of an onset–transition and thus marshall evidence for or against the proposition that hemispheric asymmetry for language sounds relates in some part to the existence of short– and long–time constant systems. Third, by determining whether EEG and/or behavioral response latencies vary systematically according to the stimulus conditions, we may be able to validate our notion that speech-like sounds are processed at higher levels of the auditory system than are other kinds of

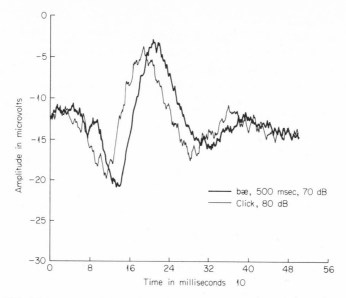

FIG. 1.7.   Average evoked responses at C₃ - A₁ site to a 70 dB synthetic / bae/ sound of 500 msec duration (____) and an 80 dB click stimulus (_ _ _) in one normal adult. In these data, derived from Research Institute Contract NO1-4-2816 (Marmarou, A. & Eisenberg, R. B. Manuscript in preparation) the interval between each of the 100 replications in each condition was 3 sec, and data have been smoothed. Note the consistently greater latency of the AEP to / bae/ as compared with a click of greater intensity.

signals. As a matter of fact, exploratory data on subjects older than 2 years (see Figure 1.7) suggests that the latency of certain components of the average evoked potential to sound (AEP) varies systematically according to whether the signal employed is a click or a synthetic speech sound, so we already have some preliminary support for this last notion.

The question of whether hemispheric asymmetry for speech and nonspeech sounds exists in earliest life seems to me entirely open. Although Molfese's (Note 6) thesis data suggest that the left hemisphere is specialized to process speech sounds at birth, his results have to be viewed skeptically because of procedural and other problems. There is no reason to assume that functional asymmetries exist in the auditory system simply because anatomical asymmetries in the area of the temporal planum can be found (Wada, Clarke & Hamm, 1975; Witelson & Pallie, 1973; Yeni-Komshian & Benson, 1976); nor can it be assumed that dichotic listening studies measure the same kinds of processes as are measured by evoked potentials. Whatever the facts may be, however, I think it useful, – if not critical, – to explore the AEP under well controlled stimulus conditions and at symmetrical derivations. Whether or not the answers we come up with are those we would like to find, we should obtain valuable insights into auditory organization and very useful operational information on newborn hearing processes.

Having exhausted what little can said at present about EEG asymmetries, let me now tell you about some of the behavioral data we've thus far collected from the current study. I think they are exciting because, after looking at more babies than can be counted for more years than I like to think about, we are seeing a higher incidence of certain behavioral response modes than any of us ever recall seeing before. Frankly, I'm not sure what constellation of factors is operating to produce what we're seeing on the video screen since this experiment is different in form from anything we've run before: the signals are shorter, that is, 250 msec, as opposed to a previous minimum of 500 msec; the schedule is longer, - this is, 60 latin–square–randomized replications per condition for a total of 240 presentations, as opposed to a previous maximum of 100 presentations; the interval between signals is latin–square–randomized between 13 and 16 sec, rather than regular; the properties of isolated formants have never before been explored in infants; the use of whole body indices is precluded by swaddling, so we're looking at faces far more carefully than we've ever looked at them before. In any event, whatever the effects of these new procedural variables and conditions, there is no question that we are seeing what I would characterize as "affective" behavior: some of it seems to be what Lou Lipsitt calls "hedonistic" in nature; some of it clearly is attentive in nature; and some of it can only be described as "rage".

Such behavior does not occur regularly, nor even,—so far as can be determined from data on 4 babies,—in response to a given signal. However, when it does occur, there is absolutely no mistaking it. I cannot recall seeing a baby quite literally grin after hearing a sound, but unless I discount the evidence of my senses and experience, I must assume that sound to have been pleasurable. I have seen eye widening and pupillary dilatation in response to patterned signals of one kind or another, but I have never seen eyes literally pop open and pupils dilate so widely that pinpoints of light are reflected and the sclera almost obliterated. I have heard babies whimper and cry when bombarded by stimulation during a time they would prefer to sleep, but I never before have seen them glare with anger, as if to say: "What do you mean by annoying me so!"

I am inclined to think, then, that what we have is a prepotent schedule and, indeed, I am beginning to wonder whether isolated formants, which are technically easier to control than speech sounds, may not have as much potential for clinical evaluation of hearing functions as the speech sounds from which they derive. I fear this is a question we will be unable to answer adequately until our experiment is completed, if then, but it is worth mentioning that every analysis undertaken on our first 4 subjects suggests that none of the experimental signals we are working with has differential properties by the behavioral measures we're using. To put this another way, all of the signals being used, whether fully structured synthetic speech sounds or merely the f_2 bands extracted from these sounds, seem to elicit differential behavior of much the same kind and in pretty much the same degree.

Perhaps this is the place to note that we did not undertake this experiment simply to prove or disprove a theory, but with an eventual clinical end in view. That aim is to develop rational and operationally useful procedures for evaluating the integrity of CNS mechanisms, and particularly of auditory mechanisms relating to language acquisition and comprehension. I am hopeful we will learn a great deal, but I think it is obvious we have a long way to go before our clinical objectives can be met either easily or economically.

Assuming, for the sake of discussion, that the auditory system—and perhaps other perceptual systems as well—in fact are organized along the hierarchical lines of our model (Fig. 1.5), let me now consider how such organization might bear upon the development of social responsiveness. What the model says, in effect, is that the infant normally is predisposed to respond to certain kinds of sensory stimuli that are not only pleasurable, but embodied in the person of the mother–caregiver. She is the most ubiquitous object in his immediate environment and, as such, an amalgam of prepotent stimuli to which the infant, by virtue of his neuronal organization, is programmed to respond. Her voice, which constitutes a patterned stimulus, is the most important sound he hears because it is presented, under wakeful conditions and at close quarters, during feeding and other caregiving activities. Her face, which also can be considered a patterned stimulus, is the object of closest regard during these activities. Further, these auditory and visual stimuli are associated not only with other percepts, but also with physical satisfactions, that is, with tactile and taste and olfactory sensations aroused during satiation of hunger, cessation of discomfort, and so on.

It is my feeling that, given a normal neuronal organization and an adequate caregiver, these sensory perceptions of the infant constitute the roots of both social and intellectual development. It is my further feeling that, given an aberrant neuronal organization or an inadequate caregiver, we can begin to develop operational techniques for assessment of, and intervention in, developmental problems only to the extent that we can elucidate the mechanisms underlying perceptual organization in early life.

I think it probable that all of us ultimately are working toward clinical goals and that all of us are pretty much in the same position: we are engaged in basic research in the sense that we are trying to learn how infants operate in order to apply that knowledge in a sensible and cost-effective way. What constitutes a major problem for too many of us, I fear, is a funding policy (not confined to the governmental sector) that places too high a priority on targeted research of limited value and too low a priority on basic research that can provide the body of knowledge to make targeted research productive rather than wasteful.

I can speak knowledgeably only of problems that exist in my own area of expertise, but I strongly suspect that similar problems exist in the entire developmental field. In audition, for instance, there has been a massive flow of money toward high risk registers and other screening procedures for infant deafness when, as a practical public health matter, the incidence of congenital deafness is so low that a cost-benefit ratio easily could be guessed at without formal analysis. Thanks to medical advances, deafness today is largely a problem among the elderly (whom we serve expensively but poorly) and among indigent populations of all ages who, for reasons of ignorance, lack of access to suitable facilities, neglect, or similar causes, fail to receive proper care. On the other hand, though we have no rational way of dealing with that exotic constellation of clinical entities grouped under such terms as "dysphasia", "dyslexia", "minimal brain damage", "communicative disorder", "learning disability", or what–have–you, until the nature and sequence of normal developmental processes can be defined, there has been only a trickle of funds for basic research in behaviors reflecting normal CNS processes. The time is long past due to recognize that we urgently need normative information of the kind the permits pediatricians to prescribe medication according to the age and electrolytic balance of young patients; and this will not be forthcoming either easily or cheaply. Most, if not all, of the questions that can be posed relatively cheaply already have been answered. The difficult questions confronting us today very probably will have to be asked in sophisticated ways, using electrophysiological measures, computers, and whatever new technical tools become available as we go along.

It seems to me that, among other things, the members of this conference might address themselves to the question of how the public and the fund-dispensing agencies might become better informed about the real research needs in the field of child development. A child in trouble is an appealing figure, but a field in trouble, as child development is today, assures that treatment of the child's trouble will be either ineffective or unnecessarily delayed.

Having expressed my concerns about the mix of funds for targeted and basic research in the hope that I am speaking for all of us, I think I now owe you the chance to ask whatever specific questions may have occurred to you.

ACKNOWLEDGMENTS

Research considered in this paper was supported by the Public Health Service under Grant No. R 01 HD 00732 from the Institute of Child Health and Human Development.

DISCUSSION

Dr. Denenberg: What was the age of the smile?
Dr. Eisenberg: Before answering you, let me note that I've been reporting

on very preliminary data here—and by preliminary, I mean only the first four subjects we've been able to analyze. It takes a two-person team (my nurse and myself) about 25 hours to eyeball the 1-hour videotape record on a single subject because so many tasks are involved: noting the time of occurrence in hours, minutes, and seconds of 240 randomized stimulus events; scoring prestimulus state during the 2 seconds immediately prior to each event; deciding whether a response event has occurred and, if so, describing it in sequence and noting—in real time—when it began and when it was completed. It then takes us another 24 hours or so per subject to code the data in various ways on various forms, to make scattergrams, and so forth. Under the circumstances, some of the data stick in my mind pretty well, and I can tell you quite precisely that smiling, in one form or another, was scored in all four subjects. One was 3 days old, two were 11 days old; and one was 12 days old. However, I don't remember which of the babies grinned or, in fact, how many of them did so.

Dr. Denenberg: Did you say that Conditions 3 and 4, which are the random-noise ones—

Dr. Eisenberg: They're not random noise. They're selected formants that might be viewed as embedded signals. As I tried to make clear, what we did was take out of /bae/ and /ae/ the f2 bands that constitute part of their structure and consider them noise bands, which in fact they are.

Dr. Denenberg: Did some particular signals elicit the grin?

Dr. Eisenberg: I honestly can't remember—any more than I can remember whether it was present in the older infants and not in the 3-day-old. Right now I'm inclined to think that we're probably dealing with complex interactions between state and signal variables—and that signal-specific effects may not be demonstrable by behavioral measures. I am hopeful they will be demonstrable by EEG measures, but we haven't even looked at our evoked potential data yet. We don't have a computer of our own, unfortunately, so we have to ship our data tapes to Houston for processing. This creates a good many problems, the biggest of which is budgetary, and we're waiting to accumulate enough tapes for batch processing because it's cheaper to handle things that way.

Dr. Denenberg: So A1 and A2 elicited the grins. (See Fig. 1.6)

Dr. Eisenberg: It may be A3. A1, A2 and A4 all elicited the grin.

Dr. Denenberg: A3 is the second formant of "bah."

Dr. Eisenberg: Right. It may be simply that the presence of a transition determines lateralization in the brain. My prediction was that "bah" might lateralize to the left and "ah" to the right because it lacks a transition. By the same token, A3 might lateralize to the left, and A4 not at all. I don't know what the EEG is going to tell us. What I could not predict at the start of this experiment was the behavior we are seeing. In fact, it's the first time I've ever seen such behavior. I never saw grins before, and it's true they're not frequent—partially, I think, because we do everything to keep those children asleep, because what we're really interested in is the EEG data.

Dr. Lipsitt: Is there anything remarkable about heart rate during the grins?

Dr. Eisenberg: We're not running heart rate now, unfortunately. NIH didn't give me money for that, though I would very much have liked to use correlative cardiac measures.

Dr. Papousek: There's one very important notion we have to pay more attention to, and that is whether there is a differential response to the first application or to the repeated application of a stimulus.

Dr. Eisenberg: I assume from your remark that you are referring to the effects of sequence, and I can assure you that it's one of the things we've considered very carefully on the basis of our own experience. Certainly, in our experimental design, we've taken great pains to avoid both adaptation and habituation. As I noted, both the signals in our schedule and the intervals between them are latin-square-randomized.

The intervals are well in excess of 10 seconds specifically because there are data showing this amount of time to be required for full recovery of the brain wave response (Eisenberg, 1976, p. 33). More to the point, we will be taking the effects of sequence into account in data analysis, since we will be exploring not merely the functional properties of discrete signals, but also how each of our measures changes over the course of our stimulus schedule. We will be looking at changes of state over time, at whether the functional properties of signals change as a function of state and/or as a function of sequence, at whether response modes change systematically over time and repetitions.

The point you've raised is a very important one when one is bombarding a single modality or even multiple modalities, and I completely agree with you that no response in an experimental schedule is independent of preceding stimulus and response events. Indeed, I'm sorry I did not specify our concern with this issue in my presentation, and if you can suggest anything we haven't thought of to tease out the effects of sequence, I'll be more than grateful.

Dr. Korner: Are your smiling responses in any way time related, that is, did most of them happen in the beginning, or later in the schedule?

Dr. Eisenberg: I think that they're state-related rather than time-related though we don't have enough data really to make any definitive statements. I'm not sure it's fair to judge on the basis of only four subjects, but I have a pretty strong impression that the smiling responses we've scored as such have occurred primarily under waking conditions.

However, since we are quite strict about ruling out smiles when we feel they are merely a reflection of state (particularly doze) rather than stimulus-bound events, we may be biasing our data to some extent.

Dr. Watson: My question has to do with your model. What you are saying is that, in general, there is a hierarchal filtering system.

Dr. Eisenberg: I think it's a little bit oversimplified to consider the model simply as a filtering system, since it is concerned mainly with possible mechanisms for processing and storage of acoustic information.

Dr. Watson: Granted. The essential question is how you are handling the recent ripples in the field of speech perception and the concept of prepotency as it relates to lower animals like chinchillas as well as man.

Dr. Eisenberg: You refer, I think to the Kuhl and Miller data (Science 190:69-72).

Dr. Watson: Not knowing much about the area, it seems to me that's an important piece of information in that it asks the question whether or not speech is a particularly human thing, and whether the initial responses of the infant to speech are built in by the experience of language.

Dr. Eisenberg: In the first place, I do not regard synthetic "ae" or "bae" sounds as speech, and I don't think the newborn infant has any concepts whatever about speech or language. In the second place—and this is a point I discuss at some length in my book—I would expect, purely on the basis of what is known about evolution and biology, that if a chinchilla can discriminate between "ae" and "bae," a baby is going to be able to do as well—provided, of course, we employ measures sensitive enough to pick up his discriminative capacities. Personally, I have a feeling—which I trust those working in the area of feature detector systems in humans will not become too enraged about—that there is too much effort going into proving the existence of such mechanisms. Certainly, there is no particular reason to suppose that any or all feature detectors have to be high-level mechanisms: They have been reported for fish, birds, several species of lower vertebrates; and primates; and it seems to me evident they must exist in man. In other words, they're something I'm perfectly willing to accept on faith. The question that seems far more critical to me is what man's auditory system *can* do that the auditory system of lower species *cannot* do. Let me see if I can make myself clearer. All animals have communicative codes that serve well-defined biological purposes, and, in all species studied, there is evidence of a systematic relation between what goes into the ears and what comes out of the mouth. However, man has the most complicated communicative code of any species, and I know of no unequivocal evidence to show that even primates can be taught to comprehend human language by hearing alone. I therefore am making an assumption—perhaps ill-founded—that such complicated codes could not have evolved in the absence of certain auditory specializations unique to the human organism. Assuming they exist, then, I am making some guesses about what form they possibly might take and using EEG measures in the way I've described in an attempt to get at one possibility. From a theoretical standpoint, a hierarchal model is useful because it accords with what we know about how organisms function, is testable in various ways, and is neither species-nor modality-specific. From a clinical standpoint, it has implications of some importance in that control infants will show differential behavior to a hierarchy of stimulus conditions, whereas infants with pathologies of one sort or another will not. An anencephalic infant, for instance, responds in exactly the same way to a speech sound as he does to a click or a pure tone or a noise band; that is, if it's loud enough for him to hear it, he will startle. As a matter of personal experience, then, it's my feeling that such current approaches to infant auditory testing as electrocochleography, early brain stem potentials, and the like, though useful in ruling out deafness, can prove of very limited value in differentiating cerebral dysfunction or in predicting the course of language acquisition in high-risk subjects. As I see it, there must be at least three kinds of specializations underlying man's communicative behavior. The auditory system has its own specializations, which may or may not be uniquely human: That is a question that only comparative research can answer. The vocal system very probably is uniquely specialized in man in that there is evidence for structural differences among species. And finally, I am intensely biased towards the view that association cortex plays a crucial role in the development of language functions. Indeed, I wonder whether the really important questions about language development may not center about the organization of association cortex, which develops at a relatively slow rate. I say this after 15 years of work in audition and despite the fact that we also have spent a good deal of time and effort exploring prelinguistic utterance patterns in the period between birth and about 14 months. On this latter score, let me confess my doubts as to whether the results justified the efforts. We did learn that prelinguistic patterns of development were regular enough to be charted, and we still believe they represent, in some part at least, structural changes related to maturation. There is nothing much one can say beyond this, however, and I suspect that real knowledge about basic communicative mechanisms in man ultimately will derive from comparative studies. There are too few of these, partly perhaps because there are too few really crossdisciplinary programs, and certainly because there has been so little impetus for them at policy and funding levels.

Dr. Parmelee: In terms of the model, I want to propose some changes.

Dr. Eisenberg: I'm not sure I believe my model myself, but let me clarify whether you are referring to the first one (Figure 1.4) or the second (Figure 1.5).

Dr. Parmelee: I'm referring to Figure 1.4. Actually, the question is a relatively simple one. If one thinks of it in terms of decision-making processes, it would seem to me that—

Dr. Eisenberg: You mean decision-making processes in the neural sense?

Dr. Parmelee: In any sense, but for the moment—the first decision is to control the volume. It's either too loud or too soft, rather than the frequency. I'm talking about a reflex or something that sets the volume, and then the next decision is, is it patterned or not patterned.

Dr. Eisenberg: I'm not sure that I follow you. In the first place, there is a very great range between soft and loud; and I'm not sure anything I would call decision making is involved in the determination of loudness.

Dr. Parmelee: Okay. Then the real decision is whether or not a signal is patterned, and from then on, the analyses have to do with what kinds of patterns are involved—whether frequency alone, or what have you.

Dr. Eisenberg: I'm trying very hard to think of a way to answer your question simply and clearly, and I'm not sure I can. I thought I had covered the model about as well as I could in my written paper, but since my effort apparently wasn't good enough, let me give it another try here. First the model says that very low down in the auditory system, at the level of the cochlea, there's a gating mechanism such that high frequency sounds are filtered through nonspecific mechanisms to later become organized into an "affective" system. (If you want to consider this "decision making" instead of "gating," I guess you could do so, but I don't feel comfortable with such terms myself.) Further, from the standpoint of social and emotional development, I think it might be very important to study high frequency sounds in affective context—something which I don't think anybody, including myself, has looked at systematically.

Second, the model says there are storage facilities at all levels as we ascend in the nervous system—not merely in the auditory system, but in other systems as well: Thus, coded acoustic information can be retrieved in different forms and by different systems at given levels. This perhaps is controlled by biochemical specializations, but I find it difficult to relate to decision-making processes. Possibly, at the second level of the hierarchy, where neuronal mechanisms theoretically are so arranged that discrete parameters of sound, such as sound pressure level, frequency, phase, rise time, and so on, are analyzed, one could think in those terms. In any event, however you choose to think about processes, the model says that significant features of signals are extracted for further processing at higher levels, while insignificant ones, filtered through nonspecific systems, are elaborated into various kinds of subceptor systems serving a variety of purposes that bear upon how we behave in everyday life. Both models (that is, as shown in either Figure 1.4 or Figure 1.5) are concerned solely with the possible functional architecture—if I may use such terminology—of the auditory system; and they are so tentative there seems little point in trying to relate them to decision making, neural networks, or other formal theories. Our only immediate concern is whether there are specific mechanisms concerned with the processing of speech sounds that are characterized by transitions. Both models make the assumption that such mechanisms must be located at relatively high levels of the nervous system on a purely logical basis. That is to say, we feel there must be some point at which, after information irrelevant for further processing in the auditory system has been filtered out, the extracted bits of relevant information can be put back together in a bundle to be operated on at cognitive and motor levels. We arrive at this conclusion only because it is illogical to suppose that language, an organized cognitive system, could evolve in the absence of "chunked" acoustic information or that speech, as a time-locked, bundle-matched output, could exist. We don't even attempt to deal with the problems of central mechanisms, the function of associative cortex, or the nature of vocal system specializations because we're so hard put just to deal with questions about how the auditory system might work. The only real difference between Figure 1.4 and Figure 1.5 is that the second version substitutes for what we first called "ensemble" and "serial order" processing, short- and long-time constant systems that project either to the nondominant hemisphere (Level 3) or the dominant one (Level 4). It is at this point, perhaps, where "decision making" in the neural sense may be relevant, because we are saying that the nondominant hemisphere is concerned specifically with sounds that are "not speech" and the dominant hemisphere with sounds are "speech." Figure 1.5 is, if you like, simply a testable guess of where levels 3 and 4 conceivably might be located—and it may not necessarily be a good guess since it's purely an empiric one. That is to say, it's based largely on scattered bits of information about communicative function in normal and aberrant subjects and known facts about the physical properties of sounds—particularly their duration characteristics. For instance, if you study the literature on musical sounds, transitions are found to be in excess of 40 msec, and dichotic listening studies have shown musical sounds to be perceived primarily by the nondominant hemisphere; if you study what little literature there is on intonation, you come up with pretty much the same answer. On the other hand, we know that short transitions are characteristic of connected speech, and there is increasing evidence to show that patients who have difficulty in discriminating signals in the duration range for speech transitions also have severe communicative problems. I am inclined to think the basic dysfunction in *developmental* disorders of communication is probably biochemically based—as opposed to lesion-based—but that speculation is quite outside the concerns of this conference.

Dr. Parmelee: I think we shouldn't get hung up on priority. I'm just wondering if the function permitting determination of pattern-not-pattern comes in very early and then detailed analysis is achieved subsequently.

Dr. Eisenberg: I can't bring myself to believe that. You may well be right, but there is nothing in my data to support such a view. Moreover, our data on differential behaviors, on habituation rates, and on AEP latencies as a function of stimulus conditions supports the existence of hierarchy.

Dr. Parmelee: The evoked response pattern is over association areas.

Dr. Eisenberg: In newborn babies? What capability for association does the newborn baby have?

Dr. Parmelee: I'm talking about cortex. You are recording a long distance from the auditory cortex.

Dr. Eisenberg: That may be true, but if I'm using the differential symmetric placements I've already described and find that latencies for speech-like sounds quite regularly are greater than those found for nonspeech sounds (as in Figure 1.7), it can be assumed it took longer for the speech signal to arrive at cortical areas. We already have scattered data on newborns, 2- to 4-year-old children, and adults (Marmarou & Eisenberg, unpublished data) to show this. This may not be a correct assumption, and, in fact, Nelson Kiang, who thinks my model is merely a fantasy, has suggested a number of other physiological explanations that are entirely plausible. For all I know, the model indeed may be a fantasy and you may be more right than I, but until I'm proved wrong, I'm perfectly willing to stick my neck out on it. For the moment, on the basis of my clinical and research experience as well as the known facts of physiology, it seems to me the simplest and most economical guess that I can make about how the auditory system works.

REFERENCE NOTES

1. Lemkau, Paul. Personal communication.
2. Unpublished Bioacoustic Laboratory data.
3. Coleman, M. & Eisenberg, R. B. *Correlative studies of auditory behavior in autistic children and their matched controls.* Unpublished Bioacoustic Laboratory study. (St. Joseph Hospital, Lancaster, Pa. 17604).
4. Unpublished Bioacoustic Laboratory data.
5. Barnet, A. B., deSotillo, M. & Campos, M. S. *EEG sensory evoked potentials in early infancy malnutrition.* Paper presented at the Society for Neuroscience, St. Louis, Missouri, 1974.
6. Molfese, D. L. *Cerebral asymmetry in infants, chlidren, and adults: Auditory evoked responses to speech and noise stimuli.* Ph. D thesis, Pennsylvania State University, University Park, Pennsylvania, 1972.
7. Specifically, Terry Halwes, whose help with technical aspects of our work is gratefully acknowledged.
8. We additionally are using a vertex (C_z) derivation, but our sole purpose in doing so is to permit comparison between our findings for these kinds of signals and those in the literature for constant stimuli such as clicks or pure tones.

REFERENCES

Cohen, L. P., & Salapatek, P. (Eds.) *Infant perception* (Vol. 1). New York: Academic Press, 1974.

Crook, C., K. & Lipsitt, L. P. Neonatal nutritive sucking: Effects of taste stimulation upon sucking rhythm and heart rate. *Child Development, 1976, 47,* 518–522.

Crowell, D. H., Jones, R. H., Kapuniai, L. E., & Nakagawa, J. K. Unilateral cortical activity in newborn humans: An early index of cerebral dominance? *Science, 1973, 180,* 205–208.

Eisenberg, R. B. Auditory behavior in the human neonate. I. Methodologic problems and the logical design of research procedures. *Journal of Auditory Research, 1965, 5,* 159–177.

Eisenberg, R. B. The ontogeny of auditory behavior in humans. In L. Jilek & S. Trojan (Eds.), *Otogenesis of the brain* (Vol. 2). Prague, Czechoslovakia: Univsitas Carolina Pragensis, 1974.

Eisenberg, R. B. *Auditory competence in early life: The roots of communicative behavior.* Baltimore, Md.: University Park Press, 1976.

Engen, T., Lipsitt, L. P., & Kaye, H. Olfactory response and adaptation in the human neonate. *Journal of Comparative Physiological Psychology, 1963, 56,* 73–77.

Gersuni, G. V. (Ed.), *Sensory processes at the neuronal and behavioral levels.* New York: Academic Press, 1971.

Hutt, C., & Hutt, S. J. The neonatal evoked heart rate response and the law of initial value. *Nature*, 1970, *220*, 618–620.

Hutt, S. J., Hutt, C., Lenard, H. G., Bernuth, H. v., & Muntjewerff, W. J. Auditory responsivity in the human neonate. *Nature*, 1968, *218*, 888–890.

Lenard, H. G., Bernuth, H. v., & Hutt, S. J. Acoustic evoked responses in newborn infants: The influence of pitch and complexity of the stimulus. *Electroencephalograry and Clinical Neurophysiology, 1969*, 27, 121–127.

Nowlis, G. H., & Kessen, W. Human newborns differentiate differing concentrations of sucrose and glucose. *Science*, 1976, *191*, 865–866.

Peiper, A. *Cerebral function in infancy and childhood.* New York: Consultants Bureau of New York, 1963.

Wada, J. A., Clarke, R. & Hamm, A. Cerebral hemispheric asymmetry in humans. *Archives of Neurology*, 1975, *32*, 239–246.

Witelson, S. F., & Pallie, W. Left hemisphere specialization for language in the newborn: Neuroanatomical evidence of asymmetry. *Brain*, 1973, *96*, 641–646.

Yeni-Komshian, G. H., & Benson, D. A. Anatomical study of cerebral asymmetry in the temporal lobe of humans, chimpanzees, and Rhesus monkeys. *Science*, 1976, *192*, 387–389.

2 Perception of Contingency as a Determinant of Social Responsiveness

John S. Watson
University of California, Berkeley

Two general views have dominated the history of speculation on the origin and maintenance of social responsiveness in humans and other social animals. Just as has been the case for most other significant psychological traits, social responsiveness has had a history of theorizing that has swung upon the pendulum of nativistic versus empiricistic thinking. The recent growth of interest in ethological analysis of human social behavior (e.g., Ainsworth, 1967; Bowlby, 1958, 1969; Eibl-Eibesfeldt, 1970; Lewis & Rosenblum, 1973) represents a clear swing back from the empiricism of Freudian and social learning theories (e.g., Miller & Dollard, 1941; Sears, Maccoby, & Levin, 1957; Bandura & Walters, 1963), which had held sway since the fall of interest in specific instinct theory (e.g., McDougall, 1923) a half-century ago.

If we imagine that the pendulum is now midway in its swing from recent empiricistic heights, it might be useful to momentarily stop the movement and consider the potential limitations inherent in the traditional path traversed. An objective of this paper is to show that traditional definitions of simple nativistic and empiricistic mechanisms have limited our view of what may constitute the structure of experience. It is hoped that if we overcome this limitation, the timing and related productivity of future swings in our conceptual pendulum might be improved.

With specific regard to social responsiveness, the extreme nativist and empiricist positions can be stated simply as follows: Extreme nativism holds that social objects are "recognized" innately and that social response to the appropriate physical stimulus complex is produced (released) on an innate ("prewired") motor program; extreme empiricism holds that the organism learns to be especially responsive to social objects as a result of experiencing a history of contingencies wherein the physical properties of social objects are associated with stimuli that have innate potency to elicit specific behavior (i.e., classical conditioning) or with stimuli that have innate potency to reinforce behavior that has been emitted (i.e., operant conditioning). The nativistic and empiricistic perspectives are in absolute opposition as regards the necessity of prior experience in determining special responsiveness to social objects. Yet, notably, both perspectives have traditionally defined experience as composed of the physical properties of stimuli and responses (which the organism is capable of sensing). Implicit in both perspectives is the assumption that the physical properties of stimuli and responses either do or do not have inherent potency, and, if not, then the acquistion of potency may be transferred from or shaped by the experience of contingent relations to other potent stimuli. From this perspective on experience, both nativists and empiricists would traditionally concur that if an instance of behavior in a specific stimulus context required prior exposure of the organism to a contingent series of stimulus occurrences, then the behavioral reaction in question could not be termed innate.

What is overlooked in this view of experience is that a contingent relation in any history of exposure to physical stimuli may itself comprise the significant structure of the experience. That is to say, contingency may not simply be a conduit for the transfer or shaping of stimulus potency, but rather contingency may be a source of potency in its own right for eliciting social responsiveness. As one begins to consider this possibility, and questions arise as to whether special responsiveness to the perception of contingency is itself innate or acquired, then it would seem evident that some adjustment must be made to the conceptual path of our pendulum—either in our definition of innate and learned or in our definition of experience. An adjustment of the latter would seem the easiest to conceive.

Let us propose then, for the purpose of this chapter at least, that organisms may perceive contingent relations between stimuli and/or responses and the perception of contingency per se may have a special significance (innate or acquired) for some organisms. We are here beginning to treat a contingency as we have traditionally treated the concept of a stimulus. It is easy to underestimate the novelty of this vantage point. Therefore, before continuing on to a necessarily abstract discussion of how various forms of contingency might be perceived as the focal structure of experience, let us briefly consider some concrete examples of how perception of contingency per se might affect social responsiveness in man and other animals.

Recognition of Social Objects

Watson (1972) has proposed that the perception of the contingent relation between responding and subsequent stimulation is possibly the major initial influence in guiding the human infant to classify fellow members of the species as "social objects." In a set of studies of instrumental learning (Watson, 1972; Watson & Ramey, 1972) in which 8-week-old infants were provided a means of controlling the movement of a mobile over their cribs by movement of their head on a special pillow for a period of 10 minutes per day, mothers reported that exuberant smiling and cooing occurred after a few days of exposure. Mothers of infants in other experimental conditions, where no control over the mobile was possible, did not report a similar increase of these social responses to the mobile. It was concluded that these and other data on early social responsiveness make sense if one assumes the human infant is innately organized to orient towards the stimulus context of his initial experience of a clear contingency for this will most likely arise in "game" situations with fellow members of the species.

In a series of studies on the stimulus control of social attractiveness in rats, Latane and his colleagues (Latane & Hothersall, 1972; Latane, Joy, Meltzer, & Lubell, 1972; Werner and Latane, 1974) observed that social orienting toward an experimenter's hand increased with experience in "interactive" handling. The potential for interaction with a stimulus appears to hold an attraction that far outweighs that of various static physical dimensions that are associated with the biological structure of rats. These researchers have concluded that interaction with the rat's behavior is itself a major, possibly the primary, determinant of the rat's social orientation. In the words of Werner and Latane (1974):

> Rats were very attracted to other rats but, when allowed to become familiar with the hand, were equally attracted to and showed similar reactions to it. Social deprivation had equivalent effects on attraction to hands as to rats. Such results cannot be explained by theories that attribute rodent sociability to attraction to physical characteristics only. Behavioral not physical cues and the opportunity for interaction seem to be the source and the satisfaction of social attraction [p.328].

In both Watson's report with infants and Latane's with rats, it is important to note that surrogate social objects appear to have obtained social significance (i.e., become targets of social responses) solely by presentation in a context where contingent relations were existent between the subject's behavior and available stimulation. In neither case is there evidence that social responsiveness was either transferred or shaped by the contingency experience. Rather, it would seem that the contingency experience was itself the eliciting experience.

Arousal of Agonistic Behavior

The perception of contingency may serve to determine negative as well as positive social interaction. With some moderation by stimulus context and developmental level of the animal, contingency perception could well serve as a major influence in the control of defensive and aggressive behavior both within and between species. For example, it would seem to provide an answer to a curious predatory-prey relation that presents a puzzle for traditional analysis, which focuses on physical-stimulus elements alone. It has been observed that members of a herd of certain ungulates will frantically avoid a hungry lion. The large cat must work hard and craftily for its meal. Yet once the cat has made a kill, the rest of the herd stop their frantic flight and resume calmly grazing within close range of the feeding cat. The question to be answered, of course, is just how do the surviving members of the herd come to ignore a stimulus configuration (the cat) that they seemed so wildly frightened by only minutes before. Speculation could surely range from changes in the smell of the cat to subtle visual signs (e.g., ear position). The difficulty for these explanations, in addition to a lack of direct evidence for them, is that if the cat possessed such potent signals for controlling the flight behavior of its prey, then it seems odd that evolution has failed to capitalize on this fact in shaping the cat's predatory behavior.

There is one thing that cannot be altered in predatory behavior, however. To succeed it must eventuate in contact with the prey. In instances where predatory behavior requires stalking the prey, there will of necessity be a contingent relation between the behavior of the predator and the prey. It seems quite plausible that prey would use this contingency, when perceived, as a cue for flight. Thus it may be that once the cat has grounded its target, the rest of the herd stops flight because no member of the herd is excited to flight by perceiving the cat's movements as being contingent on its own. Carried to the extreme, the use of contingent behavior as a signal might even provide the sole mechanism for some species to identify its predators. It is even conceivable that some predators identify prey by their contingent avoidance—though we should expect such prey to evolve adaptive freezing.

It need be mentioned only briefly, but the plausible use of perceived behavioral contingency as a determinant of predator–prey interactions suggests a clear likelihood that the same mechanism functions in controlling agonistic behavior within a species. One might even argue that its use is made more likely by the fact that so many physical features are shared by members of the same species. Surely, specific physical stimulus configurations of visual, auditory, and olfactory cues are operative as determinants of agonistic behavior in most species, but it is not difficult to imagine that there could be yet a large role played by behavioral contingency.

Courtship

As a final example of the potential widespread use of perceived contingency in the determination of social responsiveness, the domain of courtship and sexual encounter would seem very likely. The "dances" and other interactive sequences displayed in the course of mate selection in various species may not be just interlocked chains of stimuli and responses wherein each animal's behavior is a physical stimulus configuration provocative to the other. In addition, it could be that much of such interaction is a means of displaying forms of behavioral contingency. We consider variations in contingency form later in this chapter, but the point to be made here is that the arousing and binding cues in courtship may not be so much the specific stimulus conditions as these sequentially impact upon the sensorium. Rather, it may well be that a critical aspect of the interaction is the perception of contingency within the sequence of the animal's behavior and the behavior of the candidate for mate selection.

The preceding examples should serve to at least suggest the range of possibilities in which perceived contingency might function in determining social responsiveness. The history of search for specific physical dimensional control has bypassed the question of how important perception of contingency per se might be in the origin and maintenance of social responsiveness in any social species. To examine this question for the case of humans or any other animal, however, one will need to formulate some basic notions about the process of contingency perception. It should shortly become evident that any adequate conception of this process will not be simple. An objective of this chapter is to provide a working model of contingency perception and to report some results of its use in research with infants. Let us now turn to that task.

A MODEL OF CONTINGENCY PERCEPTION

To begin, consider the case where a response, R, has some efficacy in the causal determination of a stimulus, S. This form of contingency can be represented as a case where the probability of S is a function of the probability of R, or $P_S = f P_R$. Perfect contingency would exist if R were a necessary and sufficient cause of S. Were that so, then every response would produce a stimulus. The subject could control the rate of occurrence of the stimulus perfectly by varying his rate of response.

Now consider how this contingent relationship between R and S might be diminished. There are two ways. One is by having the stimulus fail to occur on some occasions when R has occurred. When this situation of reduced contingency is arranged in a laboratory of learning, it is termed a partial schedule of reinforcement (or intermittent reward). The other way of reducing the contingency is by introducing the occurrence of the stimulus independent of the occurrence of the response. When this situation of reduced contingency is arranged, it is termed a condition of noncontingent or response-independent stimulation.

Remarkably, these two ways of reducing the contingency of a stimulus on a response have received separate and very unequal attention in the experimental literature. There has been extensive study of intermittent, or partial, reinforcement particularly by Skinner and his colleagues (e.g., Ferster & Skinner, 1957). However, the second way of reducing a contingency, involving response-independent occurrence of the stimulus, has only recently received attention as an experimental variable in its own right. Previously, the presentation of reinforcement noncontingently was introduced only as a control condition to assess "pseudo-conditioning" arousal effects of the stimulus (Brackbill & Koltsova, 1967). It has been only within the last decade that researchers have become concerned with the apparent lasting interference with later learning that may arise from experiencing a history of noncontingent occurrences of the reinforcement stimulus (Seligman, 1975; Maier, Seligman, & Solomon, 1969; Watson, 1971). Apparently, if a subject, be he human infant or laboratory rat, fails to perceive a contingency between his behavior and some recurrent stimulation, then his ability to perceive a contingency in later situations will be greatly impaired even if the stimulus is then perfectly contingent and seemingly obvious. While this recent research on noncontingent stimulation effects provides a strong impetus for the inquiry into how organisms perceive contingency, the research can offer little to this end. The universal limitation of existing research in this area is that noncontingency has always been presented in pure form.

To make this important point clearly, it is necessary to consider a method of representing the degree of contingency between a behavior and the stimuli related to it. If one considers the conditional probability of the stimulus within time following the response $P\,(S/Rt)$, then the strength of the contingency can be represented as the proportion of times the stimulus occurs (within some specified span of time [t]) following the response, that is, $\Sigma R{\rightarrow}S^{(t)}/\Sigma R$.[1] Investigations of partial reinforcement effects in studies of operant learning use this index to specify the degree of contingency (though the index is stated in reciprocal form). Alternatively, one can represent the contingency by referring to the conditional probability of the response within time preceding the stimulus, $P(R/tS)$, in which case the index would be

---

[1] The conventional way of representing this conditional probability would be $P\,(S/R)$. The choice to use $P\,(S/Rt)$ is made to allow a distinction in temporal sequence, that is, between the case where S precedes, $P\,(S/tR)$, versus follows, $P\,(S/Rt)$, the response and between the case where R precedes, $P\,(R/tS)$, versus follows, $P\,(R/St)$, the stimulus. The unconventional symbol also allows the addition of a temporal qualification introduced later. This temporal qualification is in the form of a time limit t and is essential to the perceptual structure of the model. The virtue of specifying a temporal limit to a conditional probability is perhaps easiest to recognize in considering that the answer to the question, What is the probability of s, given r? will always be 1.00 if an infinite time for assessment is allowed (e.g., if one is allowed to wait forever in the case of the question of conditional occurrence of the S following the R and each element has some probability greater than 0).

calculated as the proportion of times the response occurs (within some specified span of time [t]) prior to the stimulus, that is, $\Sigma R \leftarrow S^{(t)}/\Sigma S$. Put anthropomorphically, the first index would help answer the question, Is my behavior sufficient to cause the stimulus? and the second index would help answer the question, Is my behavior necessary to cause the stimulus? Both questions are obviously relevant to our sense of possessing control over an event. What is not obvious is the extent to which these indices may differ in a situation where less than perfect contingency exists. Yet with the help of a few illustrations the point should be made clear.

Consider the situation in which half a subject's responses are followed (within t=1 second) by a particular reward stimulus. Also assume the stimulus never occurs independent of the response. In this case, a pure case of partial reinforcement, the conditional probability $P(S/Rt)$ would be .5. But now note that when one asks what is the conditional probability of the response preceding the stimulus, one observes that every stimulus occurrence is preceded by a response. $P(R/tS)$ would be 1.00. Now consider the converse case. Every response of the subject is followed (within 1 second) by the stimulus, but the stimulus also occurs an equal number of times on its own. In this case, then, $P(S/Rt)$ is 1.00 and $P(R/tS)$ is .5. It is evident that the two probabilities are logically free to vary, with the only exception to total independence being that if one index has a positive value the other cannot be 0. All other combinations of values are possible.

When considering the range of possible values of $P(R/tS)$, it is important to note that all values between 1.00 and 0 (exclusively) require that the subject be in a situation in which the stimulus is sometimes being produced by his behavior and sometimes the stimulus is occurring on its own. It seems extraordinary, but the long history of research on instrumental learning in man and animals has apparently never examined learning in a situation of this kind. It is all the more extraordinary when one considers the likelihood that situations of this kind are the rule rather than the exception in the general experience of most animals including man. One seldom holds the sole source of control over any stimulus event. A major source of response-independent occurrence of stimuli will be the effects of the behavior of other animals. It seems likely that social species, and particularly their young, would be exposed to a great part of their contingency experience in a manner where $P(R/tS)$ would be in the range between 0 and 1.00. For example, even the most successful of babies whose vocalization consistently obtains a vocal response from its mother will yet experience instances when its mother speaks for other reasons. It is evident, therefore, that if we believe contingency experience plays an important role in human development then we will want to understand how contingency is perceived in common yet heretofore unexplored conditions where stimuli occur both contingently and noncontingently at the same time.

We have noted that a contingency situation can be seen to provide two virtually independent indices of contingency. It should be obvious, then, that one question in the area of contingency perception will be how these two indices function to determine the clarity of an existing contingency, that is, do they have separable effects and/or do they interact in their effect on contingency experience? Below we shall present some evidence that in the case of the human infant, at least, it would appear that these indices interact in a rather special way. But to properly introduce the research to be presented it is necessary to clarify an important difference between the indices of contingency as these are related to a subject's rate of behavior. The first thing to note is that the accurate perception of contingency cannot be based solely on the indices thus far described. Each index needs to be viewed in the context of its deviation from chance expectancy. That is, to appreciate $P(S/Rt) = .6$ as an implication of contingency, one needs to compare it with the probability of the stimulus S occurring within time t of the response by chance. If the probability of S following a response within time t is no different from the probability of S within time t of any moment (selected at random), then the occurrence of S would not be properly classed as contingent on R.[2]

The distribution in time of an event occurring repeatedly by chance at some given rate is known to have a distribution conforming to the negative exponential $e-\lambda t$ where λ is the event rate (e.g., events per second) and t is the interval width from any random point in time and $1 - e^{-\lambda t}$ equals the probability of an event's occurrence within that interval. (See discussion of "renewal processes" in Cox, 1962; McGill, 1963). So then, to accurately assess the existence of contingency when $P(S/Rt)$ is known, it will be necessary to contrast it with $P(S/rand.t)$ which will equal $1 - e^{-\lambda t}$ where $\lambda = \Sigma S/T$ and t is the specified amount of time from any random point in time, rand., and T is the time span of the experience. If this value is significantly different from the former, then one may conclude that a contingent relation exists.

Likewise, when $P(R/tS)$ is known, it is necessary to contrast this value with $2P(R/t\ rand.)$, which will equal $1 - e^{-\lambda t}$ where $\lambda = \Sigma R/T$ (note R is reference in this case) and t is the specified amount of time from any random point in time. If the value is different from $P(R/tS)$, then one has evidence of a contingency. If one works through the potential variation in the set of four relevant probabilities [i.e., $P(S/Rt)$, $P(S/rand.\ t)$, $P(R/tS)$, and $P(R/t\ rand.)$] the following notable deductions will be clear: (1) It is possible for one index to

---

[2]Appreciation of contingency has at times been conceived as visible in the relationship between the conditional $P(S/R)$ and $P(S/\bar{R})$ where the latter is said to represent the probability of S given not R—for example, discussions by Rescorla, 1967; Seligman, 1975. However, as usually conceived these conditionals are logically unrelatable. $P(S/R)$ is assessable on the basis of countable occurrences of R. $P(S/\bar{R})$ is *not* assessable on the basis of countable occurrences of $\bar{R}$)however. For example, one can not count the number of times one did not blink during the preceding minute. The present use of temporally based conditionals avoids this logical problem.

differ from its chance comparison by a greater amount than the other does, (2) it is possible for both to differ from chance by the same amount, and (3) it is, of course, possible for neither index to differ from its relevant chance comparison. Thus we may note that while introduction of the notion that the two indices must each be viewed in relation to chance expectancy has increased the complexity of the discussion, the same major points prevail as regards the essential independence of the two resulting indices of contingency.

If the discussion were concluded at this point, it would very likely leave the impression that the indices of contingency represent structural features of the external world, and that a contingency, like a stimulus, originates from attributes of the subject's environment. It would be unfortunate to leave such an impression for a fascinating feature of contingency perception is that an R-S contingency is an interaction of attributes of both the environment and subject—the environment's S and the subject's R.

Response Rate and Clarity of an R-S Contingency

As a subject's rate of behavior changes, so too will the indices of contingency in any situation. The environment can be said to specify the probability of efficacy of a particular response class $[P(S/Rt)]$ and to specify the general temporal probability (rate) of noncontingent occurrences of the stimulus (P_{nc}). The subject, however, is the immediate source of the temporal probability (rate) of relevant responses (P_R) in any given situation. The possibility of perceiving an R-S contingency will, therefore, very much depend on the subject's disposition to respond, his P_R. This is obvious in the case where the subject never responds in a relevant manner, that is, $P_R=0$. For in that case, there will be no manifest instance of the contingency. Yet, the effect of a positive response rate (i.e., $P_R>0$) is not as obvious as one might expect.

Consider the case where R has some efficacy. If one were to calculate the effect of response rate on the two indices of contingency magnitude $[P(S/Rt) - P(S/rand.\ t)$ and $P(R/tS) - P(R/t\ rand.)]$, two rather startling implications would become clear. The first is that the absolute magnitude of both indices eventually declines with increasing response rate. This fact is the consequence of the increase in the estimates of chance contingency, $P(S/rand.\ t)$ and $P(R/t\ rand.)$, which will increase with higher rates of R (see Figure 2.1). The second surprising implication is that the two indices are affected differently by increasing response rate. $P(S/Rt)-P(S/rand.\ t)$ declines continuously (monotonically) as response rate rises since $P(S/Rt)$ will remain virtually constant, whereas $P(S/rand.t)$ increases directly with response rate. The same continuous decline will occur for the index $P(R/tS)-P(R/t\ rand.)$ when the stimulus never occurs noncontingently ($P_{nc}=0$). However, when a subject is in a situation where the stimulus sometimes occurs for reasons other than his behavior ($P_{nc}>0$), then the

Conditional Probabilities

Perceptual Indices
of Contingency Magnitude (CM)

$$P(S/Rt) = \frac{\overset{(t)}{\Sigma\ R \to S}}{\Sigma\ R}$$

$$P(S/rand.\ t) = 1 - e^{-\lambda(S)t}$$

with $\lambda(S) = \Sigma\ S/T$

$$CM_a = P(S/Rt) - P(S/rand.\ t)$$

$$P(R/tS) = \frac{\overset{(t)}{\Sigma\ R \leftarrow S}}{\Sigma\ S}$$

$$P(R/t\ rand.) = 1 - e^{-\lambda(R)t}$$

with $\lambda(R) = \Sigma\ R/T$

$$CM_b = P(R/tS) - P(R/t\ rand.)$$

Discriminability (D) of Change in
$R \to S$ Contingency Magnitude from
Period T_1 to Period T_2

$$D_a = f\left| \frac{CM_a\ of\ T_1 - CM_a\ of\ T_2}{CM_a\ of\ T_1} \right|$$

$$D_b = f\left| \frac{CM_b\ of\ T_1 - CM_b\ of\ T_2}{CM_b\ of\ T_1} \right|$$

FIG. 2.1.   Conditional probabilities relevant to perception of contingency of stimulus (S) on response (R) during some time period (T), with focal interval (t).

relationship between increasing response rate and the index of contingency magnitude, $P(R/tS) - P(R/t\ rand.)$, will be an inverted-U function, increasing at first, then declining. The implication is clear that for situations where $P_{nc} > 0$ there will be an optimal response rate for obtaining the maximal magnitude of contingency as perceivable in the index $P(R/tS) - P(R/t\ rand.)$.

It should be noted that the discussion thus far has focused on the perception of contingency in situations where a subject's response rate is assumed to be constant. A major implication of this model of contingency perception is that a subject need not alter response rate in order to be in a position to assess the existence of a contingency. So long as the subject responds with some rate $P_R > 0$, evidence of contingency will be available in experience through time (the evidence may be more or less clear, however, as noted with respect to particular level of response rate).

However, it is worth noting that if a subject alters response rate and is capable of comparing experience accumulated under alternative response rates, then an additional index of contingency clarity will be available. The change in contingency magnitude from one span of time (T_a) to the next (T_b) would itself provide evidence of any existing contingency. It seems reasonably safe to assume that experiential contrast of this type will be discriminable in a manner much like the many stimulation contrasts that take the form of Weber's law, $\Delta I / I$ (discriminable change in stimulus intensity is proportional to initial intensity). Let us assume, then, that a change in contingency magnitude will be appreciable as some function of the proportional change in magnitude from time T_a to time T_b. For example, in the case of the index of contingency magnitude $P(S/Rt) - P(S/rand.\ t)$, a change in magnitude would be expected to have a discriminability (D),

$$D = f \frac{\left| [P(S/Rt) - P(S/rand.\ t)]^{Ta} - [P(S/Rt) - P(S/rand.\ t)]^{Tb} \right|}{[P(S/Rt) - P(S/rand.\ t)]^{Ta}}.$$

The point to be made by introducing this rather cumbersome equation is simply to record the fact that if one works through the formulation of contingency clarity for instances of varying response rate, it will again be found that contingency clarity as assessed by the two indices will be differently affected by response rate. Just as the relationship between levels of constant response rate and contingency magnitude differ for the two indices of contingency, so too the relationship between a given change in response rate and the proportional change in magnitude can differ for the two indices of contingency when $P_{nc} > 0$.

The Effect of t on Contingency Perception

The model of contingency perception as discussed thus far is summarized in Figure 2.1. With reference to that figure, a very important implication of this model can be made briefly. The size of the interval t will greatly affect both indices of contingency magnitude and both indices of magnitude contrast. As t is reduced magnitude may rise sharply. "May" is a necessary qualification because t in this model is an analytic variable, and the effect of reducing it will depend on whether it encompasses the span of time in which contingent stimulation occurs. For example, if contingent stimulation, when it occurs, occurs within 1 second of the efficacious response, then a subject who has been employing an analytic $t=2$ seconds can markedly increase the perceived magnitude of contingency by reducing t to $t = 1$ second. Perception of contingency will be clearer as the subject aligns the focal interval of contingency analysis, t, upon the "real" interval of contingency.

If one assumes that a naive subject will be likely to begin the perceptual process with one end of the focal interval set at the time of response occurrence, then an intriguing implication is evident. Delay of reward (i.e., the displacement in time of S from the efficacious R) will reduce contingency clarity. It is surely a common observation that delay of reward has a negative effect on rate of learning in most cases with animals and humans (it would seem that a delay of only 3 seconds obscures a contingency for human infants; Ramey & Ourth, 1971; Millar, 1972), but the interpretation of this effect is commonly one in which limited memory and/or intervening responses are assigned the responsibility for disruption (Terrill, 1965; Watson, 1967). In the present perceptual model, we see the possibility that delay of contingent stimulation can directly obscure the existence of a contingency even if one were to assume perfect memory and no competing responses. To highlight this perceptual issue, one need only consider the possibility of a stimulus having a narrow interval at some fixed delay (e.g., a 1-second interval at 4 seconds after the response). In this case the subject's perception of contingency would be greatly clarified by displacing the lower boundary of the focal interval from the time of the occurrence of R to some point up to 4 seconds following R. This increase in clarity derives from the fact that focusing the analytic time span t on the temporal span of contingent occurrence will not alter the calculation of $P(S/Rt)$ (because $\Sigma R\text{-}S/\Sigma R$ will remain the same), but the narrowing of t to a smaller span of time will directly reduce the estimate of chance $P(S/rand.\ t)$—therefore CM will increase in value. If a subject were capable of performing this type of displaced focus, then it would follow that a fixed delay of n seconds would create much less perceptual difficulty than a random delay of up to n seconds. This distinction between perceptual and memory effects of time (t) can perhaps be further clarified by consideration of an analogous distinction recently demonstrated in "delayed reaction" experiments with squirrel monkeys by McGonigle (Note 1) at the University of Edinburgh. Although the delayed reaction test is a classic paradigm of memory span (e.g., Hunter, 1913) the question arose as to whether the usual training of subjects with zero delay might be a setting condition that contributed to the subsequent demonstration that increasing delays produced increasing errors as subjects tried to remember where the object was hidden. McGonigle trained a group of subjects at 6 seconds delay and then tested them at shorter as well as longer times. Results showed a symmetrical decline on both sides of the 6 second delay. It would seem that much of the apparent evidence of memory loss observed in the standard training procedure could be attributed to the effect of deviation from the subject's entrained focal time for response. Analogously, it is expected that delay of reward studies may reflect more about the subject's focal t for contingency than the subject's memory for responses or rewards.

Two Alternate Models of R →S Contingency Perception

At this point the reader may wonder why such an elaborate model of contingency perception is being laid out in the absence of any set of data in special need of explanation. Is it not possible to propose that $R \rightarrow S$ contingency is perceived by a less complex process than that involving a two-part analysis of conditional probabilities? The answer is that at least two ready alternatives exist but each fails to use all the information available in a contingency experience and each introduces a risky assumption in the place of a potential perceptual act.

The first alternative is one that might be termed "perception of contingency by focus on R–S correlation." Here the subject need only assess the correlation of frequencies of R and S over a series of time spans. Given the assumption that simple correlation implies contingency, the subject would have a relatively uncomplicated process for assessing the existence of R–S contingency. However, by failing to use available information about the sequential pattern of individual S and R events, this process is blind to distinctions between cases where S is contingent on R and cases where R is contingent on S (this process would also be incapable of distinguishing what will later be termed "R–S synchrony").

The second less complex alternative to conditional probability analysis is what might be called "perception of contingency by focus on R–S contiguity."[3] Here the subject would keep track of R–S sequence and timing but then assume that greater contiguity implied greater contingency. While this process could make distinctions regarding directionality of contingency between S and R, it would be confused by a failure to distinguish chance coincidence.

Thus, while either of these models might be thought attractive because of its simplicity, to accept it is to presume that a perceptual system functions in disregard of relevant information that is available in the experiential context. Just as Gibson (1950) has argued that it is not likely that the experience of visual depth is derived on the basis of an *assumption* tacked on (via learning) to perception of two dimensions but rather that it is *perceived directly* in the available information generated by the fact of depth (e.g., stimulus gradients, form transformation, etc.), it is here proposed that it is not likely that contingency is experienced through an assumption tacked on (via learning or innately) to the perception of correlation or contiguity. Organisms with sufficient information-processing capacity to deal with conditional probabilities can be assumed to *perceive contingency directly* within the information it generates through time. To propose that a subject is set to construct the experience of contingency by making a risky assumption would itself seem a risky assumption at this point in our effort to understand the role of contingency perception in behavioral development.

---

[3]There has been a long history of concern for the roles of contiguity and temporal correlation within classical and instrumental conditioning (e.g., Rescorla, 1967). Here we are specifically limiting our concern to the potential roles of these variables in the perceptual process of recognizing the existence of a contingency.

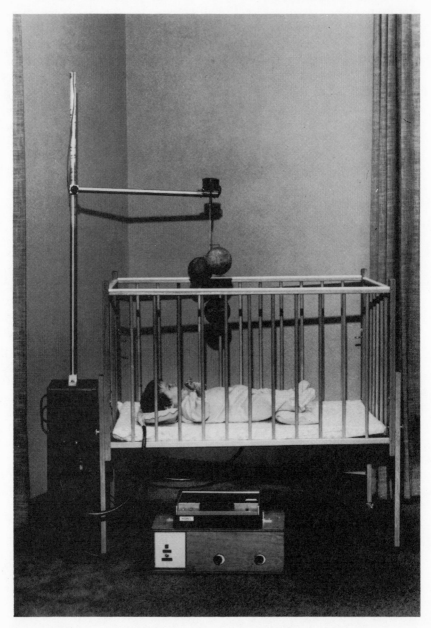

FIG. 2.2. Mobile device with pressure-sensitive pillows for head and feet.

Some Empirical Evidence

The most direct evidence for what has been proposed thus far comes from three recent studies in the author's research on infant instrumental initiative and social responsiveness. The first study was focused on obtaining direct evidence of the change in smiling to a contingent mobile. Earlier studies of this reaction (Watson and Ramey, 1972; Watson, 1972) relied heavily on interview reports from mothers of subjects. In the present study, 8-week-old subjects were exposed to a mobile in their home (see Figure 2.2) for 10 minutes on each of 7 consecutive days. On the first day the mobile did not turn. On the 6 subsequent days the mobile turned for 1 second contingent upon leg movement on a pressure-sensitive pillow. An observer was scheduled to monitor the infant's smiling during a few of the sessions. The data obtained are quite clear.

One group of 16 infants (Group A) showed a significant increase in daily response rate. Frequency of smiling also increased significantly. Notably, head movement on a separate pillow did not increase significantly, which indicates that the increase in smiling was not the result of a generalized arousal of all behavior. Of importance to the contingency perception model is the fact that another group of 8-week-old infants (Group B) were also observed in the course of this study. Group B, however, had a more sensitive pillow under their legs. On average, these pillows would sense 18 efficacious responses per minute, whereas the leg pillows of Group A were set to half that sensitivity. The sensitivity of head pillows was not different for the two groups. This contrived manipulation of efficacious response rate resulted in the high-rate group's showing a significant rise in neither response rate nor smiling rate. Rate of head movement across days was at the same unchanging level for both groups.

It would seem that the higher rate of response and stimulus conjunction reduced the infant's ability to perceive the contingency. This finding is consistent with the proposal that contingency magnitude is lower at higher levels of P_R for any case where t is greater than 0. It is clearly inconsistent with either the "perception of correlation" or the "perception of contiguity" models. If anything, this shift in rate of efficacious behavior should have increased both correlation (via increase in range of S and R across time spans) and contiguity (via increase in average density of reward following a response).

The second study represents the first time, to the author's knowledge, that an experiment in instrumental learning has been arranged to have contingent and noncontingent occurrences of a stimulus simultaneously available. Forty 14-week-old infants served as subjects. The learning situation was the same as in the previous study except that the mobile was in a laboratory room and turning of the mobile was accompanied by a bell tone. A subject had only one session that involved a 3-minute base period (during which the mobile was not activated), a 9-minute learning period (during which the mobile was activated both contingently and noncontingently), and a 3-minute extinction period (during which the mobile was again inactive). Subjects were randomly assigned to four groups, which differed in terms of the rate at which the mobile was activated noncontingently by a computer (5 per minute or 10 per minute with random intervals) and in terms of the probability that a leg move would activate the mobile (p=1.00 or p=.5). When this study was designed it was expected that both a lower $P(S/Rt)$ (i.e., p = .5) and a lower $P(R/tS)$ (i.e., as produced by the 10 per minute noncontingent rate) would have negative effects on learning. The results were curious.

An analysis of the change in rate of leg movement from the base period through the learning period resulted in a significant effect of groups (F test, $p < .05$). The weakest rise was where we expected it, in the group experiencing partial reinforcement at p = .5 and a noncontingent rate of 10 per minute. To our surprise, however, the sharpest rise in response rate was in the group with p = .5 and 5 per minute noncontingent rate. Indeed this group was the only one of the four to exhibit a significant rate gain.

An interpretation of this finding was that learning might be inhibited not only by low values on both indices of contingency but by sufficient disparity between them. This disparity would account for the poor showing of the groups experiencing $P(S/Rt) = 1.00$. As illustrated in Table 2.1, the average initial response rate of 10 responses per minute would have produced an initial average $P(R/tS) = .67$ (with P_{nc} = 5 per minute) and .50 (with P_{nc} = 10 per minute). By contrast, the group that learned best would have experienced an

TABLE 2.1

Initial Disparity Between $P(S/Rt)$ and $P(R/tS)$* in Four Conditions of Study Where Response Rate Began at About 10 per min., Values of $P(S/Rt)$ Were Set at 1.00 and .50, And Values of P_{nc} Were Set at 5 per min. And 10 per min.

		Temporal Probability of Noncontingent Occurrence (P_{nc})	
	$P(S/Rt)$	5/min.	10/min.
Probability that Response Produces Stimulus	1.00	$P(S/Rt)$ = 1.00 $P(R/tS)$ = .67 Disp. = .33	$P(S/Rt)$ = 1.00 $P(R/tS)$ = .50 Disp. = .50
	.50	$P(S/Rt)$ = .50 $P(R/tS)$ = .50 Disp. = 0	$P(S/Rt)$ = .50 $P(R/tS)$ = .33 Disp. = .17

Calculation based on initial average response rate of 10/min. and assuming t = 1 sec.

average $P(S/Rt)$ and $P(R/tS)$ which were both about .5. Yet how is one to explain the assumed positive value of matched indices of contingency?

A Hypothesis of "Striving for Perfect Control"

A hypothesis of some interest arises if one assumes that an infant may in a certain sense be a perfectionist. Consider the implications of assuming that perfect control may be possible. By definition, that situation would entail the subject's possession of behavior which stands as the necessary and sufficient condition for the occurrence of the contingent stimulus. In such a situation the subject need only discover the proper boundaries of his efficacious behavior. If the response class he is analyzing is too broadly defined, then some instances will not cause S to occur and the apparent value of $P(S/Rt)$ will be less than the apparent value of $P(R/tS)$. If the response class he is analyzing is too narrowly defined, then S will sometimes occur in the absence of the R as defined and $P(R/tS)$ will be less than $P(S/Rt)$. When the two indices of contingency are equal and positive, however, he has evidence the response class is properly defined—or at least getting on target. The only thing left is to adjust the interval value of t to create maximal contingency magnitude. This use of matching would give it a special role in contingency analysis. Matched indices would be a state of contingency experience that signaled approach to perfection. If the magnitude of contingency at equality is sufficient (it need not equal 1, since t may not be reducible to 0), then control is manifest.

One need not take this specific hypothesis too seriously. Yet it at least suggests the possibility that some special cognitive-perceptual significance might be attributed to contingency index matching (or, conversely, to the disparity that might be perceived between the two available indices of contingency magnitude).

The third study was conducted to assess the special significance of matching. Support for matching would provide the strongest evidence for a belief that both indices are being perceived by subjects. In a situation where the probability of a response is contrived to be effective less than every time it occurs (i.e., $P(S/Rt)$ is set <1.00), then matching will require some noncontingent stimulus occurrences. Likewise, if a situation involves noncontingent stimulation, matching will require something less than continuous reinforcement. Yet in such cases matching is achieved at the expense of the average values of contiguity and correlation between R and S.

To provide a sensitive test of this notion, a new learning situation was developed. Other research was indicating that our mobile situation might be subject to transfer effects from our subjects' home experience with commercial mobiles (Watson, 1977). In addition, we worried that the matching effect might have arisen in some manner related to the fact that our

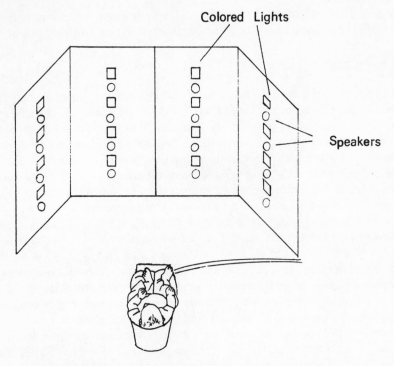

FIG. 2.3.   Display board in front of infant seat with pressure sensing device for
right leg movements.

leg pillow could be activated by both legs. The new situation is shown in
Figure 2.3. It involved a seat from which individual movement of the right leg
was monitored by a pressure-sensitive device. The seat faced a large display
board (8 x 6 ft.) of 16 pairs of lights and speakers arranged in a 4 x 4 matrix.
After pilot work with approximately 60 subjects, a reward stimulus was
settled upon, which involved a 2-second pattern of lights and sounds that
expanded upwards and outwards to fill the board with colored lights to the
accompaniment of a growing C major chord of pure tones. The session
involved a 1-minute base period, a 6-minute learning period, and a 2-minute
extinction period. At all times, except during presentation of the reward
stimulus, an "attention stimulus" was presented, which involved random
alternation each ¼ second between two white lights, and tones situated in the
center of the bottom row of the matrix.

Fifty-four 14-week-old infants were randomly assigned to 9 experimental
groups which differed on the basis of three probability levels of contingent
stimulation (1.00, .75, .50) and three rates of noncontingent stimulation (0, 4,
and 8 per minute). Each subject's record of intensity and frequency of leg
movement during the base period was used to individually set a required
intensity for an efficacious response that would predict an initial rate of

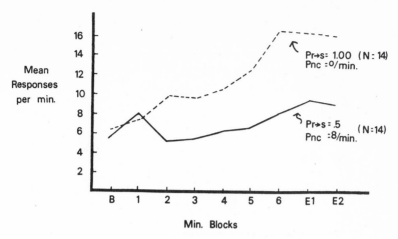

FIG. 2.4. Learning curves from Pilot Study ($N = 28$) showing mean rate of criterial leg movement across 1-minute base period, 6-minute contingency period, and 2-minute extinction period for two experimental groups that differed on probability of responses causing reward ($P_{R \to S} = 1.00$ or .50) and on probability of reward occurring noncontingently ($P_{nc} = 0/$min. and 8/min.).

criterial response at as close to 8 per minute as possible. This was done instantaneously at the end of the base period by computer and assured low variation from planned levels of $P(R/tS)$ at the start of the learning period.

Analysis of contingency perception was accomplished by obtaining a rate-change score for each subject reflecting the change from base period to the final 2 minutes of the learning period. The notion of matching plus a pilot study formed the bases of eight predictions about intergroup differences in mean rate change. The pilot study established that contingency is probably invisible in this experimental situation when partial reward is set at .5 and noncontingent rate is 8 per minute. In a pilot study (see Figure 2.4) 14 subjects experiencing this combination showed no significant change in response rate (mean change of +2.0) while 14 subjects experiencing continuous reward and no noncontingent stimulation showed a very significant rise in response rate (mean change of +8.3, difference between groups p<.01). Figure 2.5 presents the learning curves for the 9 groups. The eight predictions for the present study were those shown in Table 2.2 at the relevant cell boundaries. The table also presents the observed mean response rate change per group. Notably, all the predictions were confirmed.

The critical comparisons, however, are the four that contrast Cells b and e, c and f, d and e, g and h, for in each of these cases the increase in contingency index matching (or reduction in disparity) is clearly accomplished at the expense of contiguity and/or correlation. It should perhaps be noted that the pattern of these predictions does not lend itself to evaluation by standard

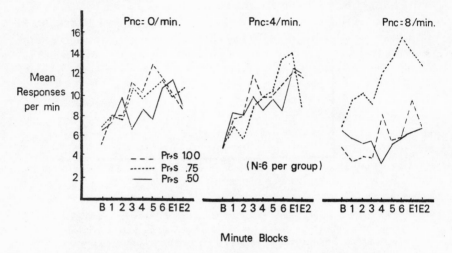

FIG. 2.5. Learning curves from experiment ($N = 54$) showing mean rate of criterial leg movement across 1-minute base period, 6-minute contingency period, and 2-minute extinction period for nine experimental groups that differed on probability of responses causing reward ($P(S/Rt)$ = 1.00, .75, or .50) and on probability of reward occurring noncontingently (P_{nc} = 0/min., 4/min., or 8/min.).

TABLE 2.2
Mean Response Rate Change From Base Period to Final
2 Minutes of Contingency Period for Nine Combinations
of $P(S/Rt)$ and P_{nc} (N = 6 per Cell)
With "Contingency Matching" Predictions ($>$)

		Temporal Probability of Noncontingent Occurrence (P_{nc})		
	$P(S/Rt)$	0/min.	4/min.	8/min.
		a	b	c
Probability	1.00	+6.1 $>$	+5.7 $>$	+1.4
that		$\vee$	$\wedge$	$\wedge$
Response		d	e	f
Produces	.75	+4.0 $<$	+7.2	+7.8
Stimulus		$\vee$		
		g	h	i
	.50	+2.6 $<$	+4.8	−.09

52

analysis of variance statistical models. A simple test of the critical contrasts was made (though with conservative bias) by testing the mean of Cells b, c, d, and g against the mean of Cells e, f, and h. The contrast was found to be statistically reliable but only for boys ($p < .05$, two tailed).[4] Just as in the preceding study, it seems that, if anything, matching the indices of contingency improves the perception of contingency even when it is obtained by reducing one of the indices.

Overall, the results of these three studies are rather consistent in their implication that human infants appear sensitive to features of contingency situations that are not reflected in simple R-S correlation and contiguity per se but that are assessable within two sets of conditional probabilities, as we have noted above. As we shall see in the following section of this paper, analysis of these conditional probabilities may also serve as a basis for perceiving other forms of contingency.

A TYPOLOGY OF CONTINGENCY EXPERIENCE

The potential variety of contingency forms is conceivably very great. The extent of conceptual distinction will depend on how many events and classes of events one wishes to consider within a single contingency structure. However, one may profitably limit one's view to the contingent relations between two events and to two classes of these events. Accepting the traditional classification of elemental experiential events as being either responses (R) or stimuli (S) and considering the temporal distribution of any two events, the logical possibilities entail three temporal pairings, that is, S and R, S and S, R and R. We shall further limit our discussion here to the first of these pairings, for the formal analysis of S and R directly implies a parallel analysis of the remaining two pairings. Furthermore, our attention to the S and R pairing is advantageous to the purposes of this chapter, because it is our assumption that the impact of contingency perception on social behavior is most salient in cases of contingency forms within the S and R pairing.

If one now introduces a concern for directionality of contingency, three potential forms of contingency arise for any given pairing. With our attention to the S and R pairing, the three forms can be described as S contingent on R ($R \to S$), R contingent on S ($S \to R$), and cocontingency of R and S ($R \leftrightarrow S$). For ease of discussion we shall label these three forms, respectively, *behavioral control of stimulation, stimulus control of behavior,* and *synchrony of behavior and stimulation.*

---

[4]Since the writing of this chapter, a replication of the comparison of cells c and f was run with 23 subjects per cell. The predicted superiority of cell f was significant across both sexes.

Behavioral Control of Stimulation

This, of course, is that form of contingency experience just discussed in detail while outlining the model of contingency perception. The only point to be added here is that care should be taken not to confuse the classification of contingency form ($R \rightarrow S$) with the perceptual index involved in assessing its existence, for example, $P(S/Rt)$. This point can be emphasized by noting that the conception of $P(S/tR)$ implies the direction of conditional probability is from R to S, and yet the index is relevant to the $S \rightarrow R$ form of contingency experience. Confusion should be minimized if one attends to the conceptual distinction between temporal order of occurrence of events in "real time" and temporal order of the conditional relation in "analytic time" (represented symbolically by the place of t in the conditional). This will serve an additional clarification of the contingency perception model by highlighting the fact that the proposed analyses of conditional probability require fundamental assumptions that the subject keeps track of real time and is capable of dealing with both directions of analytic time. There is considerable evidence that infants are very sensitive to time as a variable in experience—both short spans (e.g., Fitzgerald, Lintz, Brackbill, & Adams, 1967) and long spans (e.g., Sander, Stechler, Burns, & Lee, this book)—but the assumption that infants can deal with both directions of analytic time is purely an assumption at this point.

Stimulus Control of Behavior

This type of contingency experience is the formal opposite of the preceding. Yet it is potentially more interesting than that statement might lead one to expect. For as soon as we frame the control of behavior by stimuli as a perceptual problem, we are making a notable break with an implicit assumption in traditional views of the innate structure of reflexive behavioral systems. Historically, reflexive systems have been viewed as involving the release of an innately programmed behavior when and if an innately potent stimulus is perceived. From this traditional perspective, there would be little reason to suspect (or assume) that an organism would have an investment in attending to the resulting contingency between the provocative stimulus and the behavior it determines. Yet, as we shall see, there are important functions that perception of $S \rightarrow R$ contingency might serve. But first, we need to frame this perceptual problem briefly in the same manner as used with $R \rightarrow S$ contingency experience.

As noted in Figure 2.6, the contingency of behavior on a stimulus can be expressed by reference to the conditional probability of the behavior (R) following (within some specified time t) the stimulus occurrence (S), that is, $P(R/St)$, obtained by observing $\Sigma S \rightarrow R^{(t)} / \Sigma S$. Just as with $R \rightarrow S$ contingency, the $S \rightarrow R$ contingency is also assessable by reference to a second conditional

Conditional Probabilities

Perceptual Indices
of Contingency Magnitude

$$P(R/St) = \frac{\overset{(t)}{\Sigma\ S \rightarrow R}}{\Sigma\ S}$$

$$P(R/rand.\ t) = 1 - e^{-\lambda(R)t}$$

with $\lambda(R) = \Sigma\ R/T$

$$CM_c = P(R/St) - P(R/rand.\ t)$$

$$P(S/tR) = \frac{\overset{(t)}{\Sigma\ S \leftarrow R}}{\Sigma\ R}$$

$$P(S/t\ rand.) = 1 - e^{-\lambda(S)t}$$

with $\lambda(S) = \Sigma\ S/T$

$$CM_d = P(S/tR) - P(S/t\ rand.)$$

Discriminability (D) of Change in
$S \rightarrow R$ Contingency Magnitude from
Period T_1 to Period T_2

$$D_a = f\ \frac{|\ CM_c\ \text{of}\ T_1 - CM_c\ \text{of}\ T_2\ |}{CM_c\ \text{of}\ T_1}$$

$$D_b = f\ \frac{|\ CM_d\ \text{of}\ T_1 - CM_d\ \text{of}\ T_2\ |}{CM_d\ \text{of}\ T_1}$$

FIG. 2.6.   Conditional probabilities relevant to the perception of contingency of response (R) on stimulus (S) during some time period (T), with focal interval (t).

probability. One may consider the probability of the stimulus's having preceded (within time t) the response, as expressed in $P(S/tR)$, obtained by observing $\Sigma S \leftarrow R^{(t)}/\Sigma R$. We may wish to say that while $P(R/St)$ tells us the odds that the behavior will follow a stimulus occurrence, $P(S/tR)$ tells us the odds that an occurrence of behavior will have been preceded by the stimulus. Yet, if these probabilities are to be used to express contingency beyond chance expectancy, then they must be viewed in the light of their appropriate chance comparisons. Following the same reasoning as above with $R \rightarrow S$ contingency, we see that $P(R/St)$ needs to be contrasted with $P(R/rand.\ t) = 1 - e^{-\lambda(R)t}$ $P(S/tR)$ needs to be contrasted with $P(S/t\ rand.) = 1 - e^{-\lambda(S)t}$.

If each index is found to differ from its chance comparison value, then each will imply an aspect of how R is contingent on (is controlled by) S. As $P(R/St)$ is found to exceed its chance value, then we may wish to say this expresses the degree to which the stimulus is sufficient for the occurrence of the behavior. As $P(S/tR)$ exceeds chance we may wish to say this expresses the degree to which the stimulus is necessary for the occurrence of the behavior. However, it should be noted that the difference in either case may be one in which the index of contingency magnitude is significantly less than chance, in which case response suppression is implied and the normal use of necessary versus sufficient causation will be somewhat convoluted.

The general problem of perceiving an $S \rightarrow R$ contingency is formally (though not necessarily psychologically) the same as perceiving an $R \rightarrow S$ contingency. Following analogous reasoning to that presented in the earlier discussion, discriminability of a change in $S \rightarrow R$ contingency can be expressed as shown in Figure 2.6.

It was said earlier that the experience of $S \rightarrow R$ contingency may have important functions in the development of behavior. One of these is its potential as a source of influence in the orienting of the infant (as well as the young of other social animals) toward the stimulus objects that are its fellow species members. This proposal is parallel to a proposal that $R \rightarrow S$ contingency experience may serve to orient subjects toward what will serve as the class of "social objects," a process of special orientation that, as noted earlier, has been proposed for human infants by Watson (Watson, 1972; Watson & Ramey, 1972) and for rats by Latane (Latane & Hothersall, 1972; Latane et al., 1972; Werner & Latane, 1974).

In the case of $S \rightarrow R$ contingency, however, this proposal may be more difficult to grasp clearly. We tend to view early stimulus control as *prima facie* evidence of complete (innate) organization of the component perceptual and response components. But surely this need not be so, as is evident, for example, by our change in orientation towards certain foods after versus before we discover (sometimes through protracted medical observation) that we are allergic to them. Our "respect" for them is altered even though their potency to control our bodily comfort has not changed. In a more positive example, consider the happy confusion of puberty whereupon much attention is focused on discovering the contingent relation between stimulus events and one's sexual response.

The point is that one may experience unconditioned responses to stimulus events a number of times before perceiving the contingency. While perception of the contingency may not change the specific potency of the stimulus, it very likely will change one's general orientation toward the stimulus (e.g., increasing one's attention to the circumstances that may predict its occurrence). More notably, however, perception of contingency might itself establish a new functional potency for the stimulus and the context of contingency.

Consider the case of human infancy. The infant's behavior is controlled in many ways by its caretaker, and the infant's eventual perception of "being controlled" could well be an organizing influence in its own right. Note that this proposal is not the same as a classical conditioning proposal, where the caretaker is viewed as becoming a complex conditioned stimulus. In conditioning, the focal behavior would be expected to be transferred to stimulus features of the caretaker from naturally potent stimuli that become associated with the caretaker. From the perspective of classical conditioning, the occurrence of food is associated with the mother's presence, and eventually the orienting and attractive potency of food is in some measure aroused by the mother's presence. This conditioning presumably extends through other salient experiences of pleasure and pain (e.g., temperature regulation, stimulation of pleasurable tactile and kinesthetic sensations, etc.). What culminates from this view of social responsiveness is the establishment of the caretaker as a composite of conditioned stimuli where the special attractiveness of the social object has grown bit by bit from experience with provocative physical stimuli. In contrast to this view, we are proposing that social responsiveness, as this is displayed in potency for eliciting "social responses" and in proximity sensitivity, may be derived directly from perception of the caretaker's contextual role in a variety of $S \rightarrow R$ contingency experiences.

This contingency hypothesis is distinguished by its lack of concern for hedonic balance. The organizing influence of caretaking activity is not that it dispenses more pleasure (or pain removal) than it dispenses pain (or pleasure removal). These features of experience must surely have their own special effects (though the author would guess they are less important in early than later experience), but a principle organizing influence of caretaking activity is that it involves many instances of $S \rightarrow R$ contingency experience. Many reflexes are elicited. Some may be intrinsically pleasurable, others may be intrinsically painful (as in cleaning and changing, which commonly elicits crying), and many must surely have little hedonic salience at all (as in the Babinski, the Moro, the ear–neck, or the startle reflexes). Yet each may equally contribute to the perception of "being controlled."

The human caretaker must exercise control over the infant's behavioral system if survival is to be assured. It would seem reasonable to expect that this fact of early life may have provided a base on which selective pressure fashioned a mechanism to assure adaptive social orientation. One might even go on to speculate that the role of $S \rightarrow R$ contingency experience in organizing social behavior probably extends well beyond the initial period of establishing the proper identity of "social objects." A recent study by Becker (1977) offers some evidence that the perception of $S \rightarrow R$ contingency may participate in the development of peer orientation in 9-month-old infants.

Becker observed the change in social orientation displayed by 16 pairs of first-born infants over a sequence of 10 1-hour play sessions. Sessions were alternated between the homes of each member of a pair. An 11th session was held with a new partner. A control group of 16 pairs was observed in two sessions spaced to coincide with the 1st and 10th sessions of the experimental group. Sequential occurrences of "peer oriented" behavior by both members of a pair were recorded. It was found that frequency of these behaviors increased significantly over the 10 sessions for experimentals, though no change was observed for controls. The heightened response rate also generalized to the new partner on the 11th session. Analysis of contingency within the interchange of peer-oriented behavior showed no relationship between a subject's increase in response rate and his history of being rewarded (by response of other) for behavior. Instead, behavior rate increase was found to be a significant function of the frequency of being stimulated by one's partner and the level of motor development of that partner. It would seem, therefore, that 9-month-old infants, at least, become socially responsive to peers as a consequence of experience in being stimulated by peers. This process would seem to be some type of "sensitization," but not one of simple familiarization through passive exposure. These results are consistent with the notion that the human infant may organize his social behavior toward those social objects he has perceived to have stimulated his behavior in the past.

Stimulus–Response Synchrony

Synchrony of two or more events refers to their likelihood of occurring at the same point (within some limit, t) in time. However, synchrony is not simply coincidence. There is an implication of coordination in time that would not be expected by chance alone. This is a type of contingency in that the occurrence of one event apparently limits the likelihood of another event. But the limitation is not directional in time. If Event A is synchronous with Event B, then A will occur within some narrow limit of the time B occurs. In contrast to directional contingency, however, there is no implication about temporal order—indeed as we shall see, the perception of synchrony can be specified as entailing a judgment that consistent temporal order is not the case. If A is synchronous with B, then the tendency for co-occurrence should involve as much precedence of A as consequence of A—otherwise control rather than synchrony would be implied.

Consider that case at hand where one event is a subject's response, R, and the other is some stimulus event, S. Stimulus–response synchrony can be represented by reference to the conditional probabilities displayed in the discussions of the preceding forms of contingency experience. As with each of these preceding perceptual analyses, the perception of synchrony between stimulus and behavior would also appear to have two available indices. As presented in Figure 2.7, the first can be stated as $P(R/St) = P(R/tS) > 1 - e^{-\lambda(R)t}$. This specifies the judgment that the probability that R follows S (within time t) is equal to the probability that the R precedes S (within time t) and that both are greater than chance would allow considering the general rate of occurrence of R, $[\lambda(R)]$. One might wish to term this the index of a stimulus-synchronous response in contrast to the second index, which might

Conditional Probabilities

Perceptual Indices
of Synchrony Magnitude (SM)

$$P(S/Rt) = \frac{\overset{(t)}{\Sigma\ R \rightarrow S}}{\Sigma\ R}$$

$$P(S/tR) = \frac{\overset{(t)}{\Sigma\ S \leftarrow R}}{\Sigma\ R}$$

$$P(S/rand.\ t) = 1 - e^{-\lambda(S)t}$$

$$SM_a = f[P(S/Rt) = P(S/tR) > 1 - e^{\lambda(S)t}]$$

perhaps $SM_a =$

$$\frac{(CM_a + CM_d) - |\ CM_a - CM_d\ |}{2}$$

$$P(R/tS) = \frac{\overset{(t)}{\Sigma\ R \leftarrow S}}{\Sigma\ S}$$

$$P(R/St) = \frac{\overset{(t)}{\Sigma\ S \rightarrow R}}{\Sigma\ S}$$

$$P(R/rand.\ t) = 1 - e^{-\lambda(R)t}$$

$$SM_b = f[P(R/tS) = P(R/St) > 1 - e^{\lambda(R)t}]$$

perhaps $SM_b =$

$$\frac{(CM_b + CM_c) - |\ CM_b - CM_c\ |}{2}$$

Discriminability (D) of Change in
$S \leftrightarrow R$ Synchrony from
Period T_1 to Time Period T_2

$$D_a = f\ \frac{|\ SM_a\ \text{at}\ T_1 - SM_a\ \text{at}\ T_2\ |}{SM_a\ \text{at}\ T_1}$$

$$D_b = f\ \frac{|\ SM_b\ \text{at}\ T_1 - SM_b\ \text{at}\ T_2\ |}{SM_b\ \text{at}\ T_1}$$

FIG. 2.7. Conditional probabilities relevant to the perception of synchrony of stimulus (S) and response (R) during some time period (T), with focal interval (t).

be termed the index of response-synchronous stimulation. This second index is formulated as $[P(S/tR) = P(S/Rt) > 1 - e_{-\lambda(S)t}]$. Here we see reference to the probability that S precedes R is equal to the probability that S follows R and that both are greater than chance would allow considering the general rate of S, $[\lambda(S)]$.

One may wonder how a synchronous contingency experience might arise. Control contingencies are not difficult to conceive in that the contingency derives directly from the causal relation implied in the notion of control. The stimulus causes the response or the response causes the stimulus. However, in the case of synchrony the co-occurrence of stimulus and response is not conceived as the effect of the occurrence of one event's being the causal condition for the other—at least not with regard to the particular occurrences of the response and stimulus in any given conjunction. So, then, what mechanism might provide a means for temporal conjunction to occur at a rate beyond chance expectancy? Both events might be the causal effects of a third event, but this "secondary" or "derived" synchrony would thus arise in a context where it is possible to perceive control of the constituent events. One possibility for "primary" synchrony is for one event to be generated on the base of the temporal pattern observed in the past occurrences of the other event. In this case the synchrony would derive from a kind of temporal conditioning of at least one of the events. Yet, this would not have to be a traditional form of temporal conditioning where time becomes potent by the patterning of a potent stimulus. Indeed, that would entail the existence of direct control of one event by the other. We may imagine synchrony arising without an initial exhibition of control contingency between the events. The temporal pattern of the stimulus becomes potent for the occurrence of the behavior, whereas the occurrence of S per se may remain ineffective.

A separate question from that of the potential origin of synchrony is the question of the potential role that synchrony perception might play in the determination of behavior. Why should a subject react to the perception of synchrony as a significant form of contingency experience? One possibility is suggested by the very fact that synchrony can be viewed as a balance between the perception of "being in control" and the perception of "being controlled."

When one perceives that one is "being controlled" by the behavior of another ($P_R = fP_S$), then one has information that the other might perceive his control ($P_S = fP_R$), assuming one's behavior is perceivable, and that would mean he would have evidence that one was perceiving his behavior. When one perceives that one is "in control" of the other's behavior ($P_S = fP_R$), then one has evidence that the other perceives one's behavior (if not one's control) and that the other has information about one's existence. Now then, when one perceives synchrony, both preceding implications apply, and one has information that the other has information of one's perception of the other. Thus the perception of synchrony involves the unique state in which the subject has evidence that he can be perceived as attending to the organism to whom he is attending by the organism to whom he is attending. In short, perception of synchrony may be special because it implies mutual regard.

By contrast, consider the sight of two eyes staring at one's eyes. If one assumes that the eyes of the other sees one's eyes and that the sight of eyes implies to the other that he is seen to be in the act of looking, then the sight of eyes might be taken to imply a state of mutual regard. The same case might be made for the touch of flesh. If one assumes the flesh of the other feels one's touch and that the touch of flesh implies being felt to the other, one might go on to assume that the touch of flesh implies mutual regard. Yet in both of these apparently direct cases of mutual regard, the reciprocal state of perception must be assumed. In the case of behavioral synchrony, there is evidence of the other's perception of one's behavior in the perception of one's control of the other's behavior. Therefore it would seem that if evolution should have provided special mechanisms for certain species to react to the existence of mutual regard by way of perceiving the sight of eyes or the touch of flesh (and it is difficult to conceive of other direct physical stimuli that could serve this function), it would have been a similar and possibly a greater advantage to provide a special responsiveness to the perception of synchrony. Synchrony not only specifies mutual regard on the basis of more firm evidence, it also has the advantage of being perceivable at a distance (which the touch of flesh does not) and when vision is occluded (which the sight of eyes does not).

If the perception of synchrony is important because it specifies mutual regard, we must next ask why it would be advantageous for an organism to perceive mutual regard. That should, of course, depend largely on the species of organism one considers. For some, mutual regard may have little adaptive significance—in which case we should expect that perception of synchrony would be of little matter. However, whenever a species relies on simultaneous acts of coordinated behavior between members, then some mechanism for detecting mutual regard should prove advantageous. The various cooperative ventures of social species (e.g., hunting, feeding, nest building) and the sexual behavior of most species should be particularly dependent on the contextual signals specifying mutual regard.

The sensitivity of humans to the state of mutual regard seems intuitively obvious. The role that perception of synchrony plays in developing this sensitivity is not clear at this time. However, judging from the recent work of Condon and Sander (1974), it would seem that the human infant is capable of generating states of synchrony between his or her motor behavior and vocal sounds from the environment. It is not yet clear whether caretakers perceive this synchrony, or even whether the infants perceive it. However, it is very suggestive of perceptual sensitivity on the infant's part to what are apparently very short time cycles in adult speech.

If the infants are prone to establish behavioral synchrony with adult speech (i.e., stimulus synchronous responding), then it seems reasonable to imagine that they are guided to this state by some sensitivity to this aspect of synchrony. Since perceptual analysis of this aspect would seem no less difficult (see Figure 2.7) than the aspect arising when a stimulus source (e.g., an adult) establishes synchrony with the infant's behavior (i.e., response synchronous stimulation), it would seem only a bit more speculative to propose that infants are capable of using information from both indices of synchrony. Whether or not the infant is especially sensitive to a match in indices, as he appears to be with indices of R→S contingency, there is at least a tenable, if tenuous, basis for expecting that future research will find the infant as capable of perceiving synchrony as he is capable of perceiving the contingencies of control.

CONCLUSION

The major point of this paper has been to propose that our progress in understanding the origins of social responsiveness in humans and other social animals will benefit by a close examination of contingency perception and its determinants. It is not clear at this time whether better understanding of the effects of contingency perception will accelerate or retard the current swing of the conceptual pendulum from empiricism to nativism. What is more important, of course, is how attention to contingency perception helps increase our accumulation of basic data on the development of social responsiveness. With that objective in mind, the present paper has put forth five rather major theoretical proposals: (1) Contingencies of stimulus and response occurrence can be viewed as structures of experience that have functions in the determination of social responsiveness in addition to the functions of their component physical stimuli per se; (2) contingency experience can be perceived directly in the temporal distribution of stimuli and responses by any animal capable of analyzing the relevant conditional probabilities that are observable through time; (3) contingencies can have different structural forms (e.g., R→S, S→R, S↔R), and each of these forms may be perceived by more than one analytic index; (4) the various forms of contingency experience probably have somewhat different specific effects from one species to another and from one ontogenetic level to another; and (5) if we are to eventually understand the process of contingency perception and its effects, new research procedures will be necessary that allow that the subject is in a world in which events that are occurring contingently may also be occurring noncontingently.

ACKNOWLEDGMENTS

Work reported from the author's laboratory was supported by grant (MH 24283) from the National Institute of Mental Health. Assistance from Mark Bronson, Georgia Chouré, Richard Ewy, and Paul Karrawanny in data collection and analysis is gratefully acknowledged. Thanks are extended to Dr. Gordon Bronson and Dr. J. Barnard Gilmore for their suggestions on improving a previous version of the conditional probability notation.

REFERENCE NOTES

1. McGonigle, B. O. Personal communication. Psychology Department, University of Edinburgh, Scotland. August, 1976.

REFERENCES

Ainsworth, M. D. S. *Infancy in Uganda: infant care and the growth of attachment.* Baltimore: Johns Hopkins Press, 1967.

Bandura, A., & Walters, R. H. *Social learning and personality development.* New York: Holt, Rinehart, & Winston, 1963.

Becker, J. M. T. A learning analysis of the development of peer-oriented behavior in nine-month-old infants. *Developmental Psychology,* 1977, *13,* 481–491.

Bowlby, J. The nature of the child's tie to his mother. *International Journal of Psychoanalysis,* 1958, *39,* 350–373.

Bowlby, J. *Attachment and loss* (Vol. 1), *Attachment.* London: Hogarth Press, 1969.

Brackbill, Y., & Koltsova, M. M. Conditioning and learning. In Y. Brackbill (Ed.), *Infancy and early childhood.* New York: Free Press, 1967.

Condon, W. S., & Sander, L. W. Synchrony demonstrated between movements of the neonate and adult speech. *Child Development,* 1974, *45,* 456–462.

Cox, D. R. *Renewal Theory.* London: Methuen, 1962.

Eibl-Eibesfeldt, I. *Ethology: the biology of behavior.* New York: Holt, Rinehart, & Winston, 1970.

Ferster, C. B., & Skinner, B. F. *Schedules of reinforcement.* New York: Appleton-Century-Crofts, 1957.

Fitzgerald, H. E., Lintz, L. M., Brackbill, Y., & Adams, G. Time perception and conditioning an autonomic response in human infants. *Perceptual and Motor Skills,* 1967, *24,* 479–486.

Gibson, J. J. *The perception of the visual world.* New York: Houghton Mifflin, 1950.

Hunter, W. S. The delayed reaction in animals and children. *Behavior Monographs,* 1913, *2,* 1–86.

Latane, B., & Hothersall, D. Social attraction in animals. In P. C. Dodwell (Ed.), *New Horizons in psychology 2.* New York: Penguin, 1972.

Latane, B., Joy, V., Meltzer, J., & Lubell, B. Stimulus determinants of social attraction in rats. *Journal of Comparative and Physiological Psychology,* 1972, *79,* 13–21.

Lewis, M., & Rosenblum, L. (Eds.), *The effects of the infant on its caregiver.* (Vol. 1) *The origins of behavior.* New York: John Wiley, 1973.

Maier, S. F., Seligman, M. E. P., & Solomon, R. L. Pavlovian fear conditioning and learned helplessness. In B. A. Campbell and R. M. Church (Eds.), *Punishment.* New York: Appleton-Century-Crofts, 1969.

McDougall, W. *An Introduction to Social Psychology.* Boston: Luce, 1923.

McGill, W. J. Stochastic latency mechanisms. In R. D. Luce, R. R. Bush, & E. Galanter (Eds.), *Handbook of mathematical psychology* (Vol. 1.) New York: John Wiley, 1963, 309–360.

Millar, W. S. A study of operant conditioning under delayed reinforcement in early infancy. *Monographs of the Society for Research in Child Development,* 1972, *37*(2), (Serial No. 147).

Miller, N. E., & Dollard, J. *Social learning and imitation.* New Haven: Yale University Press, 1941.

Ramey, C. T., & Ourth, L. L. Delayed reinforcement and vocalization rates of infants. *Child Development,* 1971, *42,* 291–298.

Rescorla, R. A. Pavlovian conditioning and its proper control procedures. *Psychological Review,* 1967, *74,* 71–80.

Sander, L. W., Stechler, G., Burns, P., & Lee, A. Changes in infant and caregiver variables over the first two months of life: Regulation and adaptation in the organization of the infant–caregiver system. In E. Thoman (Ed.), *Origins of the infant's social responsiveness.* New Jersey: Lawrence Erlbaum Associates, 1979

Sears, R. R., Maccoby, E. E. & Levin, H. *Patterns of child rearing.* Evanston, Illinois: Row, Peterson, 1957.

Seligman, M. E. P. *Helplessness: On depression, development and death.* San Francisco: Freeman, 1975.

Terrill, G. Delayed reinforcement effects. In L. P. Lipsitt & C. C. Spiker (Eds.), *Advances in child development and behavior* (Vol. 2). New York: Academic Press, 1965.

Watson, J. S. Memory and "contingency analysis" in infant learning. *Merrill-Palmer Quarterly,* 1967, *13,* 55–76.

Watson, J. S. Cognitive-perceptual development in infancy: setting for the seventies. *Merrill-Palmer Quarterly,* 1971, *17,* 139–152.

Watson, J. S. Smiling, cooing, and 'The Game.' *Merrill-Palmer Quartertly,* 1972, *18,* 323–339.

Watson, J. S. Depression and the perception of control in early childhood. In J. G. Schulterbrandt and A. Raskin (Eds.), *Depression in Childhood: diagnosis, treatment, and conceptual models.* New York: Raven Press, 1977.

Watson, J. S., & Ramey, C. T. Reactions to response-contingent stimulation in early infancy. *Merrill-Palmer Quarterly,* 1972, *18,* 219–227.

Werner, C., & Latane, B. Interaction motivates attraction: Rats are fond of fondling. *Journal of Personality and Social Psychology,* 1974, *29,* 328–334.

3 Towards a Unitary Theory of Development

T. G. R. Bower
Jennifer G. Wishart
University of Edinburgh

INTRODUCTION — CONCEPTS OF DEVELOPMENT

While we hope that this paper will eventually get to some speculations about the origins of social responsiveness, our more basic subject is the nature of development. Our primary concern has been cognitive development. Our justification for presenting such a paper here is that we believe that there should be a unitary theory of development and that insights gained in one area should illuminate other areas. Most psychologists work with a concept of development that has the following characteristics. Development is seen as a cumulative process with later behavioral changes depending on earlier behavioral changes. "Higher" psychological functions depend on "lower" psychological functions. More complex behaviors are dependent on simpler behaviors. There are numerous striking developmental effects that illustrate this concept. Take, for example, the differing effects of blindness that depend on whether it occurs early or late in life. It would seem that the congenitally blind child may never be able to master concepts of space. If blinded later in life, after infancy, the child typically has no such problems (Drever, 1955; Hatwell, 1966). Concepts such as those of Euclidean geometry emerge years after infancy is over. Although blind perhaps for years before the usual age of emergence of these concepts, the late-blinded child nonetheless develops the concepts. The congenitally blind child, by contrast, probably does not develop them at all. Something that happened in the first two years of life has determined whether or not spatial concepts can appear 10 years later, around the age of 12.

Effects like these are well-known but are not well understood. A standard model to explain them would look something like that shown in Figure 3.1.

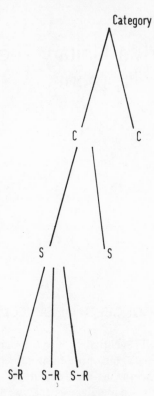

FIG. 3.1.   A possible model for the process of conversion of $S - R$ coordinations to schemas, concepts, and categories during the course of development.

On this model, young babies acquire S→R coordinations that may be amalgamated to form schemas, the schemas amalgamated to form concepts, and so on. Such a model embodies the ideas of development outlined above. It seems on the face of it that it could cope with the kind of long-term effects we mentioned above. The congenitally blind child obviously cannot have the same S→R coordinations as the sighted child. On this model he therefore cannot have the same schemas, concepts, or categories.

There are, of course, some problems in understanding how the conversion from S→R coordinations to schemas or concepts occurs. Some recent studies seem to indicate that the process might be relatively direct. Mounoud and Bower (1974), for example, found a sensorimotor form of weight conservation emerging around 18 months. It is not until years later that verbally expressed weight conservation appears. However the finding that there is a direct S→R predecessor of the verbal concept seems in principle to support the general model outlined above. Wishart and Bower (Note 1) have described a similar predecessor for concepts of space (see Figure 3.2). Younger babies are clearly egocentric, taking no account of changes in position; thus in Part B of Figure 3.2, the baby would take Cup B. This egocentrism is over by 18 months, although the concept is not attained at a verbal level until 7 years of age (Piaget & Inhelder, 1948/1956).

These studies could be taken to imply that S→R acquisitions are simply reflected up into verbal concepts. A study carried out by Sheeran (Note 2) however, rather spoils this attractive conclusion. She investigated the developmental fate of the S→R coordinations that seemed to presage verbal weight conservation. This coordination usually enters the repertoire of the child at around 18 months. What happens to it after the child begins to talk, particularly after he or she begins to understand (and misunderstand) questions about weight? Instead of correcting the verbal misunderstandings, the S→R coordination is itself undone by the erroneous verbal responses.

In these experiments, the child is presented with an object a number of times. As indexed by the change in the position of his arm on taking the object, he will overestimate or underestimate the weight the first time. With successive presentations the accuracy of the estimate improves. What if the shape of the object is then changed? A 1-year-old thinks the weight has also now changed. Figure 3.3 illustrates the reaction of such a child to shape transformation, the arm flying up as a result of the baby's overestimation of the weight of the transformed object. An 18-month old knows that the weight

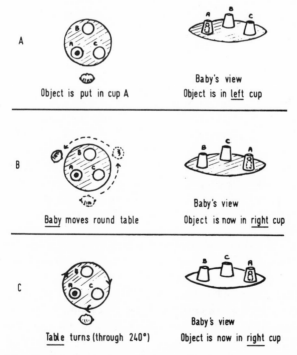

FIG. 3.2. The baby must advance from use of egocentric to geographically defined spatial labels in order to solve these problems.

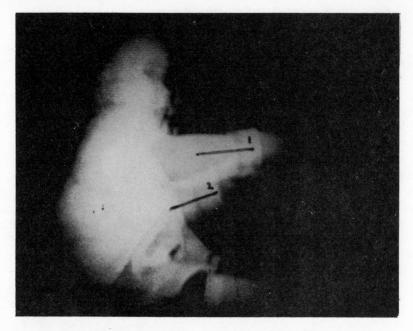

FIG. 3.3. These double exposure photographs illustrate failure of weight conservation in a 1-year-old child. The right picture, showing behavior after shape transformation, is notably different from the left picture, showing the last grasp prior to transformation.

of an object does not vary with changes in its shape and does not make this behavioral error. What happens if we do this experiment with a 4½-year-old child? He does as well as an 18-month-old. What if, before giving him the transformed object, we then ask him if it weighs the same as it did before? The child will typically answer that it weighs more, or less, because the shape has changed. He then acts as if the weight had been changed, just as a 1-year-old would. An erroneous verbal response has destroyed an S→R coordination that had been in the child's repertoire for three years. The behavioral response of a 3-year-old who does not understand the verbal problem is not disturbed (see Table 3.1).

There are other similar results to be found. Between 6 months and 2 years of age babies learn to count, albeit in primitive form, as indicated by correct choice of the greater number from displays such as those shown in Figure 3.4 (Collard & Dempsey, 1978; Wishart & Bower, Note 3). By 20 months of age babies can reliably chose the array that contains more items by making a one-to-one correspondence between the objects in each array. What happens later when the child starts to talk erroneously about number, tying words like *more* to length or density rather than number? As Figure 3.5 shows, the S→R

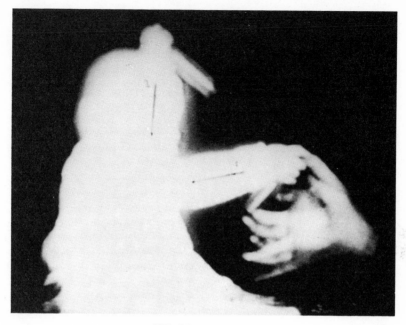

FIG. 3.3. *Continued*

coordination is lost to be regained only with success with the verbally posed problems (Mehler & Bever, 1967).

Similarly, Bower (1971a) showed that by the age of 6 months a baby believed his or her mother to be a single person (see Figure 3.6). The sight of three or more mothers shown to a baby simultaneously before 6 months is not disturbing at all, but after that age increasing understanding of object identity results in such a presentation causing upset. Gouin-Décarie (1966) and Piaget (1945/1963), however, describe how at the age of 2½ years a child when asked by his or her mother where the mother is, will point to some place where she is usually to be found, and say she is there. The advent of language seems to destroy the sensorimotor comprehension of the uniqueness of the mother that is found in infancy.

It would therefore seem that the transfer from S→R to conceptual levels is far from simple. An examination of the developmental history of correct verbal responses to such problems leads to further complications. Contrary to what we might expect, younger children do better with verbally posed number problems similar to those shown in Figure 4 than do somewhat older children (see Figure 3.7). Similarly they do better with area problems (Maratsos, 1973)

TABLE 3.1

Mean Change in Arm Position after Third Presentation Before
Transformation and on First Presentation After Transformation

Age (Years)	Before Transformation	First Presentation After Transformation
3, 2	0.3	0.9*
4, 10	2.4	7.8**

Note. The change is measured In mm by superimposing the arm
position on taking the object and its position 250 msecs later.
*N.S.
**p = .03
Data from Sheeran (Note 2).

(see Figure 3.8). Whereas younger children can use both dimensions of a
rectangle in comparing its area with that of another rectangle, older children
use height exclusively. Only when they are older still do they recover the
capacity they had when younger.

It does indeed seem that the child acquires S→R coordinations in the course
of development. The conceptual content of these coordinations can be
transferred to a verbal level of response. However, at later points in

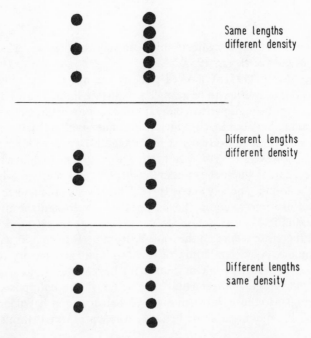

FIG. 3.4. Examples of the arrays used in the "counting" experiment.

development, both the original coordination and its transfer may well be lost. Should we then conclude that early development has nothing to do with later development? Must we accept that "development" does not really occur and that successive age-linked behavior changes are independent of one another? The studies reviewed above would seem to point to such a conclusion. We must, however, set the long-term effects described at the beginning of this paper against these. We are thus forced back to the continuing problem of developmental psychology: How can we establish that there is a connection between behaviors occurring at different ages? Bower has argued elsewhere that the only ethical research paradigm at our disposal is the acceleration paradigm (Bower, 1974a, 1974b). There are practical problems with this kind of study, since the age span covered is normally several years wide. One can get around this by using repetitive sequences occurring within infancy where the age band is months rather than years. The results obtained are, to say the least, mixed. In a continuing study of the counting abilities described above,

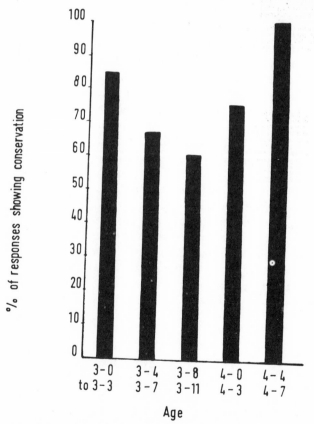

FIG. 3.5.   Correct-choice behavior in counting tasks like those shown in Figure 4 initially declines with age. Data from Mehler and Bever (1967).

FIG. 3.6.   An arrangement of mirrors allows the infant to be presented with multiple mothers.

we practiced the counting behavior of infancy (i.e., the correct choices shown in problems such as those in Figure 3.4) and looked for an effect in verbal responses. We did find an effect—the virtual abolition of the correct choice responses normally seen between 2 and 3 years of age.

Similar paradoxes appeared in our attempts to accelerate development of the object concept. The development of the object concept is essentially development of comprehension of spatial relations. Related S→R coordinations can be demonstrated with eye movements or with manual search. Successful eye movement strategies normally precede successful manual search (Mundy-Castle & Anglin, 1973; Bower & Paterson, 1973; Bower, Broughton, & Moore, 1971; Bower & Wishart, 1972).

A number of experiments were done that aimed to find out the effects of eye movement practice on competence with manual search. The results showed clearly that practice with eye movement tasks does improve performance on manual tasks; however the relationship is nonmonotonic. (Wishart & Bower, 1976, Note 9) A little practice with tracking tasks facilitates performance on manual search tasks a great deal more than a great deal of practice does (see Figure 3.9).

AN ABSTRACT→SPECIFIC MODEL — COGNITIVE DEVELOPMENT

How are we to explain such a result? We would like to propose a model based on data about short-term perceptual development. Consider a simple experiment on habituation. If we show a baby a cube in a constant orientation 10 times for 30 seconds each time, the baby will look at the cube progressively less and less. This indicates that the baby recognizes that he is seeing the same object each time and is, naturally, less and less interested in it. What if we show the baby a cube 10 times, in a different orientation each time? There is exactly the same decline in looking (Day & McKenzie, 1973). Consider what this tells us about the way a baby remembers objects. Obviously, the baby cannot have a very specific image of a cube-in-an-orientation, since every presentation is different in respect of orientation. He must remember from presentation to presentation that there is a cube out there, without remembering the orientation of the cube. This kind of memory is really rather abstract. It is almost as abstract as a word is. It also lacks detail, even detail about something as important as orientation (see also Bower, 1966). Given time, however, a baby can work up a very detailed internal description of an object, so that even very slight changes will arrest the decline in looking behavior. The baby's internal description of an object thus goes from rather abstract to very specific in short-term perceptual learning.

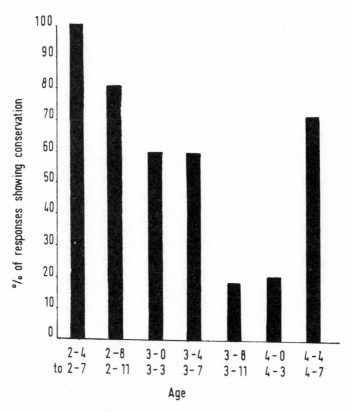

FIG. 3.7.   The probability of correct verbal responses in counting tasks initially declines with age. Data from Mehler and Bever, (1967)

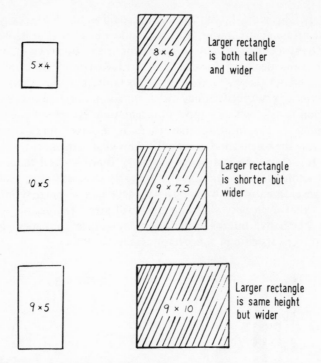

FIG. 3.8.   Comparison rectangles used by Maratsos (1973) in his study of the understanding of the word *big*.

We wish to propose a similar kind of process in conceptual development, with the baby or young child progressively elaborating his descriptions of events to make them more specific. This changes the likelihood of smooth transfer from one task to another involving the same concept, thereby increasing the likelihood of a seeming repetition in concept acquisition. Consider the problem posed to a baby by the sight of an object moving through a tunnel. Babies may initially refuse to look at this kind of display. With recognition that the object he or she sees on each side of the tunnel is the same object, the baby must then work out what is happening to the object when it is out of sight—no easy feat. We propose that the baby's first discovery is that one object can go inside another and still exist. This does not generate particularly skilled behavior in the tracking situation. Such an hypothesis will, however, allow for perfect transfer from the tracking situation to other situations. Suppose the baby sees a toy placed in a cup. He or she should know that the toy is in the cup and should therefore be able to retrieve it. This is exactly what happens if the babies are given the transfer task. What, though, if we give the babies more practice with the tracking task? They readily work out more specific sensorimotor rules that permit much more efficient tracking. Their behavior shows that they know that in order to see the object that has vanished at the left-hand edge of the tunnel they must look for it at the right-hand edge after so many seconds. Their knowledge of the spatiotemporal nature of the tracking task has become very detailed indeed. Babies who have had weeks of experience of tracking tasks do not look at the display often; they can, however, move their eyes unerringly to catch the object from any other point in space. If they are then given the transfer task, they do better than babies with no tracking experience but less well than babies who were given the transfer task after less tracking experience. The older babies seem to have to work out again that one object can be inside another. There is thus a seeming repetition of development. The cause of the repetition is, we would suggest, the increasing specification of the rules governing performance in the first situation, so that transfer to a new situation is not possible. The initial conceptual discovery is stored in memory and must be retrieved before accelerated performance in the new situation is permitted.

Such a model can explain puzzling instances of repetition in conceptual acquisition where young children give correct verbal responses, whereas somewhat older children give incorrect responses. The underlying concept in

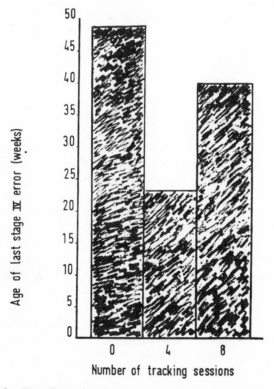

FIG. 3.9. The effects of variation in amount of practice in tracking on performance in manual search tasks.

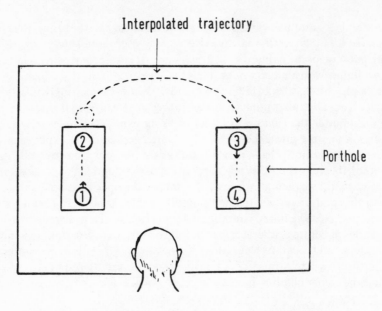

FIG. 3.10.   The tracking task used in the study by Mundy-Castle and Anglin (1973).

these cases is attained late in infancy. When the verbal tests are given first, there has not been enough time for the initial discovery to have been so specified that transfer is impossible. With older children, though, this will have taken place. Spontaneous transfer of the initial conceptual discovery will not thus occur. It will instead have to be dredged out of memory. There will thus be a seeming repetition.

There is one other experiment that fits quite well with the idea that in development abstract ideas necessarily precede specific ideas. This experiment attempted to accelerate the appearance of the trajectory interpolation effect describing by Mundy-Castle and Anglin (Bower, Note 4). In their experiment, the baby is shown an object moving upwards in a straight line to disappear at the edge of a window. After some time, an identical object appears at the top of the right-hand window and moves down in a straight line as shown in Figure 3.10. At some points of development, they found that babies will look along an "invisible" curvilinear trajectory between the windows as if looking for the object on a possible path between the windows.

The rationale behind the training conditions used is fully described in Bower (1974a) (see Figure 3.11). Both training conditions can clearly be described relatively abstractly or relatively specifically. Condition A can be described as (1) an object moves from place to place along a trajectory. A more specific description might say (2) If the object is at place x at time t, it will be at place y at time $t + n$. Description 2 is clearly more specific than Description 1. Which would tend to lead to improved interpolation performance? Clearly Description 1, applied to the Mundy-Castle situation, would produce trajectory interpolation. Description 2 would have no applicability in the transfer situation. Trajectory interpolation in the transfer situation should thus be as it is, a nonmonotonic function of amount of training in situation A (Figure 3.12).

What of Situation B? It could be described as (1) An object continues to move on an unchanging trajectory; (2) An object moves at x cycles per second on the circumference of a circle of radius r. Neither description, applied to the Mundy-Castle situation, would produce trajectory interpolation. Description 1 would, however, produce "movement" responses (Bower, Broughton, & Moore, 1971), that is, the child would look ceilingwards or floorwards depending on the movement just seen. This kind of response in the transfer situation waxes then wanes with increasing exposure to Situation B, as the results shown in Figure 3.13 show.

These transfer functions surely indicate that short-term problem solving goes from abstract to specific. The abstract solution will permit smooth transfer to new situations embodying the same conceptual problem. The specific solution will not. If the initial problem has been cracked down to specifics, we will thus get seeming repetition in development. This repetition

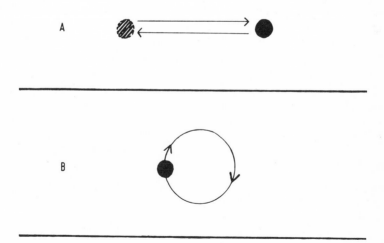

FIG. 3.11.   In Situation A the object stops briefly at each end of its movement path. In Situation B the object moves continuously.

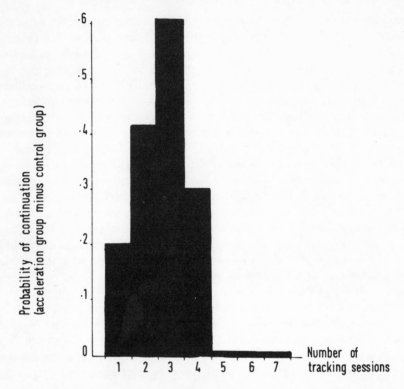

FIG. 3.12.   Trajectory interpolation is a nonmonotonic function of amount of training in Situation A.

will persist until the original solution can be dredged out of memory, or else created anew.

The problem with all of this, of course, is how to define terms like abstract. Abstract can be contrasted with *iconic* or *enactive* easily enough (Bruner, Olver, & Greenfield, 1966). That will only give us a negative definition of abstract, defining it by contrast with terms that may have little psychological validity anyway. The defnitions we now propose to offer are derived from Russell's theory of types (1910). The theory of types was first applied to psychology by Gregory Bateson (1972). For the purposes of this analysis we must assume that the process of learning and the process of development are processes in which representations or models of reality are constructed. It is these representations that control behavior. A representation can be more or less well specified. Let us consider a simple conditioning situation. When a bell rings and a baby turns his head to the right, sucrose is delivered to his mouth. A baby who has mastered this situation could have in its head a very well specified description of the form (1) I know that in this situation whenever a bell rings, if I turn my head to the right, I get sucrose in my mouth. This description amounts to a complete specification of the conditioning situation. A less well specified description might have the form (2) I know that in this situation there is a connection between my movements and the delivery of sucrose to my mouth. Statement 2 is less well specified than Statement 1. However, it is not simply a less-articulated version of Statement 1: It is a statement that is about the same state of affairs as Statement 1 but that provides no information about the truth or falsity of Statement 1, and is therefore of a different and conventionally higher logical type than Statement 1. The relationship between the levels is such that a type 1 statement can be true only if there is a true type 2 relationship to generate it. However the type 2 statement does not specify which of a family of type 1 statements is true. The relationship between levels is thus asymmetric. There are of course higher levels, which we do not propose to discuss (see Bower, 1978).

Psychologically, we are proposing that development goes from abstract to specific, whether we are talking about very short-term development or a long-term developmental effect like blindness, mentioned at the beginning.

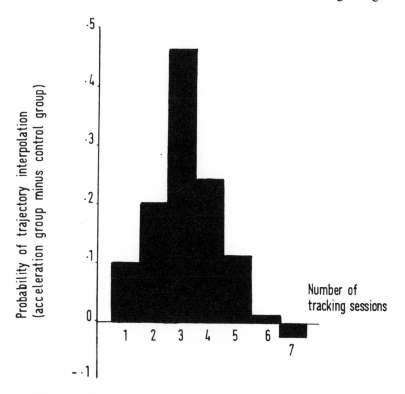

FIG. 3.13.   Continuation responses are a nonmonotonic function of amount of training in Situation B.

THE MODEL APPLIED TO
PERCEPTUAL DEVELOPMENT

Does a model of this kind have any application to other areas of development? Before coming to the primary concern of this conference, social development, we would like to take a look at perceptual development. The perceptual system of the very young child is, we know, very well organized and seems able to pick up quite detailed, specific information. Recently Dunkeld and Bower (1977) reinvestigated the infant's response to approaching objects. Bower, Broughton, and Moore (1970) and Ball and Tronick (1971) had claimed that very young infants will show a defensive response when presented with an approaching object. Yonas and Pick (1975) argued that the response was an artifact. The babies were trying to track the top edge of the object. As the object approached, its top edge went higher in the visual field, and the babies overbalanced. Dunkeld and Bower presented the babies with an approaching object where approach was correlated with a falling contour in the visual field. This was done by presenting the babies with a rotating rectangle in polar projection. What the babies saw in the two conditions is shown in Figure 3.14. The babies defended themselves in the polar condition and not in the parallel condition. This kind of differentiation indexes a high degree of specificity within the immature perceptual system. And yet there is evidence that the developmental process operates to make the system yet more specific and less plastic. If we stick with the topic of space perception, it seems possible to argue that the baby's first acquisition, possibly an intrauterine acquisition, is the very high level idea that the world has a three-dimensional structure and a temporal structure. This structural idea is then specified in terms of whatever variables are available. It is possible that the form of the variables are specified but not their modalities. Consider the recent study by Bower, Watson, and Umansky, (1976), which seemed to indicate that at least one congenitally blind child could use artificial auditory variables provided by an ultrasonic scanner to pick up spatial position and change of position. The variables given to the ear by this device are formally—at an abstract level—similar to those given to the eye by light. The immature perceptual system is quite happy to use this kind of variable. Later in development the system has been specified to use a particular set of inputs. It is very difficult for the adult to use an ultrasonic scanner of this kind. No adult has been able to make as good use of the scanner as this one baby did. The time course of this specification is not at present known. We were somewhat surprised by a second subject, a blind 13-month-old baby, who tried on an ultrasonic scanner (Bower, 1977). After only 20 minutes he seemed to be making some use of the information provided by the machine. This again is much more rapid acquisition than an adult could be expected to demonstrate. In perception then, it would seem that there is some evidence of an abstract to specific pattern in development, with increasing specification restricting the

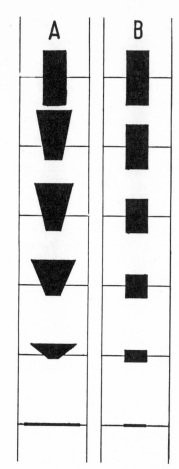

FIG. 3.14.   The baby's view of the rotating rectangle when (A) polar projection and (B) parallel projection were used.

range of the system, inhibiting "transfer" to new stimulus systems. Perception is perhaps of interest, too, since specification processes within perceptual systems have been described at a neural level. Since we know that neurones and even intact genotypes are specified from a very abstract potential by their environments, we might be able to look more kindly on the idea that the whole child in development is specified from a set of extremely abstract potentials to something functional yet much more limited.

CAN THE MODEL BE USED
TO CLARIFY SOCIAL DEVELOPMENT?

It is when we come to the origins of social responsiveness that a theory of this kind seems to face the greatest difficulties. The most influential theories of social development, theories such as those of Bowlby (1969) argue that sociability starts off as a set of specific, quasireflex responses. Since their normal focus is a human being, these reflexes coalesce to form the origins of sociability. As the theory is presented by some of its adherents (e.g., Schaffer, 1971) it is explicitly modeled on Piagetian theory of cognitive development.

There are of course other theories of the origins of sociability. Cupboard love theory though is basically a specific → abstract theory. Only the model offered by Watson at this conference would seem to fit with the abstract → specific model we are proposing. That model itself proposes extremely abstract beginnings for sociability. The amount of social information that is genetically specified is rather little within this theory. The specifics of social responses are not well described at all, according to Watson's theory.

One of the traditional battle grounds for trying to decide the original nature of the child's social responses has been the smile. Parents, at least, think the smile is a social response—a response for them, or, at least, for people. Psychologists typically have denounced them as naive. The smile is a reflex response to high-contrast stimuli, or else it signals detection of a contingency, or else perhaps it simply signals the experience of familiarity. Last year we presented 8- to 10-week old babies with the following three stimulus situations:

1. ::
2. The mother's face
3. A contingency game

All three elicited smiles. However the smiles were quite different. Situation 1 elicited short smiles, less frequently accompanied by tongue protrusion than in the other two situations. Situation 2 elicited slower smiles which lasted longer than those elicited by (1). Accompanying movements were towards the stimulus. Situation 3 elicited quicker, shorter smiles than the above two. This study, if we can replicate it, would seem to argue that, in the 8- to 10-week-old, as in the adult, there are multiple smiles, which are specific to specific situations, rather than the single response elicited by a rather loosely related set of stimuli.

Further evidence of specificity comes from studies of imitation. Imitation in our laboratory has been studied by Dunkeld (Note 5). Her results have been replicated by Maratos (Note 6) and Meltzoff & Moore (1977). If we set a baby opposite its mother or some other adult and the adult sticks his or her tongue out at the baby, the baby will begin to stick its tongue back out at the adult within a relatively short time. Suppose the adult then stops sticking his or her tongue out and begins to flutter his or her eyelashes; the baby will imitate the adult. If the adult then goes into mouth opening, for example, the baby will begin to open its mouth in synchrony. Similarly with finger waving. Babies will of course, stick their tongues out, flutter their eyelashes, wave their fingers, and open their mouths spontaneously. They do it far, far more, however, if there is an adult model present. Furthermore, unlike many of the other things we have mentioned, the newborn actually seems to enjoy engaging in this mutual-imitation game.

Let us stop for a moment and consider the level of organization employed by these behaviors. How does a baby know it has a mouth? How does a baby know it has a tongue? How does it know that its mouth and tongue are like the mouth and tongue it sees before him? There must be an incredible amount of built-in intersensory mapping for the baby to be able to look at an adult sticking out his or her tongue and transform that information so that it knows that, in this social situation, it should stick its tongue back out. The same thing goes for any of the imitations involving the face. How many very young babies have ever seen themselves in a mirror? The number must be very, very small. It does not seem to be typical or necessary to have seen oneself in a mirror for this precocious imitation to appear. The amount of built in intersensory coordination implied is more astonishing than anything we have had so far in straightforward studies of perception. The motor control involved is more precise than anything we have seen in any studies of neonatal motor skills. And all of these capacities are bent towards what is clearly, we think, a social purpose. The baby enjoys social interaction with adults. At this stage, imitation is a social game. The responses are quite specifically directed towards humans and seem to us to be testimony that newborns think they are human too. They somehow know that their face is like the adult face they see before them; their mouth is like the adult mouth they see before them.

The imitation described is very specific. When the mother's *hand* opens, the baby's *hand* opens; when the mother's *mouth* opens, the baby's *mouth* opens; when the mother's *eyes* open, the baby's *eyes* open. Confusions between the three were not observed.

With this kind of specificity, is there any point in trying to argue that social responsiveness begins with anything abstract? We think there is. For these responses, while specific enough, are subclasses of a very abstract family of responses. The baby's imitation is specific to *humans*. Presentation of a line that turns into a circle will elicit more or less rapt attention from young babies. It does not elicit imitation at all, so far as we can gather.

In the same way Condon and Sander (1974) found that interactional synchrony was elicited by human voices, but not by nonhuman noises. At the base of these two very specific behaviors there is, we would argue, a very abstract generating category—or awareness, if you like—that "I am human" and "they are human"—"I am like them." This kind of category judgment would amount to a very abstract yet surely innate specification for social responsiveness. That kind of responsiveness could be refined or perverted in numerous ways, depending on the contingent encounters experienced by the child. A particular set of encounters could obviously lead to the affectionless character (see Bowlby, 1951, for example).

A more interesting case is how "I am human" could be turned into "I am a girl" or "I am a boy." Lewis and Brooks (1975) have shown that infants by the age of 10 months will preferentially look at pictures of other infants of the same sex. As they point out this implies the kind of double categorization we implied above, "I am a girl—she is a girl—she is like me." "I am a girl" is a great deal more specific than "I am human."

We are thus arguing that social responsiveness is an innate human capacity. The earliest awareness is of nothing more specific than "humanness," a very abstract awareness that is gradually specified through categories such as gender to awareness of a specific personal identity (Bower, 1977).

This early social responsiveness is mediated by behaviors that are themselves very specific. Nonetheless, the early behaviors depend on abilities that are broader, less specific, than their descendants. For example it does seem that very young babies can segment and respond to the sounds of all human languages, including sounds that they will be unable to differentiate when they are older. Furthermore, it does seem that these early broad capacities do become very specific, occasionally producing maladaptive-seeming behavior, just as happens in the case of cognitive development. Consider the classic attachment behaviors, separation anxiety and stranger fear. Why do these behaviors occur? A variety of ingenious explanations have been offered, mostly oriented around the propositions that just as the mother's presence signals relief from discomfort, her absence signals incipient discomfort. Since a stranger is not the mother, the sight of a stranger may signal incipient discomfort too. This kind of theory has been extensively criticised by Schaffer (1971) among others, on the grounds that the target for a baby's separation anxiety may be someone who has played no part in caring for the baby at all. The most striking instances of this are child–child attachments. Babies—twins, in particular—may become more attached to other babies than to any adult (Figure 3.15). In such cases "nurture" is hardly relevant. In the same way Lewis and Brooks (1975) have shown that strange children are less fear provoking than are strange adults.

Can the kind of model presented here illuminate these processes at all? We would propose that separation anxiety and stranger fear are directly analogous to the repetition effects discussed at the beginning, that they basically represent failures of transfer due to overspecification. Overspecification of what? Previously we argued that the child is born with a very abstract awareness of "humanness" plus some very general strategies for signalling that awareness to others, strategies like imitation and interactional synchrony. It is these strategies, we would argue, that become so specified that they must produce separation anxiety and stranger fear. Right from the beginning of life, babies are ready to communicate in some fashion, with any adult around them. Typically, the baby will communicate with his mother. This communication is, of course, nonverbal, but it is communication. As

FIG. 3.15.   Child–child interaction can be as intense as adult–child interaction.

babies grow older, they and their mother develop particular individualistic communicational styles—styles of interaction that are characteristic of that mother and that baby (Trevarthen, 1975). Trevarthen has also shown that the communication routines used by a mother and her baby become more complex, more specific to them, the older the baby gets. Indeed, by 7 months or so, the age at which separation anxiety normally appears in Scotland, mother and baby have quite well-worked-out routines of communication. These routines are, as we have said, nonverbal, but they are specific to mother and baby. What happens when the mother leaves the baby with someone else? The baby is left with the stranger, someone who doesn't speak the same language as he or she does; someone who doesn't respond to his or her social gestures, social invitations, social ploys, or interactions. The baby is effectively left alone; his communication partner is gone. He is isolated from other adults by the very specificity and development of the communication routines he shares with his mother. As we know from the work of Schachter (1959) and others, human adults cannot tolerate solitude. It would seem very unlikely that babies can either. When their mothers go off and leave them they are, effectively, alone. In terms of communication they are completely isolated, because they have learned to "talk" to and interact with one specific person. Twin babies obviously learn to communicate with one another and they probably learn to communicate with each other more efficiently than with any adult. This could explain why twins characteristically show separation anxiety when separated from one another.

The newborn is ready to interact with anyone in any way. After some months with one communication figure—a communication figure who perhaps emphasizes vocalization, body contact, or a body movement, or a sequence of all three—the child comes to expect certain sorts of interchange, set patterns of interchange, and is geared to these patterns of interchange. If they are not forthcoming, the baby is alone. If we agree with William James, who said that the original source of terror is solitude, we can perhaps empathize with these babies, communicationally isolated on the departure of their primary communicational partner.

There is evidence that babies growing up in close proximity do learn to communicate with one another; they become communicationally attuned. Their level of motor skill and their own individual temperaments determine just how well they can do so. Very typically, babies of less than 1 year will exchange strings of vocalizations; they will vastly enjoy doing this. The more closely attuned they are, the greater is the risk of loss whenever a communicational partner goes, leaving the child effectively alone in a world of strangers who cannot communicate with him.

This analysis of separation anxiety can possibly illuminate the stranger fear too. By the age of 8 months a stranger is someone the child cannot communicate with, someone he has never tried to communicate with.

Schaffer (1971) has pointed out that we are more likely to see stranger fear if a stranger tries to interact with the baby. If he ignores the baby, we're not likely to see stranger fear. If, however, the stranger tries to communicate with the baby, we are very likely to get stranger fear in its fullest form. Suppose we were approached by someone much larger than us, speaking a foreign tongue, obviously expecting to be understood; such a situation it seems to us, would be fear provoking, and it is not surprising that it provokes fear in babies.

CONCLUSIONS

We have thus proposed a model of development in which "higher"(i.e., more abstract) structures precede "lower" (i.e., more specific) structures. The increasing specificity of initially abstract structures and capacities may result in seeming loss of capacity throughout development. The most useful area of application of this kind of model is cognitive development. It can be applied to personality development without violence (Bateson, 1972). Abstract to specific as a pattern may be useful in the analysis of perceptual development as well. In the realm of social development we have proposed that the child is born with a very abstract awareness of humanness. By 10 months a less abstract awareness of gender has also been acquired. During infancy too it seems possible that the child acquires abstract ideas about other people (basically nice versus basically not nice). These abstract ideas about self and others generate specific rules and behaviors for coping with people. At times the rules and behaviors may become so specific that transfer to new people is impossible. This is, for us, homologous with the processes whereby the baby in coping with the problem of "in" can so specify his representation of a situation that he cannot cope with a new presentation involving the same spatial relation.

ACKNOWLEDGMENTS

This research has been supported by grant numbers G972/982/C and G972/186/N from the Medical Research Council, Great Britain.

DISCUSSION

Dr. William Mason: Would you say that what you mean by *abstract* is more or less synonymous with *schematic*? Abstract ordinarily implies some sort of a hierarchical arrangement, to me at least. In contrast, schematic implies a lack of detailed specification of the effective elements. Will you comment on this?

Mrs. Wishart: The theory of types offers a very powerful tool for defining abstract and specific. Psychologically, I think we mean abstract firstly in terms of power of generating appropriate behavior. It's abstract in that it can cope with more situations. If babies have an abstract framework for applying to any given situation it's more powerful obviously than having only specific responses to specific situations. It's also very useful to a baby to have such an economical way of organizing input.

Dr. Mason: Would you apply that to actions as well as to perceptions then?

Mrs. Wishart: Yes. Take, for example, reaching and the comercially based attempts to intervene in this area. We all know what is bad for babies. We know that minimal social contact, for example, and few opportunities for learning is a bad environment, so we've turned to think that a good evnironment must necessarily mean increased social contact and increased learning situations. It does not seem to be as straightforward as that. Commercially available reaching aids work on the assumption that a simple increase in opportunities for reaching must improve and accelerate performance. I believe there are a great variety of these on sale in this country. Mothers are persuaded that they are good for their children. Some of them are not. they may just be irrelevant. They certainly don't affect social development or cognitive development. They might be good muscular exercisers. According to advertising claims, however, they're supposed to accelerate reaching. They don't in fact. In some cases, they may actually retard reaching and grasping, because the baby gets used to reaching for something in the same place all the time. They make a very specified movement and can't adapt it to an object in a different place. This is true, of course, only if it's used to excess—if the mother uses it as some sort of baby sitter by sticking it in the crib. Used in moderation with social interaction and bearing in mind John's points, it will, of course, not be harmful. It's just been so hard sold that it's very difficult to persuade people that in certain circumstances it *could* be harmful. The baby can overspecify his behavior and then cannot adapt to different situations requiring similar but not identical responses.

Dr. Korner: I too am wondering whether the baby really responds in an abstract way. Might it not be more accurate to view his responses as being global? At a very young age babies don't respond to the fine details of a general configuration, and they therefore do not as yet get confused by them. It is not more congruent with prevailing developmental theory to consider the infant's first response to be global or general; that as he develops, his response becomes more specific and differentiated and that only after he can look beyond the specifics, can his response become truly abstract?

Mrs. Wishart: I think babies come into the world better prepared than we are willing to give them credit for. For instance, consider the rotating object presentation—they seem to realize that it represents a threat, even though the stimulation involved is very specific. They respond immediately to adult speech with social behavior. Obviously the world must be a very confusing place for them but they are already have some sort of built-in structure that programs them to organize it in a human way. A sort of biological safeguard. Abstract generating categories are powerful but also have limitations. They produce losses, as I say, but these are only temporary setbacks resulting from reorganizations. They're getting new input all the time. That new input has to be reorganized on the basis of what's gone before. Development is not just additive. It's a matter of direction. If a baby shoots off in the wrong direction to start with, any amount of later intervention is futile if you don't know which developmental path he's taken in the first place. You're wasting your time attempting simply to give them later what they've lost earlier, because they will now interpret it in a different way completely. The input has to be modified to suit the particular child's development. That could be why Head Start failed. These children were in fact *different* by that time—they had probably developed in an entirely different direction—so the enrichment being given to them was not as appropriate and therefore valuable as it could have been.

Dr. Denenberg: There is in biology a concept that I think is similar in abstract notion to yours. This has to do with the function of the male sex hormone, which we know to be present either prenatally or neonatally in virtually all male mammals. For many years no one knew why the hormone was there. Testosterone, for example, was found in the neonatal rat, then it disappeared. So it was present, then it was not present for a long period of time, and then it was present again. And that, in a sense, is crudely like your infant being able to do something, and then the function dropping off to a poorer performance, and then increasing in adulthood. Now Jeffrey Harris, of course, came up with the concept that the function of the hormone in the neonatal or prenatal period was to organize the brain to make it either a male or a female brain. If testosterone was present in the prenatal or neonatal period, the brain was masculinized. Otherwise it became feminine. The important thing is that the brain has the potential to be *either* male or female. In that sense it is "abstract." Thereafter—that is, in adulthood—the presence of the hormone functioned to activate an already organized system.

Now let me see whether that kind of concept is similiar to what you're saying. You're saying that the infant starts out with abstract capabilities. Let me phrase it this way: The infant starts out in early life with something analogous to the presence of testosterone that acts to organize the potential for behavior in a certain fashion. Having had the organizational structure laid down, later events and stimuli activate this structure.

This raises the interesting point that it may not be relevant to study some behavior patterns between infancy and puberty. Certainly the study of sex behavior in immature rats is irrelevant. The organizational characteristics have been established in infancy but are not expressed until after puberty. Studying sex behavior in immature rats would tell you absolutely nothing. Studying the hormonal substrate in infancy would tell you a tremendous amount. It would tell you whether the animal will have a male brain or a female brain.

So we have two interesting questions. First, perhaps the focus should indeed be upon infancy, which is the function of this particular meeting. Secondly, it raises the issue as to whether we're gathering very much relevant information by studying certain behaviors at ages prior to puberty or prior to the occurrence of some other particularly defined function.

Mrs. Wishart: I'm afraid I can't claim to know a great deal about biology. It does seem to me though that there would seem to be some support from these areas for our type of analysis.

Dr. Denenberg: Let me add one more thing. The studies on those individuals who were blind and had sight restored have shown that if they had had some degree of prior visual experience, it did not matter very much when the cataracts were removed. It's as though the initial visual experience in infancy was sufficient to organize that system. I would guess the same thing is probably true of linguistic experience. Thus, I think the concept may have applications well beyond the original work on sex hormones.

Mrs. Wishart: This is very true of the spatial concepts mentioned— Euclidean geometry for instance. It seems ridiculous that experience in infancy could have any possible effect on the acquisition of Euclidean geometry, but it does seem that without certain experience in infancy, there's just no way that the concepts involved in Euclidean geometry can be understood. In the past, Edinburgh University was a very traditional university, and to be accepted there, you had to be proficient in Latin, Greek, and Euclidean geometry. There were quite a number of blind students in the university who passed the entrance test in Euclidean geometry, but they did it completely by rote learning. They could churn out the theorems, but given a really simple problem, they had no idea at all what to do. The blind seem to order the world temporally, which is how information comes in through the ear; and they're incapable of reorganizing it in a spatial way at all.

Dr. Papousek: The biological models that might be relevant to this point of view are available at least theoretically. I think that what you show with this structural hierarchy seems to be a very general model that can be applied to different situations. It has been applied in logical classification and Linnaeus's system of botany, and in animal classification. What interests me is the structure of the muscular system. That seems to be organized, in a similar way, from single units to simple parts of muscles to individual muscles to whole complex of muscles, and this is something that is relevant for the development of behavior. Now I think that you only look at a very narrow section of developmental capacities to reach such a general conclusion as you're drawing about going from abstraction to specific responses. We first have to differentiate something.

That's the way the motor system develops. If you look at prenatal development at the moment when the nervous system starts controlling the muscle, we first see nondifferentiated global responses to stimulate a whole system response. And then it becomes specific and actually creates those individual responses. Now this could be called a global response and only here would we call it an abstract response.

Dr. Denenberg: There is a different kind of efficiency involved in the two things. If you take an organism that's relatively naive and say it's got to deal with the world in some way, then you really want it to respond on the basis of fairly gross categories and dispositions and that kind of thing.

Mrs. Wishart: That's true—it's very efficient in infancy to organize input in such a way.

Dr. Denenberg: If it hears a loud noise or something moves towards it and the eyes blink, and so on, this reflects the verbalized nature of the nervous system. And at some later stage you want an organism to really respond on the basis, let's say, of the acquired significance of events or functional equivalents or that sort of thing. That, it seems to me, gets closer to what we usually mean by abstract.

Mrs. Wishart: I think it's really particularly efficient in infancy. It's perhaps only reallly plausible at this stage when new input is enormous and really must be organized in some way if they're going to be able to make sense out of it. You would have to have some structure to condense the information coming in. We did do one experiment on babies under 3 weeks which lends support to the idea of input being organized on rather abstract principles. We showed them a display that could change in position or could change in modality. For instance, a light would flash from left to right. We recorded the baby's heart rate. We would wait till the baby became habituated to the display and then it would change to, say, a light flashing from top to bottom; alternatively it could change from a light going left to right to a sound going from left to right in the same position. We were interested to see which caused a greater change in heart rate. The change in modality meant little to the babies. They did not seem to process the information as coming through any particular sense. It was as though there was just information on the position of an event. The same is true in the case of the blind child who was using an ultrasonic device. The information given to the ear is, at an abstract level, very similar to that given through the eyes—it can give size, distance, and texture, although obviously there's no light, no color. It gives much better information than self-produced echoes can. It does seem that an infant is much more capable of using this information than adults. The device itself is technically perfect, but the majority of adults don't seem to be able to make good use of the information it gives. It's just too complex. A child seems to respond—I don't like the word *spontaneously*—but they seem to respond to the input through the ears just as if it were coming through the eyes.

REFERENCE NOTES

1. Wishart, J. G., & Bower, T. G. R. *Comprehension of spatial relations in infancy.* Manuscript in preparation, 1976.
2. Sheeran, L. *Vertical decalage in weight conservation between sensorimotor and conceptual levels.* Unpublished honors thesis, Department of Psychology, University of Edinburgh, 1973.
3. Wishart, J. G., & Bower, T. G. R. *Conservation of number in infancy.* Manuscript in preparation, 1976.
4. Bower, T. G. R. *Notion d'objet et contradictions sensorimotrices chez le nouveau-ne et le tres jeune enfant.* Paper read at 26th International Congress of Genetic Epistemology, Geneva, 1971.
5. Dunkeld, J. *The development of imitation in infancy.* Unpublished Ph.D thesis, University of Edinburgh, 1973.
6. Maratos, O. *The origin and development of imitation in the first six months of life.* Unpublished Ph.D thesis, University of Geneva, 1973.

REFERENCES

Ball, W., & Tronick, E. Infant responses to impending collision: Optical and real. *Science,* 1971, *171,* 818–820.

Bateson, G. *Steps towards an ecology of mind.* London: Picador, 1972.

Bower, T. G. R. The visual world of infants. *Scientific American,* 1966, *215,* 80–92.

Bower, T. G. R. The object in the world of the infant. *Scientific American,* 1971, *225,* 30–38.

Bower, T. G. R. *Development in infancy.* San Francisco: W. H. Freeman & Co., 1974. (a)

Bower, T. G. R. Repetition in human development. *Merrill-Palmer Quarterly of Behavior and Development,* 1974, *20,* 303–318. (b)

Bower, T. G. R. Concepts of development. *In Proceedings of the 21st International Congress of Psychology,* Paris, July 1976. Paris, Presses Universitaires de France 1978.

Bower, T. G. R. *A primer of infant development.* San Francisco: W. H. Freeman & Co, 1977.

Bower, T. G. R. Blind babies see with their ears. *New Scientist,* 3rd February, 1977.

Bower, T. G. R., Broughton, J. M., & Moore, M. K. Infant responses to approaching objects: An indicator of response to distal variables. *Perception and Psychophysics,* 1970, *90,* 193–196.

Bower, T. G. R., Broughton, J. K., & Moore, M. K. The development of the object concept as manifested by changes in the tracking behavior of infants between 7 and 20 weeks of age. *Journal of Experimental Child Psychology,* 1971, *11,* 182–193.

Bower, T. G. R., & Paterson, J. G. The separation of place, movement and object in the world of the infant. *Journal of Experimental Child Psychology,* 1973, *15,* 161–168.

Bower, T. G. R., Watson, J. S., Umansky, R. Auditory surrogates for vision in sensori-motor development. Manuscript submitted for publication, October 1976.

Bower, T. G. R., & Wishart, J. G. The effects of motor skill on object permanence. *Cognition,* 1972, *1,* 165–172.

Bowlby, J. *Maternal care and mental health.* Geneva: World Health Organization, 1951.

Bowlby, J. *Attachment and Loss* (Vol. 1) *Attachment.* London: Hogarth Press, 1969.

Bruner, J. S., Olver, R. R., & Greenfield, P. M. *Studies in Cognitive Growth.* New York: John Wiley, 1966.

Collard, R. R., & Dempsey, J. R. Number concept in eight to twelve-month-old infants. *Proceedings of the 21st International Congress of Psychology,* Paris, July 1976, Paris, Presses Universitaires de France, 1978.

Condon, W. S., & Sander, L. Neonate movement is synchronized with adult speech: Interactional participation and language acquisition. *Science,* 1974, *183,* 99–101.

Day, R. H., & McKenzie, B. E. Perceptual shape constancy in early infancy. *Perception,* 1973, *2,* 315–332.

Drever, J. Early learning and the perception of space. *American Journal of Psychology,* 1955, *68,* 605–614.

Dunkeld, J., & Bower, T. G. R. Infant response to impending optical collision. Manuscript submitted for publication, October 1977.

Gouin-Décarie, T. *Intelligence and affectivity in early childhood: An experimental study of Jean Piaget's object concept and object relations.* New York: International Universities Press, 1966.

Hatwell, Y. *Privation sensorielle et intelligence.* Paris: Presses Universitaires de France, 1966.

Lewis, M., & Brooks, J. Infants' social perception: A constructivist view. In L. B. Cohen and P. Salapatek (Eds.), *Infant perception: From sensation to cognition* (Vol. 2). New York: Academic Press, 1975.

Maratsos, M. P. Decrease in the understanding of the word "Big" in pre-school children. *Child Development,* 1973, *44,* 747–752.

Mehler, J., & Bever, T. G. Cognitive capacity of very young children. *Science,* 1967, *158,* 141–142.

Meltzoff, A. & Moore, M. K. Imitation of facial and manual gestures. *Science,* 1977, *198,* 75–80.

Mounoud, P., & Bower, T. G. R. Conservation of weight in infants. *Cognition,* 1974, *3,* 29–40.

Mundy-Castle, A. C., & Anglin, J. Looking strategies in infants. In L. J. Stone, H. T. Smith, L. B. Murphy (Eds.), *The Competent Infant.* New York, Basic Books 1973.

Piaget, J. *Play, dreams and imitation.* New York: Norton, 1963. (Originally French edition, 1945.)

Piaget, J., & Inhelder, B. *The child's conception of space.* London: Routledge & Kegan Paul, 1956. (Originally French edition, 1948.)

Russell, B. La theorie des types logiques. *Revue de Metaphysique et de Morale,* 1910, *18,* 263–301.

Schachter, S. *The psychology of affiliation.* Stanford: Stanford University Press, 1959.

Schaffer, H. R. *The growth of sociability.* Harmondsworth, England: Penguin Books, 1971.

Trevarthen, C. Early attempts at speech. In R. Lewin (Ed.), *Child Alive.* London: Temple Smith, 1975.

Yonas, A. & Pick, H. L. An approach to the study of infant space perception In L. B. Cohen & P. Salapatek (Eds.), *Infant perception: From Sensation to Cognition.* Vol. 2 New York, Academic Press, 1975.

4

Maternal Rhythms and Waterbeds: A Form of Intervention with Premature Infants

Anneliese F. Korner
Stanford University

In this chapter, I am going to present the hypotheses and rationale, the methodological approaches, and some of the findings of several related intervention studies with premature infants currently under way in my laboratory. I would like to use this account to illustrate some of the theoretical issues I needed to confront and some of the methodological choices I had to make in implementing these studies.

SOME THEORETICAL QUESTIONS AT ISSUE IN INTERVENTION STUDIES WITH PREMATURE INFANTS

In considering an intervention study with premature infants, the first and most fundamental issue one must address is the question of whether providing extra stimulation to premature infants is indeed relevant for their development. If it is, what kind of stimulation is theoretically apt to be the most relevant, delivered in what form, and to achieve what end?

The question of whether stimulation given to premature infants has any relevance for their development is indeed a controversial one. This controversy is perhaps less alive in the United States than elsewhere for there are currently a number of intervention studies with premature infants under way in this country. The controversy centers around the issue of whether the natural course of brain maturation is not mainly responsible for the infant's developmental progress, or whether benefits accrue from environmental stimulation and experience that will materially affect this progress. The premature birth of an infant represents an experiment in nature that potentially could shed some light on this controversy. By comparing the behavioral performance of infants born at term with that of two-to-three months prematurely born infants that have grown to term, one may gain some insight into whether extrauterine experience materially affects behavioral development. Parmelee (1975) recently reviewed the evidence from studies making this comparison and found this evidence to be largely contradictory and inconclusive. Many behavioral and psychophysiological studies point to developmental similarities between infants at comparable postconceptual ages regardless of age from birth. Other studies point to both selected areas of precocity and to areas of developmental delays among premature infants when compared to infants born at term. Parmelee concluded from much of the conflicting evidence that the development of many premature infants is characterized by a certain unevenness that is apt to lead to difficulties later in life.

If one accepts, as I do, the overriding importance of brain maturation in governing behavioral development, is it nevertheless possible to believe that the uneven development among premature infants may be due, in addition to the obvious morbidity in this group, to the peculiar environment in which these infants are raised? Dreyfus-Brisac (1970), who by virtue of her studies of the ontogeny of sleep patterns is a strong proponent of the paramount influence of brain maturation on development, nevertheless thinks that the particular kind of extrauterine environment in which premature infants are treated may hamper the natural unfolding of maturation. Until recently it was thought advisable to minimally handle premature infants; the stimulation they received was largely limited to medical procedures, thus constituting stressful stimulation. The incubator and the intensive-care nursery environment, with its continuous bright lights and its monotonous, loud white noise generated by the incubator motor and by other nursery equipment, have alternately been described as an environment of sensory deprivation and sensory bombardment. A good case can be made for both descriptions: The sheer monotony of light and sound and the lack of patterned stimulation in the nursery have been considered as creating an environment of sensory deprivation, whereas the intensity and persistence of these stimuli have been described as a source of sensory bombardment. While nothing is known about how premature infants deal with either sensory deprivation or sensory overload, we know from studies with adults that overstimulation and understimulation have a disruptive and disorganizing effect on the physiological and psychological functioning of the organism (e.g., Frankenhaeuser & Johansson, 1974). We also know from studies with full-term babies (Brackbill, 1971; Schmidt, 1975; Wolff, 1966) that continuous monotonous stimulation lowers the infants' arousal level and is sleep inducing. We do not know whether premature infants react the same way to such stimulation, nor can we be certain that lowering these infants' arousal level is a desirable goal. One may conclude from the above that the premature infant may not now be raised in an environment that optimizes the natural course of brain maturation, and that there may be room for improvement of this environment, particularly in the area of providing more patterned stimulation that is not connected with stressful medical procedures.

Few investigators engaged in intervention studies with premature infants explicitly state the specific goals they wish to achieve with intervention. Implied in many intervention studies is the aim to accelerate the infants' development. One may question to what extent behavioral and neurological acceleration is feasible, and if it is feasible, whether it is desirable. We do know that physiological development can be hastened, as exemplified by the administration of cortisone-type substances to mothers prior to giving birth in order to hasten the formation of surfactant in the premature infant's lungs. Such intervention substantially reduces the risk of the infant's developing severe respiratory distress. Here, the potentially life-saving benefits offset the risks of disrupting the orderly sequence of the infant's physiological development. But in situations where the priorities of needs are less obvious and clear-cut, do we want to risk interfering with the orderly sequence of the infant's development through our intervention? Do we know enough about this sequence to intervene in a functionally appropriate way? Most importantly, does a *faster* rate of developing certain functions guarantee a *higher* level of functioning in the long run? I think not.

What then is my rationale in doing an intervention study with premature infants? Obviously my goals are not to accelerate development, but they are to create conditions in which the infants' maturation can take place with a minimum of interference. My model is designed to offset certain deficits within the environment in which premature infants are currently raised and also to compensate for certain forms of stimulation that are presumably highly prevalent *in utero* and that are minimally provided in premature infant care. My goals then are to create conditions which facilitate, consolidate, and optimize the infants' development and, if possible, to make it more even. The issue is not whether intervention can raise developmental quotients that are measurable months or years after its completion, for we know from many studies that the home environment and family circumstances over which the investigator has no control exert an overriding influence on developmental outcome (see, for example, Sameroff's 1975 review on this topic). The issue is to produce a child that is as intact as possible and that, by that token, is more capable of coping with whatever home environment he or she may be entering. What may count the most is what gets set in motion between parent and child, and I assume that what the infant presents to the parent by way of robustness and intactness is an important factor in this equation.

If we assume that intervention may benefit premature infants, are there certain forms of intervention that may be more relevant than others? Here, too, much controversy exists. Several studies including that by Scarr-Salapatek and Williams (1973) have used multiple forms of stimulation, including patterned visual stimuli, handling, rocking, and exposure to the human face and voice. In presenting their rationale for the choice of these forms of stimulation, Scarr-Salapatek and Williams argued pursuasively that even though the fetus would not be exposed to any of these types of stimuli *in utero,* "at birth it seems likely that sensory systems change in their organization and functioning just as respiratory and digestive systems alter their mode of operation [p. 95]." It is quite true that the event of birth is irreversible and changes the functioning of the infant in fundamental ways. However, within the realm of sensory or neurological behavior we know nothing as to how the infant's functioning changes with the advent of birth. In my view, just as good an argument can be presented that the event of birth does not change the preterm infant into an organism that responds to the visual or social environment like a full-term infant. We do know from many studies that psychophysiologically and neurologically the preterm infant does not function like a full-term baby, which must mean that some of the forms of stimulation to which full-term infants are highly responsive may have very little relevance for the premature baby.

A case in point is the preterm infant's apparent inability to profit much from visual experiences. Parmelee and Sigman (1976) recently reviewed their own work and that of others on the development of visual behavior in pre- and full-term infants. The authors concluded that from all the evidence accumulated, the preterm infant does not seem to benefit from visual experiences before the expected date of birth. Neither their usually extended stay in the newborn nursery nor the longer periods these infants spend in their own homes prior to the time of testing seems to give the prematurely born infant an advantage with regard to his or her visual development over the full-term infant of the same postconceptual age. Parmelee and Sigman suggested as a result of their comparisons that the maturation of the nervous system is the predominant determinant of visual responses in the early months of life. The premature infant does not seem to respond much to social stimulation either. Studies that have used social stimulation as a form of intervention with premature infants through early mother–infant interaction have shown that although early exposure and interaction with her young greatly facilitates the mother's bond formation and commitment to her child (Barnett, Leiderman, Grobstein, & Klaus, Jerauld, Kreger, McAlpine, Steffa, & Kennell, 1972), such interactions seem to have very little direct effect on the infant (Barnett et al, 1970; Powell, 1974). This does not mean that there are not potentially long-range effects on the child's development as mediated through the mother's involvement with the child (see, for example, the study by Kennell, Jerauld, Wolfe, Chesler, Kreger, McAlpine, Steffa, and Klaus, 1974). What it does mean is that the small preterm infant's development is not sufficiently differentiated for her or him to respond differentially or specifically to his *mother's* interventions.

What then might be relevant forms of stimulation for the preterm infant? In my view, for stimulation to be relevant one must consider the infant's level of neurophysiologic development and such stimulation must be transmitted through functions that ontogentically mature early. According to Hooker's (1952) studies of prenatal behavior, the fetus responds earliest to tactile and vestibular–proprioceptive stimulation. Many intervention studies with premature babies have used tactile stimulation, usually not for the above reasons but because child-care practices and much of the literature emphasize the importance of contact and touch for the early development of very young infants. The results of these studies vary. What is of interest from our studies with full-term infants (Korner & Thoman, 1970, 1972), is that in almost all instances in which an infant is provided contact or tactile stimulation he is also moved in the process. The effects of tactile and vestibular-proprioceptive stimulation are thus confounded in most stroking studies.

In my view, there is a good deal of rationale for providing vestibular–proprioceptive stimulation to small premature infants. Premature infants do not receive much of this type of stimulation during intensive care nor during their frequently extended period of stay inside the incubator. Also, while we do not know precisely what kinds of stimulation the fetal infant receives *in utero,* I do assume that he is exposed to considerable amounts of vestibular–proprioceptive stimulation mediated through his flotation in the amniotic fluid, caused by his own movements and by the postural changes of his mother. Furthermore, the reason that I view vestibular–proprioceptive stimulation as particularly relevant ontogenetically for the preterm infant is that according to the literature, the vestibular system matures very early in fetal life, both anatomically and functionally. According to Hooker (1952) the vestibular apparatus is anatomically complete in the $9\frac{1}{2}$-week-old fetus. Langworthy (1933) demonstrated that myelinization of the vestibular system begins at 4 months gestational age, is well underway in the fetus of 6 months, and is quite heavy at term. While the presence of myelin does not necessarily indicate that a system is functional, Minkowski (1921) and Humphrey 1965) showed that the vestibular system begins to function at about the same time myelinization commences. Minkowski demonstrated reflexes that he thought to be of labyrinthine origin in fetuses as young as 3 to 4 months, and Humphrey described the vestibular nuclei as unquestionably functional at 21 weeks of gestation. Although there is some debate on the extent to which the reflexes elicited this early in fetal life are of vestibular or of postural origin

(Parmelee, 1975, personal communication), there is no question that the postural and righting reflexes do have a vestibular component. Certainly, by the time the infant has reached 32 weeks of postconceptual age, he is able to respond with both a rotational and postrotational nystagmus to rotation according to Pendleton and Paine (1961). As he nears term, the awake infant's rotational and postrotational nystagmus is quite similar to that of the adult, according to these authors. Also highlighting the early maturity of the vestibular system is the fact that in conditioning experiments, vestibular stimulation is the earliest conditional stimulus that is effective with neonates (Kasatkin, 1972). It is thus the early functional maturity of the vestibular system that makes me view this system as an ontogenetically relevant mediator of early stimulation.

Only a few intervention studies with premature infants aiming to facilitate behavioral development have used vestibular–proprioceptive stimulation exclusively or as one of the main forms of stimulation. Neal's (1967) and Barnard's (1972) studies are notable exceptions. Neal randomly assigned 62 premature infants whose gestational ages ranged from 28 to 32 weeks to an experimental group that received a regimen of vestibular stimulation or to a control group that received routine care. Vestibular stimulation was given in a hammock within the incubator, for three 30-minute periods a day. The hammock moved in a compound motion horizontally and vertically. When assessed through the Rosenblith revision of the Graham Test at 36 weeks postconceptual age, the babies from the experimental group showed significantly greater overall behavioral maturation, particularly in the visual, auditory, and motor spheres. Also, the mean weight gain of the infants in the experimental groups exceeded that of controls. Barnard combined vestibular –proprioceptive and auditory stimulation by providing mechanical horizontal rocking in the incubator and the sound of a heartbeat to 7 premature infants. This was done for 15 minutes every hour during the 33rd and 34th weeks of postconceptual age. Barnard found significantly greater increases in quiet sleep in the experimental group than in the 8 control subjects. Also, the experimental group showed a trend toward more weight gain and higher maturational scores.

I should probably state at this point that my interest in providing compensatory vestibular–proprioceptive stimulation to premature infants did not originate from a long-standing commitment to doing an intervention study with premature babies. Instead, this interest grew out of the results of 10 years of developmental research, which alerted us to the potency of vestibular–proprioceptive stimulation in producing both behavioral and developmental changes in the newborn. Our intervening with premature infants can thus be viewed as a logical extension of these earlier studies, the results of which furnished the rationale for our current work.

BACKGROUND STUDIES LEADING TO
INTERVENTION WITH PREMATURE INFANTS

About 12 years ago, I was primarily engaged in studies of individual and sex differences in normal neonates (e.g., Korner, 1964, 1971, 1973, 1974). In the context of these studies, I naturally became interested in the types of stimulation neonates are most responsive to, and this inevitably led to studies of the kinds of stimuli that are most soothing to newborns. Needless to say this issue has great relevance for the beginning mother–infant relationship. Rather than studying various forms of soothing in a laboratory context as had been done by others, we wanted to determine what forms of stimulation typically provided by maternal interventions were most effective in soothing newborns (Korner and Grobstein, 1966; Korner and Thoman, 1970, 1972). In imitating various maternal ministrations, we found, not surprisingly, that one of the most effective interventions with a crying newborn was to pick him up and put him to the shoulder. What we did not anticipate was that this intervention, in addition to promptly soothing infants, almost invariably made them bright-eyed and alert and caused them to scan the environment. The reason we got excited about this observation is that it predictably produced a state that many investigators of newborns feel to be the one most conducive to the earliest forms of learning. It is through visual exploration that the motorically helpless infant is most apt to get acquainted with his environment, including his mother. In two studies we were able to produce this state of visual alertness in over 75% of all trials; still, it should be noted that this state occurs spontaneously only infrequently. Wolff (1966) who monitored infant states around the clock, found that the newborn spends only 11% of his day in the state of visual alertness.

As a result of this unexpected finding we became curious as to what exactly produced the soothing effect and the activation of visual exploration. We wondered whether it was mostly body contact, which is usually considered such an important form of stimulation for very young infants, or whether it was the vestibular–proprioceptive stimulation and the activation of the antigravity reflexes that produced this effect. To answer this question we embarked on an experimental study in which we tested the relative efficacy of body contact and of vestibular–proprioceptive stimulation with and without the upright position in both soothing and evoking visual alertness in the infant (Korner and Thoman, 1970, 1972). These types of stimulation were given singly and in combination in the context of what mothers commonly do with infants. The following six interventions were made in random order with 40 normal newborns, equally divided as to males and females, breast- and bottle-fed infants. The types of stimulation given in each intervention are listed in parentheses.

1. The infant was lifted from the examining table and put to the shoulder, head supported (Upright, vestibular–proprioceptive, contact).

2. The infant was lifted horizontally and cradled in arms as if nursing (Vestibular–proprioceptive, contact).

3. The infant was embraced, held close. In this position, great care was taken not to move the infant in any way (contact).

4. The infant who had previously been placed in an infant seat, was raised to the upright position with the back of the infant seat at a 55-degree angle to the examining table (Upright, vestibular–proprioceptive).

5. The infant, having been previously placed in the infant seat, was moved to and fro horizontally as if in a perambulator (Vestibular–proprioceptive).

6. The infant lying supine on the examining table, was talked to at a standard distance in a high-pitched female voice, simulating "mother talk". The voice was used as a marker to indicate when to observe, after a preliminary study had shown that the voice elicited no more alerting than occurred spontaneously without any intervention. (None of the above types of stimulation).

The results of this study clearly indicated that the interventions entailing vestibular–proprioceptive stimulation evoked significantly more visual alertness than contact, and that contact alone had no greater effect than hearing a high-pitched voice, which in turn, judging from preliminary work, had no greater effect on alerting than would have occurred by chance. Very similar results were seen with respect to the soothing effects of the interventions. Vestibular–proprioceptive stimulation was significantly more effective than contact, but at least contact was a better soother than the voice.

We were struck by the implications of these findings. It seemed that infants whose mothers respond to their crying by picking them up, not only must derive comfort and gradually a feeling that their actions have an effect on their environment, but they are also given many more opportunities for visual experiences than they would have had if they were left unattended. We were also struck by the fact that the anthropological and early-stimulation literature has stressed primarily the importance of body contact and tactile stimulation for early development, whereas the less visible, vestibular–proprioceptive stimulation, which is involved in almost every contact between mother and child, had largely been overlooked.

Next we undertook a study that sought to clarify the differential efficacy of vestibular–proprioceptive stimulation and the upright position in bringing about visual attentiveness in neonates (Gregg, Haffner, & Korner, 1976). This study was prompted, in part, by the fact that others interpreted our findings to mean that it is the upright, rather than the infant's being moved that produced the alerting effect. Since vestibular–proprioceptive stimulation is a much more pervasive form of stimulation in the interaction between mother and child, it seemed important to us to sort out whether it was this form of stimulation or the upright position that brings about the infant's attentiveness to the environment.

This was not a naturalistic study; it was done under well-controlled laboratory conditions. An apparatus was used that permitted horizontal and upright positioning of an infant seat as well as displacement of the infant in both these directions. There were many different aspects to this study, but our main question was tested by randomly assigning 24 normal, awake, motorically inactive newborns to four conditions:

1. The infants were placed in the supine.
2. The infants were placed in the upright at a 52-degree angle.
3. The infants were placed in the supine and moved horizontally on lubricated tracks six times.
4. The infants were placed in the upright and were moved up and down on the same tracks six times.

In each condition, the infants viewed a black vertical line on a white field, which was moved slowly 10 inches before the infants' eyes and which, in each position, was perpendicular to their line of vision. Quality of visual tracking was rated on a 7-point scale from video tape that was taken by a concealed camera directly overhead.

The major finding of this study was that the upright per se had no effect in improving the infant's visual behavior, and that only when the infant was moved, either horizontally or vertically, was his visual-tracking performance significantly enhanced. Infants who viewed the visual stimulus from a stationary upright position performed no better than infants lying in the supine. We concluded from this study that it is *not* the upright position that significantly influences the infant's visual behavior, but that it is the vestibular–proprioceptive stimulation that enhances that response.

In the process of conducting the above studies, we began to read the embryological, developmental, and clinical literature in an attempt to understand the role of the vestibular system in growth and development. We soon became aware of the early maturity of that system as discussed above, which led us to postulate that vestibular–proprioceptive stimulation may be ontogenetically one of the most adequate and relevant forms of stimulation at the pre- and full-term infant's level of neurophysiological development. It also became clear to us that vestibular dysfunction was implicated in some of the most severe developmental deviations. This is probably because the malfunction of the vestibular system exerts an important influence on all other sensory experiences. Vestibular dysfunction has been invoked as an important factor in the development of dyslexia and other learning disorders (Frank & Levinson, 1973; DeQuiros, 1964) and as a contributory factor in schizophrenia and infantile autism (Schilder, 1933). In her early studies with schizophrenic children, Lauretta Bender, who worked with Schilder, noted the prevalence of vertigo and self-rocking and twirling in these children. More recently, Ornitz and Ritvo (1968) and Ornitz (1970) have postulated that perceptual inconsistency resulting from faulty vestibular–proprioceptive feedback may be at the root of some autistic children's difficulties. Also, there are numerous studies of adult schizophrenics that demonstrate vestibular dysfunction in that group.

Severe *deprivation* of vestibular–proprioceptive stimulation may also be an important factor in bringing about developmental deviations. (For a review of this literature, see Prescott, 1971). Erway (1975), who works on otolith defects in mice, recently stated that "deficiency of vestibular input either for reasons of congenital defect or for lack of motion stimulation, may inpair the early development and integrating capacities of the brain, especially that of the cerebellum [p.20]." Mason's work (1968) with nonhuman primates seems to bear out Erway's statement. Mason, like Harlow (1958), isolation-reared infant monkeys on surrogate mothers. Harlow, as may be recalled, produced highly abnormal monkeys who engaged in autistic-like, self-mutilating, and rocking behavior as a result of these rearing conditions. Mason, by providing isolation-reared monkeys with *swinging* surrogate mothers, offset the most severe developmental deficits typically seen in Harlow's monkeys.

As we continued our studies, and particularly in the light of Mason's findings, we too became interested in the *developmental* effects of supplementary vestibular–proprioceptive stimulation (Thoman & Korner, 1971). To assess this effect we used 181 newborn rats from 19 litters and assigned them to one of three groups:

1. Reared under standard laboratory conditions.
2. Swaddled snugly in acetate batting for 10 minutes a day for the first 14 days of life.
3. Swaddled in the same way as the Group 2 rats and slowly rotated on a small drum for 10 minutes a day for the first 14 days of life. To avoid habituation, the pups were rotated for 45 seconds each minute, with 15 seconds nonrotation interspersed at random intervals.

We used Sprague-Dawley miltiparous females, who for two weeks prior to impregnation, were handled or gentled for 1 minute every day. This was done because Thoman and Levine (1969) had found that merely disturbing the nest produced a significant "early experience" effect on the pups, which apparently is mediated through the mother. By using multiparous mothers and gentling them first, we could be more certain that the effects produced were a function of the stimulation given and not merely of the pups being handled.

It is interesting that behaviorally the rat pups response to vestibular–proprioceptive stimulation was very similar to the response typically elicited in human newborns. During rotation, the rat pups almost completely stopped their distress calls, whereas the swaddled rats engaged in a chorus of distress calls while swaddled, as did the rotated rats during the 15 seconds of nonrotation.

A number of developmental assessments were done as the rat pups grew older. At 15 days, the rotated group had the highest percentage of eyes fully opened. Next was the swaddled group, with the control group having the lowest percentage. These differences were, however, not statistically significant.

At 20 days, the rotated group was significantly more exploratory on a visual cliff test and at weaning, that group was significantly heavier than the swaddled and the control group.

The overall results of this study thus showed that vestibular–proprioceptive stimulation given to newborn rats, produced not only behavioral, but also developmental, effects. Again, as in our studies with human infants, the vestibular–proprioceptive stimulation was much more potent in bringing about these changes than was contact.

WATERBED FLOTATION AS A MEANS FOR IMPARTING VESTIBULAR–PROPRIOCEPTIVE STIMULATION TO PREMATURE INFANTS

It was thus the results of our previous developmental studies that provided the rationale for our intervening with premature infants. I view our studies with waterbed flotation as merely a logical extension of these previous studies. We not only felt that waterbed flotation was a naturalistic way of imparting vestibular–proprioceptive stimulation to premature infants, but also that such a change in the infant's environment might provide a number of clinical benefits. In particular, we thought that a waterbed might help preserve the fragile skin of very small infants. By providing the soft head support of the water mattress, we hoped we might be able to reduce the incidence of the infants' developing assymetrically shaped heads and perhaps even the frequency of intracranial bleeds. Further, we postulated that waterbed flotation might reduce the infants' need to cope prematurely with the full impact of gravity, thus conserving their energy.

The Waterbeds

Development of the infant waterbeds began in 1972. Since the levels of vestibular–proprioceptive stimulation that are optimal for our purposes were unknown, two types of waterbeds were developed for use inside the incubator. The basic waterbed provides slight containment for the infant and is highly responsive to each of his movements. The second type of waterbed is identical in design and consistency, but in addition to the stimulation generated by the infant's own movements, it provides gentle oscillations. The rationale for providing these oscillations was to insure that very inactive infants would at least be exposed to some passive movement stimulation. Waterbed flotation with or without the oscillations does, of course, provide both vestibular and proprioceptive stimulation, since vestibular input cannot be dissociated from an activation of the proprioceptors. Judging from Purdon Martin's (1967) work it would appear that the stimulation on the waterbeds is primarily vestibular inasmuch as the organism is greatly dependent on his vestibular mechanisms when his supporting base is unstable. As Martin put it, "under conditions of stability, proprioception is dominant and the vestibular reactions are suppressed; under conditions of instability, the vestibular influence predominates and proprioceptive reactions are relatively in abeyance [p. 96]."

The basic waterbed consists of a high-impact styrene shell, and a vinyl bag covered by a latex membrane in a stainless steel frame which attaches to the top of the shell. This unit is designed to replace the foam-rubber matress usually used in incubators. The temperature of the waterbed is maintained entirely by the incubator's heating system. When a waterbed is prepared, a vinyl bag is filed with 2¼ gallons of warm tap water treated with algecide and blue dye. The water temperature chosen is 2 degrees above the incubator's environmental temperature, since thermal tests have shown that the water temperature stabilizes at that level. The blue dye in the water is designed to alert the caregiver in the event of a leak (which has occurred only once during the four years that the waterbeds have been in use, as a result of a hyperdermic needle that accidentally penetrated both the membrane and the waterbag). Blue was chosen so as not to be confused with urine, emesis, or blood. Repeated cultures of the water inside the vinyl bag have been negative even after continuous use for more than a month. Between uses, the waterbeds are readily gas autoclaved. The frame of the bed provides anchor points to restrain the infant as needed. When the infant requires elevation or percussion, a plastic-covered styrofoam wedge, which sits on the waterbed frame, provides a stable surface.

In designing the *oscillating* waterbed, we were confronting all the issues one typically faces when setting up an experimental study involving stimulation. We had to decide on the wave form, the rise time, the frequency, and the amplitude of the oscillations. We also needed to decide whether to have the oscillations occur continuously or intermittently, and in regular or in random intervals. In making these choices I tried to stay away from completely arbitrary decisions. Instead, I attempted to make choices that I felt had some clinical, experiential, or biological rationale.

In the light of these considerations, I decided that the direction of the oscillations should be from head to foot, rather than from side to side. The choice of head-to-foot oscillations was predicated on the studies by Lee (1954) and by Millen and Davies (1946), which suggest that the direction of this motion may benefit the infant's respiratory effort. Since the infant would be exposed to the oscillations for a long period of time, it was important to make the oscillations very gentle. The amplitude of the oscillations was thus determined by clinical considerations. This was done by exposing several infants to various amplitudes of motion, by ascertaining that the infant had no untoward reactions, and by soliciting input from the nursing and medical personnel regarding the feasibiity of care for the infants on an oscillating surface. As a result of these preliminary studies, a very gentle, barely visible amplitude was chosen. In order to make these very small oscillations more perceptible to the infant, a wave with a rise time of only ½ second was chosen. This has the effect of producing a very gentle jolt, which sets the wave in motion and is followed by a period of quiescence during which the wave attenuates.

In deciding on the frequency of the oscillations, we had, of course, an infinite number of choices. Rather than making an arbitrary decision, I looked for a biologically relevant rhythm. I felt that it would be safest to provide a *maternal rhythm,* since such a rhythm would probably not interfere with the developing organization of the infant's own rhythms and would, at the same time, expose the infant to a rhythm that he would have been exposed to anyway, had he not been born prematurely. The rhythm of maternal respirations in the third trimester of pregnancy is such as experientally relevant rhythm. According to Goodlin (1972), maternal respirations at that stage of gestation are 16 ± 4 per minute. In choosing the frequency of oscillations, I decided on the lower rates of this range, namely between 12 and 13 oscillations per minute. I also felt that the oscillations should occur at slightly irregular intervals, partly because irregular pulses would more nearly resemble maternal respirations and partly because they would reduce the chance that the infant would habituate or adapt and therefore tune out the stimulus.

Finally, we had to decide whether to provide continuous or intermittent oscillations. In the first two studies, we used a continuous pulse; this was an arbitrary decision. As it turned out, the continuous oscillations were, I believe, largely responsible for unanticipated *clinical* benefits, which I shall describe later. For *developmental* purposes, I have since come to appreciate that intermittent stimulation may be far more effective. Intermittent stimulation allows the organism periods of rest and of activity, both of which are probably equally important for the well-being of the infant. Intermittent rather than continuous oscillations also would provide the infant with the opportunity to activate the waterbed through his own spontaneous movements during periods of nonoscillation, while, at the same time, insuring that some of the more placid infants would receive passive movement stimulation, at least during part of the day. In deciding on intermittent oscillations, I was also strongly influenced by Denenberg's (1975) review of the early stimulation effects reported in the animal literature, from which he concluded that stimulus variation, rather than sensory constancy, is an important, if not indeed necessary, condition for adequate development.

Once it was decided to use intermittent oscillations, it was still necessary to decide on the kind of intermittency to be used. Rather than chosing arbitrary intervals of stimulations as is usually done, I again chose a maternal rhythm that the infant would have been exposed to had he not been born prematurely and that by virtue of that fact, would probably not interfere with the developing organization of the infant's own rhythms. The basic rest–activity cycle as described by Kleitman (1969) is such a maternal rhythm. In the adult, the average length of this cycle is 90 minutes. According to an increasing number of sleep researchers, manifestations of the basic rest-activity cycle persist throughout the day and express themselves at night through the cycles of REM and NREM sleep. From Sterman's (1967) research pointing to a strong relationship between maternal sleep stages and intrauterine fetal activity it is clear that maternal cycles exert a regulatory influence on fetal behavior. The prematurely born infant is clearly deprived of the potentially organizing influences of maternal cycles. The lack of exposure to the maternal cyclicity of physiological and motor activity and rest may very well be one of the contributing factors to the poor organization of sleep seen in premature infants. By superimposing a 90-minute cycle, as we are doing through 30 minutes of oscillations within each 90-minute period, we may perhaps provide an external aid to the infants' own developing rest–activity cycles. This hypothesis is supported to some extent by Hofer's (1975a) research with young rats. Separated from their mothers, 2-week-old rats showed fragmentation in the organization and rhythmicity of sleep and a reduced cycle length. In another study (Hofer, 1975b), separation from the mother produced behavioral hyperactivity in the young rats, which was reduced to the level of nonseparated pups by administering external stimulation over a variety of sensory pathways with a time patterning similar to the mother's periodic stimulation. Hofer (1975a) concluded that perhaps the "rhythmicity of maternal behavior acts as a Zeitgeber, a rhythm-giver, for the infant [p. 153]."

In the first two studies described below, we used an Emerson respirator connected to a small inflatable rubber bladder to impart 12 to 13 oscillations per minute. This particular Emerson provides irregular pulses that admirably suited our purposes. Since then, a small, compact unit built on the same principle has been developed. While we have chosen maternal rhythms for our studies for the particular theoretical reasons outlined above, this unit provides the option of using a variety of other frequencies and amplitudes of oscillations, if desired.

In using both the oscillating and the nonoscillating waterbeds, the nurses have quickly adapted to attending the infants on this surface. At Stanford, the waterbeds have been used with infants on restraints, IV's, and even on assisted ventilation.

Study 1

Since the waterbeds change the infant's environment on a 24-hour basis, it was important to first demonstrate that they are safe to use. In our first study (Korner, Kraemer, Haffner & Cosper, 1975) which was prompted by these considerations, all infants with gestations of 34 weeks or less, and weighing less than 2000 grams, who were patients in the Stanford Intensive Care Nurseries between January and November 1974 were considered for inclusion in this study. Infants with moderate or severe RDS requiring any form of assisted ventilation, small-for-dates infants and babies with congenital anomalies or severe postnatal complications were excluded. Thus this sample included infants with mild RDS, apnea of prematurity, elevated bilirubin, mild hypoglycemia, and hypocalcemia.

Twenty-one subjects were assigned to an experimental or control group by a totally random process. When a premature baby who met the above criteria became available, consent to include the infant in the study as either a control or an experimental subject was obtained, first from the pediatrician in charge, then from the mother and/or father of the child. Until both consents were obtained, the group to which the baby was to be assigned was known to no one (including the persons obtaining consent), lest knowledge of the group would influence in any way the decisions made, or the treatment the infant would receive.

The study subjects ranged in gestational age from 27 to 34 weeks and had birth weights ranging from 1050 and 1920 grams. The sample included 11 males and 10 females. The experimental and control groups did not differ significantly from each other in weight or gestational age.

The 10 babies in the experimental group were placed on the waterbed before the 6th postnatal day. The infants remained on the waterbed for 7 days and nights.

The results reported here are based on a comparison of the clinical progress of the two groups during the first 9 days of life, after which, 2 subjects were transferred back to their referring hospital. The data collected were drawn from the nurses' daily progress notes and other entries in the infants' medical charts. To avoid inadvertent bias in recording, the nursery personnel was unaware of the measures of interest to us.

We were reassured in finding that the oscillating waterbed in no way affected the babies' vital signs. Pulse and respiration rates and temperature ranges did not differ significantly between the two groups, nor did weight changes or oxygen requirements. Furthermore, the oscillating waterbed did not increase the frequency of emesis.

We did find one very highly significant difference between the experimental and control infants, and that was in the incidence of apnea, with infants on the oscillating waterbed having significantly fewer apneic spells ($p < .01$). Apnea is monitored routinely in the Stanford Intensive Care Nurseries, and the monitor alarms were set to go off when the baby's heart rate dropped below 100 per minute and/or when the respiration stopped for 20 seconds or more: Figure 4.1 shows descriptively the pattern of apnea frequency of the two groups.

Figure 4.1 compares the mean daily frequency of apnea, starting with the baseline average for the first two postnatal days. The differences in the first 2 days were not significant between the two groups. But as can be seen from Figure 4.1, after the babies in the experimental group were put on the oscillating waterbed, the incidence of their apneic spells tended to drop, whereas it continued to increase in the control babies.

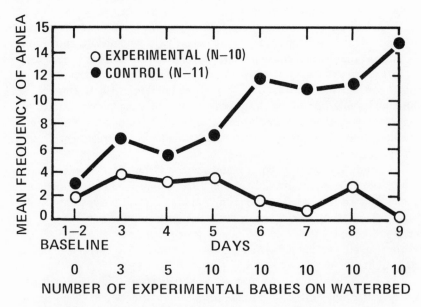

FIG. 4.1.   Comparison between experimental and control groups in the mean daily apnea incidence. (From *Pediatrics*, Vol. 56, No. 3, September 1975, pp. 361–367.)

Study 2

In our first study we had not preselected infants for apnea. Our next question was, of course, does apnea decrease as a function of waterbed flotation in infants who are preselected for having this symptom. We soon had a unique opportunity to test this question. When Dr. Christian Guilleminault from the Stanford Sleep Disorder Clinic read the results of our first study, he proposed that we do a polygraphic study in which each apneic infant would serve as his own control on and off the oscillating waterbed. I naturally welcomed the opportunity to have an independent investigator from a separate laboratory test the validity of our observations regarding the apnea-reducing potential of the oscillating waterbeds.

In this new study, the infants' sleep and respiratory patterns are polygraphically recorded over a 24-hour period. Participants in this study are Johanna Van den Hoed, M.D., Marianne Souquet, and Roger Baldwin, all of whom work under the direction of Christian Guilleminault, M. D. The 24-hour recordings are divided into four 6-hour blocks, with the infant being placed on the waterbed during alternate 6-hour periods. To avoid an order effect, half the infants are recorded on the waterbed during the first 6 hours, half during the second 6-hour block.

To date, we have recorded seven infants. We sought to include in this study only infants with true apnea of prematurity and to exclude infants whose apnea was a symptom of other major complications such as CNS damage, septicemia, major cardiac pathology, and so on. Four of the infants were Anglo-Saxon and three were Mexican-American in origin; six of the seven subjects were male. Birth weights ranged from 1077 to 1650 grams, and gestations from 27 to 32 weeks. On the day of the study the infants' weights were between 1115 and 1600 grams, and their postnatal ages ranged from 7 to 28 days. None were on any medication other than antibiotics at the time of the study.

Before the study of each infant began, electrodes were applied. Recordings of each child began within half an hour of noon. They included an electroencephalogram ($C_3/A_2 - C_4/A_1$), electrooculogram, chin electromyogram, and electrocardiogram; respiration was monitored by two mercury-filled strain gauges (one abdominal and one thoracic) and two thermistors positioned in front of each nostril. Behavioral criteria were systematically checked by an observer and noted on the record during the entire monitoring.

Since this is still an ongoing study, the results must be considered preliminary. The sleep records are only partially scored at this time; thus only the apnea data will be presented here.

Table 4.1 compares the number of apneas exceeding 10 seconds of each baby, combining the incidence during the two periods on and the two periods

TABLE 4.1
Apneas > 10 Seconds On and Off Oscillating Waterbed

Baby	Off	On	Change	t_6
1	158	132	−16%	
2	141	111	−21%	
3	39	23	−41%	
4	36	22	−39%	2.66*
5	28	39	+28%	
6	32	16	−50%	
7	33	28	−16%	

Matched Pairs t Test, 1 tailed
*$p < .025$

TABLE 4.2
Number of Apnea Alarms On and Off Oscillating Waterbed

Baby	Off	On	Change	t_6
1	10	8	−20%	
2	16	7	−56%	
3	1	0	to 0	
4	15	9	−40%	
5	14	13	− 7%	3.03*
6	13	10	−23%	
7	5	3	−40%	

Matched Pairs t Test, 1 tailed
*$p < .025$

TABLE 4.3
Apneas With Severe Bradycardia (Below 80 Beats/Minute) On and Off Oscillating Waterbed

Baby	Off	On	Change	t_6
1	8	5	−38%	
2	20	9	−55%	
3	5	2	−60%	
4	17	10	−41%	1.50 NS
5	11	20	+45%	
6	16	9	−44%	
7	5	2	−60%	

Matched Pairs t Test, 1 tailed

off the oscillating waterbed. Match-paired *t* tests were used for statistical analysis. Since reduction of apnea was anticipated from the results of Study 1 one-tailed tests were appropriate.

As Table 4.1 shows, apneas exceeding 10 seconds were reduced in six out of seven infants while they were on the oscillating waterbed. The waterbed seemed to benefit some babies more than others. Reductions in apnea ranged between 16% and 50%.

Apneas of longer durations, as indicated by the apnea monitor alarms, were reduced in each of the babies studied while they were on the oscillating waterbed (see Table 4.2). The alarms in the Stanford Intensive Care Nurseries usually ring when apneas exceed 20 seconds. Reductions in apnea again varied depending on the infant.

In most babies, the severest types of apnea as defined by their association with bradycardia of below 80 heart beats per minute were reduced much more sharply on the oscillating waterbed than were apneas in general. In six out of seven infants, reductions ranged from 38% to 60%.

Baby 5 was a notable exception in not showing the general trend of apnea reduction on the oscillating waterbed seen in all the other study babies. From the history of his apnea prior to the polygraphic study, we should have suspected that this baby was not a typical case of apnea of prematurity, and we would therefore have been wise not to include him in the study. Aside from his atypical apnea history, he had a very stormy medical course from the start. He had a difficult birth, which resulted in asphyxia in spite of a Cesarean section done for a frank breech presentation and an abruptio placenta. He had an Apgar of 1 at 1 minute and of 6 at 5 minutes. On the fourth day of life, a diagnosis of necrotizing enterocolotis was made. He was on assisted ventilation for the 1st week of life. When he was extubated, he showed severe bradycardia in the absence of apnea. Only after several days did apnea begin to be associated with bradycardia but the frequency of bradycardia by itself continued to predominate. It is this pattern that should have alerted us to the fact that this baby was not a typical case of apnea of prematurity. When on the 19th day of life he was polygraphically recorded, his record showed a pattern quite different from the rest of our subjects. His bradycardia with apneas was much more severe and had a much earlier onset than in any of the other infants. Also, this infant showed a much larger proportion of obstructive, upper-airway apneas than any of the other babies. In fact, 19% of his apneas were of the obstructive type, and an additional 6% were a mixture of obstructive and central apneas. Obstructive apneas are relatively rare among premature infants whose apneas are mostly central (Guilleminault, Peraita, Souquet, & Dement, 1975). The pattern of Baby 5 of early onset of severe bradycardia associated with a high incidence of obstructive apnea has been found to occur in older babies who have been identified as "near-miss sudden infant death babies" for having survived episodes of prolonged cessation of breathing (Guilleminault, Souquet, Ariagno, & Dement, 1976). One of these babies actually was found dead the day after he was recorded. To follow up on Baby 5 who lives in a distant city and who is now 6 months old chronologically and 4 months post-term, we called his mother and his pediatrician. He continued to have a difficult medical course, which included milk allergies, surgery for pyloric stenosis, and emergency treatment for gastroenteritis and chronic upper respiratory infections. It is the latter and the fact that in his sleep this infant "snores" (a symptom frequently seen in "near-miss" babies) that makes us wonder whether this infant does not continue to have obstructive apnea at this time.

In conclusion, the preliminary results of our polygraphic study confirm that the oscillating waterbed significantly reduces the frequency of apnea in infants with apnea of prematurity. Some of the sharpest reductions occurred in the most severe apneas, associated with bradycardia. Had we excluded from analysis the one infant whose apnea was probably not a typical manifestation of apnea of prematurity, reductions of the most severe types of apneas would have been statistically highly significant. ($t = 4.25$, $df = 5$, $p <$ .005, one-tailed).

Mechanism of Action

One can only speculate about the underlying mechanism that brings about reduction of apnea on the oscillating waterbed. The most plausible explanation appears to be that the continuous irregular oscillations provide afferent input to the respiratory center, thus aborting a number of apneas. This hypothesis was put forth by Kattwinkel, Nearman, Fanaroff, Katona, and Klaus (1975) in an attempt to explain significant reductions of apnea in their sample of prematures as a result of periods of 5 minutes of cutaneous stimulation followed by 10 minutes of nonstimulation. I would postulate that, had we not fortuitously chosen continuous oscillations when we began our first study, and had instead used a simile of the maternal rest–activity cycle with 30 minutes of oscillations and 60 minutes of quiescence, we would not have found the pattern of apnea reduction seen in our two studies. We shall find out in our developmental longitudinal study, in which we are going to use the 90-minute cycle, from those infants who happen to develop apnea.

Clinical Observations

The nonoscillating waterbed has been used extensively for clinical purposes. These beds are frequently requested by the Stanford nursing or medical staff. Sometimes they are used very briefly to relieve acute conditions; but at other times a small baby may stay on the waterbed for close to 3 months. The nonoscillating waterbed was found particularly useful with infants recovering from abdominal surgery or for babies who are on a regimen of parenteral nutrition for emaciation. As anticipated, the waterbeds are very helpful in the care of very small premature babies, such as infants between 600 and a 1000 grams, in that they preserve the infants' fragile skin. The waterbeds are undoubtedly soothing in cases of painful skin conditions. Not long ago, we had a request from the University of California Hospital in San Francisco for a waterbed for a full-term infant who was born with blisters all over her body. Attending physicians observed that the infant became more quiet when placed on the waterbed, that she required less sedation and that from then on, skin breakdown on her back was halted. In order to make an infant more comfortable, we recently used the waterbed in the case of disseminated herpes. We have not as yet systematically tested the hypothesis we originally had that the waterbeds would reduce the incidence of assymetrically shaped narrow heads, which are so frequently seen in premature infants. The waterbeds undoubtedly have this effect, for this is the primary reason that the nursing staff requests these beds. Our hypothesis was recently confirmed by Kramer and Pierpont (1976), who found that infants placed on waterbeds had more rounded heads. It seems logical that, just as waterbeds have proved to be useful in preventing decubitus ulcers in geriatric patients, the fluid support would be helpful in any condition in prematures where pressure points to the skin or to the skeletal structure are to be avoided.

In watching infants on the waterbed, we have the subjective impression that their motility is more modulated and less random. There seem to be fewer overshooting movements of the limbs, fewer jerks and startles. The infants seem to be more able to establish hand–mouth contact. It is as if the slight containment provided by the waterbeds, and perhaps the relaxation that attends waterbed flotation, have a binding or organizing effect on the infants' motility. These impressions do, of course, have to be objectively verified. We intend to do so through TV monitoring of the infants' motility in the course of our developmental longitudinal study, which we are about to begin.

SUMMARY

Waterbeds oscillating in maternal biological rhythms were developed in order to impart vestibular–proprioceptive stimulation to premature infants. The rationale, the underlying hypotheses, and the goals of such intervention were first reviewed, as were our developmental studies, which prompted the subsequent studies using waterbed flotation with premature babies. In designing the oscillating waterbed, instead of using arbitrary intervals and rhythms of oscillations, it was decided to use rhythms that may have experiential and biological relevance for the infant. We postulated that it might be safest to use maternal rhythms, for such rhythms would probably not interfere with the developing organization of the infant's own rhythms, since he would have been exposed to these rhythms had he not been born prematurely. In fact, the premature birth deprives the infant of the possibly organizing effect of maternal cyclicity of rest and activity, and of REM and NREM sleep. The latter have been shown to exert a regulatory influence on fetal behavior (Sterman, 1967). With these considerations in mind, we have chosen the rhythm of maternal respirations in the third trimester of gestation to provide slightly irregularly timed oscillations and the 90-minute basic rest–activity cycle of the adult to impart 30 minutes of oscillations and 60 minutes of quiescence. It is hoped that by superimposing the 90-minute adult rest–activity cycle on the infant it will be possible to provide an external aid to the infant's own developing biological rhythms. Evidence from the animal literature suggests that superimposing maternal rhythms of stimulation on rat pups separated from their mothers has an organizing effect on the behavior of the young, reducing their hyperactivity to the level of nonseparated pups (Hofer, 1975a, 1975b).

Results from the first two studies using waterbed flotation with premature infants were presented. In the first study, 21 infants ranging in gestational age from 27 to 34 weeks were randomly assigned to experimental and control groups. The experimental group consisted of 10 infants who were placed on the oscillating waterbed before the 6th postnatal day, where they remained for 7 days. Their clinical progress was compared with that of a control group of 11 similar babies. Flotation on the oscillating waterbed was found to be a safe procedure, not affecting any of the infants' vital signs, weight, or frequency of emesis. Highly significant differences were found in the incidence of apnea, with infants on the oscillating waterbed having significantly fewer apneas. The preliminary results of the second study—which uses 24-hour polygraphic recordings, with each infant serving as his own control, on and off the oscillating waterbed,—confirm that apnea is significantly reduced on the oscillating waterbed. In these two studies, continuous irregular oscillations were used in the rhythm of maternal respirations. The intermittent oscillations in the pattern of the maternal basic rest–activity cycle will be used in a developmental longitudinal study with premature infants, which we are about to begin.

ACKNOWLEDGMENTS

Preparation of this chapter was supported by The T. W. Grant Foundation. The research presented was supported by The T. W. Grant Foundation, Public Health Service Grants HD-08339 and HD-03591, the Boys Town Center for Youth Development at Stanford, and Grant RR-81 from the General Clinical Research Centers Program of the Division of Human Resources, National Institutes of Health.

DISCUSSION

Dr. Stern: One of the first thoughts I had was, is there any way to make the water mattress do even more, since you have shown that it does so much already? You've made the point that it is important that the stimulation be variable, and you've done that by having on and off 90-minute cycles and a variable rate of wave frequency, either 12 or 13 per minute. I have two questions and two suggestions. I wonder if the infant can discriminate between a rate of 12 and 13 beats per minute, and why you chose the lower limit? I don't know how the Goodlin study was done, where they chose 16 ± 4. I gather that's the standard deviation of the resting respiratory rate for 6 to 9-months pregnant mothers. Is that right?

Dr. Korner: I think so.

Dr. Stern: I suspect it probably is. My point is that the average mother, who is sometimes walking or working hard and at other times resting, will present the infant in utero with much more respiratory variability than 12–13 beats per minute. Secondly, if she spends say 10% of the day talking, that introduces another variable, because inspirations during talking are very fast and expirations are very long, compared to not talking. So if you wanted to introduce greater variability that was still within the range of the intrauterine environment, you might both vary the wave rise time as well as increasing the range of rates. Together or separately these increases in variability, which are probably within the natural range, might give you even better results.

Dr. Korner: Our oscillator has the capability of providing oscillations ranging from 6 to 20 per minute. The rise time of half a second is built into the electronic design and therefore is invariable. This interval was chosen because a faster rise time provides too much of a jerk to the baby, which then results in ripples rather than a smooth head-to-foot waveform; a slower rise time provides practically no wave at all. I chose the lower rates of Goodlin's range of maternal respirations because I felt intuitively that the lower rates might provide a more peaceful and a less restless environment. Speaking of peaceful, I should reiterate that these oscillations are so gentle they are barely visible. Sometimes, when we stand in front of the incubator when the apparatus is on, we wonder whether it is really working. The reason I chose such gentle oscillations is that I felt that since the infant is exposed to those oscillations all day, I would rather err on the side of caution and be too gentle. The problem with this kind of research is that you have to make an intuitive choice and then you have to stick with it. This is particularly true with a longitudinal study, which is usually an undertaking of many years. Were one to try to use several different rhythms or amplitudes and compare their differential effect on development, one would have that many more cells to fill, and with the limited number of subjects available, that is quite unrealistic. The issue is quite different in the case of studies testing the apnea-reducing potential of the oscillating waterbed. In these studies it is important to find out which rates or amplitudes of oscillation are clinically most effective. We plan to do just that.

Dr. Stern: I understand that and I agree with you. It's so impressive what you've already found. As the old saying goes, "Good, better, best, never let it rest, until the good is better and the better best"—something like that. I felt like that about your design and results. If in fact the variability is important maybe one should make sure—you know.

Dr. Korner: It would be nice if one could use an animal model to determine what parameters are optimal. But obviously, an animal model, even if one could create one, would not be applicable to apnea in humans. In choosing the stimulus parameters for a longitudinal study, one obviously has to place one's bets intuitively, and then one has to stick to one's decision. Since we haven't started our longitudinal study yet. I am still open to suggestions.

Dr. Eisenberg: One of the things that I found particularly fascinating about your data is the relation between the apnea episode and the bradycardia in excess of a certain amount. It occurred to me as you were talking that the implications of these kinds of studies for particular kinds of pathological groups may be enormous. For instance, a large number of Down's syndrome babies are known to have bradycardia or other defects of the cardiac system; and it seems to be that some kind of study of the relation between apnea episodes and heart defects in Down's syndrome children might be very productive. They are so many ways to go at this, it's just fascinating.

Dr. Korner: Do Down's syndrome babies have apnea associated with the bradycardia?

Dr. Eisenberg: I don't really know enough about apnea. I know that the incidence of cardiac problems is very high.

Dr. Kennel: I don't think they're related problems.

Dr. Korner: Judging from the reaction of one baby, I would be concerned to use the oscillating waterbed with children who have cardiac problems.

Dr. Eisenberg: You're right.

Dr. Kennell: You had to make some difficult decisions to carry out your work, and I think it's remarkable how you used the mother's rhythms and cycles as the guide for your intervention. Your point about mechanism—I wonder if you have had experience using the waterbed right from birth to find out whether you can prevent prematures from ever developing apneic episodes; that would be an important finding. And then in regard to your earlier comments about the effect of the waterbed on the infant's proprioceptive and vestibular systems, do you believe you have produced a different baby as a result of this stimulation? Do you see any difference in the responsiveness of one of your waterbed babies when the mother comes to visit than with an infant that has not been on a waterbed?

Dr. Korner: To your first question, it would be very nice if a baby in the experimental group could be placed on the waterbed immediately after birth, because then he would not have to get used to a stationary environment. However, by the time consents for study are obtained from the pediatrician and the parents, and until it is determined whether a baby is going to live or die or go on a respirator, sometimes considerable time elapses. As to your second question: Are we producing different babies? We are going to try to find out. Built into the design of our longitudinal study are a number of development substudies. One of these involves time-lapse TV monitoring of sleep-wake cycles through a technique developed by Anders and Sostek, a method Kathy Barnard is also using in monitoring premature babies. While this technique will give us a much grosser estimate of the infant's sleep states than does our polygraphic study, it will nevertheless yield a weekly 12-hour record of the frequency, duration, and sequencing of the infant's sleep and awake behavior. In line with the findings of our earlier studies, this technique will also furnish us with information as to whether the infants on waterbeds spend longer periods in alertness. In another substudy, we will use TV monitoring in real time to compare the qualitative differences in the motility of infants in the experimental and control groups. We want to test our subjective impression that the motility of the babies in the experimental group is more modulated, that in moving their limbs they don't overshoot as much, that they startle less and produce fewer jerks, and that they have greater facility in hand–mouth coordination. We are also going to do a substudy of the development of nonnutritive sucking. Sucking is an important sensori-motor coordination early in life, and we will be interested to see whether the babies in the experimental group develop differently in this respect than do the infants in the control group. If they differ, we will be interested in what way. If they do not, we will have a nice study of the ontogeny of nonnutritive sucking. In fact, if there are no differences between the experimental and control groups in any or all of these behaviors, we can use the information from both groups and thereby derive our conclusions from twice the number of subjects. In other words, the study is designed in such a way that it is a no-lose situation in that we will be getting useful information whether there are differences or not. We will also do a substudy of the frequency and amplitude of movements and the development of the rest–activity cycles with the help of an activity monitor that was developed in our Laboratory. In this study we will compare the groups 3 days after the babies in the experimental group have been removed from the waterbed in order to give the latter a chance to get used to a stationary environment. Before discharge from the hospital, we shall make neurological and behavioral assessments, and these will be done by someone who is unaware of the group to which a given baby belonged. We also plan to do some follow-up studies. We thus hope to find out whether we are producing different babies.

Dr. Lipsitt: Your clever use of the within-subjects design in your last study raises an additional methodological problem and an empirical question: Is it possible that the waterbed merely displaces the time when the baby is going to have apneic episodes, rather than truly diminishing their frequency? That is to say, it is possible that every baby has to engage in a certain number of apneic episodes, perhaps even bradycardia, and that the waterbed simply displaces these to another time, namely the time when he's off the waterbed?

Dr. Korner: How would you speculate this would come about? What do you think the mechanism would be?

Dr. Lipsitt: The question is whether they may be having a few more apneic episodes in the off periods than they otherwise would have.

Dr. Eisenberg: What you want is the sum of all babies on waterbeds versus the sum of all the babies not on waterbeds for your baseline—or vice versa.

Dr. Lipsitt: You would need a new kind of control to go along with that comparison.

Dr. Korner: What would you use?

Dr. Lipsitt: You would take babies who were not at any time on the waterbed and some who were on all the time.

Dr. Watson: The experimental babies were on the bed 24 hours a day, is that correct?

Dr. Korner: That was true in Study 1. In that study we randomly assigned babies to the waterbed 24 hours a day for 7 consecutive days and others who were not on the waterbed at any time. If I understand you correctly, Study 1 used the design you are suggesting. The results of that study showed that the infants who were on the waterbed for 24 hours a day had significantly fewer apneic spells than the infants who were not. In Study 2, we used the within-subject design with each infant serving as his own control. Polygraphic recordings were made over a 24-hour period divided into four 6-hour blocks, with each infant being placed on the waterbed during alternate 6-hour periods. To avoid an order effect, half the infants were recorded on the waterbed during the first 6 hours, half during the second 6-hour block. Using this within-subjects design, we found the same thing. While they were on the oscillating waterbed, the infants had significantly less apnea.

Dr. Watson: What was the definition of apnea?

Dr. Korner: In the first study or the second one?

Dr. Watson: Both.

Dr. Korner: In the first study the number of alarms were recorded by the nurses. In the second study, all respiratory pauses in excess of 10 seconds as recorded polygraphically were counted as apneas.

Dr. Watson: No, I mean length of time. What constituted that?

Dr. Eisenberg: What was the criterion for it?

Dr. Korner: The apnea monitors were set to go off when the heart rate dropped below 100 beats per minute and respiratory pauses exceeded 20 seconds.

Dr. Watson: Pause of 20 seconds?

Dr. Korner: Right.

Dr. Denenberg: In following Lew's point about the developmental potential of the exercise, don't you have evidence before these babies are discharged from the hospital? Isn't there a period of time that they are off the waterbed? I'd expect there'd still be some time in which they'd still be monitored in terms of alarms.

Dr. Korner: Yes.

Dr. Denenberg: Do you have even a day or two in which you could look at what was the alarm rate when off the bed? If there's any disadvantage to the exercise, you should have evidence if there was any monitoring during this interim between coming off the bed and leaving the hospital.

Dr. Korner: The problem is that one cannot compare an infant with himself when he is a few days old with when he is older or getting ready for discharge. Developmentally, with respect to his respiratory adjustment, he is quite a different baby between these points in time.

Dr. Watson: But I think in relevance to Lew's point then, in fact you're saying that the problem as far as the real world is concerned is over at that time, and therefore there isn't this sort of residual period that is going to arise for the children as they come off the waterbed.

Dr. Eisenberg: You don't know that.

Dr. Watson: But I think his question was different. Within an hour's period if you deferred it to this hour would it come up the next hour, days, weeks maybe.

Dr. Korner: These babies were on apnea monitors all the time, whether they were on the waterbed or on the stationary mattress.

Dr. Watson: Therefore you do know how many times the alarm rang while the baby was on the waterbed and how many times the alarm rang when the baby was off the waterbed.

Dr. Korner: Right. There were highly significant differences in the incidence of apnea between the group that was continuously on the waterbed and the group that never was on the waterbed. The reason we did the second study was that with the small sample we had in the first study I was concerned that there was still a remote possibility that in spite of completely random assignment, one group, and in this instance the control group, could have accidentally contained a greater number of seriously ill infants. This is why in the second study we went to a within-subjects design using each baby as his own control.

Dr. Watson: But that's the kind of proof that I think meets the objections, except that clinically it isn't the same as the group later worked with. Isn't that right? Assuming that the incidence was less in some general way, that is, it wasn't just while the bed was operating; you monitored at all times and those two groups were different. That would certainly be presumptive evidence that—

Dr. Korner: Yes, the two studies used different babies. And in both studies there was a reduction of apnea as a function of the oscillating waterbed. In the first study there was a group difference, with the experimental group having significantly fewer apneic spells. In the second study, six out of seven babies had less apnea while on the oscillating waterbed as compared to when they were on a standard mattress. One of the reasons that I think the within-subjects design is much better and certainly more parsimonious is that the condition and pathology of premature babies varies so much that it is very difficult to have a comparable population in two groups, even when randomly assigned.

Dr. Thoman: This dramatic reduction in the levels of apnea should be expected to have some long-term effects.

REFERENCES

Barnard, K. E. *The effect of stimulation on the duration and amount of sleep and wakefulness in the premature infant.* Ann Arbor, Michigan: University Microfilms; 1972.

Barnett, C. R., Leiderman, P. H., Grobstein, R., & Klaus, M. Neonatal separation: The maternal side of interactional deprivation. *Pediactrics,* 1970, *45*(2), 197–205.

Brackbill, Y. Cumulative effects of continuous stimulation on arousal level in infants. *Child Development,* 1971, *42,* 17–26.

Denenberg, V. H. Effects of exposure to stressors in early life upon later behavioural and biological processes. In L. Levi (Ed.), *Society, Stress, and Disease: Childhood and Adolescence* (Vol. 2). New York: Oxford University Press, 1975.

Dreyfus-Brisac, C. Ontongenesis of sleep in human prematures after 32 weeks of conceptional age. *Developmental Psychobiology,* 1970, *3,* 91–121.

Erway, L. C. Otolith formation and trace elements: A theory of schizophrenic behavior. *The Journal of Orthomolecular Psychiatry,* 1975, *4*(1), 16–26.

Frank, J., & Levinson, H. Dysmetric dyslexia and dyspraxia. *Journal of the American Academy of Child Psychiatry,* 1973, *12,* 690–701.

Frankenhaeuser, M., & Johansson, G. On the psychophysiological consequences of under-stimulation and over-stimulation. *Reports from the Psychological Laboratories of the University of Stockholm,* 1974, Supplement 25.

Goodlin, R. C. *Handbook of Obstetrical and Gynecological Data.* Los Altos, California: Geron-X, 1972.

Gregg, C. L., Haffner, M. E., & Korner, A. F. The relative efficacy of vestibular–proprioceptive stimulation and the upright position in enhancing visual pursuit in neonates. *Child Development,* 1976, *47,* 309–314.

Guilleminault, C., Peraita, R., Souquet, M., & Dement, W. C. Apnea during sleep in infants: Possible relationship with sudden infant death syndrome. *Science,* 1975, *190,* 677–679.

Guilleminault, C., Souquet, M., Ariagno, R., & Dement, W. C. Abnormal polygraphic findings in near-miss sudden infant death. *The Lancet,* June 19, 1976, pp. 1326–1327.

Harlow, H. The nature of love. *American Psychologist,* 1958, *13,* 673–685.

Hofer, M. A. Infant separation responses and the maternal role. *Biological Psychiatry,* 1975, *10*(2), 149–153. (a)

Hofer, M. A. Studies on how early maternal separation produces behavioral changes in young rats. *Psychosomatic Medicine,* 1975, *37*(3), 245–264. (b)

Hooker, D. *The Prenatal Origin of Behavior.* University of Kansas Press, 1952.

Humphrey, T. The embryologic differentiation of the vestibular nuclei in man correlated with functional development. In *International Symposium on Vestibular and Oculomotor Problems*. Tokyo: Nippoon-Hoeschst, 1965.

Kasatkin, N. I. First conditioned reflexes and the beginning of the learning process in the human infant. *Advances in Psychobiology*, 1972, *1*, 213–257.

Kattwinkel, J., Nearman, H. S., Fanaroff, A. A., Katona, P. G., & Klaus, M. H. Apnea of prematurity. Comparative therapeutic effects of cutaneous stimulation and nasal continuous positive airway pressure. *Journal of Pediatrics*, 1975, *86*(4), 588–592.

Kennell, J. H., Jerauld, R., Wolfe, H., Chesler, D., Kreger, N., McAlpine, W., Steffa, M., & Klaus, M. H. Maternal behavior one year after early and extended post-partum contact. *Developmental Medicine and Child Neurology*, 1974, *16*, 172–179.

Klaus, M. H., Jerauld, B. S., Kreger, N. C., McAlpine, W., Steffa, M., & Kennell, J. H. Maternal attachment: Importance of the first post-partum days. *The New England Journal of Medicine*, 1972, *286*, 460–463.

Kleitman, N. Basic rest–activity cycle in relation to sleep and wakefulness. In A. Kales (Ed.), *Sleep Physiology and Pathology: A Symposium*. Philadelphia and Toronto: J. B. Lippincott Company, 1969.

Korner, A. F. Some hypotheses regarding the significance of individual differences at birth for later development. *The Psychoanalytic Study of the Child*, 1964, *19*, 58–72.

Korner, A. F. Individual differences at birth: Implications for early experience and later development. *American Journal of Orthopsychiatry*, 1971, *41*(4), 608–619.

Korner, A. F. Sex differences in newborns with special reference to differences in the organization of oral behavior. *Journal of Child Psychology and Psychiatry*, 1973, *14*, 19–29.

Korner, A. F. Methodological considerations in studying sex differences in the behavioral functioning of newborns. In R. C. Friedman, R. M. Richart, & R. L. Vande Wiele (Eds.), *Sex Differences in behavior*. New York: John Wiley & Sons, Inc., 1974.

Korner, A. F., & Grobstein, R. Visual alertness as related to soothing in neonates: Implications for maternal stimulation and early deprivation. *Child Development*, 1966, *37*, 867–876.

Korner, A. F., Kraemer, H. C., Haffner, M. E., & Cosper, L. M. Effects of waterbed flotation on premature infants: A pilot study. *Pediatrics*, 1975, *56*, 361–367.

Korner, A. F., & Thoman, E. B. Visual alertness in neonates as evoked by maternal care. *Journal of Experimental Child Psychology*, 1970, *10*, 67–78.

Korner, A. F., & Thoman, E. B. The relative efficacy of contact and vestibular stimulation in soothing neonates. *Child Development*, 1972, *43*(2), 443–453.

Kramer, L. I., & Pierpont, M. E. Rocking waterbeds and auditory stimuli to enhance growth of preterm infants. *The Journal of Pediatrics*, 1976, *88*(2), 297–299.

Langworthy, O. R. Development of behavior patterns and myelinization of the nervous system in the human fetus and infant. *Carnegie Institution of Washington, Contributions to Embryology*, 1933, *24*, 1–57.

Lee, H. F. A rocking bed respirator for use with premature infants in incubators. *Journal of Pediatrics*, 1954, *44*, 570–573.

Martin, J. P. Role of the vestibular system in the control of posture and movement in man. In A. V. S. de Reuck & J. Knight (Eds.), *Myotatic, Kinesthetic and Vestibular Mechanisms*. Boston: Little, Brown and Company, 1967.

Mason, W. A. Early social deprivation in the non-human primates: Implications for human behavior in environmental influences In D. C. Glass (Ed.), *Environmental Infuences*. New York: Rockefeller University Press and Russell Sage Foundation, 1968.

Millen, R. S., & Davies, J. See-saw resuscitator for the treatment of asphyxia. *American Journal of Obstetrics and Gynecology*, 1946, *52*, 508–.

Minkowski, M. Sur les mouvements, les réflexes et les reactions musculaires du foetus humain de 2 à 5 mois et leurs relations avec le systeme nerveux foetal. *Revue Neurologique*, 1921, *37*, 1105–1118.

Neal, M. V. *The Relationship Between a Regimen of Vestibular Stimulation and the Developmental Behavior of the Premature Infant.* University Microfilms: Ann Arbor, Michigan, 1967.

Ornitz, E. M. Vestibular dysfunction in schizophrenia and childhood autism. *Comprehensive Psychiatry,* 1970, *11*(2), 159–173.

Ornitz, E. M., & Ritvo, E. R. Perceptual inconstancy in early infantile autism. *Archives of General Psychiatry,* 1968, *18*, 76–98.

Parmelee, A. H. Neurophysiological and behavioral organization of premature infants in the first months of life. *Biological Psychiatry,* 1975, *10*(5), 501–512.

Parmelee, A. H., & Sigman, M. Development of visual behavior and neurological organization in pre-term and full-term infants. *Minnesota Symposia on Child Development,* 1976, *10*, in press.

Pendleton, M. E., & Paine, R. S. Vestibular nystagmus in newborn infants. *Neurology,* 1961, *11*, 450–458.

Powell, L. F. The effect of extra stimulation and maternal involvement on the development of low-birth-weight infants and on maternal behavior. *Child Development,* 1974, *45*, 106–113.

Prescott, J. W. Early somatosensory deprivation as an ontogenetic process in the abnormal development of the brain and behavior. In I. E. Goldsmith & J. Moor-Jankowski (Ed.), *Medical Primatology.* Basel, London, New York: S. Karger, 1971.

Quiros, de, J. B. Dysphasia and dyslexia in school children. *Folia Phoniatrica,* 1964, *16*, 201–222.

Sameroff, A. J. Early influences on development: Fact or fancy? *Merrill-Palmer Quarterly,* 1975, *21*(4), 267–294.

Scarr-Salapatek, S., & Williams, M. L. The effects of early stimulation on low-birth-weight infants. *Child Development,* 1973, *44*, 94–101.

Schilder, P. The vestibular apparatus in neurosis and psychosis. *Journal of Nervous and Mental Disease,* 1933, *78*, 1–23; 137–164.

Schmidt, K. The effect of continuous stimulation on the behavioral sleep of infants. *Merrill-Palmer Quarterly,* 1975, *21*(2), 77–88.

Sterman, M. B. Relationship of intrauterine fetal activity to maternal sleep stage. *Experimental Neurology,* 1967, Supplement 4, 98–106.

Thoman, E. B., & Korner, A. F. Effects of vestibular stimulation on the behavior and development of rats. *Developmental Psychology,* 1971, *5*, 92–98.

Thoman, E. B., & Levin, S. Role of maternal disturbance and temperature change in early experience studies. *Physiology and Behavior,* 1969, *4*, 143–145.

Wolff, P. H. The causes, controls and organization of behavior in the neonate. *Psychological Issues,* 1966, *5*, 1–105.

5 The Pleasures and Annoyances of Infants: Approach and Avoidance Behavior

Lewis P. Lipsitt
Brown University

The newborn human arrives in the world with a large repertoire of sensorimotor capabilities. Many of the psychophysiological responses of the neonate, moreover, are mediated by a hedonic "screen" that signals to others that the baby finds its experience either pleasant or unpleasant. The "pleasures of sensation," as Pfaffmann (1960) called them, are immediately evident to even the casual observer of the young infant. Unfortunately, the hedonic basis of human responsivity has been too often ignored (Young, 1936). Empirical purists have presumed that to say the baby is enjoying something is to project a mentalistic attribute where a mere descriptive account of the observations would do as well or better.

Skinner (1971) has a point in urging us to divest our scientific language of excesses. Still, one is unhappy with shunning the question of joy entirely. When you hear a baby cry furiously, you know that this is not a state in which he wishes to remain, and you know (perhaps the Skinnerians know best) that the baby will readily learn responses that will reduce the unhappy condition and terminate the cry. Similarly, when we watch a newborn actively rooting in response to a touch near the mouth, quickly zeroing in on the attractive object, then latching on and sucking it avidly, we are aware that there is pleasure going on in there. The human newborn is an approaching and avoiding creature. Some responses seem to be attempts to perpetuate the stimulation, and others to terminate it. While identification of the observer with the observed can lead easily to projection or anthropomorphism, one does have the impression that the neonate is rather adept in pursuing and perpetuating pleasurable stimulation and avoiding aversive stimulation. The hedonic flavor of this presentation, and of my orientation in general, has its precedents in the writings of other psychologists such as Young (1936). The approach–avoidance characterizations are, of course, compatible with the writings of Lewin (1954), Miller and Dollard (1941), and Schneirla (1957), among many others.

This paper will emphasize the processes and mechanisms of psychophysiological change over the course of repetitive experiences. I will further suggest that pleasure and pain, or enjoyment and annoyance, serve as the "screen" through which sensory stimulation passes and by which it is either appreciated and perpetuated, or censured and expelled. I am speaking of a hedonic continuum, of course, and not of a dichotomously judgmental screening mechanism.

Some types of neonatal experience may be both enjoyable and annoying. When such a condition prevails, a situation of ambivalence arises. Most infants do endure ambivalence-generating experiences, often in the arms of their loving relatives. I will want to suggest, in fact, that infants' responses to annoying or aversive stimulation may be important in setting the ontogenetic stage for the eventual acquisition of "voluntary" or operant behaviors important for the viability of the organism. For example, infants must have experience in retrieving themselves from respiratory occlusion, an eventuality which is quite frequent in the normal life experiences of the baby. By the time the baby is 2 or 3 months of age, most infants will have learned "coping" behaviors which reduce the possible dangers inherent in respiratory blockage. If they have not learned such responses by the time that the congenital neonatal reflexes have waned, as so many of them do, the threats to survival may be redoubled.

The young infant is a reciprocating organism from the outset, and both the baby and its mother (or whoever is caring for and interacting with the baby) have the capacity to affect each other. Appreciating this goes a long way toward understanding the essence of infancy (and motherhood) and also toward appreciating the importance of infancy as practice for the future. The view of the infant, even the newborn, as a reciprocating social creature necessitates that we try to understand learning disabilities and other developmental problems in terms of their earliest origins.

The lessons from recent research with infants indicate that normal newborn humans arrive in the world with all of their sensory systems functioning, and even with some specific abilities to learn (Lipsitt, 1976). There is some controversy, of course, concerning the particulars. While there are motoric and perceptual limitations, and newborns cannot learn everything, there is no question that the human neonate is a more responsive creature than has generally been supposed, possibly throughout the history of mankind. At the same time, the individual differences among newborns—in motoric precocity, in sensory functioning, and in learning ability—undoubtedly have bearing on their response to environmental constraints and indulgences.

SILENT ASSENT OF THE NEWBORN:
SUCKING AND HEART RATE

Our recently acquired knowledge about the considerable sensory and learning capabilities of the newborn has been accompanied by an increasing reliance upon polygraphic recording of various psychophysiological processes and the use of the computer in analyzing multiple parameters simultaneously affected by specific and manageable stimulation.

In recent years, many advances have been made in the technical aspects of psychobiological recording.[1] This new expertise has found its way into the maternity hospital where it is being used to monitor the condition of the mother and fetus prior to birth. Subsequently, it is used to explore the psychophysiology of the neonate in considerable detail. There is growing disenchantment among child psychologists with traditional modes of behavioral assessment, including the developmental tests that, in their time, have established growth and development patterns as a function of chronological age. The dismay comes in part from the emerging realization that an active and advancing science of human development must go beyond describing normative behavior, and even beyond the use of its techniques for the definition of aberrations and anomalies. Increasingly, developmental scientists are interested in the processes of development, and a process science requires manipulation or intervention. Studies of sensory and learning processes in young infants involve the arranging of specific environmental conditions for purposes of studying the effect on the child of repetitive or successive experiences with stimuli. Such experimental manipulative procedures can the be used to enhance developmental performance, particularly in those born with, or destined for, physical or social handicaps.

THE POLYGRAPHIC STUDY OF THE NEWBORN

The use of the polygraph for the documentation of infantile responsivity can facilitate the study of processes involving changes in the infant's condition over time and in response to specific sensory stimulation. Recent studies utilizing polygraphic recording of newborns' responses enable much finer detection of sensory and neurological capability. This is just as one would

---

[1]Much of this section has been appropriated verbatim, with permission, from a previous private publication: Lipsitt, L. P. The synchrony of respiration, heart rate and sucking behavior in the newborn. In J. C. Sinclair, J. B. Warshaw, & R. S. Bloom (Eds.), *Biological and clinical aspects of brain development. Mead Johnson Symposium on Perinatal and Developmental Medicine,* 1975, No. 6, pp. 67–72.

expect of techniques that are highly sensitive to individual differences. In addition, such procedures enable the simultaneous documentation of multiple responses, yielding a written record of the infant's response. The recording, and the stimulation associated with it, may then be "replayed" to provide the opportunity for further statistical analyses of the episode.

We were concerned in the present studies with the interrelationships among several response characteristics, such as sucking, respiration, and heart rate. Our intent was also to document the way in which sensory stimulation, taste in this case, serves to alter what might be called the basic congenital responsivity of the infant. In these studies we explore the earliest contributions of the environment to the newborn's response repertoire. The circumstances in which we accomplish this do not deviate sharply, of course, from the range of stimulation that infants ordinarily experience within the first few days of life in the ecological niche that is the normal nursery of the modern maternity hospital. Even so, the techniques are very sensitive to individual differences in newborns. They enable the documentation both of commonalities among infants with respect to their response to environmental change and of the stability of individual reactions over a period of time.

Testing is done in a special crib, housed in a white sound-attenuated chamber with temperature about 80° F. Ambient light is about 50 foot candles. Breathing is monitored by a Phipps and Bird infant pneumobelt around the abdomen. Respiration and body activity are recorded continuously on a Grass polygraph. Hewlett-Packard electrodes are placed on the chest and leg, permitting polygraphic monitoring of the primary heart rate, which is integrated by a Hewlett-Packard cardiotachometer and recorded on another channel. The testing situation is shown in Figure 5.1.

Sucking is recorded on another polygraph channel. The "suckometer" consists of a stainless steel housing with a pressure transducer, over which a commercial nipple is pulled. A polyethylene tube runs into the nipple from a pump source and delivers fluid under the control of the experimeter and on demand of the subject. When delivering, the pump ejects into the nipple end a .02-ml drop contingent upon the execution of a sucking response of preset amplitude.

In these studies, the situation may be arranged in such a way as to allow the infant to receive no fluid for sucking, or to receive a fluid such as sucrose or dextrose, in any desired concentration, contingent upon sucking, with one drop being ejected onto the tongue for each suck. A polygraph event marker records fluid ejections during fluid delivery periods, or the occurrence of a criterion suck during no-fluid conditions. To insure a constant acoustical environment, a 74-db background white noise is produced from a noise generator continuously through a speaker enclosed in the infant chamber.

A nurse applies the electrodes and pneumobelt to the infant, who is then swaddled and placed on its left side. The nipple is then inserted, supported by

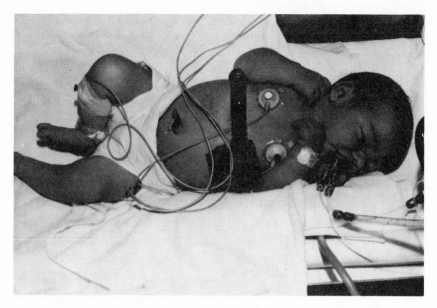

FIG. 5.1. A two-day-old child with the pneumobelt attached for the recording of respiration, EEG electrodes for recording of heart rate, and the automatic sucking apparatus in place for recording and for delivery of fluid contingent upon sucking behavior.

a cushion to enable recording without touching the infant. During the first few sucking bursts on the nipple, no fluid is delivered and the equipment is calibrated. Preamplifier sensitivity is adjusted for each infant so the average sucking amplitude results in a 5-cm excursion of a polygraph pen. The threshold criterion is then set at 2.5 cm, so that only responses causing a pen sweep greater than 2.5 cm meet the criterion of a suck and are counted.

An exemplary polygraph record showing respiration, heart rate, the cardiotachometer transformation of the basic electrocardiogram (EKG), and sucking can be seen in Figure 5.2. Newborns characteristically suck in bursts of responses separated by rests. The burst lengths and the rest lengths both constitute individual difference variables under no-fluid conditions. But both of these parameters as well as the sucking rate within bursts (as will be seen later) are importantly influenced by the conditions that are arranged as consequences of the infant's own response. For example, with a change from a no-fluid condition to a fluid-sucking condition, or with a change from sucking for a less-sweet solution to a sweeter solution, there is a tendency for the sucking bursts to become longer, for the interburst intervals to become shorter, and for the intersuck intervals to become longer (i.e., for sucking rate within bursts to become slower.) Because of these regularities of response in relation to the conditions imposed upon the infants during testing, it is

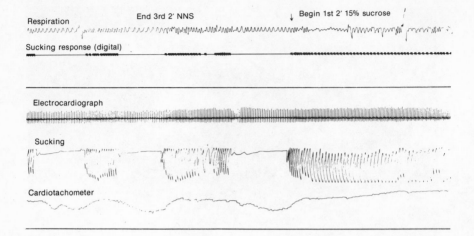

Respiration   End 3rd 2′ NNS   ↓ Begin 1st 2′ 15% sucrose

Sucking response (digital)

Electrocardiograph

Sucking

Cardiotachometer

FIG. 5.2.   Exemplary polygraph record from 38-hr-old normal male, showing the last two bursts of no-fluid sucking preceding introduction of the sucrose-sucking condition without interruption. Total polygraph record shown runs for 2 min. Top channel records respiration, pen marker shows digital representation of criterion sucks, which receive .02 ml drop of fluid during sucrose period. Next operating channel is the electrocardiograph (EKG), then the cardiotachometer transformation of the inter-beat intervals, followed by the sucking record. Long sucking bursts are characteristic of sucrose-sucking. No-fluid sucking occurs in short bursts of more rapid sucks. Heart rate during sucrose may be seen to go to a higher level (and remain there) than during no-fluid sucking.

possible to (1) explore the effects of one period of taste experience upon the response of the infant during a subsequent taste experience. and (2) investigate the interrelationships of these various sucking-response parameters with one another and with certain other response measures, such as heart rate. The two studies reported here relate to those objectives.

SUCKING FOR SUCROSE, WATER, OR NOTHING

In a study by Kobre and Lipsitt (1972), the infants were first tested for 2 minutes on the nipple without any fluid delivery whatever. Subjects in this study were rejected for further study if they had a mean sucking rate lower than 30 per minute during the 2 minute period. The 25 subjects remaining were divided into five groups. A total of 20 minutes of responding was recorded for each subject, four successive periods each of 5 minute duration. Between each period the nipple was removed for 1 minute to allow the tube to be flushed out with water and the child to be picked up.

The 25 infants, most in the 3rd day of life, received one of five reinforcement regimens for the 20-minute period. One group (Suc-Suc)

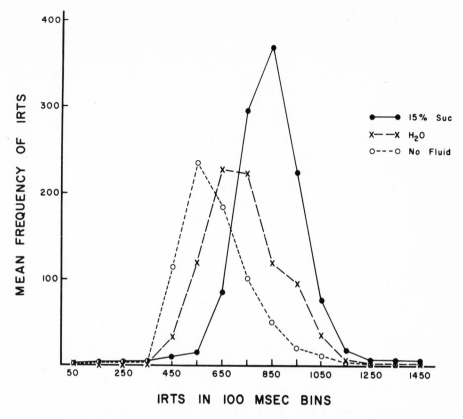

FIG. 5.3. Mean incidence of interresponse times (IRTs) for each of the 100 msec bins. Each curve represents the combined IRT distribution for the five subjects in that group (Suc-Suc: H_2O-H_2O; NF-NF) over the twenty minute session. Sucking is slower for sucrose than for water, on average, and slower for water than under the no-fluid condition.

received only sucrose throughout the 20-minute period. A second group (H_2O-H_2O) received water throughout, and a third group (Suc-H_2O) received sucrose and water alternated twice, in 5 minute units. In a second portion of the experiment, one group (NF-NF) received no fluid throughout the four 5-minute periods, and a second group (Suc-NF) received sucrose alternated with no fluid in 5-minute periods.

It is of interest first to compare the frequency polygons representing the sucking behavior of the three groups that received a constant reinforcement condition throughout the 20-minute sucking period. These are the groups that got either sucrose, or distilled water, or no fluid for that 20 minutes. Figure 5.3 provides a graphical comparison of the three groups as represented by the computer-generated polygons, which threw the intersuck intervals accumulated during the 20-minute period into bins representing 100-msec intervals. This shows clearly that sucking rate within bursts slows down for a fluid-sucking condition relative to no-fluid sucking and that sucking rate slows still further for sweet-fluid-sucking relative to sucking for distilled water. Thus there is an orderly progression from no fluid to plain water to 15% sucrose sucking, with the sucking response becoming slower and slower with an apparent increase in the incentive value of the reinforcement delivered contingent upon the response. It may also be noted, parenthetically, that under the sucrose condition the infants invested a larger number of responses during a comparable period of time than under either the water or no-fluid condition. A somewhat larger number of responses was emitted for water, moreover, than for no fluid.

As has been indicated earlier, rather interesting interplays between various response parameters occur in neonates. For example, whereas infants suck more slowly within bursts for sweeter fluids, as if to savor them more, it is also

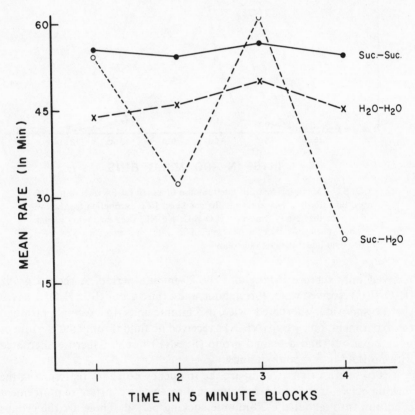

FIG. 5.4.   Mean sucking rate over four 5-minute blocks for each of the three groups; sucrose alone (Suc-Suc), water alone (H₂O-H₂O) and sucrose and water alternated twice (Suc-H₂O). N = 5 in each group.

the case that when sucking for sweet they tend to take shorter rests. Thus, they suck more times per minute for sweet than for nonsweet. This effect may be seen in Figure 5.4, wherein the comparison is shown of mean rates per minute for the group that got sucrose throughout with the group that got water throughout. Then both of these are compared to the group that got sucrose and water alternated in 5-minute blocks. Here it may be seen that the sucking rate per minute for the sucrose group is higher than for the water-sucking group. The trend shows that sucking rate over the 20-minute period is remarkably stable, and the difference between the two groups is a reliable one. More important, however, is the obvious indication of an experiential effect in the alternated group. When sucking for sucrose, this group was essentially comparable to the group sucking for sucrose throughout. When switched to water, however, response rate during each of those 5-minute periods was significantly lower than their counterpart controls in the water-throughout group. Thus, when newborns have experience in sucking for sucrose, an immediately subsequent experience with water "turns them off." They display their apparent "aversion" for the water by a marked reduction in instrumental behavior that would put that fluid in their mouths. As can be seen from the figure, when the response consequent is changed, as from water to sucrose, response rate goes right back up to a normal level. There is even a suggestion there (though not reliable) of a positive contrast effect counterpointing the negative contrast effect shown during the second and fourth blocks (both of which effects are reliable).

The comparable comparison showing a similar effect in the relations between sucking for sucrose and sucking for no fluid is shown in Figure 5.5. This figure shows the no-fluid group to suck at an essentially constant rate of about 40 sucks per minute throughout the 20-minute testing session. The group that was alternated between sucrose and the no fluid in succesive 5-minute bocks, however, goes from a sucking rate of almost 60 under sucrose to a rate of about 30 sucks per minute under the no-fluid condition. This is a drop to a level significantly below that of the group receiving no fluid throughout. Thus the negative contrast effect occurs under conditions in which the lower-incentive condition involves either no fluid at all or plain distilled water. There is reason to suppose at this point that the phenomenon is widespread throughout the range of incentive conditions and that it would occur whenever the infant is called upon to compare two levels of incentive, such as breast milk versus formula, or formula versus plain water.

More important from the standpoint of the psychologist interested in behavioral changes due to accruing experiences is the fact that the newborn is strikingly affected in his subsequent behavior by his experiences within the immediately previous 5 minutes. Surely the negative contrast effect demonstrated here is one of the most rudimentary types of behavioral

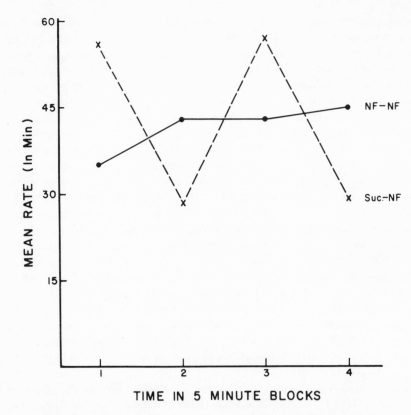

FIG. 5.5. Mean sucking rate over four 5-minute blocks for each of two groups: no fluid (NF—NF), and sucrose and no fluid alternated twice (Suc— NF). N = 5 in each group.

alteration, however temporary, due to experiential circumstances. As in the case of neonatal habituation to olfactory stimulation (Engen & Lipsitt, 1965), there is the strong suggestion that memorial processes are already working during the newborn period, such that there is a lasting impression made, admittedly of unknown duration, of the experience endured. These are the beginnings of learning processes.

RESPIRATION, HEART RATE, AND SUCKING

In a study involving 44 normal full-term newborns, 24 males and 20 females, testing was conducted on 2 consecutive days, using the polygraph recording techniques previously described. Mean age on initial testing (Day 1) was 54 hours (27 to 120 hours) and , on Day 2, 78 hours (51 to 144 hours). All infants, 33 bottled-fed and 11 breast-fed, were seen between 8:30 and 9:30 a.m. Infants in this study were part of a long-term longitudinal study; only some aspects of the newborn data will be considered here. The procedures described here constituted only a portion of the total battery of testing done on each infant, but they were administered, under identical standardized conditions, to all infants in the study.

A total of 10 minutes of sucking was recorded for each infant immediately following calibration of the apparatus, five successive periods each of 2 minutes duration. Three of these were sucking for no fluid, followed by two periods of 15% sucrose-sucking. About 35 second intervened between periods, during which a computer printed out the interresponse time data (IRT) for the preceding period. The nipple was not removed between periods. The infant continued sucking under the same condition as in the preceding period. The beginning of a period following the 35 second printout was initiated after the infant stopped sucking for at least 2 seconds after the end of a burst.

At the end of the second sucrose period, the nipple was removed. There then ensued a 2-minute period of polygraph recording during a "resting" state, defined as quiescent and with regular respiration, in which the infant neither sucked nor was stimulated in any way.

The results (Lipsitt, Reilly, Butcher, & Greenwood, 1976) of this part of the longitudinal study have suggested a very interesting interplay between the sucking response and heart rate. They further substantiate a process that suggests a "savory mechanism," which seems already to be present during the newborn period.

The computer printout at the end of each 2-minute period provided a frequency distribution, for intersuck intervals under 2 seconds, of sucking IRTs in 100-msec bins. The mean IRT could be calculated from the printout, using the midpoint of the bin as its numerical representation. Figure 2, shown earlier, is a polygraph record from this study, showing the final phase of nonnutritive (no-fluid) sucking in comparison with the first phase of sucrose-sucking for an exemplary subject of this experiment.

Table 5.1 shows the five sucking parameters under the no-fluid and sucrose-sucking conditions. The mean and modal IRTs are greater when sucking is for sucrose than when sucking under a no-fluid condition, and the number of responses per burst is twice as large. Also, more rest periods (IRTs more than 2 seconds) occur under the no-fluid condition. Consequently, despite the faster rate of sucking within bursts under the no-fluid condition, more sucks per minute are emitted under sucrose. All these effects are reliable.

Table 5.2 compares the heart rate of infants during sucking periods with basal heart rate without the nipple. Very interestingly, the mean heart rate under no-fluid sucking was significantly higher than the basal rate. In turn the mean heart rate under sucrose-sucking was higher than under the no-fluid condition. Although sucking rate within burst is *reduced* when the infant sucks for sucrose, then, heart rate nevertheless increases reliably.

TABLE 5.1

Comparison of the Means (2-min units) of Five Sucking Parameters
Under No-Fluid and Sucrose-Sucking Conditions Over a 2-day
Period, and Correlation Coefficients (r) Comparing Day 1 and Day 2

	Day 1		Day 2		Day 1/Day 2	
	Mean	SD	Mean	SD	r	p^r
No-fluid sucking (N=41)						
Total responses	88.3	23.2	96.6	30.9	.62	.001
IRTs > 2″ (rests)	8.1	2.6	8.7	2.8	.65	.001
Responses/burst	12.9	15.5	11.2	6.1	.79	.001
Mode IRT	620.3	99.0	572.8	61.9	.37	.05
Mean IRT	657.8	81.7	611.9	56.0	.42	.01
15% Sucrose sucking (N =40)						
Total responses	103.0	28.2	106.2	27.6	.08	—
IRTs > 2″ (rests)	5.3	2.7	5.9	3.5	.13	—
Responses/burst	29.7	34.2	24.2	21.7	.03	—
Mode IRT	838.1	109.9	771.3	115.7	.63	.001
Mean IRT	855.8	105.3	786.9	85.8	.71	.001

Adapted from Lipsitt, Reilly, Butcher, and Greenwood (1976).

TABLE 5.2

Heart Rate (bpm) During Resting and When Sucking for No Fluid or Sucrose, and
Correlation Coefficients (r) Comparing Day 1 and Day 2

	N	Day 1		Day 2		Combined		Day 1/Day 2	
	N	Mean	SD	Mean	SD	Mean	SD	r	p^r
Basal	44	113.8	16.7	118.7	18.1	116.3	14.2	.29	.05
No-fluid sucking	40	124.0	14.5	123.4	13.6	123.8	12.2	.46	.01
Sucrose-sucking	39	145.7	15.5	147.4	12.3	146.6	13.1	.71	.001

Adapted from Lipsitt, Reilly, Butcher, and Greenwood (1976).

FURTHER STUDIES

The more we study the human neonate under rather precise response
measurement conditions afforded by the polygraph and associated apparatus
such as the computer, the more we are impressed, first by the fine interplay
between the various congenital responses of the newborn, and second, by the
extent to which the newborn's behavior and psychophysiological indices are
affected by the environmental resources available to the infants at any given
moment. Thus, the manual introduction of 10% sucrose into the infant's

mouth in the presence of a refusal to suck will almost immediately generate sucking behavior that will persist even upon the subsequent withdrawal of that sucrose incentive. Similarly, and as has been demonstrated in the first experiment reported here, experience in sucking for a sweet substance for 5-minute period will affect the infant's subsequent behavior, at least for the next 5 minutes, when offered a less-sweet incentive.

An important feature of the present experimental techniques is that the infant has been studied not just in the presence of stimulating features of the environment that were under the control of the examiner or experimenter, but also under conditions where the infant is offered the opportunity to self-regulate. Our incentive conditions were such that we simply made available to the baby different reinforcing conditions, to which we studied the response. The newborn through its instrumental or operant activity either made it happen or didn't, or did something in between. We think that we are formulating a model for the interaction between an infant and its environment. The model will be quite specific eventually, for there is a limited domain of responses that the newborn can make and to which the adult can generate reactions, and the documented responses of adults to newborns thus far seem, even though there is a good deal of creativity in the process, quite manageable. Involved is not merely a stimulus–response relationship in which the environment or the infant's caretaker serves as stimulus and the subject responds, or even one in which the infant serves as stimulus and the environment responds. Rather, it is one in which there is constant reciprocity between the organism and the environment, between the infant and the caretaker, in which each serves as stimulus and each responds. Both operate at least in part according to incentive principles that can and will be discovered. This too simple view of human nature and human development will yield to more complex models as we learn more, but we can learn more only by starting at the beginning.

Lending credibility to the assumption that stable sensory functions in the neonate will ultimately yield to an orderly understanding of the effects of experience on the developing brain and being is a further experiment conducted in this laboratory, in which the magnitude of the reinforcer was varied rather than the sweetness of the fluid. This study showed that certain incentive conditions are virtually collapsible in their effects on behavioral output. Crook (1976) was interested in whether the changes in infantile behavior that we had obtained to variations in sweetness of the fluid delivered would be similar under conditions in which sweetness was held constant (at 10% sucrose concentration) but amount of fluid for which the babies sucked differed. In some instances the babies received a .01-ml drop, and in other instances a .03-ml suck. To our own pleasure, the functional relationships that had been previously established for sweetness held also for amount, for both sucking behavior and heart rate. Each infant was tested over two 4-minute periods. One group of newborns experienced only the larger amount, a second experienced the smaller, and two other groups received both in counterbalanced order. Cumulative pausing time and intersuck intervals (sucking rate within bursts) were affected both by the amounts of fluid delivered at each response and in the direction that promotes the collapsibility of the sweetness and magnitude operations. Babies paused more and for longer periods of time when sucking for the smaller amount of fluid than for the larger, and their interresponse times or intersuck intervals were longer when sucking for the larger amount of fluid. As would be expected, those infants who were switched from the small to the large, or from the large to the small, reinforcing condition altered their sucking rhythms accordingly, whereas the infants who were left on the previous condition continued sucking with essentially the same rhythm. Thus both sweetness and magnitude may be conceived as incentive–motivational variables with common consequences.

In the Crook study, at the start of sucking bursts, heart rate accelerated to a stable level. Within-burst heart rates were higher with increased quantity of the contingently delivered fluid. Controls were introduced into this study across all conditions, which removes the possibility that the changes in heart rate commensurate with the fluid taste and amount on the tongue are due to different lengths of sucking bursts.

Figure 5.6 shows the data from this study on two measures of sucking, pause time and interresponse time.

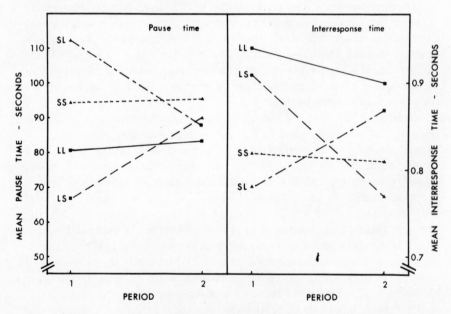

FIG. 5.6.   Mean total pausing times and mean interresponse times for each group during the two experimental periods.

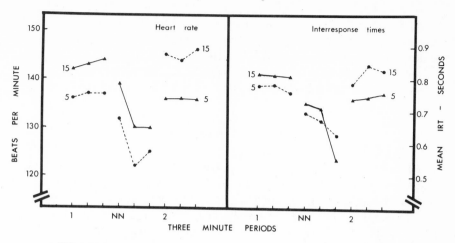

FIG. 5.7   Mean heart rates and mean interresponse times during each minute of the three experimental periods. *Solid lines* represent group 15-5, *broken lines* group 5-15.

In another study (Crook & Lipsitt, 1976) the sucking behavior and heart rate of 22 full-term newborns were recorded. Half of the infants sucked for 9 minutes in three blocks of 3 minutes, first receiving a .02-ml drop of 5% sucrose for each criterion suck, then no fluid contingent upon such sucks, and finally a .01-ml drop of 15% sucrose for each suck. The other half received these conditions in reverse order. Regardless of the order in which the two nutrient conditions were administered, intersuck intervals were longer under the sweeter condition, but heart rate was also higher. Possible interpretations of this and the foregoing effects must include a hedonic explanation suggesting that sucking rate is modulated to facilitate savoring of the sweeter fluid. The results of the Crook and Lipsitt study for both heart rate and sucking interresponse times are shown in Figure 5.7.

Finally, a recent study has investigated the relevance of the human voice in recruiting attention of the newborn (Ashmead and Lipsitt, note 1). The voice of female, actually the mother of a newborn talking to her own infant, was recorded while she was addressing her baby. This recording was replicated by a male speaker who said the same words, and the two recordings were used in a counterbalanced study with decibel level controlled, to assess whether there would be different heart rate responses of newborns to the male and female voices. These two recordings were used along with a recording of a newborn cry, which was previously shown (Simner, 1971) to produce aggravation and crying in other newborns. The results were clear, from two associated studies, in showing that the female voice tended to generate cardiac deceleration responses, usually associated with orienting and attending behavior, whereas the male voice and the infant cry produced only accelerative responses. Thus it appears that the newborn may be selectively attuned to the frequency range of the female voice, or at least more so than to the male voice range. The first few interbeat intervals in response to the female voice were decelerative, following which the accelerative pattern was evident. It appears that the response pattern to the female voice is biphasic, and that to the male voice monophasic and accelerative.

RESPONSE DEVIATIONS IN THE NEWBORN

The techniques, tools, and results represented in the foregoing should have diagnostic significance in relation to the newborn, inasmuch as such normative findings can be utilized to assess "response deviation" in individual infants tested by the same techniques. The 24-hour test–retest stabilities of certain of these measures, given in Table 1, lend credibility to their utility for tagging the "deviant newborn." We have been conducting further studies to determine the validity of these psychophysiological measures in assessing degree of fetal, obstetrical, and other perinatal distress. We recognize that the "scales" that we have been using (those of Prechtl, 1969, and Hoebel, Hyvarinen, Okada, & Oh, 1973) for our identification and "quantification" of degree of perinatal distress are not the refined instruments that we will some day need and will no doubt have. For now, a simple enumeration and rough weighting of "hazardous" or "nonoptimal" perinatal conditions has been used as a first approximation to a continuum of distress that, hopefully, will have some psychophysiological validity. Moreover, longitudinal studies will be required ultimately to determine the long-term usefulness of the neonatal measures of sucking, heart rate, and other parameters for purposes of assessing prognosis. With empirical luck, we might be able someday to identify, then intensify our remedial efforts on behalf of, infants with aberrations or deficits for which compensatory training techniques either are available now or will be later.

For now, it can be reported in a preliminary way that listings of risk factors at birth do seem to bear a relationship to psychophysiological measures that can be obtained from the essentially normal newborn. In a recent study by Kittner and Lipsitt (1976) it was shown that two groups of newborns differing only in the number of nonoptimal factors in their obstetric history showed a significant disparity in the direction of the average heart rate response to an auditory stimulus. The "high risk" group showed more heart rate acceleration and less deceleration compared with the "low risk"group. The heart rate responses were significantly related to the number of nonoptimal obstetric conditions and to parity, but not to the maternal predelivery medication score. The greater the "risk" at birth, the less the deceleration; the greater the maternal parity, the less did acceleration occur in response to auditory stimulation. Both groups, interestingly, showed reliable diminution of decelerative heart rate responding over trials. Habituation of response in the newborn is often taken as a "good sign" in neurological and behavioral assessments. The infants studied here were, it should be repeated, essentially normal children, being cared for routinely in the normal nursery, but differing in their exposure to presumably stressful perinatal conditions.

NEGATIVE HEDONICS

Our emphasis thus far on the "savoring behaviors" of the newborn must be counterbalanced with an acknowledgment that even newborns sometimes display "distaste" of certain types of stimulation. This can be observed anecdotally, of course, in the frowning and crying behavior of the baby when subjected to very loud noises or other sudden stimulation, such as rapid onset of a bright light, a pin prick in the heel, or other apparently noxious environmental input. Crook (1978) has provided some systematic documentation of aversive behavior in the baby under entirely innocuous conditions. He adapted the taste-stimulation and sucking apparatus, previously described, to deliver fluid only on demand of the experimenter,

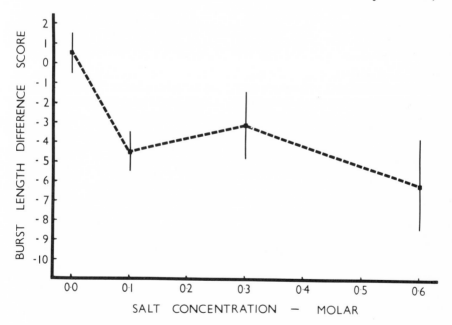

FIG. 5.8. The burst shortening effect of salt stimulation as a function of concentration. The mean length of water potentiated bursts is subtracted from the mean length of salt potentiated bursts for each subject. Group means and ± 1 standard error are shown.

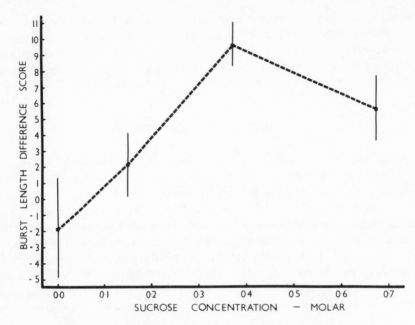

FIG. 5.9.   The burst lengthening effect of sucrose stimulation as a function of concentration. The mean length of bursts containing a water stimulus is subtracted from the mean length of bursts containing a sucrose stimulus for each subject. Group means and ± 1 standard error are shown.

and not contingent upon the baby's own sucking behavior. Thus the infants were studied sucking nonnutritively (that is, for no fluid). but were administered .02-ml drops of salt solution during the interburst intervals. Using this technique, and varying the concentration of the salt solution, he was able to derive meaningful psychophysical data from the infants using only three trials per subject, for a total of .06 ml of solution. The response parameters utilized were the time transpired from administration of the salt drop to the onset of the next sucking burst and the length of that subsequent sucking burst. Figure 5.8 shows the data obtained under these conditions. A reliable effect of salt concentration was obtained, and this effect mirrored the effect obtained under identical conditions when various concentrations of sugar, in .02-ml dosages, rather than salt were used. The sugar effect is shown in Figure 5.9.

AVERSIVE BEHAVIOR IN THE NEWBORN

Aversive behavior occurs in human infants under conditions in which biological threat exists. In its milder forms, such behavior is manifested in the autonomic and withdrawal responses to intense stimulation, such as bright lights, noxious tactile stimuli, unpleasant odorants and tastes, trigeminal stimulants, and loud noises. The amount of active response occurring to such stimulation is directly proportional to stimulus intensity, with very intense stimulation culminating in crying.

Angry behavior may be defined in terms of the presence and vigor of autonomic and withdrawal response to noxious stimulation. I believe it warranted to say that angry behavior does occur in the newborn and that what we subsequently call aggressive behavior in infants and young children may have its ontogenetic roots in these congenitally bestowed "angry reactions." Aggressive behavior might, in this view, be taken as responses of the baby, in the presence of anger, that have the function of thwarting perpetuation of the instigating noxious stimulation (Lipsitt, 1976). In ordinary feeding circumstances, such defensive behavior can be fortuitously directed against the mother.

A particularly striking pattern of aversive behavior can often be seen in the newborn's response to the threat of respiratory occlusion. Stimulation that supports or threatens respiratory occlusion tends to elicit a response pattern consisting of five components, which might be viewed as a fixed action pattern beginning with mild responsivity and proceeding toward extreme arousal if the stimulus condition is not removed. The five steps involved are (1) side-to-side head waving, (2) head withdrawal, with backward jerks and grimacing, (3) facial vasodilation, (4) arm jabbing, and (5) crying. It is this continuum of response that is here regarded as angry behavior. It may be seen to abate when the threatening or noxious stimulation is reduced.

Such behavior often occurs in the natural course of infant feeding. When anger is elicited in the newborn to respiratory occlusion, the action pattern has the effect of freeing the respiratory passages, by displacing the offending object or by impelling the mother to adjust her feeding position. The freeing from occlusion constitutes a reinforcement condition that can increase the probability of its occurrence under this and similar future conditions. The anger response may occur subsequently with a shorter latency, or even anticipatorily to less intense, but similar stimulating conditions. Still later in ontogeny, it may occur without direct (exteroceptive) instigation at all. Such "aggressive behavior" may be mediated, moreover, by anger generated from circumstances entirely different from those in which the behavior has been first learned. The learning mechanisms involved in the acquisition of aggressive behavior are those presumed implicated in other forms of instrumental learning. Initially, a congenital response pattern (anger) is elicited by experiential circumstances conducive to its expression. Components of that action pattern are selectively reinforced, following which these behaviors (now called aggressive) are learned and perpetuated through reinforcement consequences.

The foregoing comments are to a great extent speculative and theoretical, except for their evidential basis in the observations of Gunther (1955, 1961) and others who have documented the infantile response to brief respiratory occlusion in the natural feeding situation. The reciprocating relationship between mother and infant has been well described by Gunther, who has made close observations of the fascinating ways in which the nursing mother and her infant affect each other reciprocally, immediately after birth, and quite possibly with lasting effects. When the newborn is suckling at the breast, its nostrils periodically and fortuitously become occluded. This results in an aversive reaction from the baby, involving various manifestations of withdrawal from the nipple and breast. The threat to nasal occlusion generally produces the pattern of aversive behavior previously described, involving swaying of the head and pulling backwards. Gunther has described some infants who seemed reluctant to reattach to the breast after such aversive experiences. Although Gunther does not phrase the sequence of activities as such, the stimulating event, the resulting reaction, and the subsequent aversion to the feeding situation may be conceptualized easily as one of operant learning. It is a type of aversive behavior that warrants much more extensive study than it has thus far been accorded.

CONCLUDING REMARKS

The newborn child does engage in systematic congenital patterns of behavior from the earliest moments after birth. These behavior patterns are mediated in part by hedonic mechanisms that screen stimulation, whereupon further approach behavior ensues or defensive reactions supervene. A plausible case can be made for the presumption that part of the function of early infancy is to provide a period in which the baby receives and endures a fair range of stimuli—positive and negative, pleasant and unpleasant—and to which the baby can rehearse its congenital response repertoire in relative safety. During these first 2 months, the infant modulates its behavior to accord with the "palatability" of the stimulation, perhaps in preparation for a later period (which we might speculate to be that between 2 and 6 months of age) when so many previously reflexive behaviors become voluntary and operantly guided. This overly simplistic view of the first half-year of life derives some support from the neurophysiological evidence for rapidly accelerating myelination and dendritic development during this later period. Many of the neonatal reflexes, too, seem to undergo marked transformations compatible with this view by about 2 months of age. We need studies of differential experience in infants prior to 2 months of age, with follow-up assessments of the infants' reflexes and operant capabilities between the ages of 2 and 6 months of age. Short-term longitudinal studies are crucial for discovery of the effects of early experience upon later (but still early) behavior.

DISCUSSION

Dr. Papousek: How old were your infants?

Dr. Lipsitt: Newborns, 2 and 3 days of age.

Dr. Eisenberg: When you say voice, exactly what were the stimuli? Were the speakers talking to the subjects?

Dr. Lipsitt: Yes, we recorded an actual mother talking to her infant, saying something like "Come on, baby, I know what you want. Put your head down."

Dr. Eisenberg: And the male voice said the same thing?

Dr. Lipsitt: The male voice said precisely the same thing. The two were played at the same intensity, both voices to the same subjects.

Dr. Watson: What's your conclusion?

Dr. Lipsitt: Well, that's a fair question. My conclusion is, rather like my introduction, that the newborn child is a hedonic screener of stimuli, that the pleasures of sensation are already operative in the newborn child, and that the pleasure the baby experiences and is accorded in the hands of his caretakers, including his mother and his father, have an effect upon his behavior. This includes, as we just saw, cardiac deceleration from the mother's voice at least. The hedonic screen set the baby up, if you will, for reinforcing learning experiences.

Dr. Eisenberg: One also finds cardiac deceleration, and very marked deceleration, in response to synthetic speech sounds that have nothing whatever to do with maternal voice, so I would find it very difficult to draw any conclusions from your findings. Aside from this, I have a problem in interpreting your data in that, given beats rather than real time, I'm not even sure what time span your analysis deals with.

Dr. Lipsitt: Well, the heart rate is approximately 120 beats per minute, so you can figure out about how much time. It would be 4 or 5 seconds during which cardiac deceleration was occurring—4 or 5 seconds after the onset of the stimulus. In response to your suggestion that one shouldn't make much of it, I would say two things. First, that we have data with the same infants using the male voice, which did not elicit cardiac deceleration, at least under our conditions; and secondly, I'm not sure what in the world the synthetic voices are all about-it doesn't distress me that a real live human voice produces a different effect than does a computerized simulated voice!

Dr. Eisenberg: The point I've been trying to make is that a real live human voice *does not* seem to produce different effects from synthetic vowels, CV syllables, or even tonal patterns. We have gotten decelerative changes of 20–30 beats to these kinds of stimuli across substantial populations of newborns ($N = 40$), as well as smaller but equally systematic changes in adolescents and young adults.

The reason I asked you about the time characteristics of your responses is that it has been our experience, which is in agreement with your data, that such decelerative changes to patterned sounds tend to have very long latencies: In a majority of cases, they appear at least 4 seconds after stimulus onset and persist for relatively long periods of time (see Figure 15, p. 100 in Eisenberg, 1976). Your analysis, however, covers only about 6 seconds, which tells you that deceleration has occurred, but not always: nor does it necessarily tell you how long it has persisted.

Further, given the sentence material you specified, which contains more acoustic variables that I can consider offhand and would cover about 5 seconds of real time, as best I can judge, there is an almost complete overlap between your stimulus period and your analysis period that makes it impossible to determine which variables were operating for you. It could be merely an onset effect relating to differences in fundamental frequency between male and female voices: it could be differences in intonation or phrasing related to the fact that one speaker was a mother talking to her own child and the other a male stranger simply repeating a phrase; it could be differences in pauses between phrases or syllables in the sentence material; it could, in fact be any combination of these and other factors. On the other hand, our data on decelerative responses to speech-like sounds were obtained with short and exactly defined physical stimuli, which permit one to define exactly which variables are operating, and in analyzing our date, we took into account matched amounts of heart rate data deriving from either side of signal-onset time (Eisenberg, 1976).

Dr. Lipsitt: Those are speech sounds simulated by people who are very good at simulating speech sounds, is that right?

Dr. Eisenberg: No, they were synthetic stimuli, generated by electronic equipment at Haskins Laboratories...and the virtue of such stimuli (whatever one's intuitions about their differences from real speech) is that they can be specified exactly and replicated exactly by any investigator who chooses to work with them. Whatever stimuli one uses, however, it seems to me that analysis must take into account whatever period of time is required before the heart rate returns to baseline: It is not uncommon for cardiac responses to be diphasic—that is , deceleration followed by acceleration, or the reverse—and the use of an arbitrarily chosen short postsignal analysis period may mask similarities in heart rate response patterns that occur later in time.

Dr. Stern: How do you interpret that?

Dr. Lipsitt: Well, it makes some ethological sense that stimuli that particularly grab the attention of the newborn will produce cardiac deceleration.The dichotomy between defensive behavior, which is presumably associated with cardiac acceleration, and orienting behavior. The Sokolovian orienting behavior indexed by cardiac deceleration, is relevant here.

Dr. Stern: It's hard for me to understand why the baby wouldn't orient to father's voice as well as to the mother's.

Dr. Lipsitt: This is the first study we've done with the voice. Admittedly— it's not preliminary data—it's a complete experiment, but it's our earliest data on the effect of the human voice on the baby's cardiac responsivity.

Dr. Stern: I had one other question. When you introduced saline that was aversive, was the rate of sucking slowed? I know you said the bursts were shorter, but how about the rate?

Dr. Lipsitt: If by that you mean the number of sucks per minute or per unit time for a time after the presentation of the stimulus—it is lower for salt.

Dr. Stern: As well as for sugar?

Dr. Lipsitt: No. It's greater for sugar. The number of responses that the baby puts out for sugar is greater.

Dr. Stern: I thought you said he slowed down.

Dr. Lipsitt: Let's get all the measures straight then. There are five different parameters.

Dr. Stern: The one that I'm most interested in is the slowing of the rate, because that's the one that you're attributing savoring to. So my question is , when you introduce the aversive solution is there a slowing of the rate?

Dr. Lipsitt: A slowing of the rate? That is, you're referring then to the amount of time between sucks?

Dr. Stern: That's right.

Dr. Lipsitt: There is a marked disruption in sucking, a foreshortening of the next sucking burst. I think the pacing of sucking within the burst thereupon becomes difficult to define or quantify.

Dr. Stern: I think it would be important, because otherwise you can't interpret slowing or savoring.

Dr. Lipsitt: We're just using the measure having to do with the length of this burst. The length of the next burst following the drop of fluid on the baby's tongue. That's the index that's being used. I won't hazard a guess as to what happens to the interresponse times.

Dr. Stern: That would be very important if you're talking about savoring. Which way would you think it would go?

Dr. Eisenberg: They should go the other way, or at least not change. I mean if the rate is hedonically interpreted as a positive response called savoring, then you have to assume if you put something aversive on the tongue something different will happen.

Dr. Lipsitt: Yes, alright. And you would want it to speed up. Perhaps the baby would suck less, but suck faster, just as they suck faster for water than for sucrose.

Dr. Eisenberg: Or else he'd quit.

Dr. Parmelee: When you gave just water and increased the volume, what happened? I want to know how much the act of swallowing contributes to increased heart rate.

Dr. Lipsitt: As a matter of fact, Patrick Burke (1977) did his doctoral dissertation in my laboratory precisely on swallowing, using an apparatus with an electric recording device on the neck. He was able to record swallowing coincident with sucking. Swallowing behaves lawfully just as do these five sucking parameters in response to both sweetness and magnitude. That is to say, regardless of whether you increase the sweetness of the fluid or increase the magnitude of the drops that the baby gets contingent upon each of the sucking responses, swallowing is greater for the sweeter fluids than it is for the less-sweet fluids.

Dr. Parmelee: Just swallowing, itself, can increase the heart rate. And heart rate increased as a function of volume of water. It's conceivable, that sucrose in the mouth generates a greater volume by inducing salivation.

Dr. Papousek: As far as I know, the newborn hardly salivates at all.

Dr. Lipsitt: My response to your question would be this: The heart rate effect takes place so quickly that this effect couldn't possibly have anything to do with ingestion, nor with the number of swallows. This effect occurs virtually coincident with the first swallow. This is such a tiny drop of fluid on the tongue that it takes a while for the baby to accumulate enough to place it on the back of his tongue, which will then trigger the swallow response. It's a miniscule drop of fluid, and even four of them don't make the usual drop of water. It's not much like the real life sucking situation in which the baby is usually drawing large dollops of milk.

Dr. Sander: What happens with the parameters if you have a large amount?

Dr. Lipsitt: That, as a matter of fact, is a question that fascinates me. Dr. Burke, just mentioned a moment ago, studied heart rate in infants while they were being breast fed by their mothers or being bottle-fed, and he found what was previously reported by Israeli researchers (Winter, Samueloff, Cohen, Porges, and Gross, 1966) namely that in some normal newborns an enormous bradycardia takes place when the baby gets a large amount of fluid at once in his mouth. It must be taking place all the time in newborns, only one doesn't notice this unless the baby is hooked up to a polygraph. Their heart rate goes down to below 80 beats per minute for the time it takes them to get that large bolus of food out of their mouth and into their stomach. It's almost as if the baby is startled by the sudden intake of a large amount of food. It doesn't take place in all infants. Many show cardiac acceleration, but in some, there is this almost frightening bradycardia that takes place. I believe that newborns learn to modulate their sucking behavior on the basis of experiences such as these.

Dr. Korner: Have you by any chance looked at sex differences? I am reminded of Nisbett and Gurwitz's study (1970), which showed that females increased their intake when there is sucrose available significantly more than males: which in your terms would mean that females are more hedonistic?

Dr. Lipsitt: Well, I wouldn't deny the conclusion!

Dr. Korner: Have you looked at any sex differences at all?

Dr. Lipsitt: Not very much. Most of the time that we look at sex differences in the newborn we get none. We have not replicated the Nisbett and Gurwitz sex-difference effect in sucking and ingestion (Engen, Lipsitt, and Robinson, 1978), but our testing situation was somewhat different from theirs.

Dr. Watson: Given the fact that you pursued a "convergent validity" assessment of the hedonistic model using both intensity of the solution and the amount, I worry that these may not really provide two separate pieces of information. Have you ever tried sucking on the nipple yourself and finding out whether there was any distinction with such a small amount of fluid between a tiny bit of higher solution versus a little more—two teeny bits—of a lower solution?

Dr. Lipsitt: Yes, I have.

Dr. Watson: Could you distinguish the different volume levels?

Dr. Lipsitt: It's very difficult to distinguish the volume level. It's very difficult for me, and every adult, to distinguish between the sucrose concentrations that we use on the babies—and get differences to. Between 5 and 10% sucrose is very difficult for me, and every other adult in my lab, to discriminate. Yet the baby shows regular effects of this. But it should be no surprise that the adult tongue is not the best calibration device or standardization procedure.

Dr. Watson: I'm wondering whether it's really the same effect—that, with such small amounts, the fact of having a higher volume or having a higher intensity would be essentially the same variable for the infant, in which case you wouldn't really have two convergent pieces of information supporting hedonism. Not that one isn't enough in this world, but two pieces would be nicer.

Dr. Lipsitt: You're saying that the two variables I've talked about, amount and sucrose concentration, might in fact be collapsible. Increased amount stimulates more receptors and increases the sweetness in the system. That is certainly a possibility. However, operationally the two produce the same behavioral effects and that's what is important.

Dr. Eisenberg: Could we go back for a moment to your findings for the effects of male versus female voices? What did you use as your baseline for the prestimulus heart rate pattern? And how long a period did you consider?

Dr. Lipsitt: Six beats before. The baby's heart rate preceding the onset of the tone is measured for the six beats before, and that becomes baseline against which any heart rate change upward or downward gets measured. There is deceleration to the female voice. The data in this study also show a parity effect. The children who are of high-parity mothers show significantly more deceleration than the children of low-parity mothers.

Dr. Parmelee: That wasn't the child's own mother?

Dr. Lipsitt: No. We recorded a mother while she was talking to her infant.

Dr. Thoman: And who was the "he"?

Dr. Lipsitt: The "he" was simply a male visitor to our laboratory with a good recording voice.

Dr. Thoman: But surely a mother-person would talk very differently from a male-person who was not a parent? As I noted before, when you're dealing with phrase or sentence material, things get very complicated. If you record a mother who's talking to her own baby—and that is quite a different way, I would think, from the manner in which a passing stranger talks to the same baby.

Dr. Lipsitt: But this was a mother with a 2-day-old infant.

Dr. Eisenberg: I'm not denying this, but the man wasn't in the same situation, and I would suggest that it may not be the mother's voice per se but rather the pattern of intonation or any number of other variables that could have been operating aside from the fact that one happened to be a mother's voice and the other one happened to be a stranger's voice. The thing that's bothering me, on the basis of all the headaches we had with analyzing heart rate data, is that when we tried to analyze our heart rate data using difference measures we got very variable results, and we didn't get good across-the-group trends. It is precisely because we were unsuccessful with parametric techniques that we ultimately arrrived at using nonparametric techniques, such as Kolmogorov-Smirnov (K—S) testing: It is a means by which we can look at heart rate distributions over equal periods of time prior to and subsequent to stimulus onset and derive what, in my opinion, is pretty unequivocal evidence of stimulus-related accelerative or decelerative change. I suppose it is largely a function of my own unhappy experiences with the analysis of heart rate data, but it seems to me possible that your findings could reflect merely chance effects.

Dr. Lipsitt: I think the import of these data is in showing deceleration to *some* kinds of stimuli in normal newborns. For a long time, you may remember, it was believed that you couldn't get cardiac deceleration from the newborn. The view was that this was something that the system develops with time, with experience. Now, increasingly, there are data indicating that under some very special conditions, you can get cardiac deceleration, or what Sokolov calls orienting behavior. This has been obtained in my laboratory under the conditions that I just reported to you.

Dr. Eisenberg: You misunderstand me: I am not arguing against the fact that decelerative responses can be obtained in newborn life, and indeed, I have cited our own data showing they can be obtained. What I am arguing against is the premise that cardiac deceleration is, in all cases, a measure of maturational change or that the direction of stimulus-related heart change differentiates between "orienting" and "defensive" reactions. Despite the intellectual appeal of the Graham and Clifton (1966) hypothesis that so many people have been trying to prove experimentally with such equivocal results, I have never been able to buy it more than half-heartedly. I tend to favor a more biologically based hypothesis relating to whether or not stimuli have some sort of built-in significance reflecting the constitution of an organism. Assuming this to be the case, one might suppose, as your data as well as ours suggest, that biologically significant signals will elicit decelerative responses even in the newborn period, whereas insignificant ones will elicit them only after the organism has matured sufficiently for them to have acquired associational values that make them significant. I think that as systematic studies of infant responses to various signals that logically ought to be significant are pursued further, this notion may obtain considerable support. Insofar as work at our laboratory constitutes a valid index, sounds that we have considered to be biologically significant—that is, patterned signals— regularly have elicited decelerative responses in newborns. Furthermore, these changes in heart rate have been found under any and all conditions of state, and for the most part, in association with orienting and attentive behavior as well as EEG desynchronization. In our experience, in fact, about the only time you can't elicit decelerative responses to synthetic speech sounds is when the infants are screaming so loudly the signals effectively are masked out.

Incidentally, although I mentioned earlier that our video data show instances of what can be characterized as "rage" behaviors, I don't believe I mentioned how rapid and striking were the state changes associated with those behaviors. In some cases, for instance, where an infant was dozing and heading downwards into irregular sleep, he would open his eyes and look angry at an initial stimulus-onset and, by the time of the next state-rating period (in the 2 seconds immediately prior to the next trial), would have run the whole gamut of our arousal scale to be scored as actively upset. In other words, whether we choose to call the response *rage* or something else, the infant changes his state from something approaching sleep to loud screaming within a time span of something like 30 seconds. I must say, having looked carefully at our video records, I have often had the feeling that if our babies were not swaddled and could free their hands, they would reach out to hit at whatever or whoever was nearest.

Dr. Lipsitt: I would just add that Stechler and Latz (1966) had a study of the rage reaction of newborns to being engaged in an obligatory relation to visual stimuli.

Dr. Eisenberg: As I remember, the term used was *obligatory attention*, and I have always considered the phrase singularly descriptive: I wish I could have thought of it myself.

REFERENCE NOTES

1. Ashmead, D., & Lipsitt, L. P. *The newborn's heart rate response to voices.* In preparation.

REFERENCES

Burke, P. Swallowing and the organization of sucking in the human newborn. *Child Development,* 1977, *48,* 523–531.

Crook, C. K. Neonatal sucking: Effects of quantity of the response-contingent fluid upon sucking rhythm and heart rate. *Journal of Experimental Child Psychology,* 1976, *21,* 539–548.

Crook, C. K. Taste perception in the newborn infant. *Infant Behavior and Development,* 1978, *1,* 52–69.

Crook, C. K., & Lipsitt, L. P. Neonatal nutritive sucking: Effects of taste stimulation upon sucking rhythm and heart rate. *Child Development,* 1976, *47,* 518–522.

Eisenberg, R. B. *Auditory competence in early life: The roots of communicative behavior.* Baltimore: University Park Press, 1976.

Engen, T., & Lipsitt, L. P. Decrement and recovery of responses to olfactory stimuli in the human neonate. *Journal of Comparative and Physiological Psychology,* 1965, *59,* 312–316.

Engen, T., Lipsitt, L. P., & Robinson, D. O. The human newborn's sucking behavior for sweet fluids as a function of birthweight and maternal weight. *Infant Behavior and Development,* 1978, *1,* 118–121.

Graham, F. K. & Clifton, R. K. Heart-rate change as a component or the orienting response. *Psychological Bulletin,* 1966, *5,* 305–320.

Gunther, M. Instinct and the nursing couple. *Lancet,* 1955, *1,* 575.

Gunther, M. Infant behavior at the breast. In B. M. Foss (Ed.), *Determinants of infant behavior* (Vol. 1). London: Methuen (New York: Wiley), 1961.

Hoebel, C. J., Hyvarinen, M. A., Okada, D. M., & Oh, W. Prenatal and intrapartum high-risk screening. *American Journal of Obstetrics and Gynecology,* 1973, *117,* 1–9.

Kittner, S., & Lipsitt, L. P. Obstetric history and the heart-rate response of newborns to sound. *Developmental Medicine and Child Neurology,* 1976, *18,* 460–470.

Kobre, K. R., & Lipsitt, L. P. A negative contrast effect in newborns. *Journal of Experimental Child Psychology,* 1972, *14,* 81–91.

Lewin, K. Behavior and development as a function of the total situation. In L. Carmichael (Ed.), *Manual of child psychology.* New York: Wiley, 1954.

Lipsitt, L. P. Developmental psychobiology comes of age. In L. P. Lipsitt (Ed.), *Developmental psychobiology: The significance of infancy.* Hillsdale, New Jersey: Lawrence Erlbaum Associates, 1976.

Lipsitt, L. P., Reilly, B. M., Butcher, M. J., & Greenwood, M. M. The stability and interrelationships of newborn sucking and heart rate. *Developmental Psychobiology,* 1976, *9,* 305–310.

Miller, N. E., & Dollard, J. *Social learning and imitation.* New Haven: Yale University Press, 1941.

Nisbett, R., & Gurwitz, S. Weight, sex and the eating behavior of human newborns. *Journal of comparative and physiological psychology,* 1970, *73,* 245–253.

Pfaffmann, C. The pleasures of sensation. *Psychological Review,* 1960, *67,* 253–268.

Prechtl, H. F. R. Neurological findings in newborn infants after pre- and para-natal complications. In J. H. P. Jonix, H. K. A. Visser, & J. A. Troelstra (Eds.), *Aspects of prematurity and dysmaturity.* Leiden: Stenfert Kroese, 1969.

Schneirla, T. C. The concept of development in comparative psychology. In D. Harris (Ed.), *The concept of development*. Minneapolis: University of Minnesota Press, 1957.

Simner, M. L. Newborn's response to the cry of another infant. *Developmental Psychology*, 1971, *5*, 136–150.

Skinner, B. F. *Beyond freedom and dignity*. New York: Alfred Knopf, 1971.

Stechler, G., & Latz, E. Some observations on attention and arousal in the human infant. *Journal of the American Academy of Child Psychiatry*, 1966, *5*, 517–525.

Winter, S. T., Samueloff, M., Cohen, N. J., Porges, A., & Gross, E. Neonatal cardiac deceleration on suckle feeding, *American Journal of Diseases in Childhood*, 1966, *112*, 11–20.

Young, P. T. *Motivation of behavior*. New York: Wiley, 1936.

6

General Discussion

Arthur H. Parmelee
U.C.L.A.

GENERAL DISCUSSION

Dr. Parmelee: I would like to hear a dialogue between John Watson and Lou Lipsitt about the motivating forces in the contingent responses of infants. I could not determine the place for anticipatory cues in the contingent response diagrams of Dr. Watson. Mother and baby both anticipate responses from cues in context of the environment, their body posture, facial expressions and so on. I think we should discuss the definitions of a contingent response and a transaction. We also need to discuss further the place of pleasure in motivation.

Something that used to be discussed a lot, and hasn't been discussed here so far, are body responses associated with pleasure or fear, such as blood-pressure and heart-rate changes, the autonomic responses. These may contribute to learning. Maybe that's part of the affective component that Stern mentioned.

As a clinician I don't see how the contingent response system can encompass the intrusive mother who's always doing something to her infant. There are certain babies that we see who are rather apathetic and seem to need an intrusive mother to keep the thing going. Perhaps Dr. Watson can help me understand how this situation fits into his model.

Dr. Lipsitt, I know what you're talking about when you refer to risk infants, and I know Prechtl's system. We use one derived from this. I don't like the word risk, because I don't know what the nature of the risk is. Risk-scoring systems were designed to determine risk for mortality or morbidity in the neonatal period, bear a very limited relationship to later behavior. Social and environmental factors are so powerful, as identified by such gross indices as socio-economic status that biological risk items, even with associated deviant neonatal behavior, aren't very predictive of later behavior. This does not mean they don't have an effect, and we do need to know all the behavior processes that you're now investigating. We also need to know what the compensating mechanisms are. There are many self-righting mechanisms. In our own study, Dr. Beckwith and Dr. Cohen have found that the babies who are sickest in the neonatal period often get the best mothering scores at one month. What cues the mothers were reading that induced them to provide compensatory mothering we don't know. The difference in later performance seems to be dependent to some degree on whether or not these mothers and babies can sustain these positive interactions or transactions. There are many behavioral contradictions to biological risk. For example, in any obstetric risk-scoring systems being a firstborn increases the risk. In the first 2 years, however, being a first and only child seems to be beneficial as far as behavioral assessments are concerned. There are more opportunities for adult interaction with the firstborn infant. There are probably many more such contradictions between perinatal biological risk for immediate mortality and morbidity and later behavioral and environmental compensatory processes.

Now I would like to discuss Dr. Korner's paper. I have tremendous admiration for the work she is doing and for the related studies of Dr. Bernard. I think, if I were to do anything in the preterm period, I would probably use their approach. I would, however, like to suggest for purposes of discussion that the stimulation Dr. Korner is providing preterm infants in their nursery may not have a long-term effect. What we know about full-term infants' responsiveness doesn't necessarily carry over to preterm infants. Remember again that the word "preterm" includes babies born 12 weeks early as well as babies born only 4 weeks early and they are by no means the same in their behavioral responsiveness. I submit that the evidence is that the neurological systems of preterm infants of less than 35 weeks gestation is so immature that it is not significantly altered by environmental stimulation. This is a useful "fail safe" adaptation; otherwise few preterm infants could have done as well as they have; most actually develop quite normally. In our studies and those of Dreyfus-Brisac and Roffwarg and even in Dr. Barnard's studies, preterm infants all come to the same level of organization of state by their expected date of birth. This is achieved in a nursery environment that seems to run counter to sleep organization. Preterm infants' sleep organization at term is not easily distinguished from that of term infants.

There is animal evidence for this postulated "fail safe" period. This comes from the basic work of Hubel & Wiesel (1970). In the kitten in the first 3 weeks there is an insensitive period when visual deprivation or stimulation does not alter occipital cortex cell firing as it will after 3 weeks. Guenther Rose (Rose and Collins, 1975) has extended this further by demonstrating that kittens could not learn a visual discrimination task until after 3 weeks of age. Huttenlocker (1967) has also demonstrated that the spontaneous firing of single neurons in the kitten occipital cortex occurs infrequently until after 3 weeks. Adrian & Roffwarg (1974) also found the same in the lateral geniculate ganglion and found an association of rate of neuronal firing only when the kittens were 2-3 weeks of age. I believe that the organization of sleep states in both man and animals may be an index of when environmental stimulation can have an impact on the nervous system and behavior. Verley's work suggests that the kitten is a nice animal model for the study of the neurological organization of preterm infants, in the sense that the kitten at birth is similar to the 25-week-gestation preterm infant in neurological organization and then matures at a rate of about 1 to 5 so that at 3 weeks the kitten is like a full-term infant, and at 6 weeks like a 3-month infant. I'm not saying that sleep state organization is the cause of the environmental impact on the nervous system, I'm proposing that state organizations is a marker that tells you something about the elaboration of cybernetic systems that seem to be necessary before one can get learning or even alteration of structure or neuronal activity as a result of environmental stimulation, (Parmelee & Sigman, 1976).

It is of course possible that some types of stimulation may have some effect on the nervous system early in gestation. Whether or not vestibular stimulation is of this nature I don't know. First of all the term *vestibular stimulation* as commonly used is confusing. We often test vestibular function by stimulating the semicurcular canals by acceleratory motion, such as rotation. The vestibular system also includes the utricle and saccule that are involved in static posture. Thus in every position of the head there is vestibular neuronal activity, not just during acceleratory movement of the head. I would submit that most of the time the vestibular system is involved in static postural control and not in responding to accelerated movement of the semicircular canals. So that to put a baby into a system of constant movement in order to get semicircular canal stimulation may or may not be appropriate. Unless, the primary goal is prevention of apneic episodes. The respiratory nuclei; the respiratory cells are rather scattered through the reticular activating system. A certain amount of input to this system is necessary to sustain respiration and in the mature nervous system this can be generated internally. In the very immature preterm infant some external input is often necessary. Humphrey regarded the fifth nerve nucleus as the brain of the fetus. We have already been talking about the sensory stimulation of the face about the mouth, via the fifth nerve, as an organizing input for the fetus and newborn. Facial stimulation of the fifth nerve is also a good way to interrupt apnea. Of concern is the problem that apnea has different causes at different conceptional ages. At very early conceptional ages respiration is semiregular and does not adapt easily to need, and excessive sensory inputs into the reticular activating system can induce apnea. At later conceptional ages periodic breathing is common, though it is uncommon in full-term infants. The old preterm infants have a new level of respiratory organization. This is when their sleep states are also beginning to become well organized. In these babies, apnea may occur more commonly during transitions from one state to another. These can be readily interrupted by a variety of external stimulation of the infant. It well may be that water beds as used by Dr. Korner provide the gentlest and most effective stimulation for all conceptional age groups.

With respect to Dr. Lipsitt's discussion of sudden infant death, I would say there are as many hypotheses as there are people. The immunologists point out that the protective gamma globulins from the mother drop off during the first 3 months as the baby's own immunological protection is slowly developing, leaving the baby somewhat more vulnerable around 2 months. If you talk to the biochemists, they indicate ontogenetic changes in the liver metabolism of glucose that might make the baby more vulnerable in this same time period. I think Dr. Lipsitt's is as good an hypothesis as many of the others.

Dr. Denenberg: I would like to take strong exception to the statement that one cannot affect the behavior of animals prior to a certain date. There are many studies showing that animals can be affected at all ages in development starting at conception or even before conception. Let me summarize 15 years of research in 5 minutes. I'll restrict my comments to research with rats since that's the major animal we work with, and Dr. Parmelee referred to rats in some of his comments. Without going into references or details, I'll make the following statements. One can handle or shock rat pups during the first 5 days of life. When measured in adulthood, there will be differences in open-field performance, in avoidance learning behavior, and in the adrenal response with respect to corticosterone. There are around 50 papers in the literature on those findings. Furthermore, if one shocks rat pups in the first 2 days of life and then, at 21 days , looks at the mother of these animals (with appropriate controls), the mothers are different. The shocking of rat pups will make their mothers less emotional, that is more active in the open field. Therefore, there is a dyadic feedback relationship between the mother and the pup. It is necessary to use a systems concept to describe this relationship.

We have also taken female pups, handled them in infancy, bred them, and then studied their offspring and grandoffspring. We have found effects as a function of what happened to that pup's mother and grandmother when they were infants. Other people have shown that stress effects prior to pregnancy will influence the subsequent behavior of the offspring. Also a number of researchers have shown that stimulation during pregnancy will affect the open-field performance of offspring.In these studies, pups were crossfostered at birth, therefore separating the prenatal from the postnatal effect. Now John Dobbing has argued that the rat at birth is sufficiently premature relative to the human that it should be viewed as being similar to a 2–4 week premature human being. Wilhelmina Himwich has presented summary data on CNS development showing that the rat at birth is immature relative to humans with respect to total amount of CNS development. Dobbing's argument is that the rat at 5 days of age is approximately equal to a full-term human. On that basis then the effects I'm talking about would be equivalent to prenatal stimulation with the human over the last 2 weeks of life or so. And finally the fact that researchers fail to get measurable differences in CNS morphology is not particularly exciting because it is a null hypothesis statement. This failure to find something doesn't necessarily mean it's not there. It may mean that we haven't been able to measure it.

Dr. Parmelee: I see these studies as not directly relevant to what I was discussing because by and large they deal with stressful stimuli. If there's anything that all preterm infants may have in common it is that they are intensely stressed. They are pouring out cortical steroids to stay alive. That isn't the issue here.

Dr. Parmelee: The issue is whether the particular form of environmental stimulation is intended to change behavior through structural change in synapses or dendrites, rate of electrical activity of neurons possibly through biochemical change, or by learning. Nobody has indicated he or she was increasing stress in the preterm infants' environment in order to change behavior.Preterm infants are probably intensely stressed by the type of general care they receive. I don't think we are talking about stress as one of the environmental stimuli we wish to add. I think the waterbed is a tremendous innovation in the care of preterm infants, and I am in favor of reducing the incidence of apneic episodes by this means.

Dr. Denenberg: Early experiences are multidimensional, and one dimension that has been hypothesized is stress. Other hypothesized dimensions include stimulus change, learning, and mother–infant interaction. Thus, to dismiss the effects of early experience because of the single concept of stress is not reasonable.

Dr. Parmelee: I agree, but I don't think either one of us has proved the point.

Dr. Thoman: Ten years ago, I demonstrated that behavior of infant rats could be modified during the first days of life (Thoman, Wetzel, & Levine, 1968).Other studies since then have shown learning in the infant rat at an early age. So, if you can use the rat as a model--indicated by relative brain weight, a rat pup the first 5 days is at the same level of development as the premature human--then I think it is reasonable to expect that we might modify the behavior of the premature human infant.

Dr. Parmelee: I'd have to know whether it was a stress item.

Dr. Thoman: No, the stimuli were composed of the feeding conditions for the pups. Groups of infant rats were fed from the time of birth either artificially by oesophageal intubation, or they were nursed by the mother. By 3 days of age, the artificially fed group of pups showed approach responses and suckled the polyethylene tubing when it was presented to them. The mother-nursed animals showed rejecting responses to the polyethylene tubing; and they were much more likely to approach and suckle on an anesthetized, lactating female. This is clearly not a stress kind of paradigm, and that is why I think it is relevant to the issue of the possibility of modifying behavior in the premature human infant.

Dr. Kennell: I would like to mention our observations of mothers of two groups of low-birth-weight infants. The first group are very tiny premature babies. It is extremely difficult for a mother to find a way to interact with or get a response from her small, immature, premature infant. That's one group. Another challenging group are those premature infants who are on respirators for long periods, or very sick for an extended period, who are unresponsive and extremely difficult to relate to when the tubes or respirator are removed. The effects of proprioceptive–vestibular stimulation that Dr. Korner has reported suggest that babies become more responsive and appealing-for example, the infants have their eyes open more. Isn't it likely that this would make it easier for a mother to start an interaction with her infant and gain positive feedback that might pay off with increasing interaction and more attachment as the baby becomes progressively better organized, and more alert and responsive. I think that this might be an extremely important consequence of this stimulation—the effect of a more responsive, alert infant on the mother and then progressively greater interaction of the mother—infant dyad.

Dr. Parmelee: Indeed, if that is what happens. It's not clear that they have more awake states. The reason that it's difficult to make strong statements about state is that preterm babies are usually sent home at about 36 weeks conceptional age, a month before term. This is just when states are becoming well organized. Then they are at home and the mother is indeed interacting with them. Thus at term it is too late to assess the specific effects of stimulation in the nursery. So far we do not have the technique for assessing behavior at 36 weeks conceptional age. Dr. Korner is gathering this information to help develop such techniques.

Dr. Kennell: Do you think it is harmful practice sending premature babies home at 35–36 weeks? How do you balance the advantages of continuous contact at home versus the disadvantages of caring for a baby that is very difficult to figure out, worrisome in its fragility, sleepiness, slowness of feeding, and irregularity of respiration.

Dr. Parmelee: The critical issue for me is that the behavior of the baby has to be judged on the basis of time from conception. With full-term babies the first 3 months of life is a struggle for survival for the parents, particularly the mother. The frequent feedings, disrupted sleep and 24-hour care are a difficult burden. With the full-term infant after about 6–8 weeks, life improves, crying lessens, sleep periods are longer, and the baby gives a rewarding smile, so that by 3 months life is tolerable. The mother of the preterm infant sent home 4 weeks before term has an extra month of this difficult struggle in addition to her concern about the baby's survival. The key issue is the organization of support services for the parents of preterm infants. If you do provide that service then there is much to be gained by having the mother and the baby together this extra month. If you don't provide support service the mother can fall apart under this stress, and you lose what you tried to gain.

Dr. Thoman: There are studies that demonstrate learning in the premature infant.

Dr. Parmelee: I know of none.

Dr. Thoman: The only study I know of was reported by Einar Siqueland, (1969).

Dr. Parmelee: I think these infants were about 35 weeks conceptional age when stimulated; at least they were older preterm infants. They were not preterm in the sense that Dr. Korner defines preterm.

Dr. Thoman: I assume *preterm* means pre–40 weeks gestational age, or at the extreme, prior to 37 or 38 weeks gestational age.

Dr. Parmelee: I'm saying that sleep organization comes in between 35 weeks and term conceptional age, so you're already in the period where you can do something.

Dr. Thoman: So you are talking about preterm prior to 35 weeks?

Dr. Parmelee: Right.

Dr. Thoman: But then you are making a distinction among preterm infants?

Dr. Parmelee: Preterm infant stimulation in nurseries that we're talking about is prior to that time.

Dr. Thoman: Prior to 35 weeks.

Dr. Denenberg: You're saying that prior to sleep organization—as defined by some sort of criterion. There's no evidence of learning?

Dr. Parmelee: That's right. And sleep organization is not the cause. It's an index of a certain level of development of cybernetic feedback systems.

Dr. Thoman: So your beginning point then is 35 weeks, not 40 weeks.

Dr. Parmelee: I wouldn't want to make it so specific.

Dr. Thoman: But in general—you're talking about what we consider—

Dr. Parmelee: State organization comes in more strongly at that time.

Dr. Denenberg: There's good data from Rosenblatt's lab that the kitten at 2 days of age has learned the particular location of a nipple—it will seek that nipple out and go to it and not go to other nipples. That's within the second or third day, which is, I believe, prior to evidence of sleep organization in the kitten.

Dr. Parmelee: That's true.

Dr. Rheingold: If you examine nipple preference carefully in the kitten at 2 and 3 days of age, you find that it is not yet well organized. A good deal of shifting goes on for the next week or so.

Dr. Denenberg: True, but there are data on feeding. I can't recall how early Walt Stanley found evidence of sucking preference.

Dr. Eisenberg: It was during the first few days of life, I believe.

Dr. Denenberg: So I think that's also prior to the evidence of strong sleep organization.

Dr. Parmelee: I don't want to push this too hard although I still believe the general thesis. I think that one has to be careful in interpreting feeding studies as evidence for early durable learning from limited early experience since this learning is constantly reinstated with each feeding. This kind of learning probably does take place at home. What is done in the nursery may not be reinstated in this fashion and the learning may not last; there is little evidence of long-term memory even in the full-term infant.

Dr. Lipsitt: I think it's a bit unfair to disparage those data, whether they are from normal newborns or 35-week-old premature infants. What we are trying to do here is to get a sense of what the newborn child, including the premature newborn, is capable of, and especially in the arms of his caretakers. And any evidence that has to do with the learning precocity of the kind that has been cited here in both humans and animals is information that will help us to understand what the baby is capable of and of what the mother is capable of responding to.

Dr. Parmelee: I am in complete agreement. I am just trying to point out that one needs to think about the fact that there may be some limits to how far back that can go. That's all I'm saying.

Dr. Lipsitt: In that connection I think that it's unfair also to redefine the definition—to change the definition of prematurity.

Dr. Parmelee: I'm not changing the definition. I specifically said sleep state organization is my index, and it comes in strongly between the 35th week of conceptional age and term. I don't think it's a single-step process. I think it's a continuum.

Dr. Lipsitt: But the point is that prematures as traditionally defined—

Dr. Parmelee: An infant of 37-week gestation or less is usually defined as preterm. I have not studied Siqueland's data in detail, and that's the only data that I know of, and you know it well so I will take your word for it.

Dr. Papousek: In regard to learning in prematures, you may be interested in two of our own studies. In one carried out back in Prague, learning in 10-week-premature infants was compared with learning in full-term infants of the same post-conceptional age. No difference was found in palpebral conditioning. Head-turn conditioning was slower in prematures. Since the premature infants were already comparable with the full-term ones at the time of conditioning, our data do not confirm any prenatal capacity for learning, of course. Rather, they contradict the argument of some Soviet authors that an additional extrauterine environmental impact leads to faster conditioning in the premature infant.

The other recent study concerns habituation in sleeping premature infants at the gestational age of 32 to 40 weeks. If you are ready to accept habituation as a very simple form of learning, then this study would give you an evidence of prenatal learning. As far as I can say now, habituation appears only in non–REM sleep, not in REM sleep, and depends on the organization of sleep states, as we can observe habituation around 36 weeks at first when the non–REM sleep becomes organized as well.

Dr. Parmelee: Of course I'm trapped in my own system if the techniques that Doctors Korner and Barnard are using speed up the organization of sleep states. Since I'm so organically oriented I don't think it will.

Dr. Papousek: It is very difficult to say which of the newborn's capacities are learned. Let us say we know that the newborn is capable of detecting contingency. It is innate or learned? If learned, then he had to learn prenatally. This cannot be excluded. He did a lot of movements prenatally that led to contingent consequences, for example, in tactile modality, to different touches and 'double touches' if he once hit the uterine wall and another time his own body. His movement also elicited remarkable acoustic consequence in the maternal bowel noise, as you can hear yourselves with a stethoscope.

Dr. Parmelee: One of the interesting recent developments in neurobiology is stated by Victor Hamburger. He provides evidence in the chick embryo that sensory input is not necessary for the development of motor organization. At what point in development sensory input effectively contributes to neurological organization in the chick is not known.

Dr. Sander: I'd just like to say that if we did have a picture of the 24-hour organization of states—that these inputs might very well change the picture of organization between or before the 35-week level. One of the things that doesn't usually come to mind is the 24-hour pattern, for example, during the day the fetus is standing on its head and during the night it's horizontal. If you're thinking of postural proprioceptive inputs—there may be an important 8-, 12-, or 14-hour period. I'm just adding to what you say, that there are different ways we might be able to influence the organization of states in a 24-hour pattern. I think one of the things I may be able to show later is that there is organization of REM or non-REM cycling, but there's a great deal of difference between babies at birth in how they do this, how well organized, how well differentiated, and so on.

Dr. Parmelee: Not only between babies, but within a baby at different times.

Dr. Sander: Yes.

Dr. Parmelee: The large standard deviation in this type of data is a reason why it's going to be very hard to use such data to determine the effect of intervention.

Dr. Sander: Unless you are looking at variation as the variable.

Dr. Lipsitt: May I come back to a point that was raised by your discussion yesterday and that I still wanted to comment on. It concerns your reservations, Hawley, about the use of perinatal hazard scales, perinatal stress scales such as those of Prechtl and Hobel et al. and, I think, some others as well. You pointed out in alluding to your reservations that yes it seems as though there are very early behavioral differences between so-called high-risk child and the low-risk child, but that you weren't sure what all of this means because later on it turns out, for example, that firstborns who seem to be in jeopardy, or are in greater jeopardy than laterborns early in life, show some later superiorities, or show some benefits of having been the first born. I don't see why that sort of thing should bother us in trying to assess the effects of risk at birth. It's quite conceivable to me that risk may have alternative effects upon different children. It may have deleterious effects on some children, and it may have some salubrious effects on other children. That sort of lawfulness isn't unknown in science. It's simply for us to figure out in which children we're going to have the effects in one direction and in which ones we're going to have the effects in the other. Moreover, in the very same children one may have deficit early and benefits later. It's easy enough to construct a model in which the high-risk child is in fact attended to differently by its mother and other caretakers in such a way that their risk actually becomes a benefit. It's quite possible that some infants who are at risk are given a different kind of care that can possibly be beneficial.

Dr. Parmelee: We're in complete agreement. The only disagreement is the fault of doctors who want to see one-to-one relationships between neonatal events and 7-year outcomes. That's not a reasonable expectation. It is because "risk infant" has gotten that connotation that I would like some other word. Babies are different in the neonatal period, and they're cared for differently. We have to look at all the interactions between infants and caretakers in a series of short-term studies. I'm sure there are effects of neonatal hazardous events on the behavior of neonates and subsequently on the type of care they receive. I don't think we will find a one-to-one relation between neonatal hazards and later behavioral outcomes.

Dr. Lipsitt: I think that our research has to be directed toward teasing apart what the elements of the relationship are.

Dr. Parmelee: I have no quarrel with your using the Prechtl scale or using it the way you do. I only quarrel with the word "risk," which has in the medical literature an implication beyond our current information.

Dr. Lipsitt: Well these conditions are perinatal hazards that are incorporated in "risk scales."

Dr. Parmelee: Which alter their neonatal behavior, which alter mothering, but these can balance each other.

Dr. Kennell: I would like to interject a question about the effect of labeling. If you took 100 normal mothers and babies and labeled half of them as high risk, I would expect a difference in care, concern, attention.

Dr. Parmelee: That's true too, and the problem for us has been that babies in our study who have had no such events also get into all kinds of trouble in the first year of life. This makes it difficult to predict at high levels from a given event to later behavior. You have to take the total family context into consideration. We're just beginning to look at such factors.

Dr. Eisenberg: I would like, if I may, to raise what might be a peripheral issue. In Anneliese's discussion yesterday, and in our current discussions as well, we've been concerned mainly with direct measures, such as the extent and frequency of apnea episodes; and I wonder whether this is the best way to look at questions of organization. As I think about premature infants in relation to work at my lab, for instance, it seems to me that our most intractable problem in studying their overt responses to sound has been differentiating those responses: prematures, as we all know, seem to be almost constantly in motion, and because this is so, it is enormously difficult to establish solid criteria for scoring stimulus-bound behavior. It occurs to me, therefore, that the waterbed, in fact, might have certain kinds of organizing effects that extend beyond sleep patterns: Perhaps they serve more generally to reduce irritability levels in prematures, which would be important in itself and also a methodologic boon to those of us trying to assess the sensory capacities of preterm babies. By the same token, it seems possible that these kinds of organizing effects might be explored systematically by using sensory stimuli as probes: For instance, one could measure differences in stimulus-bound behavior between a group of prematures on waterbeds and a control group on conventional beds. The nature of such differences seems to me a relatively unimportant issue right now, but their demonstration might be very important in terms of our thinking about organizational mechanisms in early life and, more specifically, in terms of what Anneliese may be getting at with the waterbed technique.

Dr. Parmelee: I'm sure Dr. Korner has thought about this a great deal, and she'll be the first to tell you it will be difficult to control all these variables.

Dr. Eisenberg: Have you tried it?

Dr. Korner: No, we have not tried any auditory experiments with prematures on the waterbed. That seems like a very good idea. Hawley, you mentioned in your discussion that the premature baby has fail-safe mechanisms.

Dr. Parmelee: I would like to believe that.

Dr. Korner: That is a hypothesis, of course. Certainly your review of the premature baby's being unable to profit much from visual stimulation bears out your hypothesis, at least as far as the visual modality is concerned. My whole point is that while the visual system seems to mature relatively late, the vestibular system develops very early. That's why I think the baby may profit from experience in that modality. There is a lot of evidence in the literature that the vestibular system matures early, evidence that I reviewed in the first part of my chapter.

Dr. Parmelee: I don't think that evidence exists. First of all, if you look at the work of Minkowski and Hooker whom you cite, you will see that they did not test visual or auditory sensation. All they tested was touch. All they saw was that with movement there was a startle. That's not proof of early vestibular function. The structure of the organ itself is also not proof of the degree of its functioning. Sporadic neuronal activity may carry little or no information or have little influence on other structures. We need to have recordings from the vestibular nuclei in animals at various gestational ages. We also need electron-microscopic studies of the vestibular system, including the utricle and succule, to know the level of organization of the receptor organs. These are not nearly as advanced as the gross anatomy.

Dr. Eisenberg: Why do you have to assume it's the otoliths? Why can't you just as well assume vestibular mechanisms controlled by the cerebellum?

Dr. Parmelee: The cerebellum is in fact one of the latest of the brain structures to mature in the human organism.

Dr. Eisenberg: But not in terms of myelinization. If you look at the data on myelinization, you see that the vestibular system is one of the first to develop.

Dr. Parmelee: Myelin was an important marker in the past because it was easily stained, but myelin by no means tells you that there is or is not function or the degree of the function.

Dr. Eisenberg: Well, you do know that in certain nervous mechanisms you simply don't have response before the nerve is myelinized.

Dr. Parmelee: Yes you can have neural response before the nerve is myelinized. Myelin simply serves to increase conduction velocity.

Dr. Korner: In the case of the vestibular system, there is evidence that myelinization and function begin simultaneously. They both start at about the fourth-month gestational age. In our past discussions about this, you expressed the feeling that the fetal responses obtained at that age were primarily postural responses. But does not each postural response also have a vestibular component?

Dr. Parmelee: Function in the sense of occasional neuronal firing is not necessarily functioning that gives you a great deal of information.

Dr. Korner: The fetal responses that I am thinking about are the startles that have been noted in the young embryo.

Dr. Parmelee: A startle has been observed in a baby without a vestibular apparatus secondary to intrauterine thalidomide damage. A startle or Moro reflex is best obtained from neck proprioceptive stimulation by suddenly shifting the position of the head in relation to the trunk.

Dr. Korner: In terms of my hypothesis—and this is a hypothesis, just as it is your hypothesis that premies have fail-safe mechanisms—providing stimulation mediated by a relatively mature system may have an effect, whereas visual stimulation mediated through an apparatus that matures relatively late might not.

Dr. Parmelee: Where is the effect? What kind of effect? I can't envision the synapses changing, and I don't envision learning. How does it have an effect on motor development of the baby?

Dr. Korner: I am not talking about learning. I am wondering, for example, whether we won't improve the baby's motor development.

Dr. Parmelee: What kind of an effect? Where would the effect be?

Dr. Korner: We have some very preliminary indications that the waterbed, with the slight containment it provides, may help in the development of motor inhibition of the random, jerky, overshooting kinds of motions of the limbs that are so characteristic of premature babies. We will study longitudinally what happens to the motor patterns of these babies. Now I am perfectly open to think that perhaps we will have no effect on the infant's motor patterns, or for that matter on several other developing behaviors, but at least our studies are set up in such a way that whether we have an effect or not, we will learn a lot about the ontogeny of these behaviors. However, I am also open to the notion that perhaps we will have an effect, even if no other way than to provide an environment that may be more conducive to comfort, to maintaining the infant's fragile skin, or for that matter an environment that reduces the incidence of unesthetic, asymmetrically shaped heads among these infants. I think the latter may have a real impact in facilitating the beginning mother–infant relationship. The mother will get a child who is less odd-looking when he comes home from the hospital. I think that we are making such enormous interventions by maintaining the life of many of these babies that I believe it is time that we also think about improving the quality of life for these infants.

Dr. Parmelee: If the outcome, though, as the collaborative project and Werner's studies show, is so greatly affected by social class, as compared with any neonatal factors, we're talking about relatively small influences. As I told Dr. Korner earlier, I generally turn out to be wrong, and I'm pleased that she is doing the study in just the way she has organized it.

Dr. Korner: I could not agree with you more regarding the impact of later environmental factors in obscuring what might have occurred early on. All one has to read is Sameroff's and Chandler's (1975) review on this subject for one to realize that environmental influences have an overriding influence on developmental outcome, no matter what occurred early. This is why it is almost irrelevant to expect follow-up studies a year or two later to show any persistent effects of an early intervention. And yet, in spite of all the evidence that is accumulating about the overriding impact of environmental conditions, there is an expectation among investigators, as well as nationally, that a persistent effect on intervention should be measurable or the intervention is not worth doing. Without the appropriate alterations of the environmental factors, I believe this is an unrealistic expectation. The experience with Headstart is a good case in point where improvements did occur, which, however, later washed out because there was no follow-through either by the schools or by changing the environmental conditions in which the children lived. The goal of my intervention at this time is to see whether we can help a baby become as intact as possible so that he is able to cope more adequately with whatever environment he enters than he would if he were less well put together. That, to my mind, is a desirable goal by itself, for that would mean that given adequate environmental conditions, the infant is in a position to consolidate and build on the gains he has made. From a public health point of view it would, of course, make sense to provide follow-through after the infant goes home through some kind of continued support system. However, such a course of action would not only make an already complicated intervention study more so, it would also make it extremely difficult to sort out whether the benefits, if any, are due to the hospital or the home intervention. So my goal for now is to see whether by altering the baby's incubator environment in the way we are proposing, we are able to create a baby that is more intact. I don't know whether we will be able to succeed, but I certainly think it is worth a try.

Dr. Parmelee: I can't quarrel with that goal.

Dr. Thoman: I really have to address myself to Dr. Korner's statement. We all recognize that environmental influences may intervene and thus make it difficult or even impossible to measure the effects of an intervention—such as the waterbed stimulation. Clearly, her data indicate that the stimulation improves the condition of the babies over the period of time during which it was given. I object to the arguments that have been put forth against even studying the early infancy period because we cannot identify long-term effects. I think one thing Dr. Korner is saying is that the quality of life during any period in infancy is important, and thus the short-term effects are also important. In due time, with more refined measures, and longitudinal studies, it should be possible to assess longer-term consequences.

Dr. Parmelee: I'm in complete agreement with you and with Dr. Lipsitt, but the problem is that we frequently imply that it's going to be beneficial at age 7.

Dr. Thoman: If we do we're wrong.

Dr. Parmelee: We're talking now about short-term changes, and they are terribly important to study. Let's keep it that way. That was the only reason I was quarreling with the word "risk." Risk for what? If you want to talk about risk for some difference in early infancy, that's clear enough for me.

Dr. Kennell: When we caregivers deviate from what has happened to mothers and their newborn infants under natural circumstances, we have to think carefully about the consequences. And if we consider full-term babies and mothers, it is really very recent in the sweep of human existence that we have had all those things that we now think of as normal and natural. For example, beds where infants sleep apart from their mothers, incubators where infants lie horizontally and quietly and are fed on a schedule. Observations of present-day hunter–gatherer tribes suggest what probably went on with humans up until 2 to 3 to 4,000 years ago. For example, in these tribes babies are carried on their mother's bodies, which keep them warm, and provide vestibular–proprioceptive stimulation and almost continuous opportunities for nutritive and nonnutritive sucking from the time of delivery until 3 to 4 years of age.

Dr. Parmelee: There's vestibular input when you're standing still, when you're lying down. It doesn't have to be motion. Let's get that straight.

Dr. Kennell: But there is motion, there are changes and shifts with unending variety. I would like to make an argument about this from the other side—in intensive care nurseries, we put a baby in a situation where there are elements of overstimulation and also deprivation. To put a baby in a regular incubator where he is just lying on a flat surface without any postural shifts—

Dr. Parmelee: But you see sometimes they're lying flat, then on their side, and maybe prone. These position changes provide vestibular inputs. How many position shifts occur daily in the care of the preterm should be carefully documented.

Dr. Kennell: Wouldn't it seem reasonable to try to duplicate the natural situation?

Dr. Parmelee: But how do you know it's not duplicated? We have to sit down and document preterm postural changes with observations; this is my point.

Dr. Mason: It seems to me that two things are implied. One is that babies in this society, at least for the past 50 or 100 years or so, have been raised under conditions that are quite different physically and socially from those that have presumably existed not only since the beginning of man as a species, but exist still in the nonhuman primates. And that that produces effects is pretty obvious. For example, under natural conditions, nonhuman primates don't show thumb sucking; and if you raise a nonhuman primate as you would a human baby, in 95% of the cases it becomes a chronic and habitual thumb sucker. The behavior is far more persistent and stereotyped than it is in man. The dentition is displaced, the conformation of the mouth is altered, and so on. That then brings up my other point, which is that the human organism seems to be in some ways buffered or more tolerant of variations in rearing conditions, so that one can get away with a great deal more before one produces obvious changes in the developing individual. Another example that is quite common in nonhuman primates—in fact, all of the old-world primates that I have information about, baboons, gibbons, chimpanzees—is the development of stereotyped body rocking in most individuals raised apart from the natural mother. We know that in human infants that seem to be perfectly normal in all other respects, rocking sometimes develops. I suspect we're dealing here with individual differences in tolerance for this particular form of maternal deprivation. In institutions where the children are not carried about much, the incidence of body rocking is very high. The noninstitutionalized child that rocks, but shows no other abnormalities, may simply require a different amount of input than other children who are perfectly able to tolerate being alone in the crib or are satisfied with a relatively small amount of handling, as compared to what a child would receive in a hunter–gatherer society. My point is that our caretaking practices in Western society depart from what is normal for mankind as a whole and for the nonhuman primates. Some of these departures increase the likelihood of certain developmental outcomes, such as thumb sucking or stereotyped body rocking, but it only makes the outcome more probable, whereas in the nonhuman primates, we can predict with some confidence what the outcome will be. This says that there is something about the organization of behavior in the developing human infant that makes it quite different from other primates.

Dr. Stern: I feel that there is an underlying issue. The pediatrician, through his experience, generally and rightfully occupies a conservative position from the point of view of interventions and fooling around with "natural" mechanism. This comes in great part from his experience with the fail-safe and self-righting tendencies of the infant and of growth and development that generally proceed such that one doesn't mess around with the process. However, a central point here is that the situation is really reversed, in that preemies that we're talking about are to a large extent the product of medical advances, that is, interventions. In a sense, we're talking about an iatrogenic human condition that is non-"natural". The burden of proof now lies on the pediatrician. I don't feel that pediatricians can afford, morally speaking, to maintain the conservative noninterventionist position given that this is the situation.

Dr. Parmelee: I'm coming from some difficult experiences of my own, as we all do. One is that we have not yet had careful documentation of what exactly does happen behaviorally in preterm nurseries. What is the behavior in the setting that we're decrying. Such data are now being collected, I understand. I'm concerned that we're going ahead with interventions when we can't measure the outcome. We haven't yet the measures to say that it's worked. We've gone through the period of making babies blind because we thought oxygen was exceedingly good, of crippling babies with jaundice because we thought a lot of vitamin K was good. In other words, there have been many things that we've done that were easily justified but were wrong. We need to document exactly what it is we're doing. Why we're doing it. Where we're starting from. How we're going to measure the outcome, and when we're going to measure the outcome. That's all I'm asking for.

Dr. Kennell: Perhaps I can be excused for using data from one of our studies that may have relevance to what we're discussing. It is a study with full-term normal babies of normal mothers, mainly lower socio-economic level from the inner city. One group of mothers received routine care, the other group of mothers had their babies for 1 hour shortly after birth and for 5 extra hours during each of the first 3 hospital days. There were significant differences between the behavior of the mothers in the two groups at 1 month and at 1 year. At 2 years, the group of mothers with early and extended contact were talking differently to their children. They had much richer speech with more words per proposition, more adjectives and many more questions; whereas, in contrast, the routine group used many more commands. We brought the children back when they were 5 years of age and found that the children of the mothers who had early and extended contact had a significantly higher IQ of 97 on the Stanford–Binet test and the other group mean IQ was 89. The early contact group was also more advanced on a number of language tests. Now this is a tiny study and needs to be replicated in a larger population, but let me go to the point I would like to make. I am so familiar with the experience of our premature babies, going home to two different environments, the private patients going to an environment where they will usually have a mean IQ of 120 or more in 5 years and the others going to the inner city where the average IQ will often be 80 or below. The same has been true with the full-term babies. The influence of the socio-economic background has been mentioned. I would just like to bring up the possibility that what we do very early about keeping the mother and baby together might be an equally important determinant of how the infant's subsequent development will proceed. Of course, the situation with a premature infant is very different. Usually a mother does not develop a strong attachment to her premature infant until days or weeks after the baby is born. But if the baby is better organized and more responsive, if its eyes are open more so that the mother can understand the needs of her baby better, an earlier and stronger attachment may be achieved and there might be more of the effect that is suggested in the study I mentioned with full-term infants.

Dr. Parmelee: These data concern normal mothers and normal babies. There's no quarrel with that. The minute the baby is sick or the mother is sick, you have disrupted the potential for attachment. That's a given. For the preterm infant that's a given. The attachment problem is distorted. You can't necessarily go the other way around though and assume that putting a very sick baby in the mother's arms is going to promote attachment. It's a much more difficult process that probably extends over the whole first year or longer. I don't know how long. The question then is how to generate support services long after the baby has left the nursery to help solve that problem. I have no quarrel with the baby who responds well. The problem we're facing is that preterms are not born without incident and so their obstetric history, their neonatal history, and how imminent death was, affects what they'll do and how their mothers perceive them. These are factors influencing mothers that we're trying to deal with. If you think you can help by making the infants somewhat more alert, that's certainly a positive step.

Dr. Barnard: I too have a great deal of concern for the environment of the preterm infant. I can't really add much new information. We're now in the midst of a replication phase of the rocking—heartbeat previously mentioned by Dr. Parmelee. I would love to be able to say something, but the data are in the computer and they won't be out till later. In addition to a fixed-interval schedule, we now are testing a self-activated rocking-heartbeat program. We have proposed that this self-activated stimulation will show more environmental support for the infant's emerging organization of sleep state. I am concerned about the matter of stressing the infant; what we're doing in no way matches the magnitude of what's going on in pediatric nursing and medical intervention now occurring. For instance, I read a report recently from Canada; within the hospital period it's estimated that the average preterm infant has 70 caretakers. Also, there is a very erratic schedule of stimuli available to the infant. In one present Premature Infant Refocus Study, we're doing 24-hour video recordings of study babies in the nursery. It is interesting to observe how and when staff interact with these infants. The last area I'd like to mention concerns a bit of data we have and infants to test out what observations and information from the first year of life would relate to later developmental states. We only had by Dubowitz's exam 11 babies out of 193 who had a gestational age below 37 weeks. We did Brazelton exams at 2 days on all the babies, and it was of interest to me to calculate, using the dimension profile of interactive processes, that half of these preterm infants (mean GA at birth = 35 weeks) scored in the category of markedly deficient interactive behavior at the time of discharge from the hospital nursery.

Dr. Parmelee: Is this testing at term?

Dr. Barnard: Before discharge from the hospital. In those 11 babies, 6 out of the 11 were at the III level (markedly deficient) for interactive process. We're also using the Brazelton scale in our study of prematures at 34 weeks then at a term equivalent age. It appears that the preterm infant in this population too is rather poor in orienting, alerting to his or her mother. I am interested and fascinated by the question of who initiates and who imitates; in the interaction of the mother with her premature infant, there is perhaps some confirmation of the fact that there is early initiation from the infant, and the imitation is by the mother. In the premature infant–mother dyad, you see much less interaction in feeding, play, and so on. Compared to the term infant, there is simply less behavioral responsiveness from the infant.

Dr. Thoman: As a matter of fact the points that have just been made provide a very nice transition to the next section of participants, whereby we will deal with the whole baby in his environment, and of course the primary source of environmental stimuli is the parent. It's very clear that we need to know something about the course of the interactional relationship as it develops, taking into account also the various things that we've been talking about with respect to what the baby can process.

REFERENCES

Adrien, J., & Roffwarg, H. P. The development of unit activity in the lateral geniculate nucleus of the kitten. *Experimental Neurology*, 1974, *43*, 261–275.

Hubel, D. H., & Wiesel, T. N. The period of susceptibility to the physiological effects of unilateral eye closure in the kitten. *Journal of Physiology*, 1970, *206*, 419–436.

Huttenlocker, P. R. Development of cortical neuronal activity in the neonatal cat, *Experimental Neurology*, 1967, *17*, 247–262.

Parmelee, A. H., & Sigman, M. Development of Visual Behavior and Neurological Organization in Pre-term and Full-term Infants. In A. D. Pick (Ed.), *Minnesota Symposia on Child Development* (Vol. 10). Minneapolis: University of Minnesota Press, 1976.

Rose, G. H., & Collins, J. P. Light-dark discrimination and reversal learning in early postnatal kittens. *Developmental Psychobiology*, 1975, *8*, 511–518.

Sameroff, A. J., & Chandler, M. J. Reproductive risk in the contiuum of caretaking casuality. In F. D. Horowitz, M. Hetherton, S. Scarr-Salapatek, & G. Siegel (Eds.) *Review of Child Development Research* (Vol. 4) Chicago: University of Chicago Press, 1975, 187–244.

Siqueland, E. R. The development of instrumental exploratory behavior during the first year of human life. Paper presented at SRCD, Santa Monica, California, March, 1969.

Thoman, E. B., Wetzel, A., & Levine, S. Learning in the neonatal rat. *Animal Behavior*, 1968, *16*, 54–57.

II DEVELOPING DESIGNS FOR VIEWING THE INFANT AS A SOCIAL BEING

The Infant's Fundamental Adaptive Response System in Social Interaction

Hanuš Papoušek
Mechthild Papoušek
Max Planck Institute for Psychiatry

INTRODUCTION

What I am going to discuss in this paper could almost be called a synthesis of by-products, since in designing our experiments, our primary objective was not in the analysis of those general aspects of behavioral regulation that we have given as the title for this presentation. If a student today did what we had done 20 years ago, he would be asked to be more cautious in selecting experimental parameters to study. At that time, however, many things looked differently than they do now. Indeed, in terms of advancement of knowledge, the last two decades in infancy research deserve the status of an historical epoch.

When we started our research, we wanted to look at the early postnatal development of adaptive behavioral processes. But at that time, such an attempt was still theoretically and methodologically premature, and thus we were compelled to approach this task almost *de novo*.

First of all, we were interested in human neonates and infants, but they were not among the standard laboratory subjects. The experimental and theoretical work in learning, even though very rich and extensive, was obviously based upon adult animals or adult humans, and it was difficult to find implications for human infants by extrapolation.

In choosing the human infant for study, we hoped to find a developing young organism that would be more predictable than the adult, in accordance with the principles of neural intergrative development, but we were perplexed by the small amount of knowledge about human infancy. We found textbooks on their biochemistry, metabolism, and pathological abnormalities, but very little on their normal behavior, perception, learning, or cognition. Thus, we had to keep our eyes open and observe carefully, almost like ethologists do now when studying the behavior of an unknown species.

As to the experimental methods, the situation seemed to be simpler. We had a choice between associative (classical) and operant conditioning, and the choice seemed to depend almost entirely on the geographical location of one's laboratory. However, for both physiological and ethical reasons, we did not try to adapt the common experimental methods for use with the fragile young human organism.

By selecting conditioning methods, we were not obligated to confine ourselves to studies of the simple forms of learning. Strict operant conditioning did help to elucidate some crucial questions of intervening variables, such as concept formation (Fields, 1932; Tolman, Ritchie, & Kalish, 1946; Herrnstein & Loveland, 1964). Similarly, strict Pavlovian conditioning was applied to children to study logical operations as well.

Quite another question was whether the natural learning situations of babies—that is, their play and their social interactions with adults—could be reduced to the laboratory forms of conditioning. Here, the theories left us helpless. And yet, we were interested in the ecological aspects of early development and particularly in the infant's natural interactions with his biological and social environments.

Our approach to these issues owed much to the first author's studies at Purkinje's University, where he had learned about Purkinje's equal respect for both empirical observation and laboratory experiment; and from Babak—a pioneer in developmental biology in Prague—he also learned much of what would today be considered an ethological approach. Another important event for him was the inspiring experience of seeing the late Krasnogorskij using the same salivatory conditioning procedures with children as had originally been used with dogs, but designing experiments like the one in Table 7.1 (Volkova, 1954; Krasnogorskij, 1958).

We include that study since these experiments are not well known in the American literature. Here in a 14-year-old pupil, a conditioned salivation response elicited by cranberry candy (the unconditioned stimulus) was associated with the number 18 as a conditioning signal. The pupil was then given simple arithmetic tasks leading to results equaling 18. Changes in the latency and intensity of the conditioned salivation served as indicators of the course of mental operations, relationships between motor–verbal and autonomic responses, and so on.

Even when we used conditioning designs, an explicit interest in the development of individual personalities in our studies required various deviations from the available procedures. Let me mention the main ones:

1. We combined operant and associative elements of conditioning in one design, to make the design more nearly comparable with natural learning situations where a subject learns to obtain a relevant reinforcement through

TABLE 7.1
Classical Salivary Conditioning Used to Evaluate Logical
Operations

	Parameters of Conditioned Salivation:	
	Latency (in Seconds)	Amount of Salivation (in Drops)
Arithmetic tasks:		
9 + 9	2	17
90 : 5	6	13
72 : 4	11	7
Too difficult	general inhibition and/or chaotic responses	

Note. CS (verbal) = "18", UCS =cranberry candy, CR = salivation

his own activity, but where certain environmental constraints allow him to do so successfully only under certain conditions. In our design, the contingent reinforcement was available to the subject only in the presence of a conditioning signal.

2. We were interested in the complex coordination of adaptive behavioral changes. Therefore, in addition to the main response in question—head movement in most studies to be mentioned—we also recorded general motor behavior, vocalization, facial expressions, respiratory movements, and heart rate.

3. In order to be able to analyze the course of learning per se, and to detect interindividual differences, we decided not to follow the usual procedure of testing each subject for a constant block of trials. Instead, we defined learning as the achievement of a given criterion.

4. In addition to the acquisition of a conditioned response, we also paid attention to simpler adaptive processes, for example, to the orienting responses and to their habituation, as well as to more complex processes, such as conditioned differentiation of two signals, a reversal of such differentiation, or concept formation in relation to operant conditioning.

5. Simultaneous with the experimental studies, which were run daily for several months, we observed our infants in everyday situations, for example, in their interactions with mothers or caretakers. Other members of our team studied their waking and sleep cycles, health state, sensorimotor development, and so on. We were able to carry out long-term studies because of the unique opportunity we had: keeping the infants and their mothers at a special research unit free of charge.

Thus while collecting data on the early development of learning, we also gradually obtained considerable information on the interrelationship between learning and changes in behavioral states; we discovered meaningful parallels between experimental learning and play activities or social interactions; and we learned more about accompanying emotional behavior, autonomic responses and communicative responses in vocalization, and facial expressions. In other words, there slowly emerged the interesting concept of a fundamental regulatory system underlying different categories of behavior.

In the following parts of our communication, we shall comment on several aspects of this fundamental system of adaptive responses with respect to the observations and to their theoretical interpretation. Our comments will first refer to two main features of what have often been called intervening variables: processing of informational input and organization of adaptive responses. Different models have been developed for these processes, and we shall try to view them in their natural unity. We shall then discuss the significance of these processes in two important categories of the infant's natural activities: play and social interaction.

INTERVENING VARIABLES

Intervening Variable 1: Perception and Its Processing

From information theory (e.g., Shannon & Weaver, 1949), we know that the content of any information input is a function of the probablility with which the receiving system can carry a given number of signals in a given spatial and temporal distribution. We also know that any environmental situation always consists of a large number of relational units moving in space or, at least, in time. The perception of the situation involves even more important relational aspects: the relationships of the information input to the general behavioral state of the organism, to other ongoing activities, and to the engrams of past activities and experience that have equal or similar information inputs. The combination of these various aspects will result in the current information being perceived as familiar, or as unknown and novel, to the perceiving person.

Obviously, perception is a complex and active process. It depends partly on innate capacities. In addition, the contribution of experience to perception has been amply documented. Gibson (1969) has shown that perceptual learning improves the capacity to detect accurately and economically the relevant features in the structure of the information input. Futhermore, a perceiving person also responds to environmental stimulation with changes influencing perception, for example, with increased attention and the search for invariants in the information input. Such changes have been described as components of orienting responses (Sokolov, 1963), which were originally discovered by Pavlov (1953). Sokolov's model postulates a comparative subsystem for the detection of potential relations of new informational input to past experience, and an amplifying subsystem increasing, for example the velocity of nerve conduction and/or decreasing thresholds. From a different perspective, cognitive psychology believes that the important contribution of experience is to establish cognitive processes—including cognitive mediation, use of hypotheses, and problem solving (Miller, Galanter & Pribram, 1960; Bruner, 1957)—which act to supplement the perceptual process.

Our own studies helped us to elucidate the early postnatal development of the infant's perceptual capacities and drew our attention to aspects that are seldom discussed. These involved the investigation of proprioceptive, particularly kinesthetic perception. Research on these modalities in relation to perception has been neglected, since psychology has no easy methods for their study, although the integration of motor acts plays a major role in such important theories of cognitive development as those of Piaget (1954) and Bruner (1966). Our findings stemmed from the procedure we used to study learning. As mentioned above, we made the infant's head movement an instrumental act; by head movement, and by it alone, he could obtain reinforcement. If he made the proper head movement after hearing an acoustic conditioning signal, he received a portion of milk. By means of this procedure, we were able to determine the infant's capacity to discover the relationship between a relevant environmental change and his own motor activity.

We discovered that even the newborn was able to detect the relationship between his own motor activity and the nutritional reinforcement and is able to learn the appropriate head movement within the 1st week of life on the average. In addition, the rate of conditioning increases significantly every month between birth and 5 months (Papousek, 1961 a,b; 1967), although it is not possible to separate the contributions of prior learning experience and maturational development of the perceptual capacities themselves in bringing about this increase. Unlike other authors (Sameroff, 1971), we ascribe the ability of the newborn to cope with instrumental conditioning, even though still unable to cope with associative conditioning, to the particular power of contingent stimulation in structuring perception.

Whether this special power of contingent stimulation can be attributed to genetically determined preferences in the newborn is difficult to say, since we cannot exclude the effects of prenatal intrauterine learning. We know that the fetus is capable of movement, and it is possible that his movements may elicit different detectable contingent environmental stimulations. For instance, the fetus might learn that his movements increase bowel sounds in his mother, or lead to tactile self-stimulation resulting from touches of the uterine wall and from "double-touches" if the fetus touches his own body.

In any case, by four months the infant demonstrates complex cognitive processes, such as the capacity to detect various rules by means of which he could switch on an attractive color–light display through his head movements. Some of the rules were to make two, three, or four consecutive head movements to one side, or to regularly alternate left and right head turns (Papousek & Bernstein, 1969). These were relatively simple rules, but even adults needed some experience if they were to detect them without any instruction.

We also found some interesting relationships between orienting responses and contingency. Before we made the visual display contingent on the infant's head movements, it took 8 to 12 exposures to habituate out the orienting responses. However, once the infants detected a potential contingency, the display elicited much more attention and exploration. Such an increased orienting was resistant to habituation, even after 30 to 40 repetitions.

An interesting example of the simultaneous operation of two different perceptual processes was shown in our study of mirror behavior in 5-month-old infants (Papousek & Papousek, 1974). Using two television monitors, we simultaneously showed the infants (1) a mirror image of themselves which precluded eye-to-eye contact, and (2) a comparable playback of themselves allowing eye-to-eye contact. Both the eye-to-eye contact offered in the playback, and the contingency of the behavior as seen in the mirror image appeared to be powerful determiners of perception. However, as indicated in a preference design (see Figure 7.1), the infants detected the possibility of eye-to-eye contact very rapidly, paid most attention to it, and only gradually—as if first by trial—and—check—discovered the contingency in the behavior of their mirror image and then began to pay increasing attention to it, while their attention to eye-to-eye contact gradually decreased.

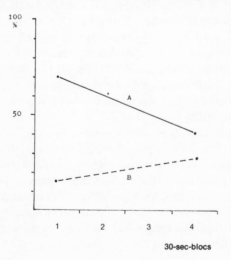

30-sec-blocs

FIG. 7.1.   Percentage of time spent by infants looking at video-movie of self with eye-to-eye contact (A), and at videoed mirror-image of self where eye contact was precluded (B).

These observations led us to the following categorization of environmental events with respect to the infant's adaptive processes (Papousek & Papousek, 1975):

1. Random external change, whether it occurs once or repeatedly, that is completely independent of the infant's activity, and that does not signal any other relevant change, elicits attention or orientation that habituates quickly.

2. External change that is independent of the infant's activity but is regularly associated with another relevant change (e.g., nutritional supply or social contact) may function as a signal for the latter change and may facilitate the infant's adaptation to his environment. As soon as regularity is detected, the infant shows intensive orientation and learns a conditioned response to such a conditional signal.

3. External change that is contingent on the infant's own activity elicits the most intensive of orienting reactions, involving approach or manipulatory exploration. These reactions may be resistant to habituation and will cease only after different forms of operant learning have enabled the infant to reach the relevant external change repeatedly.

4. External change that depends on the infant's own activity, but in which the dependency is difficult to perceive, represents a problem situation. In immature and inexperienced infants, the search for the right solution may tax the limits of the capability of the nervous system, even though these are situations that older infants may solve easily and rapidly.

Intervening Variable 2: The Organization of Adaptive Responses

The usual approach when analyzing adaptive behavior is to consider only particular observable responses and to concentrate on the question of whether they belong to the set of genetically determined responses or whether they result from learning. This, however, is often an oversimplification, because adaptive behavior consists of large numbers of behavioral units that are spatially and temporally arranged into very complex structures. It is the interrelations among external stimulation, the central processing of the informational input, and the organization of adaptive responses that give behavior the character of a dynamic process of interaction. Even though it is difficult to record and analyze all aspects of such a complex process, modern theoretical models are attempting to take all of these factors into consideration, thereby delineating important directions for the development of new experimental measuring procedures. Such a complex conceptual view, together with new mathematical models for describing discontinuous processes (e.g., Markov chains or the models of Thom, 1975), helps us to understand what used to seem unpredictable and uncontrollable. This approach is particularly useful in studying infants, who still "talk with the whole body," since—other things being equal—their behavior is more predictable, a circumstance that facilitates the testing and verification of models.

A great number of adaptive responses involve different kinds of muscles. The somatic muscles themselves represent an amazingly complex and integrated system. At the level of motor activity, a vast number of simple elements are integrated into functional units of higher orders, from the simplest reflexes of single muscles up to the more complex coordinations of many synergists, antagonists, and concurrent positional or locomotor adaptations; and from the shortest of reactions up to the extremely long and exhaustive performances requiring multilateral autonomic adaptation and intensive metabolic transport. In fact, the hierarchical integration of the motor system offers an analogy, if not a model, for cognitive integration of single perceptions into concepts, categories, and classes. It could even be that the development of embryonic motor integrations is the necessary prerequisite for cognitive processes and motor acts.

But adaptive responses include more than the motor acts involved in specific responses to environmental stimulation. They also involve the central nervous system of the responding subject itself, the autonomic system, and the internal milieu. We have already noted that different mechanisms activate attentional and perceptual processes, scanning in the memory system, exploration, and decision making. Just within the decision-making act alone, there is the choice of potential response alternatives, the choice of hypotheses with predictions on the outcome of selected alternatives, and the use of reafference as a way to test the validity of such hypotheses. While these actions are going on, other ongoing activities are often interrupted or terminated. We may look upon the changes in the degree of conscious control of such processes as upon one of the adaptive responses directed at one's own nervous system.

In addition to the observed specific responses upon which we focus, there are other accompanying nonspecific responses that change the general state in the responding organism. These include changes in the actual readiness to perceive and to respond, as well as the prospective readiness to respond to the next analogous situation on the bases of the actual experience coded and stored in memory. Other nonspecific responses are located in the autonomic system and provide the necessary energetic supply and metabolic adjustment.

One aspect of adaptive responses is their function as a means of communication with the social environment. It seems to be beyond doubt that during the phylogenetic development of humans, some of their behaviors attained particular significance as messages, alarming or quieting other members of their social environment and informing the other members of their experience.

The organization of adaptive responses may sometimes involve a mere structuring of unconditioned responses, whereas at other times it may involve learning or cognitive processes. The choice among them again is determined by the structure of the environmental stimulation: If an environmental change is contingent on the subject's activity, then a particular category of operant learning is called for; if the detection of a more complex form of contingency represents a problem situation requiring a difficult solution, then various other cognitive processes will be set into gear.

The Fundamental Adaptive Response System and Its Motivational Aspect

There are two important features of the way we have described the organization of adaptive responses: (1) In addition to particular responses appropriate to certain relevant biological situations—such as seen in nutritional, social, or aversive situations—the organism also responds with more general responses, which act to facilitate the regulation of information input, information processing, and the organization of adaptive responses; and (2) these fundamental adaptive responses, including many cognitive processes, have been described almost as a category of unconditioned responses. In fact, at least one of the adaptive responses belonging to this fundamental category has always been viewed as an unconditioned reflex by Pavlov and his followers, and that is the orienting reflex. Unlike the other categories of unconditioned responses, the orienting reactions lack specific unconditioned eliciting signals, or triggering signals in the ethological sense. The eliciting power lies in the relational character of any signal: Any signal can elicit orienting responses if it can be perceived and if it is new to the perceiving subject.

The novelty feature is, of course, a product of the organism's active perceptual processes. If the perceptual processes indicate that an environmental change is unfamiliar, this leads to the activation of orienting responses, even if the novelty is in fact only relative and caused by a failure in the memory system. In a similar vein, if the perceptual processes indicate the contingency of an environmental change on the organism's motor activity, this leads to the activation of operant learning or of problem solving, even if the contingency only seemingly exists.

Indeed, if this topic had been discussed at the time that drive theories were popular, the fundamental adaptive response system could have been classified as a basic drive, because it participated in all other categories of drives. For example, in any biologically relevant situation connected with the satiation of hunger, avoidance of pain, or reproduction, the organism first has to activate the mechanisms controlling informational input and processing and all other subsequent cognitive or learning processes up to the evaluation of the final outcome.

In human infants, the presence and the significance of such general adaptive responses is particularly obvious because they occur slowly and manifest themselves in the total motor behavior, and because their interpretation is not yet complicated by an uncontrollable amount and variety of preceding experience. In newborns especially, we were able to observe the activation of orienting responses, the gradual organization of individual components of a newly learned response (Papousek, 1967), and the participation of autonomic and communicative changes in behavioral states.

In 2 to 3-month-old infants, we were able to study more complex behavior. Their task was to learn to respond differentially to two different acoustic signals with two symmetrical but contralateral head movements or to relearn such a differentiation when we reversed the sides of reinforcement. In trying to solve these tasks, we saw attempts by the infants to apply different strategies, frequently false and reminiscent of superstitious behavior. It was amazing to see how much effort these infants exerted in order to find solutions in learning situations that were obviously problematical for them.

Naturally, we became interested in the underlying motivation, for the efforts of the infants sometimes seemed to threaten them with exhaustion. We were surprised to discover that the motivation was independent of hunger in learning experiments where milk was used as a reinforcement. During the average session of conditioning or conditioned discrimination, which in fact represented one of the normal feedings of a hungry infant, there was no significant change found in either the probability of a correct response or the latency of a correct response as a function of the gradual satiation of hunger (see Figure 7.2).

We tried to analyze the role of satiation more closely in a group of 4-month-old infants. Following the standard conditioning session, we added another 10 to 20 trials, in which an unlimited amount of milk reinforcement was made available (Papousek, 1967). As Figure 7.3 shows, even after complete satiation of hunger, at a time when the infant refused drinking and turned his head away at the offer of milk, successive conditioning signals elicited quick and intensive correct head movements and signs of pleasure. The performance of the correct adaptive response motivated the infant more strongly than reinforcement with milk.

Another example can be given from the studies of concept formation in 4-month-old infants who learned to switch on a 5-second display of blinking colored lights with a head turn to a given side. Having acquired this skill, they were exposed to situations in which different rules were introduced into the

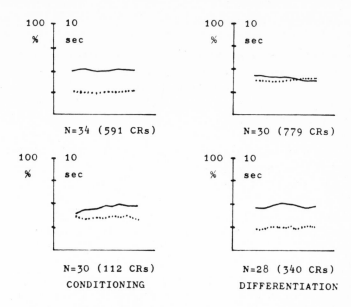

N=34 (591 CRs)　　　　　　N=30 (779 CRs)

N=30 (112 CRs)　　　　　　N=28 (340 CRs)
CONDITIONING　　　　　　DIFFERENTIATION

FIG. 7.2.　Effect of satiation of hunger upon the course of conditioning (left graphs) and conditioned differentiation (right graphs) within one session (10 trials).

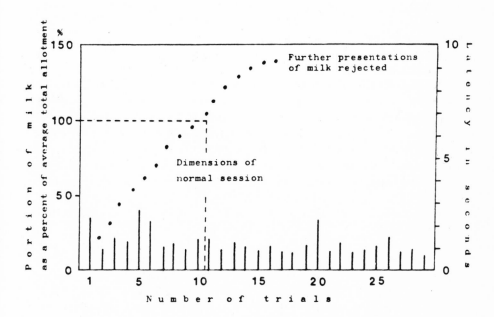

FIG. 7.3.　Temporal course of a prolonged conditioning session with appetitional reinforcement. Thick vertical lines: latencies of the conditioned head movements. Dots: milk portion as a percent of average milk quantity per session. (From Papousek and Papousek, 1975).

reinforcement system, and the infants were to find out those rules by themselves. Figure 7.4, for instance, shows the polygraphic record of the infant's behavior in the experiment in which he could switch on the reinforcement only by regularly alternating head movements to the left and to the right on a 1:1 ratio.

The record in Figure 7.5 shows another behavior in a later stage of the same experiments. Here the infant turns up to 90° degrees to the left, switches on the blinking lights, but leaves his head in this position, even during the visual display coming from the midline, and observes other things. As soon as the reinforcement is finished, the infant turns his head back to the midline and carries out the next correct response to the right. Again he is not interested in the visual display but seems to be pleased by having performed the correct responses. In fact, he becomes upset when the reinforcement is omitted and starts searching for it. Obviously, the infant expects a certain result to follow from his motor act, and the congruency between his expectation and the real outcome pleases him, whereas an incongruency upsets him and elicits new exploration.

If we accept a relaxed facial expression, smiles, and quiet vocalization accompanied by quiet and well-coordinated motor activities with open palms as sufficient parameters for pleasant emotional feelings in the infant; and likewise, a fussy face and vocalization or crying accompanied with uncoordinated or chaotic movements, usually with firmly closed fists, as parameters of unpleasant emotional feelings—then we find much evidence on the motivational significance of the course and outcome of intervening processes belonging to the fundamental adaptive system.

In analyzing the course of instrumental conditioning in infants, we drew attention to some regular changes in emotional behavior (Papousek, 1967): We described signs of unpleasant feelings during the initial occurrence of conditioned responses, during initial extinction of them, and during reversal of reinforcement schedules that caused conflicts between the infant's expectation and the actual outcome in reinforcement. On the other hand, we observed signs of pleasure regularly associated with exposure to familiar objects, with the acquisition of a stabler and well-coordinated conditioned response, and with the acquisition of a good level of conditioned differentiation.

When students of motivation moved beyond the external motivators that were stressed so exclusively in former drive theories and became interested in intrinsic sources of motivation, they mainly emphasized phenomena of incongruency or dissonance. Hebb (1949) postulated an "incongruous receptor input" to disrupt the sequential organization in "cell assemblies" responsible for concepts. Hunt (1966) considered incongruity the essential feature of novelty, and the right amount of incongruity to be one of the most important factors in the epigenesis of intrinsic motivation. Both Hebb and

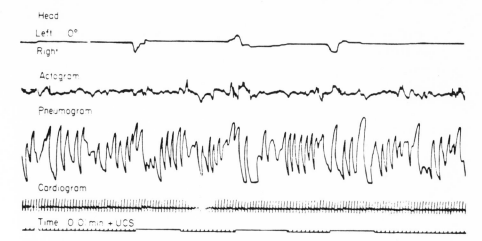

FIG. 7.4. Alternating head turns to left and right, when reinforcement is provided for this sequence. The polygram represents from above downwards: head movement, general body movement, breathing, heartbeat, and time. The time at which a stimulus was applied is shown on the time marker. The infant switches on a rewarding visual display by turning head to the correct side. Then, he turns head back to midline where the visual reinforcement is offered. (From Papousek, 1969.)

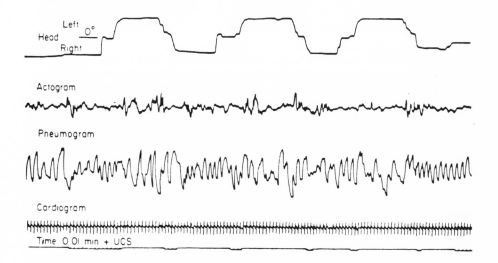

FIG. 7.5. A similar situation as in Figure 7.4. Here, however, the infant keeps his head turned sharply towards the side that has produced a reward, despite the fact that the visual reinforcement is offered in the midline. As soon as the reinforcement ends, he turns his head to the midline and then to the opposite side, as necessary for attaining the next reinforcement, but again, he does not pay attention to the reinforcement itself. (From Papousek, 1969.)

Hunt also stressed the pleasure resulting from encounters with something new within the framework of the familiar (Hebb) or resulting from a recognition of familiar encounters in general (Hunt). In our observations, we have seen so much evidence of joyful experience resulting from the outcome of the fundamental adaptive processes in infants that we are inclined to believe, from the point of view of motivation, that the infant is as strongly pulled by the expectation of pleasure connected with successful adaptation as he is pushed by unpleasant feelings resulting from incongruency, dissonance, or failure in adjustment.

The Fundamental Adaptive Response System as a Unifying Concept

Our attempt to conceptually integrate several different response patterns into one overall category called the fundamental adaptive response system can be seen either as a useful abridgement of redundant theoretical alternatives or as the creation of another "wastebasket category" for phenomena still eluding a reasonable interpretation. A certain formal unity may be seen in the sense that from the point of view of stimulus–response theories, the all fundamental adaptive responses represent mediating or intervening variables. Since we are observers of early human behavior rather than experimental neurophysiologists, we cannot examine the anatomical unity of underlying neurophysiological substrates of such a system. However, for us the unity of this system is represented by the quality of relations that unite all its individual parts. We assume that this relationship is a dialectic one, determined by probabilistic laws, and that it is bidirectional, having the character of a dynamic interaction.

We have already pointed out the interactional character of perceptual processes and its relationship to perceptual learning (Gibson, 1969). We have found similar relationships between the regulation of behavioral states and measures of learning or cognition (Papousek, 1969). Not only could we demonstrate how the behavioral state preceding a conditioning signal influenced the course of the conditioned response, but we could also describe the effects of the course of learning or cognitive processes on the subsequent behavioral states.

Thus in our concept of the stimulus–response relationship, we should hardly admit a less-contracted abbreviation than $\Sigma S \rightleftharpoons IP \rightleftharpoons AO \rightleftharpoons \Sigma R$, where ΣS stands for the whole structure of environmental stimulation, IP for information processing, AO for organization of adaptive responses, and ΣR for the complex response of the whole organism.

Furthermore, we believe that the mechanisms included in the fundamental adaptive response system are not regulated by on–off switches that activate or terminate certain functions. (Such an on–off principle, for instance, has often been applied in models of orienting responses.) We suggest, rather that this regulation works in both directions, so that both the processing of information input and the organization of adaptive responses can either be positively activated or actively decreased and inhibited.

An organism has at its disposal two sets of mechanisms. One set is for orienting towards something, for facilitating the input or processing of information, for approach and exploration; the opposite set of mechanisms is involved in turning away from unpleasant or noxious situations, avoidance, and reduction or interruption of informatinal input and processing. The latter set corresponds to the biological needs of the organism to be protected against a flood of information, particularly of information that is difficult to process.

The assumption that the fundamental adaptive response system also has a protective role helps us to interpret the infant's behavior in terms of avoidance mechanisms. A good example is found in our analysis of head movements in our learning studies, which is a good model for simple approach–avoidance behavior. Sudden head turns in the "incorrect" direction, which we originally described as a "paradoxical reversal of the conditioned response" now appear to be much better interpreted as an avoidance mechanism.

This response is found in newborns (Papousek, 1967). The avoidance function of this response became more evident in relatively difficult problem situations in 4-month-old infants (Papousek & Bernstein, 1969) and also offered a better interpretation for the baby's avoidance of the mother in situations when her behavior violated the infant's expectancy, and which other authors have interpreted as an "oversatiation phenomenon" (e.g., Koch, 1968). (The significance of such internal or external detachment in social interactions has become an object of particular interest in our present studies, which we shall return to later.)

In our studies, we saw a developmental change in the form of reduction of information processing. Infants younger than two months responded to difficult stimulations more frequently with a sudden temporary change of behavioral state reminiscent of "playing possum" (Papousek, 1969). For a few seconds or minutes, they would lie motionless and silent, the eyes remaining open but staring without convergence; the respiration and heart rate are slow and regular as in sleep (see Figure 7.6). Older infants, on the other hand, responded with active redistribution of interest, avoiding behavior, or rejection that did not necessarily change the behavioral state in general.

On the whole, we conceptualize the fundamental adaptive response system as a complex set of processes concerned with the regulation of behavioral states, attention, perception, memory, orienting, exploration, learning, and cognition. It is a system consisting of unconditioned responses to stimuli external to the nervous system as well as to the internal products resulting from the processing of external stimuli within the nervous system. It is also a system integrating those internal products in different forms of learning, from

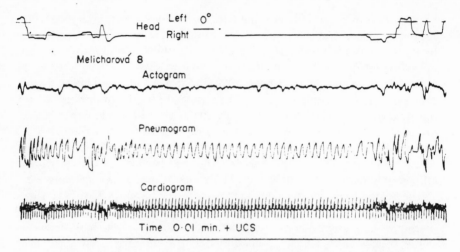

FIG. 7.6.   Changes in behavioral state observed during operant conditioning (a "biological fuse" phenomenon). Channels of polygram as in Figure 7.4. Note a decrease in head movement, general body movement, heartbeat, and the slow, regular breathing like in sleep. (From Papousek and Bernstein, 1969.)

the simple biological phenomenon of habituation, through different forms of conditioning, and up to complex concept formation, problem solving, verbal symbolization, and consciousness. This system operates in both directions, either activating all analytic and integral mechanisms or inhibiting them in accordance with the adaptation of the organism to environmental changes. This system encompasses all other behaviors elicited by external motivators such as nutritional, aversive, social or reproductive behaviors. This system is common to all of them, perhaps collateral to them, but no less significant. The motivation for this system of responses derives from the "intervening" or "mediating" outcomes within the nervous sytem, which also include a sort of intrinsic "reward" or "punishment" in the form of a pleasant feeling in successful adaptation and an unpleasant feeling in unsuccessful adaptation. The purpose and biological sense of this system is to provide the organism with a control of informational input and its utilization as well as control of the general readiness to realize adequate specific adaptive responses in the present or in the future.

We fully appreciate that all the individual processes comprehended in the fundamental system deserve the specialized interest of appropriate branches of scientific disciplines. We are also convinced that they all stem from simpler biological functions and thus deserve another approach, namely an attempt to detect their common pathways and the interrelations among them. We have found this approach particularly useful for our field of activity, the study of human behavioral development from the very beginning of postnatal life.

We have hardly been able to do more than combine our own observations with the theoretical models that fit best and perhaps stress certain new aspects. We have taken these models from studies based on much better experimental evidence, although they involve adult animals or humans, rather than infants. The combination of these various models and their application to human infancy required certain modifications which, hopefully, were justified.

Figure 7.7 illustrates, with roughly simplified descriptive symbols, the direction of general behavioral changes resulting from some processes involved in the fundamental adaptive system. Most of these symbols point to observable phenomena. Movement is possible in both directions, meaning either an increase (ascent) or decrease (descent). Under normal conditions in waking subjects, this movement takes place within the narrower limits of fluctuations in attention, or orientation and habituation of orienting responses. Signs of both ascent and descent may, however, be seen in overt approaching or exploration (in autonomic changes connected with the energetic supply, for instance) and in the emission of signals toward the social environment. In both directions as well, ascent or descent may reach the border of maladaptation, as indicated in the scheme. According to age, of course, some of the behavioral changes may be only foreshadowed, for example, "escape" before locomotion develops at all. In an interaction with a

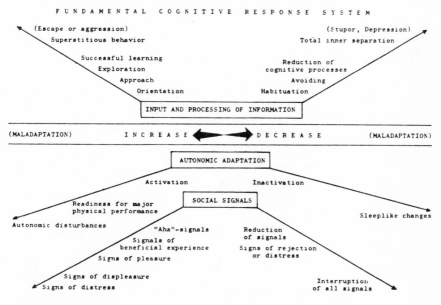

FIG. 7.7. The fundamental adaptive response system in infants. (From Papousek and Papousek, 1975.)

caretaker, the infant's own lack of skill can be compensated for by the adult's intervention, which is in turn manipulated by the infant. To suggest aggression as one of the potential exits of problematic situations is not to speculate on the origins of aggression. Any behavioral changes observed in our infants that resemble aggressive behavior might simply be interpreted as disturbances of response coordination in situations in which other signs of coordination disorders were present anyway.

As mentioned in the introduction to this communication, we collected evidence for our concept in studies of learning and cognitive development under laboratory conditions on the one hand, and in the analysis of infant–adult interactions on the other. The logical bridge between these two types of studies was given by our hypothesis that play and social interaction represent the most important of all natural learning situations for the infant. Therefore, we would like to suggest certain possible implications of the concept of fundamental adaptive responses for both play and social interaction.

Play: From Unknown to Known, and Between Stress and Boredom

Play—a term easily understood on the level of intuitive, common-sense psychology—is actually extremely difficult to define. It is too broad a category, presenting real difficulties in the logical search for substantial invariants where common sense does not seem to have any problems.

If we pay more attention to the way in which common sense deals with the question of play, we come to two interesting conclusions: (1) The play of a child is viewed as the opposite of the work of an adult, and yet there is no sharp distinction that can be made between them, as if a dialectic relation between play and work should not be excluded a priori; (2) to play with ideas is generally admitted as one kind of play so that some relation between play and cognitive processes has already been acknowledged in general. Interestingly enough, the saying that somebody played with an idea usually concerns a problem for which he or she has no solution as yet.

Present scientific trends seem to be on the way to confirming these two common assumptions about play. However, the biological explanation of play still lacks a satisfactory interpretation. From comparative studies of animal play, we know its descriptive features, such as incomplete sequences of motor patterns, the presence of play-specific patterns that are functionless outside of play, and the intermingling of functionally diverse patterns or atypically distributed intensity of movements in sequences (Hinde, 1970). We also know some of the key features signaling play behavior to social partners, such as the "play-face" (van Hooff, 1962), for which the analogy in human children may be the wide-mouth laugh (Blurton-Jones, 1967). According to ethological criteria, since many activities of the infant are incomplete and often inappropriate to external situations, most infant behavior would be classified as play activity. However, such patterns may result either from the fact that the infant has not yet acquired complete sequences of motor patterns or from the fact that he has already acquired them but now playfully modifies them into new sequences. Those who see the elements of creativity in play (e.g., Huizinga, 1962) would, of course, interpret only the latter alternative as play.

Classical drive theories failed to explain the motivation for play, even when postulating a special drive for it (Hall, 1904). Modern theories pay more attention to intrinsic sources of motivation and stress the cognitive processes involved in play.

We have made an attempt to go one step further and to explore how far we could conceptualize the biological meaning of play from the point of view of fundamental adaptive processes. The essence of cognition is to increase the degree of knowledge of objects and events around us and in us, that is, to alter the degree of novelty (McCall & Kagan, 1967), incongruity (Hunt, 1966), or uncertainty (Musinger & Kessen, 1964). Cognitive processes represent, therefore, a movement from "unknown" to "known." However, those who study this movement agree that it should not exceed certain optimal limits. Too much novelty, incongruity, or uncertainty elicits fear or stress, while too little appears to result in boredom.

According to our assumption (Papousek & Papousek, 1977b), there are two strategies involved in the fundamental adaptive processes that direct the movement from unknown to known (see Figure 7.8). One tends to integrate available information into a complete and closed concept of an unknown incongruent event. This strategy utilizes different forms of learning and acquisition of skills, and it corresponds to the trivial goals of formal education. The other strategy works in the opposite direction as soon as the first strategy reaches its aim, and it tends to open the seemingly complete concepts, to view the already known events from nontraditional aspects, to bring them into unexpected new relations, simply to make the "known" more "unknown" again. This second strategy is included in play, and is also essential for the creative arts and for humor.

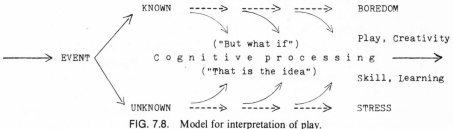

FIG. 7.8.   Model for interpretation of play.

As a matter of fact, both strategies seem to complement each other, leading to higher and higher levels of knowledge. The first one protects the organism against stress from too much uncertainty or the inability to solve problems, whereas the second one helps to avoid boredom.

According to this concept, play can only start at the point where a certain amount of integrated knowledge has already been accumulated. Thus, play can hardly be expected to function from the very beginning of postnatal life. It is interesting to see that parental behavior at that time, in fact, provides the infant with stimulation that may fully compensate for his lack of playful or creative activities. We shall describe some examples in the next section.

Infant-Adult Interaction: A Perfect Learning Situation

The theoretical concept of a fundamental adaptive response system appeared to be a particularly helpful tool when we turned our attention to the infant's social interactions to find out in which ways they might influence the development of learning and cognitive capacities in the infant.

The role of the mother in this respect has mostly been deduced from deprivation situations (see Lowrey, 1940; Goldfarb, 1945; or Spitz, 1945) concerning the effects of the absence of adequate caretakers. Less attention has been paid to the functions of maternal behavior that prove effective in supporting the infant's cognitive growth. As in the case of play, maternal love was categorized as a drive and thus left unexplained. or it was viewed by learning theories as a source of enriched stimulation and a set of rewards, before more autonomy and competence was ascribed to the infant and before the interactional character of his interplay with the adult was appreciated. The role of the infant in social interaction was simply underestimated for a long time. It was not until the 1960's that experimental research established evidence of learning in the newborn, enriching our understanding of the learning processes in infants (e.g., Reese & Lipsitt, 1970). Indeed, only in the last decade have more complex cognitive processes and their relation to social interactions become the subject of intensive study (Bruner, 1966; Lewis & Rosenblum, 1974; etc.).

From observations in animals we can learn more about the biological bases of parental behavior (Hinde, 1974) than we can learn from the observation of humans. At least we find there a description of typical parental behavior patterns and their triggering signals, or analyses of their regulation and consequences (e.g., Harlow & Harlow, 1969; Rosenblatt, 1975; Mason & Berkson, 1975). However, the repertoire is not extensive enough to allow conclusions on the main question raised here, namely, which functions of parental behavior are favorable for the infant's cognitive development.

Social interaction is now commonly interpreted as a chain of interlocking behavioral patterns that represent responses and simultaneously act as stimuli eliciting the next step in the interaction. Each element gains new dimensions resulting from its position in such a chain, but also from its preceding history in similar interactions and from the outcome of the cognitive processing of this element in the perceiving partner. In our opinion, two aspects require particular attention from the viewpoint of the infant: the degree of familiarity with such an element and the contingency of that element of the infant's own activity.

According to all that we know about learning in the newborn, the fundamental processes for familiarization are functioning, although at this early age they still require many repetitions of the stimulation. Interestingly enough, when interacting with infants, parents tend to modify their behavior into repeated simple patterns: this is seen in all modalities. Such repeated patterns may have very different effects upon the infant. Sometimes they become merely repetitious; they may elicit expressions of pleasure due to recognition, although once they are too familiar, the response to them can decrease and become habituated. In other situations, the repetitions become signals for other rewarding events and function as conditioned signals. Finally, the repetitions may also depend on the infant's activity, and he may learn to operate them. The tendency of the parent to repeat simple behavioral patterns results in frequent learning situations or different types that are appropriate to the limited capacities of the infant.

Paying attention to the development of adaptive processes in the infant, we have to keep in mind that at the beginning of his life, it is mainly the adult who must adapt his or her behavior in favor of effective interaction. The adult may represent the main source of external stimulation at the beginning, and he or she mediates the infant's interaction with the rest of the environment, either by bringing different objects to the infant or bringing the infant to the more important objects, and by naming individual objects and explaining their meaning. As to the extent to which the adult can facilitate learning and cognitive processes in the infant it is, therefore, biologically relevant, e.g., whether the stimulation takes place at the optimal waking state and or whether it attracts the infant's attention. The adult's ability to allocate and time stimulation is particularly important during the first months after birth when the behavioral states change more frequently and irregularly.

Film analyses of mother–infant interactions showed us that the mother evaluates the infant's behavioral state, tries to maintain it at the optimal level, and makes decisions, based upon the infant's attention, as to whether to continue, modify, or stop her repetitious stimulation. She is seldom aware of her reasons for making these decisions, as we see from subsequent interviews, but while talking to the infant she often very distinctly reveals what cues she is using and how she evaluates them. Surprisingly, she often uses the same criteria we have been recording as indirect evidence of the functions involved in the fundamental system of adaptive responses in the infant: the state of the eyes, muscle tone, the position and activity of the infant's hands, his facial expression, the type of vocalization, and the level of visual attention. Thus, in film records, the mother may be seen touching the infant's hands; trying to open the closed fists; trying to elicit the grasping reflex; touching the chin and testing how easily she can open the infant's mouth; touching the lips, which eventually elicits signs of hunger; and lifting his legs. These signs are familiar to those who study behavioral states in infants. We ourselves chose some of them as criteria for distinguishing four levels of waking (Papousek, 1961a, 1969).

Visual contact is a particularly important cue in the infant's interaction. Unlike other mammals, direct eye-to-eye contact is a powerful means of communication in man from the earliest age. We described a series of behavioral patterns in the mother that help to achieve and maintain mutual visual contact, for example, behaviors that adjust for the newborn's capacity to focus and convergence only within the limited distance of 20–25 cm (Papousek & Papousek, 1975, 1976a). Visual contact is also a basic mechanism of orientation and thus indicates what the infant pays attention to or what he wants to avoid. Here is an important cue to which the mother very distinctly responds in the first months after delivery. For instance, she changes her repetitive behavioral patterns to regain the infant's attention if he stops looking at her, or she checks his general behavioral state and interrupts her stimulation if the infant seems to be sleepy.

Our experience thus indicates that the infant's visual contact is an important means of feeding back information to the mother, telling her whether her mothering has been performed at the right time and in the proper way.

Facial expression and vocalization are further powerful cues for eliciting adult attention. Let us consider, for example, the role of signs of pleasure. As we explained in the preceding sections of this communication, in cognitive terms the infant obtains two sources of pleasure in social interactions that elicit smiling and joyful vocalization. Firstly, it is the familiarization with repeated stimulation, particularly that offered by the behavior of his parents or caretakers. Secondly, it is successfully learning how to bring about a relevant contingent event through his own activity. Signs of pleasure in the infant may thus first appear as responses caused by fulfillment of his prediction that an event is going to be repeated or, in other cases, that his own activity will elicit a relevant event. At the same time, of course, those signs of pleasure also function as stimuli eliciting changes in the mother's behavior. Therefore, we see that the role of smiling becomes very complex and can hardly be understood without insight into its initial postnatal development.

Two more important factors of the infant cognitive growth resulting from forms of parental responses to the infant's behavior have attracted our attention: the playful character in the repetition of stimulation and imitation of the infant's behavior.

We mentioned in the preceding section that playful processing of information can be expected only after a certain amount of integrated experience has already been accumulated. However, in successful forms of parental interactions, we often see that parents themselves compensate for an initial inability on the part of the infant. They repeat simple behavioral patterns first and then add new surprising elements or modify their repetitious behavior in other ways as soon as the behavior pattern becomes so familiar that it stops eliciting enough attention, that is, when it starts to become boring. Thus, the infant repeatedly learns to recognize the performed event and, at the same time, to expect a new surprising change that again increases the attractivity of that event. In fact, he may really be learning how to prevent boredom, and later he may find that the same behaviors also lead to better knowledge. This assumption may seem too speculative, but in fact it is based on empirical analyses of parental behavior in families of infants who showed an increased capacity for inventive modifications of repetitious activities or repetitious vocalization in particular. Such an infant, when following a repetitious stimulation performed to him by his parent, smiles after a certain number of repetitions and then, as if having picked up signs of a coming change—such as a longer pause or a slight frowning in the parental face—stops moving and shows very intensive attention, often combined with a wide open mouth resembling the play face. In the second half year of life, he may then respond to the predicted surprise with a burst of laughter.

The parent's tendency to imitate the infant's facial expressions, vocalizations, and movements may also play a more important role than commonly assumed. From the beginning of life, the infant is offered what we call a "biological mirror" by his parents, the mother in particular (Papousek & Papousek, 1977a). On the one hand, he has a chance to associate his interoceptive information about his own movements with their visual representation, particularly when he produces sounds that his mother imitates. These may be the first steps leading to the later development of self-awareness as well as to the development of intellectual processes. The connection between imitation, play, and intelligence in the child was stressed by Piaget (1951).

More examples could be given confirming the significance of fundamental adaptive responses in social interaction, and many more are still to be discovered and elucidated. At present, we can conclude that the social interaction between the infant and his adult caretaker consists of a great number of natural learning situations in which not only the acquisition of a new skill, but—equally important—the course and outcomes of the fundamental adaptive processes in the infant play a major role. Above all, these processes elicit meaningful responses in the adult that represent crucial components in the interaction. In addition to that, they provide the adult with feedback information, helping him to allocate and time his stimulation in an optimal way, and they also represent elements of nonverbal communication between both partners. All of these aspects facilitate and accentuate the processes of learning and cognition in the infant. Although we can still only guess as to how relevant this is with respect to longitudinal consequences, we believe that a better understanding of the functions underlying the early regulation of behavior requires further analysis and verification of the individual aspect of responses described by us as the fundamental adaptive system.

ACKNOWLEDGMENTS

The preparation of this report was kindly supported by grants from the Deutsche Forschungsgemeinschaft (Pa 208/1) and from the Stifterverband für die Deutsche Wissenschaft. We also owe special thanks to Prof. Victor H. Denenberg for his criticism and important suggestions as well as to Anne Fernald for her helpful assistance during the preparation of this manuscript.

DISCUSSION

Dr. Watson: How long were the mothers' eyes closed?

Dr. Papousek: Two minutes. That's our experimental situation.

Dr. Watson: Does the mother in the eyes-closed situation keep interacting?

Dr. Papousek: It is very difficult for her to maintain behavior fully comparable with her baseline responsiveness. But no matter how she may change her behavior, the question is how the infant responds to her abnormal behavior.

Dr. Watson: My question has to do with whether or not it was specifically the loss of the sight of the mother's eyes, which it might well be, or whether it's the fact that when closing her eyes the mother goes out of phase with the baby because she hasn't seen the cues that guide her interactions. Thus she begins to move what essentially becomes noncontingent presentation of her voice.

Dr. Papousek: Exactly.

Dr. Watson: That could be a variable without the eyes getting involved.

Dr. Papousek: The mother's closed eyes may not be the crucial variable, but they were an easy way to make the mother's behavior discrepant from the infant's expectance. The crucial variable is the discrepancy between how the mother really behaves and how the infant expects her to behave.

Dr. Stern: I'm curious if you would speculate on affect or affective drives as they relate to these cognitive processes. The cognitive processes certainly do get triggered by events, as you mentioned, but once again the payoff is always either some affective response, either the "aha" or just pleasure or getting away from something. My question is, how you might bring affect back to the model. I don't know how to do it, and I'm wondering what your thoughts are about it, or why you stayed away from attempting it.

Dr. Papousek: I have already mentioned how one could conceptualize affective behavior in relation to a cognitive drive if we still felt like using the concepts of drives. We could, of course, also draw flowcharts and interpret the same aspects from the point of view of cybernetic simulation models of social interaction or from the point of view of system theories. In fact, our models are primarily derived from simple learning situations in which affective responses appeared independently of social interaction, and for which the models presented allowed the best theoretical interpretation. The generality of our models may be another question. We cannot do any comparative studies; we have observed only human babies and have good reasons to stick to this early age.

Dr. Korner: I wonder in studying your babies whether you found any self-consistent individual differences in the infants' tendencies to preferentially use increasing or decreasing mechanisms. If you found such self-consistent tendencies among your infants, you would have a beautiful base for studying the analog for the development of all sorts of characterological differences, particularly in the area of preferred coping strategies and the choice of future defense mechanisms.

Dr. Papousek: That's the right question to ask. This is how we came to our problems. My former co-worker and the most experienced psychologist in our group, Janos, designed most of his studies for the purpose of the analysis of individual differences. One step was to differentiate age differences from the other differences. We did a lot of studies of that kind. The next step was to try to understand what else could have contributed to the individual differences. We analyzed all possible aspects: the seasons of the year, the somatic development of the baby, the caloric intake of the baby, sexual differences. Partly we saw a little evidence but most of these factors appeared to be ineffective. Then we paid attention to differences in the degree of activation or inactivation in the fundamental adaptive responses. You can evaluate them more easily in newborns where most adaptive processes occur slowly, like in a slow-motion film. However, it is impossible to evaluate such individual differences with any simple parameters. We may come to some more operational criteria if we first learn enough about the most relevant fundamental responses. Then we could perhaps measure individual variability in them as well.

Dr. Barnard: I'd like to go back to slides—when the baby was looking at the mother and the mother was looking at the baby talking versus when she closed her eyes. There seemed to me to be symmetry of posturing and tone in the baby's arms when the baby was looking at the mother with the eyes opened, and then as the baby became more distressed in the eyes-closed condition there was more asymmetry both in posturing and in tone. Even asymmetry in the fingering. Is this a phenomenon you've noticed often?

Dr. Papousek: You may have noticed on that diagram of hand positions in different behavioral states (Papousek & Papousek, 1977a) that there was more asymmetry to be seen in fully waking babies. Similarly there would be a lot of asymmetry in crying babies. On the other hand, more symmetry appears in the states of transition to sleep when the muscle tone gradually decreases. You are right as to the fully waking baby. His hands are more or less in a symmetric position, but he may communicate with the mother with very different and asymmetrical movements of fingers.

Dr. Denenberg: There are a couple of things which I find very exciting about today's papers and the others I've been reading. First, we're viewing the infant in a biological–ethological context, and this is something most researchers have not done before. In the studies of learning, for example, we're talking about such things as milk, human voices, and picking the baby up. We're using stimuli that are part of what the baby normally experiences and that are necessary for its survival. Getting to Dan's point, when these kinds of stimuli are used, they seem to be pleasurable, as indicated by the baby's vocal response and facial expression. And of course what an infant has to do in order for it to survive is to signal information back to the caregiver, and therefore the infant's emotional response going back to the caregiver— particularly the mother—now closes that loop. And this leads us into tommorrow's discussion, where I will talk about general systems theory. None of us now is talking about conditioning and learning in the simplistic S–R model. I think we've got to talk about learning and other behaviors in the context of biological adaptation, and in the context of feeding back information to an adult caregiver for purposes of keeping the system of the mother and the infant integrated for the survival of the infant. This is what I find extremely exciting about what's taking place at this conference.

Dr. Stern: When we go back to what is observed, we observe a stimulus event, then we postulate a variety of cognitive processes, such as stimulus–schema matching. Then the next thing that we really see is an affect. That's why I'm asking you, Why is it that we talk about cognitive processes without talking about affect, which is in fact the only observable result of an assumed process?

Dr. Papousek: You raise a whole set of questions. One concerns the preceding paper of Rita Eisenberg as well. Is there a prepotency in some signals? Or, do some signals gain an extra effectiveness due to familiarization if applied repeatedly, or perhaps due to contingency on the infant's behavior? To answer such questions we have to know enough about the preceding history of the stimulus and examine the role of every stimulus in the structure of the whole stimulational situation.

This is particularly true about affective responses to social stimuli. Does the infant smile because of some prepotency of the human face and voice, or does he smile because a particular social stimulation has been repeated, has become familiar and predictable, so that the smile is now elicited by the fulfillment of the infant's prediction? To answer this question you have to observe the neonate from the very beginning of life. Once the mother's face has become familiar to him, it is too late to analyze why he smiles. The infant may soon associate the first pleasant experience with other conditioning signals and the determination of smiles becomes too complex. Observing parent–infant interaction, we see for sure that parents do everything possible to make themselves more predictable. Look at the mother during interaction. She stimulates her baby in quite specific ways, repeats simple patterns in a special rhythm, whether by tactile stimulation, visual stimulation, or speech, but mostly in combinations of modalities. When doing so, she keeps observing her baby and adjusting the duration, gradation, rhythm, and melody to the infant's capacity to attend her stimulation.

Or take the puzzle of imitation and the sense for identity. If we look at the very beginning we see that it is the mother who imitates first and from the first day after delivery. It may well be that the baby first learns that a part of its behavior regularly elicits a particular behavioral pattern in its mother. No matter how capable the baby is to sense identity, it may learn in an operant way how to manipulate maternal behavior, and the baby may enjoy this capacity without knowing that they both do the same thing.

Dr. Mason: It seems to me that in the animals I've worked with imitation is very selective. The sight of another individual engaging in activities involving mouth-and-food has a very compelling effect. There is a strong tendency to watch and to show similar behavior; perhaps social facilitation is a better term than imitation to describe the effect. In any event, you see it in animals in virtually their first opportunity to interact with each other socially. And yet there are other responses that are seemingly quite simple and clearly in the individual's repertoire that are not nearly as susceptible to social influences. In fact, you would have to engage in some very intensive training to get anything that you would be willing to call social facilitation or imitation. The belief that monkeys and apes will imitate almost any response simply is not true. There are some things that they will mimic readily, and others—sticking out the tongue, for example, which is certainly an available response, easy to perform—that are difficult to produce through social facilitation.

Dr. Eisenberg: We've noticed on our video films a great deal of spontaneous tongue thrusting among newborns babies in the absence of any particular stimulus to thrust out the tongue. Have you done this type of experiment with the baby not in such a wakeful state, say it was in doze?

Dr. Papousek: No, only wakeful infants have been observed in this experiment.

Dr. Eisenberg: I must confess I am very stuck by the amount of spontaneous tongue thrusting we are seeing in our current study with newborns. I don't recall anything approaching this high incidence in our earlier work and am not sure what it relates to. It doesn't seem related to state, since we see it in all states, and whatever my biases, I'm hard put to explain it on the basis of our stimulus conditions. I wonder, however, whether it may not have to do with current patterns of infant feeding: that is, we now are dealing primarily with breast-fed babies where we formerly dealt primarily with bottle-fed ones, and it seems clear that breast-and bottle-fed babies differ from each other in a variety of ways. Moreover, some of our longitudinal observations suggest that these differences persist much longer than might be suspected.

Perhaps, to help me clarify my thinking, you could get into the state question in a little more detail. Have you done experiments different from that shown in your film, where the baby was wide awake? Specifically, have you investigated the baby behavior when it was in doze or when it was awake, but not alert?

Dr. Papousek: Sometime around 1959 I wrote a short paper on stereotypic head movements related to change in behavioral state. By chance, we saw during extinction of conditioned responses that in some infants the former conditioning signals now acted as inhibitory signals eliciting drowsiness with stereotypic head turning. That alarmed us, since such head movements are known to signal hospitalism. However, most careful observation revealed no similar signs outside the laboratory. There is, therefore, some evidence in our data that a lower level of wakefulness may be related to another level of coordination in motor responses leading to more frequent stereotypic responses.

Dr. Eisenberg: My interest relates to a question previously raised about symmetry, because one of the things we've been noticing in our video records is that there are a great many asymmetrical response behaviors. For instance, when babies in doze states open their eyes responsively, most often only one eye will open while the other remains closed: and when they widen their eyes in waking states, one eye tends to open more widely than the other. I don't know whether this is partly a state-related phenomenon, though I think it must be; and I don't know how far it would extend in age or to another situation. I am wodering, therefore, whether you have seen anything similar in your more challenging situation where the baby continues to get stimuli whether or not he's responding or interacting in any way.

Dr. Watson: If you set up a specific rule for some instrumental behavior of an infant and he learns it, then rather than shifting the rule as you did in some of your earlier experiments, what if you kept the rule constant and watched behavior carefully. Would you see a shift from a stereotypic pattern to some novel behavior? Could you see some kind of behavioral variance introduced that would be evidence of that "creative shift" in the infant's reactions to specific instrumental situations?

Dr. Papousek: I hope so, although we have to be very cautious in regard to as broad a category as play. We have to do many a priori decisions to eliminate what does not concern infants. And we have no criteria to tell when the infant does or does not play. In "Animal Behavior," Hinde (1970) quotes a list of behavioral parameters characterizing animal play. Hooff (1962) describes a typical "play face." Piaget (1951) discusses the proportions of accommodation and assimilation in play. However, no such criteria help us to decide whether a younger infant plays or not. Therefore, we tried hard to derive some ideas on the most fundamental steps in behavioral regulation that might have something to do with the essence of play. Observations of infants inspired us as much as our logic and introspective speculations. We are presenting our model, but we are aware that it is going to be a long and very difficult way to an experimental analysis of its validity. As we have already suggested in our paper, I think that at the beginning, parents show the infant how to play with things. They repeat some stimulation, make it familiar, and then they modify it. This has often reminded me of what Bach does with us adults so well. He presents a melody, repeats it, then just at the moment when the melody becomes predictable he varies something in it, and this something gives us a real kick.

Mrs. Wishart: Dunkeld and Meltzoff's studies of imitation were, I think, in a more controlled setting than Maratos's. "Imitation" of the kind you describe in fact would seem to come later in infancy. It seems that the baby does the initial imitating and then later turns to preferring the mother to imitate. It starts off with the baby in fact doing the imitating, but later he likes to get the mother to imitate him. It becomes a social game for him. I haven't seen your film of imitation, but you said there was one period and then there was a natural break and the mother was told not to initiate the first response. What actually happened in the very first period? Was there no imitation in this first period of the mother by the baby?

Dr. Papousek: Well that was exactly what everyone would otherwise call an imitation. The mother stuck out her tongue, and the baby responded in a similar way. But of course we knew in that case what preceded, that is, that the mother imitated the baby from the very beginning.

Mrs. Wishart: How old was this baby?

Dr. Papousek: Two months.

Mrs. Wishart: We've seen it in 6-day-old babies and it's difficult to believe...

Dr. Papousek: And I say that from the first day the mother imitates the things that the newborn baby carries out for the first time.

Mrs. Wishart: Some of the behaviors are so specific. It's difficult to believe, for instance, that the mother can have already conditioned the baby to respond to finger wiggling.

Dr. Papousek: I think that is the next step. By then, a lot of learning has been involved, and it is difficult to detect eliciting factors. But as to the imitation of hand movements, here the infant can already compare the outcomes; he sees both his and the mother's hands. Similarly, he can compare the identity of outcomes in imitated vocalization. Such cases are different from those where oral responses are involved, as at the very beginning of life.

Mrs. Wishart: As I say, we looked at the development of imitation. The baby's imitation of the mother seemed to stop after a certain period, and then in fact we got the opposite pattern, the mother imitating the baby. This presumably also happens in the early period but was not initiated by the baby. In the second period, however, you don't get the imitation by the baby of the mother's activities. It takes time for them to learn the social implications of getting the mother to respond back with imitation. I really do believe that they imitate the mother rather than vice-versa at the beginning.

Dr. Papousek: I don't think that we know the solution. I don't know any study; we haven't yet done any study to confirm that either. I'm just offering another alternative that does not pre-assume any mystic capacities of the infant. The necessary step is now to take all alternatives into consideration and do studies that will look at imitation from the very beginning; what I know for sure is that the mother does imitate before the baby starts imitating. She imitates the very first things that the baby does for the first time.

Mrs. Wishart: And you think operant learning can account for all behaviors? The very first appearance of a baby imitating, for instance, this sort of movement? I woudn't have thought very many babies spontaneously make this sort of movement for the mother to imitate.

Dr. Papousek: At what age with the fingers?

Mrs. Wishart: With the fingers, I'm not sure. Certainly we've seen imitation of tongue protrusion very clearly at 6 days.

Dr. Papousek: That is something else. The coordination of oral activity comes very early. Operant conditioning would probably occur there much earlier than in hand movements. If you know how much some babies do with their hands and fingers during the periods of wakefulness, particularly during social interaction, you realize how difficult it is to say what is imitation and what is not. Even if you eliminate visual control in both partners, you will get a lot of similarity in finger movements, I guess.

Dr. Watson: In the studies of imitation by Jane Dunkeld at Edinburgh and by Moore and Meltzoff at Oxford, they had crosscontrol comparison groups for all the stimuli. When they did tonguing, mouth opening, head nodding, or hand opening, they assessed all those behaviors under each of those stimulus conditions. The disproportionate feedback, as it were, by the baby of doing what was done was found for all the input signals. That being so, then an explanation of this as chance rate hits doesn't hold.

Dr. Kennell: They also videotaped the adult who was sticking his tongue out and eliminated any situation where there was any reinforcement. We see it at a day or two in such situations where the baby may not have been to the mother. Of course, there may have been someone else.

Mrs. Wishart: I'm sure you can get them on brand new babies. I believe Meltzoff has good evidence of imitation of tongue protrusion at 17 minutes and 1 hour, but we haven't yet had the opportunity to verify that in our own lab.

Dr. Lipsitt: This so-called imitative behavior has been described and has been replicated in two fairly well controlled studies so that we have to assume that it exists. I don't know exactly how early it exists. There are anecdotal reports of it existing very early. More importantly, we don't know what its etiology is. We don't know what the ontogeny of this behavior is. There is an interpretive problem with the data rather than with whether it exists or not.

Dr. Papousek: There's no doubt that it exists. We have very good evidence for imitation. I'm just thinking of the very beginning.

Dr. Lipsitt: I'm sure it's observable that mothers do engage in imitative behavior with their infants even in the very first day. That is, when the baby opens its eyes and looks at the mother, the mother herself widens her eyes. When the baby opens its mouth, and it's very much on the first day of life like it is when mothers can be observed feeding their babies with a spoon. As the baby opens its mouth, the mother also opens her mouth. And it goes on from the earliest moments of the infant's life, so there is the opportunity for learning processes to occur, such that this behavior that is documentable at 6 weeks or 6 days of age is actually a learning phenomenon. I think that the appropriate studies have yet to be done of who's doing what to whom and who's paying for it.

Dr. Mason: I'm still curious as to what sort of limits there are on this sort of behavior. I don't know this literature. What is happening, specifically? Is it a matter of sticking out the tongue and waving fingers and that's it, or what? I take it that there are a number of different responses, mostly involving the face.

Dr. Kennell: They're all motions that a baby would do naturally.

Dr. Stern: I think that from an ethological point of view these imitated behaviors are prepotent, and I wonder to what extent we are talking about some kind of releasing phenomenon, at least from the infant's point of view. I don't question the mother is imitating. There is something quite striking about mouth opening and tongue thrusting. We showed to mothers films of them interacting with their infants and asked them when the baby appeared to be the highest from the point of view of excitement and positive affect. It turned out to be not when the baby was smiling, but when the baby threw his head up and back, opened his mouth, and thrust out his tongue. This was the highest point. If any two adults in this room get their faces within 19 cm and one of them throws his head back, opens his mouth and thrusts out his tongue, it would elicit an extremely potent emotional experience. I think there's some ethological prepotency in these behaviors, and this aspect of the problem should be considered also in the experimental design.

Dr. Mason: That's essentially what I meant by selectivity. The young organism is disposed to imitate some behaviors and not others. For example, freshly hatched chicks will peck green corn, if they see a crude model pecking the corn; the tendency to imitate in this case seems to be independent of any prior social experience. We know very little actually about the parameters that the model is able to control. Does it influence the actual rate of pecking? How close is the degree of matching between subject and model? Suppose you made a really wierd kind of facial expression that a baby might make now and then but had no particular social relevance: would it imitate that?

Dr. Eisenberg: Probably not.

Dr. Yarrow: But if it means something to the baby in relation to the feeling that he is mastering the environment or controlling the environment, it wouldn't matter what kind of response that he was getting. It seems to me that you did emphasize this aspect too, and other people have talked about mutual visual regard in the context of mutual visual regards being a baby's first experience in learning to control his environment.

Dr. Parmelee: The idea of being born with some predisposition to contingent responding is a very fascinating idea to me. I wonder if the ability of the baby to respond to patterned sound, such as speech, is in anticipation of the probability that these patterned sounds will occur in much contingent situations than unpatterned noise or sine waves. In all of the discussions everybody seemed to dance round the problem of motivation. Pleasure seems to be not quite acceptable because it is ill defined. At least, this is the way I heard the discussions. To be born with the ability to see the third dimension seems to me to add a powerful capacity to get some understanding of the environment very early. I would like to hear Dr. Wishart talk about contingency as a way of advancing the understanding of object concept. For me, it's easier to think of object awareness, object constancy, object permanence, and finally object concept as the order of development.

REFERENCES

Blurton Jones, N. G. An ethological study of some aspects of social behavior of children in nursery schools. In D. Morris (Ed.), *Primate ethology*. London: Weidenfeld & Nicolson, 1967.

Bower, T. G. R. *Development in infancy*. San Francisco: Freeman, 1974.

Bruner, J. S. Going beyond the information given. In H. E. Gruber, G. Terrell & M. Wertheimer, *Contemporary approaches to cognition.* Cambridge, Massachusetts: Harvard University Press, 1957.

Bruner, J. S., Olver, R. R., & Greenfield, P. M. (Eds.) *Studies in cognitive growth.* New York: Wiley, 1966.

Fields, P. E. Studies in concept formation. I. The development of the concept of triangularity in the white rat. *Comparative Psychological Monograph.* 1932, *9*, No 2.

Gibson, E. J. *Principles of perceptual learning and development.* New York: Appleton-Century-Crofts, 1969.

Goldfarb, W. Effects of psychological deprivation in infancy and subsequent stimulation. *American Journal of Psychiatry*, *102*, 18–33.

Hall, S. G. *Adolescence.* New York: Appleton, 1904.

Harlow, H. F., & Harlow, M. K. Effects of various mother–infant relationships on rhesus monkey behavior. In B. M. Foss (Ed.), *Determinants of infant behavior* (Vol. 4). London: Methuen, 1969.

Hebb, D. O. *The organization of behavior.* New York: Wiley, 1949.

Herrnstein, R. J., & Loveland, D. H. Complex visual concept in the pigeon. *Science*, 1964, *146*, 549–551.

Hinde, R. A. *Animal behavior* (2nd ed.) London: McGraw-Hill, 1970.

Hinde, R. A. *Biological bases of human social behavior.* New York: McGraw—Hill, 1974.

Hooff, van, J. A. R. A. M. Facial expressions in higher primates. *Symposia of the Zoological Society London.*, 1962, *8*, 97–125.

Huizinga, J. *Homo ludens. Vom Ursprung der Kultur im Spiel.* Hamburg: Rainbek, 1962.

Hunt, J. McV. The epigenesis of intrinsic motivation and early cognitive learning. In R. N. Haber (Ed.), *Current research in motivation.* New York: Holt, Rinehart, and Winston, 1966.

Koch, J. Conditioned orienting reactions to persons and things in 2-5-month-old infants. *Human Development*, 1968, *11*, 81–91.

Krasnogorskij, N. I. *Higher nervous activity in the child.* (Russian). Leningrad: Medgiz, 1958.

Lewis, M., & Rosenblum, L. A. (Eds.). *The effect of the infant on his caregiver.* New York: Wiley, 1974.

Lowrey, L. G. Personality distortion and early institutional care. *American Journal of Orthopsychiatry*, 1940, 10, 576–586.

Mason, W. A., & Berkson, G. Effects of maternal mobility on the development of rocking and other behaviors in the rhesus monkeys: A study with artificial mothers. *Developmental Psychobiology*, 1975, 197–211.

McCall, R. B., & Kagan, J. Attention in the infant: Effects of complexity, contour, perimeter, and familiarity. *Child Development*, 1967, *38*, 939–952.

Miller, G. A., Galanter, E., & Pribram, K. H. *Plans and the structure of behavior.* New York: Holt, 1960.

Munsinger, H., & Kessen, W. Uncertainty, structure, and preference. *Psychological Monographs*, 1964, *78*, No. 9.

Papousek, H. Conditioned appetitional responses in infants. (Czech). *Thomayer's Collection*, 409. Prague:

Papousek, H. 1961. (a) A physiological view of early ontogenesis of so-called voluntary movements. Plzensky lekarsky sbornik Supplementum 1961, *3*, 195–198.

Papousek, H. Experimental studies of appetitional behavior in human newborns and infants. In Stevenson, H. W., Hess, E. H. & Rheingold, H. L. (Eds.) *Early behavior: Comparative and developmental approaches.* New York: Wiley, 1967.

Papousek, H. Individual variability in learned responses in human infants. In R. J. Robinson (Ed.), *Brain and early behavior.* London: Academic Press, 1969.

Papousek, H., & Bernstein, P. The functions of conditioning stimulation in human neonates and infants. In A. Ambrose (Ed.) *Stimulation in early infancy.* London: Academic Press, 1969.

Papousek, H., & Papousek, M. Mirror image and self-recognition in young human infants: I. A new method of experimental analysis. *Developmental Psychobiology*, 1974, *7*, 149E157.

Papousek, H., & Papousek, M. Cognitive aspects of preverbal social interaction between human infants and adults. In M. O'Connor (Ed.), *Parent-infant-interaction.* Amsterdam: Elsevier, 1975.

Papousek, H., & Papousek, M. Mothering and the cognitive head-start: Psychobiological considerations. In H. R. Schaffer (Ed.), *Studies in mother-infant interaction.* The Loch Lomond Symposium. London: Academic Press, 1977. (a)

Papousek, H., & Papousek, M. Das Spiel in der Frühentwicklung des Kindes. *Supplementum Pädiatrische Praxis*, 1977, *18*, 17–32. (b)

Pavlov, I. P. *Sämtliche Werke. III/2.* Berlin: Akademie-Verlag, 1953.

Piaget, J. *Play, dreams and imitation in childhood.* London: Heinemann, 1951.

Piaget, J. *Origins of intelligence.* New York: Basic Books, 1954.

Reese, H. W., & Lipsitt, L. P. *Experimental child psychology.* New York, London: Academic Press, 1970.

Rosenblatt, J. S. Prepartum and postpartum regulation of maternal behavior in the rat. In M. O'Connor (Ed.), *Parent-infant interaction.* Amsterdam: Elsevier, 1975.

Sameroff, A. J. Can conditioned responses be established in the newborn infant: 1971? *Developmental Psychology*, 1971, *5*, 1–12.

Shannon, C., & Weaver, W. *The mathematical theory of communication.* Urbana: University of Illinois Press, 1949.

Sokolov, E. N. *Perception and the conditioned reflex.* Oxford: Pergamon Press, 1963.

Spitz, R. A. Hospitalization: An inquiry into the genesis of psychiatric conditions in early childhood. *Psychoanalytical Study of the Child, International Universities Press Inc. 1945, 1*, 53–74.

Thom, R. *Structured stability and morphogenesis.* Reading: Addison-Wesley, 1975.

Tolman, E. C., Ritchie, B. F., & Kalish, D. Studies in spatial learning: II. Place learning versus response learning. *Journal of Experimental Psychology*, 1946, *36*, 221–229.

Volkova, V. D. On some problems in the acquisition of conditioned responses to verbal signals. Dissertation, University of Leningrad. Leningrad, USSR, 1954.

8 Procedures For Studying Parent–Infant Interaction: A Critique

Leon J. Yarrow
National Institute of Child Health and Human Development

Barbara J. Anderson
St. Louis Children's Hospital

Our research findings are always intimately bound up with our research methods, especially our procedures for data collection and our techniques of analysis. We have made great progress in methods for studying parent–infant interaction in the past twenty years. Our knowledge of parent–infant relationships is no longer derived exclusively from interviews; we have been moving increasingly toward direct observation as a replacement for the interview or as a supplement. Despite the changes in technique and dramatic advances in technology for observing parent–infant interaction, we have as yet no systematic rationale for our methods of observation. Techniques for observing parents and infants have been developed, for the most part, without clear articulation of the guidelines. There has been little conceptual basis for the choice of categories or for the specific techniques used to collect data. At times, the observational techniques and categories have been dictated by the specific objectives of a study, sometimes they have been loosely tied to the conceptual framework of an individual investigator. Most frequently, the categories seem to "emerge" out of a particular investigator's general awareness of frequently occurring parent and infant behaviors. The many variations in methods for observing and recording behaviors seem almost randomly determined. This unsystematic approach to observation of parent–infant interaction has a number of obvious deficiencies. Although there are no simple solutions, perhaps recognizing the issues will help in eventually dealing with the problems.

In this paper we shall focus our discussion, limiting it to a critical analysis of methods for observing parents and infants in the home. Within this framework, we shall consider three basic issues: the choice of settings or contexts for observing parent and infant behavior, the selection of categories for indexing parent-infant interaction, and the choice of strategies for sampling behaviors and recording interaction. Decisions about contexts, categories and strategies are interrelated. We are distinguishing them only for purposes of exposition. The issues seem basically simple, but they are fundamental; perhaps because of their apparent simplicity they have not been given serious attention. Some of these considerations are not unique to assessing parent-infant interaction; many are larger methodological problems of observational research. This critique is intended to heighten awareness of these issues; we shall attempt simply to summarize our basic concerns and to suggest some areas in need of further methodological investigation.

CONTEXTS IN WHICH INTERACTIONS OCCUR

The behaviors of parents and infants are very much influenced by the physical, the cultural, and the interpersonal contexts in which they are observed (Thomas & Martin, 1976). They are also influenced by another type of context, the child's temperament and his changing states (Korner, 1974). Yet research on parent-infant interaction has not systematically controlled for the influence of environmental contexts or infant states. Studies of parent-infant interaction have been carried out in a variety of contexts, sometimes in the familiar surroundings of the home (the natural setting), sometimes in the unfamiliar laboratory environment, and sometimes in a laboratory setting designed to approximate the home (naturalistic setting).[1]

The contexts differ in a number of important ways. They differ in relative familiarity and thus may influence the spontaneity of infant's and mother's behavior; the differences in degree of structure influence the extent to which the behavior of mother and infant is regulated.

In the natural setting, even when there are no obvious attempts to elicit any particular behavior, there are many subtle ways in which the interaction may be influenced. The mere presence of the observer has effects which are difficult to define precisely. Some parents, for example, are not capable of being spontaneous when observed, whereas others may adapt readily to the presence of an observer; some parents are stimulated to be more active with the infant while others may be greatly inhibited.

Certainly the ways in which the observer defines the purpose of the observation and the extent to which he emphasizes his interest in the parent or the infant will influence parental behavior. The constraints placed on parental behavior may vary from simply asking them to remain in the room and

---

[1] *Natural* and *naturalistic* have often been used interchangeably. We think it is important to distinguish between the home and situations approximating the home.

interact "normally" to asking the parent to feed or play with the infant. The latter may not be essentially different from a procedure that attempts to measure curiosity by using a "highly structured" situation in the laboratory in which, for example, the parent is asked to attract the infant's attention to an object. Clearly there is a wide range in the degree of structure that may be imposed. We do not know how these varying degrees of structure may distort or mask typical parent–infant exchanges.

The effects of the situation on interaction have generally been ignored. Most studies in the home observe behavior in multiple situations, during feeding, bathing, playing (Lewis, 1972; Moss, 1967; Yarrow, Rubenstein & Pedersen, 1975). Frequently, we do not know whether comparable situations have been observed for all families in a given study or whether there is any comparability between studies in the situations observed. Other studies deliberately focus on only one or two situations (Brody, 1956; Brown et al., 1975). We have neither controlled for the influence of situational contexts nor often analyzed behaviors separately by context. It is likely that very different parent-infant behaviors are elicited in a feeding situation than a play situation. Beckwith, Cohen, and Parmelee (Note 1), who analyzed feeding and nonfeeding separately as contexts for maternal and infant behavior, found strong situational effects. According to these investigators, "To have assessed mother-infant transactions in only one context—either feeding or non-feeding—would have resulted in misleading conclusions [p. 12]." There are many dimensions on which situations may differ: in the constraints placed on behavior, in their psychological meaning to the parent, and in the implicit goals of interaction. We need more data on how these situational differences affect parent and infant behavior in order to control and account for them in designing observational studies.

A second influence that has largely been ignored is the parent's personal definition of the observation situation. The parent's perception of an unstructured observation in the home is difficult to evaluate. Most studies have not attempted to understand the parents' definition of the situation nor their expectations and biases. These idiosyncratic definitions and expectations are influenced by feelings of security about being observed as well as by a number of specific personality characteristics. In addition to the general interaction between parental characteristics and situations, we know that specific settings and situations have idiosyncratic meanings to different parent-infant dyads. Some situations, feeding, for example, may be conflict-ridden for particular parent-infant pairs, whereas for other dyads feeding may be a very pleasurable situation.

Another contextual influence on parent-infant interaction is the infant's state of consciousness as influenced by physiological variables such as degree of hunger or thirst and the time within the sleep-wake cycle (Brazelton, 1973). Infant state has recently received attention as an influence on the behavior of newborns and the performance of older infants in laboratory settings.

Although there is increasing agreement on observable criteria of state, for example, whether the infant is in deep sleep or is alert-awake (Korner, 1972), infant state has rarely been monitored as a potential influence on parent-infant interaction in the home. Korner (1974) has described several dimensions of infant state that affect the caregiver's behavior in the laboratory, such as, the distinctiveness or clarity with which the infant expresses state, the smooth gradations or abrupt transitions between states, the ease with which state is modified by parental stimulation or intervention. In an observational study in which infant state was carefully recorded concurrently with maternal and infant behavior, Thoman, Becker, and Freese (Note 2) clearly demonstrate how an infant who gave "mixed signals" regarding sleeping and waking states and who made rapid shifts from sleep to wakefulness elicited behavior from the mother that indicated she often misinterpreted infant sleep as wakefulness. Similarly, Brazelton (1962) has described the devastating effect on the mother-infant relationship of an infant who expressed only two states--deep sleep during which it was extremely difficult to arouse him with stimulation, and crying in which he was unresponsive to any maternal soothing.

In addition to the observations by Thoman et al. and by Brazelton on the early and continuing influence of deviations in state organization on dyadic interactions, Jones and Moss (1971) have shown that infant state affects the probability of maternal vocalizations to the infant as well as the infant's vocal activity. Yet we know very little about how accurately parents "read" different states and how these perceptions guide their choice of stimulation. Moreover, we have not assessed the meaning for the parent of different infant states, although we know that different interpretations of state will elicit quite different repertoires of parental behavior. Caudill (Note 3), studying 3-month-old infants and their mothers in Japan and in the United States, found cultural variations in response to infant state. He found that infant irritability and sleep states were *perceived* differently by Japanese and American mothers and elicited vastly different maternal responses. Thus, given what we know about the possible effects of state on the infant's level of responsiveness and on parental behavior, it seems important for observational studies to include infant states as contextual variables within which interactions of parent and infant are studied and to sample infant behavior in a variety of states.

BEHAVIORAL CATEGORIES TO INDEX INTERACTION

Clearly the choice of categories and the variables derived from these categories will significantly influence what one finds, yet there has not been systematic consideration given to the selection of categories and the choice of variables. This deficiency is partly a result of a lack of a comprehensive theory of parent-infant interaction. There are many hypotheses about early experience that emphasize certain variables, but there are no clear guidelines for the choice of behavioral categories to index these variables.

If we attempt to order the variables in studies on parent-infant interaction within some framework, we are impressed by the many theoretical frames of reference and the many different levels of inference reflected in the variables. There are categories for observation on the concrete level, describing simple behaviors that can be directly observed, for example, talking, touching, or holding the infant. Other variables cannot be directly observed, but can be derived from combinations of observable behaviors. For example, Yarrow et al. (1975) used a variable, "level of social stimulation," a composite measure that included providing opportunities for, and stimulating, the infant's visual attentiveness, encouraging the practice of motor skills, and engaging the infant in vigorous play. Other variables are on a much more inferential level; they are derived from a great number of cues, which the observer must organize and synthesize (Ainsworth & Bell, 1969). An example of a variable on this level is the degree to which the mother individualizes the child and is sensitive to his special likes and dislikes and unique characteristics (Yarrow, 1963). Maternal attitudes or feelings are difficult to infer from simple behavioral categories. Often we can assess such qualitative aspects of the relationship only through ratings made by observers after a long series of observations, sometimes the observations need to be supplemented by interviews.

A very fundamental limitation of our categories of observation and the variables derived from them is their unidirectional character. For some purposes, it may be sufficient to describe the experiences of the infant in unidirectional terms, to record the frequency with which the parent speaks to the infant. Such data may indicate that the infant receives a large amount of verbal stimulation. However, if one does not know whether the infant is listening attentively, babbling back to the parent, becoming excited or being soothed by the parent's verbalizations, one cannot legitimately assume that the intended stimulation is being registered by the child. For example, if we want to investigate the parent's influence on the infant's vocalizations, it is not sufficient to know that the adult talks a lot in the infant's presence. We also need to know whether the infant is attentive to the adult's speech. Moreover, it is important to know if the parent continues to speak when the infant is unresponsive, as well as how the parent responds when the infant is very attentive. Similarly, we cannot make inferences about the quality of the relationship unless we observe the behaviors of both infant and parent at the same time. We cannot simply assume that the parent who talks extensively to the infant is sensitive or responsive to him.

Our unidirectional categories cannot capture the reciprocal nature of the parent-infant relationship. They cannot adequately characterize an interaction in which the behavior of one person is conditional upon a response from the other and the other person's behavior is in turn influenced by the partner's response. To study parent-infant reciprocity, a systems orientation is necessary. Such an orientation characterizes interactions in terms of mutual regulation of *patterns* of behavior: "the behavior of any one individual in the interaction becomes a part of the cluster of behaviors which interacts with a cluster of behaviors from the other member of the dyad. No single behavior can be separated from the cluster for analysis without losing its meaning in the sequence" (Brazelton, Koslowski, & Main, 1974, pp. 55-56). The implication of this orientation for observational systems is that we must not only consider the behavior of one member of the parent-infant dyad in relationship to the behavior of the other, but that we must also look at configurations of behavior for both members of the dyad rather than at single categories.

To characterize parent and infant as a social system, we need a vocabulary to describe interactional processes. Presently we have categories for describing only the elements of the interaction. Our primary vocabulary consists of monadic categories that partial out the elements of the interactive process; because they do so, we lose any sense of the process or cyclical clustering to which Brazelton et al. (1974) refer. For instance, play may be elicited in response to the infant's initiation or it may be initiated by the parent. Certainly some level of response from the infant is required for the parent to maintain a playful interaction.

Some recent observational studies are attempting to shift from a monadic to a dyadic description of parent and infant behavior through the use of categories which describe contingent and co-occurring parent and infant behaviors. These approaches represent an advance in categorizing interactive behavior, but they also have limitations. Contingency codes such as "baby takes an object offered by mother" (Clarke-Stewart, 1973) and "mother responds verbally to infant's positive vocalizations" (Yarrow et al., 1975) have been used to describe short sequences of dyadic exchanges within a brief time interval. This type of contingency code preserves the sequence of at most two or three behaviors and does not distinguish behaviors that follow one another from overlapping or co-occurring behaviors. These codes, moreover, are restricted to descriptions of brief sequences of discrete behavioral acts; they provide no flexibility in characterizing the repertoire of maternal behaviors that may precede or follow an infant behavior. For example, a code such as "contingent response to infant distress" (Yarrow et al., 1975) gives no information about the variety of behaviors the mother shows in trying to soothe the infant nor of the variations in the infant's response.

A second type of dyadic category describes co-occurrences of parent and infant behaviors. Categories of co-occurrence have been used relatively infrequently, because of the difficulty in observing and recording behavior of parent and infant simultaneously except with film, videotape, or event or digital recording devices. Without these technologically advanced recording systems, the only category of co-occurring parent and infant behavior that has been frequently used is mutual visual regard. Eye-to-eye contact between parent and infant is considered one of the most important behavioral indicators of a positive relationship between parent and infant in the first months of life (Robson, 1967). Although categories of contingency and of co-occurring parent and infant behavior have been significant improvements over monadic categories, they are still limited to describing isolated elements of the total parent–infant exchange. More detailed information about the process of reciprocal interaction between parent and infant has been obtained when systems for the continuous recording of behavior have been used. For example, observational studies which continuously record mutual regard have documented the predominance of asymmetry between a mother's gaze and that of her infant during the early months of life. The mother provides a "gaze frame,"continuously looking at the baby while he visually cycles in and out (Fogel, 1976). The significance of this pattern of visual interaction is that it may be one of the infant's earliest experiences in controlling environmental stimulation. Some ways in which methods for continuous recording of interactive behavior have gone beyond dyadic categories will be discussed later.

STRATEGIES FOR SAMPLING AND RECORDING INTERACTION

The choice of variables and strategies for recording are closely linked. Both directly affect the behaviors and the processes that can be studied as well as the interpretations that can be made of the data. Most observation systems record behavior as though one response occurs in isolation from other responses. A single discrete response is segmented from the cluster of responses in which it is embedded. Reciprocal social interaction is much more complex as pointed out by Condon and Ogston (1967):

> In essence, the fundamental problem involves finding an empirical, decisional basis for the analysis of an ongoing process across the multiple and interlocking levels of that process as it occurs naturally...[p. 222].
> Behavior, to reemphasize, occurs as patterns of whiles; a person speaks connecting segments of sound, while eyes and brows move, while arms, hands, and fingers move, while the other person or persons move. Behavior is what they all are "while" they occur. We are seeking to illustrate that the components of behavior are not discrete and isolated events which are then combined to form behavior, but are regular and predictable patterns of change within an ongoing process [p. 225].

There are several considerations that influence our recording of reciprocal interactions between parent and infant. One important question regarding the strategy of recording is which aspects of time need to be noted and in what detail. Decisions must be made concerning the precision with which the onset, duration, ending, and overlap of responses are to be recorded. For some behaviors that are momentary, such as burping or the smiling of a very young infant, a concern with onset, duration, and termination of response may not be as relevant as for other behaviors such as crying or visual attention. Inasmuch as the behavioral repertoires of parent and infant are not similar with respect to frequency of occurence or duration of individual behaviors, there are special problems in recording the temporal dimensions of behavior. For example, the vocalizations of the parent are likely to be much more frequent and of longer duration than the young infant's vocalizations, yet precise recording of the timing of the vocal behavior of both mother and infant is critical for understanding the importance of vocal communication in their early dyadic relationship (Stern, Jaffe, Beebe, & Bennett, 1975).

A fundamental issue in recording behavior concerns the ways in which the observer breaks into the ongoing stream of behaviors. The problem of segmentation of ongoing behavior has been approached from two different perspectives: time-independent strategies and time-dependent strategies of recording (Collet & Semmel, Note 4). Each of these methods has its own unique advantages and limitations, and more importantly, each yields different kinds of data. Time-dependent strategies, often called event sampling, preserve the frequency and sequence of preselected behaviors (Wright, 1960), but the duration and time between behaviors are usually not recorded. Event sampling has not been widely used in parent-infant interaction research in the past decade, mainly because it is not appropriate for studying reciprocity. Therefore, we shall limit our discussion to time-dependent strategies.

There are two basic time-dependent methods: time-sampling and continuous recording. Traditionally, investigators using time-sampling methods have observed for a specified time interval and then taken time out to record. There are a great many variations in the intervals of time designated for observing and the time for recording. For example, Caudill (Note 3) observed for 1 second and recorded for the next 14 seconds, whereas in a study by Yarrow et al. (1975) the observation time was 30 seconds and recording time was 60 seconds. There have been no guidelines for determining the cycle for observing and recording or the length of time most appropriate for sampling parent-infant interactive behavior. There are several reasons why this is an especially important consideration. Segmenting the ongoing flow of parent and infant behavior into 5 or 10–second units makes it difficult to see the interrelatedness of behaviors of both members of a dyad; we lose the pattern of behaviors as well as the sequence. We are left with frequencies of small units of behavior. These frequencies are presumed to be representative samples of usual behaviors, yet the absolute frequencies would be quite different in the two studies mentioned above.

The practice of recording the behavior of each member of the dyad separated from the interactive context grew out of the model implicit in observational studies attempting to answer questions about the effects of different types of parental stimulation on the child's development. With the recognition of the importance of the bidirectional model of parent–infant interaction (Bell, 1968), it became imperative to use techniques for observing behaviors-in-sequence.

Recently some investigators have used a modified time-sampling procedure for observing short consecutive intervals without "taking time out" to record. Several investigators employing this method have devised techniques for indicating the sequence of parental and infant behaviors within continuous short time intervals. Using 10-second observation units, Clarke-Stewart (1973) recorded maternal and infant behaviors, indicating the sequence of occurrence on alternate lines of the recording form. Similarly, Lewis (1972) used the numbers 1 and 2 to specify the sequence of maternal and infant behaviors within a 10-second period. These innovations in recording sequence within a specified time unit represent progress in measuring interaction as compared with techniques that simply record behavior of one partner in the presence of the other.

A more refined and precise procedure for measuring interaction has come about with the second method of time-dependent sampling of behavior, continuous recording. With this method, the frequency, sequence, and duration of the behavior of each member of the dyad are preserved. New devices such as videotape, event recorders, and more recently, portable electronic digital units have made this type of recording possible in observational research. Moreover, they have stimulated analytic and statistical models for handling continuous streams of behavior (Bakeman & Brown, 1977). These methods have enabled us to move beyond static descriptions of parent and infant responses and arbitrary designations of brief contingent exchanges; they are providing ways for studying parents and infants as a reciprocal social system.

SUMMARY AND INTEGRATION

We have pointed to the need for methodological studies of various sources of influence on observational data: our approach to sampling behaviors, the contexts in which we observe, the categories we use to observe behavior and the interpretation of variables derived from behavioral categories, as well as our techniques for recording behavior.

Central to the problem of obtaining a representative sample of behavior is the question of day-to-day or hour-to-hour consistency in the behavior of the parent and of the infant. Our sampling procedures implicitly accept the assumption that the behaviors of parent and infant are consistent across time and in different contexts and situations. We know that there are great diurnal variations in infant state, and individual differences in infants' regularity and rhythmicity (Brazelton et al., 1974). Some infants in fact may be characterized most accurately by their variability. Even if there may not be great stability on all dimensions of infant behavior, some parents may see their infants as more consistent than they actually are. Thus, their behaviors towards their infant may be determined by their relatively stable perception of the infant far more than by his changing day-to-day behavior. Some parents may also be quite variable in their behavior toward infants. Obtaining a representative sample of the behaviors of two changing organisms and a changing dyad present basic methodological problems. These methodological questions need to be investigated. For example, we do not know the answers to such fundamental questions as whether a 30 minute behavior sample on 3 days is in any way comparable to a 90-minute sample of behavior on 1 day. The length and number of observations and their spacing require careful consideration in relation to the generalizations one hopes to draw from the data.

There are many contextual influences in the natural setting that are not easily identified; sometimes we are not aware of them, or minimize their importance. Investigators have assumed that the home environment as distinguished from the laboratory is a situation in which there are no constraints. Yet we know there are many subtle effects on the behavior of the parents that are associated with being observed and with their definition of the situation. There are also many variations in home settings that influence parental behavior. We must analyze the demand characteristics of different situations in an effort to understand the meaning of these environmental contexts for the parent, the infant and the dyad. We need descriptive data on the modal characteristics of different contexts, for example, feeding and play. Similarly, we must consider variations in infant state and the effects of these organismic contexts on parental behavior. We need methodological studies of parent-infant interaction in a variety of settings, analyzing the behaviors occurring in each setting separately so that we might better understand the relations of setting and parent and infant behavior. Such methodological research should help us in designing more adequate studies of parent-infant interaction and should enable us to look beyond single variable relationships.

With regard to the choice of categories, we must give consideration to the meaning of our variables for the infant and for the parent. We need to consider individual differences in infant sensitivities to various modalities and intensities of parental stimulation. We cannot conclude too simplistically that the infant who receives 46 touches during one observation session obtains twice the amount of effective stimulation as the baby who receives 23. An infant who is more sensitive to tactile stimulation, may experience the same amount of touching very differently than a baby with a higher threshold for tactile stimulation. Similarly, we cannot simply conclude that a parent who gives more tactile stimulation than another is more highly stimulating or more responsive and sensitive to the infant. Our need to make sense of our data often leads us to draw broad and often erroneous conclusions from very simple findings such as these. In addition, the patterning of tactile, visual, and kinesthetic stimulation is more important than the total amounts of stimulation in any one modality. We need to develop categories and to record our data in ways that preserve the configurations of parental and infant behaviors.

There are similar difficulties in interpreting more abstract and subjective variables. For example, a high score on a variable such as the parent's respect for the infant's autonomy may have different meanings for different parent-infant dyads. For some parents, it may indicate they value and encourage the infant's need to be independent. For other parents, it may mean a reluctance to become engaged with the infant. We cannot make any simple interpretations of the effects on the infant of encouraging autonomy; some babies may feel challenged, while others may experience such parental behavior as frustrating and understimulating.

No one strategy for observing and recording the behavior of parents and infants is inherently preferable to another. The method for recording determines the kinds of processes that can be studied and the interpretations that can be made of the observational data. If an investigator were interested in the relations between the level or intensity of parental stimulation and infant behavior, she would use methods different from those of a researcher whose interest is in the reciprocal interactions of parent and infant. Few studies of parent-infant interaction have presented a theoretical rationale for their techniques of observation. Moreover, as Rosenthal (1973) notes when a theoretical rationale is stated, there is often a lack of correspondence between the theory and the method for observing behavior.

In our search for objectivity, we have simplified our categories and techniques of observing parent and infant behavior, and in this process we have often adopted an oversimplified view of parent-infant interaction. We have emphasized in this paper the importance of accounting systematically for the complexities of parent-infant interaction. The methodological issues raised are not sterile scientific concerns. Our methodology and our concepts are closely related to our findings. We can no longer ignore these thorny issues because they are too complex and too difficult to handle. They have direct relevance to substantive questions of the role of early parent-infant interaction in development.

DISCUSSION

Dr. Papousek: You really did outline a series of important problems. If we do nothing else but discuss maternal behavior now, we shall fill the conference with a meaningful content. First comes the question of naturalistic observation. My problem also was how many elements of maternal behavior we knew in man, and thus, I had to combine naturalistic observation with experimental analysis of every detected individual element. We would like to have measurable parameters of maternal behavior, such as crouching, which Rosenblatt can use in rats. However, in human research, we first had to look for them, that is, we first had to observe and film naturalistic situations. The second step led to exact laboratory analyses, and then again, the next important step was to return to naturalistic interaction in order to verify the validity of models derived from the experimental analyses.

We often forget to do the last step: We like to stick to experimental—that is, very artificial—situations. Nevertheless, we should be able to detach from them, go back to natural observation, and try to apply there what we found in experiments in order to be sure that our theoretical model fits.

My second point concerns behavioral states you mentioned. We also pay a lot of attention to them, not only because they influence behavior on both sides, but also because they provide important feedback cues. Particularly, the mother's ability to evaluate changes in the infant's behavioral state has a strong biological relevance, in my opinion. That is one of the elements of maternal behavior we observed in naturalistic situations.

The next point is rather philosophical and concerns system theories in fact. We all speak of interaction now, but here, as well, there may be a dichotomy in how we conceptualize it. We can define both the mother and the infant either as static interacting systems that do not change or as dynamic systems. The static view may easily come with our tendency to standardize and immobilize sets of stimuli and responses in strict experimental conditions. But in mother–infant interaction, only dynamic concepts are acceptable, I think, with the view that both partners are developing and changing systems. Nowadays, some speak of transaction rather than interaction. A dynamic interaction concept becomes necessary as soon as you start longitudinal or repeated observations.

My last point concerns definitions and categories of mother–infant interaction. Although I know well how disadvantageous it is to use labels polluted by previous theories and interpretations, I would still wait a while with any revision, because we do not yet know all relevant components of behavior involved in such interaction. Recently, we analyzed maternal movements adjusting the mother–infant distance in order to facilitate visual contact with the newborn. We also described modifications of maternal voice during interaction with the newborn. Other previously unknown control mechanisms have been reported from other laboratories. It would be premature to suggest a new vocabulary now.

Dr. Mason: About this sort of dialogue between the laboratory and the field, essentially that never stops, and one has to assume that once some ideas have been obtained in the laboratory, you try to validate them, the field turns up new ideas, and this goes on continuously, and we're deluding ourselves if we say now the basic normative data are in and we can go ahead and do the analytic studies. Because once the analytic studies are done, you say, well things have turned up that we would now like to look for in a normative situation, and it goes on continuously.

Dr. Lipsitt: It isn't necessary that one individual carry this on, but I think we have to be prepared to see it go on indefinitely, and rather than thinking of it in terms of historical phases or that part of the discipline is now complete. And if that's true, then I think it also follows we have to be prepared for the same kind of change with respect to methodology. Categories are going to change, units are going to change, different individuals will be working with units of different sizes, not because one is wrong-headed and the other has the truth, but because the particular things you're seeking at the moment are different. There's obviously going to be a place for very fine-grained studies with small categories and microanalysis, videotapes; and it seems to me there's going to be a place for people who are still using rating scales and working with very global kinds of things where they talk about a transaction, perhaps in units that run into minutes or even hours, episodes during the day, rather than units that can be measured in terms of seconds or discrete movements or whatever. I personally don't think there's any way we'll ever reduce all of that complexity to a single method, a single set of categories.

Dr. Yarrow: I don't think so either, and I recognize there are different levels of questions that are asked. The categories are very much determined by those questions too, but if you're asking on one level what the quality of the relationship is, the more comprehensive question, then you really get into problems with the categories.

Dr. Lipsitt: Of course there are many different ways of looking at people, so there are many different ways of a mother's looking at her child and the child's looking at its mother. Certainly there are many different ways of touching people. Sometimes you might touch affectionately, and sometimes you might touch hurtfully. I don't think that should distress us at all in trying to refine the concept of touching or of gazing or whatever other parameters we're looking at in connection with the mother–child relationship. I think that in our study and in your review of parent–child interaction and methods of looking at these, we are at a stage in child development now that is rather like the stage physics must have been in shortly after Ohm's law was discovered; but people could not figure out that you had to make a slight change in the arithmetic if you wanted to make Ohm's law work in parallel circuits as well as it works in series. All it took was for somebody to notice that you had to reciprocalize the resistance in the circuit in order for Ohm's law to hold for both series circuits and parallel circuits. I don't think that is a distant analogy. I think that in any scientific endeavor one goes through a stage in which one uses relatively crude concepts, and indeed the concept of gaze is a crude concept. The concept of touching is a crude concept, before one gets to the point of refining the concept and having Touch 1, Touch 2, Touch 3 types of concepts in order to further refine our knowledge about antecedent–consequent relations. Our pursuit of knowledge about the way certain aspects of parent–child interaction cause certain differential consequences is a gradual process. I got a certain pessimistic flavor from the discussion about the ambiguities involved in our definition of observable behaviors and the use of such concepts as "touch" and "gaze." Our problems are not so much with this stage of our scientific endeavor as they are with a later stage when objections begin to be heard over the increasing refinement of our dependent variables. That is when people start saying we've become too mechanistic, too precise, too objective, and that we've lost sight of the child we started to study.

Dr. Denenberg: Given our focal interest in mother–infant interactions, I am very skeptical that using the typical correlational group data or factor analytic approach would be fruitful whatsoever. I think we're going to have to go to single-subject longitudinal-intensive data to understand it, and we will mask it by group averages.

Dr. Yarrow: That was an issue that I mentioned briefly in the paper that I skipped in the presentation about what individual case analyses can contribute.

REFERENCE NOTES

1. Beckwith, L., Cohen, S., & Parmelee, A. H. *Risk, sex and situational influences in social interactions with premature infants.* Paper presented at the meeting of the American Psychological Association, Montreal, September, 1973.
2. Thoman, E. B., Becker, P. T., & Freese, M. P. *Individual patterns of mother-infant interaction.* Paper presented at the Conference on Application of Observational/Ethological Methods to the Study of Mental Retardation, Lake Wilderness, Washington, June 1976.
3. Caudill, W. *Tiny dramas: Vocal communication between mother and infant in Japanese and American families.* Paper presented at the Conference on Culture and Mental Health, Honolulu, March 1969.
4. Collet, L. S., & Semmel, M. I. *The analysis of sequential behavior in classrooms and social environments: Problems and proposed solutions* (Technical Report 3.23) Center for Innovations in Teaching the Handicapped, Indiana University, Bloomington, Indiana, 1973.

REFERENCES

Ainsworth, M. D. S., & Bell, S. M. Some contemporary patterns of mother-infant interaction in the feeding situation. In J. A. Ambrose (Ed.), *Stimulation in Early Infancy.* London: Academic Press, 1969, 133-170.

Bakeman, R., & Brown, J. V. Behavioral dialogues: An approach to the assessment of mother-infant interaction. *Child Development*, 1977, *48*, 195–203.

Bell, R. A. A reinterpretation of the direction of effects in studies of socialization. *Psychological Review*, 1968, *75*, 81–95.

Brazelton, T. B. Observations of the neonate. *Journal of the American Academy of Child Psychiatry*, 1962, *1*, 38–58.

Brazelton, T. B. *Neonatal behavioral assessment scale*. Clinics in Developmental Medicine, No. 50. Philadelphia: J. B. Lippincott, 1973.

Brazelton, T. B., Koslowski, B., & Main, M. The origins of reciprocity: The early mother-infant interaction. In M. Lewis & L. A. Rosenblum (Eds.), *The effect of the infant on its caregiver*. New York: Wiley, 1974, 49–76.

Brody, S. *Patterns of mothering*. New York: International Universities Press, 1956.

Brown, J. V., Bakeman, R., Snyder, P. A., Fredrickson, W. T., Morgan, S. T., & Hepler, R. Interactions of Black inner-city mothers and their newborn infants. *Child Development*, 1975, *46*, 677–686.

Clarke-Stewart, K. A. Interactions between mothers and their young children: Characteristics and consequences. *Monographs of the Society for Research in Child Development*, 1973, *38*, (6–7, Serial No. 153).

Condon, W. S., & Ogston, W. D. A segmentation of behavior. *Journal of Psychiatric Research*, 1967, *5*, 221–235.

Fogel, A. Temporal organization in mother-infant face-to-face interaction. In H. R. Schaffer (Ed.), *Studies in mother-infant interaction*. London: Academic Press, 1976.

Jones, S. J., & Moss, H. A. Age, state, and maternal behavior associated with infant vocalizations. *Child Development*. 1971, *42*, 1039–1051.

Korner, A. F. State as variable, as obstacle, and as mediator of stimulation in infant research. *Merrill-Palmer Quarterly of Behavior and Development*, 1972, *18*, 77–94.

Korner, A. F. The effect of the infant's state, level of arousal, sex and ontogenetic stage on the caregiver. In M. Lewis & L. A. Rosenblum (Eds.), *The effect of the infant on its caregiver*. New York: Wiley, 1974, 105–121.

Lewis, M. State as in infant-environment interaction: An analysis of mother-infant interaction as a function of sex. *Merrill-Palmer Quarterly of Behavior and Development*, 1972, *18*, 95–121.

Moss, H. A. Sex, age, and state as determinants of mother-infant interaction. *Merrill-Palmer Quarterly of Behavior and Development*, 1967, *13*, 19–36.

Robson, K. S. The role of eye-to-eye contact in maternal-infant attachment. *Journal of Child Psychology and Psychiatry*, 1967, *8*, 13–25.

Rosenthal, M. K. The study of infant-environment interaction: Some comments on trends and methodologies. *Journal of Child Psychology and Psychiatry*, 1973, *14*, 301–317.

Stern, D. N., Jaffe, J., Beebe, B., & Bennett, S. L. Vocalizing in unison and in alternation: Two modes of communication within the mother-infant dyad. *Annals of the New York Academy of Sciences*, 1975, *263*, 89–100.

Thomas, E. A., & Martin, J. A. Analyses of parent-infant interaction. *Psychological Review*, 1976, *83*, 141–156.

Wright, H. F. Observational child study. In P. H. Mussen (Ed.), *Handbook of research methods in child development*. New York: Wiley, 1960, 71–139.

Yarrow, L. J. Research in dimensions of early maternal care. *Merrill-Palmer Quarterly of Behavior and Development*, 1963, *9*, 101–114.

Yarrow, L. J., Rubenstein, J. L., & Pedersen, F. A. *Infant and environment: Early cognitive and motivational development*. New York: Halsted, 1975.

9 Wanting and Knowing: A Biological Perspective on Maternal Deprivation

William A. Mason
University of California, Davis

From a biological perspective the two great themes in the evolution of behavior are "wanting" and "knowing." Natural selection provides the key to the evolution of behavioral variety and increasing complexity; wanting and knowing provide the basic functional dimensions within which these changes have occurred. And surely it will be apparent that these themes are interwoven throughout evolution. Knowledge, for the vast majority of organisms, is pragmatic and utilitarian: Animals are prepared to know what they need to know in order to survive. Knowledge is at the service of the primordial requirements of organismic equilibrium and integrity—of preserving the individual intact and functioning until such time as it has made its genetic contribution to future generations. This is basic, axiomatic. Except in the rather special circumstances of kin selection, which I will not go into here, the individual who does not meet these elemental requirements is an evolutionary failure, the terminal point in its family line. Knowledge for its "own sake," if it exists at all, is a rare bird indeed in the evolutionary scene; rather than being taken for granted as a common and widespread attribute, it should be treated as a biological anomaly that requires detailed analysis and explication—wherever it seems to occur, whether in mouse, monkey, or man.

The interplay between the processes subserving wanting and knowing can be seen in all phases and facets of the life cycle, but it is nowhere more evident than in the developing relationship between parent and young. Obviously, cognitive and motivational elements are closely interwoven from the very beginning of this relationship. Various mechanisms have evolved to insure that in normal circumstances each participant comes rather quickly to "know" the other and "wants" to maintain the relationship. It is also obvious that the basic framework for these developments is present at birth, and that many of the elements are specialized, buffered, and overdetermined, as one would expect in view of the critical role the parent–offspring relationship plays in survival. Indeed, the close functional interdependence of cognitive and motivational processes in the early phases of the relationship is partly what we have in mind when we refer to maternal patterns or filial responses as *instinctive*.

In many species, however, the interplay of wanting and knowing in the parent–offspring relationship has implications that extend far beyond the giving and receiving of care and questions of the immediate survival and well-being of the offspring. We recognize this in our descriptions of the parent as "teacher" or "model" or "socializer." What we refer to of course is not to the parent's effects on the offspring's immediate chances of survival, but to its effects on long-range prospects, on the *preparation* for survival. For such species, the relationship between parent and offspring has a paradigmatic quality. It partakes of, or foreshadows, the nature, not only of future social relations, but quite possibly of relations with the environment as a whole. It can properly be described as a pivotal relationship, for it includes what is peculiar to the conditions and requirements of infancy and what is representative of the larger world. It is this combination of specialized and generalized (or paradigmatic) features that make the mother–infant relationship so intriguing an object of study in the nonhuman primates that are the subject of most of my research.

One way of attempting to sort out the various kinds of influences that the parent–offspring relationship exerts on the developing individual is to observe mothers and infants as they interact in a naturalistic setting. Such normative data are indispensible. Among their other virtues, they often suggest particular hypotheses about cause-and-effect relations. A familiar example is the hypothesis that young chimpanzees at the Gombe Stream Reserve acquire skills in termite "fishing" from observing their mothers at work. In spite of their unique importance, however, naturalistic data are usually not suited to the kind of hypothesis testing that is required to establish cause-and-effect relations. For this, some sort of experimental intervention is usually required.

It will be obvious that any radical intervention in the natural relationship between mother and offspring will have serious developmental consequences. This in itself is of no great theoretical interest. The point of altering the natural relationship, however, is not to produce behavioral "deviance" but to shed new light on how normal development proceeds. Exposing a newborn animal to conditions that it is unlikely to encounter in nature is a way of altering the normal transactions between the organism and its surround; it is an attempt to alter the dialogue in instructive ways. Intervention does not eliminate the dialogue, for this is impossible short of the grave; but it can change it so that its structure is more clearly seen. The organism, after all, is at every moment of its career an organized ongoing enterprise, and the interesting question is not *whether* development will be altered by abnormal circumstances but *how*. The nature of the organization is the central concern.

In the remainder of this essay I will examine some of the effects on the developing rhesus monkey of various forms of intervention in the natural mother–infant relation. A major thesis will be that one of the most basic and significant consequences of depriving an infant monkey of its natural mother is a disruption of the normal intimate interplay between the processes subserving "wanting" and "knowing," which may lead to fundamental changes in the way the infant relates to the world in the later stages of its life.

Let us begin with an extreme example, the infant rhesus monkey separated from its mother at birth and raised with a cloth artificial mother. Now such a monkey "wants" to cling to something and its early behavior is exquisitely organized to permit it to do so. We also know from Harlow's celebrated research that clinging plays a critical role in the formation of the filial bond. The monkey "knows" from the moment it enters this world what its mother "feels like"—it is equipped with a tactile maternal schema, if you will—but it does not know how she will look; or at least the specifications are not detailed. Consequently, virtually any claspable object, regardless of its appearance, can become the focus of attachment. In time the maternal figure becomes known through vision, of course. It is recognized at a distance and from various angles of regard; and its presence becomes a powerful source of emotional security. As a security object—the "wanting" part of the relationship—an inanimate surrogate may be as effective as the real mother, at least in early developmental stages. What is conspicuously lacking in the relationship with an inanimate surrogate, however, is the presence of those dynamic attributes that facilitate and support the development of knowledge and skill. With an inanimate mother life is all too easy. A cloth mother holds no surprises; she engenders no conflicts, makes no unexpected demands, sets no conditions, neither placates nor punishes. She is simply there, available and inert.

MOVING AND STATIONARY ARTIFICIAL MOTHERS

We have found that even a fairly modest increase in the dynamic properties of an artificial mother, such as mechanizing her so that she moves somewhat unpredictably up and down and around the cage, can have abiding effects on various aspects of psychological development, including visual curiosity and social behavior (Mason & Berkson, 1975).

Visual curiosity was measured when the monkeys were on the average about 2 years old, more than a year after they had been permanently separated from their artificial mothers (Eastman & Mason, 1975). They were placed in a situation in which they could look through a peephole at other monkeys. Various stimulus conditions were used—such as a mother with her infant, a juvenile male, a monkey of a different species, and the like—and each condition was presented on several different days (sessions). Figure 9.1 presents the results by sessions, summed across the various viewing conditions. The data clearly indicate that monkeys raised with mobile artificial mothers (MS) showed a higher level of looking behavior than did those raised with stationary surrogates (SS), and only a slightly lower level than did monkeys born in the wild (WB).

Social behavior was investigated when the monkeys were about 4 years old by pairing them with wild-born monkeys of the opposite sex. Previous research by myself and others has shown that the development of normal sexual patterns in both male and female rhesus monkeys is dependent on prior social experience (Mason, 1960). Although the sexual behavior of

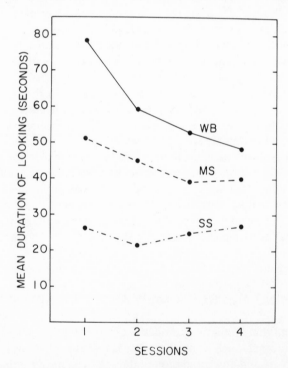

FIG. 9.1. Differences in duration of looking by wild-born rhesus monkeys (WB) and monkeys raised with mobile (MS) and stationary (SS) cloth surrogates. (After Eastman & Mason, 1975.)

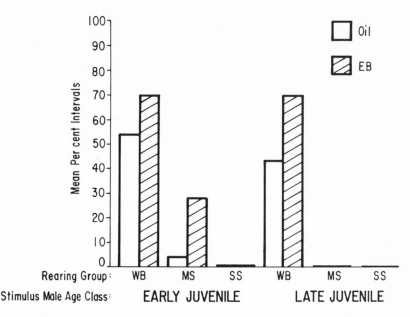

FIG. 9.2.   Bracing in support of male's mounting attempts by wild-born female
rhesus monkeys (WB) and females raised with mobile (MS) and stationary (SS)
cloth surrogates. In half the pairings the females were treated with estradiol
benzoate (EB), and in half with oil vehicle. (After Anderson, Kenney & Mason,
1977.)

neither of our surrogate-raised monkey groups can be considered normal,
those raised with mobile artificial mothers showed more adequate sexual
performance than those raised with the stationary devices. This was most
clearly the case with females. In this experiment, each female was tested with
relatively large juvenile males (late juveniles) and with relatively small
juvenile males (early juveniles). They were also tested following treatment
with the female sex hormone estradiol benzoate or with an oil vehicle as a
control (all had been ovariectomized previously). Figure 9.2 shows that
females raised with mobile dummies were the only ones in the two surrogate
groups to brace and support the males during their mounting attempts,
although they did so only with the smaller males and mostly following
treatment with estradiol benzoate (Anderson, Kenney & Mason, 1977).

Obviously, however, a cloth-covered dummy, even a mobile one, is a far cry
from a real monkey mother, and if one is seeking a more representative view
of the effects of maternal attributes on the interplay between wanting and
knowing, a different approach is required. It was for this reason that we
turned to canine mother substitutes in our developmental research with
rhesus monkeys (Mason & Kenney, 1974).

DOGS AS SURROGATE MONKEY MOTHERS

Our current project includes animals raised either with cloth surrogates (Figure 9.3) or with dogs (Figure 9.4). All monkeys are housed outdoors with their surrogates in spacious kennels that afford them frequent visual contact with people, dogs, other monkeys, and a variety of other ongoing and occasional events. Moreover, from the 3rd to the 15th month of life every monkey was regularly allowed to roam in several different complex outdoor enclosures, which contained a variety of playthings, puzzles, and climbing devices. The aim was to provide all monkeys with a generally "enriched" experience, while withholding from some (those raised with cloth surrogates) the opportunity for give and take with an object that really mattered—to separate, if you will, the attachment per se, from the dynamic (and paradigmatic) properties of the attachment figure. For the monkeys raised with canine mother surrogates, of course, these attributes were present.

We used dogs rather than real mothers for several reasons. Of particular importance was our knowledge that dogs were tolerant, accepting, and highly social attachment figures and yet did not display the typical primate-specific patterns of maternal solicitude or restraint. In fact, we have no indication that our dogs (all females, incidentally) respond maternally to the monkeys. They like them, yes; play with them, to be sure; they even growl at them on occasion, particularly as the monkeys grow older and more rambunctious. But on the whole they are remarkably gentle and indulgent. Our hope was that such a "generalized" companion would as surrogate mother throw more light on the broader effects of social stimulation than would a natural mother, whose behavior has been shaped by evolution to complement, support, and direct the development of her offspring along species-typical paths.

We have one group of six monkeys raised with inanimate surrogates and two groups of six monkeys each raised with dogs. The inanimate surrogates are plastic hobby horses mounted on wheels, and they carry a "saddle" of acrylic "fur." The dog-raised monkeys differ in that in one group, the free-dog group, dog and monkey were free to roam together in the complex environments, whereas in the other, the restricted-dog group, the dog was confined to a small region in the exposure environment that was visually isolated from the rest of it. The condition for exposure to the complex environments for monkeys raised with inanimate surrogates was precisely the same as that for monkeys in the restricted-dog group. Although the research is still in progress, sufficient data have been collected to establish differences between all groups. The most pervasive and abiding differences, however, are between the dog-raised monkeys and those raised with inanimate surrogates, and I will limit myself to comparisons of these two groups.

What intrigues me most about our findings is the suggestion that the monkey's basic stance toward the environment, its characteristic approach to

FIG. 9.3.   Monkey with inanimate substitute mother.

FIG. 9.4.   Monkey with canine substitute mother.

the world, is significantly altered by the kind of mother substitute with which it has been raised. Consider first how this is reflected in relations with the surrogate itself. One of the simplest measures we have obtained is the amount of time the monkey spent looking at the surrogate under baseline conditions. These results are presented in Figure 9.5. The finding that monkeys raised with dogs spent considerably more time looking at their surrogates throughout the first year of life than did monkeys that were raised with inanimate surrogates is not surprising, of course, but it does illustrate how the properties of the attachment figure impinge on a basic kind of "knowing" activity.

When the monkeys were about 4 months of age we began to test them in a delayed response situation. The reward for a correct response was contact with the substitute mother. As the monkey watched, a handler led the surrogate through one of four differentially colored doorways where it disappeared from view. The disappearance of the surrogate started a delay period ranging up to 45 seconds in duration. At the end of the delay, the monkeys were allowed 30 seconds in which to select and enter one of the goal boxes; if they failed to enter within this period, a "balk" was scored for the trial. The most striking difference between groups in the first phase of testing was the much higher level of balks in the inanimate surrogate group. They refused to respond to 46% of the trials, as compared to less than 2% for the dog-raised monkeys (see Figure 9.6). Because we were also interested in the accuracy of performance, in the next phase of testing we set up various

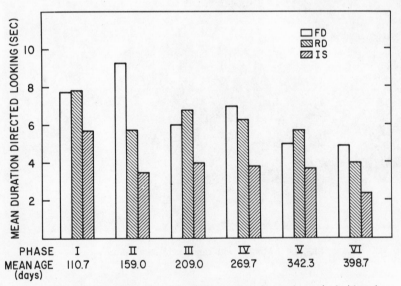

FIG. 9.5.   Mean duration of looking at surrogate by monkeys raised with canine (FD, RD) or cloth surrogates (IS).

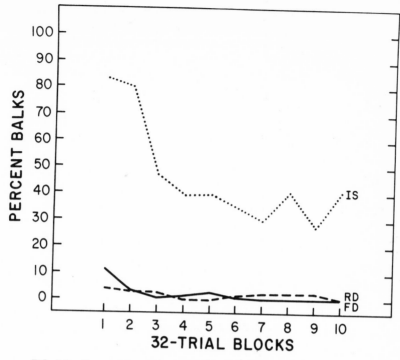

FIG. 9.6.   Percentage of balks in first phase of delayed response testing by monkeys raised with canine (FD, RD) or cloth surrogates (IS).

procedures to encourage the monkeys in the inanimate surrogate group to leave the start compartment, the aim being to increase the number of completed trials. These procedures were effective, and when groups are equated for number of trials completed, they do not differ significantly in accuracy.

In the delayed-response test two cues were present, of course, the surrogate and the handler who led the surrogate into the correct goal box. After completion of the final phase of the regular delayed-response test we omitted the surrogate as a cue, leaving only the handler (although contact with the surrogate continued to be used as the reward for a correct response). The immediate effect of requiring the monkeys to rely entirely on the handler as a cue to the correct door was a substantial decrement in the level of correct responses by dog-raised monkeys (a loss of 33.1%), whereas little change (8.7%) occurred in the performance of the inanimate surrogate group, suggesting that in the situation in which both handler and surrogate were available as cues, they are attending more to the handler than to the surrogate. These results are presented in Figure 9.7.

We also completed a variety of tests in which the monkeys were observed in novel surroundings. In some of these, presence or absence of the surrogate

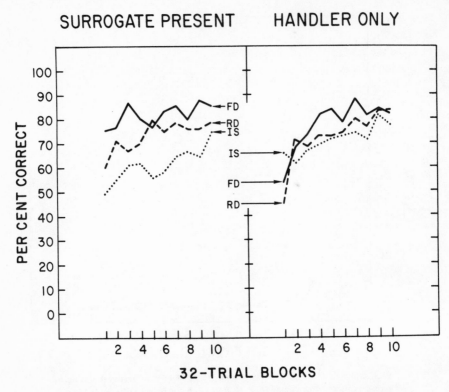

FIG. 9.7.   Effect on delayed response performance of eliminating the surrogate, leaving only the handler as a cue to the correct goal box.

was manipulated systematically to determine its influence on reactions to an unfamiliar environment; in others, the surrogate variable was a constant element, either being present or absent under all conditions, depending on the particular test.

Consider first the effects of the surrogate on emotional reactions to a novel situation. In one of the tests directed at this question, the monkeys were observed in an unfamiliar room on three separate occasions approximately 50 days apart, starting when they were 4 months of age. On each occasion the following five test conditions were presented: the monkey's surrogate available for contact, the surrogate enclosed in a plastic box (so that it could be seen but not touched), an unfamiliar surrogate (dog or hobby horse, corresponding to rearing groups) available for contact and enclosed in the plastic box, and the empty test chamber. The results for the five conditions are presented in Figures 9.8 and 9.9. Two features are of interest: First, monkeys raised with inanimate surrogates did not differentiate the social conditions as sharply as did monkeys raised with dogs, particularly as measured by heart rate. Second, when they were entirely alone in the test chamber, their levels of heart rate and distress vocalizations were much lower than those of the monkeys raised with dogs. We have different measures from similar tests that point to the same conclusion. For example, as shown in Figure 9.10, the level of plasma cortisol (a physiological indicant of stress) was also substantially lower following 40 minutes of confinement within an empty room in monkeys raised with inanimate surrogates than in those raised with dogs.

Do these results indicate that monkeys raised with inanimate surrogates are generally calmer or less susceptible to stress than those raised with dogs? I do not believe so. I think it is more accurate to conclude that characteristic ways of coping with novel situations are different in the two groups. In thinking about the monkeys raised with inanimate surrogates I am reminded of Seligman's discussion of learned helplessness (Seligman, 1975). I do not mean that the monkeys were helpless to control their inanimate surrogates. On the

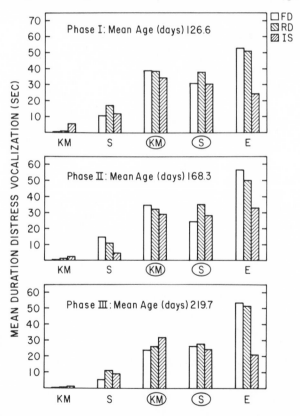

FIG. 9.8. Mean duration of distress vocalizations (coo, screech) in a novel room. KM and S indicate the familiar surrogate or stranger, respectively. Ovals indicate that these objects could be seen but not touched. E indicates the absence of surrogates. Groups FD and RD were raised with dogs, group IS with inanimate surrogates.

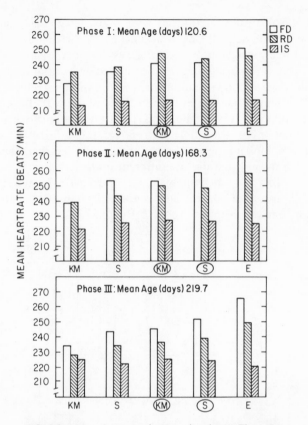

FIG. 9.9.   Mean heart rate in same situation as Figure 9.8.

contrary, they had virtually complete control over them and soon became quite proficient at moving their hobby horses about the cage, getting them into a comfortable position, and so on. And of course they were "reinforced" (by clinging, presumably) whenever they chose. It could certainly be argued, however, that the inanimate surrogates did not require much "control." The monkeys raised with hobby horses surely experienced much less response-contingent feedback in their relations with the attachment figure than did the monkeys raised with dogs. Inanimate surrogates did not routinely create circumstances in which attentional processes or the acquisition of specific instrumental behaviors were encouraged.

If, as I have suggested, the attachment figure is in part paradigmatic, an exemplar of how the larger world behaves, then monkeys raised with inanimate surrogates received a most peculiar sample of what the world is like. I doubt that they have "learned" to be helpless. Certainly, we did not teach them to be helpless by subjecting them to the traumatic conditioning procedures that characterize the experimental paradigm for creating "learned helplessness." Apparently, the critical factor is that they failed to learn in their relations with inanimate surrogates that the environment required and was amenable to control. Hence, when faced with a novel situation, such as solitary confinement in an unfamiliar room, they were less likely to try to escape from the situation or attempt to change their condition than were the monkeys raised with dogs; they were more likely to accept the situation passively and therefore were less distressed by it than the dog-raised monkeys. This contrast between rearing groups could reflect nothing more than a specific difference in the direction of greater tolerance for stressful situations (or reduced susceptibility to stress) by the monkeys raised with inanimate surrogates, rather than more generalized differences in patterns of coping with the environment. If this were true, however, one might expect monkeys raised with inanimate surrogates to be less distraught in situations in which an adaptive outcome was possible and, hence, to enjoy some advantage over

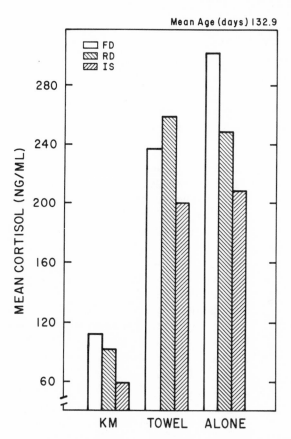

FIG. 9.10.   Mean levels of plasma cortisol in monkeys raised with canine (FD, RD) or cloth (IS) surrogates.

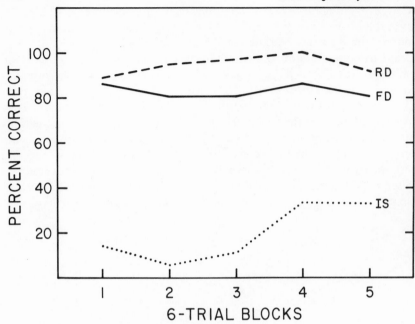

FIG. 9.11. Percent success in monkeys raised with canine (FD, RD) or cloth
(IS) surrogates.

monkeys raised with dogs. This does not appear to be the case. On the
contrary, in situations such as the delayed response test, as we have seen, on
nearly half the initial trials the monkeys raised with inanimate surrogates
refused to enter the goal boxes. If achieving contact with the surrogate had
been a factor in survival, then their chances of achieving an adaptive outcome
would have been slim.

Perhaps this indicates only that the strength of attachment was less in the
inanimate surrogate group, that their motivation to regain contact with the
surrogate was low. I doubt this, even though I do not insist that strength of
attachment is equal to that of the monkeys raised with dogs. But there is no
need to resolve this question here, for we have other data showing striking
contrasts in relations with the environment in situations in which the
surrogate plays no direct role. We have completed a number of simple
problem-solving tests in which the surrogate is present in the situation (so that
the potentially disruptive effects of separation are not involved) but cannot
contribute in any direct way to successful performance.

One test series began by presenting food in an open box of clear plastic
suspended 30 cm above the floor; after 30 trials, this condition was altered by
raising the box to 60 cm above the floor and providing a wooden step. The

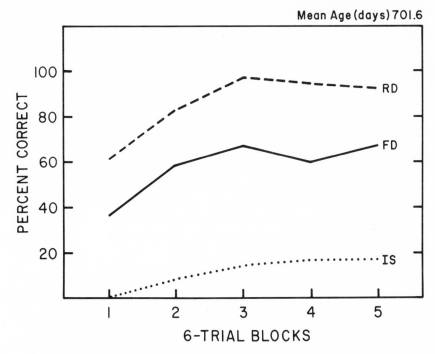

FIG. 9.12.   Percent success in monkeys raised with canine (FD, RD) or cloth (IS) surrogates.

results presented in Figures 9.11 and 9.12 show that the level of successful performance of the monkeys raised with inanimate surrogates was consistently below that of the monkeys raised with dogs.

We have also examined another aspect of adaptive behavior with similar outcome. For the nonhuman primates, as for man, keeping in touch with the world is very much a visual affair. We were therefore interested in discovering how this basic activity might be affected by our rearing conditions. The monkeys were tested in an apparatus similar to that described by Eastman and Mason (1975). Essentially, the animals were placed in an enclosed test chamber containing peepholes, through which they could look at projected colored transparencies. In the first test series the procedure was to present a single slide (e.g., landscape, interior of a room, etc.) for 9 trials, and on the 10th trial to introduce a new slide. The results are presented in Figure 9.13. It is clear that monkeys raised with dogs demonstrated a much higher level of visual curiosity in this situation than did monkeys raised with inanimate surrogates. Moreover, should there be any question that they were in fact looking at the projected pictures, their performance on the 10th trial (in which a novel slide was presented) removes all doubt. They not only showed a sharp increase in duration of looking, as compared to the immediately preceding trial, but, in fact, showed a definite contrast effect: The duration of looking at the test slide was nearly twice that elicited by the repeated stimulus even on its first presentation, even though it was also completely novel on that trial.

Partly to confirm this incidental finding, and partly to determine whether or not additional experience with the situation would induce increased looking in the inanimate surrogate group, a second experiment was completed, in which a different picture was presented on each trial (variable series) or the same stimulus was repeated for 9 trials with a novel stimulus on Trial 10, as in the first experiment (constant series). The results, presented in Figure 9.14, confirm the contrast effect, show that a variable series produced

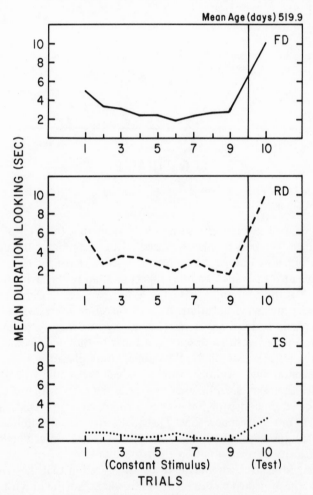

FIG. 9.13.   Duration of looking at colored transparencies by monkeys raised with canine (FD,RD) or cloth (IS) surrogates. A novel stimulus was presented on Trial 10.

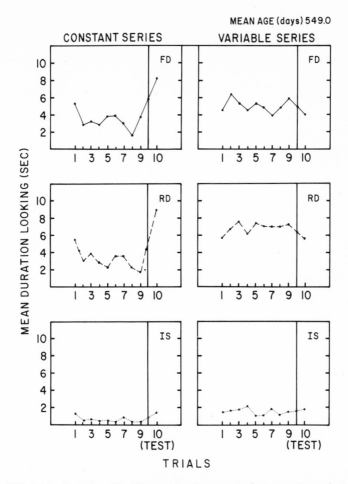

FIG. 9.14.   Duration of looking at colored transparencies by monkeys raised with canine (FD, RD) or cloth (IS) surrogates. Constant series: Same stimulus presented on each trial except 10, which introduced novel stimulus. Variable series: Different stimulus presented on every trial.

essentially no intrasession decrement in looking behavior, and provide no evidence that additional experience in the test situation had any positive effect on the behavior of the monkeys raised with inanimate surrogates.

COGNITIVE IMPLICATIONS OF THE ATTACHMENT FIGURE

On the whole, these results provide a convincing demonstration of the central importance of early social experience to the interrelations between "wanting" and "knowing" in the developing macaque. Merely "enriching" the environment is not sufficient to override the effects of having a live companion as a mother substitute. Although all our monkeys experienced a high level of incidental environmental stimulation, differences between rearing groups are clear.

The fact that the attachment figure was a dog rather than the natural mother is significant, for it suggests that the critical dimensions in early social life are not closely tied to the highly specific structure of the natural mother–infant relation. This is not to say that the particularities of the natural relation are without influence, of course, but only that they are apparently superimposed on rather generalized developmental systems.

For nonhuman primates the propensity to form a strong emotional attachment to a maternal figure is a conspicuous and well-nigh universal characteristic. In these animals the "selection" of an attachment figure sets the scene for much that will follow as development proceeds. "Wanting" in the context of filial attachment leads naturally to an elaboration of those processes subserving "knowing." This is patently inherent in the organization of behavior in the very first stages of development, at least in the rhesus monkey. What is elaborated will depend on the attributes of the maternal figure, of course, and how they impinge on the developing individual. Our results give some indication of the different consequences that follow from having an attachment figure that is living or inert. But even when the object of attachment is a cloth dummy, surely not a propitious vehicle for the development of complex cognitive dispositions and skill, "knowing" processes of a simple order are plainly involved. Such a "mother" becomes recognized on sight, and the attachment to her is specific and preferential.

For the nonhuman primates this means that the maternal figure occupies a privileged and influential position, one particularly well suited to shape the early development of behavior. Is the primate mother unique in this respect? This seems unlikely. Data on a host of species demonstrate the broad range and subtlety of maternal effects. The details vary with species, of course, but the thesis of privileged influence is fully supported by the facts.

Having given the mother her due, however, it is important to recognize that her effects on development may sometimes reflect sufficient rather than necessary conditions. We need no reminder that the developing individual is neither a lump of clay, passively shaped at the whim of any potter's hand, nor a clockwork automaton with machinery set and ready for entrainment. Once embarked on his brief career, we know that the developing individual plays an active role in all that transpires. He selects from the environment the best that is available to him, as dictated by his existing structure and organization, and he is altered as a consequence of his acts. This is the basic dialogue in which all living systems are endlessly engaged, and it is carried forward at every functional level. While life goes on, the dialogue continues in some form, regardless of what the environment offers. Natural mothers, like dogs and dummies, produce their effects as participants in this process.

ACKNOWLEDGMENTS

Support for this research was provided by National Institues of Health Grants HD 06367 and RR 00169. Unpublished data reported here was obtained in collaboration with Mr. D. DeSalles, Ms. M. Kenney, Dr. E. N. Sassenrath, Mr. S. A. Williams, and Dr. B. J. Wood.

DISCUSSION

Dr. Rheingold: What is the age of your animals?

Dr. Mason: This starts off in the first week of life. And those are 20-week observation blocks, 5 days a week, so at this point they were about 8 to 9 months old.

Dr. Eisenberg: Does this refer to any kind of play?

Dr. Mason: No, this is what is called social play. Rough-and-tumble play.

Dr. Rheingold: Upon the surrogate.

Dr. Mason: Yes. Chiefly on the surrogate. It is an indication that the surrogate would elicit the play and also would support it.

Dr. Rheingold: How rough-and-tumble play?

Dr. Mason: For example, pouncing on it, mouthing it, bouncing off of it, pursuing it, and so on.

Dr. Rheingold: What is the ratio as far as age is concerned, between the rhesus monkey and the human infant? Is the factor 4 or 5?

Dr. Mason: Something like that. But such comparisons are really not too meaningful. You're dealing with an animal that is not only more precocious but also is differently organized. At 15 days, the rhesus monkey is capable of walking very nicely. And by 40 to 50 days, you're getting the first signs of this rough-and-tumble play. By this age the sexes are beginning to separate with respect to frequency of play behavior. By 3 months it's pretty clear, and so on.

Dr. Lipsitt: It looks as though at about 40 days of age there's a sharp jump up, and this early behavior remains about the same ever after.

Dr. Mason: Yes. It does in this situation. It doesn't increase, that's true. Whether that's true in natural groups I don't know. Probably not. After all, the surrogate is a pretty limited device for allowing any real development of this activity.

Dr. Eisenberg: There are only certain amounts of activity you can indulge in with surrogates.

Dr. Mason: Absolutely, but more than I anticipated. For example, this surrogate moved by motor 50% of the time. It had a universal joint in the rod that suspended it from the ceiling so that the surrogate would swing as it was moving, and in the course of moving around it might bump the animal; sometimes this would elicit a sex present or pursuit or play. I didn't anticipate that sort of thing. Although it's a rather limited device from the standpoint of its physical properties, the use that the animals made of it was more complex than I had anticipated.

Dr. Watson: Was the rapid shift upward an effect of simple mobility? Of the infant? Or was there mobility long before that?

Dr. Mason: They're mobile very early. They become more mobile as they get older, of course, but they will traverse a runway to get to the surrogate when they're only 8 to 10 days old.

Dr. Eisenberg: Yes, but in your first block, if I remember right, it was fairly flat.

Dr. Mason: Yes.

Dr. Eisenberg: And that's simply because they can't do very much.

Dr. Mason: That's true.

Dr. Eisenberg: Obviously, if they don't walk before 5 days, there are many things they can't attempt.

Dr. Mason: Yes, but these are 20-day blocks and 5-day weeks, so actually each block includes more than 20 calendar days.

Dr. Rheingold: I'd like to know your conclusion.

Dr. Mason: Well at this point I'm just saying, Look, they're playing more.

Dr. Rheingold: Because?

Dr. Mason: I'll come to that in a moment.

Dr. Stern: You didn't answer Harriet's question of why.

Dr. Mason: Okay. What I'm really thinking about now is first if you just look at the behaviors of these animals, the inanimate surrogate group, it suggests very much the kind of thing that Seligman calls learned helplessness. Second, if you look at the relation to the surrogate it suggests a lack of response-contingent feedback. Now it is not terribly helpful to say that these monkeys learn to be helpless. We didn't put them through a traumatic conditioning procedure or teach them that they could not control the environment. Rather they failed to learn that the environment could be controlled. They failed to learn to attend to significant events, and so on. For the monkey, the most significant object in its early life is the mother. If you give it a mother substitute that doesn't do anything, doesn't make any demands, that doesn't need to be predicted, I think—and this is why I'm excited by these results—you create an animal whose basic stance towards the environment is altered. The monkey is not curious about what's happening around it. It doesn't act upon the environment in situations where you might expect it to, even when there's some modestly worthwhile payoff, such as a small piece of food. What we're looking for now is more evidence to corroborate that kind of interpretation in animals that are now approaching the third year of life. We'll eventually move into social situations where we expect similar effects to be found.

Dr. Stern: Have you tried putting in a stimulus with a stationary surrogate that in fact does change? For instance suppose a stationary animal or whatever it was made a sound, a monkey-type sound, and then you did a habituation task to that sound. If it worked for sound but not for a visual or a motoric task, that would lend a lot of credence to the generalizations you've made.

Dr. Mason: Yes, right. That's a good suggestion. Although I feel quite secure when I say we've altered the general stance towards the environment, there are usually one or two individuals—and it varies across situations—who seem to say, What the hell, there's a piece of food; and they pick it up, and in this situation receive a high score while the others do nothing. Now we might be able to sharpen the differences between groups, or eliminate that kind of variability, by making the situation more stringent. I have tried to avoid that thus far. Instead, we have put them in situations in which they can do something that would be considered adaptive but in which the monkey doesn't really have to mobilize everything it's got in order to perform.

Dr. Eisenberg: Are these animals in individual cages and isolated from each other so that they have no sensory input?

Dr. Mason: No. They're all raised in kennels outdoors.

Dr. Eisenberg: So they *do* have sensory input, including the auditory input of their own species.

Dr. Mason: The monkeys raised with inanimate surrogates see dogs being led back and forth—

Dr. Eisenberg: That means they also hear the vocalizations of other species.

Dr. Mason: Yes. And they can even touch each other.

Dr. Eisenberg: Well, one certainly can't argue that they're deprived of sensory input.

Dr. Mason: No. In fact, what we tried to do is to eliminate that factor, because it's been a confounding variable in most of the work that's been done before. If you look at our environments, I think you would have to say that even compared to a mother-raised monkey in a laboratory environment, the general level of environmental stimulation the monkeys received is far richer. And it doesn't seem to make that much difference. It certainly isn't sufficient to swamp the effects of this inert maternal figure.

Dr. Eisenberg: When Jim Sackett was at Wisconsin, he and I once discussed the possibility of providing newborn monkeys with all stimuli save species-specific sound to see whether and how their vocal and other behaviors might be affected during the course of development. Unfortunately, since there was no way to set up such an experiment properly, we never could test out our hypothesis that vocalization patterns at least would be disrupted by species-specific auditory deprivation during early life. I don't suppose you've ever gotten around to looking at this, have you?

Dr. Mason: No, I haven't looked at it. About all I can say here is that if you give them a cage, 8 feet long, 6 feet high, and 4 feet wide, allow people to walk back and forth, allow them to touch other monkeys between cages, put them for an hour a day from about the fourth to the 15th months of life into complex outdoor environments, the monkeys raised with inanimate surrogates nevertheless develop the syndrome I've described.

Dr. Watson: Do you have any sense of any control relationship that the infant managed to establish with the dog—the dog surrogate mother?

Dr. Mason: It's hard to describe any explicit forms of social control, but it is probably present and works in both directions.

Dr. Watson: Would the dog posture when it was leaped on by the monkey?

Dr. Mason: Well, they'd play together, for example.

Dr. Watson: They would play.

Dr. Mason: Oh, they'd play together. I have a film we might have a chance to look at. The dog will lick the monkey's behind, the monkey will groom the dog. There's social facilitation. The dog goes and drinks and the monkey approaches looking intently at the dog's mouth. It's a true social relationship. But it does not seem the case that these dogs are responding maternally to the monkey. They're just very very tolerant, lovable animals.

Dr. Thoman: I am curious to know whether the monkey who went in and picked up the piece of food may also have been the one who showed variability in terms of the looking measures.

Dr. Mason: There is some consistency, but it's not so great that you can really say this is the individual who seemed least vulnerable. At the same time, I believe that if we had 20 animals in a group, which is a luxury I never expect to be able to afford, then one might be able to do something with individual differences. They're real, they're important in these animals, and they're tantalizing because they just don't really add up to this is the extrovert, this is the introvert.

Dr. Thoman: You are quite right, it would be far too much to expect you to have a large enough group to do correlational analyses. It is just that, in addition to the very dramatic group differences you find, you have individual monkeys, individual dogs, and thus individual transactions. For me, the excitement would also be in the nature of the individuality in dog–monkey interactions—with the possibility of abstracting information about their ways of relating to each other that might suggest commonalities one does not get from group analyses.

Dr. Lipsitt: I wouldn't quarrel with the interpretation that you're putting on your data—that is, in terms of the Seligman hopelessness hypothesis—but as I think about all of your data together, as a constellation of findings, it seems to me that the picture of these aberrant animals who were raised on the inanimate surrogate is one more of imperturbability, including in their heart rate behavior. Imperturbability, rather than the picture of depression and despair that Seligman draws for his "hopelessness syndrome." I hesitate to suggest this—because it's so terribly clinical, in the sense of speculative and *ad hoc*—but I wonder if you are not really dealing with something like the etiology of psychopathy. Imperturbability, rather than the sadness found in the etiology of depression, which is what Seligman deals with.

Dr. Mason: Yes, your point is certainly well taken. If one goes back and looks carefully at Seligman's ideas, I think one will find that the kinds of distinctions he makes are not totally relevant to my situation, partly because the basic paradigm for Seligman is traumatic avoidance conditioning. His interpretation emphasizes that susceptibility to depression is greatest in animals that have been stressed in situations in which they were actively prevented from coping. He also suggests, however, that animals that have no opportunity to learn to cope are more susceptible to depression. As I see the thrust of your remarks, we have no evidence of depression. What we have here are animals that are passive, that have insulated themselves from the environment. I think that's reasonable. They have developed self-directed behaviors that serve to buffer them against the environment, rather like cutoff mechanisms. If we prevented them from using these buffering techniques, which the animals raised with live surrogates direct toward the dog, then they might show depression or excessive stress. They're not perturbed, because they've developed ways of coping that allow them to be secure just by sitting in a corner and clutching themselves and rocking. Seligman's ideas may be compatible with what you're saying, but he apparently hasn't considered the distinctions that are most pertinent to the data I've presented.

Dr. Lipsitt: These animals of yours do not go and mope in a corner very much.

Dr. Mason: They do show occasional rocking behavior, but the clinical impression is that they are more normal than the typical isolation-raised monkey.

Dr. Lipsitt: If you throw them the food rather than make them solve a little problem to get the food, they eat it avidly?

Dr. Mason: Yes. Even in the test situation, one or two animals may take food on every occasion.

Dr. Lipsitt: Those aspects of their behavior don't sound to me like the kind of syndrome that Seligman was describing, at least in humans, but to borrow a page from Hawley Parmelee's book, your hypothesis is as good as anybody's.

Dr. Barnard: You mentioned that the dogs did not engage in what you would call mothering behavior. By this what do you mean?

Dr. Mason: I mean that they don't show any protective behavior. Moreover, they don't seem particularly concerned with what the monkey is doing usually, except as it affects them. They don't show any sort of suckling postures or anything of this sort. If I had to characterize the dogs' relationship to the monkey, I would say it is very much like what you'd expect to find in a household pet in its relations with children in the family. Tolerant up to a point. They don't accept abuse. They will snap at the monkeys, and yet they don't savage them. They control, and they're controlled. For example, we have a few dogs that won't tolerate the monkey's feeding with its head in the same dish, and in those cases you see the monkey sitting about a foot from the dish and reaching its hand in. The dog will tolerate that. And there are other dogs that are quite tolerant in that respect, and so the two feed together.

Dr. Barnard: If the infant monkey is distressed, caught in something, does the dog go to it?

Dr. Mason: No. It's not obvious, at any rate. Some dogs show evidence of distress. That may be partly the result of our shaping. We shape the dogs.

Dr. Barnard: What does shaping mean?

Dr. Mason: The monkeys were about 3 to 4 weeks of age when they started their first exposures to the dogs. We would try to shape the monkey so that it would cling to the dog's neck, because that seemed to be the most comfortable place; and to shape the dogs so they wouldn't step on the monkey, or whatever. In some cases, in what we call the first overnight, we would muzzle the dog if we had any doubts about whether it was going to be safe. Or we would stay overnight and monitor the pair. It sounds very mysterious, and I don't know what it's all about, but one gets the feeling that the dog rather quickly comes to understand that that monkey has a special status, perhaps only in the eyes of the experimenter.

Dr. Barnard: Would you do that again?

Dr. Mason: That same procedure? Yes. I don't see any other way.

Dr. Barnard: You wouldn't just put the dog and the monkey together.

Dr. Mason: You can't assume in this case that the dog is going to respond at once as if to say: Here is a nice cuddly little thing that I must treat tenderly. The remarkable thing, however, is that they seem to pick up that message very quickly.

Mrs. Wishart: You talked about the infant–dog interaction. Do you think it changes over time?

Dr. Mason: Surely. It's basically misleading to refer to the relative importance of the contribution of the mother, of peers, and so on to normal development. The parts of maternal behavior that we eliminated by not using the real mother were all these highly structured species-typical things that the normal mother shows. The natural mother retrieves, she restrains, she punishes. Many of those acts are probably specially suited to the status of the infant and to its needs. Not that the natural mother says I've got to do this for baby, but she has been shaped by evolution so that she performs these acts in a predictable way. In addition, she also has what I would call paradigmatic features, and these paradigmatic effects are the ones that are most influenced by the dog or the inanimate surrogate. The mother represents how other animals are, how the environment is, and so on. If you're willing to accept that view, then an age-mate has some of the same properties as the mother, in addition to some specialized features of its own. It will cling when clung to, but it also represents social objects in general. So we're not really going to be able to get much help in sorting out what's involved in social development by treating peers, mothers, or whatever as though they were simple "variables" producing independent effects.

Mrs. Wishart: Could that account for the difference in intensity between your studies and Seligman's studies—that there was this possibility of infant–infant interaction? Another infant may not be as competent as a mother, but it could be enough.

Dr. Mason: We've also done research in which baby monkeys were fostered on each other. It is a terrible preparation for trying to do any systematic assessment, because each monkey clings fiercely to the other, even if the other doesn't want to be clung to. And so each is treating the other like a mother surrogate. Everybody is messed up.

Dr. Korner: There are a couple of corollaries in the human literature that come to mind in relation to this unresponsiveness that you were referring to. One of them is an early study by Greenberg that showed that infants raised in a very drab orphanage were generally less reactive to events. Their heart rate was less responsive to changes in the environment, and their emotional responsiveness was dampened. The other study that comes to mind is that by Provence, Lipton, and Ritvo. This study also involves infants in an institution. In a meeting Ritvo reported that they tested object permanence and object loss with these infants and that they found that the children raised in this institution just were not interested in pursuing or looking for the lost object. What of course interests me very much in your presentation is that your results clearly show the tremendous importance that movement stimulation has on the development of your animals.

Dr. Mason: There's no question about that.

REFERENCES

Anderson, C. O., Kenney, A. McM., & Mason, W. A. Effects of maternal mobility, partner and endocrine state on social responsiveness of adolescent rhesus monkeys (*Macaca mulatta*). *Developmental Psychobiology,* 1977, *10,* 421–434.

Eastman, R. F., & Mason, W. A. Looking behavior in monkeys raised with mobile and stationary artificial mothers. *Developmental Psychobiology,* 1975, *8,* 213–221.

Mason, W. A. The effects of social restriction on the behavior of rhesus monkeys: I. Free social behavior. *Journal of Comparative and Physiological Psychology,* 1960, *53,* 582–589.

Mason, W. A., & Berkson, G. Effects of maternal mobility on the development of rocking and other behaviors in rhesus monkeys: A study with artificial mothers. *Developmental Psychobiology,* 1975, *8,* 197–211.

Mason, W. A., & Kenney, M. D. Re-direction of filial attachments in rhesus monkeys: Dogs as mother surrogates. *Science,* 1974, *183,* 1209–1211.

Seligman, M. E. P. *Helplessness: On depression, development and death.* San Francisco: W. H. Freeman, 1975.

10 Paradigms and Paradoxes in the Study of Behavioral Development

Victor H. Denenberg
University of Connecticut

The study of behavioral and biological processes during development is probably at least one order of magnitude more difficult than the investigation of these same processes after the organism has reached the relatively steady state of adulthood. This is so because the developing organism has inherent biological changes programmed in via the genes, and its transactions and interactions with its environment change dynamically as the organism's physical, physiological and behavioral characteristics change. Thus, those of us who wish to investigate developmental processes, either descriptively or by use of an experimental intervention, are involved in studying a biobehavioral preparation that is undergoing many marked changes both endogenously and as a function of exogenous stimulation, brought about by direct excitation as well as by multicircuit feedback loops involving the internal environment, the external environment, and interactions between these two systems. These types of changes are less likely to be present when one works with the adult organism, whose behavior and physiology have achieved a rough asymptotic level (at least until the effects of aging begin to set in).

Because of these differences between the developing and the mature organism, I believe that it is necessary to use somewhat different research strategies in investigating developmental processes. In addition, the routine application of paradigms or models that we have found to be successful when working with adult organisms may lead us to make erroneous conclusions when working with developing animals. The purpose of this paper is to discuss some of the paradigms that we use in developmental research, show how these can lead to paradoxical conclusions, and then suggest ways by which we can improve or modify the paradigms so that we do not lead ourselves into logical cul-de-sacs. I will first discuss research using groups of subjects in the usual experimental design framework and will then talk about general systems theory; after that I will comment on the correlational model and will then turn to a discussion of the use of single subjects in a longitudinal context. I will keep this discussion at a sufficiently general level so that the arguments I put forth are equally applicable to those doing human developmental research as well as those who study development with animal preparations.

EXPERIMENTAL DESIGNS AND DEVELOPMENTAL RESEARCH

The simplest kind of experimental design needed to study a developmental process is shown in Table 10.1. It consists of an experimental group and a control group, with the assignment of the subjects to the groups done by random allotment. At some time in early life, which is designated as T_1 in Table 10.1, the experimental subjects are given a treatment (i.e., an independent variable is administered). After that a gap of time exists during which all animals are treated alike. This time gap is very important because any effects obtained afterwards have to be related to the experiences that occurred early in life, thus establishing that the difference obtained is of a relatively long term (often called "permanent") nature; if, on the other hand, no time gap were present, any differences obtained could be viewed as transient rather than permanent.

Some time later in life, often in adulthood but not necessarily so, at a time designated as T_t, both groups of subjects are given a criterion test on the endpoint, or dependent variable, chosen by the researcher for investigation.

The treatment effect is defined as the difference between the means of the control and experimental groups, as indicated in Table 10.1, and this

TABLE 10.1
An Experimental Design to Study the Effects of an
Experimental Treatment Administered in Early Life Upon
Later Performance

Group	Experimental Treatment at Time T_1	Time Gap T_1-T_t	Criterion Test at Later Time T_t
Control	C		$\bar{X}_c$
		All conditions kept constant	
Experimental	C + Trt		$\bar{X}_e$

Experimental Treatment Effect = $\bar{X}_e - \bar{X}_c$

difference is usually evaluated by a *t* test or the analysis of variance. If we find a significant difference between the means, we generally draw the following types of conclusions:

1. The treatment at time T_1 caused the difference found at time T_t.
2. The treatment had an additive (i.e., linear) effect upon the criterion test measured.
3. The treatment resulted in the experimental group being better than (or poorer than) the control group.

Thus, from the design shown in Table 10.1 we draw conclusions about causality and additivity (linearity); and we also make a value judgment as to whether the experimental treatment made our subjects better than or poorer than the control subjects.

To give some substance to the design in Table 10.1, let me cite some examples from the developmental literature. With respect to animal studies, the design is a standard one used to evaluate the effects of early experiences. One form of early experience that has been extensively studied is called handling (Denenberg, 1977a). Our typical procedure is to handle animals 3 minutes per day for the first 20 days of life while control animals are not disturbed. At weaning (21 days) all animals are placed into laboratory cages, where they are kept under constant conditions until later testing. One of the common endpoints that we use is the open-field test, and our usual findings are that experimental animals are more active and defecate less in this situation (Denenberg, 1969). The open-field test has been used as a measure of the construct of emotionality, and a typical conclusion that we would draw is as follows: Handling in infancy brings about a reduction in emotionality as measured by open-field performance. Note that this sentence has several implications to it. First of all, the statement "handling in infancy" really means "the presence of handling in infancy" and suggests the concept of additivity; that is, the addition of handling to the experience of the animal is the key event. Next, the statement that the independent variable "brings about a reduction in emotionality" is a direct statement about causality. There is no value judgment as such in the sentence. That does not occur until the discussion section of the paper, where there is either an implied or explicit statement that the less emotional animal is better adapted to its environment than is the more emotional animal, and therefore the conclusion is drawn that handling makes for a "better"animal.

As another example, at weaning rats have been placed in groups into a large cage containing playthings, ramps, ladders, and other objects. Such a unit is called a free or enriched environment (Hebb, 1949), and animals are kept for several weeks while controls are reared in the usual laboratory cage. After that, all animals are maintained under constant conditions and are then tested. In many studies, those reared in the enriched environment have been found to make less errors in a problem-solving maze than controls (e.g., Denenberg, Woodcock, & Rosenberg, 1968). The conclusion is that the enriched experience caused the improvement in problem-solving behavior.

Turning to human studies, there are only a few developmental experiments in which subjects were randomly assigned to a treatment or a control condition and were then tested for the effects of the experimental treatment at some later time (e.g., see Rheingold, 1956; Rheingold & Bayley, 1959). However, many researchers have conducted studies that they have interpreted *as though* they were working within the design in Table 10.1. For example, Spitz (1945) had a group of babies that presumably did not receive sufficient "mothering." When compared to a control group, these babies were reported to have a number of psychological and psychiatric disturbances, and some of the infants died. The conclusion Spitz drew was that the lack of mothering was the cause of the subsequent psychological disablement or death of the children.

Using a somewhat similar design Goldfarb (1943) compared children who had been reared until about 3 years of age in an institution and then in foster homes with children who had been reared continuously in foster homes. When tested in later life, the institutional children were found to be inferior to the foster home controls on a number of variables including measures of IQ, concept formation, and personality. The conclusion was that the institutional experience in early life was the cause of the later difficulties.

In terms of more recent literature, Operation Headstart is an example of an intervention at the preschool level with subsequent evaluations by means of academic achievement measures. Other independent variables studied within the framework of the paradigm in Table 10.1 include whether there has been a presence or absence of nursery school experience, whether children have had interactions with adults or not, and whether infants have been kept within dark huts for the first year of life or not. Indeed, in a number of these studies there is no control group. When this happens, the subjects under investigation are usually compared to some set of population norms.

The examples given above could be multiplied many times over. The important point here is that the paradigm shown in Table 10.1 is *the prototype* used by many developmental researchers whether they work with animal preparations or with humans, whether they have randomly assigned subjects to treatment groups or not, and whether they have control group or not. Thus it is necessary to examine the logic of the conclusions drawn from Table 1 concerning causality, additivity or linearity, and the value judgment of better than or poorer than to see whether these conclusions follow logically from the design. If not, then the conclusions drawn become suspect.

When the structure of the experimental design in Table 10.1 is examined in detail, it becomes clear that when a significant difference between the group means is found, the *only* conclusion possible is that the independent variable caused the observed difference by adding (or subtracting) an amount, thus making the experimental group quantitatively better than (or poorer than) the control group. *The nature of the experiment does not allow the researcher to draw any other conclusion.* Thus we are confronted with the very likely possibility that our interpretations of data are nothing more than an artifact of our paradigm, and that these interpretations have nothing to do with the actual nature of the relationships between our independent and dependent variables. I believe this to be the case for much of the field of behavioral development. In order to document this statement, I will now discuss how one can test for causality and additivity and how one can validate one's value judgments.

THE CONCEPT OF CAUSALITY IN
DEVELOPMENTAL RESEARCH

Philosophically cause is defined as the necessary and sufficient condition to bring about an effect. This definition is rarely if ever used by empirical researchers. Instead, for the experimentalist a cause is typically defined as a sufficient condition to produce a particular result. The concept of necessity is not employed by the experimenter for the simple reason that it cannot be made to apply. For example, depriving an animal of water, placing it in a heated environment, or injecting the animal with saline are all sufficient conditions to cause an animal to drink water, yet none of these conditions is necessary. Thus, the concept of causality as discussed here will be in the context used by researchers rather than by philosophers.

Typically we think of a cause in experimental research as a temporally proximal event rather than a distal event. In the example given above, the animal will begin to drink water within a few minutes to a few hours after the initiation of the experimental treatment. The nearer in time the independent variable is to the criterion measure, the more easily are we able to control other events that can impinge upon the organism during that time gap, and thus the more confident are we that we can talk about a causal relationship. However, the concept of proximity definitely does not apply to the experimental design shown in Table 10.1. Here we are talking about something that occurred in early life with a test of the consequences much later on. We are talking about days, weeks, and months in the life of animals; or months, years, and decades in the life of humans. There is not only the enormous time gap, but there are also occurring during this interval of time the vast number of developmental changes referred to previously.

When the design in Table 10.1 is viewed in perspective, it is clearly very dangerous to draw the causal conclusion that a particular event occurring in early life over a limited time span is sufficient to bring about a measured difference in performance in adulthood. On the other hand, if such a conclusion can be validly drawn, then this is extremely important and has great implications for developmental research.

I can think of two ways to test for causality in developmental studies. The first is by means of the proper experimental design, and the second involves independent verification in different laboratories. In essence, both of these are extensions of the design in Table 10.1 to include a test for interaction. Let me discuss each in turn.

An Experimental Design to Test for Causality

A factorial design, in which qualitatively different experiences occur at different ages in development, permits one to test for causality.[1] The presence of a robust main effect and the lack of strong interactions are sufficient to tentatively conclude that the variable with the significant main effect can be viewed as a casual variable. Contrariwise, the presence of strong interactions with weak or no significant main effects is sufficient to reject the idea that the independent variables have casual consequences.

An experimental design illustrating these points is shown in Table 10.2. In the table there are three time periods in early life, T_1, T_2, T_3. At each of these time intervals the organisms receive different experimental treatments. In this design the experimental treatments are symbolized by the letters A, B, and C. To keep this as simple as possible, I have let each independent variable take one of two levels, either 0 or 1.

To make the independent variables a little more concrete, let me give two examples. For an animal researcher working with rats, T_1 could be the prenatal interval between conception and birth, T_2 could be the lactational interval between birth and weaning at 21 days, and T_3 could be the interval between 21 days and 42 days of age. The A variable could be the presence or absence of conditioned anxiety on the part of the mother during pregnancy (Thompson, 1957); the B variable during T_2 could be the presence or absence of handling; and the C variable could be whether the animals are reared in laboratory cages or in enriched environments.

For a human example, T_1, T_2, and T_3 could refer to the 1st year, 2nd year, and 3rd years of life. The A variable could indicate whether the baby was breast or bottle fed during its 1st year; the B variable could indicate whether the mother stayed home with her child during the 2nd year or went to work;

---

[1]This kind of design should not be confused with an experimental design in which the *same* experience is given at different ages in development. The purpose of such an experiment is to try to isolate critical periods in development. See Denenberg (1968) for a discussion of this concept.

TABLE 10.2

An Experimental Design Showing How Three
Qualitatively Different Independent Variables (A, B,
and C) Are Administered at Three Different Time
Periods (T_1, T_2, and T_3) During Development

Independent Variables Administered at Times:			Dependent Variable Measured at Time T_t	
T_1	T_2	T_3	Individual Subject Score	Group Total
			15	
A_0	B_0	C_0	5	20
			40	
A_0	B_0	C_1	20	60
			30	
A_0	B_1	C_0	50	80
			10	
A_0	B_1	C_1	30	40
			45	
A_1	B_0	C_0	35	80
			30	
A_1	B_0	C_1	10	40
			5	
A_1	B_1	C_0	15	20
			25	
A_1	B_1	C_1	35	60

and the C variable could specify whether the child received nursery school experience or not during its 3rd year of life.

In the design of Table 10.2 we are again restricting ourselves to measuring one dependent variable at time T_t, which will be some time after the termination of the C variable at T_3. In the example in Table 10.2 there are 16 hypothetical subjects making up the eight experimental groups. The analysis of variance of these data is shown in Table 10.3.

The analysis reveals that the three variables taken singly have no main effect components; the AB interaction has an F value of 3.2, which is not significant, and the AC and BC interactions are 0; the ABC interaction has an F of 12.8, which is significant beyond the .01 level. Since variable A at time T_1, variable B at T_2, and variable C at T_3 did not have any effect upon the criterion measured at T_t, the only conclusion we can draw is that none of these variables taken alone is sufficient to bring about a change in performance. Thus, since no main effect was found to be significant, we cannot conclude that any of these variables causally influence our endpoint at time T_t. However, even though no single variable has a causal relationship to our dependent variable, there is still evidence of important significance effects as

TABLE 10.3
Analysis of Variance of Data in Table 10.2

Source	df	SS	MS	F
A	1	0	0	
B	1	0	0	
C	1	0	0	
AB	1	400	400	3.2
AC	1	0	0	
BC	1	0	0	
ABC	1	1600	1600	12.8
Error	8	1000	125	

indicated by the triple interaction. That is, varying combinations of different levels of the three independent variables over a time domain result in patterns of experience during early development that are sufficient to yield performance differences in later life. Unless we are willing to extend our definition to think of configurations of experiences over time in a particular context as being "the cause," we see that the concept of causality becomes useless when these kinds of findings are obtained.

It is important to note that I am not talking about "compound causes" here. By a compound cause I mean a particular combination of sequential events (e.g., $A_1 B_0 C_1$) that will always (or, at least, very often) bring about a predicted change. No such configuration is seen in Table 10.2. This kind of pattern could be revealed in the analysis of variance by the presence of a significant main effect in combination with a significant interaction. It could also be found by visual inspection of one's data.

Note that it is possible to draw causal conclusions, albeit erroneously, by modifying the design in Table 10.2 to conform to the experiment shown in Table 10.1. Suppose we have chosen, as we typically do in experimental research, to fix certain parameters rather than manipulate them systematically. Suppose we investigated variable A, with variables B and C held constant. Let us assume that B is held constant at level 1 and C is held constant at level 0. Then A_0 has a total score of 80 units while A_1 has only 20 performance units, and we would draw the conclusion that the presence of A_1 causes a significant *decrease* in performance. However, suppose variables B and C were both held constant at level 0. Then the value for A_0 is 20 units while the value for A_1 is 80 units, and we would now conclude that the presence of A_1 leads to a significant *increase* in performance.

Since we live in a world in which variables interact with each other across time, to talk about a variable having a causal consequence in later life may be meaningless. We can, of course, create and maintain the illusion of causality by limiting our research to single independent variables, as in Table 10.1. Note that this is not an argument for the use of factorial designs in research.

Indeed, I think that for many reasons single variable designs are quite useful in developmental studies. However, I think it most important to emphasize that conclusions concerning causality cannot be logically derived from single variable designs because of the extremely high likelihood that experiential and biological variables interact over an organisms' developmental life history.

Testing for Causality by Independent Verification in Different Laboratories

The experimental design described above is a way to make an approximate test for causality within one's own laboratory. Another approach is to look for interlaboratory validation by seeing whether other laboratories can obtain the same findings when they carry out independent tests of the experiment. Each laboratory would have its own constellation of environmental variables, subject pool, testers, procedures and apparatus, and so on, and these conditions would differ from one laboratory to another. In addition, each laboratory would choose its own set of variables to hold constant in an experiment while randomizing others. Thus the context and boundary conditions would be markedly different between laboratories. If, under these circumstances, a particular experimental variable were found to have the same significant directional effect in many or most of the laboratories, then one could conclude that the experimental variable is a causal variable.

The Concept of Additivity in Developmental Research

The statement that our experimental treatment has an additive effect is a consequence of the assumption in our statistical model that all components contributing to an individual's score (i.e., main effects, interactions, and error variance) are additive. Given that assumption, the proper way to determine the increment due to the treatment is to subtract the control mean from the experimental mean as was done in Table 10.1.

A way to test the additivity assumption is to take groups of subjects who received different experimental treatments in early life and measure those subjects on the same variable at various times in adulthood, that is, at different values of T_t. (It may be necessary to use independent groups for the adult measurement at differing ages, rather than use a repeated measures design, if there is danger of carry-over effects.) If the additivity assumption is true, it necessarily follows that the performance curves in adulthood should be roughly parallel to each other. That is, if the experimental group has a higher score than the control group at one time in adulthood, then it should continue to have higher scores at other adult times. Thus, if the means reverse themselves so that the curves cross each other, this is sufficient evidence to reject the assumption of additivity, because we are faced with the paradox of trying to rationalize how a treatment effect in early life can add an increment of a positive nature at one time in adulthood and then add a negative increment at another time.

Also note that if the means do cross over, this is sufficient to reject the assumption that the independent variable is of a causal nature. That is, how can the same factor, in and of itself, cause opposite effects to occur in adult life when the organism's behavior and physiology are in a relatively steady state?

Value Judgments of Better or Poorer in Developmental Research

Probably the major reason that we often make wide sweeping statements to the effect that an independent variable results in better or poorer performance is that we measure only one endpoint. Given a single criterion measure and a numerical scale that lends itself to interpretation in the context of better or worse, when we find that one group is significantly different from another group, it is a natural next step (but not a logical one) to conclude that one group is "better than" the other group (logically all we can conclude is that one group is different from the other group). There is a subtle but important distinction to be made between stating that one group has higher scores than another and concluding that one group is better than another. For example, consider the following two statements: "White students generally score higher on intelligence tests than do black students." "White students generally are more intelligent than black students."

If we wish to conclude that our experimental treatment has a generally pervasive "good" or "bad" effect, it is necessary to administer a variety of tests to our subjects in adulthood. These tests should tap a variety of behavioral and/or biological dimensions so that they include a fair sampling of the capabilities of the organism. If, under such circumstances, those who received the experimental treatment were found to perform consistently better (or worse) on the test battery, then it would be appropriate to draw the general conclusion that the experimental treatment had an overall effect of making the organisms better than (or poorer than) the control subjects.

Two Examples of Causal and Additive Variables

I do not know of any variable in the human developmental literature that has been subjected to sufficiently rigorous tests to warrant the conclusion that the variable has causal consequences. I only know of a few instances in the animal literature and will describe two briefly. The first involves the procedure first reported by Hebb (1949) of rearing rodents from weaning in a complex enriched environment while controls are reared in laboratory cages. When such animals are tested on a variety of problem-solving, perceptual, and learning tasks, the typical finding is that those reared in the enriched environment have better performance scores than control animals. In a number of experiments, the animals were tested immediately after they had been removed from the enriched environment, and so there is no evidence as to the long-term consequences of this experience. However, in other experiments, an interval of time intervened between the termination of the enrichment experience and the initiation of testing, thus establishing that the effects are long-term in nature. On the assumption that animals who perform better on learning, perceptual, and problem-solving tasks are better adapted to their environment, we may make a strong statement to the effect that enriched experience immediately after weaning is a sufficient condition to bring about (cause) long-term improvement in a variety of cognitive and perceptual tasks.

The second example concerns a different period in the organism's developmental history, that between birth and weaning. Again using rodents as the primary source of information, the procedure called handling has generally been found to reduce emotionality as measured by a variety of endpoints in adulthood. In addition, handling has also been found to lead to earlier sexual maturation, a change in adrenal responsivity to novel or stressful stimuli, greater adult body weight, more rapid learning in an aversive conditioning apparatus, and greater capability to survive terminal stressors. The strongest causal conclusion we can draw from these findings is that handling in infancy will reduce emotional reactivity in adulthood. Whether a reduction in emotional reactivity is "better" or "poorer" than not reducing emotional reactivity cannot be answered simply because of the complex interactional nature of emotional processes with other behavioral and biological processes. Nor can we conclude that having greater body weight or being sexually precocious is either better or worse than the opposite since this also depends upon the context in which the animal is living.

Some cautionary notes are needed here. We should not expect even the most robust of causal variables to always have the same effect because of the sampling errors involved in any one experiment. Thus, I am using causality in a probabilistic sense in that the likelihood is quite high that in any experiment, handling or enriched experience will have the predicted effect. Also note that the conclusions were limited to the species studied and to the kinds of endpoints measured. There is no evidence, for example, that handling improves cognitive processes in rats, nor is there any evidence that enriched experience modifies adrenal activity.

An Example of Interactional Effects

As indicated above, only a few variables in the developmental literature with animals have been found to be sufficiently robust to warrant the conclusion that they may be called causes. A more typical finding is that variables will interact rather than being sufficient unto themselves to stand alone (Denenberg, 1977b). One example of this is a set of studies with rats using a variation of the design in Table 10.2 (Denenberg & Whimbey, 1968; Denenberg, Karas, Rosenberg, & Schell, 1968). Four experimental variables were combined in a 2 x 2 x 2 x 2 factorial design. These were A, infantile handling *versus* no handling of the mothers of our subjects; B, infantile handling *versus* no handling of the subjects themselves; C, rearing of the subjects in either a maternity cage or a free environment between birth and weaning; and D, rearing of the subjects in either a laboratory cage or a free environment between weaning and 42 days of age. Starting at 220 days, when the animals were tested for exploratory behavior, one major finding was that the interactions involving BCD, ABD, and $ABCD$ were all significant (Denenberg & Whimbey, 1968). In the other study, rats were tested at 70 days in an open-field apparatus, followed by avoidance learning testing. Analysis of the activity scores in the open field found significant interactions for AC, BC, and ABC; for the avoidance learning data, the AC interaction was significant (Denenberg, Karas, Rosenberg, & Schell, 1968).

We see from these data that even though handling has main-effect consequences with respect to emotionality, and the free environment has main-effect consequences upon cognitive processes, they function in an interactive manner rather than a main-effect manner when other dependent variables are examined.

Implications for Developmental Concepts and Theories

The general findings obtained when we carry out experiments similar to the ones depicted in Table 10.2 is that qualitatively different experiences at different ages in development will interact with each other rather than summate in an additive fashion. My thesis is that the presence of strong interactions precludes our drawing any main-effect conclusions concerning our independent variables, and the lack of any meaningful main effects prevents us from using the concept of causality in interpreting our findings. For this reason we have to assume that we are not able to discuss developmental phenomena in a causal context unless we have very strong evidence that a particular variable (or compound variable) is sufficiently powerful to have similar consequences whenever applied, independent of other intervening experiences.

The finding in experimental studies of interactions with variables across time is important for another reason. It reveals the effects that uncontrolled variables can have upon developmental processes. This is particularly true with human research, where it is impossible to control most environmental variables, in contrast to research with animals, where much greater control is possible. To illustrate this point, suppose that we view the design in Table 10.2 from a human perspective. Let us say that we are interested in evaluating the effects of variable A in early life upon later behavior. We have individuals classified with respect to whether they are at level A_1 or A_0; however, we have no information about the levels of B and C that these individuals have experienced while growing. Our usual assumption is that these experiences are randomized across our subjects. However, it is very important to be aware that even if the assumption of randomization is correct, this in no way says anything about the nature of the interactions of variable A (which we have measured) with other variables that we have not measured. The function of randomization is to assure the validity of the test for significance for the effect of A; randomization does not eliminate interactional effects of A with other variables. Figure 10.1 portrays this situation schematically.

If B and C are randomly distributed with respect to A, we see from Tables 10.2 and 10.3 that, depending upon the particular sample we happen to draw, we could find that A_1 has (1) no effect, (2) a positive effect, or (3) a negative effect. It is also apparent that if enough researchers did enough independent experiments investigating the effects of A, the overall conclusion would be that A has no effect, since many of the experiments would show a zero difference between A_1 and A_0 and approximately half of the remaining experiments would show that the presence of A_1 yield positive effects while the other half would show that the absence of A_1 yields positive effects.

I submit that the characterization I have given above is probably very close to being a real-life description of developmental processes with humans. That is, the most reasonable assumption for us to make is that unknown events over which we have no control, as well as known phenomena that we chose

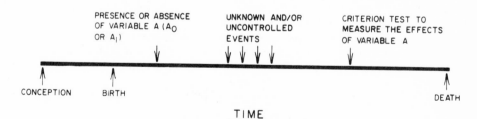

FIG. 10.1. Showing the relationship between the presence or absence of Variable A in early life, the occurrence of unknown or uncontrolled events, and the criterion test to assess the effects of Variable A.

not to control, are in all likelihood going to interact with our experimental variable. Thus, when we find that our independent variable has no effect, this tells us very little.Nor do we have much useful information from any one experiment that shows that the variable had either a positive or negative effect. Only when we have replicated the experiment on a number of occasions and found consistent results can we begin to make meaningful statements about the nature of the variable.

If the concept of causality is not sufficent to describe developmental data, we need another framework within which to view our results. Such a framework is offered by general systems theory.

BEYOND CAUSALITY:
GENERAL SYSTEMS THEORY

General systems theory is concerned with problems of organized complexity (Bertalanffy, 1969). This field developed because the two central concepts that had been used to explain the phenomena of science—linear causality and random probability—were not sufficient to account for the events observed in an organized structure. In discussing this Bertalanffy (1969) states:

> Organisms are organized things, with respect to both structure and function, exhibiting hierarchical order, differentiation, interaction of innumerable processes, goal-directed behavior , negentropic trends, and related criteria. About these, the mechanistic approach...is silent...[T]he conventional categories, concepts and models of physics and chemistry do not deal with the organismic aspects that I have mentioned. They seem to leave out just what is specific to living things and life processes; and new categories appear to be required [p. 58].

Thus, understanding the properties and principles of "wholes" or organization is the objective of general systems theory.

Weiss (1969) has also addressed the general systems question from the perspective of a biologist. He contrasts a machine and a system with the statement that "in the system, the structure of the whole determines the operation of the parts; in the machine, the operation of the parts determines the outcome [p. 13]." Thus, the use of the analytical method, which is the sine qua non of experimental science, will not lead to an understanding of a system, though it will lead to an understanding of a machine. Weiss (1969) flatly states "We are concerned with *living organisms*, and for those we can assert definitely, on the basis of empirical investigation, that the mere reversal of our prior analytic dissection of the Universe by *putting the pieces together again...can yield no complete explanation of the behavior of even the most elementary living system* [p. 7, italics in original]."

Anderson (1972) has also discussed this issue from the perspective of a physicist; he points out that to accept the reductionist hypothesis does not mean that its converse, a "constructionist" hypothesis, must also be true. He states, "The ability to reduce everything to simple fundamental laws does not imply the ability to start from those laws and reconstruct the universe [p. 393]."

A system, therefore, has an integrated wholeness of its own, and the laws that govern a system have to be obtained by studying the system as a complete entity, rather than deriving them from a study of the system's component parts. The relationship of the parts to the whole has been incorporated in a formula by Weiss that is sufficient to define a system. Let parts of a complex, which may have systems properties, be designated by the letters A, B,...N. If part A is studied in isolation, and its behavior is measured, we can obtain the variance of that behavior (v_A). Similarly, parts B, C, and so on can be studied in isolation yielding their variances v_B, v_C,...v_N. When these parts are now part of a total complex (S), the complex as an integrated entity can be measured and its variance obtained. This will be designated as V_S. If the complex is a system, then it will be found that the variance of the complex (V_S) is significantly less than the variance of the component parts (v_A,...v_N). This can be expressed in the following formula:

$$V_S \ll \Sigma (v_A + v_B + v_C + \ldots\ldots\ldots\ldots + v_N)$$

The principle underlying this formula can be illustrated with a simple example of a control system. Suppose we have a furnace turned on and off by a thermostat. We can measure, on several occasions, the temperature of the heat coming out of the furnace. This would range from the ambient temperature of the room in which the furnace is housed (say, 65° F) to a high value (say, 120° F). This is a range of 55°, and thus the variance of the temperature at the duct leading out of the furnace would have a high numerical value. This would be V_A, or the variance in isolation. However, when we measure the temperature in the room which is controlled by the thermostat, we find that the range is from 68° F to 72° F. The variance of these scores reflects the variability of the system when functioning as an integrated entity. With a range of 4° the variance of the complex (V_s) is markedly smaller than the variance of the isolated component (V_A). This satisfies the equation for a system given above.

We can see, therefore, that one basic property of a system is that it *acts to restrict the degrees of freedom of the components*. Algebraically, the formula for a system can only be true if the average intercorrelation among the component parts is *negative*. Only then can the sum of the variances of the parts be more than the variance of the total. (The concept of a negative correlation is also seen in the terminology used to describe the thermostat–furnace complex: It is called negative feedback system.)

When the thermostat-furnace system is viewed from the perspective of experimental design, some interesting relationships are found. Imagine that we know nothing of the "mechanism" of the system, but that we have carried out observations which permit us to make the following statements:

(1) when the furnace is on, the room gets hotter;
(2) when the furnace is off, the room cools down;
(3) manipulating the dial setting of the thermostat can turn the furnace on or off and thus influence the temperature in the room.

These descriptive statements show that there is a correlation between the thermostat and the furnace, but the nature of the relationship is unknown. To gain more information we decide to carry out an experiment in which we independently vary the presence or absence of each of the two components in a factorial design. Thus, the furnace will be at two levels: *off* (A_0) or *on* (A_1). The thermostat will also be at two levels: *not present* (B_0) (i.e., excluded from the circuitry) or *present* (i.e., included in the circuitry) (B_1). Our dependent variable or endpoint is the temperature in the room.

In doing the experiment it is easy to obtain data when the thermostat is in the circuit: we simply record temperatures in the room when the furnace is on and when it is off. When we now remove the thermostat we note that the furnace is off, and the room temperature drops until it levels off at the ambient temperature of the environment. However, unlike the prior situation, it does not go on again (a valuable piece of information). We find that we are able to turn the unit on by throwing a switch, and the temperature in the room then gets quite hot. The graph of our data would be similar in form to the curves shown in Figure 10.2. When the furnace was not on (A_0), the room temperature was lower when the thermostat was not in the circuitry (B_0) than when it was present (B_1). When the furnace was on (A_1), just the opposite pattern was obtained: the temperature was higher without the thermostat present (B_0) than when present (B_1).

The most important feature of Figure 10.2 is that the *curves cross*. Because of this the rank order of the temperature values at level A_0 is the reverse of the rank order at level A_1. Thus, the rank order correlation between the two components, A and B, is -1.0. This is a simple demonstration of the principle that the average intercorrelation among the parts of a system must be negative.

Because the curves cross in Figure 10.2, if we did an analysis of variance we would find that the interaction term was numerically large. Even though we would also find a large mean square for the main effect of the Furnace variable (higher temperature with Furnace On than with Furnace Off), we could not draw any general conclusion concerning this variable because of the crossing of the curves and presence of interaction. That is, the presence of a

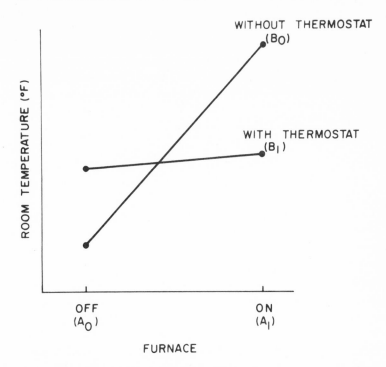

FIG. 10.2. Showing the interactional effects upon room temperature of a furnace being on or off in combination with a thermostat being in or out of the circuitry.

thermostat in a system will "cause" the room to be warmer when the furnace is off (i.e., at level A_0), but the presence of the same thermostat will also "cause" the room to be less warm when the furnace is on (i.e., at level A_1).

It will now be illustrative to return to the data of Table 10.2 and look at the group totals in graphic form. This is shown in Figure 10.3. All the curves cross each other in a symmetrical manner. The intercorrelations between A and B, A and C, and B and C are all –1.0.

We see, then, that the data of Table 10.2 and Figure 10.3 have the same graphic pattern and the same correlational pattern as the furnace–thermostat system in Figure 10.2, and that these patterns are sufficient to state that these parts, when functioning together, act as a system. We have also seen, from the quotes of Bertalanffy and Weiss, that one cannot talk about causes when discussing a system, but must view the system as a whole in organization terms (or, to use the language of experimental design again, the system must be viewed in interactional terms). It is for these reasons that I stated earlier that the presence of strong interactions (i.e., the curves cross) with weak or no significant main effects is sufficient to reject the idea that the independent

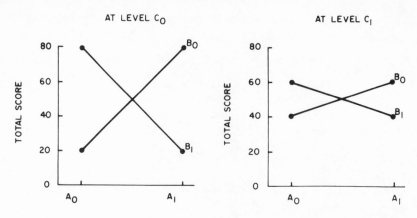

FIG. 10.3.   A graphic portrayal of the data in Table 10.2.

variables have causal consequences. Instead, the set of independent variables have to be viewed within a systems framework.

To return more specifically to the topic of behavioral development, we have already seen that results obtained by experimental procedures can only be interpreted in causal terms if there is good evidence that the variable is sufficiently robust to be not strongly affected in an interactive manner by other independent variables. If relatively strong interactions are present, then a systems interpretation, rather than a causal interpretation, is necessary.

Examples of Systems Principles

A characteristic of many systems is a "fail-safe" feature. That is, even though one or more components of the system fail, the system will still maintain its integrity and continue to function. In the context of Weiss's definition of a system, we see that the variance of the components can be large (the components may be operative or nonoperative) but the variance of the system remains small (the system continued to function appropriately).

A classical example of a fail-safe system in psychobiological research is the work of Beach and Jaynes (1956) who studied, in the rat, the effects of various sensory cues (i.e., components) upon maternal retrieving (the system response). They found that no one type of stimulation is essential (i.e., "causal") for retrieving to occur. Animals could be blinded, made anosmic, or have their tactile sensitivity destroyed and they were still able to retrieve pups. Beach and Jaynes had used experienced mothers. Herrenkohl and Rosenberg (1972) extended their findings to the naive rat: They destroyed vision, smell, or hearing and measured retrieving, crouching, licking and sniffing of pups. Although some of the response components were altered, the maternal behavior pattern remained intact. This capability of maintaining itself is an example of Bertalanffy's statement that systems have organizational properties of their own.

Another characteristic of a system is that it has emergent properties that cannot be derived from a study of the component parts. This occurs when the parts are interdependent rather than independent. Odum (1977) illustrates this point in a recent discussion about the field of ecology viewed from a general systems perspective. As an example, he describes an ecosystem-level study of a coral reef. The metabolism of the intact reef was measured by monitoring oxygen changes in the water flow. The researchers then charted the major energy flows by means of a nutritional analysis, and from this they were able to construct what they called an energy budget for the entire system. Odum (1977) writes:

> It became evident from the latter [the energy budget] that corals and associated algae were much more closely linked metabolically than had previously been supposed, and that the inflow of nutrients and animal food from surrounding ocean waters was inadequate to support the reef if corals and other major components were functioning as independent populations. We theorized that the observed high rate of primary production for the reef as a whole was an emergent property resulting from symbiotic linkages that maintain efficient energy exchange and nutrient recycling between plant and animal components [p. 1290].

The principle discussed above is that a system has emergent properties that cannot be derived from a study of the component parts. It follows, therefore, that an understanding of the functioning of the component parts is not sufficient to allow one to predict the behavior of the system. An example of this is seen in the work of Doolittle (1961), who studied the effect of a single gene and its mutation upon the mouse's resistance to lethal doses of irradiation. The dominant form of one gene that Doolittle studied is symbolized as *Se*, and the recessive form is *se*. Doolittle found, in one mouse strain, that males that had no recessives or one recessive (i.e., *SeSe* or *Sese*, respectively) lived equally long (24.2 and 24.3 days) while those with two recessives (sese) died after 17.3 days, a significant difference. This suggests that two recessive genes (or components) enhanced the lethality of the irradiation. However, when the same genes were studied in females of this strain, Doolittle found that the *more* recessives present, the longer did the mice live: Those with no recessives lived 17.3 days, mice with one recessive lived 19.8 days, and those with two recessives lived 23.9 days. Therefore, knowing the functioning of the recessive genes in one context (males) did not permit the researcher to generalize to another context (females) even though the mice were genetically identical except for the sex chromosome.

Finally, for examples of the use of systems theory in the study of infant development, see the chapter by Thoman, Acebo, Dreyer, Becker, and Freese in this volume.

CORRELATIONAL STUDIES AND DEVELOPMENTAL RESEARCH

In addition to the experimental approach, we have another major set of procedures that we employ in the study of behavioral development. These are correlational procedures. The application of correlational techniques is probably the most widely used approach to the study of developmental events with human subjects. I should like to discuss two concepts here: the question of how to interpret a nonsignificant correlation and the matter of the relationship between correlational data and individual subjects.

Interpreting a Nonsignificant Correlation

A common statement often found in the developmental literature is that some variable measured in early life *is not related to* later performance. For example, one can find statements to the effect that Bayley Developmental Test scores are not related to later IQ scores; that experience in Operation Headstart is not related to later school achievement; that experiences during the first 3 to 6 months of life is not related to subsequent cognitive or perceptual measures: and that the experiences that Guatamalan infants have during their 1st year of life is not related to various psychometric scores in later life.

It is apparent that such conclusions can have great impact upon the research activities within the developmental sciences, as well as influence social and political actions nationally. Thus, it is quite important to examine the underlying logic concerning these conclusions to see whether they are justifiable. When we examine the logic concerning the conclusion that something in early life is "not related to" something in later life, three things become apparent.

Nonlinear Relationships.   The statistic we almost always use to determine whether two variables are related is the Pearson product–moment correlation coefficient. As is well known, this statistic is sensitive only to linear, or at least monotonic, relationships. A significant nonlinear relationship (e.g., a U-shaped function) will not be revealed by the use of the Pearson statistic. One can determine whether two variables have a linear relationship by either visual inspection of the scatterplot or by carrying out a statistical test for linearity. It is rare that either of these procedures is used. Since much correlational work is done via computer, it would be possible, with a graphics terminal, to have scatterplots printed out; it is also possible to write a simple program to determine whether the relationship between any two variables has a significant nonlinear trend to it. If the researcher has not evaluated his or her variables with respect to linearity, then the conclusion that a particular variable "is not related to" another variable is very weak.

Accepting the Null Hypothesis.   To conclude that something is not related to something else is the same as accepting the null hypothesis. We also know that the null hypothesis can never be proven, since one significant (and replicable) departure from a chance relationship is sufficient to negate that hypothesis. The usual response that a researcher will make to this argument is that if there have been sufficient replications of the same variables in different places and at different time, and no one has found a significant relationship, then it is reasonable to accept the null hypothesis that the variable under question is not related to the criteria that we have measured. There are three responses to this statement: (1) That may indeed be the actual state of affairs in the population, that is, the variables are not related to each other; (2) however, replication of negative findings cannot be used logically as a method of establishing proof that a relationship does not exist, and (3) the argument that replication may be used as a basis for supporting the conclusion that two variables are not related involves the assumption that there are no interactions in the population; this concept is discussed below.

The Effects of Interactions.   The comments involving the null hypothesis and the assumption of linearity are quite well known to anyone who has had one course in statistics, and researchers typically take these into account, at least to some extent, when interpreting their insignificant correlations. However, there is a third condition that can bring about an apparent lack of relationship between two variables, which is not discussed in most statistical texts or book concerned with research design. This condition is the presence of interactions between the X variable (i.e., the "independent" variable) and other variables that may be impinging upon the developing organism. A likely consequence of the presence of interactions is that the relationship between the independent variable and some criterion measure appears to be zero when it is actually significant.

This can be shown by returning to Table 10.2. If we consider each of the three independent variables separately, and compute the Pearson correlation (which in this instance is the same as the point biserial correlation) between the two levels of A (or B, or C) and the scores of the individual subjects, we find the numerical value of the correlation coefficient is 0. In addition, all partial correlations of the variables A, B, and C against the criterion scores are 0; as is the multiple correlation of A, B, and C against the criterion values.

It is not necessary to actually compute the correlations to verify this. The critical information is already contained in Table 10.3. In that table we found that the main effects for *A*, *B*, and *C* were all equal to 0. Thus, the Pearson correlation between the two levels of *A* (or *B*, or *C*) against the individual scores must also necessarily be 0. In other words, *a significant correlation coefficient is identical to a significant main effect in the analysis of variance.* Similarly, the lack of a significant main effect also means that there is no significant correlation between the two variables. However, we have already seen from Table 10.3 that there is a significant relationship among particular combinations of levels of *A*, *B*, and *C*, as indicated by the presence of a significant triple interaction. Yet that significant relationship cannot be found by the use of conventional correlational procedures, as was previously shown. This information, of course, is extracted when the data are cast into a factorial design framework as in Table 10.2 and analyzed by the usual procedure as summarized in Table 10.3.

Therefore, a third major reason that variables measured in early life may not appear "to be related to" variables measured in later life is that the early variables may interact with subsequent (or prior) events to yield a configuration that appears to be zero as measured by our usual correlational procedures (i.e., zero-order, partial, and multiple correlations) or by main effects in the analysis of variance, but in which important relationships are present as indicated by one or more significant interactions in the analysis of variance.

My conclusion from this analysis is that it is not possible to make *any* meaningful statement concerning developmental relationships in humans based upon the lack of significant correlations between early variables and later variables unless a test for interactional effects has been made. Even when a significant correlation has been obtained, unless the numerical value of the coefficient is very high, there is a good likelihood that the variable is being influenced interactively by other variables. Thus, we also see here, as in the case of experimental research, that a general systems approach is a more accurate framework within which to interpret our data than a linear causal (or correlational) model. For those doing correlational studies, it is quite important to be cautious and not to draw insignificant conclusions about nonsignificant correlations.

Correlational Data and Individual Subjects

A characteristic shared by the experimental and the correlational model is that both paradigms measure groups of subjects on a common variable. This procedure allows us to partially characterize the individual in a statistical or actuarial sense. That is, by knowing to which group a subject belongs, we can say something about his future behavior. This is easily seen in the

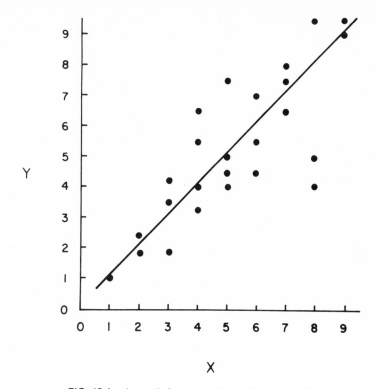

FIG. 10.4.   A correlation scatterplot and line of best fit.

experimental model where we randomly assign subjects to groups and then evaluate the group means as shown in Tables 10.1 and 10.2. It may not be so apparent that the correlational model also uses group means for predictive purposes.

In correlational research we have a sample of subjects that are measured on two variables, X and Y, as shown in Figure 10.4. Even though it appears that we are working with only one group, or with a collection of single individuals, this is actually not the case. Instead, the underlying assumption is that we have many groups of individuals with each group having a particular score on the independent or X variable. This is shown in Figure 10.5, which is an expanded version of Figure 10.4.

In both experimental and correlational designs we are dealing with the means of groups of subjects, whether those groups are systemically assembled by an experimenter or randomly selected and measured by a psychometrician. Our prediction about the expected performance of an individual is obtained by knowing the subgroup of which he or she is a member and then predicting the mean of that subgroup as the most likely score for the single individual. It is for this reason that this is a statistical or actuarial approach.

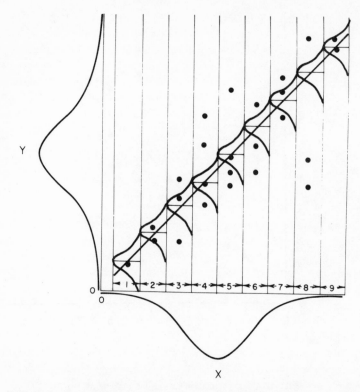

FIG. 10.5.   Expanded version of Figure 10.4 showing that each X-score covers a range of values and that each score range is composed of a group of subjects.

These statements are quite obvious when using the experimental model, but they do not appear to be so obvious when using the correlational model. In part, I think this is due to the expression "individual differences," which is deceptive in that the phrase leads one to think that correlational studies focus upon the individual *per se*. As is shown in Figure 10.5 this is not so. The expression "individual differences" actually means "when groups of individuals who differ in their mean performance on variable X are found to differ in their mean scores on variable Y, then we can make predictions that are better than chance."

LIMITATIONS OF EXPERIMENTAL AND CORRELATIONAL APPROACHES

In summary, both the correlational and experimental approaches (1) measure each organism on the same variable, and (2) use group average statistics for purposes of (a) finding general laws, and (b) characterizing the individual in a statistical or actuarial sense. If our interest is in general laws applying to populations of subjects, then this is a fine approach. However, if our interest is in the single individual, then there are some inherent limitations in using group average statistics to characterize single subjects.

One difficulty has to do with the effects of averaging. For example, if individuals learn something in an all-or-none fashion, but different subjects take varying lengths of time to shift from none to all, the average learning curve will appear as smooth and continuous even though each person has a stepwise function. Another common example is that the average growth curve typically will not show the pubertal spurt characteristic of single individuals, because different people start the growth spurt at different ages and the averaging smooths out and hides the rapid increase in growth during puberty.

A second problem has to do with the requirement that all subjects have to be measured on the same variable. This is necessary for statistical comparisons among individuals or among groups, but if we limit ourselves to studying only those variables that are common to everyone, our view of the individual will be extraodinarily narrow, albeit important. That is, we do have a better understanding of a child when we know that person's sex, socioeconomic status, growth rate, IQ, school achievement scores, aptitudes, interests, and so on. However, these kinds of measures tell us nothing about the child's style of communication, his or her play behavior, food preferences, the nature of the interactions with the mother and father, and many other behavioral characteristics that we must know to describe the child as an "interesting" human being (in contrast to describing the child as a "statistical" human being).

The third limitation to using the group approach to study behavioral development is that it is extremely difficult to do a general systems analysis with group data. The developing infant and its caregivers constitute a dynamic system in the sense that Bertalanffy and Weiss use that concept. In order to gain an understanding of the laws that govern the infant–caregiver system, it is better to study each system separately rather than work with group averages. As an example of this, one would gain a quicker and deeper understanding of the systems dynamics of the furnace and thermostat discussed earlier by studying one such system in depth, in contrast to drawing a random sample of furnaces (which would vary with respect to latency to start up, rate of generating heat, asymptotic heat level achieved, and latency to turn off) and thermostats (which would differ in set point, tolerance range of sensitivity, and response latency) and studying the group of furnaces and thermostats by either correlational or experimental procedures.

We see, then, that there is information to be gained from the study of single individuals that cannot be derived from group averaging procedures. Let me now turn to a brief discussion of that topic.

SINGLE SUBJECT RESEARCH

Case Histories

One purpose for studying single subjects is to understand an individual per se as in a case history or clinical context. The focus is upon idiosyncratic (i.e., unique) facets of the person as well as upon characteristics held in common with others, with the objective of portraying that individual in as much depth and roundness as possible. The kinds of people who would study a single individual in this fashion would be a biographer or psychobiographer trying to depict an important personage, or a clinician concerned with the well-being (both mental and physical) of an individual. In this context, the person studied is *the population* of interest.

This approach to studying a person is generally considered to be "unscientific," since the biographer or clinician is not seeking general laws but is only concerned with the one case under study. However, we are all aware that biographers and clinicians, as well as many other human beings, do extract general principles from their detailed study of single subjects and are able to test these principles on other individuals. An outstanding example of this is Sigmund Freud and his theory of psychoanalysis.

General Principles and General Systems Theory

Thus we see that a second purpose for studying single subjects would be to attempt to derive broad principles which may apply to a general population of subjects.[2] Many, though not all, of these principles will be concerned with organizational structure and function during development, and thus will fall within the rubric of general systems theory. The rationale for the use of general systems theory as a frame of reference for studying the development of infants is discussed in detail by Thoman et al. in this volume. They also present longitudinal data from several of their infants to illustrate the use of systems theory.

Measuring and Generalizing from Single Subjects

Regardless of one's theoretical position regarding experimental research, correlational methodology, and general systems theory, there are some major obstacles to overcome if one wishes to work with single subjects. For one thing, it is quite difficult to separate, within any one person, the unique features of that person's behavior pattern from those features shared in common with others in the population. Meaningful generalizations can be

---

[2]For a general discussion of the use of experimental designs for single subjects, see the book by Hersen and Barlow (1976).

obtained only from communality, not from uniqueness. Once the obstacle of uniqueness is overcome, so that we are dealing with common processes across persons, we then have the problem of determining how general our generalization is. In essence, this means we have to define the population to which the generalization is applicable.

What I wish to discuss in this section is an approach to obtaining information about single subjects and a method to test for generality (i.e., nonuniqueness) of the findings. In the comments that follow, I am assuming that subjects have been studied longitudinally in a naturalistic or semi-naturalistic setting and that the observations are sufficiently detailed so that quantitative values can be derived, including frequency of occurrence of an event, duration of an event, and latency until an event has occurred. It is also assumed that a sufficient number of subjects have been measured (say, 10 to 20); this is necessary in order to test for generality.

The principle involved in this analysis is that each subject is a separate experiment. Given an extensive data base for each subject, it is possible to perform statistical tests with an individual and to obtain parameters that characterize the person. If the parameters, or pattern of parameters, obtained on one subject (i.e., in one experiment) can be replicated in other subjects (i.e., in other experiments), this will be sufficient to establish that the phenomenon generalizes beyond one person, thus eliminating the problem of uniqueness within an individual.

Let me now describe some of the kinds of statistical parameters one can look for within subjects.

Single Value Constants.   Several forms of invariance may be present in one's data. One such form of invariance is constants that typify an individual. As an example of this, Thoman (1975) reported the following in an analysis of six infants. If the infant cried and was picked up in less than 90 seconds, then the baby stopped crying very quickly. However, if the baby cried for more than 90 seconds before being picked up, then it took a long time before it stopped crying. This 90-second value was found in five of Thoman's babies (the sixth one was always picked up in less than 90 seconds and thus yielded no information concerning prolonged crying). Here, then, is an example of a statistical parameter that clearly generalizes beyond any one infant to a wider population.

Even though Thoman found the same constant—90 seconds—for her sample of infants, it is not necessary that all subjects have the same value (though that makes the conclusion more powerful). All that is needed is that each infant have a constant (i.e., a measure of central tendency) that remains very much the same from one set of observations to another (i.e., has a small measure of dispersion).

Another kind of constant is suggested in the report of Thoman et al. in this volume of a mother–infant pair in which the baby was held less than most of the infants in a sample. However, this particular mother–infant pair had a great deal of pat and caress. This suggests the hypothesis that the amount of mother–infant contact (as defined by touching, talking to, or looking at) is a constant. This hypothesis could be tested by determining the percentage of contact time (out of wake time) over several observation sets for each infant. If an infant had very similar values from one observation to another (i.e., a small dispersion around the central tendency value), this would be consistent with the hypothesis. If this were found to be true for a significant number of infants, this would establish the generality of the hypothesis.

Trends over Time.   Given an extensive set of observations on a number of occasions (i.e., at different ages), one can look for developmental trends within an individual. For example, the percent of time spent in sleep decreases as the infant matures. This can be plotted for each subject and the curve used as a measure characterizing the infant. If all infants show the same form of curve, this is also an invariance. If there are a few major trend patterns, this suggests a potentially useful taxonomy. If no discernible pattern is seen among the various curves, then this would not be a worthwhile parameter to pursue.

As another example Freese (1975) describes a mother–infant dyad in which the baby cried a lot during the 2nd week of life. Over the next 3 weeks, it cried less and less. Analysis of the data revealed that at first the mother did not pick the infant up when it started crying (i.e., in less than 90 seconds), but over the successive weeks she learned to do so. Thus the reduction in baby crying was a function of a change in the mother's behavior over time. This form of "learning curve," if found in general form in some other mother–infant pairs, might be useful as a taxonomic category.

Within-Person Comparisons.   If infants are observed for enough time over sufficient occasions, there will occur "natural experiments," which the researcher can use to advantage. For example, one can ask about the relationship (if any) between a baby's disposition prior to going to sleep and its subsequent pattern of sleeping behavior. Thus, if a baby fussed or cried on some occasion prior to sleeping, and cooed and smiled on other occasions, an analysis could be made of the sleep states after each antecedent condition.

Having found a pattern that describes one infant, the researcher can see whether this same pattern is present in other infants. If so, this establishes the generality of the phenomenon.

A Statistical Test for Generality.   As noted previously, a serious problem when working with single cases is whether the results obtained have any degree of generality or whether they represent part of the unique constellation of the individual studied. A rational argument would be that finding several other persons with the same pattern of results should suffice to indicate that the results are not unique. That is essentially what one finds when a statistical test is applied to evaluate uniqueness. The reasoning for the test is as follows. Suppose that the data of one subject are extensively analysed. Any pattern of findings that the researcher would obtain has to be viewed with suspicion because of the likelihood that it represents (1) unique aspects of the person studied, and/or (2) a chance event because of the large number of analyses done. In this instance the null hypothesis is that this particular pattern of results does not exist in the population. In other words, the proportion of people in the population who would exhibit this pattern of results is zero, if the null hypothesis is true. This hypothesis can be tested (Walker and Lev, 1953, pp. 43–55 and Chart 4). It is necessary to find only 1 or 2 additional cases to reject the null hypothesis that the population proportion is zero. If one finds the same pattern occurring in only 1 additional case out of 50 or less, this is sufficient to reject the null hypothesis at the .05 level. And if one is sampling between 51 and 350 cases, it is necessary to find only 2 additional instances of the phenomenon to reject the null hypothesis at the .05 level.

Normally we do not ask whether a population proportion is greater than zero because we are working with groups of subjects. Yet this is a necessary question when studying single individuals. It is rather surprising to find out that the occurrence of the phenonmenon in only one or two cases is sufficient to reject the null hypothesis. Thus, two of the arguments leveled against the use of single subjects—uniqueness and chance relationships—can be readily tested and easily rejected. There is a parallel between testing an observed proportion to see if it is significantly different from zero and testing a correlation coefficient to see if it differs from zero. Neither finding yields very much information, but it is information needed in order to proceed with one's research.

Determining Degree of Generality.   We see from the above discussion that finding the same phenomenon in one or two additional cases will usually be sufficient to cause us to reject the hypothesis that the phenomenon does not exist in the population. This tells us that the proportion is some non-zero value. The actual value of the proportion in the population would define the degree of generality of the phenomenon. If this is the question of interest, it is necessary to carry out a study using large numbers of cases in order to obtain a reliable estimate of the population proportion with a relatively small standard error.

PERSPECTIVES AND TACTICS IN
THE STUDY OF BEHAVIORAL DEVELOPMENT

It is important to keep separate the tactics we use in conducting research in behavioral development (and other areas as well) and the perspectives we have about our research. The most powerful research tactics we have involve the skillful design of experiments and the use of the statistical procedures of the analysis of variance and the Pearson correlation coefficient to evaluate our data. Every procedure has certain basic assumptions underlying its use. Thus, *causality* is the assumption involved in elemental experimental designs, *additivity* is a necessary assumption in the use of the analysis of variance, and *linearity* of relationship is an assumption we must make in order to use the Pearson correlation coefficient. We are willing to accept these assumptions because doing so permits us to use procedures that are not otherwise available. We also know that *to a first approximation* the assumptions are valid. We know this because we are able to replicate our findings statistically in other experiments and in other laboratories, and because we can use or apply our findings to events in the everyday world around us on a probabilistic basis. However, we also know that these assumptions are not ultimately true because we have found too many discrepancies between our data and our models or expectations—and these discrepancies have occurred too often and too consistently to be rationalized away as chance happenings due to sampling error.

Many years ago physicists gave up the belief that the universe could be described or explained in simple mechanistic and causal terms, and they were compelled to turn to more complex models in order to account for their findings. Recently Engel (1977) has argued convincingly that medicine has to give up the reductionistic biomedical model that it has been using for centuries because this model is insufficient to account for known medical phenomena. He proposes, instead, a biopsychosocial model with a general systems theory perspective.

I believe that we have also advanced in our study of behavioral development to a point where the basic assumption of mechanistic causality no longer offers us a perspective of sufficient breadth and depth to integrate the many findings we have obtained. I believe that general sytems theory offers us a far better perspective for viewing developmental phenomena; and that a powerful tactic, which we are just beginning to exploit, involves the intensive study of individual units (which include the single subject, the infant-caregiver dyad, and the family constellation) in a naturalistic or seminatural setting, over some portion of the developmental time span. To use this tactic efficiently it is necessary to sample a wide range of behaviors in a sufficiently quantitative manner to allow for extensive statistical analyses *within* the individual unit. I am fully confident that the application of the concepts of general systems theory to such data will widen and change our perspectives and will suggest other research directions for us to follow; and that such an approach will aid in giving us a richer and fuller understanding of behavioral development.

SUMMARY AND CONCLUSIONS

The most common experimental design used in the study of behavioral development involves a control group and an experimental group that receives some treatment in early life. After an interval of time both groups are given a criterion test. If a significant effect is obtained, the findings are interpreted in terms of the experimental treatment's *causing* the difference because of the *additive* effect of the experimental variable, and there is usually a further interpretation based upon a *value judgment* as to the merits of the treatment (i.e., did it make the experimental group perform better or worse than the controls.) An examination of the structure of the experimental design show that such conclusions are unwarranted, and other procedures are suggested as ways of testing for causality, additivity, and judgments of better or poorer.

Evidence is presented to support the thesis that the presence of strong interactions among qualitatively different variables across a developmental time domain will make it very unlikely that one can draw any causal conclusions from the findings. In place of the concept of causality, it is proposed that the perspective of general systems theory is a more appropriate one for viewing developmental data.

For those using correlational procedures to study developmental processes, a common statement is that some variable(s) measured in early life *is not related to* some variable(s) obtained in later life. The logical difficulties in drawing such a conclusion are discussed, and it is emphasized that one must make the assumption that the variable measured in early life does not interact with any other variable before it is possible to talk meaningfully about nonsignificant correlations. A general systems theory framework is shown to be helpful in viewing correlational data as well.

The limitations of experimental and correlational procedures for the understanding of the behavior of single individuals are discussed, and procedures are suggested that will allow the researcher to determine meaningful statistical parameters for individual subjects.

ACKNOWLEDGMENTS

The preparation of this paper was supported, in part, by Research Grant HD-08195 from the National Institute of Child Health and Human Development, NIH. I should like to express my appreciation to the following individuals, who read over and commented on drafts of this paper; Stephen Chorover, Glyn Collis, Herman Epstein, Robert Hinde, John A. King, and Melvin Konner.

DISCUSSION

Dr. Watson: My understanding, although I can't give you the references, is that multiple regression analysis proposes in its modern form to have all the power of analysis of variance to deal with all the interaction terms. It strikes me then that the initial part of your presentation about the limited use of correlational techniques in the analysis of cause and effect is possibly wrong, or at least possibly not up-to-date with the present state of the art. On top of that, the general proposal about statistical interactions having an implication for the nature of one's causal attribution—one's statement of lawfulness—is something that if we accept then we accept your following arguments, but if we don't accept that premise we don't have to accept what follows. And at the moment, I see no reason to accept that premise.

Dr. Denenberg: I did not say that there were no correlational procedures available for the analysis of interactional effects. My statement was that the usual correlational procedures employed by the vast majority of researchers—namely, zero-order, partial, and multiple correlations—are not capable of isolating interactional effects. This is really not an argument about analytical procedures, since I showed that the data could be cast into a factorial design and analyzed that way; it is more a matter of the way of thinking about the nature of the relationships among the variables under investigation. If researchers believe that a single variable, occurring in early life, can have such powerful impact that it will have a significant influence upon later behavior, independent of other experiences that occur throughout one's life history, then those researchers will continue to seek for such variables and will use the Pearson correlation coefficient as their statistical evaluator. That search has been remarkably unsuccessful insofar as human behavioral development is concerned. Given that simple notions of causality (tested via correlational procedures) are not yielding much meaningful information, we have to look for another model, and I have proposed general systems theory as such a model. This leads me to your second point—the relationship between statistical interaction and causal attribution. When we have a strong interaction effect, we have to conclude that the effects of A are in part dependent upon the levels of B, C, and so on present in the study. When you have to talk about the effects of one variable as being dependent upon the values of other variables, then you are out of the realm of direct cause and effect and into systems theory, whether you want to admit it or not.

Dr. Watson: Well you might have a compound cause. Causes that are labeled as A_0 versus A_1 are classification statements about a dimension of life or of the world we call A, which if we analyzed it more fully we might end up seeing as itself composed of constituent dimensions. When you deal in cross-classification of the world as being both A and B and then find that there's an interaction of these dimensions, all that you've found is that when levels of A

and B are compounded (e.g., A_1 and B_1) a different outcome occurs than you would have expected, given a simple additive model of causality. An additive model of causality is not the only model of causality. To say that you must give up causality when finding an interaction of the components of what could be termed a compound cause strikes me as a special use of the word *causality*, which I don't see a reason to accept as yet.

Dr. Denenberg: If, by a compound cause, you mean that a particular combination of variables (say, A_1B_1) will have a high likelihood of producing a particular outcome, independent of other variables in the experiment, then I agree with you. And such an effect would produce a significant interaction. However, not all interactions are alike. Another kind of interactional pattern could be one in which the effect of the combination A_1B_1 is dependent upon the levels of C and D in the experiment. If that were the case, we could not talk about A_1B_1 being a compound cause.

I would like to make another point, which has to do with the way we use words. When we make interpretations and when we recommend social policy, we talk in causal terminology. Thus, many people think that Operation Headstart was a failure because it did not cause a significant improvement in school achievement.

Dr. Watson: Now you're talking about the null hypothesis, which is not the same as the issue of compound cause or of how interaction might prohibit a statement of causality. I mean I would give you the point regarding the null hypothesis. On the other hand, I'd say there's a limit there. If you look and look and look and don't find anything, it makes no sense to hold it up as a legitimate powerful option. Not that this proves the null hypothesis. It is just a fact that as far as we can extend energy it doesn't make any sense to dig any further. So in some sense there's a limit on that statement, but indeed logically it's perfectly right. When you haven't found it, you can't say it doesn't exist. That's a different point, however, than the point about the limits on a statement of causality of a main effect being dependent on the condition of whether it was interacting with other variables.

Dr. Denenberg: It is my sense of general systems theory that as soon as you have to make the statement that everything depends upon something else, you are into general systems theory. Maybe it's just a matter of degree where one stops and the other begins.

Dr. Lipsitt: May I put John Watson's disagreement with you, with which I agree, in a different way. If you were to do an experiment with rats and were to show that your frustrating condition that you implemented for the rats produced aggression in your rats but more in the males than in the females, would you say this compromises the lawfulness of the relationship between frustration and aggression?

Dr. Denenberg: In your example there is a significant main effect for sex, with the males being more aggressive than females. There is no difficulty in dealing with this situation, since the presence of a strong main effect will allow us to draw causal conclusions within the sex dimension. My focus is upon these situations where we do not find powerful main effects but do have strong interactional effects.

Dr. Mason: Maybe the problem is that our experimental models really assume linear causality, although none of us really takes that assumption very seriously. At the same time, having set up the model and done the experiment, it's not very satisfying to go back and say that the conditions made a difference, but God knows why. There are a lot of things happening and 3 or 4 subjects out of a group of 15 didn't show the effect, even though it's highly significant statistically or whatever it is. Partly it's a matter of just economy of expression and getting through the thing and communicating, and at the same time there's always that trap that we'll really be led to believe that the system is that tidy and neat and there's a kind of direct relation between what you put in and what comes out.

Dr. Denenberg: We always make assumptions in research. We assume linearity because if we do not, it is very difficult to do correlational studies. We assume additivity because this allows us to use analysis of variance procedures. Likewise, in research studies we assume causality and use that as the basis for our experiments. However, there is a difference between a set of assumptions that we use as first approximations and the underlying philosophy that we have about the nature of the world. My philosophy is that the world is much more complex than what we are led to believe from our linear, additive, and causal assumptions. But since these assumptions allow us to use the powerful tools of correlation and analysis of variance procedures, we are willing to go along with them. I think, however, that there is the strong danger that we will deceive ourselves into converting our strategic assumptions into our underlying philosophy.

Dr. Thoman: But I think we are easily deceived. A case in point: If you look at Anneliese's data where there was one baby that had *more* rather than *less* apnea on the waterbed. Without that subject it would have been very easy to draw the general conclusion that being on the waterbed causes apnea to be reduced; whereas being on the waterbed is associated with a reduction in apnea under certain circumstances for certain kinds of babies. We tend to focus on our data and overgeneralize what we find in terms of linear causal relations.

Dr. Yarrow: Those are lawful relationships even though we know that we haven't considered all the interactions that occur. We still can say that that's a lawful relationship. You can't say that we identified *the* cause for *the* causes. It is a meaningful lawful relationship.

Dr. Denenberg: Consider all the data on all-or-none learning curves in the literature. The statistical average gives you a lawful cumulative smooth function for the population, even though for each individual you have a stepwise function. So I think there are some dangers in taking group averages and then applying them to the individual.

Dr. Eisenberg: I'm sorry, but I'm not clear about what you're getting at...despite the fact that I've found systems theory very useful in my own work. It seems to me that one virtue of systems theory is that you don't have to specify the processes intervening between stimulus and response with any specificity. As I understand it, whether living systems theory or some other aspect of automatic process control, it's simply a series of constructs permitting you to regard the organism as a "black box" incorporating feedback mechanisms. Thus, if you provide a known input that pushes the organism into disequilibrium, you can make certain inferences respecting what's going on inside the organism by measuring changes in output. Systems theory is simply a strategy one can use, either in the design of experiments or in the analysis of them, that provides flexibility precisely because you don't have to specify variables that, in some cases, are not specifiable. I'm not at all sure I buy your argument that system theory is superior to any other approach, even though I find it so in my own work. However, that is because the auditory system has many attributes of an automatic control system. The choice of an experimental approach, it seems to me, is dictated by the systems one is dealing with and the questions one is asking; and I don't believe all questions can best be answered by systems theory.

Dr. Denenberg: As I see the research in human development, concepts of causation are insufficient to account for the kinds of data we obtain. We have to move beyond that kind of thinking to a more complex form of thinking.

Dr. Eisenberg: Even in living systems theory, you can't escape causality: You can just escape specifying it. However, if you introduce something into the black box system and you thereby effect a change in output, that something you introduced certainly must be regarded as causal in nature. It may result in interactions or even specific internal reactions one can't specify, but nonetheless, something happened.

Dr. Denenberg: General systems theory does not assume that there has to be a cause.

Dr. Eisenberg: The cause is the input.

Dr. Denenberg: No. Not as I read it, anyway.

Dr. Eisenberg: In the experimental system it has to be.

Dr. Denenberg: As Weiss points out in his complex diagram tracing some of the relationships between the fertilized egg and the central nervous system, any one of the many small boxes that are connected by arrows has a cause–effect relationship. But in order to account for how an egg turns into a central nervous system you cannot use causal connections. You have to assume there is a supra-organizational principle, a hierarchical arrangement that the system itself has and that controls and governs the parts of it.

Dr. Mason: I think the thing that you're talking about is sufficient cause—

in the sense that not only does the particular thing you do cause the obtained outcome, but nothing else is involved. It doesn't assume any particular state of the organism, any existing organization, or whatever. Rita's point is we don't know much about the existing state or the existing organization or how that interacts or whatever, and what systems theory says is that that's going to make a difference somewhere.

Dr. Eisenberg: I don't know what the organization is.

Dr. Mason: Yes. It's going through all of this, but whatever you put in is causing that change in outcome as a result of these interactions or whatever it is. It seems to me that's where you are. So that you can't say, given any organism at any state at any developmental age, and this treatment—this is the outcome that's bound to occur. That's the kind of generalization we always used to try to aim for.

Dr. Papousek: I explained to you our concept of playfulness. Allow me to be playful now in the same sense, to re-open concepts we would like to close, and to come up with the question, But what if. The theory of systems re-opened our old and quite well closed learning concepts with the question of interaction. We re-opened the static concepts of interaction with the notion of dynamic systems and also with probabilistic aspects. However, until now we have considered only those mathematical and statistical concepts that reduce relations to those that can be expressed with two-dimensional lines and curves, and we have had considerable troubles with unexpected and unpredictable discontinuous trends in behavior. Now Rene Thom comes to re-open our concepts with his theory of discontinuous or catastrophic trends. He simply projects the trajectories of, let's say, decision-making upon uneven planes controlled by four dimensions: the three spatial ones and time. Here, as soon as the trajectory moves on the surface of a folded plane, it can suddenly make a sharp curve and run in the opposite direction, something unusual in our two- or three-dimensional even-plane models. Perhaps something a Marxist would call a jump in quality after a successive change in quantity.

Dr. Eisenberg: It forces you to think about feedback, which is something completely overlooked in classical work. The minute you get into systems theory, you get into feedback, which brings us all back to the question Hanus brought up at the beginning when he asked me whether I had considered the effect of my entire schedule and how that affected the organism. One must consider the sequence of events as well as the discrete stimuli when one looks at an organism; one must consider the effects of experimental interventions as they occur in time and change in time. And the real value of systems theory, in my opinion, is that it literally forces you to look at all of the variables you're dealing with: It becomes impossible to reduce complex events to simple cause–effect or stimulus–response relations. I don't disagree with you about the value of systems theory, and as I noted before, it's very useful for my particular purposes. I just don't think it's the only useful strategy around or, indeed, the best strategy for all purposes.

Dr. Denenberg: That's why I said one of the best strategies we have now is to treat data as though it were in a causal framework, because we know how to deal with that.

Dr. Mason: I think it's probably complicating things unnecessarily to argue systems theory on the basis of statistical considerations. The intuitive notions can be expressed verbally. A system is nothing more than a set of elements and their relations to each other. You can define the elements and you can define the relations in any way you want. It then becomes a question of how you measure the relations, and at that point you're into questions of statistical devices. But it seems to me that one problem with the approach that Vic is advocating is that you determine whether you're going to think in systems terms on the basis of the appropriateness of statistical techniques, and I don't think that's correct. I think you start with a systems orientation, then you ask what statistical techniques are appropriate to what I want to do here, and that's quite different. On the one hand you start with a perspective that doesn't require any very high level of criteria at all. You're simply saying the mother and infant are a system, presumably because they are two entities in relationship to each other. Now how do we express that relationship? It may be in terms of some fairly simple kind of behavioral measure. You remove the mother, and the infant cries more. You remove the infant, and the mother shows an increase in heart rate, or whatever. It seems that would be the way to start with it. The problem analysis, I agree, is a very serious one and the lack of analytic techniques is one of the things that's held up the application of systems theory to behavioral research. It seems that that's where the contribution that you're moving towards could be most important to people who want to work within this perspective.

Dr. Watson: A point that I don't want to take too long in saying: The statistics that we have available at present are statistics that are very sensitive in assessing lawfulness in the world. Their sensitivity to lawfulness (e.g., that variables A and/or B relate lawfully to the occurrence of R) is assisted by making an assumption about the potential "form of law" (e.g., $R = fA + B$). However, the usefulness of this assumption is not dependent on its validity regarding the real form of law. An example is the additive assumption that exists in correlational and analysis of variance statistics. If you try using these statistical methods as measures of the "form of law," they can lead you into very problematic states. These statistics are extraordinarily insensitive to the form of law. For example, one can assume an interactive form (e.g., $R = A \times B$) and then use it to simulate data arrays. Analysis of variance of these data will commonly tell you that there is no significant interaction, that there are only main effects with a miniscule interaction even though you've generated the data out of an interactive model. Statisticians will say that's the state of the art. The future is hopefully going to bring us something better in the way of procedures to assess the relative likelihood of statements about contrasts in form of law. The best we have now are maximum likelihood procedures, which in fact are not good procedures for telling us the degree of difference that exists between form of law *A* and form of law *B*. Why all this is relevant is that I see the difference between a systems approach and a non–systems approach as really a difference in perspective on the form of law as opposed to a fundamental difference in perspective on lawfulness. The systems approach may be an advantage heuristically. Yet its accessability for generating thought should be separate from any dependence on the structure of our existing statistical models. In the end, one presumably wants to find out things that one can tell other people that will convince them according to the rules of the game. When we come down to provide a statement of probable truth value of our claims, we then turn to statistics. However, there are really two separate games going on, one trying to assess the form of law, and the other, the existence of lawfulness. The question of lawfulness per se is appropriately one for the array of statistics that we have. But we do not yet possess statistics to help us make firm confident statements for a claim about the form of law.

Dr. Thoman: I don't think the search for main effects will get us anywhere with respect to understanding *process*. The variables we have defined in our study are assumed to be process variables—many of them involve behaviors of both mother and infant, and all are assumed to reflect their interaction even where only one member of the dyad is described. For example, the state of the infant while sleeping alone in the crib is an infant process and one that is affected by and, in turn, has an effect on mother–infant behaviors both before and after the sleeping period. Thus, the sleeping process is part of the larger interactive process. Our summary variables are, therefore, assumed to reflect process, even though we have not yet used them to describe changes over time. While we are searching for even more sophisticated statistical procedures for helping us to depict process changes with age, it seems to me most important that we express verbally how we conceptualize the development of behavioral interactions—and let our ideas in this respect guide us in the development or utilization of analytic procedures, rather than rushing into the use of statistics that may violate our most basic assumptions about the nature of the baby's development as we can see it in the real world.

REFERENCES

Anderson, P. W. More is different. *Science*, 1972, 177, 393–396.

Beach, F. A., & Jaynes, J. Studies of maternal retrieving in rats. III. Sensory cues involved in the lactating female's response to her young. *Behaviour*, 1956, *10*, 104–125.

Bertalanffy, L. v. Chance or law. In A. Koestler and J. R. Smythies (Eds.), *Beyond reductionism*. Boston: Beacon Press, 1969.

Denenberg, V. H. A consideration of the usefulness of the critical period hypothesis as applied to the stimulation of rodents in infancy. In G. Newton and S. Levine (Eds.), *Early experience and behavior*, Springfield, Illinois: Thomas, 1968.

Denenberg, V. H. The effects of early experience. In E. S. E. Hafez (Ed.), *The behaviour of domestic animals.* London: Bailliere, Tindall & Cassell, 1969.

Denenberg, V. H. Assessing the effects of early experience. In R. D. Myers (Ed.), *Methods of Psychobiology* (Vol. III). New York: Academic Press, 1977. (a)

Denenberg, V. H. Interactional effects in early experience research. In A. Oliverio (Ed.), *Genetics, environment and intelligence.* Amsterdam: Elselier/North-Holland Biomedical Press, 1977. (b)

Denenberg, V. H., Karas, G. G., Rosenberg, K. M., & Schell, S. F. Programming life histories: An experimental design and initial results. *Developmental Psychobiology,* 1968, *1,* 3–9.

Denenberg, V. H., & Whimbey, A. E. Experimental programming of life histories: Toward an experimental science of individual differences. *Developmental Psychobiology,* 1968, *1,* 55–59.

Denenberg, V. H., Woodcock, J. M., & Rosenberg, K. M. Long-term effects of preweaning and postweaning free-environment experience on rats' problem-solving behavior. *Journal of Comparative and Physiological Psychology,* 1968, *66,* 533–535.

Doolittle, D. P. The effect of single gene substitution on resistance to radiation in mice. *Genetics,* 1961, *46,* 1501–1509.

Engel, G. L. The need for a new medical model: A challenge for biomedicine. *Science,* 1977, *196,* 129–136.

Freese, M. P. *Assessment of maternal attitudes and analysis of their role in early mother–infant interactions.* Ph.D. dissertation, Purdue University, 1975.

Goldfarb, W. The effects of early institutional care on adolescent personality. *Journal of Experimental Education,* 1943, *12,* 106–129.

Hebb, D. O. *The organization of behavior.* New York: Wiley, 1949.

Herrenkohl, L. R., & Rosenberg, P. A. Exteroceptive stimulation of maternal behavior in the naive rat. *Physiology and Behavior, 1972, 8,* 595–598.

Hersen, M., & Barlow, D. H. *Single case experimental designs.* New York: Pergamon Press, 1976.

Odum, E. P. The emergence of ecology as a new integrative discipline. *Science,* 1977, *195,* 1289–1293.

Rheingold, H. L. The modification of social responsiveness in institutional babies. *Monographs of the Society for Research in Child Development,* 1956, *21,* (2 Serial No. 63).

Rheingold, H. L. & Bayley, N. The later effects of an experimental modification of mothering. *Child Development,* 1959, *30,* 363–372.

Spitz, R. A. Hospitalism: An inquiry into the genesis of psychiatric conditions in early childhood. *Psychoanalitic Study of the Child., 1,* 53–74; New York: International University Press, 1945.

Thoman, E. B. How a rejecting baby may affect mother–infant synchrony. In *Parent–Infant interaction.* New York: Associated Scientific Publishers, 1975.

Thoman, E. B., Acebo, C., Dreyer, C., Becker, P. T., & Freese, M. P. Individuality in the interactive process. In E. B. Thoman (Ed.), *The Origins of the Infant's Social Responsiveness.* Hillsdale, New Jersey: Lawrence Erlbaum Associates, 1979.

Thompson, W. R. Influence of prenatal maternal anxiety on emotionality in young rats. *Science,* 1957, *125,* 698–699.

Walker, H., & Lev, J. *Statistical inference.* New York: Holt, 1953.

Weiss, P. The living system: determinism stratified. In A. Koestler & J. R. Symthies (Eds.) *Beyond reductionism.* Boston: Beacon Press, 1969.

11 Mother–Infant Behavior: Description or Explanation?

Harriet L. Rheingold
University of North Carolina at Chapel Hill

In their diversity, the three papers I am to discuss very nearly box the compass we need to direct our studies of parent–infant interaction. I am indeed grateful to the authors for providing the occasion to present some further directions for research in this area.

THE NEED FOR A FIRM DATA BASE

To Doctors Yarrow and Anderson we owe the portrayal of how disorderly in fact is the data base on which we draw inferences about the results of observational studies of parent–infant interactions. The variability among studies in setting, directions and explanations to mothers, the state of the infant, the behaviors recorded, the schedules and units of observation, is indeed so great as to render well-nigh impossible general statements of principles. A survey of the field may well lead an impartial reviewer to the conclusion that no further justification for the studies is required than that one is studying the relation between mother and infant behavior. How one conducts the study and the rationale for each decision would seem to matter less.

Yet many of the questions they have raised are testable and would yield to empirical study. Comparisons can be made between behaviors in different settings. The effect of different instructions to mothers can be assessed. The differences between event sampling and time sampling, as well as between different units of time, can be measured. Without knowledge about these elementary facts we cannot build firm statements of relationships. Are we too individualistic to repeat another's procedure? Are we in such a hurry to make the great discovery that we cannot pay attention to the trustworthiness of the bricks out of which we build our structures? Or do investigators hope that they alone by chance will choose correctly among the many possibilities? We seem not to have the will to do the hard work.

By now the issue of the home or the laboratory as the more suitable and productive setting for gaining knowledge should have been laid to rest. Dr. Mason has already spoken cogently to the issue. However, given the current tendency to elevate the study of parent–child relations in the home, I may be allowed a more extended treatment of the matter.

The choice of the environment in which the study is to be carried out depends on the question or questions the investigator sets out to answer. No environment in and of itself holds any special claim without regard to the question. It cannot be held that only observations made in "natural" environments are valid. What is a natural environment? What are the special advantages of studying infants and their parents where they spend all of their time, most of their time, or some of their time? As for laboratories, although they may conjure up images of Skinner boxes in the minds of some, they in fact may present quite ordinary and even homelike settings. The question to be asked here is "more natural for what?"

In neither of these two types of settings can one obtain a "true" record of how people behave when they are not being observed. Laboratory studies provide an unfamiliar setting; homes provide an unfamiliar observer. There are ways, however, to reduce the influence of both types of departure from what would occur in "enduring" environments when the actors are not under observation. In homes, the effect of the observer's presence can be minimized, but never completely eliminated, by the conduct of the observer and by sheer familiarity. In laboratories, the effect of its unfamiliarity can be minimized by its furnishings and by increasing its familiarity. Laboratories have the advantage of eliminating the presence of observers from the participants' view, of having the same setting for all participants, of permitting a greater number of observers, as well as a greater number and variety of recording instruments. Homes, in contrast, vary so much in physical characteristics and routines that more variability in behavior is to be expected.

The suitability of settings should be judged by two main criteria. First, is the behavior of the actors in this or that setting, with or without an observer's presence, representative of how they would normally behave? For this difficult question, seldom faced, no suitable criteria yet exist. The other main criterion concerns the extent to which the setting yields behavior that would occur in all similar settings and in different settings as well. We can only talk about these criteria because we never really use them.

We assume that that behavior is representative that would obtain when people are "adapted" to the environment and the people in it. How would we ever know? In one sense, behavior is natural wherever displayed or obtained.

To test how representative it is, one could compare behavior during the second half of an observation period with that during the first, or compare behavior during a second exposure to the setting with that during a first. Such a procedure, however, yields only a partial answer because familiarity brings its own changes and, also, because we are dealing with biological organisms with their own rhythms.

The criterion of generality can be faced at different levels. The first might be the relative extent to which the findings can be generalized from one home setting to another and from one laboratory to another. Here the laboratory environment is more likely to meet the criterion of that kind of generality.

But how about the generalizability of findings from laboratory to home, or home to laboratory? My belief is that any behavior observed in a laboratory must also occur outside the laboratory; thus laboratory findings are generalizable. Rather, it is a feat to design laboratory studies to reproduce behavior that occurs outside a laboratory. It is a feat, however, that has often been accomplished. There is no sound reason for thinking that behaviors in the laboratory are not normal, natural, representative, and generalizable. Infants and mothers do not have one set of behaviors for the laboratory and a totally different, mutually exclusive set for outside the laboratory. In the last analysis, to do more than describe behavior, to set up cause and effect relationships, the laboratory may provide the better setting. Ideally, of course, one ought to move freely between environments.

Studies of human children in the laboratory are not to be equated with studies of animals in the laboratory (which is not to say that I decry the latter). It is understandable that the behavior of an animal raised in an unnatural environment, a cage, will not resemble that of a member of its own species living in its natural environment in the field. However, no matter where conducted, studies of children in many ways do resemble field studies. Children are not reared in cages, nor in isolation, and for them laboratories need not represent an environment very different from the many places they are already familiar with.

The setting by itself, then, possesses no special merit. Studies in the field are not superior just because they are field studies. Rather, some questions can best be answered in the field, some in the laboratory. Each setting has advantages, each has limitations. The novice especially is advised not to be persuaded too easily to accept without careful consideration the current elevation of field studies to the status of a summum bonum.

Answers to some of Dr. Yarrow's concerns could come from the replicating of studies. This concern speaks once again to the need for a firmer base from which to draw conclusions, a base that is largely wanting. Admittedly, in the area of parent–child studies, where truly massive amounts of data are gathered, sometimes over relatively long periods of time, replications in the exact sense often seem prohibitive of time and effort. Yet without replications, either by the original investigator or by others, the area suffers from the absence of a sound structure from which to draw conclusions or on which to build future studies. It is my belief that the necessity to replicate rests first and foremost on the original investigator. Otherwise investigators face the likely probability that the edifice they build, the principles and explanations offered, will eventually be destroyed. Some thought to this necessary part of the effort will often suggest imaginative ways to accomplish a replication short of repeating the entire study. For example, the study can be carried out in two parts, the first providing data for a set of tentative conclusions, the second providing evidence to support or disconfirm them. Or some part of the next study, asking a different question or using a fresh sample, can include a partial replication of the first. Given the variability of our subjects, both children and parents, and the variability inherent in natural events, only replications can provide a measure of precision. Only repetition can show investigators how general their conclusions may be. Precision narrows the zone of uncertainty, that zone within which we may confidently expect the true value to lie. To base conclusions and general principles on unreplicated studies, as we do every day, entails the risk of serious error.

Beyond the absolute necessity of replication for the support of conclusions lie two apparently real problems the investigator faces. First, it is said that confirmation of results by a second investigator cannot claim journal space because it is not original work. But editors and referees must eventually realize the value of confirmatory studies, even though they may relegate them to the status of brief reports. The second problem, on examination, is not as real as it seems, that is, that reporting both the original study and its replication takes more space. They need not, and furthermore, by eliminating attractive but unconfirmed hypotheses they may require even less space.

Many of the problems so vividly portrayed by Yarrow and Anderson stem I believe from the absence of clearly stated questions. If the questions are precisely stated before the study begins, then a rationale can be proposed for choices of setting, actors, schedules of observations, and the behaviors. Just to study the free flow of behavior confers no special license to proceed without hypotheses, even though at the present time it does seem to need no further justification. Nor can a study be justified solely by the hypotheses it gives rise to. Hypotheses lie all around us and in abundance. Hypotheses are to be tested; to propose them is no feat.

Going one step beyond the issues raised by Yarrow and Anderson, I would like to draw our attention to the descriptive nature of the studies reviewed. Description has an honored role in the scientific enterprise and needs no defense. But once we recognize the absence of experimental control, we realize how strongly we must oppose the tendency of placing the behaviors of either parent or child in a cause and effect relationship. Only experimental manipulation permits definitive statements about cause and effect.

THE USE OF MODELS

Dr. Mason extends our knowledge of the relationships between young organisms and their caretakers by the ingenious use of responsive and nonresponsive "companions" of a different species. His results demonstrate clearly the differences in many behaviors produced by animate and inanimate companions. Investigators of the human infant can only marvel at the possibilities open to investigators of nonhuman infants. But marvel as we do, we recognize that even the animate companion, the live dog, offered only some fraction of the stimuli, and performed only some fraction of the responses, that a caretaker would. The age of the monkeys, furthermore, moves the research past the animal's infancy; thus, in addition to the species differences are those inherent in an older organism. I note too the differences between the tasks set for the monkeys and those we set for human infants, toddlers, and preschool children. Despite these classes of differences, Dr. Mason's work provides imaginative rearing procedures for elucidating some elements of the young's relations to its caretakers.

In Dr. Mason's paper, nevertheless, I find some statements that we tend to accept but that, on further thought, deserve closer examination. I begin with the second half of his title and his opening paragraphs. It has become the custom for students of animal behavior to invoke the term "biological" and the principles of evolution in their presentations. For many years psychologists too have appreciated the biological basis of man's behavior, as well as that of the human infant's, and they also accept the theory of evolution. For these many years I have questioned the animal investigator's preempting the term and the theory. Thus I would like to ask Dr. Mason to show how his report of the monkey's behavior provides a biological perspective and what his data gain by an introductory paragraph on natural selection. At the same time I ask myself why do not students of the human infant use the same terms and, furthermore, what would be the gain?

Let me be more specific. What is gained by declaring, "Animals are prepared to know what they need to know in order to survive"? Does that statement aid in finding the causes of behavior or how behavior is modified? Rather it could very well serve to end our efforts. We want rather to know what it is that an organism needs to "know" in order to survive, and how it is "prepared." Although Dr. Mason does not rest his argument on that statement but proceeds to search for answers, I am concerned more generally when, as often, I see the questioning end with characterizations of behavior as "wired-in" or "preprogrammed."

It is time too to question a concept we have long accepted, that there is ample reason to regard the mother–infant relation as "pivotal." Dr. Mason's statement provides the occasion to point out that only once up to this moment have I heard the word *father*, and then only in passing. It is true that the word *parent* is part of the title of Yarrow's and Anderson's paper. Nevertheless, all the discussion so far has been in terms of only the mother. It is past time, at least in the case of the human infant, to pay some attention to fathers. This late in our endeavors a start is being made (e.g., Parke & O'Leary, 1976). I exempt as too limited studies of fathers' absence and of contrasts between fathers and mothers and unfamiliar persons pitted against each other in studies of attachment. I predict that future studies will show that when corrected for amount of time present, measures of the father–infant relation will not differ reliably from measures of the mother–infant relation. The father–infant relation may then be shown to be as pivotal as the mother–infant relation.

Dr. Mason's use of dogs and inanimate replicas thereof provides the occasion to suggest still another use of models. Our studies of the human infant's social behavior are hampered by ethical constraints in instituting long-term experimental treatments of consequence. But just as investigators of physiological and neurological functions turn to nonhuman species and use different systems of different animals to understand normal and abnormal processes in man, can we not entertain similar possibilities for the study of human behavior? My suggestion is more specific than using the rat or the rhesus monkey as a species for a variety of questions. Rather I have in mind choosing different species for different questions, depending on as precise a match as possible between the question and the social organization and behavioral characteristics of the species. Instead of using any one species as a model for a variety of questions about the factors influencing the genesis and maintenance of social behavior, I am suggesting the use of different species for different questions depending on the match between that species and ours. For example, if one were interested in the nature and extent of paternal care and its effect on the young, one would choose as an animal model a species in which the father stays with the mother and infant and participates in the infant's care. Similarly, if one were interested in the effect of birth order on social behavior, one would choose a species in which the offspring of successive births stay together for some period of time.

The advantages of using animals include a faster rate of development and the possibility of consequential experimental manipulation. The limitations of generalizability always remain, but the advances in knowledge in genetics, physiology, pharmacology, and medicine, to mention only a few areas, attest to the usefulness of animal models.

While the search for appropriate behavioral systems of different animals goes on, we should consider that we probably have not yet explored all the possibilities for the experimental study of infant behavior. Within the constraints of ethical standards I believe the possibility exists for many beneficent short-term manipulations. A corollary of such studies should be a more telling use of control groups; rather than no treatment, control groups might better investigate the effect of other different but still beneficent manipulations.

Although I here am favoring the intelligent use of models, I decry the use of the computer as a model for the developing infant. The use of the language of the computer, of terms like input, output, preprogrammed, and information processing, while useful as shorthand, often seems to suggest that we know more than we really do. Labels do not explain; their faddish use can persuade us that we have ended our search when in fact it has just begun. Being old-fashioned, I still hesitate to say the infant "prefers" this or that; how much harder it is for me to talk of the infant as "making decisions" or "adopting strategies."

Dr. Mason's statement that for the nonhuman primates, as for man, keeping in touch with the world is very much a visual affair, leads me to suggest that it may in fact be as much auditory as visual. For many years I too was impressed by the role of vision in the human infant's social development, but a recent observation is beginning to modify that view. We found that people, in particular hospital personnel, talk to infants from the day of birth. The observation seems obvious, of course, but I see in it the possibility that the speech of people may provide an answer to that tantalizing question of how the infant comes to distinguish between people and things, and to that more sophisticated question of comparative psychologists of how an organism comes to recognize a member of its own species. The response to visual stimuli is more easily measured and that fact, associated with our general predisposition to elevate the status of the eyes, has served to draw our attention from the extent to which what is heard also modifies behavior. This comment applies too to Dr. Yarrow's questions about the behaviors of the infant we customarily chart. Gaze, and even mutual gaze, so conspicuous in the infant's repertoire, may be receiving more attention than it deserves. In any case, we ought to recognize that the search for behaviors of consequence for later behavior is not yet ended.

THE SEARCH FOR ORDER IN DATA

Dr. Denenberg deserves our appreciation for setting forth so well the problems a developing organism poses for questions of statistical inference. He is in an eminently qualified position to view the special problems of the developing human infant, given his experience with similar problems of the development of behavior in a small nonhuman animal. Once again he helps us realize the limitations our subject imposes on us: How seldom we are able to assign the infants at random to experimental and control groups, and how unable we are to control the life experiences of infants and children between pre- and post-tests. In the case of the human infant the effect of some early treatment would have to be massive indeed to override the multiplicity of diverse intervening life experiences and for its effect to be detectable years later. For this reason more and more often these days developmentalists employing an experimental paradigm turn to studying the effects of short-term interventions. A happier outcome of experimental designs, however, would attend the use of four groups rather than two (Solomon & Lessac, 1968), and the use of control groups that specifically control for the variable or variables under study.

Dr. Denenberg's alternatives to studies employing analyses of variance and correlations, topics I shall return to, are general systems theory and the study of individual subjects. We do in general accept the principles of general systems theory: that all levels of organization within an organism are linked to each other in a hierarchical relationship so that change in one affects change in the others. It remains to be shown, however, how the principles can be applied to the study of the interaction between mother and child or the origins of the infant's social responsiveness or any other behavioral competence. The promise is there, but the operations remain to be specified. Nor, I must confess, do I find the model of the furnace and its thermostat appropriate for the infant-mother system. In passing, however, the effect of the thermostat on the operation of the furnace could as well be solved by the analysis of variance model.

The study of individual subjects can be considered more specifically. Skinner (1953) especially has defended the use of single subjects, but for the purpose of charting the process by which a behavior may be acquired and controlled, and its frequency maintained, increased, or extinguished. Here, however, Dr. Denenberg is recommending its use for descriptive rather than experimental purposes. Description occupies an honored position in the scientific enterprise, but it cannot inform us on the nature of causality. Are we indeed ready to eschew entirely the search for cause and effect relationships? Can we be satisfied to characterize such searches as mechanistic and reductionist? Granted that living systems are not simple machines, are we nevertheless prepared to give up experimental studies? Or rather have we found our efforts wanting and as a consequence turned to description? No one is more aware than I that as a science developmental psychology has much still to be described. But it is one thing to carry out descriptive studies because they are important, and another to carry them out because we do not yet know how to move on to questions of cause and effect, and still another because we question the value of searching for the causes of behavior. I can accept the first two premises, but not the third. Furthermore, I miss the link between single-subject research and general systems theory. It remains only to remind Dr. Denenberg that in the argument he presents for descriptive single-subject research he has not shown how it can answer the questions he set out at the beginning, namely, how to predict the effects of early experience on later behavior.

I return now to Dr. Denenberg's exposition of the problems posed by the usual employment of correlational and analysis of variance designs. Coefficients of correlation show relationships but of course do not provide evidence of cause and effect. Hence a significant correlation coefficient cannot be identical to a significant main effect in the analysis of variance. On the topic of correlations he touched on a problem becoming more common every day, that is, the sole reliance on the computer to do our thinking for us. The ease with which the computer can handle data has seduced us into using it to tell us the nature of our universe. Less often now do students turn first to scatterplots and standard deviations, those simple, elementary, and in fact necessary techniques for understanding the nature of the data we are giving the computer to organize. The computer in many cases has also played into the insidious tendency we now see of gathering more data than we can even think about. With all those data we feel the compulsion to make something of all of it; pretty soon we can find ourselves proposing relationships that make no sense in the real world.

In his treatment of the analysis of variance, Dr. Denenberg may be forgiven for drawing the argument in black and white for purposes of exposition. I would be remiss, however, if I did not object to the use of Spitz's and Goldfarb's findings as appropriate examples of the state of the art in developmental psychology. Better examples of the effect of early experience in that area could be drawn from the studies by Dennis (1973) and Skeels (1966). And I would include my own study of institutionalized infants (Rheingold, 1956) as a developmental experiment that tested for the later effects of a treatment assigned at random to one group and not to the other. Many more will come to the mind of any developmentalist.

I did appreciate how vividly Dr. Denenberg sketched the uncertainty accompanying the findings of interactions or of no difference. No matter how phrased, the investigator's speculations always seem no more than unhappy alibis.

Finally, Dr. Denenberg has made a strong case for the replication of studies, either by the investigator or by different investigators in different places. In the area of special interest to many of us, that of parent–child relations, the absence of replications robs us of the firm evidence so sorely needed. A requirement of every proposed study should be that it not be begun unless it can be replicated. Only by replications can a measure of error around the true value be obtained. Even a single repetition of a study can show how variable the results may be and thus promote caution in interpretation.

ACKNOWLEDGMENTS

Preparation of this paper was supported in part by NIH Research grant number HD 23620 from the National Institute of Child Health and Human Development.

DISCUSSION

Dr. Kennell: I'm going to propose that we have a unique opportunity to study all sorts of things about the human infant because of the different ways we have organized birthing and child rearing in the United States. We've organized our birth facilities and our child care facilities differently than in many other parts of the world. The real-life experiments that we have occurring in this country may not fit the way we would like to have set up an animal study, but they really provide great opportunities. We can think of many child care situations that are different in this country from those in many other countries. We can take advantage of some of the things that we do in the United States that we perhaps think are progressive and the natural way, but they're very different from what man has experienced throughout centuries and centuries.

Dr. Rheingold: What do you mean by that? The nature of man through the centuries? It seems to me that people throughout recorded history had much the same characteristics we have. Isn't it correct that human nature has not changed very much in thousands of years? Do you want to go back further?

Dr. Kennell: No further than that. It is a common event to separate mothers and babies in this country—which Bill Mason wouldn't have the heart to do with his animals. Or separating children from the rest of their family as they become young adults, moving to other parts of the country, having to live alone—there are a great many things that either occur only in the United States or occur only in a few so-called developed or industrialized nations. The move from the farm to the city is a change that occurred in our country mainly in the last hundred years. In other parts of the world this is just beginning or is just part way along.

Dr. Rheingold: Do you think that has changed our relationships with each other?

Dr. Kennell: I think so.

Dr. Rheingold: One would have to agree that man is still evolving.

Dr. Sander: Because of what is changing, I think of the old statement that you can't step into the same stream twice. I think the fact is you can't step in the same stream once.

Dr. Rheingold: But the same reasoning, if followed to its logical conclusion, would dictate that you could not study the same child over time.

Dr. Sander: But I could not repeat now at all what we did before because of social change, because of all kinds of changes that have taken place since 1954 and the present.

Dr. Rheingold: The effect of differences in cohorts can offer important information, and in many cases the differences produced by changes in the styles of rearing, diet, and so on, could be predicted before the study begins.

Dr. Barnard: I was interested in your comments about our fascination with the infant as a visual responder and the possibility that the auditory mechanism is equally important. I was wondering whether you have any thoughts about the importance of the motor system as a feedback for the caregiver?

Dr. Rheingold: Since Dr. Korner presented her findings on vestibular–proprioceptive stimulation, I have been thinking how one might test the infant's ability to distinguish between familiar and unfamiliar postures, between being held in the arms of different persons. But that is not answering your question about the feedback properties for the caregiver of the infant's motor response.

Dr. Barnard: I've been struck by how much feedback the young infant gives through motor acts. If you look at how much of the communication between the infant and the caregiver goes on in a verbal sense or visual sense, you see that it's not very much. And when you begin to look at the videotapes of mother–infant interaction over time, there's a tremendous amount of information and cues the mother seems to be reacting to that come from motions of the infant's body toward her, away from her, active, less active. I think we've missed a whole big area of signal power of the infant, if we don't look at motor cues.

Dr. Rheingold: Because of our concentrating on other behaviors that may not be as significant. You have now proposed a hypothesis that you can test.

Dr. Barnard: Right.

Dr. Papousek: You are putting us as scientists in front of a mirror. I am also concerned about the lack of replicatory studies, but I feel a more general danger behind it. It is time to have a look at the mirror and ask about the tremendous development of science: Are we growing adult? Or just fat? Or is it a malignant growth? How does the society view us? Are not all the lacks you mention just consequences of an inflation of sciences? I am worried much about certain trends of commercialization in regard to science. It seems to me that we have been treated more and more as machines that should produce big splashes. Someone puts a little money into the slot, pushes a button, and out must come a big splash, or else another machine is looked for.

Dr. Rheingold: I do agree with you that we sometimes behave as you say. But we probably should not be too critical, because we will have to make some mistakes to move ahead. We seem to be breaking out of one mold and have not yet found another productive one. I lived through the psychoanalytic period when the main technique was interviewing parents. In the meantime, you were carrying out your superb learning experiments in Czechoslovakia. Infant research here moved then into stimulus–response studies. During that period we developed some good techniques and some satisfying explanations. We knew how to proceed. Now we seem to have become disenchanted with that line of investigation and have turned our efforts, at least in studying the interaction between infant and parent, to naturalistic observations and simple assessment. Having done my share of such studies, I can defend the role of observation. But now I expect we should be ready to move on. We need some new and testable hypotheses.

Dr. Thoman: I am concerned, just as you are, with the problem of emphasizing one research methodology or another too much. We must recognize that our personal preferences for methodology reflect and fit with our own conceptualizations. It seems to me that we must be careful not to put down one methodology at the expense of another because of our individual preferences. It is just that as you can go back and forth between animal and human studies and not think you have all the answers from either level from the animal, you can derive hypotheses that can be explored at the human; and from human research you can derive models that can be given rigorous test at the animal level.

Dr. Rheingold: I agree absolutely.

Dr. Thoman: It seems to me that the same thing is true with respect to the use of experimental laboratory studies and naturalistic studies in the home. The methodologies should be considered complementary, with rigorous procedures used for hypothesis testing in the laboratory, and observations in naturalistic settings to confirm the meaningfulness of the conclusions obtained in the laboratory. Very rarely have any of the findings from laboratory research with infants been tested in the home situation. For example, from highly sophisticated laboratory studies, we know a lot about what babies *can* do, what they *can* learn. We know extraordinarily little about what they actually *do* and what they *do* learn. It seems to me it is a matter of balance in going back and forth between these two approaches if we are to achieve our objectives of understanding the infant's development.

Dr. Rheingold: The questions and solutions you propose deserve our closest attention. Ideally we should move freely between the laboratory and the field. We need only be careful not to elevate the value of findings from one setting over those from another. As I said before, the setting does not automatically confer any virtue. In general, we can accept the premise that behaviors that occur in the laboratory also occur in the field (homes, nursery schools, day care centers, etc.) and that behaviors that occur in the field may be produced in the laboratory. The latter operation is probably the more difficult one. Again, in general, control is more difficult to achieve in homes; consequently the search for general principles will depend on very precisely stated questions.

Let me bring up once again the need for studies of the infant's social responsiveness to persons other than the mother. Why do we not pay more attention to the interchanges between infant and father?

Dr. Eisenberg: Because they're never the primary caregiver.

Dr. Rheingold: What does that mean? She diapers more often than the father, but the father also diapers. Are we talking about sheer frequency only?

Dr. Eisenberg: She's the most ubiquitous object in the infant's environment and, under normal conditions, the source from which many pleasures flow.

Dr. Rheingold: But it is conceivable that caretaking by itself may make the mother a less potent stimulus than the father, who may more likely be free to play with the child.

Dr. Eisenberg: I don't really think that's true.

Dr. Thoman: I am not even sure that's a relevant issue. If we are really to arrive at any understanding of the processes involved in developing relationships, why should there be any basic principles that differ for mothers and fathers?

Dr. Eisenberg: Because mother is more ubiquitous, for one thing. I really want to thank you, Dr. Rheingold, for noting that perhaps the auditory system of the human infant has been downplayed. However, it's my considered opinion that exposure to sound is critical for the development of all infants. The human auditory system evolves at what has been termed by many a "precocious" rate: The inner ear is completely developed well before birth, and, indeed, cochlear function is demonstrable as early as the 5th fetal month. This means that auditory mechanisms are ready to "fire off" from the moment an infant emerges from the womb into this noisy world in which we live, and, very probably, before then. It means that whatever differential processing capacities a baby has are activated by the variety of environmental sounds to which it is exposed from the beginning of extrauterine life. It means that sounds, including noises as well as speech, impinge upon the infant willy-nilly and exert their influences both directly and indirectly. Their direct effects, I would think, must have to do with what we might think of as "preparing" the infant for communicative tasks of later life. Their indirect effects, which we seldom think about, bear more generally upon psycho-somatic organization. Sounds can affect sleep cycles, for instance, because sudden noises will wake up an infant whereas continuous ones will tend to exert soothing effects.

Dr. Rheingold: The auditory system does develop earlier than the visual, but I believe it is not the earliest.

Dr. Eisenberg: I was referring mainly to structural development. Both the cochlea and a number of middle ear structures are comparable to those of adults by the 6th month of gestation.

Dr. Parmelee: Not by electron microscopy. You can't take gross anatomy.

Dr. Eisenberg: I am not talking merely about gross anatomy. One has only to examine the data on hearing in prematures and to look at the Elliots' report of 1964 to recognize that the fetal cochlea is functionally specialized as well. That's a side issue, however. The point I'm trying to make is that audition is a primary avenue of information about the outside world for the developing infant from birth simply because he can't close it off.

The literature on vision, for instance, is enormous and goes back farther than I can remember at the moment. On the other hand, if you do an in-depth search of the literature on audition, you discover that there's relatively little. The first work wasn't undertaken until 1913, when Canestrini measured changes in pulse rates consequent upon sound stimulation. There was a flurry of good studies at the Iowa Child Welfare Station in the '30s; and then there was a 30-year void during which virtually nothing was done. What is worse, in my opinion, is that none of the recent work with infants except my own has been concerned with the organization of auditory mechanisms. People like Einar Siqueland and his colleagues, who are highly competent investigators, have directed their attention entirely towards proving theoretical constructs that are highly debatable and have ignored the psychoacoustic underpinnings of language processing almost entirely. People in the speech and hearing field, who are more concerned with deafness than with hearing, have directed their efforts largely towards developing infant screening techniques of limited value and dubious validity. The result is that we have precious little useful information on the ontogeny of hearing functions.

Dr. Rheingold: I think any person who has a special area of research should be happy. You should take pride in being a pioneer.

REFERENCES

Dennis, W. *Children of the Crèche.* New York: Appleton-Century-Crofts, 1973.

Parke, R. D., & O'Leary, S. E. Family interaction in the newborn period: Some findings, some observations, and some unresolved issues. In K. F. Riegel & J. A. Meacham (Eds.), *The developing individual in a changing world* (Vol. 2). *Social and environmental issues.* The Hague: Mouton, 1976.

Rheingold, H. L. The modification of social responsiveness in institutional babies. *Monographs of the Society for Research in Child Development,* 1956, *21*(2, Serial No. 63).

Skeels, H. M. Adult status of children from contrasting early life experiences: A follow-up study. *Monographs of the Society for Research in Child Development,* 1966, *31*(3, Serial No. 105).

Skinner, B. F. *Science and human behavior.* New York: Macmillan, 1953.

Solomon, R. L., & Lessac, M. S. A control group design for experimental studies of developmental processes. *Psychological Bulletin,* 1968, *70,* 145–150.

III ONTOGENY OF THE MOTHER–INFANT RELATIONSHIP

12 Individuality in the Interactive Process

Evelyn B. Thoman
Christine Acebo
C. A. Dreyer
Patricia T. Becker
The University of Connecticut

Margaret P. Freese
Indiana University

INTRODUCTION

A growing number of researchers interested in the early parent–infant relationship are expressing dissatisfaction with a uni–directional model of influence. In part, this dissatisfaction has derived from a failure to find any specific caretaking practices by mothers (or fathers, or other caretakers) that have an identifiable effect on the infant's development. Likewise, studies focused on the infant's behaviors have not been successful in specifying the impact of the child's characteristics on the parent. Additionally, and even more importantly, is the growing recognition that simplistic, single-factor models for the parent-infant relationship are not isomorphic with the complex and dynamic interplay of forces and events that go into any interaction. Thus, we are still searching for models and concepts that may provide the basis for research into the nature of the parent-infant relationship and how this developing interaction influences the development of the child.

More recently, researchers have proposed process models of mother-infant interaction. For example, Sameroff and Chandler (1975) have suggested the concept of transactional analysis for the ongoing interaction between a mother and infant. They stress the importance of the transactional process as an influence on the infant's development, an influence which is generally not predictable and, therefore, is a source of apparent discontinuity in the behavioral changes of the infant during the course of development.

Sander (1964; Sander, Stechler, Burns & Julia, 1970) has for some time conceptualized the mother-infant relationship as process. For example, he states: "The interplay of active tendencies in infant and mother in reaching a

305

reciprocal quality of relationship forms the unifying thread around which interactional accounts will be organized. The reciprocal quality in interaction is an achievement which is marked by harmony. It represents a fit or fitting together of active tendencies in each partner [p. 233]." Sander is concerned with the total relationship and the nature of the mutual adaptation in the process of interaction. His strategy for dealing with the earliest caretaker-infant relationship has been to describe the organization of the infant's activity patterns in response to the rhythm or sequencing of caretaking interventions. The nature of the interventions, and the relationship between the infant's rest-activity cycles, as well as vocalization, are recorded. Individual caretaker-infant patterns of interaction are depicted.

Jaffe, Stern, and Peery (1973) also focus on the flow and mutuality of the mother and infant behaviors, though with a much more molecular approach. They describe gazing and verbalizing by mother and infant as "conversational" coupling of the pair, and they propose that there may be a universal property of dyadic communication which can be identified by the study of mutuality in behaviors. They propose a model of interpersonal constraint which can be applied to the gross temporal patterning of mutual behaviors.

Along with the new views of interaction, a number of creative approaches and methodologies are currently being used. Brazelton's eloquent descriptions of the flow of mother and infant interaction focus on the waxing and waning in intensity of mutually attentive behaviors (e.g., Brazelton, Tronick, Adamson, Als & Wise, 1975). He presents graphically the nature of the synchrony of their rhythms of reactivity.

Lewis and Lee-Painter (1974) discuss the limitations of current methods used for studying interactive processes, and they emphasize the need for ways of depicting the non-static flow of interaction apart from its elements. Their approach involves describing patterns of mother and infant behaviors by means of Markovian sequence analyses. With an interest in process analysis, Stern (1971, 1974) and Bakeman (1977) have also used Markovian sequence analyses of epoch-by-epoch recording of mother and infant behaviors. This approach has the advantage of being useful for describing either behavior patterns of individual mother-infant pairs or overall patterns of groups of mothers and infants. However, there are also disadvantages to this approach. Only by recording a limited number of behaviors or by deriving behavior combinations is it possible to obtain a sufficient frequency of each category to permit sequence analyses. Additionally, Markov chain analysis requires the very tenuous assumptions that the probablility of occurrence of any behavior depends only on the immediately preceding behavioral event, and that the probabilities depicting a pattern are constant throughout the period of observation. The latter assumption may be appropriate for relatively short periods of an interaction sequence, but one would not expect such an assumption to apply through changes in ongoing types of activity. Jaffe, Stern, and Peery (1973) are very careful to point out these limitations, which apparently do not apply when the interaction involves relatively brief episodes of a mother and infant looking at one another during play.

Each of these investigators of the mother-infant relationship is acknowledging the complexities inherent in the interaction between a growing, changing, modifiable young organism and an organism which, although adult, is also subject to change by the relationship. Neither static nor moment-to-moment models for this process will suffice.

Premises for the Study of Individuality in the Interactive Process

In accord with these newer notions, our model for viewing the mother-infant pair (Thoman, Becker, and Freese, 1977) emphasizes ongoing reciprocity in the relationship. An absence of the role of causality in this view is a major consideration. If one adheres to an interactional framework, it becomes difficult to conceive of either partner as "causing" specific behaviors of the other. If a baby cries and the mother picks it up, it is easy to make the interpretation that the baby has caused the mother to engage in caretaking behaviors. On the other hand, the baby may cry and be left alone, or the baby may be asleep and be picked up, and a causal interpretation of these behaviors is more obviously erroneous. The immediately preceding behavior of either member of the pair often has only a trivial causal relationship to the subsequent behavior of the other member. Interaction is a process with an accumulation of its own history. The problem for the researcher is to select time segments and component behaviors that have meaning for depicting the nature of this ongoing process.

In this report we will present the guiding concepts for our study of the mother-infant interactive process and a description of the results from a longitudinal study of mothers and infants during their first year. Like other researchers we feel the urgent need for more adequate, realistic and fruitful ways of studying the infant-environment interaction and its relation to the infant's development. The project which will be described was designed to make some progress in a new direction.

The major premises for our research will be described in detail, as they provide the context within which our research questions are asked. These basic premises are highly interrelated and include: (a) the notion of the mother-infant dyad functioning as a system; (b) the assumption that the functioning of a system must be explored by means of longitudinal study; and (c) the assumption that the expression of the interactive process occurs uniquely in each mother-infant pair. In the sections that follow the relevance of these assumptions to our research will be described. An intensive, logical, and philosophical discussion of the issues inherent in the adoption of these assumptions is given by Denenberg in another chapter of the present volume.

The Mother-Infant Pair as a System

Each of the researchers referred to thus far has used the term "system" in describing the mother-infant relationship, and although the term has been applied very loosely, it points to a new conceptual framework for this area of study. General systems theory, as developed by Bertalanffy (1968) and Weiss (1969, 1971), provides a perspective which may ultimately enable us to understand and analyze the complexities of the interactive process.

In 1933 Bertalanffy maintained that the theory of development and of life in general must be a systems theory, applicable to social relationships as well as to other levels of biological organization. Systems notions have since been applied at a range of levels, from aggregates of inanimate particles to aggregates of living organisms. While there are many approaches to systems theory, we can consider here some general characteristics and how they may apply to the interactional area of study.

As summarized by Fowler, ". . . a system is a whole or a unit composed of hierarchically organized and functionally highly interdependent subunits that may themselves be systems (1975, p. 26)." Within a system, the component units, by 'systematic' coordination, preserve an integral configuration of structure and behavior, and tend to restore this configuration after non-destructive disturbances (Weiss, 1971). An important characteristic of a system is that the variability of the whole is less than that of any of the component parts. Thus, more generally, a system is an organization whose overall state is stable relative to the states of its components (Fowler, 1975). This stability, in turn, provides constraints within which the subunits function.

A primary implication of the application of systems theory is that one can no longer focus on single main effects, or causal factors, but must be concerned with the interplay of numerous interacting factors. Nonlinear relations are of the essence, and non-static models are required. As Ashby says, "Today science is developing along the lines not included in the 'classic' form. The classic method. . . dealt essentially with parts alone: the difficulties of 'interaction' were evaded. . . 'Modern' science however is characterized by an uninhibited advance into the nonlinear. It not merely studies systems with high internal interaction but also confidently tackles systems in which it is the interactions themselves that are of interest (1972, p. 80)."

Another aspect of a system is that of stability. This, as well as the concept of change, is central to systems theory. Without some stability there is not a system to study. A major problem in studying mother and infant behaviors is identifying stable aspects of the system despite the changes over time in form, meaning, and complexity of mutual behaviors. In a recent paper, Porges

(1976) examines this and other problems associated with the assessment of change in developmental research. He concludes that the most fruitful approach will be through longitudinal designs and within-individual analyses using time series statistics.

Notions of general systems have been proposed primarily by biologists. Although they have not yet fully solved the problems of definitions and questions in their own realm of research, the application of systems notions is as essential at the individual and interactive behavioral levels as it is at the level of biological functioning within the organism. Our assumption is that by taking the systems notion seriously, certain types of questions, particularly those of a mechanistic and causal nature, will become trivial. The questions asked will be designed to reveal aspects of the interactive process. As in biology, the problem of defining systems—or process—variables must be resolved. In the mother-infant dyad, behaviors of either the mother or of the infant can be recorded, but characteristics of the relationship have to be inferred or derived from some combination of the data from these two components of the system. Within this limitation in specifying process variables, we are pursuing the systems approach.

The Systems Approach and Study of the Individual Mother-Infant Pair

Despite the acknowledged difficulties in identifying systems-type variables and in developing statistical analyses appropriate for process data, some directions are clear if we are to make progress in dealing with the complexities of an interactive process. One major implication is the importance of studying the individual mother-infant pair. Process is change, which requires time; it can occur only within an individual system. Thus, the system level of interest for our research is the mother-infant dyad.

With the primary objective of identifying the nature of continuities in interaction, the focus of our study is on individual mother-infant pairs. A great deal of developmental research is carried out using cross-sectional data and drawing conclusions from group means about developmental processes. While group study is currently considered to be the most "scientific" approach, the logic of systems paradigms and a concern for process argue for an emphasis on the individual. Hoyer says, "It is important to note that the cumulative, irreversible effects of certain developmental antecedents should not be cited as support for the use of group designs. In fact, if development . . . is conceptualized as relatively permanent and irreversible behavioral change, group designs are of limited usefulness, since the irreversible cumulative change exists within the behavior of the individual and need not have continuity or generalizability from one individual to another. Thus, with small-N designs the paradox of 'discovering' laws of behavioral development that do not generalize to the individual is avoided (1974, p. 824)." Although

Hoyer is concerned with experimental manipulations, his critical evaluation of the use of group designs for inferring process variations is very timely and relevant to the study of mother-infant interaction.

The study of the individual has most often been associated with case studies, or baby biographies, which were not truly observational. Dismissal of this mode of study has been hastened by a rejection of the enormous numbers of abstractions that were made without any rigorously obtained empirical data base. In reaction against the "unscientific" use of case studies with their subjective interpretations, there has been a general emphasis on large-N studies, with a focus on single variables. While many investigators emphasize individual differences in behaviors and even individual patterning of behaviors, there has been great reticence in recent years to study individual subjects.

One apparent way of dealing with individual subjects has been the correlational approach, either across individuals with respect to the same measure over time or between a prediction variable at one age and a criterion variable at another age. Wohlwill maintains that this approach provides more information on *variables* than on the behavior of individuals. "With only very few exceptions, work on stability. . . has consisted in the endless proliferation of correlation coefficients, to indicate the degree of relationship between measures of behavior over some given time interval. We have already pointed to the limiting effect of this narrow approach. . . Even at the level of the focus on dimensions, the information contained in bare correlation coefficients is meager at best, and conveys little sense of a system undergoing change—or, for that matter, remaining invariant in the midst of change (1973, pp. 358–359)." As Wohlwill points out, we need information on developing patterns rather than correlations between single variables.

It can be asked whether it is possible to study individual mother-infant pairs without a return to the old "case study" approach. We believe the answer to be affirmative. First of all, new methodologies permit the collection of empirical data by recording behaviors with much less interpretive loading. Secondly, process questions are very different in nature from the judgmental or qualitative interpretations that were the context for research strategy used in the historical case studies.

One objection to the use of single-N designs is the effect of repeated measurements on the behaviors observed. The solution to this problem is the use of naturalistic observations in which there is minimal intervention with the ongoing behaviors of the individual observed. Thus, data from repeated observations over time can serve as the basis for inferences about the nature of specific processes. This is a major argument for observing mother-infant interaction in the home with minimal observer intrusion.

Another major issue for any single-N or small-N study is the generalizability of the results. This is a serious issue which must be confronted. It is certainly not possible to generalize from single subjects or small-N groups with respect to demographic characteristics such as sex, socio-economic level, race, etc. However, two kinds of generalizations are possible when the focus is on the individual baby or on the individual mother-infant pair. First, generalizations may be made for one individual or pair over time. These would reflect the stability of the system which was referred to earlier. For arriving at such generalizations, pattern analysis of some sort is most relevant in order to show changes in the relationship of one behavior to another over time, or changes in the relative timing or synchrony of behaviors. An example of the latter kind of analysis comes from the work of Brazelton (with Koslowski & Main, 1974; with Tronick, Adamson, Als & Wise, 1975). He describes the synchrony, or mutuality in timing, of a mother and infant in their successive approaches to one another. Given high mutuality at one stage or age, one would predict a high mutuality at a later age.

A second type of generalization from the study of individual mother-infant pairs concerns the nature of the interactive process across dyads. Although specific behavior patterns are unique to each dyad, there may be commonalities among pairs in terms of meaning or function. From common patterns described at a more general level, it may be possible to derive process-type variables not yet considered, always with the assumption that the process is expressed uniquely in each mother-infant pair.

We can begin with some of the time-honored concepts that have been handed down to us by very sensitive clinicians, for instance, synchrony or mutual adaptation, which are actually systems or process concepts. These can be defined empirically in terms of rhythms or timing of mother and infant behaviors; or they can be defined in terms of specific behaviors on the part of the infant (e.g., crying) or mother (e.g., caressing) where these behaviors are considered as part of the ongoing sequence of interdependent behaviors.

An example of asynchrony during the first month for one mother-infant relationship was given in a previous report (Thoman, Freese, & Becker, 1977) of an infant who exhibited a great deal of open-eyed REM during Active Sleep. It was apparent that the mother was mistaking this activity for wakefulness. She typically responded with extremely short latencies to many of her infant's behaviors, and often responded to the open-eyed REM by picking the baby up for feeding, not realizing he was actually asleep. The feedings tended to go poorly, and consequently there were many brief feeding episodes. Feeding became a difficult time for both. For another mother-infant pair, an equivalent amount of open-eyed REM on the part of the baby might have little or no relevance for their interactions, and synchrony or asynchrony might have to do with very different behaviors. We would know very little about the relating process in general by analyzing the amount of open-eyed REM in infants, or even by analyzing mothers' responses to this specific behavior. To understand the interactive process in any individual mother-infant pair, their behaviors must be observed intensively and the data analyzed to depict the individuality of those behaviors. Clues to generalizations regarding the nature of the interactive process will derive first from an understanding of the individuality expressed in many mother-infant pairs studied singly, and secondly from identifying commonalities in the roles played by differing behavior patterns in the process of interaction.

A NATURALISTIC AND LONGITUDINAL STUDY OF INDIVIDUAL MOTHERS AND INFANTS

The research to be described bears some similarities to that of other researchers who have taken a systems approach to the mother-infant relationship. It involves some extensions of the notions they have proposed, and it includes some original aspects which we believe make progress in assessing mother and infant behaviors in a systems perspective.

A major objective for this research was to identify the earliest individual patterns of infants and mothers in interaction. A second objective was to relate these early patterns of behavior to those observed at one year of age. In some cases, continuity with respect to specific behaviors was of interest, and in other cases more general patterns were most relevant to our purposes.

A group of 20 mothers and babies was studied during the first year of life. Consistent with the views presented, the patterns of individual pairs within the group are of primary interest. However, the total group of subjects serves two major functions. First of all, the total group provides a baseline in terms of mean measures and indications of variability on these measures, with which individual babies or dyads can be compared. Secondly, and even more important for our purposes, repeated measures on the subjects making up the total group permits a determination of the reliability with which any variable or combination of variables discriminates among individual mother-infant pairs. Researchers generally concern themselves with inter-observer reliability when making naturalistic observations, as we do likewise. However, very little attention is given to the reliability of the measures observed. This issue is not a critical one where the purpose is to use group means to describe a sample, but is a most important first step when the purpose is to focus on the level of individual descriptions.

The purposes of this portion of the report are: first, to describe procedures by which the mother-infant interactions can be reliably described: second, to illustrate one approach to exploring patterns of interaction by using two selected mother-infant pairs; and finally, to identify relationships between early patterns of mother-infant interaction and the later development of the two selected infants.

One mother-infant pair of primary interest in this report was described to some extent in a previous report (Thoman, 1975). During the first five weeks of life, beginning with the earliest mother-infant contacts after birth, this infant showed an unusual response to being held or carried. When the mother picked the baby up, he typically became dazed, drowsy, or fretful. In contrast, when left alone in the crib, he showed a great deal of alertness and spent time scanning his surrounds. At various times, the parents expressed their concern about the baby's "not liking to be held." The data in the earlier report indicated a dramatic difference between this mother-infant relationship and the others in the group in terms of the amount of alertness when the baby was held and the amount of alertness when the baby was in the crib. From those results, one could have readily identified this as a "relationship at risk."

Despite the apparent difficulties offered by the baby's unusual response to social stimulation, we reported (Thoman, 1975) that the mother's interaction with her baby appeared to be extremely sensitive; our prediction was that the baby and the relationship would develop quite adequately. The prediction was based on subjective judgments arrived at during the course of the series of observations. At that time, we had not made the one-year observations, nor had the data analyses been completed on most of the early interactive behaviors for our subjects. Since analyses of these data are now available, we can provide evidence relevant to the optimistic prediction. The data from this mother and infant, Pair *13*, will be compared with the total group and also with another dyad in the group in order to highlight the characteristics of this seemingly special relationship. The mother and baby selected for comparison, Pair *16*, was one for which the prediction at 5 weeks had been that the relationship would develop with difficulty. This early prediction was based primarily on subjective impressions gained during the early observations, as there were little supporting data available at that time.

The methods of study for the group will be described first, and then the methods for depicting the individual patterns of interaction in the two selected dyads will be presented. Behaviors of these two mother-infant pairs will be compared using data obtained over the first five weeks after birth and over a 3-week period at one year.

METHODS

Subjects

The subjects for this study were 20 healthy, full-term infants and their mothers. The mothers, all primipara, were enrolled in the project during their last trimester of pregnancy. Thirteen of the mothers delivered males and seven delivered females.

The two infants considered individually were Pair *13* and Pair *16*. Baby *13* was male and Baby *16* was female.

General Procedures for the Early Observations

Prenatal assessments of the mothers were obtained, and mothers and infants were observed in the hospital during the early postpartum period (Freese, 1975). Procedures for those observations will not be described in detail in the present report, which focuses on the observations made in the homes when the infants were 2, 3, 4, and 5 weeks old. However, it should be mentioned that each mother fed and interacted with her infant in the presence of an observer on at least two occasions during her postpartum hospital stay and thus was familiar with the intensive observation procedures and the presence of a noninteracting observer prior to the first home observation.

The first home observation was made when each infant was 8-14 days of age, with subsequent home observations made at approximately weekly intervals. Each observation consisted of a continuous 7-hour period. Two observers participated in the observation, each recording for 3-½ hours. The changing of observers in the middle of the observations was accomplished without interruption of either the observational procedures or ongoing household activities.

During the observation period, the observer avoided interaction with anyone in the household. She selected locations which permitted a clear view of the infant's face but where she was as unobtrusive as possible in the household setting. Whenever the infant was moved about the house, the observer followed. During long sleep periods when the infant was in the crib, the observer remained with the infant and recorded sleep patterns.

Recording Procedures for the Early Observations

The occurrence of any of 75 mother or infant behaviors was code-recorded every 10 seconds throughout the 7-hour observation. The behaviors recorded are listed in Table 12.1. A small electronic timing device provided the observer with a signal through an ear microphone every 10 seconds. At each signal the necessary codes were recorded, with no formal pause in the observational process. In this way, nearly continuous recordings of the occurrence of each variable was possible.

Several factors make it possible to reliably record this large number of mother-infant behaviors. First, many of the coded behaviors occur only in limited contexts. For example, Suck Stimulation, Not-Sucking, and Not-Attached occur only when the infant is feeding or has been given a pacifier. Secondly, the detail with which certain variables are recorded varies within the observation. For instance, distinctions among the sleep states are made

TABLE 12.1
Mother and Infant Variables

Mother Location
Out
Far
Near
In Contact
Hold
Carry

Infant Location
Crib
Cardle Board
Other

Infant Position
Prone
Supine
Up
Up at Shoulder

Mother-Infant Activity
Feed
Change
Bathe
Non-Caretaking

Feeding Subcategories
Breast or Bottle
Water
Solids

Bathing Subcategories
Head
Immersion

Maternal Behaviors
Provide pacifier
Suck-Stimulation
Vis-a-Vis
En Face Position
Look
Talk
Talk to Other
Noise
Smile or Laugh
Pat
Caress
Move
Rock

Infant Behaviors
Not Attached
Not Sucking
Rhythmic Mouthing
Hand-Mouth
Spit Up
Suck
Mouthe
Smile
Frown
Grimace
Yawn
Breath-Hold
Vocalize
Noise
Grunt
Sigh
Sigh-Sob
Cough
Bowel Movement
Eyes Open
Rapid Eye Movement
Stretch
Large Movement
Small Movement
Startle
Poor Startle
Jitter
Jerk

Infant Behavioral States
Quiet Sleep (2 categories)
Active Sleep (3 categories)
Uncertain
Drowse
Daze
Alert Inactivity
Waking Activity
Fuss
Cry

*These are mutually exclusive categories for code-recording purposes.

only when the infant is alone in the crib. Also, the variables include a number of totally inclusive and mutually exclusive categories of behavior which require code-recording only when a change occurs within the category. For example, an infant's position is coded as Prone, Up, at Shoulder, or Supine. Once a position has been recorded, it is not re-coded until the position changes. Finally, economy in recording is aided by the use of standard inferences which eliminate the actual marking of some variables. For instance, if the mother carries the infant, this implies that the infant is being moved, and consequently the Move category is not marked.

Reliabilities among the three observers who carried out these observations were calculated for each variable using the following formula:

$$\frac{2 \text{ (number of agreements)}}{\text{number of occurrences recorded by both observers}}$$

The interrater reliabilities among the three observers for variables to be reported in the present study ranged from .75 to .99.

Procedures for the Observations at One Year

Three weekly home observations were made encompassing the first birthday. Observations were begun no earlier than 11-½ months, and all three observations were completed before the infant was 12-½ months of age.

For a number of reasons, but primarily because subjects moved from the area, it was possible to complete the 3 observations on only 7 of the 20 original mother-infant pairs. Three additional subjects observed at a later time were included in the group in order to have a sample of 10 pairs, with 5 male and 5 female babies.

Each observation consisted of a two-hour period without sleeping or major caretaking activities (bathing or feeding). If any of these activities occurred, the observation was discontinued and then resumed after the excluded activity was completed.

For these observations, two observers were in the home recording simultaneously. This procedure permitted code-recording every 10 seconds of the 71 behaviors listed in Table 12.2. Since the baby is very mobile at this age, one observer or the other was at a vantage point to view or to follow the baby with less movement than would be required with only one observer. The procedures were generally the same as those described for the early observations.

Within a week after completing the home observations, the Bayley Developmental Scales were administered to each baby. Eighteen subjects were available for this assessement.

TABLE 12.2

	Mother	Baby	Mother and/or Baby
Location	Hold	Crib	Out
	Carry	Hichair	Far
		Playpen	Near
		Other	Follow
			Hug
			Body Contact
Movement	Move Baby	Vertical	Rock
		Horizontal	Hand-in-hand walking
		Climb	Physical game
		Travel	
		Hold on	
		Fall	
		Struggle	
Play		Object:	Peekaboo
		reach for,	Read together
		throw, hold,	Play with object
		mouthe, examine	Game
Visual	Look at baby	Look at mother	Vis-à-vis
			Game
Verbal	Order	Fuss	Talk
	Ask	Cry	Noise
	Praise	Shriek	Sing
	Negative	Attention	Imitate
		vocalization	Game
Nonverbal			Smile
			Laugh
			Appropriate gesture
			Take
			Offer
			Show
			Point
			Reach for person
			Game
Touch	Tickle		Kiss
	Restrain		Caress
			Negative touch
			Game
Caretaking	Change		Feed or eat:
	Bathe		Bottle
			Cup
			Finger food

RESULTS OF THE EARLY OBSERVATIONS

For the 20 mother-infant pairs observed on weeks 2, 3, 4, and 5, 209,751 ten-second epochs were recorded over the four home observations, with presence-absence information on 75 behaviors during each epoch. During the course of the observations for this project, a large number of hypotheses were generated concerning the nature of continuities in mother-infant relationships. Therefore, rather than randomly exploring the innumerable relationships that are undoubtedly to be found in this quantity of data, we have chosen to use analyses and summary statistics which are selected to answer specific questions about individual or groups of mother-infant pairs. The data analyses presented are designed to describe continuity in the interactive patterning of the two mother and infant pairs who were selected because of contrasting predictions following the early observations.

Variables Analyzed for Observations Made on Weeks, 2, 3, 4, and 5

From the list of recorded behaviors present in Table 12.1, meaningful combinations of mother and/or baby behaviors were grouped together, and a more general label was given to each of these behavior combinations. Definitions of the variables, defined as behaviors occurring concurrently, are as follows:

Total observation. The number of epochs in any home observation.

Awake. The infant is in one of the following behavioral states: Drowse, Daze, Alert Inactivity, Waking Activity, Fuss, Cry.

Fuss or Cry. The infant is in either of the following behavioral states: Fuss, Cry.

Social Interaction. All of the following are occurring: (1) the infant is in an *Awake* state; (2) mother location is *Hold or Carry*; (3) mother-infant activity is *Non-Caretaking*.

Hold or Carry. The mother is in either of the following mother locations: Hold, Carry.

Asleep. The infant is in either of the following behavioral states: Quiet Sleep, Active Sleep.

Caretaking. The mother-infant pair is engaged in one of the following mother-infant activities: Feed, Change, Bathe.

Stimulation. The mother is engaged in any of the following maternal stimulation variables: Pat, Caress, Move, Rock.

Looking. The mother is engaged in any of the following maternal variables: Look, En Face Position, Vis-à-Vis.

State Sleep. The infant is in the crib or elsewhere, but not being held, and sleep states are recorded, including: Quiet Sleep, Active Sleep, and Uncertain.

This set of combined variables encompasses 35 of the 75 individual mother and infant behaviors recorded, as listed in Table 12.1. Some of the variables include both mother and infant behaviors. This is completely consistent with our view that whether the behaviors are the mother's or the infant's, they are all expressions of the mother-infant system, and therefore mutually interdependent. Thus, independence of variables is not an objective for measurement in this study.

Individual Differences in Early Behaviors: Reliability of Variables

Absolute frequency of occurrence was not an appropriate base for analyses of these data, as the total number of epochs in an observation was never exactly equivalent to the 2520 that make up a seven-hour period ($\overline{X} = 2495$; SD = 110). In most instances, the total number of occurrences (of 10-second epochs) of a variable was expressed as a percent of the total number of epochs in the observation. In some cases, however, we were interested in the number of epochs of a behavior expressed as a percent of another variable. For example, it may be of interest to know how much time a baby spends fussing *or* crying during the total observation; or it may be of interest to know how much time the baby fusses *and* cries as a percent of the time the baby is awake, or as a percent of the time that the baby *and* mother are engaged in social interaction. Table 12.3 presents the mean percentage value for each of the variables used for this report. The group means are based on individual means across the four home observations.

The four successive weekly observations permitted the assessment of reliability, or individual differences, among mother-infant pairs for each of these measures over the four weeks. An analysis of variance was used to assess change in percentages over weeks for the entire group, differences as a function of sex of the infants, and individual differences. There were no significant sex effects for any variable. For four variables, there were significant monotonic trends over weeks and these are indicated in Table 12.3. Individual Differences, however, were highly significant for each of these variables. Thus, for any variable, the mean score across the four weekly observations reliably depicts the measure for each mother-infant pair, and the measure is, therefore, a potential predictor of later behavior. Table 12.3 also presents the total-test reliability (reliability over observations) for each variable based on the formula $r_{tt} = (1 - 1/F)$, and the standard error of measurement based on the formula $SEMeas = S.D. \times \sqrt{1 - r_{tt}}$.

As mother-infant Pairs *13* and *16* were of special interest for this report, their individual means for each variable are presented in Table 12.3. Since these two subject pairs were separated from the group for special consideration *post hoc*, they were included in the total group scores. *t* values

TABLE 12.3
Summary Data for Observations Made on Weeks 2, 3, 4, and 5

Variable	r_{tt}	Group $\bar{X}$	SEMeas	Pr. 13	Pr. 16	t^a
Fuss or Cry/Total	.73	3.8	(0.95)	3.0	1.2	1.34
Fuss or Cry/Social Interaction	.76	9.9	(3.87)	12.8	3.8	1.64
Looking/Fuss or Cry	.78	60.9	(9.20)	70.6	55.0	1.20
Talk/Fuss or Cry	.84	41.2	(7.50)	46.5	23.8	2.14*
Stimulate/Fuss or Cry	.82	35.4	(7.78)	58.8	28.9	2.72**
Hold or Carry/Total	.84	26.9	(3.95)	28.5	28.4	0.02
Caretaking/Hold or Carry	.82	56.8	(5.74)	25.0	57.4	3.99**
Caretaking/Total	.80	14.3	(2.26)	11.9	19.3	2.32*
Social Interaction/Total	.73	10.4	(2.39)	13.7	6.3	2.19*
Social Interaction/Waking	.80	29.5	(4.86)	35.0	20.9	2.05*
Talk/Social Interaction	.86	46.1	(6.16)	43.0	15.3	3.18**
Stimulation/Social Interaction	.74	81.2	(4.63)	86.0	71.0	2.29*
Vis-à-vis/Total[b]	.59	2.6	(0.81)	2.3	1.1	1.05
Vis-à-vis/Looking and Waking[b]	.71	12.4	(3.55)	8.5	4.8	0.74
Caress/Total	.83	8.4	(1.50)	13.3	4.2	4.29**
Pat/Total	.79	3.5	(0.99)	8.0	0.5	5.36**
Asleep/Total	.50	65.5	(4.81)	61.4	70.4	1.32
Runs of Sleep	.39	2.7	(0.46)	3.0	3.0	0
Quiet Sleep/State Sleep	.70	33.0	(3.44)	42.0	32.1	2.03*
Open-eye REMS/REM[b]	.84	16.2	(3.52)	8.3	19.2	2.19*

[a]t values for comparisons of Pair _13_ and Pair _16_.   [b]Significant increase over weeks, $p < .05$.
For t, df = 54, See Denenberg chapter.
*$p < .05$, two-tailed test.
**$p < .01$.

for the differences between the means of Pairs _13_ and _16_ were computed and these are also reported in Table 12.3. In the following chapter, Denenberg discusses the logical issues of statiscal comparisons between individuals within a group.

Comparisons of Pair 13 and Pair 16

The characteristics of the mother-infant relationships for Pairs _13_ and _16_ are highlighted in the series of figures 1-5, where _z_-scores for these two mother-infant pairs are plotted for each of the variables reported in Table 12.3. The relative levels for Pairs _13_ and _16_ on these variables can thus be compared with each other and with the mean of the entire group.

Figure 12.1 presents the measures which indicate the infant's irritability. From this figure, it is apparent that Baby _13_ fussed more than Baby _16_ throughout the total observation and during interaction as well. Also, whenever the baby was fussing or crying, Mother _13_ was more likely than Mother _16_ to be looking, talking, or stimulating her baby.

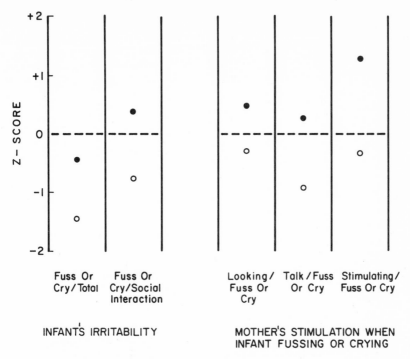

FIG. 12.1.   For mother and infant Pair 13 and Pair 16, z-scores for the means over weeks 2, 3, 4, and 5, for measures related to the infants' irritability and measures relating to the mothers' stimulation when the infant was fussing or crying.

Figure 12.2 pertains to interaction involved in holding or carrying the baby. It can be seen that the two mothers held their babies approximately the same amount of time; they are both close to the group mean on this measure. However, Mother *16* spent a much higher percent of holding or carrying time in caretaking. Mother *16* also spent a higher percent of the total observation time in caretaking activities.

Figure 12.3 presents comparisons with respect to social interaction, defined as: "the baby is awake while the mother is holding or carrying the baby but not engaged in any caretaking activity." This measure reflects much the same information as that in the preceeding figure. Primarily, Mother and Baby *13* had more social interaction during the total observation than Pair *16*, and a greater percent of Baby *13*'s waking time was spent in social interaction. In addition, Mother *13* was more likely to talk and stimulate her baby during social interaction than Mother *16*.

Figure 12.4 pertains to mutual attention, and it can be seen that Pair *13* had more vis-à-vis in the total observation, and also more vis-à-vis during the time the mother spent looking at the baby when the baby was awake, than did Pair *16*.

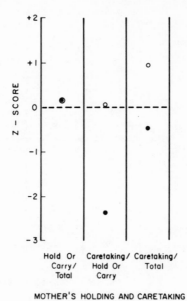

FIG. 12.2. For Pairs 13 and 16, z-scores for means of weeks 2, 3, 4, and 5, from measures related to the mothers' holding and caretaking of the infants.

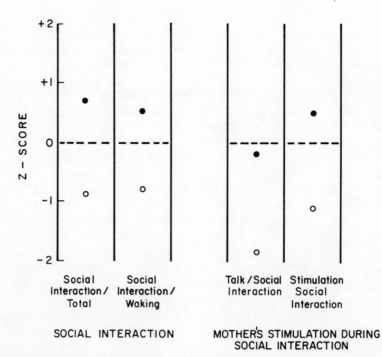

FIG. 12.3. For Pairs 13 and 16, z-scores for means of weeks 2, 3, 4, and 5, from measures of social interaction and measures of the mothers' stimulation during social interaction.

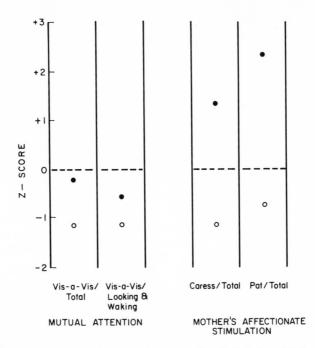

FIG. 12.4. For Pairs 13 and 16, z-scores for means of weeks 2, 3, 4, and 5, for measures of mutual attention and measures of mothers' affectionate stimulation.

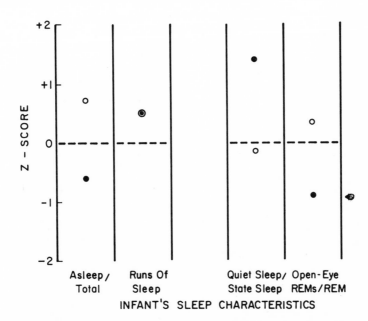

FIG. 12.5. For Pairs 13 and 16, z-scores for means of weeks 2, 3, 4, and 5, from measures of the infants' sleep characteristics.

Figure 12.4 also indicates the relative level of affectionate stimulation for these two pairs: Mother *13* was very high with respect to both patting and caressing her infant, and Mother *16* was low on both forms of stimulation.

Figure 12.5 presents the comparisons of the infants' sleep characteristics: Baby *16* slept more than Baby *13*. Although the babies did not differ in the number of sleep periods, Baby *13* was relatively high with respect to the percent of sleep that was Quiet Sleep and relatively low with respect to the amount of open-eyed REMs.

RESULTS OF THE ONE-YEAR OBSERVATIONS

For the 10 mother-infant pairs, there were a total of 21,580 ten-second epochs recorded over the three weekly home observations, with presence-absence information on 71 behaviors during each epoch.

As for the early observations, combination-variables were selected for analysis.

Variables Analyzed for Observations Made at One Year

From the behaviors listed in Table 12.2, the following combination-variables were used:

Fussing or Crying. The baby is engaged in one of these behaviors.

Interaction. Within an epoch, the mother (or father) and infant are engaged in mutual behaviors, such as looking, talking, touching, or playing together. When the mother moves the baby, as in holding or carrying, this is also included.

Physical Contact. The parent (mother or father) and baby are in Body Contact.

Mother-initiated Contact. The mother is engaged in one of the following behaviors: Hold, Carry, Hug, Body Contact. In each case, there is body-to-body contact.

Baby-initiated Contact. The baby is engaging in Body Contact, by hugging mother's legs.

Mother Available to Baby. During a non-*Interaction* epoch, the mother engages in any behavior directed to the baby.

Baby Available to Mother. Baby behaviors are directed towards the mother, including: looking, touching, offering objects, talking while looking, reaching for mother, showing objects to mother, etc. Baby's Fussing or Crying is also included. Applies to non-*Interaction* epochs only.

These combined variables encompass all of the 71 individual mother and infant behaviors recorded, as listed in Table 12.2. The percent of total time (epochs) spent in each of these parent-infant behaviors was analyzed in the same way as the data for the early observations.

TABLE 12.4

Summary Data for the Three Weekly Observations Made at One Year (Based on Percent of Total Observation Time for Each Variable)

	r_{tt}	Group $\bar{X}$	SEMeas	Pair 13	Pair 16	t^a	
Fussing or crying	.550	6.8	2.45	1.7	14.3	3.64	**
Interaction (Includes father)	.79	40.7	4.34	47.1	41.5	.91	
Interaction (Mother only)	.84	37.79	3.94	37.7	41.5	.69	
Physical contact (Includes father)	.76	21.2	3.32	22.6	34.7	2.58	*
Physical contact (Mother only)	.80	19.63	3.03	16.0	34.7	4.36	**
Mother-initiated (Body-to-body)	.86	10.3	1.83	5.2	8.1	1.12	
Baby-initiated contact	.87	9.4	2.76	10.9	26.7	4.05	**
Mother available to baby	.74	10.0	1.95	9.3	16.0	2.43	*
Baby available to mother	.57	8.4	2.63	4.4	12.0	2.04	*

[a]t value for comparisons of Pairs 13 and 16.
df for t = 18, see Denenberg chapter.
*$p < .05$.
**$p < .01$.

Individual Differences in Behavior Patterns at One Year

The analyses of variance indicated significant Individual Differences among subjects on the variables listed in Table 12.4 with two exceptions: *Fussing or Crying* and *Baby Available to Mother*. For all of the variables, total-test reliabilities (r_{tt}) based on the F values are presented in Table 12.4. The table also presents the group means for each of these variables over the three weeks, as well as the means for Pairs *13* and *16*. Pairs *13* and *16* are compared on each measure, and the *t* values for these comparisons are presented in Table 12.4

Additional Comparisons of Babies 13 and 16

Since both of these babies initiated a relatively high percent of mother-infant contact, a count was made of the frequency of fussing and crying epochs that elicited contact. Over all 3 weeks, there were only 5 such epochs for Baby *13* and 67 epochs for Baby *16*.

Additionally, for these two babies a sequence analysis was made of the frequency of fussing or crying during each 2-minute period preceding a run of *Hold, Carry,* or *Body Contact,* during all three weekly observations. For Baby *13* there were only 12 epochs and for Baby *16*, 185 epochs of fussing or crying prior to one of these contact interventions by the mother.

TABLE 12.5
Summary of Results from Developmental Assessments at One Year, Using
Bayley Mental and Motor Scales (N = 18)

	Group $\overline{X}$	(S.D.)	Baby 13	z Score	Baby 16	z Score
PDI (motor)	103.3	(13.0)	104	0.06	99	–0.34
MDI (Mental)	104.7	(12.4)	112	0.59	74	–2.47
Mental Sub-scales						
Language	10.2	(1.5)	12	1.17	7	–2.12
Adaptive	71.9	(3.4)	75	0.89	69	–0.85
Personal-Social	23.1	(1.0)	24	0.93	20	–3.24

Results of Developmental Assessment at One Year

The results of the one year developmental assessment using the Bayley scales are summarized in Table 12.5. Most notably, Baby *13* is slightly above the mean on the mental scales and the three sub-scales, whereas Baby *16* is below the mean on each of these scales. Both babies are within the normal range on motor development.

DISCUSSION

Mother and Baby *13* were selected for special study because preliminary analyses of their interaction behaviors during the first five weeks had indicated that their relationship might be at risk. We were interested in evidence at one year relevant to our prediction that despite early indications of interaction difficulties, the relationship would be a very adequate one, facilitative of the infant's development (Thoman, 1975). The strongest confirming evidence for that very optimistic prediction was the finding at one year of age that Baby *13* cried less than any other baby in the group throughout the home observations. Other data from the one year observations were also supportive of the optimistic prediction for this pair. The father was home during a portion of the observation period, and with his presence, the total interaction time for Baby *13* was well above that of the total group. The mother interacted with the baby about the same amount as other mothers. However, her interaction clearly reflected an adaptation to the infant's early avoidance response to body contact: the mother and baby had, overall, less physical contact than other mother-infant pairs. But in even greater contrast to the general group pattern, physical contact occurred primarily as a function of initiation on the part of the baby, and this form of contact was baby's-body-to-mother's-legs rather than body-to-body contact. Thus, actual body-to-body contact between this mother and baby was extremely low (5.2% of the observation, in comparison to 10.3% for the total group). This is one part of the picture of mutual adaptation of Mother and Baby *13*.

The data on availability for interaction at one year provide additional indications of mutual adaptation between Mother and Baby *13*. While the mother did not differ from the total group in the percent of time she was available for interaction with the baby, the baby was very low with respect to crying or other attention-seeking behaviors when no interaction was ongoing. Thus, the mother seemed to be allowing the baby to pace the interaction. And finally, the success of this relationship is further suggested by the results of the one year developmental assessment, which indicated that Baby *13*'s cognitive and motor functioning were very adequate at that age.

The satisfactory outcome for Baby *13* and for the mother-infant relationship is even more dramatic when this pair is contrasted with the other mother-infant pair selected for individual description—Pair *16*. Pair *16* had been selected because, following the observations during the first five weeks of life, the prediction was very different from the optimistic one proposed for Pair *13*. Based in part on preliminary data but primarily on subjective judgments of the observers, the prediction had been made at five weeks that the relationship would develop with some difficulty. It was therefore of interest to explore the patterning of this relationship more fully during the first five weeks and also following the one year observations.

Several comparisons suggested difficulty in this mother-infant relationship. Baby *16* cried more than any other baby in the total group during the one year observations. At one year, there was more mother-infant interaction for Pair *16* than for Pair *13*. Although there was a great deal of physical contact between Mother *16* and her baby, an unusually large percentage of the contact consisted of the mother holding or carrying the baby in response to her crying. Baby *16* initiated a great deal of body contact by approaching the mother, much of the time while crying. A very interesting aspect of this relationship was that, despite the high level of physical contact and a great deal of mother-infant interaction, both the mother and baby were very high on behaviors indicating availability for interaction at times when there was no response from the other member of the dyad. Thus, each was apparently seeking even more interaction from the other, but their seeking occurred at separate times. This high level of unilateral availability seems to be a clear expression of asynchrony in the relationship.

The results of the developmental assessment of Baby *16* further suggest difficulty in this system. The baby's functioning, as indicated by the mental scales, was low and this was especially marked with respect to the personal-social scales.

The results from the one year observations and assessments confirmed the earlier prediction that Pair *13* would develop an adequate relationship, one that would be facilitative of the baby's development. The results also confirmed the early prediction that the relationship for Pair *16* would not fare so well.

Interaction During the Early Weeks as a Prelude to the Interaction at One Year

Examination of the data obtained during the early weeks provided information about these two relationships which was quite consistent with the picture observed at one year. However, consistency was not found at the level of specific behaviors. For example, during the early weeks of life, Baby *13* was rather irritable and fussed a great deal even while the mother held him. In contrast, during the early weeks, Baby *16* fussed and cried the least of any of the 20 infants in the study—a completely reversed picture from that at one year, when Baby *16* cried *more* than any other baby. Baby *16* was also highly soothable during the early weeks, as she cried very little while being held. Thus, irritability on the part of the baby was not an apparent source of difficulty for Pair *16* early on. The observers' impressions of a lack of synchrony in this relationship were based on other aspects of their interactive patterns during their early weeks together.

An examination of the network of behaviors of the two mother-infant systems, rather than individual behaviors, is necessary to depict the qualitative differences between them. Although during the early weeks Baby *13* was an irritable infant, especially when held, this mother was not deterred in her attentiveness even when the baby was fussing: she looked, talked, and stimulated the baby when he was crying much more than most mothers under the same circumstances. In contrast, Mother *16* looked, talked, and stimulated her baby very little during crying—despite the fact that the baby was generally less fussy than others.

Neither of these two mothers was distinctive with respect to the amount of time they spent holding their infants. However, there was a major distinction in their activities while they were holding their babies: Mother *13* held her baby primarily for non-caretaking activities, whereas Mother *16* held her baby primarily for caretaking purposes. By the same token, Mother *13* engaged in a great deal of social interaction with her baby; and Mother *16* spent relatively little time in social interaction with the baby. Additionally, Mother *13* utilized a greater percent of her baby's waking time for interaction than did Mother *16*, and when interacting, Mother *13* talked to and stimulated her baby much more.

Other interaction variables were also consistent with the differential patterns presented so far. Mother and Baby *13* had more vis-à-vis than Pair

16. The variable vis-à-vis/ Looking and Waking is a significant one because it reflects the role of the infant in the occurrence of vis-à-vis. It is a measure of the amount of vis-à-vis as a percent of the time that the baby's eyes are open *and* the mother is looking at the baby. On this measure, Baby *13* was lower than the group mean. As most vis-à-vis occurs when the baby is held, this is consistent with the baby's negative response to being held. However, Baby *16* is even lower than Baby *13* on this measure. Thus, Baby *16* was very unresponsive to her mother's visual availability.

Two major affectional variables further highlight the differences in the early interaction patterns of these two mothers and babies: Mother *13* patted and caressed her baby a great deal, whereas Mother *16* patted and caressed her baby very little throughout the observations.

Many of the variables reported seem to be focused on the mother's side of the interaction. Also relevant to the system is the organization of the infant's endogenous behaviors as indicated by sleep state measures. Baby *13* slept less than the other babies in the study, and Baby *16* slept a great deal more; Baby *13* spent a very high percent of sleep time in Quiet Sleep, and had an unusually low amount of open-eye REMs in REM sleep. Each of these measures provide indications that, from the beginning, Baby *13* had a neurophysiological advantage which should suggest a positive prognosis for the baby's development and for the mother-infant relationship. Although Baby *16* had a relatively high level of open-eye REMs, the percentage of Quiet Sleep was equal to the mean level of the total group. Thus, Baby *16* does not appear to have had any major disadvantage as indicated from the state measures.

The picture during the first weeks of life is quite consistent with that found at one year with respect to developmental synchrony in the two relationships. Despite the early interaction handicap deriving from the baby's negative response to being held, Baby *13* was well organized with respect to behavioral states, the mother was attentive and affectionate, and Mother and Baby *13* were highly responsive to one another. Despite an apparent lack of handicap with respect to behavioral states during the early weeks, and an apparent advantage with respect to soothability, Baby *16* was visually unresponsive to the mother and the mother was generally inattentive to the baby. This pattern continues to one year, when there was still an unusually high level of unresponsiveness on the part of both mother and baby. The pattern of relational difficulty is further indicated by the relatively low level of performance of Baby *16* on the developmental test at one year, which is most marked in the items related to personal social behaviors. At one year, Mother and Baby *16* appear to be the relationship at risk. The data are consistent with the early prediction, as they indicate how difficulties in the very first weeks together were the prelude to difficulties in this relationship-system at one year.

In this paper, only two babies and their mothers have been described in great detail. Yet, it has taken very intensive, longitudinal observations and, relatively speaking, a vast amount of data on 20 babies in order to provide an empirical base for describing the nature of the continuities in these two individual relationships. By analyses of data from intensive, longitudinal study of an increasing number of individual mother-infant pairs, we hope to find commonalities in patterns that will give clues to the nature of some of the processes involved in the ontogeny of the infant's social responsiveness.

ACKNOWLEDGMENTS

The research described in this paper was supported by The Grant Foundation, Inc., NICHD Grant HD 08195-01A2, and NIMH Predoctoral Fellowship 5268-81-13645. This project was carried out with invaluable assistance from Emelia DeMusis, Linda Abramson, Leslie Gerber, and Margaret Becker. John Sieval provided the specialized programming for input and processing of the voluminous data.

DISCUSSION

Dr. Watson: Baby 13 presumably is not autistic.

Dr. Thoman: Most definitely not. The data present the picture of a baby at one year who is mentally well above average, emotionally a very happy child, and socially well adapted. The child is much older now, and this happy picture has not changed.

Dr. Watson: Do you know Michael Lewis's data, which were reported a number of years ago? Lewis assessed crying around 3 months and then around a year in a longitudinal study and found the switch, that is, that noncrying babies became criers later on and vice versa. I think the finding was one of his illustrations of "why developmental psychologists should be Oriental metaphysicians." It had to do with the potential transformation of relative positions about a group mean and the implication of that for our interpreting the meaning of a particular response at different ages. That might be a relevant finding to consider.

Dr. Thoman: Yes, it is very important to recognize that the same behaviors at different ages do not mean the same thing. However, it seems a little simplistic to talk about total reversals in behaviors. While we find a high level of consistency in the amount of crying over the first 5 weeks, the level of crying during this period is not correlated negatively with the amount of crying that was observed during the observations at 1 year.

Dr. Lipsitt: You must have had some good reason for selecting those particular 2 to show us, out of 20 children.

Dr. Thoman: We selected the two babies for comparison because at 6 weeks of age we were willing to make predictions about the subsequent development of their two systems; and the predictions were very divergent ones. We were especially interested in analyzing the data for Mother and Infant 13 because the very positive prediction was made despite some indications of difficulty in the relationship during the first week—especially the infant's apparent aversion to being held.

Dr. Lipsitt: You must have some children there with Z scores far more deviant from O.

Dr. Thoman: Sure. On *some* measures. We did not expect that these two babies would fail on extreme positions with respect to *all* measures. The idea was to depict the nature of the relationship through the patterning of measures. In order to test the accuracy of our predictions with respect to these two dyads, we expected the patterning of behaviors that would depict the nature of their relationships to be very different. And in fact, that's the way the data turned out.

Dr. Lipsitt: Although these two kids are quite different from each other, neither one of them is terribly "deviant" in terms of departure from the mean. That is, they are close to the mean on many of the measures, so I would wonder, can you tell us anything about some infant that was three standard deviations away from the mean on those particular measures you just talked about?

Dr. Thoman: There were no subjects so extreme. We reported on a total of 20 variables to describe the relationships for these two babies. I could talk about the babies that fall on the extreme end of each of these measures, but no one baby will be deviant on many of these scores. The whole idea of determining the reliability of the variables we used for describing the babies was that the patterns could be described by saying "on this measure, Baby 13 is high" and we can know that this is a reliable statement about the baby. So the various measures for any mother-infant pair can be presented as a reliable "profile" for that pair, one which does not consist of only extreme measures.

Dr.Lipsitt: These two are rather unique in the sample because of the consistent patterning.

Dr. Thoman: The consistency I refer to applies to the measures we have used over the 4 weeks. Yes, each of these babies and their mothers had a unique interactive pattern, which we depicted by means of the data presented. I am sure that *each* individual mother–infant pair will have behavioral patterns that are unique, as well as some aspects of their patterning that will be in common with other mother–infant pairs. The basic idea is not just to understand these two interactive pairs, but to begin with these two, and add additional individual analyses of individual pairs for the purpose of beginning to understand the nature of the development of interaction. Our approach is to abstract from successive individual relationships, rather than to try to understand the process of interaction from group data. Group means and group correlation can tell us very little about the nature of an ongoing process in any individual system.

Dr. Stern: One of the problems has to do with the systems theory approach to looking at this. You invariably talk about one or the other of the mother–infant pairs or groups making a better fit, or as you say, being more synchronous. We all know what you are talking about. However, the systems approach simply says how a particular mother and baby go about making the best adaptation to one another given what they have got, that is, who they are. In which case you really cannot compare different pairs or groups the way you have been. I question what that comparison is going to tell you with regard to the process of adaptation over time.

Dr. Thoman: Although we are not interested in group means as a way of getting to *process,* the group means provide a baseline for comparison. We have compared the two mother–infant dyads with each other and with the total group in order to contrast the ways in which dyads may adapt to each other. For instance, one mother may stimulate her baby 10% of the time the baby is fussing and crying; and if mothers generally stimulate their babies 75% of the time during crying, this gives us a clue as to the behavioral relationships to explore in the one mother–infant pair in order to understand how they are coping with one another. It may turn out that, overall, the baby cries very little and the amount of stimulation during crying is irrelevant because crying so rarely occurs. On the other hand, it may turn out that the baby cries a very great deal—and cries regardless of stimulation. Whereas other babies give indication from the data that stimulation is associated with noncrying. In each of these cases, comparisons between an individual baby and the group provides a context, or window if you will, for looking at the individual pair. Through research in our laboratory now being carried out by Christine Acebo, we are observing babies weekly—throughout the first year. This is very time-consuming work; and we will have only a very small number of babies that can be studied. With these data, we will be able to look at changes in behavioral relations over time—within each mother–infant pair. This will be an even more individually focused kind of study. But the data now being obtained on the larger sample will provide clues as to the significant behavioral changes to explore.

Dr. Rheingold: It concerns me when you say what kinds of changes are related to what kinds of changes. That sounds like a mathematical procedure. If it is such, then you have *A, B, C,* and you have to make some predictions about *A* greater than *B, B* less than *C,* and so on. How does systems analysis handle that?

Dr. Thoman: From a systems analysis point of view, it would simply not be meaningful to take the measures of the 75 behaviors we have observed and to correlate some measure of each of those behaviors with every other one. This would give us a huge matrix of linear relations. First of all, relationships among variables may not be linear; and secondly, correlations do not tell us about the behavior of individual subjects in the correlated group—in this case, mother–infant relationships.

Dr. Eisenberg: You also would have a very big headache.

Dr. Rheingold: You said this is related to that. How do you determine they are related? How does one determine that variables are related in systems analysis theory? Do you put mathematical values on them?

Dr. Eisenberg: What she is saying, I believe, is that the mother and the child together constitute a system.

Dr. Watson: They're the same set; therefore, they're related.

Dr. Thoman: Right.

Dr. Eisenberg: That's all she's saying.

Dr. Watson: I have a difficulty whether to respond to the presentation as a clinical sort of evaluation and therefore disregard the statistical difficulties that I think I see, or whether you mean to present it as a basis for inference about other things in the world, or even as a basis for secure statements of knowledge about these inferences, in which case then the statistical reservations rise quickly. Do you view yourself in dealing with your data as a clinician generating hypothesis about life?

Dr. Thoman: No. I am not sure what you are referring to by statistical difficulties. However, I can respond to your question about the data providing clinical information. This question relates to some of Harriet Rheingold's (see Chapter 11) statements about our "going back" to naturalistic study. As we indicated in our manuscript, we are not going *back* to anything. The commonality between present-day naturalistic studies and those of the past are only to the extent that a single subject at a time may be of interest. Methodologies for naturalistic studies have changed dramatically. We are no longer making clinical judgments about subjects and giving nonsystematic descriptions of their behaviors. Naturalistic studies can now be made by means of objective and reliable recordings of behaviors. The data are then available for us—or anyone else—to make whatever analyses and interpretations they will. Although we do make interpretations of a "fit" or lack of "fit" in the relationship, that interpretation can be challenged and the data remain intact. This is the major difference, then, between present-day naturalistic studies and clinical studies of the past. We are trying to get at the process of mother–infant relating, a process that is expressed uniquely in each mother–infant pair. A process is not a group affair, and group means as well as group correlations will not provide an understanding of this process. If we can look at enough mother–infant pairs individually, we will begin to pull out some process characteristics that will then serve as hypotheses as to the nature of the process of the developing relationship. The present study reports only the beginning for us, as we intend to explore additional mother–infant pairs intensively.

Dr. Eisenberg: But exploring to what end? Granted that it's a fishing expedition, I suppose what John is really asking and what I'm asking is, what are you fishing for? Eventually—way down the line.

Dr. Thoman: We're searching for commonalities in the ways by which mothers and infants do adapt to one another, how they cope with what they elicit from each other, and how a system may develop over time—despite the unique qualities of expressed behavior in each mother–infant pair.

Dr. Mason: It seems to me that one step you have to confront along the way is to construct some sort of taxonomy of systems. I think what you're saying must be true. The particular patterns are going to be unique in some respects, so you can't say that if this is two standard deviations above or below, and this one is such and such, the outcome will always be this. You might find that the deviations are in one case largely the result of changes in the mother's behavior; and in another, of changes in the infant's behavior. In fact, most often it is probably some combination. But that seems to me an added source of uniqueness. I think one would have to move to a place where you're talking in such terms as, This is a system that is synchronous or conflictual, and so on. I don't know what taxonomy you would attempt, but it seems to me you will have to do that, or every one of these outcomes will have to be treated as though it were completely unique.

Dr. Thoman: Yes, that's very helpful. To the extent that each relationship is actually unique and can't eventually be fitted into some kind of abstraction or higher level pattern, then the findings or descriptions are trivial. Expressing the notion of abstractions in terms of a taxonomy of systems is very helpful. That indicates exactly the direction we hope to go in. We have started with two subjects, as we have to start somewhere.

Dr. Yarrow: Could you give some examples of the kinds of predictions you would make about the process of adaptation? That's where I'm still stuck.

Dr. Thoman: Well, that's where we are struggling. In the present study, the data clearly pointed to the notion of synchrony, or fit, with a great deal more in one pair than in another. Of course, synchrony is not an all-or-none category; and it will be expressed in different ways in different mother–infant pairs. For example, in pair 13, there were indications of asynchrony very early on as indicated by the baby's fussiness when being held. By looking just at Baby 13 early on, the prognosis would have undoubtedly been a relatively poor one for this baby's development. And this case is a good example of why we cannot predict in a linear fashion from early assessments of infants. We have to look at the total system within which the infant is functioning. Then we can have a better chance of predicting for the individual, which is ultimately our objective in any case.

Dr. Eisenberg: You're saying, then, in fact that the mother had an effect on the baby's having a mental score of 112? And that the mother of the other baby had an effect on the baby's having a mental score of 74?

Dr. Thoman: I'm saying that the baby's relatively low level of functioning at 1 year of age was the outcome of the infant's developing within the particular mother–infant system.

Dr. Watson: You're also saying though that that system had a property, one property you're calling asynchrony.

Dr. Thoman: I have used the category "asynchrony" to describe generally the nature of the relationship. I am sure that other categories for description can be abstracted—a "taxonomy," as Bill Mason puts it—of patterns of behavior that reflect the mother–infant relating process.

Dr. Watson: And how many such properties do you need in order to come up with a workable scheme?

Dr. Thoman: I can't know—as yet we only have such clinical, and general, terms as "synchrony" to go with. But I like Bill Mason's term *taxonomy* as the concept that describes our objectives. The data could be ordered in meaningful ways by means of a taxonomy. It may turn out that we come up with relatively few taxonomic terms—as there may be a multitude of patterns of interaction that may be categorized as "asynchronous." In which case, we may have to derive or identify categories of asynchrony.

Dr. Watson: The synchrony is defined by its position relative to the group, which seems to me odd given your perspective—that what you want is a system function. You could still deal with all 20 of your pairs, but look at each of them with respect to themselves.

Dr. Thoman: Yes, as we have dealt with the data so far, synchrony, or mutual responsiveness, is indicated by comparing the patterns of interactions of two babies—one with the other and also of each of these babies with the total group. The total group provides a base level in a very meaningful way. For instance, one might say that in this mother–infant pair, the baby cried "a lot," and this statement can only be made if we know the level of crying of the group of babies. We can also make comparisons such as "Baby A cries more than Baby B." On the other hand, one can look at individual mother–infant pairs to see what each mother does when her baby cries and how this may change over time in relationship with changes in total crying, total sleeping, or other characteristics of the infant. This is a within-pair question. Both types of questions should be useful ones for describing and highlighting the nature of the relationship in any one mother–infant pair.

Dr. Watson: To see the relative pattern you need to get the deviation with respect to self, and with respect to the mother's own general pattern. Then you could look at the provocative value of mother's changes in behavior vis-à-vis the baby and vice versa. You could look at the commonality of such individual systematic patterns as they might be then seen again replicated across your 20 dyads. But it seems to me you're going right past that by using the relative group score on each variable as being your base to start from.

Dr. Denenberg: That's a very important point. What she has done is just get a percentage—the total time in certain hours or out of a particular subclass for each individual pair. It's not a matter of getting averages over the group. You get a statistic that states: for this particular mother in 15% of the time during which the baby was crying, it was being attended to. That's the kind of numerical value that's obtained. Each of the 20 subjects have that kind of score available. That's the kind of comparison that's now being made, which, as far as I can see, is a valid comparison. Now I think another comparison, and the one to which you refer, is to do an analysis *within the mother* and find out, of all the time that she spends caretaking, what percent of that time is involved in caretaking when the baby is fussing and crying, so you can say relatively where she is at. Okay, but that's a different kind of analysis. I don't see, though, why the first analysis is one that you're questioning.

Dr. Watson: Because in that analysis you're defining the system by values external to the system values. And it seems to me you just might miss the way in which there is a conditional relation between the behaviors of the two parties in this dyad, because you'll look at it in terms of the overall group and see group-relative statements and you won't see conditional behavior within dyads. For example, it might be the case that Baby A's mother attends to her baby 35% of the time he or she is fussing and that Baby B's mother attends to her baby 15% of the time he or she is fussing. To interpret Dyad A's percent of fussing episodes that are combined with caretaking on the basis of its contrast with Dyad B's is to base the interpretation on an external relation (i.e., that Dyad A is "high" or "low" depending on level of Dyad B). Thus, in this case, one might be led to say Dyad B is low in synchrony of caretaking and fussiness in relation to Dyad A. If one were to interpret this contrast as reflecting the closer relation between fussiness and caretaking as a system feature of Dyad A, however, one could be misled. For example, one might look and find that percent of caretaking during episodes of nonfussiness remains 35% in Dyad A but drops to 5% in Dyad B. With this information, we see that the relation of fussiness and caretaking as a system feature is clearly higher in Dyad B than A. The behavioral events of fussing and mother-caregiving are related within Dyad B, but unrelated within Dyad A. I would think an analysis guided by systems theory would wish to have features defined by relations of variables internal to the system. Once features are so defined, systems might then be compared in terms of these features (e.g., synchrony of fussiness and caretaking is higher in Dyad B than A).

Dr. Thoman: You are quite right—and I'm agreeing because we did exactly what you suggest. In Table 12.3, of the manuscript, you can see the actual percent of time spent by the two individual mother–infant pairs, 13 and 16, in a large number of activities. For example, Pair 13 spent 28.5% of the total observation holding (or carrying) the baby; and Pair 16 spent 28.4% of the time holding the baby—virtually the same figure. However, if one looks at the percent of Hold or Carry time that was devoted to Caretaking, the figures are: 25.0% and 57.4% for Pairs 13 and 16 respectively. Thus, though both mothers held their babies for the same amount of time during the day, one mother was holding the baby for caretaking purposes a great deal more. So we know something about each system by these comparisons.

Take another example using mother–infant Pairs 13 and 16 again. Pair 13 had vis-à-vis during 8.5% of the time when the-baby-was-awake-and-the-mother-was-looking-at-the-baby. The same figure for Pair 16 was 4.8%. The contrasting figures for the two systems make it clear that there is less mutuality in one system than another in one way, as the baby in the latter pair was much less responsive to the mother's visual availability. Then, by comparing both pairs to the group, one can talk about a low level, or a *lack,* of mutuality in Pair 16, as the level for this pair is far below the mean for the group. The group mean provides the normative baseline for general comparative statements of "much" or "little," "high" or "low," for any pair on a systems measure.

REFERENCES

Ashby, W. R. Systems and their information measures. In G. J. Klir (Ed.), *Trends in general systems theory.* New York: Wiley-Interscience, 1972.

Bakeman, R. Untangling streams of behavior: sequential analysis of observation data. In G. P. Sackett and C. C. Haywood (Eds.), *Application of observational/ethological methods to the study of mental retardation.* Baltimore: University Park Press, 1977.

Bertallanfy, L. von. *Modern theories of development: an introduction to theoretical biology.* Translated and adapted by J. H. Woodger. London: Oxford University Press, 1933.

Bertallanfy, L. von. *General system theory* (rev. ed.). New York: Brazillier, 1968.

Brazelton, T. B., Koslowski, B., & Main, M. Origins of reciprocity: the early mother-infant interaction. In M. Lewis and L. A. Rosenblum (Eds.), *The effect of the infant on its caregiver.* New York: John Wiley & Sons, 1974.

Brazelton, T. B., Tronick, E., Adamson, L., Als, H., & Wise, S. Early mother-infant reciprocity. In *Parent-infant interaction.* New York: Associated Scientific Publishers, 1975.

Fowler, C. A. A systems approach to the cerebral hemispheres. *Status report on speech research.* Haskins Laboratories, 1975.

Freese, M. P. *Assessment of maternal attitudes and analysis of their role in early mother-infant interactions.* Unpublished doctoral dissertation, Purdue University, 1975.

Hoyer, W. J. Aging as intraindividual change. *Developmental Psychology,* 1974, *10*(6), 821–826.

Jaffe, J., Stern, D. N., & Peery, J. C. "Conversational" coupling of gaze behavior in pre-linguistic human development. *Journal of Psycholinguistic Research,* 1973, *2*, 321–329.

Lewis, M., & Lee-Painter, S. An interactional approach to the mother-infant dyad. In M. Lewis & L. A. Rosenblum (Eds.), *The effect of the infant on its caregiver.* New York: John Wiley & Sons, 1974.

Porges, S. W. Ontogenetic comparisons, International Journal of Psychology, 1976, *11*, 203–214.

Sameroff, A. J., & Chandler, M. J. Reproductive risk and the continuum of caretaking casualty. In F. D. Horowitz (Ed.), *Child development research* (Vol. 4). Chicago: University of Chicago Press, 1975.

Sander, L. Adaptive relationships in early mother-child interaction. *Journal of American Academy of Child Psychiatry,* 1964, *3*, 231–264.

Sander, L., Stechler, G., Burns, P., & Julia, H. Early mother-infant interaction and 24-hour patterns of activity and sleep. *Journal of the American Academy of Child Psychiatry*, 1970, *9*, 103–123.

Stern, D. N. A microanalysis of mother-infant interaction: behavior regulating social contact between a mother and her 3-½-month-old twins. *Journal of the American Academy of Child Psychiatry*, 1971, *10*, 501–517.

Stern, D. N. Mother and infant at play: the dyadic interaction involving facial, vocal and gaze behaviors. In M. Lewis & L. A. Rosenblum (Eds.), *The effect of the infant on its caregiver*. New York: John Wiley & Sons, 1974.

Thoman, E. B. How a rejecting baby may affect mother-infant synchrony. In *Parent-infant interaction*. New York: Associated Scientific Publishers, 1975.

Thoman, E. B., Freese, M. P., & Becker, P. T. Individual patterns of mother-infant interaction. In G. P. Sackett & C. C. Haywood (Eds.), *Application of observational/ethological methods to the study of mental retardation*. Baltimore: University Park Press, 1977.

Weiss, P. The living system: determinism stratified. In A. Koestler and J. R. Smythies (Eds.), *Beyond reductionism*. Boston: Beacon Press, 1969.

Weiss, P. The basic concept of hierarchical systems. In P. Weiss (Ed.), *Hierarchically organized systems in theory and practice*. New York: Hafne, 1971.

Wohlwill, J. F. *The study of behavioral development*. New York: Academic Press, 1973.

13 Analysis of Variance Procedures for Estimating Reliability and Comparing Individual Subjects

Victor H. Denenberg
University of Connecticut

There are two purposes for this note. The first is to describe the analysis of variance procedure for estimating test reliability by means of the intraclass correlation. This will include estimating the reliability of a single set of observations as well as the reliability of the scores obtained by summing over observations. The second purpose is to present a method for making a statistical test between pairs of subjects to determine whether they differ significantly on some criterion measures.

ESTIMATING RELIABILITY

We start off with the data matrix shown in Table 13.1 in which n subjects are observed and measured on k occasions. There must be at least two sets of observations, but there is no upper limit (i.e., $k \geq 2$). It is assumed that there are no missing values in the matrix. The subjects are assumed to be a random sample from a population to which we wish to make inferences, and the obtained observations are a random sample from a population of observations. At the bottom of Table 13.1 are the formulas for computing the total sums of squares of the raw scores within the matrix (which are designated by the X's), as well as the sums of squares for Subjects, Observations, and the Subjects × Observation interaction. We will make use of those formulas shortly. First, however, it is necessary to define reliability.

The general definition of reliability in the population (which we will designate by the Greek letter rho, ρ) is that it is the ratio of true variance to

Table 13.1
Layout of Data Matrix in Which n Subjects are Measures on k Occasions

	Observation						
Subject	1	2	·	·	·	k	Total
A	X_{A1}						ΣS_A
B	X_{B1}						ΣS_B
·							·
·							·
·							·
·							·
n						X_{nk}	ΣS_n
Total	ΣOb_1	ΣOb_2	·	·	·	ΣOb_k	ΣX

N = Total number of raw scores = kn
ΣX = Sum of all the raw scores
ΣX^2 = Sum of the squares of all the raw scores
CT = Correction term = $(\Sigma X)^2 / N$
$SS_{total} = \Sigma X^2 - CT$
$$SS_{subjects} = \frac{(\Sigma S_A)^2 + \cdots + (\Sigma S_n)^2}{k} - CT$$
$$SS_{observations} = \frac{(\Sigma Ob_1)^2 + \cdots + (\Sigma Ob_k)^2}{n} - CT$$
$SS_{sub \times obs} = SS_{total} - SS_{sub} - SS_{obs}$

total variance where total variance is defined as true variance plus variance due to errors in measurement. In the context of an analysis of variance the mean square for Subjects can be used to estimate the true variance, while the mean square for Subjects × Observations is an estimate of the population error variance. From these sample estimates one can obtain a value for the reliability. The letter r will be used for this sample value.

In order to estimate these population parameters, it is necessary to know the expected mean squares of the model. The expected mean squares for the design of Table 1 are listed in the upper part of Table 13.2 (in the right column) along with the sources of variation, degrees of freedom, sums of squares, and mean squares.

The lower portion of Table 13.2 gives general population and sample definitions of reliability followed by definitions and formulas to obtain the reliability of a single observation (designated as r_{11}) and the reliability of the total test score (r_{tt}). We will discuss each in turn.

Table 13.2

Showing *df*, SS, MS, and the Expected Mean Squares for the Design in Table 1; and Giving Definitions of Reliability for the General Case and for Two Specific Cases

Source of Variation	df	SS	MS	E(MS)
Between				
Subjects	$n - 1$	SS_{sub}	MS_{sub}	$\sigma_e^2 + k\sigma_{sub}^2$
Within				
Observations	$k - 1$	SS_{obs}	MS_{obs}	$\sigma_e^2 + n\sigma_{obs}^2$
Subjects × Observations	$(n - 1)(k - 1)$	$SS_{sub \times obs}$	$MS_{sub \times obs}$	σ_e^2

General Definition of Reliability

$$p = \frac{\text{variance due to true scores}}{\text{variance due to true scores} + \text{variance due to measurement errors}}$$

$$r = \frac{\text{between subject variance}}{\text{between subject variance} + \text{error variance}}$$

Reliability of a Single Observation (r_{11})

$$\sigma_{sub}^2 = \frac{MS_{sub} - MS_{sub \times obs}}{k}$$

$$\sigma_e^2 = MS_{sub \times obs}$$

$$r_{11} = \frac{MS_{sub} - MS_{sub \times obs}}{MS_{sub} + (k - 1) MS_{sub \times obs}}$$

Reliability of the Total Test Score (r_{tt})

$$k\sigma_{sub}^2 = MS_{sub} - MS_{sub \times obs}$$

$$\sigma_e^2 = MS_{sub \times obs}$$

$$r_{tt} = \frac{MS_{sub} - MS_{sub \times obs}}{MS_{sub}} = 1 - \frac{MS_{sub \times obs}}{MS_{sub}}$$

RELIABILITY OF A SINGLE OBSERVATION

We can define the reliability of a single observation by the formula

$$\rho_{11} = \frac{\sigma_{subjects}^2}{\sigma_{subjects}^2 + \sigma_{error}^2}$$

From the expected mean squares in Table 13.2 we see that we can obtain an estimate of $\sigma_{subjects}^2$ by subtracting the Subjects × Observations mean square from the Subjects mean square, and dividing by k, the number of observations taken on each subject. We also see that $MS_{sub \times obs}$ can be used as an estimate of σ_{error}^2. When these values are substituted in the foregoing formula, we find that we can estimate the reliability by

$$r_{11} = \frac{MS_{sub} - MS_{sub \times obs}}{MS_{subjects} + (k - 1)\, MS_{sub \times obs}}$$

RELIABILITY OF THE TOTAL TEST SCORE

We often sum over our k observations to obtain one numerical score that typifies the individual. To obtain an estimate of the reliability of the total score, we proceed as follows. If we have k observations on a group of individuals, then the true subject variance in the population will be $k\sigma_{subjects}^2$. That is, the true variance is now k times larger than it was when we estimated the reliability for a single set of scores. However, the population error variance does not increase. Therefore, the total test reliability in the population may be defined as

$$\rho_{tt} = \frac{k\sigma_{subjects}^2}{k\sigma_{subjects}^2 + \sigma_{error}^2}$$

By appropriate substitution of the various mean squares from our analysis of variance table, we obtain the following formula to estimate reliability from our sample:

$$r_{tt} = \frac{MS_{sub} - MS_{sub \times obs}}{MS_{sub}} = 1 - \frac{MS_{sub \times obs}}{MS_{sub}}$$

THE SPEARMAN–BROWN PROPHECY FORMULA AND TOTAL TEST RELIABILITY

In the psychometric literature, an important question has to do with the effects upon test reliability of lengthening or shortening a test. Suppose that one has a reliability estimate, r, and one wishes to change the test length by the amount k. If k is less than 1, the new test will be shorter than the original test, and if k is greater than 1, the new test will be longer than the original test. To estimate the reliability for the revised test, the Spearman–Brown prophecy formula may be used. This formula is

$$r_k = \frac{kr}{1 + (k - 1)\, r}$$

If we substitute for r in the above formula the definition of r_{11} for estimating the reliability of a single observation (or its equivalent, ρ_{11}), let k equal the total number of observations, and then go through the algebra, we will find that we end up with the formula for r_{tt} (or for ρ_{tt}). In other words the algebraic relationship between r_{11} and r_{tt} as defined in analysis of variance terms, is identical to the relationship specified by the Spearman–Brown formula.

THE STANDARD ERROR OF MEASUREMENT

Imagine that we had tested one subject over a very large number of trials using equivalent forms of the same test. If we computed the standard deviation of those scores, we would have an estimate of how much that subject would vary from one test session to another. If we were to do this for many subjects, we would find that the standard deviations within subjects were approximately the same. The average of all of these standard deviations is called, in the psychometric literature, the standard error of measurement, and it is defined as follows:

$$SE_{meas} = s\sqrt{1 - r}$$

where s = the standard deviation between subjects
r = the test reliability

We see from the above formula that if a test has zero reliability then the variability within an individual subject will be as great as the variability among subjects. As the reliability increases, the within-subject variability gets progressively smaller.

Within the context of the analysis of variance, r_{tt} may be used as the estimate of reliability, and the square root of $MS_{subjects}$ may be used to estimate the variability between subjects. (It should be noted that the square root of $MS_{subjects}$ is the standard deviation of the *mean* scores of the subjects, not of their total scores.) Thus, the standard error formula can be rewritten as

$$SE_{meas} = s\sqrt{MS_{sub}(1 - r_{tt})}$$

However, it is actually not necessary to go through this computation since it can be shown algebraically that $SE_{meas} = \sqrt{MS_{sub \times obs}}$. In other words, the square root of our estimate of error variance obtained via the analysis of variance procedure is identical with the standard error of measurement as defined in correlation theory.

A NUMERICAL EXAMPLE

To illustrate the use of the formulas and principles we will use a set of data from the previous chapter by Thoman et al., which gives the percent of total

TABLE 13.3
Percent of Total Observation Time that 20 Infants
were Asleep over Four Weekly Observations

	Observation				
Subject	1	2	3	4	Total
A	74	60	44	63	241
B	69	71	71	45	256
C	69	46	61	71	247
D	64	82	77	71	294
E	58	64	59	53	234
F	64	73	65	56	258
G	69	69	71	42	251
H	66	63	61	68	258
I	63	79	93	76	311
J	65	59	66	55	245
K	61	66	58	74	259
L	48	54	46	66	214
M	68	64	60	49	241
N	62	57	75	59	253
O	55	55	56	68	234
P	83	64	66	63	276
Q	80	87	68	84	319
R	81	71	65	64	281
S	60	74	72	60	266
T	85	70	79	68	302
Total	1344	1328	1313	1255	5240

observation time that 20 infants were asleep during a 7-hour observation period. The infants were observed four times at weekly intervals. Table 13.3 presents the raw data of the 20 subjects, Table 13.4 summarizes the computations of the various sums of squares and directly parallels the definitions given at the bottom of Table 13.1, and Table 13.5 is the final analysis of variance summary table.

Note in Table 13.5 that the mean square for Subjects is significant at the .01 level. This signifies that there are significant individual differences among the subjects. The F test on $MS_{subjects}$ is also the test of significance of the reliability coefficient, and thus we may conclude that we have reliability beyond the .01 level.

We can estimate the reliability of any one weekly observation by using the formula for r_{11} from Table 13.2 and substituting the appropriate mean squares from Table 13.5. When we do this we get

$$r_{11} = \frac{MS_{sub} - MS_{sub \times obs}}{MS_{sub} + (k-1)\ MS_{sub \times obs}} = \frac{189.39 - 80.00}{189.39 + (3)\ 80.00} = .255$$

Table 13.4
Calculations for Determining the Various Sums of
Squares for the Data in Table 3, Using the Formulas
from Table 1

$N = (4) (20) = 80$
$\Sigma X = 5240$
$\Sigma X^2 = 351604$

Correction Term $= CT = (\Sigma X)^2 / N = 5240^2 / 80 = 343220$

$SS_{total} = \Sigma X^2 - CT = 8384$

$SS_{subjects} = \dfrac{(\Sigma S_A)^2 + (\Sigma S_B)^2 + \cdots + (\Sigma S_T)^2}{k} - CT$

$\qquad = \dfrac{(241)^2 + (256)^2 + \cdots + (302)^2}{4} - 343220$

$\qquad = 3598.5$

$SS_{observations} = \dfrac{(\Sigma Ob_1)^2 + \cdots + (\Sigma Ob_4)^2}{n} - CT$

$\qquad = \dfrac{(1344)^2 + (1328)^2 + (1313)^2 + (1255)^2}{20} - 343220$

$\qquad = 225.7$

$SS_{sub \times obs} = SS_{total} - SS_{sub} - SS_{obs}$

$\qquad = 8384 - 3598.5 - 225.7$

$\qquad = 4559.8$

In a similar fashion we can estimate the reliability of the total test score based upon the summation over four weekly observations. This turns out to be

$$r_{tt} = 1 - \frac{MS_{sub \times obs}}{MS_{sub}} = 1 - \frac{80.00}{189.39} = .578$$

To demonstrate the use of the Spearman–Brown formula, we can take the value obtained for r_{11}, which was .255, and ask what reliability we expect to get if we increase the test length to four observations. This results in

$$r_4 = \frac{(4)\ (.255)}{1 + (3)\ (.255)} = .578$$

which is the identical value we obtained when we solved directly for r_{tt}.

We can also use the Spearman–Brown formula to estimate k. For example, suppose we desire to have a reliability coefficient of .70 for this measure. We

TABLE 13.5
Analysis of Variance Summary Table of the Data in Table 3

Source	df	SS	MS	F
Between				
Subjects	19	3598.5	189.39	2.37*
Within				
Observations	3	225.7	75.23	
Subjects × Observations	57	4559.8	80.00	
Total	79	8384.0		

can substitute .70 into our Spearman–Brown formula and solve for k. The reliability for one weekly observation is .255, and after substitution we get

$$.70 = \frac{k(.255)}{1 + (k - 1)\,(.255)}\,, \text{ and } k = 6.82$$

Thus we would need to have about seven weekly observations on each infant in order to have a reliability coefficient of .70.

To obtain an estimate of the standard error of measurement we take the square root of $MS_{\text{sub} \times \text{obs}}$. This is found to be 80.00 in Table 13.5, and the square root equals 8.94. To show that this value is identical to the definitional formula for SE_{meas} we may substitute as follows:

$$SE_{\text{meas}} = s\,\sqrt{1 - r} = \sqrt{MS_{\text{sub}}\,(1 - r_{\text{tt}})}$$

$$= \sqrt{(189.39)\,(1 - .578)} = 8.94$$

COMPARING PAIRS OF INDIVIDUALS

At times we may wish to compare two individuals to see whether they differ significantly from each other. The decision to make such a comparison cannot be based upon inspection of the criterion data but must be based upon additional outside information.

The formula for a comparison is

$$SS_{\text{comparison}} = \frac{(\Sigma S_i - \Sigma S_j)^2}{2k}$$

where

ΣS_i = the total score for one of the subjects to be compared
ΣS_j = the total score for the other subject to be compared
k = the number of observations on each subject

This comparison has 1 df associated with it, and thus $MS_{comparison}$ is numerically the same as $SS_{comparison}$. The usual error term is employed to test for significance.

We will illustrate the use of this procedure with two hypothetical examples. Suppose that at one year of age Subjects J and R are found to differ from each other with respect to their body weight, and that Subjects I and L are found to be at the two extremes in terms of a neurological examination. We may have reason to believe that these differences may be related to their sleep states during infancy. To test this idea, we carry out a special comparison for each pair of subjects, as shown below, using the data from Table 13.3.

$$\text{Subject J versus Subject R: } SS_{comp} = \frac{(245 - 281)^2}{(2) \quad (4)} = 162.00$$

$$\text{Subject I versus Subject L: } SS_{comp} = \frac{(311 - 214)^2}{(2) \quad (4)} = 1176.12$$

These sums of squares can be incorporated into the standard analysis of variance summary table. This is done in Table 13.6, which is an extension of Table 13.5. The degrees of freedom and the sums of squares of the two special comparisons are enclosed in brackets to indicate that they are portions of the overall Between Subjects sums of squares and degrees of freedom. When tested against the error term of $MS_{sub \times obs}$, the comparison of Subjects I and L is significant, but not the one involving Subjects J and R.

A note of caution is needed here. The procedure described above must be used judiciously and sparingly, and it is necessary that the decision be based upon evidence external to the measure itself. These precautions are needed because the level of significance (i.e., the a level) goes up numerically with repeated comparisons, and thus there is the danger that one is capitalizing on chance variation. If only a few tests are made, the change in the level of

TABLE 13.6
Analysis of Variance Summary Table Incorporating the Special Comparisons
Involving Two Pairs of Individuals

Source	df	SS	MS	F
Between Subjects	19	3598.50	189.39	2.37*
Sub. J vs. Sub R	[1]	[162.00]	162.00	2.02
Sub. I vs Sub. L	[1]	[1176.12]	1176.12	14.70*
Within Subjects				
Observations	3	225.70	75.23	
Subjects × Observations	57	4559.80	80.00	
Total	79	8384.00		

$*p < .01$

significance will not be important. However, if many comparisons are made, then there can be a marked increase in the alpha level.

For more detailed discussions concerning the use of analysis of variance procedures to estimate reliability, see Haggard (1958) and Winer (1971, pp. 283–296).

REFERENCES

Haggard, E. A. *Intraclass correlation and the analysis of variance.* New York: Dryden Press, 1958.

Winer, B. J. *Statistical principles in experimental design* (2nd ed.). New York: McGraw-Hill, 1971.

14 Change in Infant and Caregiver Variables over the First Two Months of Life: Integration of Action in Early Development

Louis W. Sander
Gerald Stechler
Padraic Burns
Austin Lee
Boston University Medical Center

The contributors to the conference that gave rise to this volume conceived their presentations in a social and research climate of deepening commitment to the understanding of early human development. In this current context, as rapidly as one group arrives at any new findings, there are others waiting and eager to apply these findings to facilitate early development in a variety of situations that threaten to cause difficulty. The bulk of the new information has been won as a result of a step-by-step process of tearing apart influences, defining functions, and narrowing causality by ever more precise specification. As it comes now, however, to the *application* of such information as a means of facilitating development by programs of intervention, the worker is faced with the necessity of adopting an orientation for the *use* of the information quite different from the one that led to its discovery. The research orientation is traditionally *analytic;* the developmental process is essentially *integrative,* a process of synthesis of highly complex determinants. For success of the early intervention program, the synthesis provided by the longitudinal *clinical* perspective of developmental course and process must complement the diversity introduced by the increasingly complex array of contributing factors that are coming to light. To augment the clinical perspective, it is to be expected that research strategies that are aimed at clarifying mechanisms of synthesis and integration in the coordinations between infant and caregiver will be forthcoming.

In this chapter is reported a relatively pioneering effort directed toward the clarification of integrative mechanisms in early developmental processes. The research, which extended from 1965–1969 and which has led to our current investigations, originally aimed at describing change in the organization of interaction between infant and caregiver as they gained coordination over the first two months of life. Obviously adapted action represents the integration of many infant functions. We are well acquainted with arguments attempting to define the extent to which coordinations between infant and caregiver are part of the endowment with which each begins and the extent to which these coordinations depend on the course of their interaction together. The data to be presented here of the course of change in variables measured under three different caregiving situations provide an opportunity to consider an ontogeny of integration of regulatory mechanisms as an initial conceptual framework for those expecting to facilitate adapted action (Sander, L., 1975, 1976).

"Organization" and the process of change over days will be approached from the perspective of the infant–mother or infant–caregiver *system* rather than from the point of view of organization as characteristic of an individual's activity. The research strategy for description of a "system" has, in general, aimed at employing a combination of methods of continuous or repeated measurement on several categories of variables. In the case of the human infant, these categories are related to the different functional or behavioral systems that belong either to the infant or to the caregiver, for example, sleeping, feeding, looking, crying, picking up the baby. Part of the strategy has been to compare samples of infants reared under different caregiving environments, samples of infants reared by the same caregiving individual, or samples of infant–caretaker systems (pairs) given a perturbation (for example, by masking the caretaker's face or by introducing a visual stimulus or by substituting a strange caregiver temporarily or relatively permanently, either with or without a change in the rest of the environment,) Variables are repeatedly or continuously measured then over hours and/or days from preperturbation through the perturbation period and to recovery. For the longer observational spans, effects of perturbation must be distinguished, when possible, from developmental trends. The data so assembled can be discussed in terms of (1) *regulation* of events in the system and of the functions and behaviors of infant and caregiver; (2) the process of mutual modification or *adaptation* between infant and caregiver; (3) the stabilization of infant and caregiver functions or activities in relation to recurrent contexts for exchange, or *organization* of the system.

Those acquainted with our work will be aware of our long preoccupation with the organization question—an area of concern that can quickly become nebulous and abstract if it is not related to empirical data. However, it is a subject we all think about and have thought about in one way or another. It is a subject difficult to take up directly: partly because the great investigators of biology, embryology, genetics, animal behavior, and psychology have already said so much on the subject, partly because each of us approaches the problem from a slightly different point of view, partly because one's own comprehension and grasp of the matter undergoes continual modification as one encounters new data that must also be included, and partly because whatever one says can so easily appear either obvious or irrelevant. However, we are convinced that it is time to begin talking directly about the matter in relation to research in human infancy. The aim for the discussion today is to make some beginning contribution to the subject rather than seek for conclusive formulations. After briefly describing the events and some of the work that has led up to the viewpoint presented here, we shall try to lay out some of the data that have intrigued us and have pushed us to ask new questions, develop new methods, and design new research.

The work of the Boston University Child Development Unit over the years since 1954, which we shall be touching on most briefly, can be thought of in relation to three large project areas. The first was that of a naturalistic, multidisciplinary and multivariable study of 30 firstborns and their families followed longitudinally over the first 6 years of life; the second involved other samples of normal infants over the first 2 months of life. This included another sample of 30 normal infants constituted in three groups, each group reared under different conditions. The third project area has focused on still other normal infants studied over the 1st week of life and includes our present work over the 2nd and 3rd days of life comparing normal infants and certain infants-at-risk for developmental pathology. Because of the difficulty that systems research presents to methodology, and especially because of the bias of different investigators toward either a mechanistic or an organismic viewpoint, it seems essential that a word be said here of our position.

Our attempt has been to replace a causal with a descriptive strategy, one that makes possible the contrastive analysis of the longitudinal course of change in different infant-caregiving systems as a way of investigating the problem of organization in early development. The position from which we began our research was that of clinical child psychiatry rather than that of the animal behaviorist or experimental psychologist. Our questions arose from experience with clinical problems, and we were seeking information related to our needs in coping with them.

A description of the perspective of the clinical psychiatrist in relation to the problem of synthesis and organization provides background for our preference for a systems approach and our interest in the matter of integration.

> The clinical situation confronts one with a person, a single individual, a unity of more or less coherent functions, made up of a unique combination of characteristics, having unique potentialities for action under different circumstances, and having reached the present moment over a unique historical journey. The person is there before us because of some threat to, or deficit in, this essential coherence in the face of the adaptive demands of a particular life

context. The therapeutic task, at least from the point of view of psychotherapy, is to facilitate both coherence and adaptive effectiveness of the patient vis-à-vis his life situation by means of the actions, interactions or exchanges between the patient and that therapist. In other words, a new set of interactions is expected to change the organization of the patient's adaptive resources.

The matter of organization confronts the clinician immediately and inescapably: the traditional psychiatric formulation with all its mystique is but an effort to define that essential configuration which describes the individual *in action* in his context of life support, or in relation to his potential for action in a particular context. The formulation or dynamic description attempts to include both the organization of action and the organization of reflection—the outer and the inner. The clinician's effort to assemble such a formulation demonstrates to him, as nothing else does, that the person as a whole is something more than the sum of his component parts. It is easy to see that the clinician who begins with the task of organizing a diversity of information in some order of importance, might give primary attention to the organismic viewpoint, to the understanding of mechanisms of integration, their compromises, and the means by which integration can be facilitated within a given individual's particular environmental context.

Psychoanalysis traditionally has had a position of interest in the matter of the organization of human personality, viewing its development as in relation to an environmental context and as extending over the life span. By the 1950's psychoanalytic literature had proposed (1) the relation of adaptation to personality organization (e.g., Hartman 1939); (2) systematic effects of parental rearing practices on infant character organization (Erikson 1950), and (3) more specifically related deficits in the developing character organization of the infant to the age level at which disturbances in the interactions between mother and infant occurred, i.e., disturbed "object relations" (Spitz 1958). The bias here was overwhelmingly in favor of the impact of parent and especially *maternal* influence on the exchange with the infant. It has only been with the realization of the equally powerful influence of infant effects on the exchange with mother that the concept of the systems network or infant-environment system has become a helpful tool.

THE FIRST MAJOR RESEARCH AREA

In the first project, we asked the question, In what way does the mother's character organization affect the interaction she then has with her new baby? Will it be possible to relate the actual details recorded of this interaction to the way the behavior of the infant becomes established and to its subsequent organization. These questions were investigated in the first research entitled "The Effect of Maternal Maturity and Immaturity on Child Development." Maternal character organization was formulated in terms of three profiles of possible behaviors that a mother might show in interaction with her family, husband, and social group. These were intended to facilitate selection of three samples that would be representative of the best organized group, the most poorly organized group, and a middle group of subjects that could actually be selected from the population of a general hospital prenatal clinic. Although we had neither the concepts nor the labels at the time, we were beginning to define characteristics of three interactional systems represented by those profiles and to think in terms of hierarchical systems arrangements as we planned the definition of variables by which we would then assess the infant in relation to its mother, its family, and its later social milieu, that is, school.

As soon as we began trying to place our mothers in terms of the three organizational profiles (based on data of six to twelve tape-recorded prenatal interviews), we were faced with the fact of uniqueness in the configuration of each. As soon as we began our detailed observations of the newborn infants in terms of our predefined behavioral variables, we were faced with the fact of uniqueness in the combination of characteristics each possessed at the outset; obviously detailed observation of the interaction in each mother–infant pair, and its course of change over months, confronted us with both uniqueness and commonality at different points. As we struggled to compare the mother–infant pairs and the course of change each was following over time, our strategy turned from an attempt to determine cause to an effort to describe a sequence of changes over time in the various categories of variables and to identify (if possible) process, or steps, in the sequence that could be generalized to a sample of unique pairs. This eventuated then in the formulation of the negotiation between infant and mother of a sequence of adaptive interactional issues, or coordinations, each related to a particular chronological span of time. The hypothesis was that the way these coordinations were finally actually settled between a mother and her infant would determine persistent relatively stable exchanges which would then be characteristic of that particular infant-caregiving system. We looked to further observation to settle the matter of how these relatively stable exchanges or interactional strategies *within* the system would then relate to the later, more stable, character organization of the child when he was functioning *independently* of the system, that is, to be revealed in the later observations of the child in the school situation.

There was parsimony in viewing later adaptations as but extensions of the basic regulation initially effected by caregiving interactions between infant and mother. It became evident that our research strategy should turn to the attempt to define the basic mechanisms of regulation in a systems model from the outset of life postnatally. Actually, our scaled assessments of the way the first adaptive issue was negotiated—the one concerned with the establishing of a mutually comfortable *regulation* of sleeping, feeding, crying, and elimination—had correlated significantly with our assessments of the way subsequent issues of coordination between infant and mother were negotiated over the first 18 months (independently assessed by different raters). We took this to mean that there were fundamental connections between mechanisms of regulation of basic physiological functions of participants and the adaptive behavioral coordinations they later made possible. In other words, one of the origins of social behavior is in the mutual regulation of physiologic states. Adaptations required for initial regulation of states ultimately would define the organization of those relatively stable exchanges by which the infant-caregiver system would be maintained and by which it could be characterized. Stabilities were first of all systems characteristics. In this light then we viewed our sequence of hypothetical issues as shifts in mechanisms of regulation marking the gradually increasing complexity of behavioral exchanges in the infant-caregiving system.

THE SECOND MAJOR RESEARCH AREA

The wide range of behavior that we encountered over the first 3 years of life limited our efforts in the first project to a clinical type of research. In order to identify regulatory mechanisms and adaptive processes more specifically, the next logical step seemed to be that of beginning again with the infant–environment system at its very outset, in other words, at birth. This time, however, we wanted only variables that could be quantified so that description of change could be defined in terms of numbers. The idea was to develop noninvasive methods for continuous or repeated measurement of both infant and caregiver variables and to apply these methods concurrently. The aim was to obtain measures on a range of functions, day by day over the first weeks of life as characteristics of the infant–caregiver interaction changed. It was our hope to begin to construct a model for regulation and adaptation based on these continuous and repeated measures. A model so based might then be more instructive in understanding changes later in life in the organization of behavior than would models of organization derived from data of physical systems, animal behavior, computer simulation, and so on.

Continuous 24-hour bassinet monitoring of infant activity, quiescence, crying and caregiver intervention on a real time-basis provided the first methodological point of departure for this second major project area. (Sander L et al 1972) Experience with one's own new baby in the post partum period is a convincing argument that the initial task of adaptation for the new baby and the family is that of dwelling together around the clock, 24 hours a day. Initially baby and parents are disparately organized in relation to the 24-hour day—for example in relation to a time to eat and a time to sleep. Until some degree of comfortable synchrony is established at this gross level, a sense of confidence in the enduring harmony of the system is not achieved.

A second point of departure was provided by the strategy of keyboard event recording in obtaining a quantitative look at a number of different infant and caregiver functions in their immediate day-by-day interaction. It was quickly apparent that there was a kind of semi-independence between functions in the endowment profile of an infant. A high crying baby might have long sleep periods and be a strong sucker. A poor sleeper might be a low crying baby but a good feeder. As one began to view the organization of each infant's complement of behaviors in terms of such a profile of semi-independent functions—that is, subsystems—variables describing each subsystem could then be followed in the interaction with caregiver to study their integration as the system progressed over days.

These two methodological points of departure set the stage, then, for the overall research question for this second project area. How does adaptation or synchrony achieved in relation to recurring 24-hour patterns of sleep and wakefulness relate to adaptations achieved in the fine linear sequence of sensorimotor interactions between mother and infant–interactions which we could record on a keyboard event-recorder?

A new avenue of thought and a new question emerged: "might a conceptual solution to the relation between regulation, adaptation, and organization of the infant–environment system lie in the domain of time?" In nature, that is in the biological system, the organism is integrated in the domain of time by phenomena of rhythmicity. Even at the level of the single-celled organism, various functional subsystems of the cell can be identified, each with its characteristic rhythmicity. Obviously coherent function of an organism as a whole requires the temporal harmonizing of its complement of subsystems. In the same way at the next level the *adaptation* of the organism as a whole to its environment of life support requires a next order of synchrony. This is the synchrony between activity rhythms of the organism as a whole and periodicities inherent in the surrounding environment. Both levels of synchrony are essential to the enduring existence of the organism.

These basic facts of biology provide a simple model, which we applied to mother and infant now viewed as a biological system. At birth, infant and mother are already complexly organized in terms of endogenous rhythmicities. As components or semi-independent subsystems of the larger, infant–mother dyadic system, each, to begin with, is already running by itself, so to speak. We have viewed birth as introducing a profound perturbation in the temporal organization of each. For the fetus, all the entraining cues provided by cycling maternal functions are suddenly lost. At the same time, the newborn is exposed to new rhythmic inputs both from his own endogenous sources and from new exogenous sources. The infant and mother after birth must be *interfaced* with each other anew in terms of a wide spectrum of rhythmicities, from circadian and ultradian to infradian (e.g., the latter including the relatively higher frequency rhythms of sucking or the microsecond rhythms of linguistic–kinesic synchrony). At the present it seems clear to us that the pre-empting task for the caregiver over the first 3 to 4 weeks of life is that of re-establishing or restoring temporal organization of the infant within its new system of life support.*

But how can "temporal organization" be visualized in an infant–caregiver system? In what way would one begin to investigate it? In the following presentation of data, we will be attempting to illustrate the combination of the two methodological approaches, namely, continuous 24-hour monitoring of infant states and event recording of sequential interaction between infant and caregiver. If we could *combine* data of 24-hour patterns of sleep and wakefulness with data of the adaptive employment of specific sensorimotor functions, would we find that disturbances in the one domain affected the developmental course taken in the other? If this were the case, how might the changing organization of the developing system be conceptualized to account for such an effect?

PRESENTATION OF RESEARCH

In a project limited to the first 2 months of life,* "Adaptation and Perception in Early Infancy," we investigated three groups of infants with an N of 9 in each group. Only infants meeting our rather stringent criteria for normality of pregnancy, labor, delivery and postnatal examination were accepted. The 2 months of the study were divided into three time periods: Period I was the first 10 days of life, Period 2 Days 11 to 29, and Period 3 days 30 to 59. The three groups, which will be labeled A, B, and C, each represented infant–environment systems, which were constituted differently in the relation of the infant to the caregiving environment. Group A differed from Group B only over the first 10 days. Group C differed from both A and B over each of the three time periods. The description of the three caregiving environments will be more instructive if it follows the presentation of data and of results for each of the 3 groups of infants.

Data collection was carried out over the 2 months of the study by the two principal methods. Bassinet monitoring around the clock, day after day, provided the real-time framework of 24-hour cyclic pattens of infant activity, quiescence, crying, and caregiver intervention. On the other hand sequential events between infant and caregiver were observed during feedings and keyboard event-recorded. The combination of the two methods provided concurrent measurement of a number of categories of infant and caregive variables either continuously or by regularly repeated observations. This made possible the plotting of the day-by-day or week-by-week course of change in infant and caregiver variables, a means by which progress of the

---

*In work published elsewhere we have presented some of the data of this second major project area and some of the conceptualizations which they have given rise to. Sander et al, 1975, 1969, 1972, 1970, 1976; Burns et al 1972, Stechler et al 1969, 1973.

three groups could be compared using repeated measurement analysis of variance or trend analysis.

These data already reported in the papers referred to above provide the empirical background for a conceptualization of regulation in the infant-caregiving system. The different courses followed by the three caregiving groups posed the task of generating a concept of state regulation to account for them. It is not possible to review this material within the scope of this presentation, but it is hoped that it will be possible to review some of the major points in the discussion period that follows. In sum, the conceptualization of initial state regulation that has emerged, proposes that sensorimotor mechanisms which regulate the interaction between infant and mother over the *linear* sequence of the awake period provide the entraining cues, or cue framework, that synchronizes *cyclic* infant-sleep and awake states with corresponding daily cyclic environmental periodicities. The course of development of the sensorimotor systems, such as the visual system, would thus be associated with the way stable 24-hour state regulation was achieved.

The only data that will be presented in this chapter is that related to differences between the three groups in the changes in the infants' visual behavior over the first 2 months of life under experimental stimulus presentation and under naturalistic conditions. The experimental stimulus data was collected under the direction of Dr. G. Stechler (1973), and the data collection for the study of visual behavior under naturalistic conditions was carried out under the direction of Dr. P. Burns (1972). A conceptualization of integration in early development will then be suggested, based on the differences in the longitudinal course of basic 24–hour activity, quiescence, and intervention patterns for the three groups.

We will turn now to the description of the infant visual behavior under both experimental and naturalistic conditions. Consideration will be given only to three variables: infant "looking" time, infant crying with stimulus presentation, and "infant regard" of caregiver's face and head during feedings. Data of the experimental condition will be described first, the caregiving environments will be described second, and the results from the naturalistic observations will be described last.

The Experimental Condition

Under the experimental condition, approximately twice weekly for the first 8 weeks of life, the infant was presented a set of visual stimuli systematically, while lying supine in his familiar crib in a state of optimal quiet alertness. The analysis was based on a total of some 360 observations for the 27 infants. The observer recorded the occurrence of a number of precoded infant behaviors on a four–key event–recorder: behaviors such as looking at stimulis, looking away, fussing, closing eyes, and so on. Three visual stimuli were used, each presented at a distance of 15 inches for 60 seconds with a 15-second interstimulus interval (or if fussing supervened, until the state of quiet alertness had been resumed). The three stimuli consisted of a black and white line drawing of a face, the face of the experimenter (male), and the face of the caregiver. The face of the experimenter and the face of the caregiver were presented in a fixed sequence: still, nod, and social. The latter included every effort by expression, movement, or voice to engage the attention of the infant and to gain a response. Since we were primarily interested in group differences under the experimental conditions and group-by-stimulus interactions, we were not so concerned with order effects of stimulus presentation; and so we presented the stimuli consistently in the order just described.

From pilot work with these stimuli and on the basis of other research being carried out concurrently by Doctors Stechler and Carpenter, (Carpenter et al 1970) it was clear that confrontation with the human face provides a highly exciting stimulus for the alert awake infant—a level of excitation the infant must then regulate (Stechler & Latz, 1966). Behavior may be that of avoiding that is, going from looking at the stimulus to peripheral looking, looking away, closing the eyes, or turning the head. With persistent confrontation, behavior may reflect increasing excitation with motor activation, flailing of arms and legs, or twisting of body and head, finally perhaps eventuating in fussing or crying. Our experience with this design of stimulus presentation led us to regard a 60-second duration of presentation as a test of limits. After the first 30 seconds even, many of the infants became uncomfortable or distressed, especially with the face under the "still" condition—truly a most disturbing experience for the infant. The "nod" condition was disturbing also, although to a lesser extent. The black and white line drawing was almost invariably quieting. However, as a test of limits, the experimental 60-second stimulus presentation of experimenter and caregiver faces did reveal the infant's repertoire of regulatory mechanisms and their effectiveness.

An illustration of the infant's regulatory versatility is provided by the behavior of one of the infants, who by the beginning of the second month would begin fussing almost as soon as the stimulus presentation began. As was the procedure, we tested her in her familiar bassinet. This was always kept by the parents' bedside in their bedroom, the shades always being partly drawn. We had noted that the mother, upon picking her baby up, invariably took her at once to the bathinet top in the brighter kitchen before doing anything further with her. Having become aware of the caregiving sequence, we tested her the next time on the bathinet top in the kitchen instead of in her familiar bassinet. It was only upon testing her that we finally noticed that the bathinet was by a wall which had a 1½" black stripe about 8" above the level of the bathinet running horizontally along the wall. As the infant began looking at the stimulus and began to get excited, she turned at once to the wall, gazed steadily at the black stripe, quieted down, and then could turn back to the stimulus, from then on regulating herself as she needed by looking at the black stripe.

A very similar observation was made quite consistently in relation to the onset of responsive smiling. When the smile became available for the infants, sometime around the 5th week of life, they would, in a similiar way, begin to activate and become excited with the stimulus confrontation as before in behavior which often preceded the onset of a fuss. However, at this point, a smile would now break out and the infant would be able to continue looking without distress, the excitement now apparently channeling into smiling behavior.

Results for Groups A, B, and C (visual stimulation under experimental conditions)

Among the several variables recorded, only looking time and fussing time will be presented. Over an 8-week span, correlations for reliability between independent observers recording these variables averaged .79. Some of the overall features of the groups and the stimuli will be considered first.

Figure 14.1 shows the expected fairly linear increase in looking time from Week 2 through 8 for all stimuli and all infants combined. The overall increase, although highly significant is not dramatic, going from 39 to 46

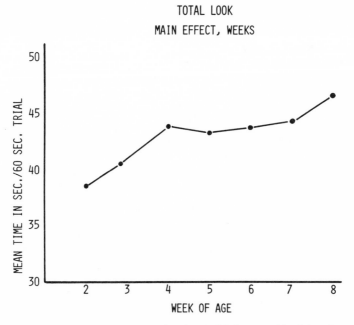

TOTAL LOOK

MAIN EFFECT, WEEKS

FIG.14.1.   Looking time for all stimuli and all infants combined, based on weekly means, Weeks 2 through 8.

seconds out of a possible 60. When all stimuli are combined, there are no significant differences between groups for the total 8-week span.

Figure 14.2 shows the breakdown for looking time for all infants by stimulus. The picture (line drawing of face) is virtually as high at Week 2 as it will get within the first 2 months. All increase in looking time occurs in the reactions to the live faces. Furthermore, the still condition for the live face fails to produce increased attention over the 8 weeks as do the nodding and social conditions (see Figure 14.3). This was particularly true for the experimenter's face (male) for all babies. If the social stimuli are considered alone, which would be the most natural conditions under which a caregiver would engage a baby, again no group differences are seen.

Differences begin to emerge as we consider the course over weeks of total looking time, by caregiving groups Figure 14.4 shows that all groups begin to steady down by the 6th week and end up in close proximity. However, in the first 5 weeks, Group C gets off to a slower start and Group A is quite erratic, reaching a high peak in Week 4 and dropping sharply in Week 5, while Group B maintains a very steady and even course with no drop in Week 5 at all. If only Weeks 2 through 5 are analyzed (see Figure 14.5), the difference in trends

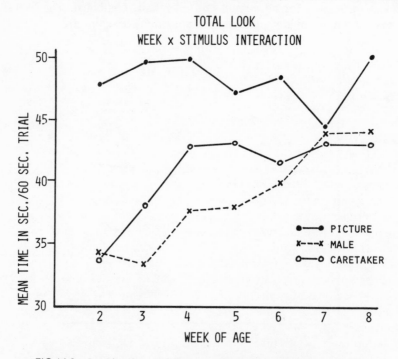

FIG.14.2. Looking time, all infants combined, for three stimuli: a black and white line drawing of a face, the experimenter's face (male), and the caregiver's face (female) based on weekly means, Weeks 2 through 8.

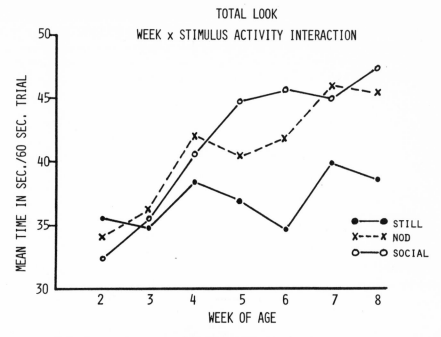

FIG.14.3.   Looking time, all infants combined, for three different movement conditions: still, nodding, and social, under which the live face stimuli were presented, weekly means, Weeks 2 through 8.

becomes significant at the P. < .05 level. If the difficult "still" face stimuli only are considered (see Figure 14.6), differences reach the P < .025 level with essentially the same curves.

Group C infants were the only infants that showed overall a significant discrimination between the male face and the caregiver's face. When data for all three movement conditions were combined, the caregiver was looked at longer by Group C infants. It is in fact a *reduction* of regard for the male face that accounts for the discrimination between male face and caregiver face by Group C infants, an *avoidance* of looking, occurring particularly in the early weeks of the study. Group C infants appear to be more specifically able, and at an earlier point, to regulate visual impact by visual system behavior alone, that is, by looking away or closing eyes. For whatever reason. The visual system of the Group C infant appears to mediate a more differentiated adaptive response.

If we turn now to time spent fussing and crying during stimulus presentation, there were highly significant differences between the three groups. Group A infants could not tolerate the stimulus condition as comfortably as the other 2 groups. This was especially true in the first 4 weeks.

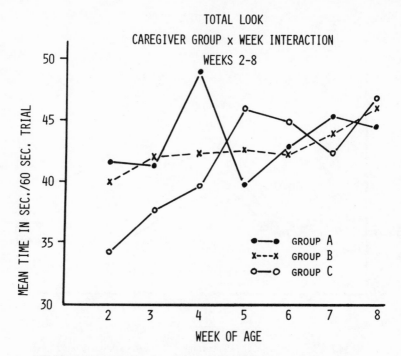

FIG.14.4.   Looking time for all stimuli combined comparing the course of change followed by each caregiving group using group weekly means, Weeks 2 through 8.

In other words, the regulatory mechanism for Group A infants in response to the visual stimulus more often involved a change of state.

Finally, in order to look at the question of individual steadiness of performance from week to week within groups, analysis of the coefficient of concordance (Kendall's W) was performed (see Figure 14.8). This was done for all stimuli pooled, and separately for each stimulus. For Group A, neither the overall W nor the W for any individual stimulus ever achieved significance. This means that Group A the relative rank order for attentiveness for any baby as compared to its same group peers varied widely from week to week. This can be viewed as an instability of individual differences, since the test depends on comparing week-to-week rank ordering of babies within a group. For Groups B and C, overall W's were significant, as were the W's for each individual stimulus, save for one in Group C. Interestingly enough, that unique instability in Group C was for the male face. A similar analysis by Kendall's Coefficient of Concordance was carried out also for fussing time, comparing rank order of the infants within groups week by week. Again the same result was found: no significant stability of infant differences in Group A and a highly significant stability in Groups B and C. In

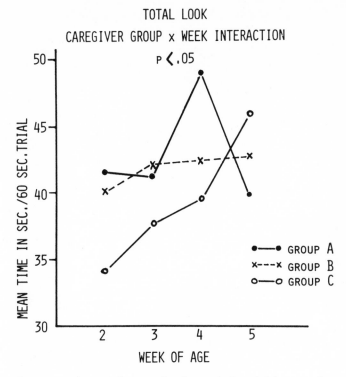

FIG.14.5. Trend analysis comparing Groups A, B, and C in terms of total looking time for all stimuli over Weeks 2, 3, 4 and 5.

sum then there were differences in the way the infants of the 3 groups regulated their behavior in the experimental situation when confronted by face stimuli.

What then were the differences in the caregiving environments of the three groups? If the caregiving experience of Group A differs from B only in the first 10 days, the effect of these days is profound over the rest of the 2 months. If Group C differs from A and B over the 2 months, a different course is apparent in the first weeks, and a greater differential response or discrimination is achieved in relation to live-face stimuli.

Description of Caregiving Environments
of Groups A, B, and C

All infants met our criteria for normality of pregnancy, labor, delivery medication, anaesthesia, and post partum examination, and all were bottle fed; still, there were differences in their environments both prenatally and postnatally. The infants of Group A and B were firstborns of unwed mothers

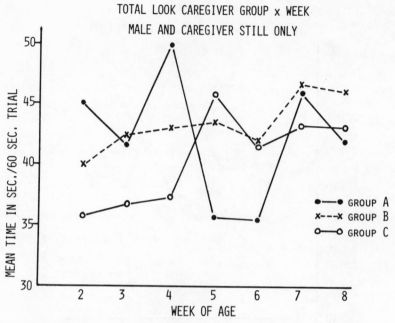

FIG.14.6. Comparison between Groups A, B, and C in terms of looking time for the experimenter (male) face in the "still" condition only. Group means Weeks 2 through 8.

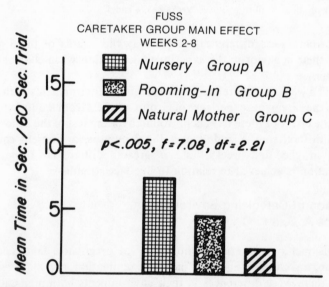

FIG.14.7. Comparison between Groups A, B, and C for fussing in response to visual stimulus presentation, all presentations combined: ANOVA group main effect $p < .001$.

released for adoption. The prenatal care of these mothers was optimal, insofar as they all resided in well-run homes for unwed mothers. The infants of Group C were secondborns, cared for by their natural mothers over the 2 months of the project. The mothers were selected on the basis of a stable marriage, a previous normal and uneventful pregnancy, a normal firstborn with successful rearing to date, and an uncomplicated pregnancy with the study infant.

In period 1, the first 10 days of life, caregiving differed for Groups A and B. Group A infants were boarders in the hospital neonatal nursery until the morning of the 11th day of life. In the nursery they received standard newborn care on a 4-hourly fixed feeding schedule by multiple nurses. By contrast, the Group B infants went directly to a surrogate mother nurse 12 to 24 hours after birth, who then roomed with the infant, around the clock, to the morning of Day 11; each nurse was on an individual basis with each infant and bottle fed on an infant-demand regimen.

Period 2 began on the morning of Day 11 of life and extended to Day 29 of life. Group A infants first began individual rooming in with surrogate mother nurses on Day 11, Group B infants continued from Day 11 onward in their same rooming-in unit, receiving individual surrogate mothering around the clock; but on day 11 they began with a *different* foster nurse from the one they had had during the first 10 days of life. The surrogate mothers were middle-aged registered private duty nurses, each having successfully raised two children of her own and having experience in pediatric nursing and 24-hour duty. They had no other duties during the caregiving period but that of the single infant's care, and they were paid at private duty rates.

For Groups A and B, there were therefore two changes of environment during the 2 months of the study: On day 11; and then on day 29, when each A and B infant went to a different agency foster home until Day 59. Agency foster mothers, most of whom had children of their own, were highly experienced caregivers, some having cared for as many as 10 to 12 foster infants over previous years, providing their care until adoption. All infants of Groups A, B, and C were bottle fed on an infant-demand regimen, except for Group A infants during Period I the first 10 days, durng which they were fed on a *fixed* 4-hourly schedule.

The newborn nursery experience over the first 10 days for Group A infants was viewed by us as a most stressful time for them largely because of the fixed schedule of interventions, betweeen which times the infants might be allowed to cry for long periods unattended, especially between the 4th to 6th or 7th day. Over those days, bouts of crying were severe, continuing steadily for up to 2 hours or more until someone came or until exhaustion supervened. After the 7th day, if the infant was unattended, the crying became more intermittent and occurred in briefer bursts, with brief episodes of closed eyes and quietness between, from which the infant soon stirred and resumed crying.

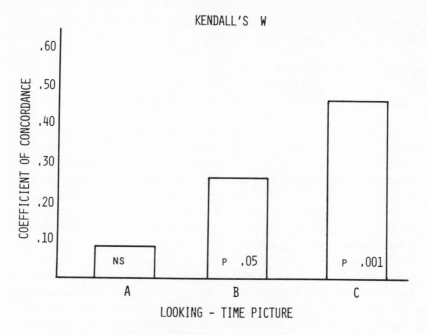

FIG.14.8. Comparison between Groups A, B, and C in terms of the rank order of subject's stability within each group from week to week for time spent looking at the line drawing of the face as visual stimulus.

Data pertaining to sleep and awake *state* variables for the three groups is reviewed in the conference discussion of the paper. The data derived from the continuous monitoring and from 24-hour observations of sleep and awake onset can be briefly summarized for each group as follows: During the first 10 days of life Group A showed (1) marked asynchrony in timing, between time of change of infant state and time of caregiving response, (2) high and prolonged crying output, (3) high distress in feeding, (4) absence of any progress in day–night differentiation over the first 10 days. There was (5) a persistent effect on 24-hour state organization over the rest of the first month of life with (6) auto correlational analysis showing a range of circadian rhythms for Days 11 to 29 from 23 to 26 hours, in contrast to Groups B and C, which showed clearcut 24-hour peaks within Days 11 to 29. Group B, on the other hand, showed (1) a very gradual achievement of day–night organization, beginning well within the first 10 days of life, (2) a much lower crying output during this time, (3) less within-subject variation and stable week-to-week individual differences in crying, visual, sleep, and other categories of variables. Group C differed from Group B in showing early stability of ultradian (nap periodicity—4 to 6 hours) as well as circadian rhythms, so that the entire 24 hours began to possess a temporal structure. Individual variation between mother–infant pairs was great for Group C, but week-to-week stability of individual difference was also high, that is, the unique characteristics of interaction and regulation for each "natural" mother–infant system became evident and established early.

Visual Behavior in the Naturalistic Observation

Let us turn now to the way infants of Groups A, B, and C used their visual apparatus in the naturalistic situation of the feeding interaction. Presentation of data will be limited to the variable of "infant regard," defined as the time during which the infant gazed in the direction of the mother's face. The time measured included gaze of infant directed at hair, hairline, chin, ear, or mouth and was not restricted to eye-to-eye contact. The question being asked was, How does the infant use its eyes in the context of the feeding interaction? And how does this use change over the first month of life? Our initial observations in the natural mother situation had impressed us with the intense and prolonged orientation of gaze in the direction of the mother's face during feeding interactions of the first few days of life that many infants displayed, especially during the first few bottle feedings. After an initial period of the first few days of prolonged intensisty of gaze, a number of the infants could be observed only at the start of the feeding to look attentively and briefly to the mother's face and then appeared to need to gaze only occasionally or randomly back to the face for the remainder of the feeding. Later on, furthermore, infant gaze behavior, in relation to feeding distress events in the feeding interaction, raised the question of the role of infant visual input as an assist in the regulation of the infant's feeding behavior.

In Groups A and B one feeding was observed daily over the 4-week hospital stay (Periods 1 and 2) and twice a week for the foster home period (Period 3). Group C infants were observed daily for the first 10 days, both in the hospital and at home, three times a week for the remainder of the first month, and twice a week thereafter. The single observer sat or stood 4 to 5 feet from the feeding infant, recording a number of variables, such as feeding time, nipple-in time, sucking time, state changes, time looking at caretaker, amount of milk taken, position change, stimulation, and distress. The duration variables were recorded in real time on the portable 4-key Rustrak event-recorder. Reliability between two observers over 20 feedings for these variables ranged from $r = .68$ to $r = .99$ with 7 out of 9 variables recorded being $r = .9$ or better (Pearson r correlation). Agreement for looking time at caregiver, which is termed here "infant regard," was $r = .90$. Measurements reported here of "infant regard" time included only those occurring during the time of the feeding proper, measured from the first insertion of nipple in the infant's mouth until the feeder rose from the feeding chair.

By taking only one new infant at a time into the project, we found that only two surrogate mother nurses would be sufficient to do the caregiving for all the Group A and Group B infants, so that each new infant was assigned in strict alternation to one nurse or the other without bias. This means that half the Group A infants were fed by Nurse X during Period 2 (Days 11–29) and half were fed by Nurse Y. For Group B infants, those who had Nurse X as caregiver during the first 10 days of life (Period 1) now had Nurse Y as a caregiver during Days 11–29 (Period 2) and vice versa. All A and B infants then went to different but experienced foster mothers in Period 3, Days 30–59. Although now the numbers for each cell are small, it is possible to have two subgroups for Group A: namely Ax and Ay depending on which nurse was the caregiver for Period 2. There were two subgroups also for Group B, Bx and By, also depending on which nurse was caregiver in Period 2 (Days 11–29). Each Bx baby in Period 2 then had Nurse Y in period 1 (first 10 days) and vice versa. The daily observations, however, gave a data base for the 27 subjects of Groups A, B, and C of over 800 feeding observations.

There were differences in the caretaking styles of the two nurses which were documented, both by strongly agreed-upon clinical impressions, and by quantititive differences revealed in data on other areas of infant care (Sander, Julia, Stechler, & Burns, 1969, Sander, Stechler, Burns, & Julia 1970). Nurse Y appeared to give the more specifically infant-oriented care. She remained attentive to the infant's behavioral characteristics and insisted on giving priority to discovering individual differences and allowing them to guide her decisions about infant care. This included an ability to manifest her displeasure at interruptions or disruptions caused by the needs of the researchers to awaken or otherwise stimulate the infant in a way or at a time she felt was out of synchrony with the infant's needs. She tended to hold the infant cradled in such a way that it was easy and direct for the infant to see her face upon opening its eyes during a feeding. She was attentive to the infant's face for cues indicating the infant's progress in the feed.

Nurse X, on the other hand, was much more oriented toward the researchers and regular hospital staff, was very successful in making herself and all concerned comfortable, and even seemed to make the research task easier. At the same time it appeared clear that she did not see the infants so much as separate individuals or note their differences, and would say the same things about each baby. She tended to hold the infants during the feeding so that face-to-face orientation was difficult. It was more difficult for the infants to see her face from the position they were in and she herself was not as attentive to the infant's face for cues as to the way the infant was managing the feeding.

The interest then is not only in the differences between Groups Ax, Ay, Bx, By, and C in the way they used their eyes during feeding. From the descriptions given above it is already evident that "infant regard" time will be some interaction between infant determinants and caregiver determinants. What may be worthy of consideration, however, is the course of each group over the 2 months of the study. Of especial interest will be the results for the second month of life for Group A and B infants *after* their in-hospital experience and while they were each with different experienced foster mothers whose variations in style of feeding were fairly balanced for the two groups.

Results for Naturalistic Observations of Infant Regard Time

Means of "infant regard" time were calculated for each infant for each 10-day block, making six 10-day blocks for the 2 months of the study. A mean of means was calculated for group mean values. Five groups were defined as above Ax, Ay, Bx, By, and C and a 2-way ANOVA with repeated measures was carried out. Significance values were obtained for three classes of trends over the 6 blocks: linear, quadratic, and unspecified higher polynomial residuals.

There were no significant differences between groups for total infant regard time over the 2 months. There was no significant correlation overall between

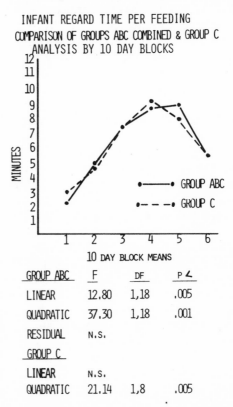

INFANT REGARD TIME PER FEEDING
COMPARISON OF GROUPS ABC COMBINED & GROUP C
ANALYSIS BY 10 DAY BLOCKS

GROUP ABC	F	DF	P ∠
LINEAR	12.80	1,18	.005
QUADRATIC	37.30	1,18	.001
RESIDUAL	N.S.		
GROUP C			
LINEAR	N.S.		
QUADRATIC	21.14	1,8	.005

FIG.14.9. Trend analysis Groups A, B, and C combined and Group C alone in terms of time per feeding spent by the infant looking in the direction of the head of the feeding caregiver. Values represent 10-day means for each group over 60 days.

"looking time" in the experimental stimulus situation and "infant regard time" in the naturalistic situation.

There were significant linear and quadratic trends in infant regard time over the 6 blocks when all groups were combined as shown in Figure 14.9.

Figure 14.9 shows the peak of infant regard of caregiver during feeding at the beginning of the second month of life, which then diminishes during the latter part of the second month of life. An almost identical curve is shown by Group C taken by itself. The latter, of course, were infants who had been fed consistently by their own mothers over the 2 months. The curve suggests the possibility that once the visual function achieves its full contribution to the regulation of the infant during the feeding interaction, its employment becomes less essential and the infant's visual attention can be given to other things. The curve of Figure 14.9 can be viewed as a trajectory of integration over the 2 months, representing the time taken to accomplish the integration of the visual system as a mechanism of regulation of the feeding interaction. Just as in the experimental condition the regulation of visual behavior showed different characteristics in the 3 groups, so in the naturalistic condition we might expect the trajectories of the 3 groups to differ.

The separate courses demonstrated by Groups A and B, combining Ax and Ay for Group A values, and Bx and By for Group B values, show significant differences in the trend analysis. When plotted in terms of means for periods 1, 2, and 3, the angle of the trajectory can be seen to be different for the 3 groups. (see Figure 14.10). Even more striking differences in the course followed by Group A and B appear when the data is plotted by 10-day means (see Figure 14.11). It is clear that by the end of the first month Group A peaks at a higher level than Group B (Days 21–30) and remains higher at the end of the 2 months, Day 51–60. This gives a significant linear trend for Group A over the 2 months. However, during the perturbation introduced by the new adaptation to foster home Group A infants do not as much use their regard of feeder's face as a mechanism of regulation. For these infants during the first 10 days of life there was no stability of visual cues during feeding, with the changing schedule of nurses in the hospital nursery. During Days 31–40 "infant regard" for Group A drops sharply, only to rise to its highest peak during Days 41-50 before dropping in the final 10 days of the study. This suggests that the trajectory of integration for Group A infants has been perturbed by the foster home adaptation. The drop in infant regard during Days 31–40 parallels, as we have seen above, the drop in looking time for Group A infants in the experimental situation also during Days 31-40. The trend analysis polynomial residual is significant for Group A, $F = 11.63$ and $df\ 3$–$15\ p < .001$.

Group B infants, although having a lower mean than Group A by the end of Month 1 (see Figure 14.11), show a great increment of visual regard during their initial adaptation to the foster home Days 31–40 and fall to a value lower

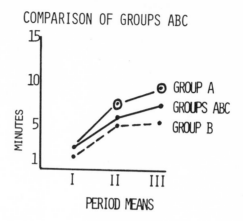

INFANT REGARD TIME PER FEEDING
ANALYSIS BY CAREGIVING PERIOD

COMPARISON OF GROUPS ABC

FIG.14.10. Trend analysis Groups A, B, and C combined, and Groups A and B separately in terms of the time per feeding spent by the infant looking in the direction of the head of the feeding caregiver. Values represent group means for each of the three major time periods of the study. Period 1 = 2–10 days, Period 2 = 11–29 days, Period 3 30–60 days.

LINEAR	F	DF	P≤
GROUP ABC	28.22	1,18	.001
GROUP A	13.66	1,5	.025
GROUP B	12.54	1,5	.025

OTHER TRENDS – N.S.

than Group A infants in the final 10 days of the study. It appears that under the stress of making a new adaptation to the foster home, Group B infants employ their visual contact with the feeder more during feeding, contrary to the finding for Group A.

As a way of examining further the effects of earlier visual experience in the feeding situation on later visual behavior during feeding, we compared the course followed by subgroups Ax and Ay. Infants of both of these groups had had the same standard neonatal nursery care over Days 1–10, but during Days 11–29 Ax infants had *not* been facilitated by their surrogate mother nurse in the use of visual cues for feeding regulation and Ay infants had. What happens during the second month of life when they each are confronted with the foster home adaptation is shown in Figure 14.12

Ax infants have in Period 3 a much greater infant regard time overall than Ay infants. One can ask whether they are compensating for the deficient opportunity they had to integrate feeding and visual experience over both the first 10 days and over Days 11–29? When results are examined by 10–day blocks (see Figure 14.13), the drop in the last 10 days, 51–60, is striking for

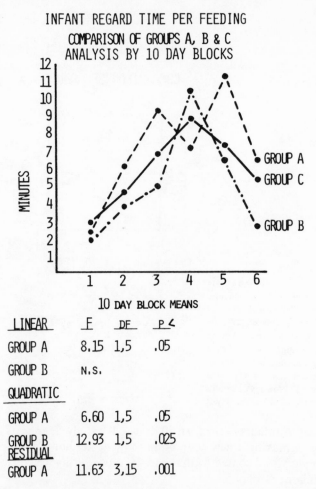

FIG.14.11. Trend analysis for Groups A, B, and C using 10-day means of infant regard time per feeding.

Ax. Once adequate integrative opportunity has been experienced, visual behavior can return to the expected trajectory.

Of equal interest is the course followed by Ay infants who had opportunity for greater visual regard of the feeder's face during Period 2 and conceivably first could begin to integrate visual and feeding behaviors during that time. The drop in visual regard for these infants soon thereafter, possibly before the integrative task has been completed upon transfer to foster home on Day 29, is striking. It is the Ay group of infants who determine the Group A curve in Figure 14.11. The newly and only partially integrated visual activity apparently cannot be utilized in the initial adaptation of Ay babies to the new feeding situation of the foster home. Regulation must be stabilized again by other mechanisms more familiar to them, a set of cybernetic mechanisms, upon which their feeding regulation first came to depend during the first 10 days in the newborn nursery when stability of visual cues was of no help.

The situation for Periods 1, 2, and 3 for Bx and By subgroups suggests further the existence of a time course for integration of visual function with feeding regulation. Although means for infant regard for Group B are lower for Periods 1, 2, and 3 and differences between subgroups do not reach significance, it is evident that infants who have had Nurse Y in Period 2 can follow the trajectory initially outlined in Figure 14.9. On the other hand, those who had Nurse X in Period 2 require further opportunity after transfer to foster home to integrate visual and feeding behavior. Bx and By arrive at the

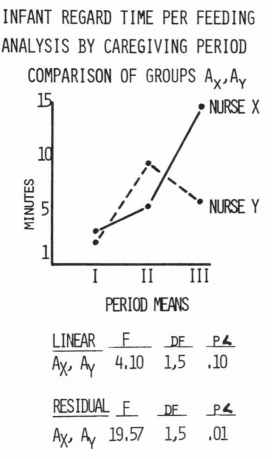

FIG.14.12.   Comparison of subgroups of Group A (by nurse caregiver) for infant regard time per feeding, using caregiving period means.

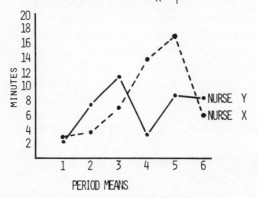

INFANT REGARD TIME PER FEEDING
ANALYSIS BY 10 DAY BLOCKS
COMPARISON OF GROUPS A_X, A_Y

GROUP A_X, A_Y - N.S. FOR LINEAR AND QUADTRATIC

RESIDUAL	F	DF	P <
A_X, A_Y	11.62	3,15	.001

FIG.14.13. Comparison of sub-groups of Group A (by nurse caregiver) for infant regard time per feeding using 10 day means.

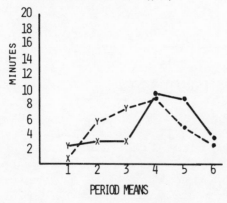

INFANT REGARD TIME PER FEEDING
ANALYSIS BY 10 DAY BLOCKS
COMPARISON OF GROUPS B_X, B_Y

GROUP B_X, B_Y - N.S. FOR LINEAR,

N.S. FOR QUADRATIC

N.S. FOR RESIDUAL

FIG.14.14. Comparison of sub-groups of Group B (by nurse caregiver) for infant regard time per feeding using 10-day means. Subgroups designated in terms of the nurse who provided care during Days 11–28.

same level in the final 10 days, the perturbation of transfer to foster home on Day 29 affecting By but little and allowing Bx more time to catch up to the trajectory apogee. The lower "infant regard" times for Group B infants overall must be reconciled conceptually with the smoother course for this group in general and their relative stability in the visual experimental condition on transfer to foster home in respect to the "looking time" variable. Transfer to foster home appears to be much less of a perturbation for Group B as a whole than for Group A.

DISCUSSION

In this presentation we have dealt particularly with the data of three groups of normal infants, each group experiencing a different infant–caregiver situation with a different history of perturbation and change over the 2 months of study. Three major categories of behavior have provided the variables that have been obtained concurrently by repeated or continuous measurement: state (asleep, awake, and crying), visual, and feeding. The task has been to consider models of regulation, adaptation and integration that account for the sequence of changes that the different variables display in each of the 3 groups over the first 2 months of life under naturalistic and experimental conditions.

Before going further in the discussion, caveats should be mentioned, which are undoubtedly already being considered by the reader. The small numbers in the samples, in spite of the relatively larger number of observations, limits the discussion more to hypothesis generation than to conclusion. The work can suggest new avenues and strategies of investigation. The implication of "good" or "bad" in relation to the courses taken by the three groups cannot be made within the confines of the 2-month span of the study. It does appear that there will be different resources for, and vulnerabilities in, the regulatory mechanisms of the three groups under the different conditions of adaptation. The *value* of the shaping effect of any particular array of early experiences is to be judged by the challenges to adaptation which that particular organism will be required to meet in its later life. The importance of understanding mechanisms of regulation, and of lawful connections between characteristics of infant–caregiver interaction and the course of integration of infant functions, is something necessitated now by the current commitment to early intervention. The possibility of improving our ability to facilitate early development of infants-at-risk for developmental pathology depends on better definition of mechanisms of integration. This is especially so for infants who begin with some compromise in one or more of the means of regulation. Mechanisms of regulation and integration specifically described for the nervous system by Sherrington (1906) are also built into the infant–caregiver system at a great many levels. We have chosen only the relationship between two broad domains of regulation for discussion in this paper. To use Ashby's (1952) terms, these are (1) the domain of the "essential variables," as represented by the 24-hour distribution of infant states; adaptive progress for this domain would relate the 24-hour distribution of infant states to the 24-hour pattern of regularly recurring events in the environment; and (2) the domain of the "reacting parts," the sensorimotor systems, such as the visual and postural; adaptation here requires the achievement of synchrony, contingency, and reciprocation in the linear sequence of exchanges between infant and caregiver. Integration of the first domain of 24–hour state *cycling* with the second domain of *sequential* infant caregiver interaction can be thought of as the integration of a circle and a line. The integration of cycles by the linear characteristics of a time sequence presents a seemingly irreconcilable paradox when considered only in terms of static imagery. When a system is in *motion*, however, the linear sequence then can serve to effect synchrony between one cycle and another.*

Ashby's concept of "ultrastability" suggests integration of "essential variables" and "reacting parts" as the consequence of interaction between cybernetic systems by which state determines selection of specific adaptive strategies. On the other hand, coordination of adaptive strategies in the adaptation between mother and infant, being effected in the linear sequence of events during caregiving, provides a framework of entraining cues that synchronize major sleep and awake cycles of the infant with major cycles of recurrent events in the caregiving environment.

In the first mechanism, suggested by Ashby's description of the ultrastable system, there are two feedback loops between organism and environment: One involves "the essential variables" (state), and the other "the reacting parts" (sensorimotor functions). The state variables, changing at a relatively slow rate in their interaction with environment, bias the regulation of the reacting parts in their more rapid rate of interaction with the environment. By step-functions, the values on essential variables determine *which* behavior of the reacting parts will be selected. This is a neatly described regulatory adaptive model integrating the state of the organism with the moment-by-moment selection of sensorimotor functions of the organism in its adaptive encounter. Cybernetic information processing models would be basic to the fine–grained interactional adaptation between infant and caregiver, including concepts of match–mismatch, orientation–habituation, or operant–schema formation. However, Ashby would propose that the particular selection of strategies in the fine–grained adaptation at any point in time is being determined by more slowly changing configurations of essential physiological

---

*See Figure 8 in symposium discussion below. The "living system obviously can be considered as in motion in terms of the flow of events over time for the component subsystems and for the system as a whole.

variables (states). This is of course, consistent with familiar clinical observation of the role of state in determining infant behavior, called to our attention 15 years ago by Escalona (1962).

Endogenous biorhythmicity, however, characterizes Ashby's "essential variables." A second important mechanism of regulation in the infant–environment system proposes that the regulation of the fine–grained linear sequence of events during the caregiving interaction, in *its* turn, acts as a mechanism to synchronize the 24–hour pattern of sleep awake states of the infant with the cycle of daily regularities of the environment. This second mechanism operates because of characteristics of biorhythms in the coordination of adapting systems, such as entrainment, phase shifting, or phase control. The effectiveness of an entraining cue is maximal when it falls, within a certain range, at the time at which the phase of the rhythm ordinarily is shifting. If it falls outside this range, it is not effective in shifting the phase of the rhythm, and the rhythm is said to be free running. We must think in terms of multiple rhythms at a range of time levels, circadian, ultradian, infradian,— each of which possesses a semi–independence and may fall under control of somewhat different entrainments. For a cue or a configuration of cues to act as an entraining input, it must *regularly* fall at a particular time in relation to a particular phase position of the cycling state.* Such *regular* recurrence in the infant–caregiver system will only emerge as a consequence of regular recurrence in the sequence of care-giving events over an awake period.

The general hypothesis of the regulatory model we are proposing, then, bases adaptation on an interaction between Ashby's two domains (the essential variables and the reacting parts), such that regulation in the one domain is a determinant of regulation in the other. (1) In the sequence of the caregiving exchange the various sensorimotor functions of the infant will be brought into play, such as the visual, kinaesthetic, postural, and so on, to achieve regulation of state over the course of the awake period. (2) The way these functions come to be employed to maintain state over the awake period will then in turn determine the recurrent sensorimotor and perceptual configurations that will come to act as entraining cues to effect the timing of the subsequent transition to sleep onset. The specific contribution of the various infant functions, for example, the visual, to the overall regulatory stability of the system will be determined by the way each becomes modified in the adaptive process through which the two domains ultimately attain optimal integration. Integration will be attained over a time course and by a configuration of relationships unique for each infant–caregiver system, thus

*From our other data, there appears to be evidence of highly specific cues and sequences of events which facilitate the infant in shifts from awake states to sleep. Although our evidence is obtained on the 7th day of postnatal life, the chronologically later appearance of "going-to-sleep" rituals, for example, in the 2nd and 3rd year of life, when the infant has acquired strategies to insist upon them, supports the formulation.

the notion of a time trajectory of integration constrained by complex deteminants. Developmental ontogeny is, of course, complexly determined. The values for a variable at any given point can be considered in terms of (1) infant determinants; (2) caregiver determinants; (3) the background, or state, determinants; and (4) the foreground, or sensorimotor determinants; (5) the historical course over which the system has traveled in its adaptation; and (6) the contemporaneous context in which adaptive interaction is currently under way. Here, in addition, we have used intentional perturbations of the system to study variables in their displacement and recovery.

One further concept of particular usefulness for regulatory conceptualization of integration is Ashby's model of the way richness of states of equilibrium in the system provide the necessary conditions for *loose-coupling*, or partial and temporary *disjoin*, of the different "semi–independent" sensorimotor subsystems which are employed by the organism in the adaptive encounter, the visual, for example. Ashby points out that adaptation time would be impossibly long if every excitation spread to all parts of the organism and each perturbation required the adaptive readjustment of all parts of the whole organism. This would be the example of a tightly coupled machine. On the other hand, in the presence of rich states of equilibrium within the organism or system, there is "loose coupling," each part having a certain leeway in its own reacting to excitation. This means that excitation tends to remain local and to perturb only the subsystem which is in specific adaptation with environmental input. Loose–coupling of component subsystems in a system rich in such equilibria decreases adaptation time by increasing the relative independence of the function, thus localizing the adaptive modification more to the subsystem in question. The different course taken by Group C infants illustrates a more localized adaptation by the visual system. These infants were able to regulate earlier in the experimental face presentation by looking away thus avoiding a general upset. A loosely coupled, more specific visual system device, is available to Group C infants, in comparison to Group A infants, who regulated visual stimulation by becoming disturbed, changing state, and crying. Group C infants were also the only infants showing specific visual system differentiation in looking significantly less at the male face than the caregiver's face in the early weeks of life. The relative richness of states of equilibrium that facilitate adaptive effectiveness by promoting loose coupling arises both from the basic synchrony of infant and environment in regard to the 24–hour pattern of sleep and awake states and from coordinations attained in the infant–caregiving exchange.

As Prechtl (1968) pointed out, "coherence" or synchrony between essential variables contributing to the regulation of states is compromised in the deviant "at–risk" newborn. On the other hand, differences in regulatory competence due to caregiving incompetence at the outset also will influence the subsequent trajectory by which integration of state regulation with the various sensorimotor functions is reached. Feeding illustrates the infant's active integration of his many sensorimotor subsystems in the adaptive encounter with caregiver. Although these subsystems begin in an often asynchronous relation to each other—that is, swallowing with breathing, feeding with falling asleep,—the different functions must all be brought together in the multifaceted, multimodal exchanges that regulate the sequential interaction taking place in the complex coordination represented by a feeding. There must be an *active* integration by the infant of semiseparate schemata that are related to the different functions in achieving the feeding coordination. Ashby's (1952) description of adaptation draws upon the analogy of learning to drive a car:

> ... it must not be overlooked that adaptation may demand independence as well as interaction. The learner–driver of a motor–car, for instance, who can only just keep the car in the center of the road, may find that any attempt at changing gear results in the car, apparently, trying to leave the road. Later, when he is more skilled, the act of changing gear will have no effect on the direction of the car's travel. Adaptation thus demands not only the integration of related activities but the independence of unrelated activities. (p. 157)

Ashby conceptualizes such independence as "loose coupling." The infant's active use of its visual function is an important mechanism for the regulation of the feeding, but it must be synthesized with all the other subsystems that are involved in the feeding coordination, such as posture and posture changes, nipple manipulations, rate of flow of milk, and so on. Our data suggest that it takes some two months for our 3 groups to achieve an integration which allows a relative independence of the visual function during feeding. Each group reaches this point by a different route and each might later show the effects of the different experience in their response to the challenge of a perturbation or stress. It is evident that if the background of state cycling is in equilibrium, an advantage is gained for the stabilizing of the different modalities coming into coordination. The richness of equlibria of basic physiological subsystems that a coherent and synchronous state cycling signifies, facilitates the achievement of loose–coupling. The various sub-systems must all be eventually integrated, as the "infant regard" data suggests, before their particular role in regulation no longer puts a demand on infant attention, and their contribution to regulation can become relatively independent.

RECAPITULATION AND SYNTHESIS

The approach to investigation of early human development from the perspective of the infant–environment system permits the application of a great many *conceptual* resources for arranging new data in comparison with an approach based only on consideration of the development of the infant as an individual. The study of the infant and caregiving environment from the systems perspective furthermore opens the way for the application of *methods* to early developmental research, which by providing continuous or repeated measurement of multiple variables over time, allow the examination of "process" and of change in the system. This is a different domain of investigation than that based on traditional correlative methods or on the concept of a linear causality in development, wherein one searches at Point B in time for an effect of a variable measured at Point A. The difference between the two approaches lies in the acknowledgement of, and the appreciation of, "organization" in the biological system and of the great complexity of variables that represent the interface of exchange between the living, actively adapting, elements making up the system. The infant and the caregiver are already highly organized; each, as organisms with a degree of relative autonomy, are already actively "running," so to speak; each is actively self-regulating; and each is capable of a degree of modification as a result of encounter with the other. The "interface" between them is an organization of time, space, and modality, representing configurations of relationships between functions, which themselves change over time and as a result of their interactions. "Organization" here means that the infant–caregiver system moves toward some optimal solution to the configuration of relationships between interfaced functions which takes into account the particular features or characteristics of the interaction. Movement of the configuration of interactions between parts toward a "configuration of optimal solution" would exert influence, in turn, over the flow of events between them. An adapted state of optimal harmony between parts must represent the criterion toward which modification of function must move each part.

For a given system, with its own set of unique characteristics, we should be able to describe a "trajectory of integration," the curve or angle of the trajectory being "set" by the unique characteristics of the partners, the rates of change and growth of which they are capable, and the particular cluster of variables making up the description. The particular trajectory one views, then, will depend on the different relationships that various clusters of variables bear to the life span of the system as a whole. Adaptation and adaptive capability can be viewed in terms of the plasticity of the elements of the system in finding compromises toward optimally resolving the configuration of exchange at interfaces within the system. These interfaces are sites at which the greater efficiency of an optimal integration of the system as a whole must exert its modifying influence as the integrative process moves towards its solution.

The differences between systems in the integrative configurations may not be evident or discovered until a particular perturbation stresses the system. The system as a whole possesses conservative, or self-righting, tendencies that exert constraints on the parts to return their relationship toward the more optimal solution after a perturbation. These tendencies are fundamentally dependent on basic mechanisms of regulation of the life process. Thus, in choosing our experimental groups, selection of systems differing in basic regulation should provide a differing "set" to the trajectories of integration. We are thinking here in terms of process and of integration always as relative, not absolute, and always in terms of the life span of the elements and of the system as a whole. On reflection, it should be evident that these are but familiar aspects of an organismic evolutionary viewpoint, cast in a slightly different context, centering attention on the way change over time in repeated measurements of several functions relates to the matter of the integration of these functions in the regulation of the system.

In contrast to the above data concerning visual behavior in the experimental and naturalistic situation, the data of the discussion which follows gives a highly condensed summary of many already published findings on the three groups regarding their early course of *state regulation along the asleep-awake continuum*. The conceptualization of a trajectory of integration was formulated to explain the combination of state and visual system data. In what way might differences over the first 10 days of life in characteristics of 24-hour state regulation, which we will now turn to, affect the integration of a specific sensorimotor function, that is, the visual over the next 2 months?

Our suggestion has been to propose that mechanisms depend on a mutually reciprocal *relation* between the achievement of synchrony of rhythms between infant and environment and the achievement of interactional coordinations in the caregiving sequence. It is hoped that the 24-hour sleep-awake data to which we turn in the discussion will help to clarify the way the two domains might relate to each other.

CONCLUSION

We have tried, then, to take up the problem of organization in early human development by searching for mechanisms of regulation in an infant-environment system that will apply also to the understanding of mutual modifications of infant and caregiver as they gain adaptive coordination over the first weeks of life. Granting the characteristics of primary activity and organization that all living matter possesses, regulation in the infant-environment system can be viewed as the active self-regulation of the participants as they negotiate the exchanges that interface their ongoing behaviors. There are many physiological and functional subsystems of each partner to be harmonized and integrated if coherence for the individual and for the system is to be achieved. These can be viewed as semi-independent subsystems—for example, sleep and awake, feeding, the various sensori-motor functions—each subsystem contributing to the adaptive process being effected at the exchange interface between infant and caregiver in terms of the modalities or categories of behavior specifically relevant to it. The adaptive process continues in the direction of reaching an optimal integration of the component contributing functions.

CONFERENCE SUPPLEMENT

As I have understood the program format this discussion—presentation is not supposed to attempt a presentation of the precirculated paper. The remarks I would like to make will represent the briefest kind of synthesis of a good many years of work by a considerable number of people at Boston University Medical Center. To the data that follow Dr. Patricia Chappell, Dr. Jeffrey Gould, and Dr. Harry Julia have made extensive contribution. As was pointed out in the paper, I would like here to present enough additional data on 24 hour sleep awake patterns to provide the basis for a consideration of mechanisms of regulation of interaction in the infant–caregiver system, especially as those mechanisms influence the course of development of particular infant functions that contribute to such regulation.

The rationale for the collection of our data comes from a different perspective than any that have been suggested thus far in the conference; namely, clinical psychiatry. It is a perspective that provides an entree to the systems viewpoint. For one reason, this is because clinical psychiatry uses a lot of words that can be given new meaning by translation into systems ideas, words such as *organization* of personality, or the *integration* of functions. The psychiatric patient is a person whose coherence or integrity is threatened in his situation of adaptation. He sits before the therapist as a patient whose personality organization is to be changed, or he wants to change it. The idea of psychotherapy seems to be for the therapist to sit with him and to interact, with the understanding that the organization of the patient's personality will change through an interactive process. Although when I started out in psychiatry I had a feeling for aspects of an interactive process, I just didn't know what to do next at a great many points, nor did the concepts of the time offer a great deal of help. One reason I wanted to look at the beginnings in early life was to search for a model of change in organization via some interactive process. Almost at the outset I was confronted by a paradox in this process of two people interacting together. In the presence of their getting together, the aim of the process was to facilitate differentiation. The process of both adaptation and differentiation had to be explained by the same events.

In my life at that time, my wife was "into" babies, so to speak. This was a kind of natural thing for her, but quite a different matter for me. I would like here to add my bit about fathers. One of the very important things about many fathers is that they have to *learn* to do what is *natural* for mothers. It only took me about 2 days to learn something very important after the baby came home from the hospital. This was that we all had to live together around-the-clock. The meaning of adaptation to me, first of all, was that both the new baby and the family had to come to terms with the organization of the 24-hour day. Entertaining the baby between 1 and 4 a.m. didn't go well with a full days work the following day. So my first approach to adaptation had to do with the task of living together around-the-clock, adjusting sleeping and waking times in respect to day and night. Then I found I had to learn how to interact with the infant in some sort of immediate way related to the moment-by-moment adjustments that go with expertise in handling a baby. Those more experienced already knew that progress in the one domain may determine progress in the other.

Out of all of this experience came the idea for our selection of the two methods of study taken up in the paper. These were descriptive methods but descriptive in a particular way, namely by numbers. One involved 24-hour continuous nonintrusive bassinet monitoring, and the other a simple four-key event recorder. For the former, the unit of observation is the entire 24-hour day and for the latter it is the full awake period, from the time of waking up until the child gets back into the first non–REM sleep.

From this sort of general beginning, our research questions gradually began to gain focus. How does adaptation on the 24-hour level relate to the moment by moment interactional sequence required for the actual caretaking procedures? In what ways does fitting together, or adaptation at these two levels relate to the development of the infant's specific functions? In the paper, I have illustrated one infant function—namely, looking behavior—basing impressions on some differences between three subject groups in regard to their use of the visual system, each group also progressing differently in regard to their regulation of states around-the-clock. We should review now just what these different courses of state regulation amounted to in the three groups, hopefully leading up to a kind of prototype model of the way regulation of the two temporal domains may be related, the one concerning recurrent or cyclic events and the other concerning the linear sequence of reciprocal or contingent events.

The general design of the project was given in the paper. Basically there were three groups, investigated over the first 2 months of life. There were three time periods: 1, the first 10 days, 2, the 11th through the 29th day, and 3, from the 30th day to the 59th day. Group A infants spent the first 10 days of life in a neonatal nursery as boarders and were subjected to traditionally scheduled, lying-in nursery caretaking. In Group B, on the other hand, there was a single foster nurse rooming in with the baby from the first 12–24 hours of life, providing a demand-feeding regimen. From the 11th day onward, both groups were cared for under the same conditions, namely, rooming in with a single nurse surrogate mother on a one-to-one basis around-the-clock and receiving contingent, or infant-demand, caregiving. At the end of Period 2 (Day 29), they both went to foster homes. There were nine babies in each group. Group C infants were babies cared for by their own mothers, roomed in over the first 5 days in the hospital and in their own homes over the rest of the 2 months. Group C represents a kind of contrast group, selected to represent a situation of presumably optimal developmental opportunity. Group C was not intended to represent a "control group" in the traditional sense of the word.

There are two points at which the developing infant–environment systems are subjected to perturbation in this design, one with the change at Day 11 for Groups A and B, and the other at the change to the foster home on Day 29. In the paper, some ANOVA group main effects were reported, which pointed to basic differences in regulation between Groups A and B. One was that of fussing in the experimental stimulus-presentation situation, in which Group A showed the greatest amount of fussing. Group A also showed the least week-to-week stability in rank ordering of subjects for looking time or fussing time. ANOVA interactions were also reported, which showed differences between Groups A and B, such as those for response to facial stimuli in the experimental situation or for "infant regard" of caregivers' face in the naturalistic feeding situation. These have all been described in the paper, as

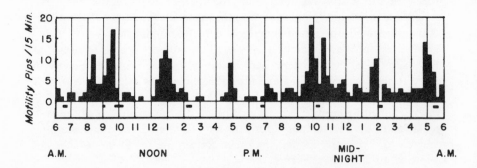

FIG.14.15. Histograms of hourly counts for 24 hours of monitor blips representing integrations of infant motility. Infant is being cared for in the lying-in nursery. Small rectangles below the histogram indicate the time spent out of the bassinet, which can be seen to occur every 4–5 hours, and not synchronized with the onset of the activity.

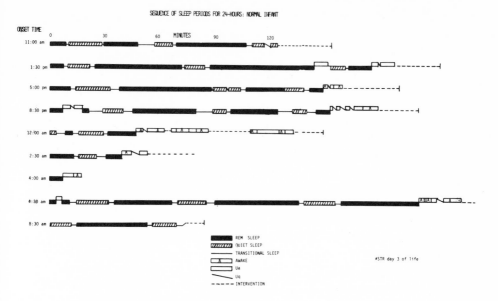

FIG. 14.16.   The organization of naps on Day 3 of life for a normal infant. The longer naps consist of two or three REM–Quiet cycles. There is a wide variation of nap duration within the 24 hours; the REM and Quiet segments are relatively unbroken by "unclassified" active or quiet states.

have the differences between the caregiving of the two nurses. The research design allows comparison of changes in variables longitudinally when one foster mother cares for different babies, one by one, over the first month of life, in contrast to the course of changes over the same time when each new baby has its own mother, as in Group C.

But to go now to the 24-hour infant state data: The monitor had been designed as a continuously recording nonintrusive observer, one that could be adapted to almost any crib. One of the earliest things that we found concerned periodicity in the motility output. Figure 14.15 shows the fourth day of life of a nursery baby in which there are six peaks of activity over the 24 hours. The black rectangle beneath the motility histogram indicates the time when the baby is out of the bassinet. The regularity of interventions so represented is characteristic for the scheduled 4-hourly caregiving of the lying-in nursery in which there is no relation of motility peaks (i.e., state of the infant) to time of occurrence of interventions. That is "noncontingent caregiving."

The relation of these motility peaks to the distribution of sleep and awake states can be examined now with the new refinements that have been made in the bassinet monitoring system. Figure 14.16 shows the 24-hour record of a normal full-term baby on the third day of life, with naps plotted in terms of the cycling of REM and Non-REM phases of sleep and the occurrence of such variations as breaks in quiet sleep or REM sleep, transitions between REM and quiet, major shifts from sleep to awake and vice versa, and so on. The cyclical nature of sleep shows clearly in such normal demand-fed infants, as does the occurrence of an even larger cycle: There is a period of the day when the naps are shorter and awake time is longer. This pattern repeats itself the next day, so that for some babies a circadian rhythm of sleep and awake states is evident almost from the very beginning, although at first the clock time of occurrence of the span of relative arousal may be in the wee hours of the morning. The repetition of such a pattern day after day of the 24-hour distribution of nap period lengths, and of the variations in nap period length at various positions in the 24 hours begins to provide for the mother a familiar 24-hour time structure, one that may be quite different from baby to baby.

Over the past year we have been looking at babies whose mothers are heavy drinkers. Figure 14.17 illustrates the record of such a baby on the third day of life. As you see, this is a much different 24-hour picture. The naps are brief, there are none of them in which the infant can cycle from one Non-REM

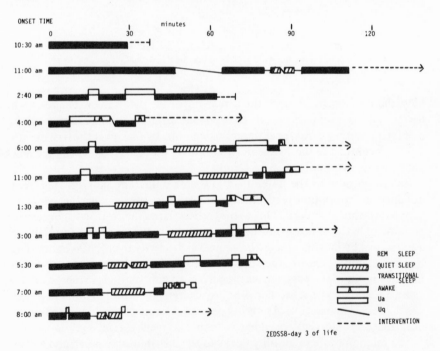

ZEDSS8-day 3 of life

FIG.14.17. The organization of naps on Day 3 of life in an infant whose mother had a high intake of alcohol during pregnancy. Long naps containing 2 or 3 R/Q cycles are absent. The variation in nap duration is less, and there are more REM periods interrupted by "unclassified" states.

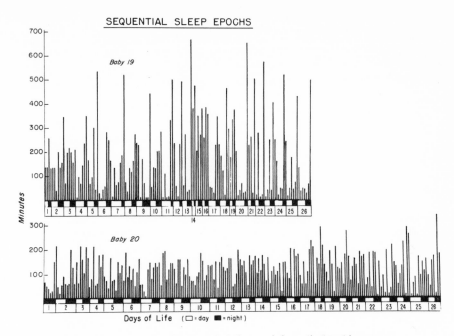

FIG.14.18.   Duration of sleep periods for two infants displayed in sequence as they occurred over the first 26 days of life. Differentiation of a longest sleep per 24 hours is seen in Baby 19 almost from the onset. This is beginning to occur only at the end of the month for Baby 20.

period to another without awakening, and there are many more breaks in both REM and Non-REM periods. An infant such as this one would present a more taxing caregiving requirement, possibly being more difficult for mother to "read" in regard to state behavior and quite unpredictable as to when awakening will occur. It is just these individual differences that the caregiver is learning over the first days, or the first week or two of life, trying to form some framework of temporal expectancy. To illustrate further the way that individual differences present quite different configurations for the caregiver, Figure 14.18 is a plot of the duration of every sleep period as it occurred in sequence over the first 26 days of life for two infants in Group B that were receiving the same caregiving regimen. The first infant, Baby 19, by 10 days of life had already differentiated its sleep over the 24-hour day into long sleep periods and short naps, while the other baby only very gradually develops this degree of differentiation at the very end of the month, relatively short sleep spans predominating throughout.

As we have gone along, we have found that the evidence points to the experience of birth as a time of profound temporal reorganization of infant functions in relation to a 24-hour day. Evidence for this was first provided us when we plotted the daily duration over the first month of life of "activity

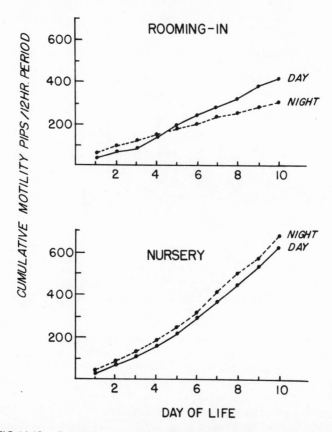

FIG. 14.19. Cumulative counts of monitor motility integrations for a groups of 3 infants reared in the lying-in nursery and 3 roomed-in with their own mothers over the first 10 days of life, showing their occurrence at night (6 p.m.–6 a.m.) or in the day (6 a.m.–6 p.m.) hours.

segment time," a variable highly correlated with awake states. There is a great deal more awake, active behavior over Days 2, 3, and 4 than occurs again until the end of the month. Other early group data (N = 3 infants in each group) obtained in 1963 and 1964 is shown in Figure 14.19, representing cumulative counts of motility blips obtained with our first monitor arrayed as daily 12-hour sums for day and night occurrence. The graph shows a switch from a nighttime predominance of activity to a daytime predominance between the 4th and 6th day of life. The switch occurs only for the contingent caregiving condition of the rooming-in caregiver and *not* for the infants in the lying in nursery. Almost exactly the same results were obtained for cumulative counts of crying blips.

The rapid reorganization that is going on during the first days of life can be studied in even more detail with our present bassinet monitor, as is shown in

Figure 14.20. The figure represents a sequential plot for one male infant of each awake period with its succeeding sleep period day after day over the first 7 days of life. The relatively long sleep periods of the first day after birth break up during Days 3, 4, and 5 into briefer and more numerous naps, and finally by the end of the week, sleep spans consolidate into the longer periods again. Other infants within the first week of life may show other days of disruption, some of which may be earlier or later in the week. For the infant of Figure 14.20, the *macroscopic* picture of napping pattern disruption on Days 3, 4, and 5 is accompanied by a more microscopic disruption within naps during days 3, 4, and 5. If one examines each nap one finds a decreased duration of REM periods, during these days, lower count of intact REM–non-REM cycles per day, and an increased number of changes of state per day. In the case of this infant, roomed-in with its own mother, the state disorganization was associated with increased crying and increased frequency and duration of caregiving interventions over Days 3, 4, and 5 as is shown in Figure 14.21. Decreased frequency and duration of intervention resumes toward the latter part of the week as the longer sleep spans reappear.

Event recording of interactional variables designed and carried out by Dr. Patricia Chappell in the Boston University Laboratory records the timing and

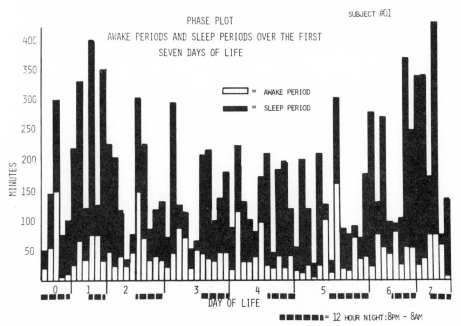

FIG.14.20.   Sequence of awake–asleep cycles as they occurred over the first 7 days of life for a normal infant roomed-in with his own mother. The initial long duration of sleep episodes disappear during Days 3, 4, and 5 to reappear on Days 6 and 7.

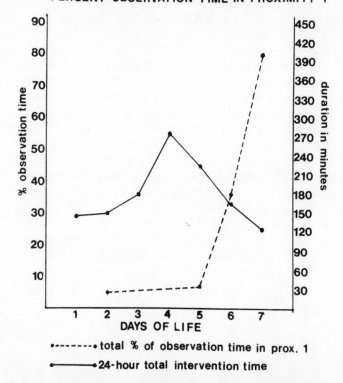

**THE CHANGING RELATION BETWEEN
DAILY INTERVENTION TIME AND THE
PERCENT OBSERVATION TIME IN PROXIMITY 1**

•------• total % of observation time in prox. 1

•———————• 24-hour total intervention time

FIG.14.21.   The graph shows for the same infant depicted in Figure 14.21 the change over the first 7 days of life in total caregiving time and in the percent of that time that the infant spends in contact with mother's ventrum (Proximity 1). During Days 3, 4, and 5 when more frequent and briefer naps are occurring, the total intervention time is greater, dropping off again during Days 6 and 7. Even though less total time is then spent in intervention on Days 6 and 7, as longest sleep periods lengthen, the percent of intervention time spent in contact with mother's ventrum rapidly increases.

duration of events such as the occurrence of contact with the mother's ventrum during the full-awake period. Her observations show that the proportion of the intervention time spent in this position of closest proximity is increasing from midweek onward. By the same method, Dr. Chappell has demonstrated that over this same time the increase in closest proximity is co-occurring increasingly with a particular state of the baby, namely the alert awake state. (Chappell P. & Sander L. 1978) (Sander L. Chappell P.) 1975 Maternal vocalization showed a similar increasing co-occurrence with the alert awake state over the first 7 days of life. We have taken all this to support the idea that particular coordinations between infant state and maternal caregiving behaviors are becoming recurrent over the recurring awake periods and are beginning to establish a familiar sequential event structure to the course of the awake period for both the infant and the caregiver. Conceivably then this recurrent sequence of coordinated events over each awake period is providing certain recurrent cues at specific times that could effect entrainment by effecting the time at which a shift from awake to sleep states occurs for the infant. Twenty-four hour regulation would then depend on a reciprocal relationship between the cycling of infant states around the clock and the stability of recurrent cues constituting the linear sequence of events being repeated each awake period.

Entrainment of the longest sleep period per 24 hours to the nighttime location may be a first mechanism by which day–night organization of sleep–awake distributions comes about. This is indicated in Figure 14.22. Here, for 9 Group B babies is plotted the position of the longest sleep period per 24 hours in terms of whether its major portion lies in the day 12 or the night 12 hours of each day of life as indicated vertically. By 10 days of life most

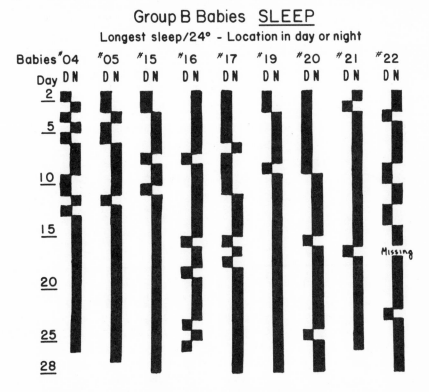

FIG.14.22.   Location of the majority of the longest sleep per 24 hours in the day or night hours over the first 28 days of life for 9 Group B infants.

all of the Group B infants have the major part of the longest sleep period falling in the night 12 hours. Obviously if the longest sleep period occurs in the night segment, that leaves only the smaller sleep periods and the awake periods for the remainder of the 24 hours. A similar plot for daytime or nighttime occurrence of the longest awake period per 24 hours over the same days for the same babies shows no such similar consistent position. Further evidence of effects of caregiving environment on ontogeny of periodicity variables is given in Figure 14.23. The two nurses who carried out the surrogate mothering for Group A and B infants had significantly different effects on the length of the longest sleep and the longest awake periods per day of the infants they cared for. There appear to be different determinants for effects on period length and for effects on day–night differentiation.

In analyzing the course of day–night differentiation during days 11–25 (Period 2) for Groups A and B, it was found that the significant determinant of the extent of day–night differentiation over Days 11 to 25 in terms of activity-segment time was whether or not the baby had had the nursery experience during the first 10 days rather than which of the two nurses provided the caregiving. Although no day–night differentiation occurs for Group A during the first 10 days, quite the opposite is found between Days 11 and 25. After the Group A infant at Day 11 begins to receive caregiving that is now contingent to change in infant state from sleep to arousal, day–night

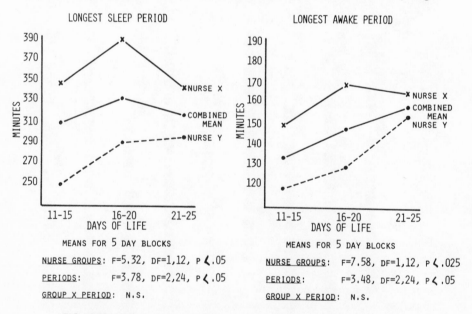

FIG.14.23.   Effect of the two nurse caregivers on the duration of the longest sleep period and longest awake periods per 24 hours, during Period 2, Days 11, 25. 7 babies cared for by each nurse.

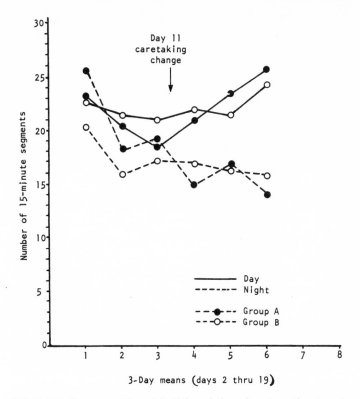

FIG.14.24.   Progress of day–night differentiation of awake–active states in Group A and Group B infants over Days 2 to 25. Group A infants do not show day–night differences in the occurrence of awake–active states while they are in the neonatal nursery (Period 1, Days 2 through 10).

differentiation becomes significantly greater for the Group A than for the Group B infants, who, nevertheless, have been showing very gradually increasing day–night differentiation over the first 10 days. (see Figure 14.24). We look upon this as the possible effect of stress during the first 10 days upon the Group A infants, which apparently tends to advance the appearance of circadian rhythmicity, as has been reported in the animal literature.

The appearance of circadian rhythmicity for the three groups can be studied also by autocorrelational analysis of 24 hour sleep distributions. Around-the-clock observations of sleep and awake period durations were recast for each day between days 11 and 20 in terms of minutes of sleep per hour for a total of 240 hours, and autocorrelations were carried out using 1-hour lags. (Days 2–10 and 16–25 were similarly recast and analyzed.) Individual differences between infants of Group A in the appearance of a 24-hour rhythm of sleep occurrence is illustrated in Figure 14.25. There is a range in the autocorrelational peaks for Group A infants extending from the 23-

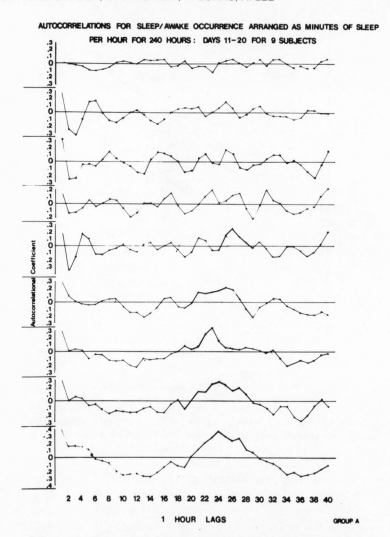

AUTOCORRELATIONS FOR SLEEP/AWAKE OCCURRENCE ARRANGED AS MINUTES OF SLEEP PER HOUR FOR 240 HOURS : DAYS 11-20 FOR 9 SUBJECTS

1 HOUR LAGS   GROUP A

FIG. 14.25.   Autocorrelations (1 hour lags) for 9 Group A infants carried out on data obtained through 24-hour observations of sleeping and waking times Days 11–20 (240 hours). Sleep data was arranged in terms of minutes of sleep per hour. Peaks in the lower 5 plots of the graph fall between the 23rd and 26th hour lags.

hour lag to the 26-hour lag. This range is not shown by the Group B infants who received contingent caregiving from birth, their peaks predominating at the 24-hour lag. Of interest is the observation that the top infants in the array shown in Figure 14.25 are the males and the lower infants are the females of the sample. In order to illustrate day by day changes in the actual pattern in real time of sleep and awake period distribution between days 11 and 25, the clock time of onset for the last infant in the array is shown in Figure 14.26. The

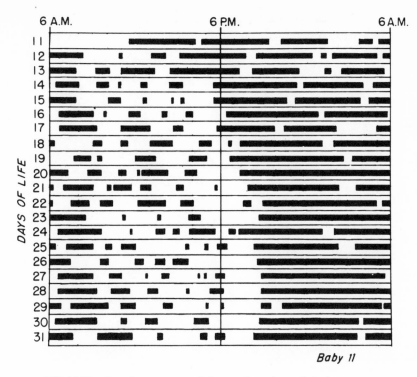

FIG.14.26. Actual occurrence of sleep and awake periods for each day between Days 11–31 for the Group A baby whose autocorrelation coefficients are displayed on the bottom line in Figure 14.25.

unpredictable events that the caregiver must cope with in this particular infant are the random occurrence of daytime naps and awake spans, some of which are relatively long.

The regularity or irregularity of occurrence of *naps* can be indicated by autocorrelational analysis. A 4- to 6-hour ultradian rhythmicity is shown for a Group B infant during Days 2–10 which is completely lost over days 11 to 20 after the change of caregiver on Day 11. Nevertheless a 24-hour or circadian peak clearly emerges during the same 11–20 day span (see Figure 14.27).

The natural-mother rearing situation, such as is found in Group C, shows still another course of emergence of rhythmicity (see Figure 14.28). Ultradian (4–6 hour) peaks appear in the Day 2–10 span, just as in Group B, and a 24-hour peak appears between Days 11 and 20. This time, however, the 4 to 6 hour ultradian regularity persists. An illustration of the actual time of occurrence of sleep and awake periods over Days 2–25 for a Group C infant is provided by Figure 14.29. In this instance, the pattern of occurrence is irregular until about Day 7, when the regular occurrence of 3 daytime naps begins in addition to the night sleep. Disorganization in pattern follows for 2 days and a

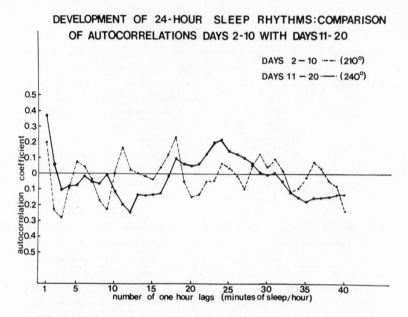

DEVELOPMENT OF 24-HOUR SLEEP RHYTHMS:COMPARISON
OF AUTOCORRELATIONS DAYS 2-10 WITH DAYS 11-20

DAYS 2 − 10 --- (210°)
DAYS 11 − 20 ·--· (240°)

FIG.14.27. Comparison of Days 2-10 with days 11-20 for one Group B infant by autocorrelation analysis. The 5-6-hour periodicity evident during Days 2-10 disappears during Days 11-20; a 24-hour peak begins to appear Days 11-20.

new pattern emerges, namely 2 daytime naps and a longer night sleep span. In following the plot further over the first 2 months, another time of disorganization is encountered, with another pattern subsequently emerging of nap period duration (one longer and one shorter, with another shift in length of night sleep duration). What seems to be happening in the group of infants reared by their own mothers is that not only are day and night getting positioned but the entire 24 hours is beginning to acquire a framework of temporal organization. By 3 weeks, in the uneventful instance, the 24 hours begins to assume a feeling of familiarity for the mother. She begins to "know" where she is with the baby and what to expect in terms of the point in the 24 hours at which she and the baby are located; an idea of what she will have to cope with in the caregiving situation is embedded in her expectations of what is coming, related to the time of day. The majority of the longest sleep span per 24 hours should be falling somewhere within the night 12 hours; the longest awake span should have migrated to later afternoon or evening often with the infant not ready to go to sleep at once after the feeding, in contrast to the rapid return to sleep characteristic of the briefer awake periods occurring at other times.

A model for the interaction of infant state with caregiver interventions over one of the longer awake periods by the third week of life when the 24 hour

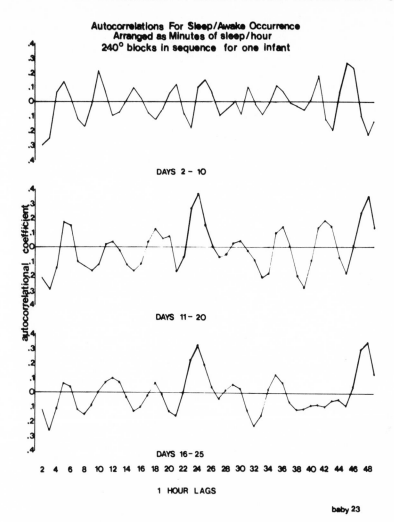

**Autocorrelations For Sleep/Awake Occurrence
Arranged as Minutes of sleep/hour
240° blocks in sequence for one infant**

DAYS 2 - 10

DAYS 11 - 20

DAYS 16 - 25

1 HOUR LAGS

baby 23

FIG.14.28.   Comparison of Days 2–10, 11–20, and 16–25 by autocorrelation analysis for one Group C infant reared by its own mother, first in a rooming-in situation, then at home.

pattern has become familiar to the caregiver might look like that shown in Figure 14.30. Here we have put together many of the points already mentioned. The heavy line represents the direction of state change in the infant as it passes from sleeping through the awake span and back to sleep again. There are both exogenous (caregiving) determinants and endogenous (infant) determinants of the specific course of state changes over any awake period. The direction of effects whether toward arousal or toward sleep of

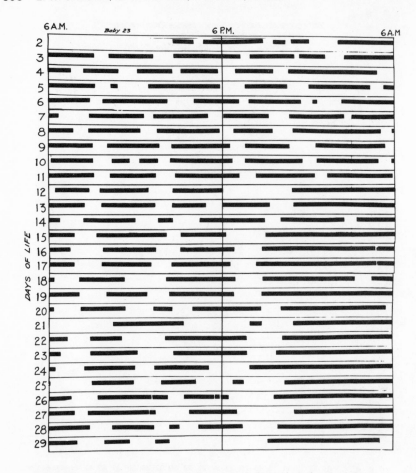

FIG.14.29. Actual occurrence of sleep and awake periods for the infant
described in Figure 14.28.

each set of determinants on state are indicated by the arrows. Coordination is
indicated by arrows pointing in the same direction.

As the infant arouses in shifting to awake on the basis of his own
endogenous rhythmicity, the effects of the caregiver correspondingly are
arousing, as she picks up the baby, changes it, bathes it, and so on. As the
feeding begins, a more finely reciprocal linear* or sequential regulation is
initiated, bringing into play the entire array of sensorimotor functions of
infant and mother. By the third week this sequential interaction is becoming
familiarly recurrent. Inasmuch as our unit of observation is from the point of
waking up to the onset of the first subsequent non-REM sleep period, we can

---

*Although we are calling it linear or sequential to distinguish it from the larger cycles of sleep
and awake, the interactional caregiving sequence itself may occur in smaller rhythmicities such as
the suck-pause rhythm of infant nursing.

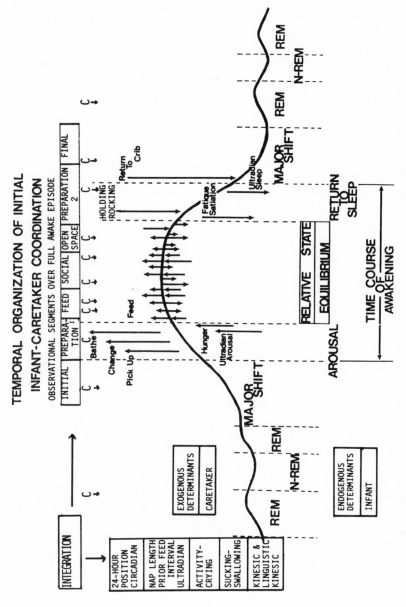

FIG. 14.30 Conceptual model of the temporal organization of interaction between infant behavior and caregiver behavior over the complete course of one awake period.

ask the question, In what way does stable regulation of this finely tuned linear sequence of interactions relate to the states of the baby across the awake period, and how does it affect the transition from awake to sleep? If the time of transition is affected, the regulation of the linear sequence of events can act as a phase setting or entraining mechanism for the onset of the subsequent sleep cycle.

The model shown in Figure 14.30 attempts to illustrate, by the vertical and horizontal lists, the various integrations that are involved in the regulation of the caregiving interaction. The vertical list includes the range of time domains that the mother is integrating in the regulation of her caregiving: One is the position in the 24 hours of this particular awake period; another is the length of the nap prior to the awakening; still another concerns the higher frequency rhythms within the awakening, such as those of sucking or body movement, and the even finer rhythms discovered by Condon of linguistic–kinesic synchrony. The horizontal list involves the sequence of events that has transpired or will transpire during the time course of the awake period. The seven segments displayed horizontally in the model represent a way of categorizing observed events for analysis and do not necessarily represent the actual sequence that will be followed in any given interaction. However, each caregiving decision is being influenced by the location of mother and infant along such a sequence of differently aimed or goal-oriented interactions. A sequence such as this should be becoming familiar to both by 3 weeks of life as the expected course of events that constitutes the awake period. We have included a category labeled "open space," which we can think of in terms of a *disengagement* between infant and mother. This is the point at which mother puts the infant into the reclining seat on the kitchen table and turns her attention to her other tasks, letting the baby "entertain itself." The infant, however, at this time is in an *equilibrium*. We might call it a "relative state equilibrium"—not hungry, not sleepy, not wet or uncomfortable. The importance of such an "open space" is the opportunities it provides for an actively organizing encounter with the world at the *initiative of the infant*. The model touches here upon two of Winnicott's notions: (1) the mother's "holding the situation in time," which relates to conditions necessary for a relative state equilibrium; (2) the "intermediate area," which provides the same opportunity for new infant initiations as does the "open-space." The contribution of a system concept of temporal organization to an ontogeny of communication is exemplified in the model by the letter C. Each C represents a point at which the infant might cry. The *meaning* of the cry at each point is read by the caregiver in terms of where it occurs in the familiar sequence. That is, the meaning of the cry can be read because the temporal organization of events in the system has become familiar.

The point we have tried to make in the paper is that the early strategies of use in the development of the various sensorimotor subsystems or functions of the infant (such as the visual) depend on their role in regulation of state. The task of regulation of infant state must be viewed in terms of the integration of two temporal domains. First, the cyclic or periodic, such as is represented by the circadian and ultradian rhythms, which make possible a recurrent, daily, regularly repeated, sequence of events. This first or cyclic domain constitutes the grosser time framework of the 24 hour distribution of sleep and awake states. This time framework provides the background of relative state equilibrium when this first level of synchrony between infant and caregiving environment is reached. Second, the sequential or linear domain, which comprises the fine synchronies and the contingent or reciprocal timings in the interaction between infant and caregiver. Within this second domain lie the specific cues, or temporally organized cue gestalts, which act as entraining inputs that facilitate major state transition again from the awake phase of the cycle to sleep.

Integrating the two time domains by mechanisms of regulation resolves the paradoxical problem of how one integrates line and circle. What we have done is to view the line and the circle as constituting essential elements of a system. We have put the system into motion and have come up with a "prototype" model (see Figure 14.31). As the system moves forward in time and space (i.e., "lives") the linear domain of interaction between mother and infant synchronizes the cyclic domains of infant and environment, just as the connecting rod synchronizes the drive wheels of the locomotive.

THE GENERAL, 1855

FIG.14.31. "Prototype" of a conceptual model by which the linear aspects of time (represented by the connecting rod) synchronizes the cyclic aspects of time in infant and in caregiver (represented by the drive wheels of the locomotive). (From the *World Book Encyclopedia.* ©1978, World Book–Childcraft International, Inc.).

ACKNOWLEDGMENTS

Dr. Sander is supported by a research Scientist Award #5K05MH20505-10. Project support was provided by NICHD #HD01766, by the Grant Foundation, and by University Hospital General Research Support Funds. Grateful appreciation is expressed to the Massachusetts Memorial Hospital, the Boston Hosital for Women, the Chelsea Naval Hospital, and the Boston City Hospital for their contributions to the project.

The initial support for the longitudinal study on the effects of maternal maturity and immaturity on child development was provided by USPHS Grants MH-898C_1C_2 and M-3923, Eleanor Pavenstedt, Principal Investigator.

DISCUSSION

Dr. Watson: Referring to the earlier part of your discussion, how do you see the contingency of the relation being in any way a cause. It seems to me to the associated shift might simply be adjustments to a new cycle.

Dr. Sander: It is causal only in providing conditions necessary for effecting entrainment, one of the conditions being a consistent relation between the timing of the event and a particular phase of the state cycle. The asynchrony in the nursery is very gross. In the contingent caregiving situation, contingency of intervention lies in its relation to a specific phase of the sleep–wake cycle. This end makes possible the recurrence of "relative state equilibrium" as the context for specific recurrent cue configurations.

Dr. Watson: I would imagine that a noncontingent presentation in the hospital situation would be temporally organized because of the "system" of the hospital. If so, then this would amount to the imposition of a time cycle on the infant's system. Perhaps the infant's system will organize itself well if it has some contingent relationship with the external world. However if one tries to impose temporal pattern on the infant's system, then it has great difficulty, even though what's getting organized by some natural inclination is a temporal pattern.

Dr. Sander: If you remember the slide of the six motility peaks—well, that's approximately every 4 hours. There's good reason for the 4-hourly scheduled nursery intervention, except it occurs with the wrong timing. We have observed babies who had been in the neonatal nursery for 10 days in terms of their awakenings over the subsequent 4–5 days, *after* they were transferred on Day 11 to the nurse who now began responding contingently to infant awakening. There was a persistent tendency to 4-hour periodicity in their awakenings, which then extinguished after 4–5 days. So the infants were already being influenced by the 4-hour nursery schedule also.

Dr. Eisenberg: The first slide you showed, as I recall, referred to two infants, one of whom had a fairly well established sleep-and-wake pattern and the other of whom did not. Can you tell me whether these individual differences had anything at all to do with their times of birth?

Dr. Sander: You mean night or day?

Dr. Eisenberg: Night or day or 2 o'clock in the morning versus 8 o'clock at night.

Dr. Sander: The difference between those two patterns—one is the pattern of a risk baby, a baby who had some problems. We've seen similar patterns in babies other than the fetal alcohol syndrome babies. That sort of thing I don't think is related to when the baby is born. We have not studied the effect of the hour of birth upon the organization of 24-hour rhythms and subsequent sleep. That's a very obvious thing, and for some reason we've just never attempted that.

Dr. Parmelee: In one of your baby's charts there seems to be a 25-hour circadian rhythm. We've reported a free circadian rhythm, as has Kleitman, in the first weeks of life. This becomes entrained gradually to a 24-hour cycle, and you show a nice example of this.

Dr. Sander: One of the interesting things about Group A and B is that actually Group B, which has had this individual caretaking, shows a spectrum of individual differences in developing their 24-hour periodicity in Days 11 to 20 similar to group A, but they are all close to 24 hours. There's a significant difference by chi square analysis between group A and B in terms of the number of infants in each group with 24-hour peaks in contrast to those with approximately 24 hours or 23 to 26 hours.

Dr. Parmelee: I think what I'm trying to say is that if you have a free rhythm it is likely to be a 25-hour rhythm. The baby is born with such a natural rhythm, which later becomes entrained to 24 hours. You're saying this can be achieved by 10 days. Babies start with a 23–26 hour rhythm and then within a few weeks have a 24-hour rhythm, whether it's 10 days or 28 days.

Dr. Sander: I think there is an effect of the caretaking environment on the organization of the whole 24 hours. That's in addition to just the 24 hour peak and includes the way naps get organized and what the expectancy of the mother is that develops from this. Dr. Chappell is analyzing our present data in terms of an expectancy model of the mother in regard to the way her caregiving actions move state in the direction one expects it to change over the awakening for that baby.

Dr. Parmelee: That I think is a critical issue. In caretaking as we see it, part of the lead is from the baby, part of it seems to come from the mother. Some mothers expect the baby to be awake after a feeding so she can play with it. Other mothers expect the baby to go to sleep the minute it's through feeding, or she wants it that way, so she comes to the baby with a definite behavioral expectation. The baby either fits or doesn't.

Dr. Sander: Right. This is where the grandmother's influence emerges and what she thinks about babies, but also how the mother begins to sense where in the 24 hours this extra-long awakening is going to be, the time when the baby's not ready to go back to sleep at once. One can almost see such a longer arousal in the first days. In the slide of the baby for whom we had the detailed state sequencing, the relative awake period came between about 11 p.m. and 4 a.m. As you watch that time of relative awake over days it scans around the 24 hours and finally settles at some particular point later in the day. By that time the mother has gotten some sense of when to expect that she's not going to just put the baby down after she finishes the feeding. It's a coordination on another level, which influences what is going on in the finely tuned sequential interaction that you can observe with event recording or other methods. The question is how does one level feed back on the other? When you take the infant whose regulation is compromised, such as the fetal alcohol syndrome babies, you wonder if it is possible to maximize the order in the 24 hours for those infants by the stability of caretaking. How will caregiving influence the way the 24 hours gets organized in a damaged baby?

Dr. Watson: Is there any chance that the organization comes with any reasonable supporting environment, but that it is in some way an echo of the intrauterine experience of the baby, for example, the metabolic cycle of the mother? My first impression of your data was that they implied the baby gets organized by extrauterine experience and it can be disorganized by certain problems. However, the case of the disorganization of infants of alcoholic mothers suggests that the organizing influence may be prenatal, but with a delayed effect on the infant cycles. One test would be—perhaps you have data on it—either people who have worked nights up until the time they had their baby, or people who came here from say New Zealand to have their baby where there would have been different time cycles during the end of pregnancy.

Dr. Sander: That's data that needs to be gotten. We just don't have anything like that. The reason that I'm interested in Kathy's and Anneliese's work and now particularly Kathy's is because these early rocking and proprioceptive or kinesthetic kinds of interventions. What will they do to this kind of organization? I don't know. One needs to follow some of these babies more closely.

Dr. Parmelee: I tend to look at larger chunks of data. If sleep state organization and cycles are disrupted in the newborn, by 3 months they've generally pulled it together, with a few exceptions. Babies seem to do this even in rather adverse environments. There's a kind of drive to get this going. When one looks at the finer details, it's possible some disorganization persists. With respect to intrauterine movements, I interpret Dr. Sterman's data, which was quoted earlier, differently than he does. Some activity cycling of the baby *in utero* seems to be independent of the mother's cycles. There may be an internal cycle in the baby that is the same before and after birth.

Dr. Sander: Are you talking about the 24-hour cycle?

Dr. Parmelee: I'm talking about short, ultradian rhythms of about 40–60 minutes.

Dr. Sander: Here's where I think Bower's notions of going from a grosser to a finer specification is interesting. It might be in some instances that only at some 24-hour level one would find these earliest organizing differences. They'd then become further specified into the ultradian and finally into the infradian.

Dr. Parmelee: Except that the circadian rhythm isn't very strongly expressed. If you look at temperature, urine output, and so on.

Dr. Watson: Yet, is it not possible that even though the intrauterine activity may not display the 24-hour cycle, there may be a 24-hour cycle timer getting organized by other things, such as nutritional or hormonal content of the fluids passing the placental barrier?

Dr. Sander: One thing I don't want to lose sight of is the relation of the stabilization of cycling and the data on infant looking behavior in both the experimental situation and the feeding situation, that is, the naturalistic situation. The two groups were different, and they used their eyes differently over the 2 months. To me that relationship offers a lot of opportunity for discussion.

Dr. Stern: In situations where you can reduce the feeding or hunger variables, such as societies in which feeding occurs every hour or two, might that change it much?

Dr. Sander: This is data that Charlie Super has obtained with one of our monitors, which he took to Kenya. He just got back this summer, and he's working on the data. After adapting the monitor to record in the native hut, what he found the first night was that the mother doesn't put the baby down at all. She just sleeps with the baby on herself, so when it wants to nurse it nurses. Obviously there's going to be a vast difference. I think it may have something to do with different rates of change. It may have to do more with how functions are integrated in relation to states.

Dr. Stern: It certainly brings up the point—and one that has certainly been at issue in Anneliese's presentation—of what constitutes an intervention. It may well be that the infant bed, as well as its being located in a different room, is an extraordinary "intervention." Perhaps sleep organizes awfully rapidly without these "interventions," and a circadian rhythm would establish itself maybe within days if the baby were left on the mother the whole time.

Dr. Sander: One of the things that's certainly true is that however we might conceal the monitor it is a perturbation to the system. We have monitored over the first 2 months in the home. As long as everything's going right, mother follows instructions; but as soon as there was a problem or whenever anything was going wrong with the baby, the baby was taken out and brought into the mother's bed, and so we have no record.

Dr. Eisenberg: Could we return for a moment to that curve you showed describing how long the infant is awake under conditions where such feedback variables as diapering, feeding, bathing, and so forth were accounted for. My interest has to do with whether type of feeding—that is, breast versus bottle—affects the length of time a baby remains in the waking state. I ask because our data on postprandial state, obtained some 10 years ago with bottle-fed babies, don't seem to match that from our current population, which consists almost entirely of breast-fed babies.

Dr. Sander: All our work has been done on bottle-fed babies. One of the factors affecting duration of awake is the time of day and which of the two types of awake period you are dealing with. I would think the breast-fed baby also has perhaps one longer period during the day that he's awake. The breast-fed baby may be different in the other periods as well, however.

Dr. Eisenberg: Let me explain what my concern is. Since we are interested mainly in obtaining good EEG data, and since such data are best obtained from sleeping babies, all our experimental arrangements are geared to getting infants to that state as quickly and as easily as possible. Our standard procedure is to have the mother (or usual caretaker) come to the lab with a hungry baby whom she immediately feeds on site. Right after this, the usual caretaking procedures (diaper changes and the like) are attended to; electrodes are attached; safety checks, calibrations, and other electronic chores are completed; and an adaptation period begins. Our problem is that the adaptation period, and, as a matter of fact, the time consumed by our experimental procedures, seems to be far in excess of anything we expected: breast feeding seems to take much longer than bottle feeding; too many of the babies don't seem very happy for some time after feeding—whether because they get too little milk or too much, I don't know; and, in general, we find it difficult to predict how long an adaptation period we should plan for. What I'm getting at is the essentially methodological question of how, in planning an experiment, you can get an infant on the down side of that curve you showed. Do you have any idea of whether and how that curve might vary as a function of type of feeding?

Dr. Sander: No. I think breast feeding is obviously an interaction: The mother's got to be letting her milk out and the baby has to be getting it. That gets into complexities of what the whole meaning of the experimental situation is for her—a "first night effect" might well be more striking with breast fed than bottle fed infants, especially if early post partum contact was more immediate and consistent in the breast fed than in the bottle fed infant.

Dr. Eisenberg: You would think it would be longer though, wouldn't you?

Dr. Sander: Well it would depend on how often the mother's breast feeding, where she is in the course of breast feeding, how many weeks along, and whether she is now supplementing with the bottle.

REFERENCES

Ashby, W. R. *Design for a Brain*. London: Chapman and Hall Ltd., (2nd ed.), 1952. Also London: Assoc. Book Publishers, Ltd., 1970, (distributed in USA by Barnes & Noble, Inc.)

Burns, P., Sander, L. W., Stechler, G., & Julia, H. Distress in Feeding—Short Term Effects of Caretaker Environment on the First Ten Days. *Journal of the American Academy of Child Psychiatry*, 1972 (July), *11:3*, 427–439.

Carpenter, G., Tecce, J. J., Stechler, G., & Friedman, S. Differential Visual Behavior to Human and Humanoid Faces in Early Infancy. *Merrill-Palmer Quarterly*, 1970, *16*, 91–108.

Chappell, P., Sander, L. Mutual Regulation of Infant-Mother Interactive Process: The Context for the Origin of Communication. In M. Bullowa (Ed.), *Before Speech — The Beginnings of Human Communication*. Cambridge, England: Cambridge University Press, In press.

Erikson, E. *Childhood and Society*. New York: Norton, 1950.

Escalona, S. The Study of Individual Differences and the Problem of State. *Journal of the American Academy of Child Psychiatry*, 1962, *1:1*, 11–38.

Hartman, H. *Ego Psychology and the Problem of Adaptation*. New York: International Universities Press, 1958.

Prechtl, H. F. R. Polygraphic Studies of the Full-term Newborn Infant. In M. Bax and R. C. MacKeith (Eds.), *Studies in Infancy*. London: Heinemann, 1968, 22–40.

Sander, L. W. Infant and Caretaking Environment: Investigation and Conceptualization of Adaptive Behavior in a System of Increasing Complexity. In E. J. Anthony (Ed.), *Explorations in Child Psychiatry*. New York: Plenum Press, 1975.

Sander, L. W. Primary Prevention and Some Aspects of Temporal Organization in Early Infant-Caretaker Interaction. In E. Rexford, L. W. Sander and T. Shapiro (Eds.), *Infant Psychiatry—A New Synthesis*. New Haven: Yale University Press, 1976.

Sander, L., Chappell, P., & Snyder, P. *An Investigation of Change in the Infant-Caretaker System Over the First Week of Life*. Paper presented at the meeting of the Society for Research in Child Development, Denver, April 1975.

Sander, L. W., Julia, H., Stechler, G., & Burns, P. Regulation and Organization in the Early Infant-Caretaker System. In R. Robinson (Ed.), *Brain and Early Behavior*. London: Academic Press Ltd., 1969.

Sander, L. W., Julia, H. L., Stechler, G. & Burns, P. Continuous 24-Hour Interactional Monitoring in Infants Reared in Two Caretaking Environments. *Psychosomatic Medicine*, 1972, *34*, 270–282.

Sander, L. W., Stechler, G., Burns, P., & Julia, H. Early Mother-Infant Interaction and 24-Hour Patterns of Activity and Sleep. *Journal of the American Academy of Child Psychiatry*, 1970 (January), *9:1*, 103–123.

Sherrington, C. S. *The Integrative Action of the Nervous System*. London: Archibald Constable & Co. Ltd., 1906.

Spitz, R. *A Genetic Field Theory of Ego Formation*. New York: International Universities Press, 1959.

Stechler, G. S., & Latz, E. Some Observations of Attention and Arousal in the Human Infant. *Journal of the American Academy of Child Psychiatry*, 1966, *5*, 517–525.

Stechler, G., & Carpenter, G. A Viewpoint on Early Affective Development. In J. Hellmuth (Ed.) *The Exceptional Infant*. New York: Bruner/Mazel, 1967.

Stechler, G. *Infant Looking and Fussing in Response to Visual Stimulation Over the First Two Months of Life in Different Infant-Caretaking Systems*. Paper presented at the meeting of the Society for Research in Child Development, Philadelphia, March 1973.

15
Temporal Expectancies of Social Behaviors in Mother–Infant Play

Daniel N. Stern
New York Hospital,
Cornell University Medical Center

John Gibbon
New York State Psychiatric
Institute
and
Columbia University

All events, including the social behaviors of mothers and infants, unfold in the dimension of time. In trying to unravel the mysteries of the infant's social responsiveness to sounds, sights, movements, and tactile experiences, it is clear that we must better understand the time dimensions and temporal patterns in which stimuli in these different modalities are presented and perceived. The examination of timing itself as a crucial variable in the understanding of social responsivity is an important subtheme of this book. Since all social stimuli to which the infant is exposed are presented in real time, his experience of these events includes the distribution of stimulus events and stimulus changes over time. This is as true for watching a human face, which is almost always in motion, as it is for hearing vocalizations or experiencing bounces or tickles.

As a starting point then, in this chapter, we shall present some evidence and speculations on how the infant might estimate time intervals, form temporal expectancies, and evaluate variations from the expected. At the same time, we shall suggest ways in which the temporal distribution of maternal social behaviors influence the infant. Lastly, we shall indicate some future directions for needed research in this area.

There are several compelling reasons for focusing on the timing and temporal patterning of social behaviors and on the infant's perception of these parameters. During the earliest months of life, the interactive social system between mother and infant is a nonverbal one in which the stimulus value and communicative content of behaviors derive mainly from their sensory properties, which includes their temporal properties, rather than from their associative or symbolic meaning. It has long been recognized that much of the affective communication of a behavior is carried in the distribution over time of one or several of its stimulus variables; for example, in the rate of change in intensity. More recently, the very phenomenon of affective displays in infants has been intimately linked to how stimuli are distributed over time. For example, Sroufe (1976), building on the work of Berlyne (1969) and Kagan (1971), has proposed that once exogenous smiling is well established, a necessary stimulus condition to generate an affective response is one that produces a rapid, accelerating increase in tension, followed by an abrupt cutoff and a rapid drop in tension.

In a similar vein, Stern (1974, 1977) has commented on the fact that infant-elicited maternal social behaviors are quite "deviant" when compared to the way that mother moves her face or body or the way that she vocalizes when interacting with another adult. One of the major differences in the infant-elicited situation lies in the way that the mother exaggerates the temporal performance of her behavior. She usually slows down, but she may also speed up changes and rates of change in tempo, rhythm, pitch, facial displays, and so on. The maintenance of infant attention often requires these exaggerated temporal performances during social interactions.

Another reason arguing for the closer examination of the timing and perception of timing of social behaviors comes from the accumulating evidence suggesting the importance, early in infancy, of the formation of expectancies based on immediately preceding experience. Most studies exploring the creation and violation of expectancies have examined visual and auditory stimuli, and they have in fact had to carefully control for the stimuli; or to put it differently, they have had to remove the temporal structure of the stimuli from consideration as a variable. There is every reason to imagine that the expectancy hypotheses of infant mental functioning should also apply to temporal intervals. The temporal dimension of social behaviors is so much part of the very "stuff" of the natural flow of mother–infant interactions that it is hard to imagine otherwise.

The major theme of this book is the origins of infant responsivity. One of the many routes to an understanding of these origins is to look at the human social environment to which the infant must be and/or becomes responsive. In this chapter, we focus mainly on how mothers naturally behave with their infants. This is a roundabout and potentially misleading, as well as a rewarding, way to proceed in understanding the origins of infant behavior. There are many possible assumptions in which we have incomplete confidence. Do the mother and infant, right from the very start, form the best possible "fit" of social behaviors such that to watch the mother behave socially toward the infant is virtually synonymous with watching the infant perceive and respond? The alternative view is that there is a fairly poor fit of social behaviors between mother and infant at the beginning and that each moves closer to a better fit through development and learning on the infant's part and learning on the mother's. We cannot resolve this issue or even approximate the correct balance, since we are focusing heavily on the mother alone. Nonetheless, mothers, in general, are the most exquisitely tuned "instruments" that nature has evolved, and that we "possess," for assessing infant social capabilities. Accordingly, the study of naturally occurring infant-elicited maternal behaviors is quite likely to tell us much about what the infant either already "knows" or is in the process of getting to know about human social behavior, and in particular for the purposes of this chapter, about the timing of human social behaviors.

METHODS

Three mother–infant pairs were studied. The infants were all normal female firstborns. Portable television tapes were taken in the home of all activities occurring during the morning waking period. Naturalistic conditions were sought and adhered to as much as possible. The mothers' only instructions were to behave as they normally do. Play periods, which we shall limit ourselves to in this chapter, were initiated whenever the mother and/or infant desired one, and play periods were terminated whenever the mother felt they had run their natural course. Data was collected at least once weekly between the infant's 3rd and 4th month of life.

Maternal utterances were scored in two different ways.

For all of the play data, the television tapes were replayed in the laboratory, and a magnetic tape event recorder was activated by push button during each continuous maternal utterance and released during each silence. The magnetic tape was then computer analyzed to give a running record, as well as the frequency distribution, of maternal utterances and pauses sampled every .1 seconds. (See Stern, Jaffe, Beebe, & Bennett, 1975, for further details of this recording and analyzing system.)

The data from this relatively crude system were used to establish criteria as to what constitutes a recognizable burst or episode of utterances and what constitutes its boundaries. Stated in another way, how long must a silence last to assume that the mother's burst or episode of vocal activity is over for the while, during which time the need to keep track of the time intervals between the onset of utterances can be temporarily suspended until a new episode of vocalizing begins?

Since we are going to suggest later that the infant has some way to keep track of the timing of maternal social behaviors, we had first better know when his "clocking" of the mother's behavior is likely to be operating.

A playful social interaction between mother and infant is hardly a smooth-running affair that unfolds with great regularity. Instead, there are bursts of activity and engagement, and there are rests when there is relative behavioral quiet and disengagement. This is true for each partner, viewed separately, as well as for the dyad. In a previous publication (Stern et al, 1977), we described these bursts on the mother's part as episodes of maintained engagement during which she maintained a fairly even level of visual attention, sustained a fairly constant rate of performance of behaviors for the infant, and held in mind some fairly obvious aim, such as getting or holding the infant's visual attention. We labeled the boundaries in between these episodes as engagement shifts. Fogel (1977), attempting a similar parsing of behavioral flow, labeled them "time outs." Since we shall be discussing mainly the timing of maternal vocal utterances, a "time out" seems to be a more appropriate term for a "long enough" silence even though it is only one of the criteria, a major one, of an engagement shift.

Since vocal "time outs" can vary from many seconds to many minutes and result from a variety of causes, we also needed a criterion of "time in" episodes when the mother was clearly engaging, or trying to engage, the infant vocally. It is clinically and statistically obvious that an examination of the timing of maternal utterances during "time in" episodes had to be conducted separately from an examination that included "time in" episodes and "time outs."

We chose a 3-second-or-longer pause as the criterion of a "time out," and anything in between pauses of this duration as a "time in" episode. The determining reason for the 3-second criterion derived from the data collected in the manner previously described. Figure 15.1 shows the frequency distribution of the duration of maternal vocal pauses for the three mothers vocalizing to their infants in the course of 33 play sessions. Three seconds closely approximates the point at which the curve levels off.

This empirical choice is supported by two different kinds of evidence. (1) A 3-second silence feels quite long to the average adult, as if the previous stream of speech and subject matter had broken off and a new one is about to begin. From the studies of Jaffe and Feldstein (1960), we know that the mean vocal pause in adult dialogue is only .60 seconds and the mean speaker-switching pause is only .64 seconds. These intervals, which are shorter than 3 seconds by a factor of almost 5, may explain in part why 3 seconds feels so long from the point of view of continuity or discontinuity of vocal activity. (2) It is known that delays of reinforcement of greater than 3 seconds significantly interfere with the contingent learning of human infants (Millar, 1972).

The previously described data-scoring method was adequate in helping to establish the boundary criteria needed, but the content of utterances as well as the mother's nonverbal behaviors and the infant's responses to both were lost. Accordingly, sections of the television tapes that included "time in" episodes consisting of at least eight separate utterances were selected and converted to 16mm film for a finer analysis. Because of the arduousness of the scoring method to be described later, we chose only the "time in" episodes of the three sessions closest to the infant's 14th week of life. This resulted in 24, 14, and 13

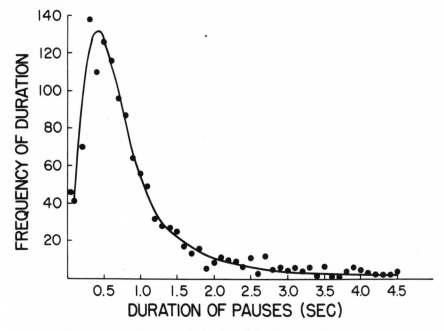

FIG. 15.1. The frequency distribution of the duration of maternal vocal pauses. The data points are the pooled pauses of three mothers vocalizing to their infants during a total of 33 play sessions.

"time in" episodes for each of the three mothers with respective mean sequence lengths of 21, 24, and 17 utterances per episode.

The films of these selected samples were then projected at normal speed. Two observers watching the films each operated, through a push button, the channels of an Esterline Angus event recorder (running at a speed of 12cm. per minute). Both vocal utterances and nonverbal behaviors were scored. Before actual scoring, (from 3 to 10 seconds) short sections of the film were replayed as many as a dozen times in succession until both observers knew the section "by heart." Accordingly, when the actual scoring run was made, each utterance or movement scored was anticipated. The experimenter's own auditory and visual perceptions and short-term memory were thus an important part of the scoring and coding "instrumentation."

During a vocalization that was continuous to the Experimenter's ears, the pens of the event recorder were activated. Each continuous vocalization (which consisted of one or many words) was considered an utterance. An utterance and its following pause together make up an onset-to-onset interval. Interrater agreement as to the presence of a vocalization was 100% with a mean error as to the start and stop of the vocalization of less than .1 second. There was 96% agreement as to the verbal content of each word.

This arduous procedure is in fact unnecessarily unwieldy for getting accurate timing and accurate recording of verbal content. However, although we shall only touch on it in this chapter, we also wished to record the mother's nonverbal phrases or kinesic "utterances," including the timing and descriptive content of the succession of her discrete facial displays, head movements, and so on. It was to capture these that the system was designed. For further details on the scoring of "kinesic phrases" see Stern et al. (1977).

The raw data, then, were collected and scored as previously described and consists of the duration of onset-to-onset intervals of utterances of two different types, successive utterances in which the same verbal content is repeated, successive utterances that are not repetitious, and the duration of onset-to-onset intervals of nonverbal repetitious movements that make up maternal games played with infants. The data included only those events occurring within the 51 "time in" episodes (no pause > 3 seconds) of the three mothers with their 14-week-old infants during play interactions.

HOW MIGHT THE INFANT ESTIMATE TIME?

Only if the infant can estimate time intervals and thus develop expectancies as to when an anticipated behavior ought to happen, can we seriously consider several communicative roles for the timing parameters of social behaviors. Infants do not have to be able to keep track of time intervals for the timing of stimulus events to be an important factor in their behavior, providing that those events are acting simply as elicitors of responses and the temporal components of those events is either unimportant or invariant. However, if expectancy and the cognitive "work" involved in the evaluation of deviations or discrepancies from the expected temporal performance are to play a role, then the infant must be able to keep track of, or evaluate, time intervals. What timing processes might the infant possess to evaluate temporal expectancies and their variations?

Imagine the infant, right after a "time in" period begins, listening to the next several utterances and the pauses between them produced by the mother. If the onset-to-onset time of utterances is fairly regular, the infant may develop a set or expectancy for the tempo of the "time" in period, which may be regarded as an estimate for the time of the next vocal production. Such a process in experimental work with the adults is similar to the method of production or reproduction (e.g., Treisman, 1962; Kristofferson, 1976), and our interest centers on how variation in these expected times on the part of the infant and variation in the interval from onset to onset of utterances on the part of the mother interact to maintain a relatively regular tempo for a "time in" period. We will later suggest that variations in timing may be "deliberately" introduced by the mother to alter attention.

Gibbon (1972, 1977) has outlined several ways in which properties of time estimation, in particular variability, might change with changes in the duration of the interval being timed. For our purposes, three different modes of timing are relevant.

Absolute timing is a process in which variability around the time interval being estimated does not change with changes in the duration of that interval. In human reproduction timing studies, this process has been found to be operative only at very short intervals of time, less than about half a second in duration (Kristofferson, 1976). For short intervals in this range, behavior is maximally accurate and is comparable to the precision with which a skilled musician executes a "riff" coming out precisely on the beat. This requires that the muscular work involved in producing the notes begin in advance and in anticipation of when the beat will fall. For durations longer than about half a second, variability in reproducing or estimating time increases with the size of the interval being timed (Getty, 1975; Gibbon, 1972). The manner in which variance increases with the size of the interval is crucial for our proposal about the way in which infants and mothers "understand" deviations from temporal expectancy. At least two different processes may be characterized.

Poisson timing is a process that has an analogue in neural energy detection mechanisms in psychophysics (e.g., McGill, 1967; Luce & Green, 1972) and might be characterized as a minimum variance time estimation process that is as efficient as possible given the variability inherent in neural organization. A schema for this process involves a count accumulator, or "neural counter," which accumulates counts of impulses emitted by one or several Poisson sources in the nervous system and estimates a given time interval by the time required to accumulate a certain number of counts. In our situation, if for example the interval from the onset of one maternal behavior to the next was 1 second and required a count of x impulses when a new tempo is established with 2-second intervals, the estimate reflects this change by "simply" doubling, so that the new time value is estimated when a count of $2x$ impulses is accumulated. In such a process, variability around the time being estimated increases slowly in such a manner that the standard deviation of the distribution of estimates is proportional to the square root of the time interval estimated.

Third and finally, a scalar timing process is one in which variance increases more rapidly with increasing intervals such that the standard deviation of estimates increases proportionally with the duration of the interval being estimated. Scalar timing might equally well be called "Weber timing," since it implies Weber's law for time discrimination. In human and animal psychophysics, Weber's law, which states that the value of the discriminable difference between stimuli is a constant fraction of the base stimulus, has been found to hold for timing in animals and humans over a broad range of time values above the minimum of around half a second, as noted previously. The estimation process underlying scalar timing may be thought of as reflecting a single time estimation distribution that is simply scale transformed for different values for the time being estimated. In our example, if maternal behaviors during one "time in" period fall about 1 second apart, the infant is regarded as setting his "unit timer" at 1 second. When a new tempo is established with intervals of 2 seconds, the unit timer is simply "stretched" to accommodate the new time interval. This means that the same proportion of estimates occur at the same relative point in the duration of the interval being timed. For example, if one-half of the time estimates were underestimates in the 1-second case, one-half of the time estimates would be underestimates in the 2-second case as well. Such a process is an extremely simple one and may be thought of as consisting of a unit timer with some minimum variability, which is "elastic" in the sense that the same *proportional* error occurs at the same proportion of the time being estimated when this time is changed.

These three alternatives differ in the way in which the standard deviation varies (or fails to vary) with changes in the mean of the estimated interval. In the absolute timing case, there is no change in variance with the mean; for Poisson timing the standard deviation is proportional to the square root of the mean; and for scalar timing the standard deviation is proportional to the mean itself.

In Figure 15.2, the standard deviation of onset-to-onset intervals of maternal vocal utterances within "time in" episodes of each mother is plotted against the mean onset-to-onset duration. The data are presented on double-log coordinates, and a small constant has been subtracted from abscissa values in each case, which is close to the one-half-second minimum, above which the scalar process is expected to operate. On a double-log plot, the scalar process implies a slope of 1.0, and the best fit lines for each mother do not differ significantly and are all close to 1.0. On double-log ordinates, an absolute timing process would be represented by a flat curve, and a Poisson process by lines with a slope of one-half. The data are in accord with a scalar process rather than the other alternatives, since the standard deviation for all three subjects is proportional to the mean. Another way to characterize these data is to say that the coefficient of variation (SD/M) is constant (equal to about one-half), and the values for this proportionality constant are surprisingly close from mother to mother.

What does this mean for the infant? We know from many sources how active is the infant's mental life. As Bruner (1975) has recently stated it, a central tendency of the infant's mental life is the formation and testing of hypotheses. The creation of expectancies (temporal as well as others), and the evaluation of deviations or discrepancies from the expected, form a crucial part of this "central tendency." Accordingly, an ideal temporal stimulus cannot be absolutely regular and fixed. If it were, there would be no deviations to evaluate and nothing to continue to engage the infant's mental

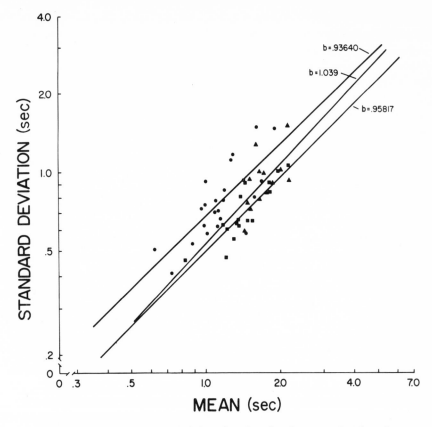

FIG. 15.2.   Log standard deviation plotted against log mean duration of onset-to-onset intervals of maternal utterances during 51 "time in" episodes. Only episodes consisting of 8 or more utterances in the sequence are included.

process. He would habituate rapidly. If, on the other hand, the deviations around the expected were too large or irregular for him to "encompass," then he would presumably be incapable of perceiving them as deviations. That is to say, they would be unrelated to the expected referent. Once again, his interest and cognitive engagement could not be maintained. Our current notion of the infant's attentional and cognitive processes thus requires that a temporal stimulus best suited to maintain interest and engagement would have a generally regular tempo (to allow for the formation of expectancy) but with a limited, or at least lawful, variability (to engage and maintain his evaluative processes).

The problem with these requirements is that the mother produces social behaviors that sometimes come quite rapidly and at other times more slowly. We have found (Stern et al., 1977) that during episodes of maintained engagement ("time in" episodes) on the mother's part, the mother generally establishes a fairly regular tempo of performing social behaviors. She may at any point suddenly change her tempo, but more generally she does so after a "time out" consisting of a shift in the nature of her engagement or strategy with the infant. The mean tempo of separate episodes of maternal infant-directed social behaviors can vary by a factor of 5 or even 10. In any event, as the mean interval between her social behavior increases so will the variability around that mean. The problem thus arises as to how the infant can deal with this common situation in which the mother, from time to time, alters considerably her tempo and its variability. For instance, if the mother is producing a mean behavioral beat of 1 per second with an SD of .5 second, and then slows to a mean beat of one behavior every 3 seconds with an SD of 1.5 seconds (as demonstrated previously), then the infant is in a situation of having to "figure out" an altered timing in which the variability itself (SD) of the new interval is larger than the previous mean interval. If the infant has a scalar unit timer, as we suggest, then the mother can switch to any tempo she wants and the infant will necessarily readjust his expectation of the mean and his range of variability appropriate to the new mean. His ability to form expectancies and to evaluate deviations from the expected will remain intact across the wide band of behavioral tempos a mother may utilize. As Gibbon and others would point out, we are simply suggesting that the infant's expectancies obey a variance-limiting process consistent with Weber's law in order to remain engaged with maternal speech, regardless of changes in the timing of her speech that may reflect emotional, cultural, situational, or other factors. The timing of maternal utterances is thus ideally suited to maintain some fairly constant high level of infant interest.

Suppose, however, she wishes to attract the infant's attention more powerfully, to capture his gaze if it is not on her, or if it is, to heighten the level or degree of ongoing engagement or arousal. We have already postulated that she cannot do it by changing tempo. She could, however, provide such a signal by adopting a different mode of timing her behavior.

SHIFTING OUT OF SCALAR TIMING AS A SIGNAL TO ATTRACT OR HEIGHTEN ATTENTION: THE USE OF REPETITION

In a previous report (Stern et al., 1977), we examined one of the more common yet striking features of maternal social behaviors, namely, the extraordinary amount of repetition in all modalities: vocal; head movements; facial expressions; tactile and kinesthetic stimulations. It was found that whether one was scoring verbal content or nonverbal behavior, as much as 30% to 40% of all vocal phrases (utterances) and kinesic "phrases" (e.g., a head nod) were repeats of the immediately preceding behavior. (The average repetitive run consisted of about three units.) The instructional use of repetition by mothers teaching older children language has been commented on by Snow (1972) and others, but the even greater use of repetition in the earlier months appears to be more related to the regulation of attention and the retuning of the degree of engagement of cognitive processes. Repetition, in this context, can have the quality of a "now hear this!" signal.

With these considerations in mind we asked whether the relationship between the means and *SD* of the interval from onset to onset of utterances was the same during repetitive runs as it was during the speech samples reported previously. An argument can be made that there is a greater likelihood that each unit in a run in which the words are repeated would have more similar temporal parameters than the units in a nonrepetitious sequence. Accordingly, there might exist greater constraints on the variability around the mean interval for repetitious runs. While this proves to be true, restraint on variability from one repeated unit to the next need not be the case,

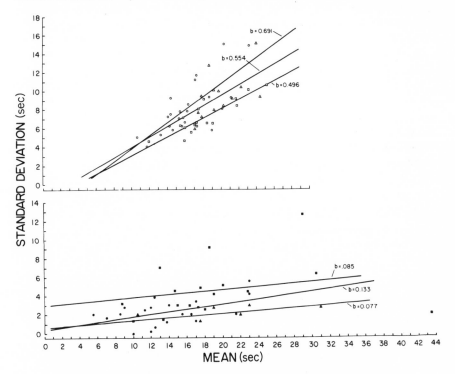

FIG. 15.3.   Standard deviation plotted against the mean duration of onset-to-onset intervals for repeating utterances (bottom panel) and for all utterances (top panel). There are 53 repeating sequences of at least 4 units in length and 51 nonrepeating sequences of at least 8 or more units in length.

and often is not. For example, "hi honey" can be repeated many ways, such as

hi...honey...   hiiiihuuuney......   hihoney   hi,

and so on. The interval from onset to onset clearly can vary greatly despite the similarity in verbal content. (Data on content repeats that are not consecutive are currently being analyzed.)

The point is not that intervals from the onset to onset of repeating units have as much temporal freedom as those involving nonrepeating units, nor that the signal value of repetition is not in large part the repetition of content itself, but rather, that if the relationship between mean and SD proves sufficiently different during repetitions compared to nonrepetitious sequences, then the infant would be forced to adopt different mechanisms of timing these two types of maternal social behaviors. The altered temporal structure in itself may contribute to the stimulus or signal value of repetition. It is important to re-emphasize that we are not trying to make a case that time is the all-important variable of social behaviors, but rather that it has been a too-neglected potential contributor to signal events in the social process.

Figure 15.3 plots on linear coordinates the standard deviation against the mean of onset-to-onset intervals for repeating utterances on the bottom and for all the data on the top. The data in the top panel are the same as those from the earlier figure but without the subtracted constant. The raw data, as may be seen here, is linear ($p < .01$) and the best fit lines for the top panel intersect the x axis at a value around 400 milliseconds. It is these constants that we subtracted for each mother from the means in the earlier figure.[1] The relationship between standard deviation and mean for repeated runs is clearly quite different from that of the scalar process exemplified in the top panel. For the repeated runs (lower panel) two features of the data are clear. First, all of the standard deviations are relatively low, with most of them falling below about 600 milliseconds, even for relatively long mean intervals. Second, the linear relationship seen in the upper panel is attenuated here, with considerably more scatter and a considerably lower slope for each subject. (Significance levels for these data are between .05 and .025 for two of the mothers, and for the third linearity is not present.) Thus, the repeated runs data may be characterized as a low variance process that is insensitive to the duration of the repeating unit. Variability for long repeated units is not very different from variability for short repeated units, in contrast to the scalar

---

[1]The data points plotted in Figure 15.2 are the same as those plotted in Figure 15.3, in which the best fit lines intercept the x axis at about .4 second. This may reflect a "reaction time"—or start-up time for a mother to begin to vocalize after she has made the decision to, or it may simply reflect a lower boundary of the scalar process. This boundary is consistent with a lower limit for Weber's law in temporal discrimination (Getty, 1975; Kristofferson, 1976). It is also fairly close to the mean non-speaker-switching pause seen in adult dialogues (.6 second).

relationship evident in the unsegregated data for maintenance of non-repeating units. The repeating run data were analyzed on the double-log transform as well, and the slopes of the best fit linear functions again were of marginal significance statistically but fell well below 1.0 and more in the range of .5 to be expected from a Poisson process (obtained double-log slopes were .42, .49, and .74).

Thus a repetitive run requires a different sort of temporal processing than the variations in tempo experienced just prior to its onset. The temporal regularity in these runs has such a low variance and bears such an unstructured relationship to the duration of the interval that the infant is likely, if you will, to "disregard" deviations from expectancies and instead attend to the run on the basis of its other stimulus values. Put another way, the attention-holding ("pleasing") level of variation experienced prior to the onset of the run has suddenly disappeared, and the infant must disengage or decrease his cognitive assessment of substantive content (stimulus properties).

This might be characterized as a low variance shift from scalar expectancies, as opposed to the high variance shift that occurs when pauses increase beyond a reasonable level based on the tempo currently in use. When a pause duration exceeds some expected level, a "time out" period is initiated, and we postulate that the infant would reset his unit timer for the next tempo value when it begins. When the variance is too *low*, that is, when a repetitious run occurs, the timing structure is altered, and attention is focused on the repeated content itself with an accompanying heightening of arousal and intensity in the communication system.

We determined the attention-getting effect of repetition by comparing all the times the infant turned to gaze at the mother when these conditions were not met. Visual attention getting was significantly greater during the 53 repetitive runs (as specified) than during the other possible times. Without electrophysiological data or far more detailed observational data, we cannot test our impression that repetition also has the effect on an already gazing infant of raising the level of his alertness or responsiveness to maternal behaviors.

AND AFTER THE ATTENTION HAS
BEEN REFOCUSED BY REPETITION?

The majority of attempts to refocus attention through repetition are failures. Failures are generally followed by the trial of a new and different repetitive run. However, these attempts sometimes succeed, and we shall focus on the successes. A repeating event with relatively little variability cannot go on for very long before the infant habituates to it. This would defeat the purpose we are proposing for these runs and could be prevented only by short sequences or by progressively introducing greater variability between successive repeating units as the sequence increases in length. Both seem to be the case, but the latter the more interesting. Figure 15.4 demonstrates that the *SD* of successive pairs of intervals, within a repeating sequence, increases as the sequence gets longer. It also shows that this is not the case for sequences of nonrepeating intervals.

The mother appears to use the timing characteristics of the early part of the repeating sequence to refocus the infant's attention. Having done that, she can then reintroduce greater and greater amounts of variability between successive units for one of two ends. By the time a sequence of 4 or 5 repeated

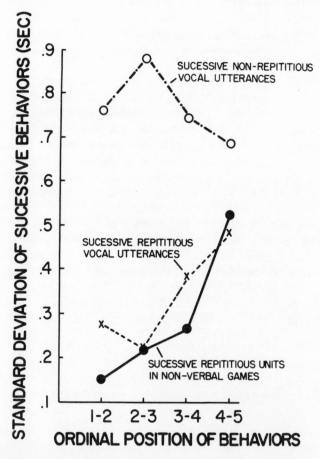

FIG. 15.4.   Standard deviation between successive pairs of intervals plotted against the ordinal position of the behaviors for: successive nonrepetitious vocal utterances, successive repetitious utterances, and successive repetitious units in nonverbal games.

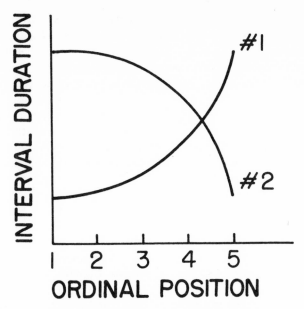

FIG. 15.5.   A schematic illustration of two different relationships between interval duration of units in a sequence and ordinal position within that sequence.

units is finished, the amount of variability that has been reintroduced begins to approach that seen in "normal," nonrepetitive utterances, and the infant has been, so to speak, eased back into a receptive position where his scalar unit timer will again begin to process the flow of maternal speech, but at a higher level of attentiveness. In a sense, the mother breaks up the temporal structure of her stimulation and then progressively reconstitutes it so as to bring the infant along with her at a different level.

The other possibility of progressively introducing greater variability into the repetitive run is perhaps even more interesting. As the run gets longer and more variable, it has unusual properties for engaging the infant—as a special unit itself, not as just a reintroduction to the normal flow of behavior. It is like the inverse of music where the beat remains the same but the words or melody keep changing. It is similar to a song where the lyrics are the beat that maintains the regularity of structure and the time intervals are the lyrics that change. This description may sound overly poetic but is being stressed because these short sequences of behaviors, with their unusual features, can be used by the mother to alter the baby's affect rapidly, not only his attentional processes. For instance, if for a repetitive run we plot the interval duration against the ordinal position of the unit, we can come up with many different curves. Two of the simplest and commonest are illustrated in Figure 15.5, in schematic form.

Each different pattern may have a different propensity for affecting the infant's level of arousal or affect in a specific manner. For instance, we found that the likelihood of the infant's smiling was greatest when Pattern 1 was followed. This could be explainable in that whereas the actual rate of stimulation decelerates, the discrepancy from expected is accelerating, and this may account for the increase in arousal that is thought to be necessary for the generation of affect. If the physical properties of the stimulus alone were the prepotent phenomena that generated affect, which might have been the case a month earlier, then we would have expected Curve 2 to be the most effective, that is, where the rate of physical stimulation accelerated. Clearly this is an area requiring far more study.

TIME EXPECTANCIES FOR MATERNAL BEHAVIORS IN OTHER MODALITIES

We know from common observation, as well as from the precise film analysis of "self synchrony" (Condon & Ogston, 1966), that utterances are accompanied by time-locked facial, gestural, and positional movements or changes in ongoing movement. Accordingly, even if the infant were deaf, so long as the mother was vocalizing to him, he might experience visually the same mode of timing and shifts in mode of timing of kinesic units of behavior that the hearing infant does with vocal units. The hearing infant, of course, is exposed to both.

As was indicated earlier in the section on methodological issues, we have been concerned with the timing of kinesic units (phrases) that are not accompanied by speech. A preliminary analysis of the relationship between the mean and SD of intervals of onset to onset of discrete kinesic phrases (facial expressions, head movements, etc.) that a mother performs in silence for her infant suggests that the temporal organization of these behaviors too conforms to a scalar process. We have also analyzed the timing of repetitive movements that constitute simple games played by mothers, such as face-presentation repetitions (peek-a-boo without a screen) and swooping down to tickle the tummy with a lip vibration, then up again, over and over. These games are a kinesic counterpart of the repetitious vocal utterances seen on the bottom half of Figure 15.3. We then asked the same "question" of the successive units that make up a nonverbal game that we asked of the successive units that make up a repeating vocal sequence. Is greater temporal variability progressively introduced into the game sequence as it gets longer? Figure 15.4 demonstrates that the SD of successive pairs of intervals within a game sequence increases as the sequence gets longer, just as it did for the repeating vocal sequences.

These similarities across modalities suggest that mother and infant may have all sensory modalities available to them to create, change, and utilize temporal structures for similar communicative functions.

SOME FUTURE DIRECTIONS

Clearly, the immediate and greatest need is to "hear directly" from the infant concerning his capabilities of forming temporal expectancies. Both physiological measures and finer behavior analysis (preferably the coordination of both) in the "naturalistic" setting, and the evaluation of the effect of the experimental manipulations of temporal parameters, will be required for this task. Without this evidence we can only describe, with a few exceptions, the infant's temporal social environment and speculate about his capabilities to decode and use it. [After reading this chapter, Dr. Eisenberg in reviewing her data on neonates' response to auditory stimuli, found that 4 out of 4 *neonates* demonstrated anticipatory responses even when the interstimulus interval was variable within a limited range, 13 to 16 seconds. The infants acted as if they "calculated" a mean and used it as the point of anticipation (Eisenberg, personal communication); see Eisenberg, Note 1.]

We know from work with adults (Kristofferson, 1976; Getty, 1975; Treisman, 1963) that the scalar process is a good first-order description of human timing. At what point in development does our infant have this capacity available to him? Is it present at birth (as Eisenberg, Note 1, suggests), and if not, what is its developmental course? Even if it is present at birth, or shortly after, what is the developmental course of its functioning? The presence of a scalar process does not of itself tell us at what coefficient of variation it will operate. Does the coefficient of variation change over development? How much life experience with time is required to permit a normal developmental course of its functioning? How long a unit can it handle at different ages?

In this chapter we have not mentioned the use of timing as a "pace setter" to alter the infant's state. The lullaby not only has a characteristic tempo, but as actually used, one of its important features is to introduce a temporal change, the progressive slowing of tempo (and loudness) at just the right point. In a similar vein, when the baby is upset and manifesting fuss–cry behaviors, the mother will frequently speed up her tempo of behavior to "top" or override the infant's and then slowly and progressively decrease the tempo of her behaviors; in doing so, she brings the baby back down to a quieter state. The reverse may also be seen. The crucial point is that we do not adequately understand the caregiver's use and the infant's perception and response to different tempos and rates of acceleration and deceleration.

Affect and timing are intimately bound. As we have previously indicated, the decoding of affective displays may require the detection of different distribution of stimulus change over time. We will need to know the developmental course of the infant's ability to discriminate these phenomena to better understand the ontogeny of his comprehension of affective displays.

Affect and temporal expectancy are linked in another way. Gibbon (1977), drawing on work with rats, speculates on the temporal distribution of "fear," over an expected interval terminated by a shock, and the temporal distribution of "hope," over an expected interval terminated by reward. One of his many interesting findings is that some rats (in the fear situation) are characteristically more "conservative" and do not "cut it so close." This raises the intriguing question of whether the level of affect associated with an expected interval can have different distributions over time depending on developmental age or "personality" tendencies. For instance, suppose one infant distributes his pleasurable expectancy over an expected interval as shown in Curve 1 of Figure 15.6 and another distributes it as shown in Curve 2; then although they both "expend" the same "amount" of pleasurable expectancy (the area under the curves), the stimulus at the end of the interval will "hit" the second infant when he is at a higher level and may thus be more

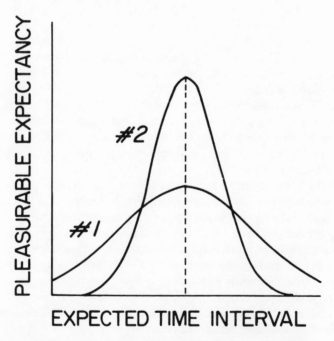

FIG. 15.6. A schematic illustration of two different distributions of "pleasurable expectancy" over the duration of the expected time interval.

likely, for instance, to make him smile or laugh than the first infant. He may thus be seen as having a different sense of humor.

An even more speculative consideration concering affect and expectancy involves the possible effect of strong emotions on the scalar unit timer. Might different emotional states create characteristic distortions in the operation of the unit timer, and if so, might it not "break up" the smooth flow of social behavioral responsiveness?

Finally, these lines of inquiry may prove fruitful in understanding abnormal infants. If an infant were unable to form temporal expectancies, or had some major deficit in that evaluative process, regardless of the intactness of all his sensory modalities and other cognitive processes, socially he would act quite differently and learn quite abnormally. Or, in a different situation, the potential for "soothing' such an infant with rhythmic song or movement may be attenuated. We have no reason to postulate such a selective abnormality, except as illustrative of the potential clinical value of understanding more the infant's social responsiveness in the fourth dimension.

ACKNOWLEDGMENTS

This research has been supported by The Jane Hilder Harris Foundation, The Grant Foundation, and The Research Foundation for Mental Hygiene, New York State Psychiatric Institute.

DISCUSSION

Dr. Lipsitt: Dan, I think you did all that without mentioning temporal conditioning once. You referred to expectancies, particularly in connection with that example about "I'm gonna get you." Temporal conditioning has got to be the basis, hasn't it?

Dr. Stern: When you say temporal conditioning, aren't you really getting around the issue? What does temporal conditioning tell you about timing processes? I agree with you I haven't used the term, but from the point of view of time estimation or reproduction issues the term *temporal conditioning* describes without explaining. It doesn't tell me anything new. It doesn't tell me how the baby will either estimate the interval or be able to evaluate what constitutes a lawful deviation.

Dr. Watson: In the extraordinarily important work you're doing, it will be necessary to distinguish between evidence of the existence of one versus another sort of timer (i.e., the time perceiving organ) and evidence of the psychological consequences of perceiving temporal pattern. At this point in your research, your evidence for the form of timing mechanism used by the infant is uncontested. However, as regards the psychological effects of introducing a transition in temporal pattern, your evidence of the mother's arousing attention to stimulus content by introducing a change in pattern is at odds with existing data derived from temporal conditioning. I just began to see and agree with Lew's earlier point that existing work on temporal conditioning is relevant here. First it should be noted that the transition in pattern you describe is one where the mother shifts from random intervals (as evidenced in the negative exponential distribution of intervals you observed) to a nonrandom pattern of intervals. This is a shift from no temporal pattern to temporal pattern of speech stimuli. In light of conditioning research, one would expect that if anything, the shift from nontemporal pattern to temporal pattern of a stimulus would shift attention from the stimulus to time. Interestingly, you are proposing that in the situation you have observed, the effect of temporal pattern shift is just the opposite for reasons I am not clear about.

Dr. Stern: No, I am proposing what you suggest plus that any such nodal change in either direction could serve as a relevant social cue. To understand human behavior we need to pay attention to the stimulus itself as well as the time structure in which it occurs. Sometimes one is more paramount than the other, depending on which social behavior we want to understand.

Dr. Watson: You're absolutely right. There are situations where timing is ultimately the thing of importance; in others, the stimulus per se is more important. However, your specific hypothesis, which is very neat and interesting, is one that should at least be clearly recognized as coming up in opposition to what one would expect from the history of learning as regards temporal conditioning. If you want to clarify the stimulus in conditioning, you wipe out time as a variable. You worry when conditioning with physical stimuli that time may become the salient variable. Brackbill and Fitzgerald's conditioning studies indicate that infants are extraordinarily sensitive to time. Indeed, one might say that if the infant comes into this world with one perceptual organ that is prearranged with tremendous facility, it's the one for perceiving time.

REFERENCES

Berlyne, D. E. Laughter, humor and play. In G. Lindzey & E. Aronson, (Eds.), *Handbook of social psychology* (2nd ed, Vol. 3). Boston: Addison-Wesley, 1969.

Bruner, J. S. The ontogenesis of speech acts. *Journal of Child Language*, 1975, *2*(1), 1–19.

Condon, W. S., & Ogston, W. D. A segmentation of behavior. *Journal of Psychiatric Research*, 1967, *5*, 221–235.

Eisenberg, R. B. Personal communication (1976) and this volume.

Fogel, A. Temporal organization in mother–infant face-to-face interaction. In R. Schaffer, (Ed.), *Studies on interactions in infancy*. New York: Academic Press, 1977.

Getty, D. J. Discrimination of short temporal intervals: A comparison of two models. *Perception and Psychophysics*, 1975, *18*, 1–8.

Gibbon, J. Timing and discrimination of shock density in avoidance. *Psychological Review*, 1972, *79*, 68–92.

Gibbon, J. Scalar expectancy theory and Weber's law in animal timing. *Psychological Review* 1977, *84*, 279–325.

Jaffe, J., & Feldstein, S. *Rhythms of dialogue*. New York: Academic Press, 1960.

Kagan, J. *Change and continuity in infancy*. New York: Wiley, 1971.

Kristofferson, A. B. Low variance stimulus response latencies: Deterministic internal delays. *Perception and Biophysics*, 1976, *20*, 89–100.

Luce, R. D., & Green, D. M. "A neural timing theory for response times and the psychophysics of intensity." *Psychological Reviews,* 1972, *79*, 14–57.

McGill, W. J. Neural counting mechanisms and energy detection in audition. *Journal of Mathematical Psychology*, 1967, *4*, 351–376.

Millar, W. S. A study of operant conditioning under delayed reinforcement in early infancy. *Monographs of the Society for Research in Child Development*, 1972, (Serial No. 147).

Snow, C. "Mother's speech to children learning language." *Child Development*, 1972, *43*, 549–564.

Sroufe, A. L., & Walters, E. The ontogenesis of smiling and laughter: A perspective on the organization of development in infancy. *Psychological Review*, 1976, *83*, 173–189.

Stern, D. N. Mother and infant at play. In M. Lewis & L. Rosenblum (Eds.), *The Effect of the Infant on the Caregiver*. The origin of behavior series. (Vol. 1) New York: Wiley, 1974.

Stern, D. N., Beebe, B., Jaffe, J., & Bennett, S. L. The infant's stimulus world during social interaction: A study of caregiver behaviors with particular reference to repetition and timing. In H. R. Schaffer, (Ed.), *Studies on interactions in infancy*. New York: Academic Press, 1977.

Stern, D. N., Jaffe, J., Beebe, B., & Bennett, S. L. Vocalizing in unison and in alternation: Two modes of communication within the mother–infant dyad. *Annals of the New York Academy of Science*, 1975, *263*, 89–100.

Stern, D. *The First Relationship: Infant and Mother*, the Developing Child Series, J. Bruner, M. Cole, & B. Lloyd (Eds.). Cambridge: Harvard Univ. Press, 1977.

Triesman, M. "Temporal discrimination and the indifference interval: Implications for a model of the "internal clock." *Psychological monographs*, 1963, V77, No. 13.

16 General Discussion

Kathryn Barnard
University of Washington

John H. Kennell
Case Western Reserve University

GENERAL DISCUSSION

Dr. Barnard: There are several points I would like to discuss. All of the papers presented have been extremely interesting and leave me at the end of this conference dealing with both a lot of unknowns and new insights. Feelings of "ahaa, that's it" have been particularly inspiring. First, to Evelyn Thoman's presentation. I have been impressed with her strategy to examine the nature of stability, consistency, and continuity in early mother-infant interactions. We have likewise been struggling with the continuity issue in mother–infant behavior for a group of approximately 200 infants and their mothers. It is hard to identify any stability over the first year of life using traditional linear models and correlational analyses. Therefore I can understand the use of systems theory as a possible model to study mother–infant interaction as a system. It is my hypothesis that since the mother–infant interaction is framed, if you will, in the window of developmental process, the most basic characteristic of the dyad's interaction from time *a* to time *b* will involve a dynamic integration of the changing and evolving behaviors of the infant and those thus elicited in the mother. I think what Dr. Thoman has stated is that even with developmental changes in rates of behavior or kinds of behavior, there is an adaptational characteristic of the dyad reflected in the responsiveness of one member to the other. Emerging from our studies we find the most impressive continuity to be measures of the mother's sensitivity to the infant's cues, her timing of providing a response; for the infant we see the kind and clarity of behavioral cues to be a central issue.

From Lou Sander's presentation I gained a new understanding of the impact the caretaker's responsiveness might have on the entire sleep–wake pattern. I knew that state is important. I have seen the reaction of infants and how it differs based on their state of arousal or tension, but I never fully appreciated what he had been saying before. Thinking of the model he presented, what the caretaker does in the period of wakefulness, the temporal sequencing of the activities of the mother, and the way she goes about bringing the infant to arousal and back down to sleep adds an influence on the whole 24-hour cycling. It is a potentially useful way to examine the link between smaller units of behavior, that is, the mother–infant interaction with larger units—the units of physiological and behavioral arousal and nonarousal. It is a tremendously fascinating model. I am reminded of the mother and the nurse we videotaped in the premature nursery. At separate times we taped the mother and the nurse taking the infant out of the incubator to feed. I was impressed, as we played back the tapes and watched the two caretakers, with what the mother did. She went through a very elaborate procedure of slowly unwrapping, touching, moving the baby's arms, stroking, jiggling, and bouncing the baby for about 20 minutes to bring the infant up to an aroused state, and then she began the feeding. When she was done feeding, she brought the infant down using nonarousal stimuli that were less intense and more regular. Whereas the nurse, when she picked up the baby, immediately began bottle feeding, with no attempt to raise the arousal level of the infant. The two approaches were markedly different in the importance they gave to this responsiveness of the infant. The premature infant in general is less responsive during the early months and as such provides an interesting sample to study when considering the origins of social responsiveness. In that regard, we have been revising the Brazelton Neonatal Assessment Scale to use with the premature. We felt that it was too exhausting to do the exam all at once, and thought, Let's divide it in half. We found the procedure for administering the Brazelton Neonatal Assessment Scale does the same temporal sequencing of stimuli the mother described did in arousing her baby. The administration technique brings the infant to a state of arousal and back down. We have determined you cannot do the exam well without going through the sequence of coming from a sleep state, doing the manipulative items in the general order prescribed, and then bringing the infant back down to a consoled state. If you try to reverse the order, try to use fewer manipulative items, you don't get an alert responsive infant. I think modulation of behavioral arousal is one of the most important qualities to consider during the first months of life. The infant's own ability to come from nonaroused to aroused states and vice versa, plus the caretaker's recognition of this process, will have a powerful influence on the quality of the interaction and social responsiveness.

We have been talking a lot about mothers. What about father involvement? I have gathered the impression over the last few years that how much the father is involved in the care of the infant really depends upon how much the mother lets him get involved. The mother in my view, seems to be the gatekeeper. I think that how easy it is for her to either keep him out or let him in may depend upon the infant. The infant's threshold for stimuli and novelty may be important. Some infants are able to deal with more variety and tempo, and some infants need more regularity; this is probably related to their whole state organization and equilibrium. I remember a mother and father where the father had gone through all the child preparation classes, participated in the childbirth, and was really into this parenting bit. At about 6 months postpartum he said, "This is a bunch of nonsense, it's no partnership." What was happening was that every time he would try to interact with the baby, she would cry, scream. When you observe the infant and the mother, the mother was using a very unique and specific tempoing in her interactions with the infant. She would approach the infant very slowly. She would gradually work up a higher tempo, whereas the father's pattern was to approach the infant without a buildup. At about 8 or 9 months the mother began to recognize this and helped the father modulate his behavior and also varied her behavior more with the infant. I think some of the sex differences brought up at this conference—the male voice, the kind of gestural differences—relate directly to this issue of arousal. Some infants need a more modulated course to get to an "interactive alert state." High-arousal techniques, larger, sharper movements, high voice variability, and so on may serve to bring infants to a high level of arousal too fast, resulting in an overload and subsequent irritabilty.

I felt conceptually Dr. Sander was talking about the overall bio-rhythmicity, and within it he suggested an opportunity to focus on the transitions between arousal and nonarousal to study the overall organization of the infant's responsiveness. From the work of Thoman and Sander we next reviewed the exciting study Dan Stern presented. His arena dealt with smaller units of behavior; however, I see the work dealing with basically the same issues—shifts and levels of behavioral arousal or attending. In Evelyn's work, I felt she was getting at both content issues and signaling powers that the parents and infants had; how they took advantage of signaling with distress, pleasure, talking, and looking. She presented a contrast of signal systems. In one system, the participants were at an advantage in that both the infant and the mother gave a lot of signals (Case 13). Whereas in case 16 there was a low level of signaling between the mother and infant, not as much crying, socializing, looking, talking in total, or interaction. Again, in preterm infants—particularly in the first 6 months after they go home from the hospital—there is a kind of depression of the signalling on the part of the infant. One thing we have found useful with mothers of preterm infants is to help them learn how to get more signals from the infant, to bring them up to a higher state of arousal without getting them overstimulated and hence fussy.

If we are to understand the origins of social responsiveness in the mother–infant pair, we probably will need to go back in time, looking for the answers that abound in the patterns of communication that the couple, the mother and father, have prenatally. The mother's or the father's ability to interact and to relate to one another will form the basic fabric for the character of the infant's emerging behavior. Therefore, if you look first at the partner's ability to signal and respond in an interaction, you already will have a beginning constant to put into the prediction equation of how the infant will respond. Dr. Stern's work on temporal expectancy is an exciting way to think about understanding how the infant begins to deal with learning to sort out the meaning that social stimuli have. Timing is an essential element of all communication. It has not been studied to the extent that content of communication has, and I would suggest that some of the most stable characteristics of behavioral interaction have to do with the sequence, duration, and tempo of the "dance." Thank you for this opportunity.

Dr. Kennell: I would like to start out with comments about a few statements that struck me as I sat through this meeting. It is necessary for us investigators to take into account the large number of perturbations and disturbances that affect the lives and behavior of parents and children in our country. We have heard that human babies have marvelous fail-safe mechanisms and, unlike the infants of other mammalian species, can do well in spite of all sorts of stress. Are we sure of this? Then yesterday, I sensed it was implied that what we do with human babies now is the way babies have been cared for almost from the beginning of time, for example, putting a baby to bed all alone on a flat surface. I would like to propose that that itself is an intervention, a perturbation. There are many, many interventions in our present care of babies that differ from what our human ancestors did. I suspect that in many of our infancy studies we should pay close attention to how the infants started out with their mothers and fathers. For example, at this point 9 out of 10 studies show that if a mother and her full-term baby are together right after birth, there will be significant effects on the mother's behavior for months and years, and in 3 studies the babies are different. When I review papers about the behavior of infants, I often wonder whether the behavior reported is due to an early mother–infant separation. My first slide shows the French painting *Bringing Home the Newborn Calf.* The painter, Millet, shows what Bill Mason and those who care for animals know—that you must keep the mother and her baby together in the period after delivery or there may be a disastrous outcome for the baby.

The next slide shows a mother and her baby on a delivery floor in an extremely busy maternity hospital in Guatemala City, where space would seem inadequate by U.S. standards. There are 60 deliveries a day here, but it is still possible to find a room where a mother can have privacy, where you can put a mother and her baby together under a heat panel to keep the baby warm in that period immediately after birth when the mother and the baby are unusually alert and prepared for interaction. The baby spends 45 to 60 minutes of the first hour in State 4, the quiet alert state. At the same time the mother is in a maximum level of arousal.

How many of the disturbances in the state and behavior of infants are due to lack of mother–infant contact in the first hours? And how many are due to babies' starting out in the standard nursery, with multiple caretakers, that Lou Sander described?

The papers and our discussions have put a strong emphasis on distance receptors, visual and auditory, how much time the mother and baby look at each other, and the response of the mother to her baby's cry. If we consider that the agricultural and industrial periods represent only 1% of the history of human existence, at most 10,000 years, then we are in a position to take a fresh look at care of the infant and consider the perturbations and stresses he experiences.

During almost all his time on earth man has lived as a hunter and gatherer. In this phase of existence, the mother carried the baby on her body all the time. The two slept together, and because the mother usually had to walk a great distance each day—about 3000 miles a year—she could carry only one baby. This had powerful influence on birth control, with the minimal spacing 3 to 4 years. It was extremely important for the mother to continue breastfeeding for a long period, probably for 3 to 4 years. Most of the foods available to hunters and gatherers are difficult for a baby to manage until he is 3 or 4 years old. So the introduction of solid foods, which practically occurs on the delivery table at present, was 3 or 4 years off for babies born in that culture.

Is the cry of the young infant that we have been talking about and that we hear so frequently peculiar to our culture? I understand that infant animals living under natural circumstances cry quite infrequently. When you visit a developing country, it is surpising to discover that you rarely hear little babies cry. Strangers to the culture may comment that this is because the baby is malnourished or sick, but the lack of crying occurs with healthy and alert infants also. Is the large amount of infant crying in our country a result of our baby care practices that differ so much from the close contact, abundant body movement, and frequent nursing of our hunter–gatherer ancestors? And in our studies have we paid too much attention to visual and auditory behavior, because we adults are interested in vision and hearing? Have we neglected other modalities of communication, such as the tactile and vestibular?

Let's look at some evidence that may give us an idea of how babies were living during the many, many previous centuries of human existence, and the types of cycles and rhythms they experienced. Ben Shaul (1962) surveyed the composition of mother's milk in more than 100 mammalian species and found that the milks differed greatly in protein and fat composition. This was not related to the size of the animals. However, there was a strong correlation between the milk composition and the frequency of feeding the young, with a distinct difference in protein and fat concentration between infrequent feeders who were cached away for long periods while the mother was away, and the composition of the milk of continuous feeders.

In certain rabbits, feedings occur once every 24 hours. The mother's milk has a high caloric density and a high protein and high fat content. In the great blue whale, feedings are widely spaced and the protein and fat content are also extremely high. In the Midwest we don't know how often a whale nurses, but it is so complicated that we can't believe it could be more than every 12 hours.

In contrast, higher primates have constant access to the nipple, feed nearly continuously and their milks have a low protein and fat content. Human milk is almost identical to that of the other primates, and according to Blurton Jones (1972), has the characteristic protein and fat content of continuous feeders. Observations of mothers sleeping with their babies throughout the night in developing countries confirm this pattern. The longest interval between feedings was 20 minutes. And, significantly, in those cultures there was almost no crying. The animals that are fed at widely spaced intervals show the fastest sucking rates. For example, the rabbit empties the breast in 4 to 5 minutes, whereas with the stump-tailed Macacque monkey, feedings last 10–30 minutes and occur at about half-hourly intervals. In addition, much time is spent with the nipple in the mouth without sucking.

In the slow rate of human suckling—I believe Rita mentioned how long mothers breast feed—provides highly suggestive support for adaptations in the baby to match those in the mother for continuous contact between them. Thus it would appear that the human is a continuous feeder. How did the change to 4-hour feedings come about in the United States? With a partial historical review, it is evident that the schedule was strongly recommended by German pediatricians who were the leaders of pediatric beliefs and practices at the turn of the century. Pediatricians in the United States, such as the senior Professor Emmett Holt and his textbook in 1914, strongly advocated this. In regard to timing influences on the infant, I wonder if the infant's timer isn't already set during the 9 months of pregnancy and then readjusted with the mother's speech to the baby, shortly after birth when mother and baby are together. Then, in spite of what we say about demand feeding, the 4-hour schedule is still an expectancy of a great proportion of mothers. We need to ask what that's doing to babies.

To go back to the hunter–gatherer, Bowlby (1969) has proposed that attachment of the infant to the mother is predominantly an antipredator device. Wasn't it perhaps necessary for the helpless newborn infant of our ancestors not to cry, and to have compellingly attractive features at birth to draw the mother to the infant so that she would hold and breast feed immediately after birth? This was probably necessary so that attachment would develop rapidly, so that the mother's desire to protect her baby from predators would override her concerns for her own safety.

Lou, if the human mother and baby were kept in constant tactile contact, that is, the baby on the mother's body during the day and in the same bed together at night, how much of a disturbance of the biorhythms would there be? Would there be the same period of perturbation, and would there be the crying that we're used to? I'm intrigued that Evelyn, in another study, showed that a baby stops crying quickly and easily if picked up by the mother in the first minute and a half after crying starts—a very important observation. But there were great difficulties in soothing the baby if the crying extended beyond that period. When the mother and baby are in close tactile contact, is it likely the baby would cry for a period as long as 90 seconds? I don't think so. Johnny Lind (see Wasz-Hockert, 1968) the Swedish pediatrician has studied the characteristics of infants' cries. He has identified a characteristic sonogram for a hunger cry and another characteristic sonogram for a pain cry. It's of interest that the characteristic hunger cry of a baby becomes converted after 4 or 5 minutes to a characteristic pain cry. In summary, I believe we have to think more about the behavior of mothers and infants through most of human existence. There is much we can learn if we take advantage of the opportunity to study the effects of care techniques in U. S. hospitals and homes that cause perturbations to babies. I also hope there can be more studies of other sensory modalities, such as smell. It's been shown by Aidan MacFarlane (1975) at Oxford that babies can identify their mother's breast pads specifically by 5 days after birth. Looking at this from the other direction, mother after mother tells me she can identify her baby by its special smell. The vestibular, proprioceptive and tactile modalities are difficult to measure, but that's a challenge for us.

Evelyn, your paper gave me the excitement of reading a suspenseful murder mystery. I came to this paper with a great interest in how to study and analyze and follow interactions, so it was intriguing to read your description of the systems approach. But just as in a good mystery, it began to seem almost impossibly difficult to apply this to the analysis of mother–infant interaction. Then the plot thickened as I thought about the fantastic amount of data to be analyzed and correlated. And you presented statements about the individuality of each mother–infant dyad, and this gave me great concerns about those things that physicians have been criticized for—subjective observations and generalizations from information accumulated from intensive psychoanalytic studies or long-term pediatric care. But as you heard yesterday, my concerns were ill-founded. I should have had faith in the great detective who had previously shown her skill at solving other mysteries of mother–infant interaction. I was impressed that detective Evelyn took an enormous risk by making predictions at an early time. We couldn't help but admire her and take a sigh of relief for the evidence of her success in the prediction. I am not sure I would have the courage to say that on the basis of high mutuality at one age you could predict high mutuality at a later age. For example, what will happen in the second year?

The description you gave of lack of responsiveness in Baby 16 in the early observations is striking to a pediatrician. I can't help but question whether the baby's contribution to this had a direct connection with the poor level of functioning at 1 year. Can we differentiate whether this was due to an innate quality of the baby or the result of the interaction that was presented so well in your paper? Was one partner responsible for the deficiencies in the interaction? Did the baby have an abnormal central nervous system? Was there a factor such as illness or the small size of the baby or a hospital rule that separated the mother and infant early and affected the mother's attachment and mothering behavior that then in turn produced a different type of baby? Was there a lack of mothering experience? Did the mother have a distorted view of the baby? These are some of the questions and factors that come to mind when we see babies who are failing to thrive. That is, not only whether the baby is not gaining weight normally but whether the baby is not developing normally. If a pediatrician saw Baby and Mother 16 at 2 to 4 weeks, what could he have done to improve the infant's personal–social development? Should he have done anything? With Mother–baby couplet 13, would an intervention have disturbed the interaction and resulted in a less satisfactory outcome?

Lou Sander, I mentioned perturbations because you have taken the opportunity to study some that occur in the course of the care of normal newborn infants. You have been helpful to physicians and nurses caring for mothers and infants because take ordinary situations and show vividly what effects they have on babies and what they do to mothers and other caretakers. I would like to ask you whether the fact that those mothers and babies were probably separated after birth—caused some of the difficulties?

Dr. Watson: I wanted to make a comment regarding your statement that you are interested in interactions and not in main effects in analysis of variance because you took this interaction to be your guide. If you're interested in interactions of variables, then you would not have a sensitive tool for guiding you, because the analysis of variance is not good at picking up Lawful interactions. It's only good at picking them up in the very special cases of crossovers in direction of effects for the particular levels of independent variables you have assessed. There can be all kinds of interactive models that it cannot sense. In others, it will end up showing 2–5% of the variance accounted for by interaction, and that will not be significant unless you've got a jillion subjects. So if you use significant interaction in analysis of variance as a guide to know where to turn because you believe it's relevant to be dealing in the terrain in which interactions appear, then you'll have a terribly insensitive tool guiding you. I think you can at best consider the logical implications of your systems prospective and use them in your decision of where to go and what to follow.

Dr. Thoman: My only response to that is that there are a number of people who are very much interested in developing statistical approaches to doing analyses of data from individual subjects. John Gettman and a number of other people have begun to explore this kind of possibility, and that's what we want to do in addition to sequential analysis and so on. With some form of pattern analysis—which is not the analysis of variance model—that one can apply to an individual subject. I don't think we're in disagreement on that.

Dr. Lipsitt: I do have a comment I want to make. In your own summary of what has happened here over the past few days, I think you left out an important issue or a constellation of issues that has arisen, and I put them all under the theme of reciprocating relationships: reciprocities between human beings in particular; reciprocities between mother and child or between infant and caretaker. Behavioral psychologists would represent this as responses leading to stimuli leading to responses leading to stimuli and so on. I think you once called it the dance that goes on between people. And Kathy talked about the mother and child waltzing to the same tune. Those are very good poetic expressions for what is going on. The behavioral way would be to try to tease apart who is engaging in what responses when, and what kinds of stimuli these responses become for the other person in the dyad. So I think there is a sixth theme that I heard in many different presentations here, which would be this notion of reciprocating relationships, and I'd like to say beyond that that reciprocities need not take place just between two humans. They can take place between one human and his environment, and this is what goes on in play behavior with toys. A child moves something in a certain way, and having engaged in that response, he changes the stimuli that he now is exposed to and appreciates in some different way. Having changed those stimuli, he now behaves differently. And having behaved differently, he has changed the stimulus situation again. So the child is constantly engaging in a reciprocating relationship with his environment even when he's engaged in solitary play. Similarly, I would say that my own studies have a lot to do with reciprocity even though I, for the most part, study infants alone in the laboratory with me, and the kind of reciprocity that I mean here is that I implement various kinds of stimulus situations to which the baby behaves, and the environment behaves back to him. This all has to do with contingent reinforcement of course. It has to do with the way in which I flip the toggle switch as to what kind of fluid the baby will get on his tongue. And when I flip the toggle one way the baby gets a sweeter fluid, and when I flip it the other way he gets a less-sweet fluid, and he changes his behavior as a consequence of that. Having changed his behavior he changes the response contingencies, so that he is, even within the first few days of life, the controller of his environment and controlled by it.

Dr. Sander: There is a difference between reciprocating relationships and co-occurrence, and I think we've also been touching on the latter.

Dr. Eisenberg: It seems to me if you want to tie in anything that I'm doing in terms of the things that Lew has just said, I'm not working with contingencies. What I'm really working with I guess ties in with what John said. It's a situation in which the child has nothing except his natural defenses to cope with what I'm doing to him, because he's on a fixed schedule and no matter what he does that schedule is going on. And if he doesn't like it he can cope with it only by those intrinsic behaviors that he possesses at the time. That is, he can scream because he hates it; he can to to sleep because he wants to go to sleep or because he wants to block me out, but it's still an interaction with the environment, and that's the way the environment is; and it's not a very good one, I'll grant you, but that's it. And it is also in the same way that Lew establishes a contingency—this is a nonnatural contingency that he establishes. The thing that concerns me is that I felt that what I had to say was really not terribly relevant to anything else that went on here because I'm not concerned with the mother–child relationship. This is something quite different, because the way the mother can respond to the child depends on what the child is, and I'm trying to define that.

Dr. Thoman: So it's highly relevant to what we were all talking about.

Dr. Eisenberg: But it isn't highly relevant to anything else that went on in the conference, it seems to me.

Dr. Thoman: This is most relevant. Because a major theme of this conference has been: What is the baby like after birth, what are the characteristics or the capabilities of this organism when he or she is born? The dramatic thing is that the baby is quite obviously capable of a great deal more even than we've even been saying, and for years we've been saying the baby's capable of a great deal more than we used to think!

Dr. Barnard: In fact we have to have that kind of information if we're going to understand—the origins of social responsiveness.

Dr. Parmelee: Dr.Stern what do you envisage as the mechanism used by the infant in timing events?

Dr. Stern: This paper was not the one I intended to give or write for this conference. What happened was I got interested in the phenomenon, and then its importance grew on me. I began to review the literature, and I haven't finished that to my own satisfaction. From what I've read so far, I cannot give you any good neurophysiological or anatomical mechanistic notions of how the timing mechanisms work with the exception of Poisson timing, which has been addressed by a number of people. With regard to scalar timing, I haven't the foggiest idea how that works. On the other hand, I'm not sure anybody really knows how Weber's law works, in the sense you are asking. As far as absolute timing is concerned, nobody has proposed how that works either, so I'm afraid I draw a blank for your question. It's something that I plan to explore further.

Dr. Parmelee: I guess what I was fishing for is a discussion of some kind of neurophysiological timing mechanism. We must have an internal clock or multiple clocks.

Dr. Stern: I suspect we do. I may be talking off the top of my head, but it seems to me that the only major advance in timing is the ability to count, learning arithmetic. What that does in a sense is it adds a learned accumulator on top of the neurobiological. I can now take a scalar unit, a second, which I've learned, which we've all learned, "one chimpanzee, two chimpanzees" or however we learn it. With that unit I can count up to 10 of them, and my variance now will be lower. It'll be I think probably somewhere between Poisson and scalar timing. That is a guess. So far as the human being versus the rat is concerned, it seems to me the only advance we've made is the ability to add and count, other than inventing watches. Actually when you think about it, even the atomic clock, which is perhaps the most sophisticated, is essentially a Poisson mechanism. What it does is produce impulses resulting from radioactive decay, and then when it accumulates so many impulses it says that a unit of time is up. An oscillator mechanism is different. That would be more like absolute timing because you know exactly what the oscillation of the crystal is, which is like the pendulum. I think the abstract notion of time rather than clocking mechanisms per se is what we first need to pay more attention to.

Dr. Sander: Is it conceivable that what we're trying to get at has to do with entirely other systems. One difference between that rat and the man has to do with the ability to become aware of inner events or one's own state. The number of different avenues for match or mismatch is really related to that. You don't need different clocks. You've just got to have a different mechanism for appreciating events with the multiplicity of components making up the systems. If you assume two highly complex organizations as being in synchrony, say they're in a reasonably stable equilibrium, and you have just the smallest component of one slipping unit of synchrony, that one small event on the background of this complexity would then make a sharp figure–ground sort of contrast. It's just that their differences may involve some other part of our evolutionary development than a difference in clocks or timing mechanisms.

Dr. Parmelee: I find Dan's ideas very exciting and think they have applications to what many of us are doing—and certainly for the kinds of work going on in Sander's lab. In terms of my own work, which mainly has to do with how the infant is organized, I find myself teased by the notion of a timing mechanism that serves as a kind of "central regulator," for lack of a better term. If one conceives of discrete systems—motor, sensory, or whatever you like—as having independent neurophysiologic characteristics that determine system(s) behavior in time, one finds oneself faced with the question of how these separate systems operate synchronously; and the only reasonable answer seems to be that there must be some kind of central mechanism, that prescribes the bounds within which any of the systems can interact. From a clinical standpoint, then, if there were such a mechanism, it should affect not just one modality or system, but all of them; and it perhaps might be important to pursue biomodal studies with a view to differentiating infants at risk of CNS dysfunction. As a matter of fact, there are so many useful avenues of inquiry suggested by the notion of a central timer that I will be hard put not to be sidetracked into examining them when I get back to my lab.

Dr. Parmelee: You're implying that a fairly well developed cybernetic system has to be present.

Dr. Eisenberg: Right. You said it more elegantly than I, but that's essentially what I meant.

Dr. Parmelee: The development of state organization might be a way such a cybernetic system is indexed.

Dr. Eisenberg: I don't know whether I would put it quite that way. I doubt whether we can be that precise right now, because I don't think there's enough data to think with. However, I do think the kind of thing Dan's doing may lead us in the direction of precision, and that's one of the reasons it seems so important to me. I know that one thing I'm going to do when I get back home is to calculate the means, standard deviations, and standard errors of the anticipatory responses we've picked up for our subjects in order to quantify what we're seeing more precisely: It's something I hadn't hitherto considered doing.

Dr. Watson: My excitement over what Dan is doing relates to a grand philosophical issue, which is that traditionally time is conceived as a variable only in the sense that it is the medium in which events occur. In our relatively recent philosophical tradition, time is disallowed as a cause per se. It is often assumed that because time is not a tangible thing, it cannot enter into our causal network. That seems to be wrong. Not only is time a potential variable that can control cycling of actions within the body but also things happen in time and there are mechanisms for perceiving coordinations of timing physical events in the world, such as sun and light and gravity shifts. I think Dan is beginning to point to perceptual mechanism for perceiving time variables directly and outside of one's body. It seems that you perceive time with an organ just as you perceive light with an organ and sound with an organ. This is a temporal organ that one is considering. It may have a counting base. It obviously has to have some basic chemical, physiological, neurological base. But its function is to perceive an event that is temporal. To anticipate is to perceive time. I think we are beginning to experience a shift philosophically about what time is. Time is now becoming a cause in the state of affairs, something that can function like a physical stimulus, truly like a stimulus–in a sense even tangible like a stimulus.

Dr. Parmelee: Are you saying the baby is matching time intervals to some internal reverberrating circuit or oscillator?

Dr. Stern: You mean when I talked theoretically. Yes, I don't see how else. I think with the scalar process the unit is given by an external source, however you want to label it. After that it gets in the head as a schema perhaps.

Dr. Eisenberg: Maybe one of the things that makes institutionalized babies different is that events are not temporally patterned in a way they can get enough practice to develop their timing mechanisms properly. One might look at it that way.

Dr. Stern: I would imagine, speaking physiologically, the most important timing mechanism is the one that's going to relate to the mother's social behavior. The macrorhythms are going to be the ones that Lou is talking about.

Dr. Eisenberg: I think that the macrorhythms also might be conditioned by maternal interventions.

Dr. Stern: One thing I'd like to add with regard to what John said concerns the 3-second criterion, which I don't really get to talk about. Once the mother has stopped vocalizing for 3 seconds she becomes so unlawful as to when she will start up again that the baby can't anticipate it. In a sense, what he's got to do is wait for her to start again to reset the unit timer, so to speak.

Dr. Thoman: That was very important.

Dr. Stern: I left that out. It's clear I believe in the paper.

Dr. Eisenberg: Say it explicitly. It's very important.

Dr. Stern: If you don't present a reinforcement for an infant within 3 seconds, as I recall the literature, learning goes down very rapidly. That seems to be the limit of whatever short-term memory is involved in contingent learning. The frequency distribution of mother's vocal pauses (Figure 1) shows a falloff by 3 seconds. And so, on that basis I chose 3 seconds as the cutoff of a time-in episode. Also, if the mother stops for 3 seconds, when she will resume becomes extremely and unlawfully variable because she may have stopped for one of a million reasons. She stopped either because she has nothing more to say or because she's changing the bottle or because she's answering the telephone or because someone else has walked into the room. Accordingly, 3 seconds may represent the point of an upward shift out of the scalar range where the baby says, "The devil with this I'm going to stop counting till I get something a little more lawful coming in."

Dr. Barnard: One of the interesting things we have found in looking at verbalization episodes and pause periods in mothers and infants over the first year of life is that a change in the mothers' and infants' verbal and pause behavior occurs in our 8 months data. The mother begins to pause twice as much, it's almost as if she's developing an expectation that the infant should verbalize. It's very fascinating, and you also see a great big jump in both infant and mother verbalizations in terms of frequency.

Dr. Eisenberg: There are any number of breaks at 8 months—just as there are at 4 months.

Dr. Barnard: This reminds me of data we were reviewing in terms of the role that the startle has in triggering a different timing mechanism in respiration.

Dr. Sander: That occurs in sleep cycling—a startle often ushers in the quiet sleep period. I don't know how to integrate that. Maybe Arthur has some notions about that. What role has the startle as you begin to get into the transition to quite sleep? Is its function to synchronize the systems that have been desynchronized in the REM sleep? It's a marker of the transition between REM and NREM sleep side stages.

Dr. Parmelee: I don't know the answer to your question Dr. Sander.

Dr. Thoman: Thank you all. We are at a point where we could be just beginning—the best sign of a productive conference!

REFERENCES

Ben Schaul, D. M. Notes on hand-rearing various species of mammals, *International Zoo Yearbook, 4,* 300.

Blurton Jones, N. In Blurton Jones, N., *Ethological studies of child behavior,* Cambridge University Press, 1972.

Bowlby, J. *Attachment and loss,* (Vol. 1). New York: Basic Book Inc. 1969.

MacFarlane, A. Olfaction in the development of social preferences in the human neonate, in *Parent to Infant Interaction,* Ciba Foundation Symposium 33 (new series) Amsterdam, 1975, Elsevier Publishing Co., 103–117.

IV CONCLUDING COMMENTARY

17 Changing Views of the Being and Becoming of Infants

Evelyn B. Thoman
University of Connecticut

"The world is full of obvious things which nobody by any chance ever observes."—Sherlock Holmes.

The papers and discussions at this conference clearly indicate an emergence of some dramatically different perspectives in the study of infancy. They reflect changes in basic assumptions about the nature of infants and the reasons for studying them from the earliest days of life. These changes in assumptions open up new doors upon the research directions of the future, and these new vantage points may enable us to perceive adaptive behaviors of infants that "nobody by any chance" has yet observed. This chapter will be devoted to clues, primarily from the Nantucket Conference, that support such an optimistic prediction.

Clues to the future rest not only in the present but in the past. Thus, it is necessary to examine the assumptions that have guided our research in the past. Some of these assumptions about infants are implicit ones, recognizable only by their influence on ongoing research. These are like myths with their hidden morality. Other assumptions, though made explicit, have been around for a very long with time with no critical concern for the extent to which they may be obstructing or distorting our perspective. These may also be no more than myths. Myths about infancy inherently involve both social and scientific components: In the social realm, they reflect the values that are held pertaining to infants; and at the scientific level they determine what we look for in the study of babies and how we interpret what is found. This is the old story of the Zeitgeist and scientific study.

The Myth that the Infant is Deficient at Birth

A major form of mythology about infancy has been that the infant, especially during the neonatal period, is an incomplete, relatively incompetent and inadequate organism; and that by a series of linear progressions, the infant becomes a complex, competent, and complete organism—an adult. Such a view is a logical and emotional heritage of the supposedly discarded notion that the infant is a miniature adult with a *tabula rasa,* helpless and passive, dependent on an imprint from the mature caretaker who provides a model for limitation and a stimulus for learning adult modes of thinking and behaving. For example, we are all familiar with the long-held notion that the newborn infant is not yet capable of learning. This conclusion was based on claims that at birth and for some time thereafter, the human infant is functionally decorticate, largely a reflex organism, controlled primarily by its internal environment and organic processes while responsive to only a small number of external inputs. As Stone, Smith, and Murphy (1973) point out, only baby biographers and mothers knew better! Now we have ample evidence from the findings of such researchers as Eisenberg, Korner, Lipsitt, Parmelee, Papousek, and Watson that the infant is capable of coping competently for his or her particular level of development. Their findings, however, are relatively new, and many people are not aware of these data— or do not fully appreciate their implications. Thus they still hold to the deficit model of infancy and thereby seriously limit their views and viewing of the human at this stage of life.

The Myth of Additive Elements:
How Many Competencies Make a Competent Infant?

The recent history of the study of infancy has been a dramatic one with a burgeoning number of studies exploring numerous facets of the infant's competency and behavior. Emde and Robinson(1976) describe this trend in the study of infants very aptly. Referring to the enthusiasm for demonstrating that the newborn infant is indeed organized, they note that researchers have used concepts such as "conditioning," "habituation," "attention," and more recently "competence" to justify research programs directed towards demonstrating a previously undiscovered capacity in the newborn. It need not matter how many infants it takes in order to find some who can reach the criterion of experimental results—it only matters that the capacity be demonstrated.

Like the college sophomore and the laboratory rat, the human infant has become a favorite laboratory subject, and highly refined techniques have been developed for exploring the infant's repertoire of sensory and response capabilities. In commenting on the numerous and diverse studies of early infancy, Stone, Smith, and Murphy (1973) say, "From our perch overlooking the vast new landscape of infancy, a landscape thrown up like a new volcanic island in the past decade and a half, we have come not only to marvel at how much new information has been produced but also to see how badly it needs to be digested... particularly needed now is research that links and relates specific, sometimes atomistic findings [p. 9]." It may be that the very atomistic nature of the accumulation of findings renders them indigestible. The unspoken assumption, or myth, seems to be that if we know enough about all the bits and pieces, we may eventually be able to put them together and be able to understand a real infant adapting to a real environment.

The bits-and-pieces kind of thinking also illustrates how our assumptions influence our methodology. Given an assumption of atomism, it follows that an acceptable methodology is the use of successive cross-sectional samples from which one infers the developmental course of *individual* infants.

Segmentation in science is a practical necessity as a strategy for selecting manageable-sized phenomena for study. However, taking the elements, viewed in isolation, too seriously is the essence of the reductionist view namely that a whole organism can be derived additively from information about the separate components.

An example from the literature illustrates this point. Highly sophisticated experiments have now demonstrated the infant's sensitivity to a variety of stimuli in all the sense modalities, including selective attention to classes of stimuli generally found in the infant's typical environment (see Eisenberg's chapter 1, this volume). Thus, we have begun to know a great deal about the baby's perception of the world. To do this research the investigator studies a single sense isolated from the other senses. However, the methodological convenience of studying the senses separately has been accompanied by a serious theoretical view that reifies the separation of the senses in the baby: a view maintaining that the infant's sensory systems initially operate independently of each other; and that the developmental task of the infant is to unify their functioning, that is, to integrate the sensations that the infant experiences in the multimodal environmental space. An opposing position, taken by Bower and Wishart, is called the "primitive unity hypothesis" and maintains that the infant is a multimodal organism from the time of birth. Although their findings and interpretations are somewhat controversial, the perceptual phenomena they describe clearly indicate a level of sensory integration that cannot be accounted for in an additive fashion.

Rejection of the additive-elements myth finds support in philosophical notions from the "hard" science of physics. Anderson (1972), in a paper entitled "More Is Different," describes the symmetric relations between analysis and synthesis. He explains that although the elements of a crystal can be separated and identified, the converse is not true—that is, it is not possible from a knowledge of the particles of a crystal to predict its symmetry. The organization of the crystal is an emergent property not present in any of the elements. As Anderson points out, some properties of every system are emergent. The total infant is such a system with emergent properties and cannot be predicted from the elements of its functioning. Thus, the complexity of an infant is far more than the total sum of all the identifiable competencies, impressive though they may be.

The Myth of Futurism:
Is Infancy only a Period of Promise?

A persisting assumption, generally implicit but occasionally made explicit, is that the period of early infancy is not of great significance because 1) the events of this stage of life are "forgotten," and 2) except in the case of extreme conditions, there are no demonstrated relations between characteristics in early infancy and those in the mature person. Despite overwhelming evidence from studies at the animal level (see Denenberg's chapter 10, this volume), the prevailing view has been that nothing of great consequence happens during the earliest period of life. It might be added that this view is also held despite the enormous amount of time and energy expended in human psychotherapy to retrieve or "deal with" critical events that have occurred during the "forgotten" ages of early infancy and childhood.

It may seem paradoxical to maintain that early infancy is not considered to be of sufficient importance to warrant concern, whereas the previous section noted that vast number of studies focusing on the early months of life. However, as was suggested, a primary purpose of these studies is to use the baby as a "handy gadget" for exploring separable behavioral processes. Implied in such laboratory studies is the assumption that the immature organism is a simplified version of the mature one; and thus perceptual, motor and cognitive processes can more easily be explored in this relatively uncomplicated organism. It should be emphasized that in such a context the infant *as infant* is definitely not the significant object of the research (in the same way that the laboratory rat is not of central significance in most pyschological studies that use this subject).

Some major characteristics of current research reflect this detached view of the infant. First, there has been relatively little interest in focusing on the early postnatal period as an important time to begin the exploration of developmental processes in the human infant. Despite the fact that numerous studies have been made during the early postnatal period, these are typically cross-sectional in nature, and the newborn period has not generally been an age for intensive longitudinal study. Notable exceptions to this general statement include the work of Papousek, Sander, and Thoman.

Cross-sectional, or time-point, studies are far more fashionable, as indicated in the previous section. These do not deal with development, and to that extent they do not deal with the infant—a very rapidly developing organism. Beginning at the time of birth when the infant is closest to its biological heritage, the rapid changes reflect *processes* involved in adaptive modifications. Process, by definition, occurs in time; and therefore in order to understand the infant's organization, it is necessary to observe and describe the many changes that occur within the earliest period of life. Only by study of the infant's earliest organizational changes will it be possible to understand the developmental processes by which the infant modifies and is modified by the environment.

Another facet of the study of infancy in which the infant, as such, is not the central core of concern, is the design and exploitation of measurement procedures with the purpose of relating infant behavior to later development. A variety of such measures have been explored, including patterns of sucking, visual attention, and behavioral state, as well as electrophysiological measures of heart rate, respiration, muscle tone, and brain activity. Along with more general developmental assessment procedures, these various measures are used to identify infants who may be at risk for developmental difficulties. Certainly, the prediction of risk status is extremely important for babies in need of early intervention. However, aside from screening for risk status, an underlying assumption for most assessment research is that if more refined techniques could be devised, later development should be more predictable even within the range of normal infants. The search for a mythical single-test tool is still on!

Since assessment procedures are typically used in cross-sectional or time-point type of studies, they are, therefore, not generally used as a means of understanding the infant as a developing organism. Except within the range of the abnormal baby, there should be little reason to expect predictability from the earliest period to the growing child or adult—when one considers the multitude of interactional events that occur during the course of development. As Denenberg, and Wohlwill (1973) have carefully pointed out, the developmental course of individual infants may not be linear nor even unidirectional. Thus, an emphasis on the refinement of assessment procedures should not necessarily be expected to lead to better prediction.

An overconcern for prediction derives from the underlying futuristic notion that the purpose of the human infant and child is to become an adult. Thus being a competent infant is of importance because it may predict a competent child and later adult. There is still far more interest in predicting and in accelerating development than there is in understanding it. Bower and Wishart (chapter 3) provide evidence that attempts at acceleration may be successful but at the risk of interfering with the later developmental course of those skills.

And finally, assessment primarily for prediction fails to take into account the great likelihood that the *present* level of the infant's functioning is of significance, that accurate description of the infant's status is important at each age. Since a person's behavior at any time is an interactive function of accumulated experience (see Denenberg's chapter 10), the neonatal stage of the life process is as important as any later age of being.

The Myth of Emotional Blandness: Does the Infant Have an Affective Life?

The infant's competence as a perceiver and performer has received a great deal of attention; whereas the infant's competence as a feeling being has received relatively little attention. Casual observation rather than scientific studies have led to the conclusion that the newborn infant has little affect, particularly of a positive nature. Although the infant's smiles are no longer considered to be "gas produced," they are only taken into account as reflexes occurring during drowsiness or active (REM) sleep. Rumblings of serious dissent with this bland view of the infant's emotional life were among the most dramatic ideas that emerged from the Nantucket Conference. Eisenberg observed smiling to auditory stimuli; Papousek found that giving a "correct response" was accompanied by a reduction in arousal, whereas arousal increased following the failure to perform the response; Watson (1966, 1967) has described a similar reaction with older infants; Lipsitt described changes in infants' sucking patterns as a function of the taste of the liquid they received—and he discussed their response in terms of the "pleasures" and "annoyances" of infants.

These findings bring to mind Wolff's (1966) suggestion that the newborn smiles in response to mild and unexpected stimuli, a suggestion that has not been followed up as yet. Given the variety of new findings, the time appears to be ripe to study this topic systematically.

Is our Sciencing Myth-Guided?

It has been noted (1) that segmental studies of infants are consistent with the myth that differing compentencies are separate and additive; (2) that research is influenced by the myth that the infant is a simplified organism that makes a convenient laboratory subject in which to study learning and perceptual paradigms; and finally, (3) that scientific detachment has been maintained by the myth that the infant has little by way of an affective life other than distress expressed by crying. It is further assumed (4) that experiences of early discomforts, of pain—or of pleasure—are so soon forgotten, or their effects so modified, that the earliest period of life is relatively unimportant. These notions all reflect a deficit model of infancy.

Additional related myths influence the study of infancy. One derives from the assumption that the infant is a pre–mature adult and that therefore adult models of behavior apply equally to infants. Researchers are still struggling valiantly to superimpose on the infant learning and other behavior paradigms that were derived from, and may only be applicable to, adult humans. As a result the adaptive capabilities of the infant have been grossly under-estimated, as the infant's lack of performance has been taken to indicate the *inability* of the infant to learn or perceive. Such findings have often reflected our inability to provide the biologically relevant stimulus conditions to elicit the infant's performance. This point was made dramatically by Gunther at the 1961 CIBA Conference, where she showed films of newborn infants during their first feeding at the mother's breast. Those infants who experienced smothering by having the nose occluded by the breast fought and struggled against being put to the mother's breast at subsequent feedings. Her films provided the first clear documentation of the newborn's adaptive modifica-tion to the circumstances of its environment. Given biologically relevant stimulus conditions, the infants showed themselves capable of an adaptive response. Such conditions would hardly be appropriate for studying the *mature* human. Gunther's work undoubtedly inspired many researchers to rush to the laboratory in the search for additional competencies of the mysterious newborn.

It has become fashionable to explore the infant experimentally, and the success of such studies has been increasingly assured by an increasing use of the infant's natural behavioral repertoire and by designing stimulus conditions more appropriate for the infant. As pointed out earlier, a basic assumption is that the findings can be combined summatively toward explaining infant behavior. This limiting perspective is related to the notion made explicit, or else held implicitly, that behavior can be conceptualized within a mechanistic, causal, and reductionistic framework. As Denenberg points out, it is necessary, important, and useful to identify causal relationships between events and behaviors in the laboratory, using relatively short time intervals. Outside the laboratory also, environmental events obviously play an important role in behavioral changes. Systematic study of short-term causal relationships is essential in identifying the responsiveness of infants to variation in stimulus conditions, and to establishing capabilities of infants for modifying their responses to stimuli.

However, cross-sectional studies of causal relations do not constitute developmental study. Development is a process which, by definition, occurs over time. As Sander says, the research orientation is traditionally analytic; the developmental process is essentially integrative, involving the synthesis of highly complex determinants. By the same logic that single assessment in infancy cannot be expected to predict to a later age, single events in infancy—whether experimentally imposed or occurring naturally—cannot be expected to have an identifiable effect at a later age. The infant does not grow in a vacuum, nor in a controlled laboratory; nor is the infant a passive victim of events. Thus, the developmental course of each infant is, in some ways, unique.

Clinicians have generally been more aware of the importance of the accumulative interactive nature of development than researchers. Emde, Gaensbauer, and Harmon (1976) explain that although it is sometimes possible during therapy to retrospectively thread out important events in the life history of a person, it is not possible to predict through a multiplicity of factors which ones will be relevant at some future time. The theoretical implications of ongoing interactional effects producing a developmental course that may not be predictable is discussed in detail by Denenberg. In light of the obvious complexities referred to only briefly here, a causal model for development is simplistic—and as limiting as any myth.

Support for this unconventional statement comes again from the science of physics. Bunge maintains that causation is just one among four different types of determination. According to Bunge (1968), the causal principle,

> even though it constitutes a very special form of the principle of determinism, . . . is part of the philosophic engine of scientific research. Every time we proclaim its universal extension we err. But every time we adopt it as a working hypothesis and as holding to a first approximation, we find something—often a noncausal relation satisfying a richer type of determinism [p. 315].

In studying infant development we may need to search for some of the richer forms of determinism.

CLUES TO CHANGE

Clues to change in our views of infants and the study of infancy are likewise in the past as well as in the present. Changes are coming about as a consequence of the demands by two types of advocates: (1) those who are advocating a science of infancy that is more humanistic in nature, maintaining that infancy is an important time of life to study in and of itself—and not because the period provides a simple prototype nor even because it is the prelude to a later stage in life (Schaffer, 1977); and (2) those who are advocating a science of early development that is holistic in nature, recognizing that newborns have been biologically designed through the evolutionary process, and that the study of infancy requires an integration of findings from the biological and behavioral sciences (Bowlby, 1977).

Changing View of Infants and the Study of Infancy

Changing Scientific Views.   The participants at this conference are, without exception, among those who have long maintained that the period of early infancy is an important one to study and understand. Some have worked primarily as researchers, others as both researchers and clinicians; all have been "advocates of infancy," with the view that infants are important as human beings and that the quality of experience during this period of life is not only of interest but of concern.

The papers and discussions reflected this combination of humanism and scientific rigor. The participants were concerned with the serious possibility that infants have a rich affective life from their earliest days; that even normal infants vary widely in their sensitivities, response capabilities, affective systems, state organization, motor behaviors, and other characteristics inherent in being a human baby; and that an evolutionary perspective is necessary in exploring the newborn infant's biological preparation for effective interaction with the environment.

The nature of these concerns was expressed most explicitly by Papousek: What is the biological–social–behavioral organization of the infant from the time of birth? The organization and coordinating capabilities of the infant are apparent in the variety of patterned events to which the newborn is responsive: patterning of sounds, particularly those present in human speech (Eisenberg); patterns of visual stimuli (Bower and Wishart, Watson), and tactile stimuli (Korner); temporal patterning of events (Lipsitt, Sander, Stern, and Watson); and patterns of various forms of social stimuli (Mason, Sander, Stern, and Papousek). Additional complex characteristics of very young infants include behaviors that reflect cognitive processes involving hypothesis making and testing (Bower and Wishart, Papousek, Stern, Watson). These characteristics of the infant were consistently linked to a second question, posed most succinctly by Sander: How does the infant achieve self-regulation as well as the tasks of adaptation? Sander pointed out that the tasks of adaptation of the infant include the development of synchrony with the mother's temporal rhythms of caretaking and interaction.

The question of adaptation becomes most complex when viewed within the context of changing interpersonal relationships. Although time-point laboratory studies of infants are as important as studies of falling objects in a sealed vacuum tube (Rheingold reminded us eloquently of the dangers of letting the pendulum of research swing too far from rigorous experimental hypothesis-testing studies), the study of the developing infant also requires an understanding of the infant's ongoing rhythms and how these are integrated with those of the mother or caretaker. As Sander pointed out, it is necessary to describe *sequences* of changes in various categories of variables in order to identify the nature of the process of change. The interweaving of mutualities constitutes a process of its own; and Yarrow gave a reasoned warning that the task of such studies is supremely difficult. Creative approaches are called for; and they are forthcoming: Stern's novel approach to the intricacies of such studies has been to measure temporal patterns of maternal forms of stimulation in order to make inferences, or derive hyptheses, about the total interactive process. He makes the tentative assumption that what a mother does reflects what a baby "can get," that is, the range of the infant's perceptual capabilities. A very different approach is that of Mason, who has removed the species-specific mother of infant monkeys in order to look at the infant's side of the ongoing adaptive process.

A related question that also persisted throughout the course of this conference was that of the nature of the biological preprogramming for selective responsiveness to social stimuli. The possibility of selective tuning is suggested by many past findings of the newborn's visual attentiveness to characteristics typical of the human face, and by Eisenberg's report that infants respond selectively to patterns of sound typically found in human speech.

An understanding of prenatal and postnatal tuning to the social environment will require very careful study of the interactive process from the moment of birth. For example, an extended discussion focused on the infant's protrusion of the tongue in response to viewing an adult protruding the tongue. The question seemed to be whether the infant at a very early age was capable of imitation, or whether certain patterned stimuli are related to patterns of responses in an obligatory fashion. As Papousek pointed out, mothers imitate their babies from their first encounter. Thus, responses that appear to be obligatory may in fact be the result of entrainment of a response that is very high in the infant's repertoire of behaviors.

It is also possible that tongue protrusion is an expression of the infant's affective state, as many of Brazelton's (Note 2) descriptions suggest. Brazelton describes the reciprocal behaviors of mother and infant as an affective synchrony reflecting psychophysiological mechanisms with which the infant is born.

The affective life of the infant is yet to be explored, both in social and nonsocial circumstances. However, the first step has been taken: a recognition of the need for such study.

Changing Humanistic Views. Recognition of the different, important, and totally human qualities of the infant will provide the context for more relevant research on how the infant develops. It can be noted that the need for recognition of human qualities has been of concern even at the adult level, as indicated by Miller's (Note 3) call for a re-evaluation of man's conception of himself. Miller predicted a psychological revolution that would be based necessarily on a change in our "conception of ourselves and how we live and love and work together... The heart of the psychological revolution will be a new and scientifically based conception of man as an individual and as a social creature [p. 9]." Such a call for a humanistic conception of man generally may have been the necessary prelude to a more human conception of the human infant. That the need persists is seen in a very recent book entitled *Toward a Man Centered Medical Science*, edited by Schaeffer, Hensel, and Brady (1977). In their introduction, concern is expressed for the limitations of conventional scientific methods and the need for broadening science to include a man-centered approach (we would substitute the term infant-centered approach): "the degree to which science is humanized will be seen in the investigator's formulation of his question, in the design of his experiment, and in the mental climate in which he carries out his work [p. i]." Schaeffer et al. call for a new type of thinking and new experimental methods to accommodate the evolving concepts of human nature. Their statements very clearly relate attitudes toward human subjects to the methods of sciencing used for understanding them.

Changing Views of the Nature of Science and Sciencing

The aforementioned quotation by Schaeffer et al. (1977) emphasizes that changing views of the nature and importance of infants is part of the process of creating new paradigms for research in infancy, a process that will supplement existing paradigms and, more importantly, replace those that are based on mythology. Denenberg's systems analysis of infant development is a proposal for a new paradigm that fits in both of these categories: Systems notions can be considered as supplementary to causal analyses: but a systems view is quite incompatible with a mechanistic analysis. A systems view is a far more complex model for the complexity of development than one that views the infant as being analogous to a machine, and it is inconsistent with the implicit assumption that the infant organism can be understood by any agglomeration of behaviors. Such a view provides a realistic context for exploring the ongoing process of changing organization at this or any other age.

The mother–infant relationship is also perceived as a systems unit, engaged in an ongoing process of mutual modification of behavior. Thus, in some respects the systems view also replaces the causal paradigm, as indicated in the work of Sander and Thoman, where neither the behavior of the mother nor the baby are considered to be causally linked to the behavior of the other member of the dyad. Synchrony, or orchestration, are more appropriate terms for referring to the patterns of behaviors that may be observed.

Such terms as synchrony or orchestration may sound amorphous, especially in the world of research where single-variable quantitative studies have been foremost and interaction effects are considered to be of secondary importance. However, recent research suggests their heuristic value. For example, Golani (1976) shows, by analysis of movement patterns, that measures of a single behavior may not reveal regularity, whereas the patterning of combinations of movement may reveal regularities of behaviors that are characteristic of an organism, animal or human. He refers to this patterning as the "orchestration of behavior." Golani's work provides a working model for the search for adaptive behaviors of individual infants and, as a next step, for the orchestration of adaptive behaviors of mother–infant systems.

At an even more general theoretical level, it is becoming clear that it may be possible to handle the complexity of systems paradigms analytically. Dawkins (1976) suggests that a good general candidate as a principle for the organization of behavior is that of hierarchical organization. He cites Simon (1962) who argues that highly complex systems that exist in the world are likely to have hierarchical structure, the nervous system being no exception. Papousek's model of early infant development combines both neural and behavioral factors in hierarchical fashion, and Eisenberg's model for central nervous control of auditory perception is also quite consistent with this view. An objective of the Thoman research is to derive a taxonomy of mother–infant behaviors, and it is reasonable to expect that taxonomic groupings can be related in a hierarchical fashion. Uzginis and Hunt (1975) describe developmental assessment based on Piagetian notions of hierarchical organization of competencies. Not only does this approach make functional and logical sense, but as Dawkins says, the hierarchy principle is one that may make the complexity of behavior manageable.

Interactional development approaches are also being proposed in the area of assessment for prediction. Parmelee (1976) has conceptualized the notion of a "cumulative risk score" whereby a broad spectrum of variables, social and physiological, are assessed at successive ages to identify patterns of deviancy at each age and patterns of changes over age. This approach reflects a realistic recognition that the infant–environment system may serve to exaggerate or ameliorate developmental handicaps from early risk factors. Likewise, Barnard has explored successive interactional assessment procedures to develop diagnostic instruments that may not only indicate the need but also provide guidelines for effective intervention.

The search for realistic research in infancy is in the head—and heart—of every research-oriented clinician. For example, Kennell and Klaus have carried out numerous interactional studies immediately after the infant's birth (e.g., Klaus & Kennell, 1970; Klaus, Kennell, Plumb, & Zuehlke, 1970) exploring the problems that may derive from the deprivation of an opportunity for mother and infant to "get acquainted" at this time. Their research represents a creative approach to some basic questions with the very practical objective of determining optimal conditions for the medical management of mothers and infants during the perinatal and early postnatal period.

Future Models of Developmental Processes

Appropriately enough, conceptual models are changing in advance of methodologies and procedures for dealing with data. This discrepancy should be expected to serve as a creative challenge to those who are not bound to conventional approaches, which so often yield significant results with insignificant implications. The challenge is apparently an effective one, and attempts are being made to deal with complex data sets in new ways.

The pattern analysis approach proposed by Golani (1976) has already been referred to. McCall (1973) has provided an example of analysis for patterns of change over age in IQ scores. He finds differing patterns of mental development that have correlates with subjects' early social experiences. The Markovian model for time series analyses and for identifying patterns of behavior sequences has recently been exploited by a number of investigators (e.g., Stern, 1974; Brown et al., 1975; Bakeman, 1977; Sackett, (Note 4); Lewis & Lee-Painter, 1974).

Even more esoteric, Freedle (1977) describes a new mathematical conceptualization for behavioral data based on the notion that differing response systems will be effective in differing states of the system (the infant, or the mother–infant). He proposes a mathematical model based on catastrophe theory by which predictions can be derived for a subject in differing states as a function of very complex forms of stimulus input. Thus the complexities of the real world of behavior may ultimately be subjected to the same standards of rigorous analysis we have come to expect in other areas of scientific study.

It should be noted that a major, inherent characteristic of these new approaches is the analyses of data for individual system units. This trend is consistent with the recognition that the dynamic process of concern in development can only occur in an individual system (see chapters by Mason, Papousek, Sander, Stern, and Thoman, in this volume), Korner has consistently stressed the individuality of infant behaviors and implications for development both directly and indirectly through interaction with the mother (e.g., Korner, 1971). Group data, although essential for some purposes, is no longer considered adequate to depict developmental processes.

Equipped with new assumptions about the nature of infants and expanding conceptual models, it may be possible to make sense of the organized complexity that we now recognize as characterizing the newborn infant.

TOWARD AN INFANT—CENTERED SCIENCE OF INFANCY

New perspectives are required, and they are appearing—in the form of new paradigms reflecting changing assumptions about the nature of the infant and about the nature of research that will provide an understanding of the infant. Like the Renaissance artist, we are finally relinquishing the myth of the infant as a miniature adult, helpless, passive, and unfeeling—in favor of the assumption that infancy is a different state from maturity; it is not necessarily a matter of moving from the more simple to the more complex, from the unfinished (incomplete) to the finished adult. The participants at this conference were in agreement that the stage of infancy is important—to the infant and to the researcher who seeks understanding of developmental processes, which may differ at each stage. The remarkable capabilities of the newborn infant already "discovered" are only an introduction to what may be expected as the infant is explored in its own right.

"Thus, the task is, not so much to see what no one has seen yet; but to think what nobody has thought yet, about that which everybody sees."

Schopenhauer, cited in L. von Bertalanffy
Problems of Life. An Evaluation of Modern Biological Thought, London: Watts & Co., 1952.

REFERENCE NOTES

1. Bunge, M. *Emergence, levels, and the mind-body problem.* Paper presented at the Winter Conference on Brain Research, Keystone, Colorado, January 15-22, 1977.
2. Brazelton, T. B., Tronick, E., Als, H, H., & Yogman, M. *Reciprocity between adults and infants.* Paper presented at the International Society for the Study of Behavioural Development meetings, Pavia, Italy, 1977.
3. Miller, G. A. Presidential address, American Psychological Association, 1969.
4. Sackett, G. P. *A nonparametric lag sequential analysis for studying dependency among responses in observational scoring system.* Paper first presented at the Western Psychological Association meeting, San Francisco, 1974.

REFERENCES

Anderson, P. W. More is different. *Science*, 1972, *177*, 393-396.
Bakeman, R. Untangling streams of behavior: Sequential analysis of observation data. In G. P. Sackett (Ed.), *Observing Behavior: Data Collection and Analysis Methods.* University Park Press, 1977.
Bowlby, J. Interview. *Washington Report*, May 1977.
Brown, J. V., Bakeman, R., Snyder, P. A., Fredrickson, W. T., Morgan, S. T. & Hepler, R. Interactions of black inner-city mothers with their newborn infants. *Child Development*, 1975, *46*, 677-686.
Bunge, M. Conjunction, Succession, Detemination and Causation. *International Journal of Theoretical Physics*, Vol. 1, No. 3, 299-315.
Dawkins, R. Hierarchical organisation: A candidate principle for ethology. In P. P. G. Bateson, & R. A. Hinde (Eds.), *Growing Points in Ethology.* Cambridge: Cambridge University Press, 1976.
Freedle, R. Psychology, thomian topologies, deviant logics, and human development. In N. Datan & H. Resse (Eds.), *Life-span Development: A Dialectical Critique.* New York: Academic Press, 1977.

Golani, I. Homeostatic motor processes in mammalian interactions—a choreography of display. In P. P. G. Bateson & P. H. Klopfer (Eds.) *Perspectives in Ethology*, (Vol. 2). New York: Plenum Press, 1976.

Gunther, M. Infant behaviour at the breast. In B. M. Foss (Ed.) *Determinants of Infant Behaviour*. London: Methuen and Company, 1961.

Klaus, M., & Kennell, J. Mothers separated from their newborn infants. *Pediatric Clinics of North America*, 1970, *17*, 1015–1037.

Klaus, M., Kennell, J., Plumb, N., & Zuehlke, S. Human maternal behavior at first contact with her young. *Pediatrics*, 1970, *46*, 187.

Korner, A. F. Individual differences at birth: implications for early experience and later development. *American Journal Orthopsychiatry*, 1971, *41*, 608.

Lewis, M., & Lee-Painter, S. An interactional approach to the mother–infant dyad. In M. Lewis & L. A. Rosenblum, *The Effects of the Infant on its Caregiver*, New York: Wiley & Sons, 1974.

McCall, R. B., Appelbaum, M. I., & Hogarty, P. S. Developmental changes in mental performance. *Monographs of the Society for Research in Child Development*, 1973, 38, (Serial No. 150).

Schaffer, K. E., Hensel, H., & Brady, R. (Eds.) *Toward a Man-Centered Medical Science*. New York: Futura Publishing Company, 1977. ·

Schaffer, H. R. (Ed.) *Studies in Mother–Infant Interaction*. New York: Academic Press, 1977.

Simon, H. A. The architecture of complexity. *Proceedings of the American Philosophical Society*, 1962, *106*, 467–482.

Stern, D. N. Mother and infant at play: The dyadic interaction involving facial, vocal, and gaze behaviors. In M. Lewis & L. Rosenblum (Eds.), *The Effect of the Infant on the Caregiver*, New York: Wiley and Sons, 1974.

Stone, L. J., Smith, H. T., & Murphy, L. B. (Eds.). *The Competent Infant: Readings and Commentary*. New York: Basic Books, 1973.

Stone, L. J., Smith, H. T., & Murphy, L. B. (Eds.). *The Competent Infant: Research and Commentary*. New York: Basic Books, 1973.

Watson, J. S. Memory and "contingency analysis" in infant learning. *Merrill-Palmer Quarterly*, 1967, *13*, 55–76. (a)

Watson, J. S. The development and generalization of "contingency awareness" in early infancy: Some hypotheses. *Merrill-Palmer Quarterly,* 1966, *12*, 123–135. (b)

Wolhwill, J. F. *The Study of Behavioral Development*. New York: Academic Press, 1973.

Wolff, P. H. The causes, controls, and organization of behavior in the neonate. *Psychological Issues*, 5(1), Monograph 17. New York: International University Press, 1966.

Index